FoxBASE+™/MAC® SIMPLIFIED

For Julie, Janelle, and Ryan—you make it all worthwhile.

FoxBASE+™/MAC® SIMPLIFIED

Michael Masterson

Windcrest books are published by Windcrest Books, an imprint of TAB BOOKS. The name "Windcrest" is a registered trademark of TAB BOOKS.

Published by **Windcrest Books**
FIRST EDITION/FIRST PRINTING

© 1990 by **Michael Masterson**. Reproduction or publication of the content in any manner, without express permission of the publisher, is prohibited. The publisher takes no responsibility for the use of any of the materials or methods described in this book, or for the products thereof. Printed in the United States of America.

Library of Congress Cataloging-in-Publication Data

Masterson, Michael.
    FoxBASE+/Mac Simplified / by Michael Masterson.
       p.   cm.
    ISBN 0-8306-3187-9
    1. Data base management. 2. FoxBASE (Computer program)
  3. Macintosh (Computer)—Programming. I. Title.
QA76.9.D3M375   1989
005.75'65—dc20   89-36606
                                                                                   CIP

TAB BOOKS offers software for sale. For information and a catalog, please contact TAB Software Department, Blue Ridge Summit, PA 17294-0850.

Questions regarding the content of this book should be addressed to:

Windcrest Books
Imprint of TAB BOOKS
Blue Ridge Summit, PA 17294-0850

Lori Flaherty: Book Editor
Katherine Brown: Production
Jaclyn J. Boone: Series Design
Lori E. Schlosser: Cover Design

Contents

Acknowledgments   *xiv*

Preface   *xv*

Introduction   *xvi*

How to Use This Book   *xviii*

PART ONE
Learning and Using FoxBASE+/Mac

1 Introducing Database Concepts   3

   Managing Information with Computers   3
      Value of Databases
      How FoxBASE+/Mac Compares
   Interactively Controlling FoxBASE+/Mac   4
      Menus
      Windows
      Dialogs
   Programs Automate FoxBASE+/Mac   5
      Programming not Required!
   FoxBASE+/Mac—A "Relational" Database   6
      Relating Tables Together
      Views

2 Database Design Considerations   *8*

Information Bins   9
     Fields
     Records
     Tables
     Related Tables
     Index Keys

Information Worth Storing   12
     Operational Data
     Categorical Data

Creating a FoxBASE+/Mac Database File   13
     Creating a New File
     Naming the File
     Entering the Data Type
     Sizing the Field
     Adding Fields and Saving the File

3 The Menu System   *16*

How to Navigate   16
     The Cursor
     Keyboard Shortcuts
     Recording Menu Choices and Playing Them Back
     Saving a Program File
     The Help System

The File Menu   20
     New
     Open
     Close
     Save
     Save As
     Revert
     Page Size
     Page Setup
     Print
     Copy File, Delete File, and Rename File
     Quit

The Edit Menu   27
     Undo
     Cut
     Copy
     Paste
     Clear
     Find
     Find Again
     Replace and Find Again

    Replace All
    Select All
    Preferences
The Database Menu   32
    Setup
    Browse
    Append From
    Copy To
    Sort
    Total
    Average
    Count
    Label
    Report
    Report/Label (Version 2.x)
    Sum
    Flush
    Pack
    Reindex
The Record Menu   41
    Append
    Change
    Goto
    Locate and Continue
    Seek
    Replace
    Delete
    Recall
The Program Menu   47
    Do
    Suspend
    Resume
    Echo
    Talk
    Compile
    Generate
The Text Menu   50
    Font
    Size
    Style
The Window Menu   51
    Hide Screens
    Command
    View
    Debug
    Help

Status
Trace
Screen

4 The FoxBASE Data Handling "Engine"   **55**

FoxBASE Program Files   55
- Interactive or Preprogrammed
- Interpreting and Compiling Programs
- FoxBASE Commands and Expressions

FoxBASE File Types Survey   58
Storing and Managing Data   59
- The Data Files (.dbf)
- Memo Picture Files (.dbt)
- Index Files
- Relations and Views

Managing Memory Requirements   62
- Containing Memory Demands

Adjusting FoxBASE Defaults   63
- Macintosh Settings
- The SET Command
- The Configuration File

5 How to Use FoxBASE   **70**

Expression   70
Work with Data   72
- Creating and Using Tables in the View Window
- Adding, Browsing, and Changing Records
- Deleting Records and Packing Files

Indexing   75
- Creating Indexes
- Data-Converting Functions
- Filtered Index
- Find and Seek

Sorting   78
Setting File Relationships   79
Listing Data On-Screen   81
Sums, Counts, Averages, and Totals   83
Replacing Field Data and Calculating Columns   84
Pinpointing Records of Interest   86
Setting Record Ranges   87
Importing Data   88
Exporting Data   88
Saving Procedures   89
Creating Data Entry Forms   89
- Artificial Intelligence?

Developing Applications   91
   Creating Successful Database Structures
   Analyzing the Information to Be Stored
   Creating a Data Model
   Relating Tables with Key Fields
   Reviewing the Design
   Creating Input and Maintenance Forms
   Creating Screen Outputs
   Building a Menu System

PART TWO
Developing FoxBASE+/Mac Applications

6 Introduction to FoxBASE Programming   97

Programming Features   97
   Commands
   Operators
   Expressions and ?
   Controls and Constructs
   Do While...Enddo
   Do Case...Otherwise...Endcase
   If...Else...Endif
   IIF( )
   Functions
Memory Variables   105
   Naming and Creating Memory Variables
   Attributes
   Public Variables
   Saving Variables on Disk
   Exchanging Variable Data with Database Fields
   Getting Information from Users
   Using Memory Variables in Programs
   Arrays
Special Features and Program Design   112
   Subroutines
   Parameter Passing
   User-Defined Functions
   Macro Expansion
Screens One through Nine   117
The Data-Handling Environment   119
   Relations and Views
   The Record Pointer
   Scopes Are Record Boundaries

Blind Record Scoping
Conditional Record Scoping

7 Developing the User Interface — 124

Introducing Interfaces   124
Introducing FoxForm and FoxCode   125
Creating Applications—A Short Tutorial   125
   Creating a New Form
   Putting Database Fields in the Layout
   Arranging the Fields and Adding Text Labels
   Saving the Form
   Generating an Application from the Screen Form
   Running the Program
Programming the Browse and Change Windows   132
   The Commands
   Options for the Browse and Change Commands
   Browse-Only Command Options
FoxForm Objects and FoxBASE Commands   135
   Looking at Objects
   Understanding Commands
   About GET and READ
   Putting Things in Their Place
   PICTURES and Pictures
Using FoxForm Menus   140
   The File and Program Menus
   The Form Menu
   The Object Menu
   The Edit Menu
Using FoxForm Tools   142
   Text Labels
   Lines and Boxes
   Clearing Parts of the Screen
   Checkboxes
   Data Entry Fields
   The PICTURE Clause
   The FUNCTION Clause
   The RANGE Clause
   The VALID Clause
   The FONT Clause
   The COLOR Clause
   The SIZE Clause
  Picture Buttons   152
  Popup Menus   155
  Radio Buttons   158
  Text Buttons   160
  Scrollable Lists   162

Text Edit Regions 165
Anatomy of an Interface Command 167
   Essential Command Parts
   Optional Command Parts
Enhancing Applications by Hand 170
Validating New Data 175
Alerts, UDFs, and Validation 176
Dialogs 179
Menus 180
   Menu Trees versus Bar Menus
   Modeless, or Nearly So
Menu-Event Handling 181
   Defining, Installing, and Handling Menus
   A Demonstration Menu
Customizing Help 186
   Helpful Hints
   Helpful Functions
Programmed Data Displays 188
Printing Reports 190
   Printing with ? and ??
   Printing with the @ SAY Command
   Printing to a File

8 FoxBASE+/Mac Commands (an alphabetical reference listing) *193*

How the Command Reference Is Organized 193
Symbols Used in the Command Reference 194
Syntax Options 195

9 FoxBASE+/Mac Functions (an alphabetical reference listing) *363*

How the Function Reference is Organized 363
Symbols Used in the Function Reference 364

10 Distributing Applications and Sharing Data *460*

Moving Data between Macs and IBM Compatibles 460
   Swapping Files
   Sharing Data
The Mac as a Development Environment 462
   Debugging
   Tracing
Creating Programs that Run on Macs and IBM Compatibles 462
   Fonts
   Keystrokes

The FoxBASE Runtime System 464
    Packaging Applications for Distribution (FoxPackage)
    Build Application
    Add Resources
    Add Config.fx . . .
    Remove Source
Multiuser Issues 466
    Why Lock Records or Files?
    Version 1.x and Version 2.x
    The Nature of Locks
    Where to Put the Files
    Exclusive Use of Database Files
    Automatic File Locks
    Automatic Record Locks
    Programmed Locking Concepts
    Using the Record-Locking Function
    Programmed File Locks
    Error-Handling Routines
    Editing Memory Variables
Managing Resources 477

11 Using FoxReport   *479*

Macintosh Printing 479
    Characters and Bitmaps
    AppleTalk and Device Drivers
Report Features 480
    Quick Report
    Bands and Body
    Page Header and Footer
    Column Header and Footer
    Group Header and Footer
    Title and Summary
Working Environments and Objects 484
    FoxReport Menus
    Thinking in Bands
FoxReport Objects 485
    Text
    Data Fields, Groups, and Totals
    Graphics
    Pictures
Manipulating Objects 490
    Adjusting the Drawing Environment
    Nudging and Micro-Sizing
    Bring to Front and Send to Back
    Fill, Pen, and Transfer Mode

Calculating and Computing 493
    Calculated Fields
    Computed Fields
    User-Defined Functions
Databases and Report Specifications 494
    Indexes and Relations
    Views and the (.frx) Report Form File
    Page Layouts
Labels 495
    New and Old Operators
    Wide Margins and Exact Sizes

Appendix A ASCII Codes   *499*

Appendix B Categorial Cross-Reference of Commands   *502*

Appendix C Error Codes and Messages   *509*

Appendix D XCMDs and XFCNs   *531*

Index   *533*

Acknowledgments

WITHOUT the generous support of my wife Julie, daughter Janelle, and son Ryan, this work could have not been finished. They gracefully managed to balance our family without all of its weights when I was hung up in work. I am also grateful to friends who encouraged and helped. I needed every bit of it. Among these special people are Jon Kennedy, Chris Veal, Dennis Dawson, and Eddie Knaack—and clients, both of and in Ernst & Young, who cared enough to prod me forward through a process that has forever upped my appreciation for all who dare to write.

And if there were a trophy for those who make, sell, and support the world's most innovative and competent database software, it should go to David and Amy Fulton, and Janet Walker, "keeper of the way," the Fox developers, Bev Grafton and the incomparable support team led by her grace, Richard Ney, Allen Mirelis, and Glen Hart, who remain human in an inhumane marketplace, and to the God who assembled and parked such an amazing pool of talent in Ohio. And, of course, to governor of the lot, Norm Chapman.

Thanks, also, to the patient souls at TAB BOOKS, namely Ron Powers and Stephen Moore, and to Lori Flaherty, a talent I desperately need.

To those who find between the covers of this book something worth its price, and to those who go even further to overlook its obvious imperfections, I owe many thanks indeed.

Preface

AS a business user of the Macintosh and of the dBase language on IBM compatible computers, I have come to appreciate some newfound qualities in both that are a product of their marriage in FoxBASE+/Mac. FoxBASE+/Mac has given the Macintosh a widely accepted, "standard," data manipulation language, and with it, more control over existing business information than it ever had before; dBase programs and data are easier than ever to manage because they now work on a Macintosh. I'm able to manage database files as large as 25 megabytes in a friendly environment because of this marriage. FoxBASE+/Mac has put a traditional database world inside the creative and comfortable Macintosh, which makes it hard for me to imagine a more powerful or more graceful database program for microcomputers.

If you know more about the Macintosh computer than about FoxBASE+/Mac, then let me, through this book, introduce you to the most popular database standard running on microcomputers. If you are more familiar with the dBASE standard than with the Macintosh, then you are in for a treat as you learn how the Macintosh can make you more productive and your work more enjoyable.

Introduction

THE traditional purpose of any database manager is to store, manipulate, and retrieve meaningful information, but that's not enough to make a program successful in today's crowded software marketplace. Microcomputer users now have powerful machines, and they demand more from expensive database software than mere functionality; a good database program should also be friendly, quick, and reliable. FoxBASE+/Mac excels in all of these things.

WHAT IS FOXBASE+/MAC?

Because FoxBASE+/Mac was designed to manage traditional database functions in a traditional way, it can be used to control large volumes of information in a business; even tens and hundreds of thousands of records are well within its reach. What's more, business users will be glad to know that many applications written in the standard dBase language will run without modification within FoxBASE+/Mac. Granted, they won't operate with the beauty of a true Macintosh design, but they will work.

While some limitations exist for IBM-PC applications run on a Macintosh, there are few limitations for those who develop applications for the Macintosh with FoxBASE+/Mac. Its programmability makes true Macintosh interfaces attainable by anyone who can learn its easy Englishlike language. Its traditional database features and power make it suitable for serious database jobs, as simple as label printing, and as complex as business accounting.

What about FoxBASE for nonprogrammers? The friendly Macintosh interface on FoxBASE+/Mac makes it as approachable as any other powerful multifile database tool. Its speed in interactive operations is significantly greater than other Macintosh DBMS (database management systems), which means that you don't have to wait for results while you learn.

WHO USES FOXBASE+/MAC?

FoxBASE+/Mac is for three types of users: database novices who are experimenting or have responsibility for database management at work; more experienced users who want to automate database tasks with preprogrammed procedures; and those brave souls who want to exploit its programmability to create complex applications for others to use. Finally, these features are available to all its users:

- New users can use the mouse and the interactive interface features, commanding FoxBASE through its menus, windows, and dialogs. All FoxBASE+/Mac users can use the mouse for some aspects of their work.
- Intermediate users can quickly master the interactive menus, as well as use the FoxBASE macrolike programming language to record procedures in command files for use whenever they are needed. Automating repetitive tasks is particularly easy with FoxBASE.
- FoxBASE power users, application developers who can create applications from scratch, can build complex programs for others to use. Finished applications have their own purpose, look, and feel. They can manage membership applications, keep track of customers and their orders, or any other task. When running such applications, FoxBASE+/Mac plays a hidden and empowering role like that of an engine in a car. FoxBASE provides the power, but is driven by the developer's prerecorded programs.

You can decide how to use FoxBASE+/Mac based on your own needs and experience. It was designed for users with all levels of experience.

WHAT YOU SHOULD KNOW

To use this book effectively, you should first be familiar with such Macintosh operations as how to select and edit text, how to open and close disk icons, size windows, click, drag, copy files, and how to start programs. Readers who have successfully completed the Macintosh tutorials provided with their computers already have those basic skills. If the Macintosh's way of working is altogether new to you, I encourage you to read the Apple-supplied owner's manual, to complete the guided tour, and then to proceed with FoxBASE. It's a good idea to have an introductory Macintosh reference book or the owner's manual handy during your first sessions with FoxBASE+/Mac.

How to Use This Book

IF you haven't designed a database for yourself or tried your hand at FoxBASE+/Mac, the first few chapters can bring you up to speed, introducing important database concepts that experienced users often take for granted. For example, if you don't know what fields or tables are, or how many fields to put in a table, then the first two chapters can teach you something about database design and supply ideas you can build on later. You can learn how to create your own databases, and even how to evaluate those you might already be using at work or home.

Chapter 1 introduces database concepts and FoxBASE, describing the difference between interactive and programmed databases, and the meaning of "relational" databases. It briefly guides you through the way FoxBASE works so you can understand how it stores information.

Chapter 2 leads you through the steps to creating your own database, and explains how databases are put together, the kinds of information they can store, and how multiple tables of information can be linked.

Chapter 3 introduces the menus in FoxBASE+/Mac where you can do many jobs without any programming. The View, Browse, and Command windows can be your tools to unlock a lot of power.

Chapter 4 discusses the concept I call a database "engine," and it outlines FoxBASE's data management strengths and technical limitations. By reading Chapter 4, you'll learn how FoxBASE works.

Chapter 5 builds on the discussion of the "engine" in FoxBASE, and goes on to discuss the specifics of working with data, such as how it gets into FoxBASE in the first place, how to manipulate it, and, finally, how to make reports and labels.

Chapter 6 is an introduction to programming in FoxBASE, introducing commands, functions, operators, and programming controls.

Chapter 7 is an introduction to user-interface programming, an all-important aspect of application development, a necessary skill to make applications in FoxBASE+/Mac for others to use.

Chapters 8 and 9 are alphabetical references to the FoxBASE commands and functions. These chapters assume that you are using FoxBASE to solve interactive data management problems with commands and functions or that you are learning to program. Anyone who is familiar with the menus and interactive features of FoxBASE+/Mac will find these chapters of lasting value.

Chapter 10 discusses distributing programs to others. Fox Software produces a "runtime" version of FoxBASE that makes distribution of finished applications easy. This chapter shows you how it works. Multiuser issues are also covered so that you can prepare programs to run on a local area network.

Chapter 11 discusses the all new report writer in version 2.0 of FoxBASE+/Mac. Learn how it works with database files to produce desktop publishing results.

PART ONE
Learning and Using FoxBASE+/Mac

1
Introducing Database Concepts

STRUCTURED information is the stuff of databases, just as words are the stuff of word processors. Gathering information from various sources, storing it away, and getting it back in a timely, meaningful way is the whole idea behind databases.

In business, paper filing cabinets are database systems, but computers do a better job because they can relate bits of information automatically, give it back quickly, and calculate figures all at the same time. What's more impressive is the cost/performance ratio of electronic databases. They're less expensive than file clerks (no offense intended) and they don't get bored doing mundane work. Many database jobs—sorting, for example—are boring work, computers earn their keep and free us to think more creatively.

MANAGING INFORMATION WITH COMPUTERS

When you think about it, manageable information is manageable because it has been cut, sliced, and diced to fit neatly into predefined categories. Computers take excellent advantage of categorical bins to remember and reproduce neat tables of information, sometimes with hundreds or thousands of individual items.

The Value of Databases

Database software such as FoxBASE+/Mac can break solid information up into little bits, but what's more useful, is that it can put it all back together in surprising combinations. Without the glue to put bits of data back together again, electronic databases would be of little good.

By storing information internally, as separate little pieces, and linking them electronically, databases provide flexible, realistic models of the information we commit to them. Their internal method of storage is of little consequence except to those who care to know and to programmers responsible for its performance.

How FoxBASE+/Mac Compares

Disk space, a keyboard, a display, and a printer are common to nearly all microcomputer database setups. Because they do the same thing, they also have the same hardware requirements. While database programs do the same thing, they don't all do them the same way; they differ in areas such as keystroke conventions and screens. Minor idiosyncracies, speed of performance, and ease of use, often set them apart from one another.

FoxBASE's internal storage methods are similar to mainframe relational database systems, yet it yields nearly all of its power through the little Macintosh mouse. It's as powerful and easy to use as a microcomputer database can be, which makes it good for novices as well as seasoned veterans. FoxBASE+/Mac has enough program flexibility and power for imposing application systems, even though many users won't need to program in order to meet their needs. In technically skilled hands, FoxBASE+/Mac can be an awesome and powerful tool.

INTERACTIVELY CONTROLLING FOXBASE+/MAC

FoxBASE+/Mac has what's been called an interactive interface, simply meaning that it interacts with users through items such as menus, windows, and special-purpose dialog screens. It lets you know what it's doing while you're using it so you can intercede and change its course. In addition, FoxBASE's menus, windows, and dialogs let you do many things—such as create a database, enter data, search, list, print, calculate, and sort or save data.

Menus

Menus offer choices on computers the same as they do in restaurants. FoxBASE+/Mac menus are called pull-down and bar menus because choices are listed in a bar across the top of the screen and more choices drop down when you make a selection. Main choices line the top of the screen; secondary choices list downward from them. To expand on the restaurant metaphor, main categories such as Chinese and Mexican food would be listed horizontally at the top of the screen, while course choices such as egg rolls and tacos would be displayed below the main choices.

Windows

Windows are FoxBASE+/Mac's main way of interacting with users and letting them get at the data it contains. For example, the Browse window gives you a direct way to view data and change it at will. Windows help you manage processes because they offer controls and report back to you the direction and progress of things beneath the surface. The View window is a perfect example, it is a virtual control center where you can open or close files, set or break file relationships, and even change the very structure of a database. The Command window accepts typewritten instructions and promptly acts on them. Finally, a Help window is available to give you assistance when you're stuck and need answers.

Dialogs

Dialogs are special windows that appear from time to time. Their name describes their purpose, which is to dialog with you—usually because FoxBASE needs information that you alone can supply. Changing the structure of a database, for example, is done in a dialog window session. Most dialogs are elementary and need no explanation. The context or process that a dialog appears in is the key to understanding its purpose. Dialogs get directions from you, the user.

PROGRAMS AUTOMATE FOXBASE+/MAC

Programs can be created using combinations of commands and functions. Commands are technically like verbs, whereas functions most often test for certain conditions or convert data from one state to another. Figure 1-1 shows a FoxBASE+/Mac program that clears the screen, then writes some text on it. Literally, it tells FoxBASE+/Mac to clear the screen, then at the screen's row number 3 and column number 15, it tells FoxBASE to place the text, "Hi, I'm a program and you are a programmer."

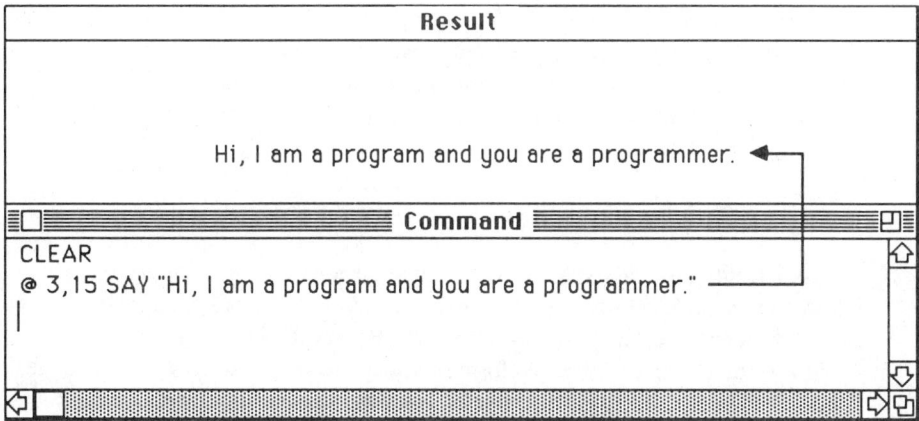

Fig. 1-1. A simple program.

Programs give FoxBASE+/Mac purpose and a new identity. Programs can be small or as large as thousands of lines. Complex programs can control the screen and the data all at once. Programs can be written to guide uninitiated users through the process of entering new data, editing it, or deleting it.

An important attribute of programs is that they can make FoxBASE+/Mac appear like a specialized software program with its own new set of menus. FoxBASE's interactive features such as the Browse window can be made to disappear and only programmed features made to appear. Programmers use FoxBASE+/Mac to create highly specialized database programs such as accounting systems, mail list managers, order entry systems, and others. Programs that customize FoxBASE+/Mac in this way are called applications because they create an applied use of the product.

Programming Not Required!

If you're not an experienced programmer, don't fret. Later in the book you'll find detailed explanations of each FoxBASE+/Mac command and function, and if you don't plan on becoming a programmer, you should know that FoxBASE+/Mac can write commands and functions for you. Programming is not required to create programs! You might want, for example, to have some macro-like programs that do specific or repetitive tasks for you. FoxBASE records all of your menu and dialog choices in the command window in a form that can be saved and repeated. It's a virtual macro recorder. If you want to learn the basic commands, you can study the program examples in the command reference sections of the book where you'll find ideas to help you accomplish your own programming goals.

FOXBASE+/MAC—A "RELATIONAL" DATABASE

The first relational databases were created several years ago by researchers at IBM's Santa Theresa research facility. Since then, the tabular-relational way of modelling information in a computer has become, by far, the most popular way to store business information. Although there are formal standards defining what a relational database is, there is little agreement on which commercial database products meet those high standards.

FoxBASE+/Mac is considered relational because it can open and relate many data tables at once. When a database software program uses the table-linking method to model information from the real world, it's a relational database program in the simplest and most important meaning of the word.

Relating Tables Together

As I mentioned, FoxBASE+/Mac is like all relational database managers that store information in tables of rows and columns. Accounting tablets and electronic spreadsheets are good examples of the basic layout of each FoxBASE file.

It's fortunate that business information can be arranged in sets that fit neatly into tables. Technically, it's easier to make efficient storage and retrieval for a table-based system, and relational databases benefit directly from this simplicity. Another advantage is the ease with which data can be analyzed and systems designed for storage. Relational databases are made up of sets. Sets for inventories, employees, receivables, and others, can all be parts of one large database consisting of related tables. The relational method allows each part of the information you store to keep its own identity and to add its significance to a larger body of information.

Views

A well-designed relational database can hold all of a company's operational information. When a salesman wants to view a customer's buying history, he can. When a warehouse worker wants to check inventory levels, he can. When managers want to check financial information, it, too, is readily available. Each of these types of information can come from one large database of tables via views.

Views virtually reconstruct data from separated tables into a model that closely resembles the form it had before it was separated into sets of tables. Lest you get nervous at the potential complexity of relational databases, remember this: customers are a table, products are another table, and sales another. Each table is stored in its own computer file that can be opened and related to other tables. Once you understand the rationale behind relational databases, these sets of real-world information are not hard to conceive, and, creating a model for them in FoxBASE is a simple matter of going through the steps.

Chapter 2 describes the internal structure of tables and the mechanisms for relating them so that there is no mystery when you're ready to start designing your own. Eventually, you should be able to design databases with the confidence that they are good models of reality, are efficient in their use of space, and efficient in their use of your computer.

2
Database Design Considerations

WHAT does it take to make a database? Does it matter if a person's first and last names are combined into one field, or should they be separated? What are the consequences of creating too little room for an address when there is no way to know exactly how many characters wide an address will be? By the end of this chapter you'll have answers for these questions, and you'll know how to create and modify your own FoxBASE+/Mac databases.

There are internal and external aspects to every database. The internal aspect is the way a computer understands data. The external aspect has to do with human understanding of the data. You need to understand both so that you can design databases that are efficient from the computer's point of view, and friendly from a user's point of view.

If the data to be stored is not familiar to you, you can't design a database to hold it; but don't worry. Databases are usually designed by people who use the information themselves, or by someone who talks with the data's owner until it's understood. Your analysis can result in a design that lets any user be the boss over data.

Database designers can spend a lot of time learning about the characteristics of information in order to make a database accurate and flexible. For information that isn't already organized, database design is like bringing order out of chaos.

If you haven't designed many databases, you'll need to understand the way databases handle information before you can effectively design systems. To experienced designers, the internal data storage concepts are second-nature; therefore, they usually start the design process for a new system by analyzing the information to be stored. The remainder of this chapter reviews those relational data storage conventions that are the foundation of effective database design. If you can benefit from a review of these concepts, or need an introduction, read on. If you know how to design systems but have not yet created a data file in FoxBASE, you can skip to the part of this chapter titled "How to create a FoxBASE+/Mac database file."

INFORMATION BINS

The internal order for a database comes from fields, records, and tables. Fields are the smallest part of a database; tables are the largest. Fields, records, and tables should be arranged to approximate the natural order of the stored information; see Fig. 2-1, where each of the two types of data has a field—also called a column—all to itself.

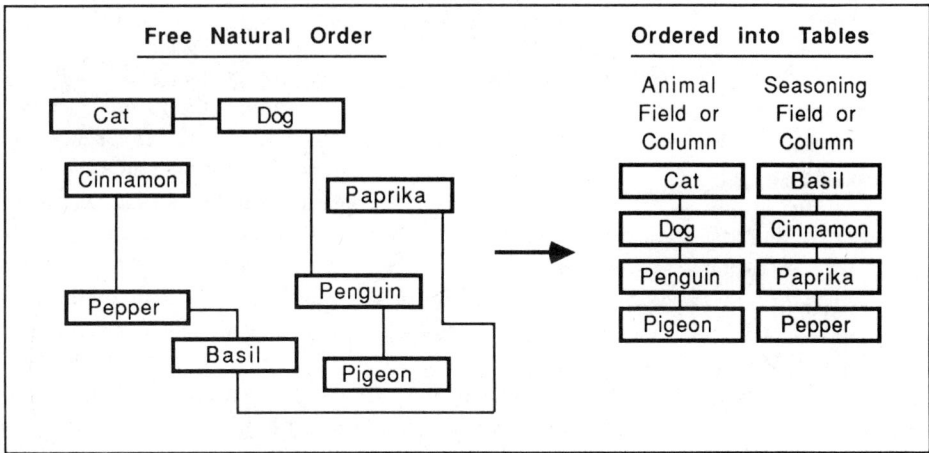

Fig. 2-1. Rows and columns to relate data.

Fields

Fields are the smallest unit of space available for storing data, therefore all the information you put into a database must be broken down into units small enough to fit into fields. Fields have a predefined width and a name to describe their contents (see Fig. 2-2). In a database that holds information about business customers, each indivisible part of the customer class of information resides in a field of its own. For example, a customer's telephone number or city would go into a separate field.

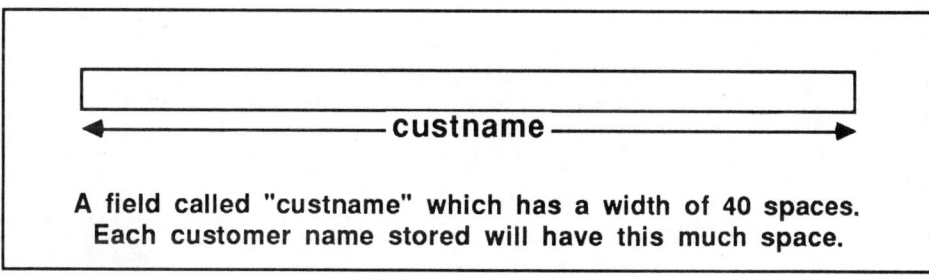

Fig. 2-2. A database field.

When you instruct FoxBASE+/Mac to make a new field, it needs to know what type of data you will store there. It's more efficient to store numbers in the type of field that's made for calculations than it is to store numbers in a field for characters, and then change their "type" every time a calculation is needed. By "typing" information ahead of time, FoxBASE can safely make assumptions about the data. This makes operations very efficient later. The inconvenience is worth it. Types of information that FoxBASE+/Mac can store in fields are numbers, characters, dates, pictures, true/false statements (called the "logical" data type), and a memo data type that's for free-form note keeping (see Fig. 2-3).

Records

Records are a predefined set of fields that are grouped together so that they can jointly describe something meaningful. Records can describe complex things such as customers, transactions, cars, sales orders, or library books. This collection of fields stores enough detail about a subject that you can learn anything you need to know about it (see Fig. 2-4).

The purpose of each field in a record is to contain a detail about the item described. Natural records can be created with 3 by 5 index cards. A research note taken on an index card is an example. Library catalog cards are also natural records, but they have a predesigned order to them, the same as computer records do. Records are sometimes called the fundamental "relation" because they are the smallest unit in a database system that is capable of representing something complex. Everything can be complex, but we don't store everything that can be known about an item in database records; it just isn't worth it. Records hold fields together, and we use records to store information that means something to us or is vital to our business.

Tables

A table is a stack of similar records. When groups of fields are arrayed like rows into records, they can be stacked—one on top of another as shown in Fig. 2-5. By stacking records, you can produce the visual effect of vertical columns which have a column for each field. Two-dimensional tables appear from this arrangement, so we call each database file a table. FoxBASE requires that we name each table so it can be saved on disk and distinquish it from other tables. The name also provides a useful way to identify a table's contents.

Fig. 2-3. There are different types of data.

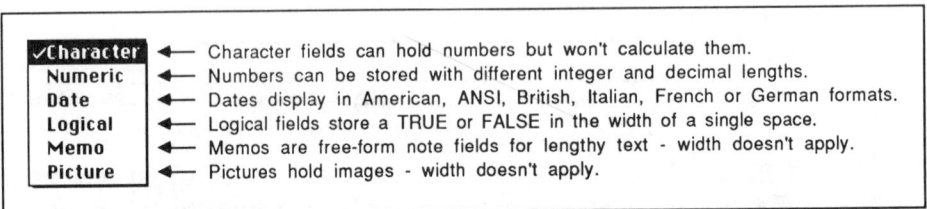

Fig. 2-4. A record relates fields of data.

Information Bins

custname	custnumber	address1	address2	city	state	zipcode
	RECORD/ROW →					
↑ FIELD/COLUMN						

Fig. 2-5. Tables group records.

Related Tables

One table is inadequate to store all of the important information to a business. Relational databases use separate tables (files) to store different sets of information. By organizing information this way, all the information that's of interest to a business can be stored in tables.

To successfully reintegrate separated tables later, a table can hold only one kind of information. Customers should be stored only in a customer file, sales orders in an order transaction file, and so on. Forcing different types of information into one table could create such a confusing patchwork of information that working with it would be more frustrating than helpful—and computers would never be able to use simple rules to tie the loose ends together. Breaking the information up into sets is called normalization.

Index Keys

Structurally speaking, relational databases keep information in separate containers; the mechanism FoxBASE uses to keep multiple data-sets, or tables, related is called an index key. An index is created for each table that can be accessed by other tables. Indexes are, in effect, the key other tables need in order to find related information. To make keys, you just select the column of information that will match in both tables and then you point an arrow from one file into the other. Indexes are made on key fields, or columns.

A key field has a special significance because it contains information that can match records in one table to records in other tables. You index them (put them in a logical order) to give FoxBASE quick access to them. In Fig. 2-6 a sales detail file is related via its customer number field to a complementary customer file. Relating two tables synchronizes their matching records by lining them up with a key-field's value.

A database structure that can support key-field relations doesn't happen by accident; key fields are carefully designed for each table. Sometimes more than one key field is put into a table so it can be linked to several other tables. Relational databases build on this simple model to create databases capable of modeling the most complex real-world information. After sets of data have been analyzed, tables created, and keys formed to relate them, FoxBASE+/Mac can interchangeably relate up to 10 of them at once. That capability provides a wide enough view into a database system that even the most complex data combinations will be satisfied—rarely are more than 10 tables needed to model real information.

Customer file

custname	custnumber	address1	address2	city	state	zipcode

Sales file

selldate	custnumber	prodnumber	price	qty	shipdate	salesrep

Fig. 2-6. Key fields link tables.

INFORMATION WORTH STORING

Generally speaking, only two types of data are needed to make a database useful. Operational data is the stuff you bought FoxBASE+/Mac for, the very information that you want to manage; categorical data defines the categories that make up operational data.

Operational Data

Of all the types of data you deal with, operational data is the easiest to understand. It's what most people think of when buying database software—information about people, inventory items, train schedules, bottles of wine aging in a cellar, music, records, or books. Operational data is the volume of information that requires a database manager in the first place.

Categorical Data

Categorical data is constant, like departments, employee classifications, inventory locations, and membership types—annual, lifetime, and so on. Categorical data doesn't necessarily need to be stored in the computer, but it can help keep operational data in order. After you discover a set of categories that exists in operational data, you can use it to decrease the actual volume of operational information you store by assigning numbers to each category and cross-referencing their descriptions. Consequently, longhand descriptions don't have to be entered repeatitively.

When categories help you make sense of operational data, their names and descriptions might be worth storing in a table. An alternative is to keep look-up sheets near the database computer, and there's nothing inherently wrong in relying on users to remember the categories that keep order. In any case, categorical data presents opportunities for designers to create order and efficiency.

CREATING A FoxBASE+/Mac DATABASE FILE

So far, this chapter has introduced the essential concepts for database design. If you have installed FoxBASE+/Mac on your computer, you're ready to create a database file. The steps that follow don't explain the FoxBASE menus—that's been saved for Chapter 5. Rather, the objective for now is to demonstrate how FoxBASE+/Mac implements the concepts you learned in Chapters 1 and 2.

Remember: you can exit FoxBASE by selecting the Quit option below File on the top menu bar. If you are in a dialog box (a boxlike window on the screen) that prevents you from using the File and Quit menu options and you want to quit, you must first leave the dialog, then quit. All dialogs have a cancel button or another equally obvious way to get out.

Creating a New File

The first thing to do to create a new database file is select the option "New" from the File menu. A dialog box like the one shown in Fig. 3-5 will appear, allowing you to select what type of file to create. The Database "radio" button (so called because they are round and because only one can be pressed at a time) will probably be already dark because this is the default selection. If it's not, select it. Press the button labeled "OK".

When you press the OK button, a Modify Structure dialog box such as the one shown in Fig. 2-7 will appear on the screen. On the right side of the dialog box are buttons that give you insert and delete options. This dialog is the way you insert, delete, and otherwise create or modify database files in FoxBASE. Like most dialog boxes, you affirm decisions by pressing the OK button. Pressing the Cancel button will close the dialog box without creating a database file, so use it only to abort.

Naming the File

At this time, you should enter names to describe the contents of each new field. When you're done entering all the fields, your choices will be visible in the dialog box. The fields in a database file describe the contents of each record that can later be added to the file when real information is put in. The fields are like bins. Follow the example shown in Fig. 2-7. Because this field will hold the customer name, we'll call it *custname*. Enter the name *custname* into the first field's Name box.

The computer doesn't care what you call a field as long as each field name is different from all of others in the same database file. For ease of use, however, you should use names that tell what the field contains.

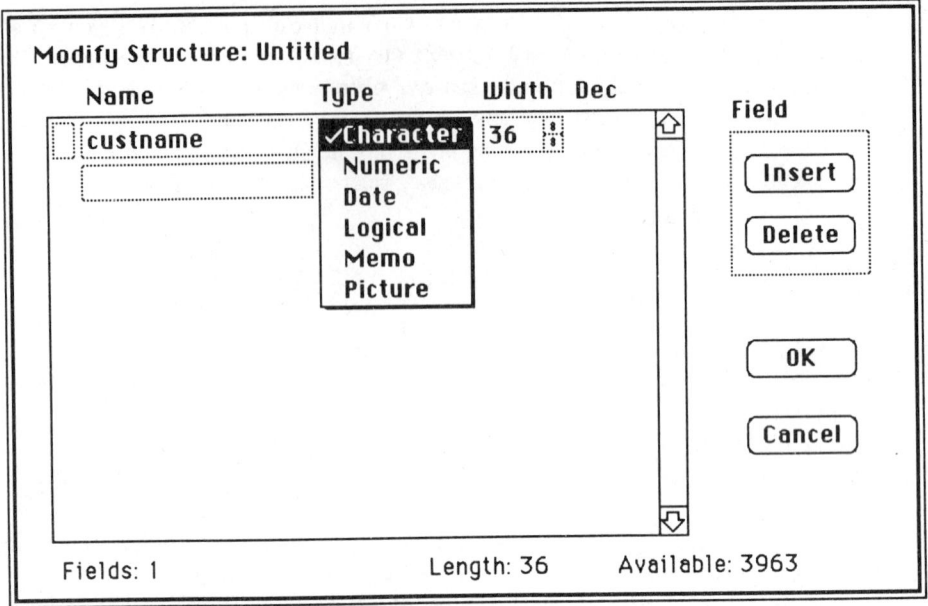

Fig. 2-7. Selecting what type of data to use for a field.

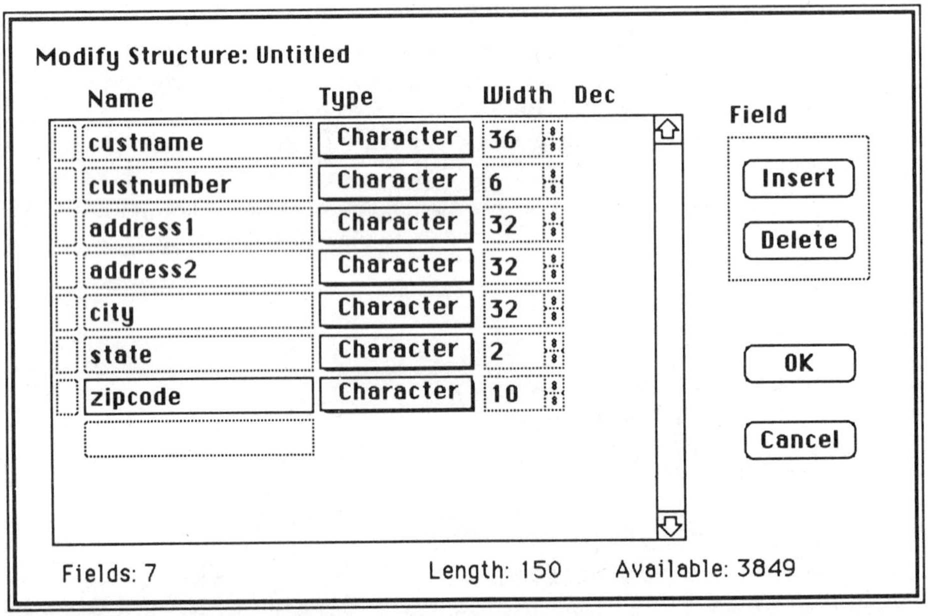

Fig. 2-8. A complete set of field column names.

14   *Creating A FoxBASE+/Mac Database File*

The Mac tutorial provided by Apple Computer can quickly make you an efficient mouse user. If you need help navigating, refer to the tutorial or experiment. Don't be afraid to explore. There's nothing to hurt that can't be replaced, so now is the time to learn by doing—mistakes are allowed.

If you cannot change fields or add new ones, that's FoxBASE's way of saying that it has already started a type of change that must be completed before another type of change can begin. It is best to press OK so it can complete the changes, then re-open the file with the File/Open menu option and select the Database/Setup menu option. When you press Modify you will be back where you started and any changes can be made.

Entering the Data Type

After you have entered *custname* into the first Name box, you need to select the type of data that the field will hold. Click in the Type box immediately to the right of the field Name box.

The Type box is called a popup menu because it gives you several options when it's selected. Data types instruct the computer what type of information will be in each field—character, numeric, data, logical, memo, or picture. A data type must be specified for each field. Select the *Character* data type.

Sizing the Field

Deciding on a width for some fields can be difficult. Nevertheless, FoxBASE needs to be told how big the biggest customer name will be. In order to supply enough room for big company names, you should select a relatively large number. In the Width box, enter *36*.

Note that, if you press one of the arrows next to the width number, it will change automatically. Fortunately, FoxBASE allows you to change the width after the file is saved. To change the width, re-open the file and select Database/Setup/Modify.

Adding Fields and Saving the File

Complete the database as shown in Fig. 2-8. When you're done, click the OK button. When you have finished defining the customer database, a file-saving dialog box will ask you to name the new file. Enter *Customer* in the box and then click the Save button.

Although you have successfully defined, created, and saved a new database file, Fox-BASE knows that it's just an empty shell without information, so the question will appear, "Input data records now?" Answer by clicking the Yes button.

Congratulations, you have just created a database file. An append screen will now appear, letting you enter actual data into the file. We'll get back to this file in Chapter 5, where you will have an opportunity to relate it to another file and to print reports and labels. You may want to try entering some sample customer information just for fun. Go for it! When you're done, save the data by pressing the Exit button in the top right corner. You can add information at any time by opening the database file and selecting the Record/Append menu options.

3
The Menu System

MACINTOSH friendliness is legendary. Part of the reason for its reputation is a menu system that lets users bounce from place to place on a whim. This chapter is designed to be a quick tour of FoxBASE's menu options and a launching pad for exploration.

FoxBASE records everything you do with the menus, then turns them into visible commands, and finally, acts upon them. After FoxBASE does an action you first selected with a menu, you can view, edit, and execute the command again in the Command window. You can also go directly to the Command window, bypassing menus altogether, to tell FoxBASE what to do. See Fig. 3-1. Another benefit of this menuing and command system is that you can save menu choices for later use by going to the Command window to run the recorded commands over and over. You can even modify commands and reissue them again.

It's good to know "the lay of the land," before launching out across it. Don't be discouraged if some of the options don't make perfect sense to you. If you're new at this, it won't be clear to you how everything works and fits together. The purpose of going through the menus for the first time is to learn what's there so you can remember it's there when you need it. Read through this chapter completely and explore the screens presented by each menu option for yourself, you'll learn what FoxBASE has to offer and how to find what you want when you need it.

HOW TO NAVIGATE

Macintosh menus have some characteristics you should be familiar with. A black menu means that option is available for selection, turning grey when it's not. The FoxBASE Program menu shown in Fig. 3-2 illustrates how menus look when they are in different stages.

Notice that the Talk option has a check mark by it. This means that the option is like a

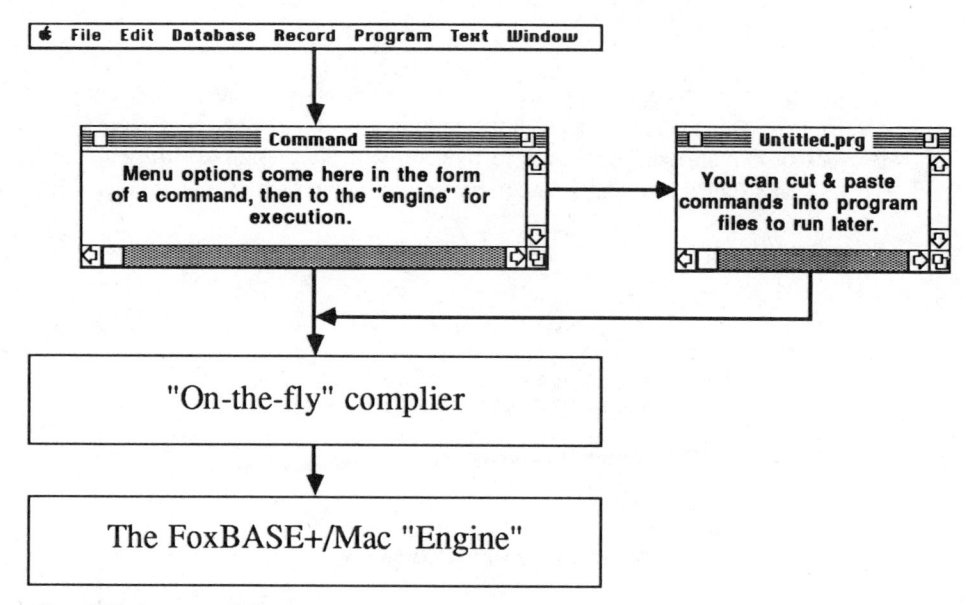

Fig. 3-1. Command-driven.

Fig. 3-2. Grey options aren't accessible.

switch. When the check mark is there, Talk is ON; when it isn't there, Talk is OFF. To turn Talk OFF, select the Talk option. Do it again and it goes back on.

    Menu choices that have three dots open a dialog box before executing. In the Program menu, for example, the Do, Compile, and Generate options all have a dialog box that asks you which program you want to run, compile, or generate. But that's not all. Look at Fig. 3-2 again, the little propeller and the "D" next to the Do option means there's a keyboard shortcut for people who would rather press keys than reach for the mouse.

How to Navigate   17

The Cursor

The cursor can be called a pointer because it moves with your mouse and has lots of personality, changing to indicate what the computer is doing. Figure 3-3 shows the different types of cursors FoxBASE uses to indicate what it's doing at different times. The Arrow, Beach Ball, Help, and Text cursors are the pointer's most common visible forms.

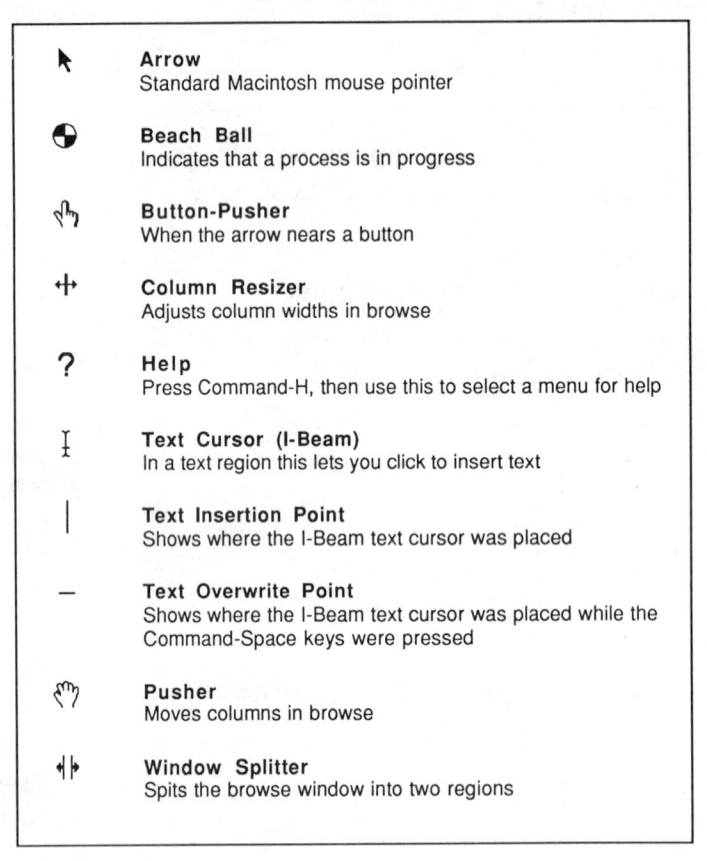

Icon	Name	Description
▸	Arrow	Standard Macintosh mouse pointer
⊕	Beach Ball	Indicates that a process is in progress
☞	Button-Pusher	When the arrow nears a button
↔	Column Resizer	Adjusts column widths in browse
?	Help	Press Command-H, then use this to select a menu for help
I	Text Cursor (I-Beam)	In a text region this lets you click to insert text
|	Text Insertion Point	Shows where the I-Beam text cursor was placed
—	Text Overwrite Point	Shows where the I-Beam text cursor was placed while the Command-Space keys were pressed
✋	Pusher	Moves columns in browse
◀▶	Window Splitter	Spits the browse window into two regions

Fig. 3-3. FoxBASE+/Mac cursors.

Keyboard Shortcuts

Power users can use a number of keyboard options to execute menu options without reaching for the mouse. The mouse, however, does have some tricks that can make your work easier, such as triple clicking to select a whole sentence or paragraph. Other shortcuts that are part of each menu are listed in Appendix D. The Option, Control key, and Shift keys are used in combination with other keys to perform menu choices and other tasks. Notice that the Command key is not labeled command, instead, it's marked with a symbol that looks like a propeller or clover leaf.

Recording Menu Choices and Playing Them Back

An incredibly useful feature in FoxBASE is automatic command recording (see Fig. 3-1). Not only is command recording useful in its own right, but it reveals the way Fox-BASE thinks. Like a court reporter who catches every word, whether you want it recorded or not, FoxBASE writes everything you do with the menus into the Command window so you can execute it later or store it in a program file. The recorder is smart enough to know exactly what to record. It filters out any unnecessary steps that you do with the menus and records only those things that are executable in the Command window. To learn how it works, try this short exercise:

Step 1. Select the Window/Command menu option. Do you see the Command window? It probably has nothing in it. Resize it so that it is a few inches wide and one or two inches tall. The resize box is in the window's lower right corner. You can move the window by clicking on the top "title" bar and dragging the mouse. Pull it into view near the bottom of your screen.

Step 2. Select the File/Open menu option so that a dialog box appears, displaying files and folders. Select and open the folder marked *Sample*. The display window will change to show the files inside the sample folder. Select and open any database file. (If you have not installed all of the sample files that came with FoxBASE, you can select any database file you like for our purposes.

Step 3. Open the View window by selecting the Window/View menu option. Adjust the windows so that you can see at least a part of each one. In the View window, the file you used should appear in the top circle, area A. You can select any window by pressing the mouse button once inside it. Click the mouse on the small browse button that appears on the lower left side of the View window. A Browse window will open. To close the Browse window, press the mouse pointer in the little box at the top left corner.

Step 4. Select the Command window again by clicking inside it once. Do you see the *USE* and *BROWSE* commands recorded? Type *CLOSE DATA* into the Command window and press return. The file that was in the View window will go away at your command.

Saving Program Files

This exercise demonstrates how the menus and the commands work together. But that's not all there is. You can also replay the commands and you can save them for later. If the Command window is still selected, click the cursor once on the line that has the *USE* command so that the little insertion bar sticks, then press return on the keyboard. You have just replayed that command. The file should reappear in the View window's work area A. Try the same thing with the *CLOSE DATA* command that you typed in earlier. It should go away. The following exercise shows you how to save a program file.

Step 1. Select all of the text in the Command window by placing the mouse pointer at the left edge of the first command line. Hold the mouse button down and drag the pointer to the right side of the last command line in the window. Release the mouse button. The text should be white on black. If it isn't, try again until it is.

Step 2. Select the Edit/Copy menu option to put the selected text into the Macintosh

How to Navigate 19

clipboard. Although you can't see it, it's being held in a temporary memory location called a clipboard.

Step 3. Select the File/New menu option and press the Program button when the dialog box appears. Click *OK* to tell FoxBASE you want to create a new program file so that it will open a text window for you. If the window is too big, resize it to match the Command window.

Step 4. Select the new window titled *Untitled.prg* by clicking inside it once; then copy the contents of the clipboard into it by selecting the Edit/Paste menu option. Did you see the text from the Command window pop in there? If it didn't, reselect the Command window and do the copy-paste again.

Step 5. Save your new program by clicking in the close box of the *Untitled.prg* Program window (upper left corner). Answer *YES* when it asks if you want to save the file. A dialog box will appear asking you to name the program. Enter any name you like where it says "Save current document," then press the SAVE button.

Step 6. Try out the new program by selecting the Program/Do menu. A dialog appears and your program will be there. Select it and press DO. All of the steps you first created with menus, and the one you typed yourself, became part of the program which executes as though you went through the same steps yourself with menus, only faster.

The purpose of this exercise was to familiarize you with the way FoxBASE "thinks." It would be sad if you learned how to do wonders with FoxBASE but always had to be there yourself to do them. With program recording and playback, you can automate complex tasks as you want. You can also repeat commands just by putting the text insertion bar anywhere on a command line in the Command window and pressing return. That's power!

The Help System

There are two ways to get help from FoxBASE. One way is to look up a command or topic by name, the other is to point at a menu option to get a description of what it does.

Developers take note: The FoxBASE help system can be customized for use in applications—see Chapter 7, Developing the User Interface.

For topical help, select the Help option under the Apple menu. Figure 3-4 shows the topic screen and the detail screen that appears when you select a topic. To use the topic window, press the Help button or double-click on a topic. When the detail screen appears, you can scan with the Next and Previous buttons, or you can return to the topic screen to select another. Much of the FoxBASE reference manual is contained in the help system.

For help with menu options, press *Command-?* to change the cursor into a question mark. Then you can use this special cursor to select any menu item and a help screen describing its use will appear.

THE FILE MENU

The file menu options are designed to let you create, open, print, and save files. At one time or another, every file you deal with will be subject to choices you make in the file

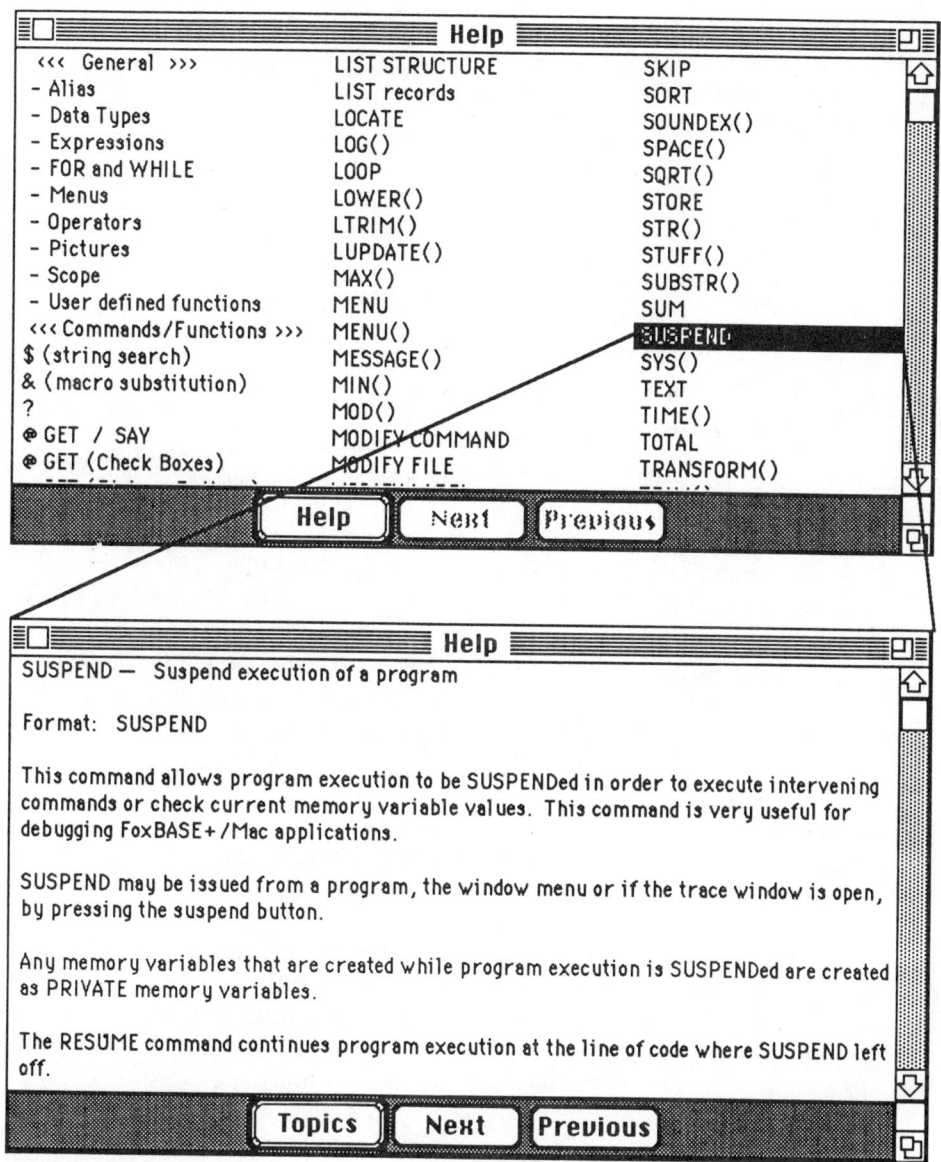

Fig. 3-4. The help system.

menu because it serves as a gatekeeper, so to speak. Each of its options is listed and explained below.

New

When you select the File/New menu, a dialog (see Fig. 3-5) will open to ask what type of file you want to create. Some menu options might be grey until at least one database file is in use because they are specifically designed to work with opened database

The File Menu 21

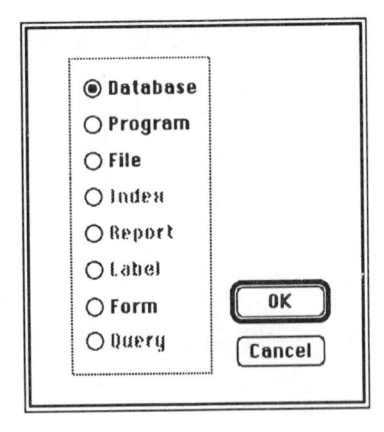

Fig. 3-5. Selecting a file type.

files. This is why Index, Report, and Label file options are grey if you haven't yet opened or created a database file. (Note: The Query file option was an unimplemented notion in version 1.x that was dropped entirely by the time version 2.x was released. You aren't missing anything by its omission. Also, report and label files differ in versions 1.x and 2.x. Version 2.x uses one button and generator to create both. Unlike version 1.x, where there is a separate generator for labels and reports.)

By selecting the Database option, you will see a dialog such as the one shown in Fig. 2-7, the Modify Structure. To create a new database file enter the field names, the type of information (data type) that will be stored in the field, and the field's width. See the entry for CREATE in Chapter 8 to learn how to create a new database file.

The Program option opens a simple text editing window (see Fig. 3-6). Program files are like other simple text files except that they contain only commands and statements that FoxBASE can understand and execute. When you save a program file, FoxBASE compiles it into object code which it alone can understand and execute, and saves it in a hidden portion of the program file.

The File option produces a window just like the Program window except that it's for text-only files. Text files have various purposes. FoxBASE can create text files with names and addresses for mail merging, and it can be used to make report files that contain anything a printed report can. Text files created by programs are called alternate files because they are an alternate way to output data, an alternative, that is, to display or print.

The File creating, opening, and saving options allow you to edit text files without having to use a word processor. Text files and program files are similar, but FoxBASE won't

Fig. 3-6. The program file editing window.

22   The File Menu

try to read and understand the text in a file that's not called a program file unless you direct it to do so from the Program/Compile menu. This turns the text file into a program file by compiling the text and saving its object code in an invisible part of the new program file called the resource fork (the other fork is called the data fork).

Index files are used to supplement database files by putting them in an apparent order. Figure 3-7 shows what the new index file dialog looks like. To create an index file, follow the directions in Chapter 8 for the INDEX command. Figure 3-8 shows how index files change the apparent order of a database file without actually changing any data at all. Index files are handy because they can be created any time they are needed. When an index file is active it's as though the database were in the physical order of the index file.

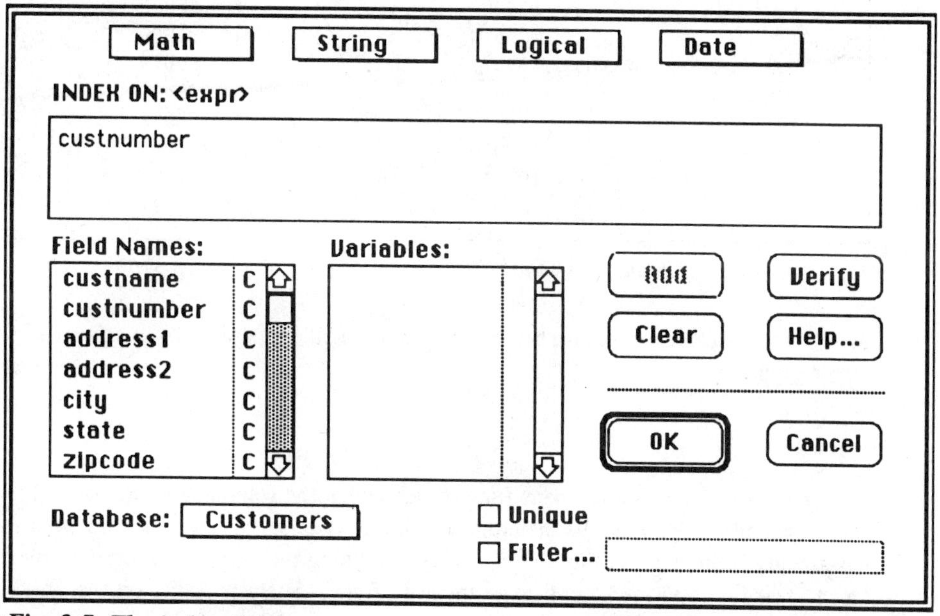

Fig. 3-7. The index dialog.

Report files are just what their name implies, output forms that print or display data from one or more files. The command CREATE REPORT in Chapter 8 describes how they're created.

Label files are like report files in that they format output to the screen or a printer, except that they print labels. See the entry, CREATE LABEL, in Chapter 8 for information about how to create and use them.

Form files, also called screen files, are covered in Chapter 7. They are special intermediate-type files that define what custom entry and editing screens should look like. The reason they are intermediate is because they are used to define and create screen forms, they are not the forms themselves. Form files are most often used when you are drawing a screen to layout fields, variables, pictures, text, and so on, and then you save the drawing as a form file. From the form file you can generate an entry and editing format (actually a program file with an extension of .FMT) from the drawing. The benefit of this approach is twofold; you can modify the form file and regenerate a new entry format from it immedi-

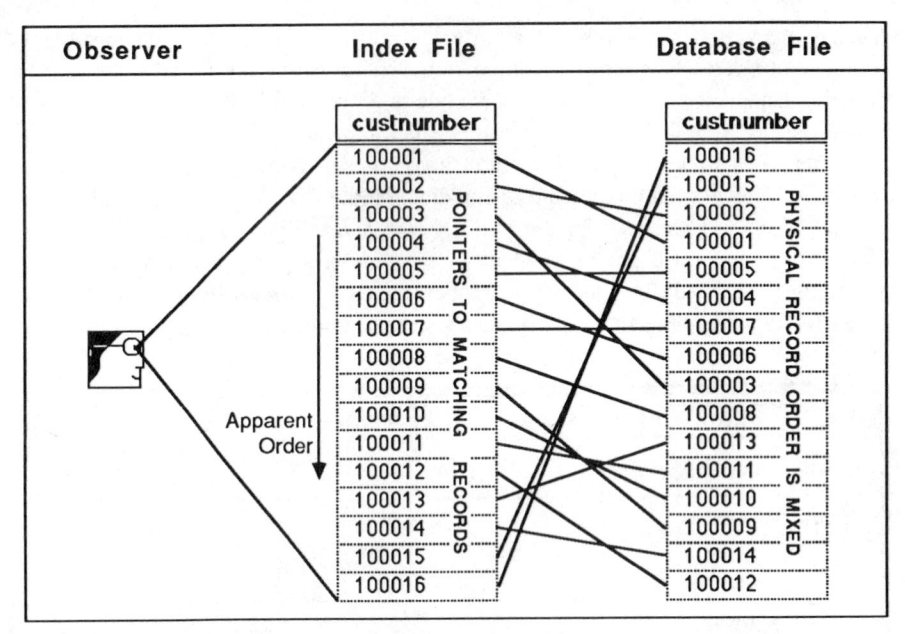

Fig. 3-8. Indexing makes a virtual file.

ately, and you can incorporate the program statements generated by the form file into a larger program.

Open

The open menu simply opens files. It does what the File/New menu does with just a few differences. One obvious difference is that it assumes that the file you want to open has already been created. Figure 3-9 shows the dialog that appears when you select File/Open. The file types are identical to those in Fig. 3-5. By pressing on the FoxBASE+/Mac bar at the top you can select a higher-level or lower-level folder. In this case, the FoxBASE name just happens to be the name of the current folder. The Eject, Drive, Open, New, and Cancel buttons are common across all Macintosh applications.

Only the type of file that has been selected by the radio button (at the bottom) will show up in the scrolling window. Files that FoxBASE+/Mac has never opened might not show up, especially if they were created on a computer other than a Macintosh.

The Macintosh records an application (in this case, FoxBASE) name with every file it saves, along with its type so that an icon can be displayed and double-clicked. You can use the All Files checkbox to make database files show up, for example, even if FoxBASE did not create them. When you select such a file and press the Open button, FoxBASE will check the file and open it for you. From that point, the file will show up as a database file in this dialog and display a FoxBASE icon because FoxBASE "brands" it when it is saved. FoxBASE is smart and will open index files as index files, program files as program files, and so on, regardless of how you open them.

24   *The File Menu*

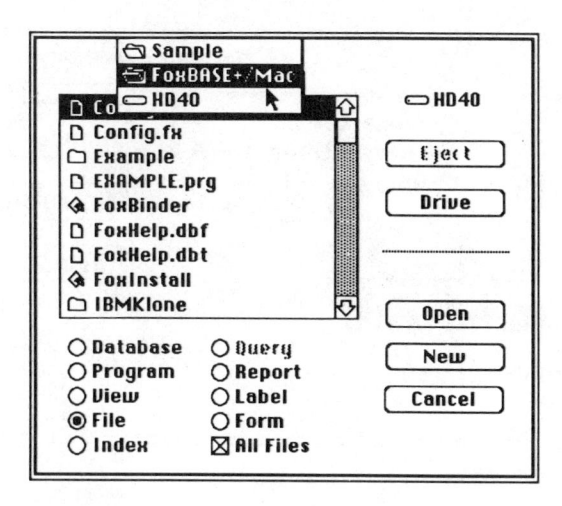

Fig. 3-9. The file picking dialog.

Close

Close is probably in the wrong place because it doesn't close any files unless they contain programs or text, and then only when the file is in a currently selected window. Close does exactly the same thing as pressing the close box in the upper left corner of an open window.

Save

Save has the same limitations as File/Close. It works only with text and program files. The difference is that it saves the file to disk without closing the window. When you're writing a program, it's a good idea to hit this menu or frequently press Command-S to save your work from being lost by a power failure or other mishap.

Save As

Save As allows you to save a file after selecting a new name for it. It works with text files like the Close and Save options, and it's also the way to save a view file. For more information about how view files work, see the *Create View* section in Chapter 8.

Revert

Revert is similar to closing the currently active text or Program window/file and reopening it so that the net result is to revert to the last saved version. Use this option when you have accidentally done something to the file you didn't intend to do. For some reason, I use options like this frequently.

Page Size

Figure 3-10 shows a special screen that appears only if the selected printer (in the Chooser) is some type of Imagewriter. The Page Size dialog box lets you select what page

Fig. 3-10. The page size dialog.

sizes you want in the Page Setup dialog box under "US Letter," "US Legal," "Computer Paper," and so on. Changes made in the Page Size dialog box won't retroactively effect setups made using the Page Setup dialog box, but subsequent changes will be affected so that FoxBASE will interpret page sizes in the Page Setup dialog as they have last been set in the Page Size dialog.

This is a powerful feature that's especially useful for making label size adjustments, because the Report/Label generator gets its page size information from page setups. In fact, you can even rename pages at will. For example, you could rename the A4 or B5 Letter choices so that they automatically reflect a name brand of labels you frequently use. This way, selecting them from the Page Setup dialog box is as easy as a mouse click.

Page Setup

Figure 3-11 shows the Macintosh page preparation dialog. Press the Help button if you want to know more about each option. Wide reports should not be printed unless you adjust the orientation to the sideways—or landscape, as opposed to portrait—mode. Print jobs follow the page setup you last established.

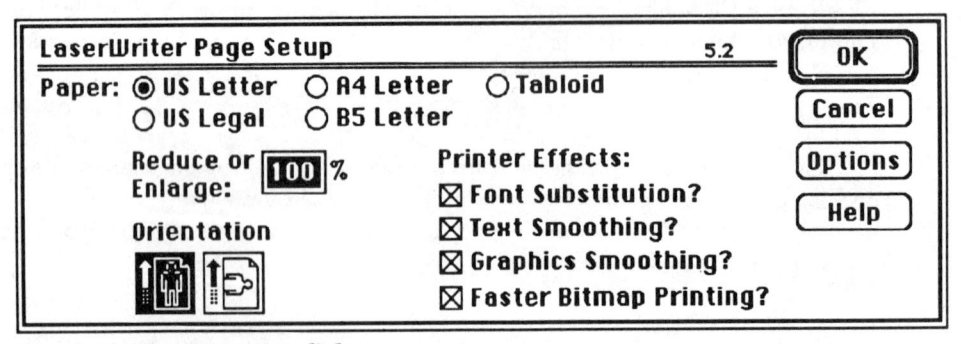

Fig. 3-11. The page setup dialog.

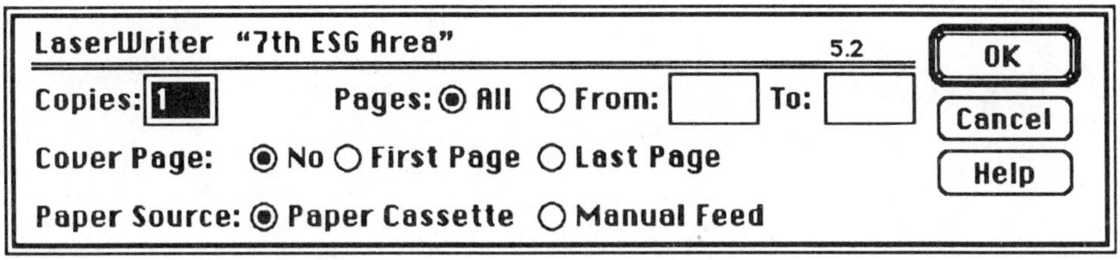

```
┌─────────────────────────────────────────────────────────────┐
│ LaserWriter  "7th ESG Area"                    5.2  │  OK   │
│ Copies: [1]     Pages: ◉ All  ○ From: [ ]  To: [ ]  │ Cancel│
│ Cover Page:   ◉ No  ○ First Page  ○ Last Page       │ Help  │
│ Paper Source: ◉ Paper Cassette   ○ Manual Feed      │       │
└─────────────────────────────────────────────────────────────┘
```

Fig. 3-12. The print dialog.

Print

Print brings forth the dialog shown in Fig. 3-12 where you can specify how many copies, which pages, and other specifics you want to print. Press the Help button to learn more about each option. Text and program files can be printed any time they're in an active window. Screen form files that are used to create screen layouts are not printable.

It's important to know that this option is not the way to get data printouts. The three primary ways to get data printed are through the Database/Report and Database/Label menus, or by using a DISPLAY or LIST command. Report and label printing requires that you first make a report or label form file for the database via the File/New menu option. The DISPLAY and LIST commands are quick ways to get information out of a file and onto the screen or printer. There are no menu options for them, however, so take a look at their entries in Chapter 8 to see how they work. When you're printing data, you don't need to select the File/Print menu at all. It will appear automatically as a result of whatever type of print request you make, such as display, list, report, or label.

Copy File, Delete File, and Rename File

The copy file, delete file and rename file options do what their names suggest. You can copy, delete, or rename files directly from the Macintosh desktop, or you can use the FoxBASE methods. The dialog boxes that appear when you select these options are shown in Fig. 3-13.

Quit

The Quit option exits FoxBASE after all open files are closed. If you have not saved and closed a text or program file that contains changes that haven't been written to the disk, you can save them before quitting via an automatic dialog such as the one shown in Fig. 3-14. Notice that the Command-Q keystrokes can also quit the program.

THE EDIT MENU

The edit menu has text editing tools that can be used whenever any window containing text is active. Editable text includes the Command window, in text files, in program files,

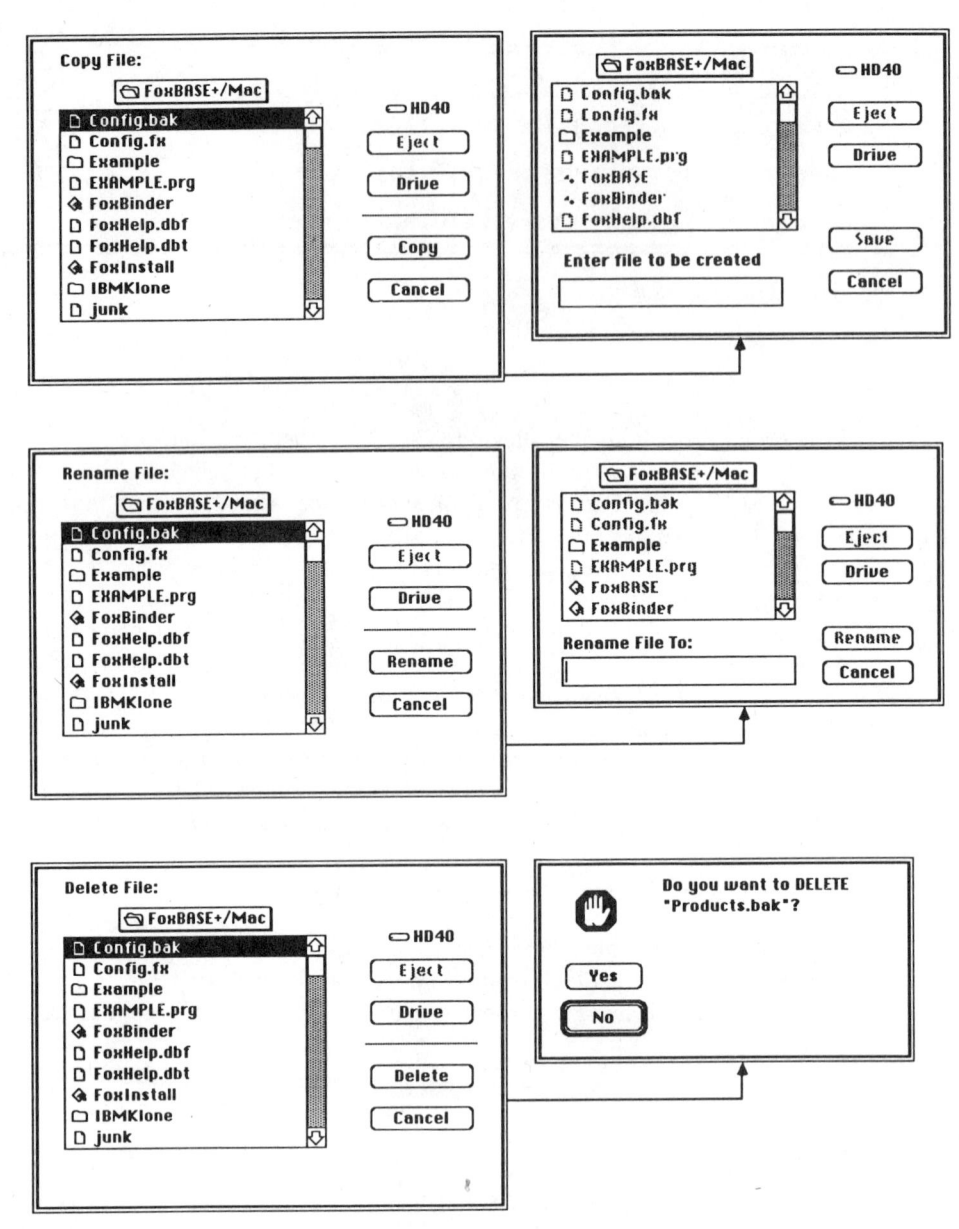

Fig. 3-13. The Copy, Rename, and Delete dialogs.

or in database memo fields. Because these tools work on any selected window containing text, you can have many windows open and use the edit menu to help you with each and every one in-turn. The cut, copy, and paste functions can even be used to move text from one window to another.

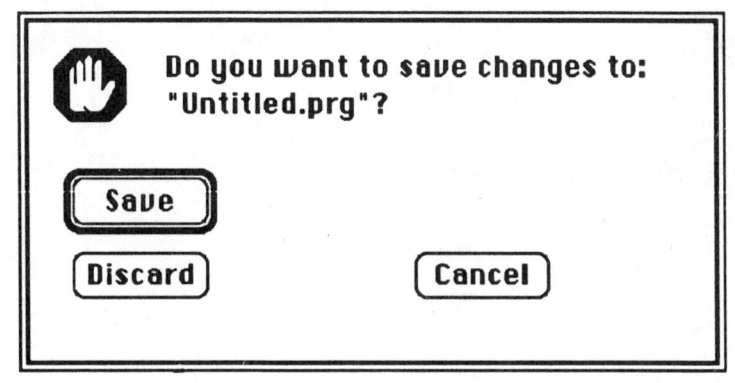

Fig. 3-14. The Save alert.

Undo

The Undo function undoes the last cut, copy, or paste that was completed.

Cut

The Cut option is used to delete or to move a selection of text. If you simply cut text after selecting it, you won't get it back—it's like selecting text and then pressing the delete key. If you cut text and then use the paste option, however, you can, in effect, move it from one place to another.

Copy

The Copy option lets you select text then stores it so you can use the paste option to place a copy of it somewhere else. It has no use except with the paste option.

Paste

The Paste option works with the cut or copy options to put text in a new location. To select the location for pasting, simply set the insertion bar by clicking once where you want text; then execute the paste option (see Fig. 3-15). The cut, copy, and paste options can move text between any text editing regions in a database file, memo fields, programs, or even the Command window. Use these options to move text from the Command window to an empty new program file for saving.

Clear

The Clear option is equivalent to pressing the delete key because it permanently erases any currently selected text.

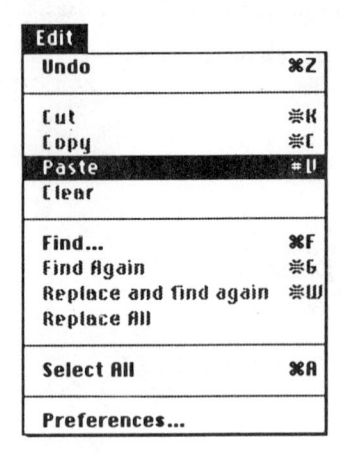

Fig. 3-15. The edit menu.

Find

The Find option lets you search for text in an active text window (see Fig. 3-16), or in a database file when you are browsing (see Fig. 3-17). You enter standard characters, numbers, and signs as they are, but to find a carriage return enter Option-D followed by an "R." To find a form-feed, enter Option-D followed by an "F," to find a line feed enter Option-D followed by an "N," and to find a tab enter Option-D followed by a "T."

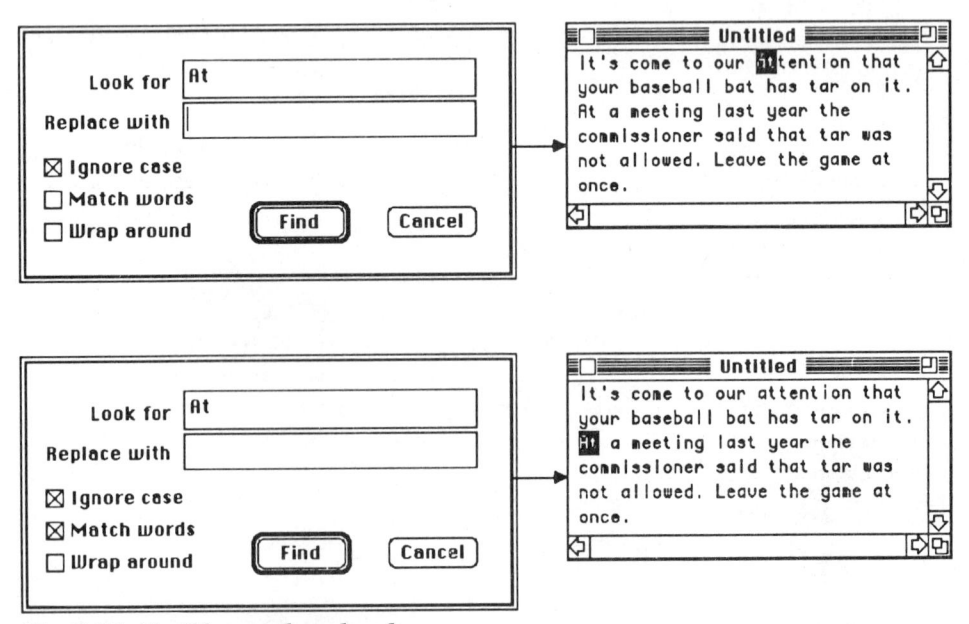

Fig. 3-16. Flexible search and replace.

30 The Edit Menu

Fig. 3-17. The find dialog can be used when browsing data.

Ignore case, means it doesn't matter if letters are entered in uppercase or lowercase. Match words means that the text you are looking for must be a whole word, not part of a word. Wrap around means that it doesn't matter if a group of words are split between two lines by line feeds or carriage returns. The find starts from the location of the insertion point, looking through the document to the end of the file.

The special find dialog shown in Fig. 3-17 can locate any number or a string of characters in an open Browse window. It ignores the case of characters, and always starts searching from the topmost record in the browsed file.

Find Again

The Find Again option is equivalent to doing a find again from the spot where text or numbers were last found.

Replace and Find Again

The Replace and Find Again option lets you look for the next occurrence of the search text and replace matching text all the way through a file. When you have to make global changes throughout a file, this is handy and safe because you approve each replacement by pressing Command-G (a keyboard shortcut).

Replace All

The Replace All option is similar to replace and find again, except that it's automatic and doesn't ask your approval for each replacement. Use this option with caution.

Select All

The Select All option does what its name implies. This is a handy option when you want to cut or copy all of the text in a file and paste it into another one.

Preferences

The Preferences option menu lets you adjust some default text editing options to your liking (see Fig. 3-18). You can make the options affect all text files, or a file in a currently active window:

- Wrap words makes sentences fit inside the window by splitting them up into as many lines as needed. This is usually preferable for narrative text or reports on file. Programs are more readable when each command starts and ends on one line, even if it is inconvenient to scroll left and right to see it.
- The Auto indent option causes a new line to start in the column (from the left) that the line above it started in. Programs are sometimes easier to write this way, especially if they use a lot of indentation.
- Make backup, makes a copy of the file (stored with the extension ".bak") you are editing when it opens it so that you can go back to it if problems occur with the one you're editing.
- Add line feeds is useful when Macintosh and DOS (or other) computers frequently share files by disk swapping, and particularly by network access. DOS computers expect that a line feed control code exists next to every carriage return, but Macintosh computers don't, so they can wrap text dynamically to fit into moveable windows. If you are creating program files to be used by DOS FoxBASE users, you need to set this option before saving them. If you receive program files from a DOS computer, the Macintosh will read them without any problem, even though they have line feeds. For more information, see Chapter 10.

THE DATABASE MENU

The database menu will be a hot spot of activity after you've built a database and are busy using it. Some of the options here are also available in the View window, but import and export options and controls to print reports and labels are found only here. Figure 3-19 shows the menu in version 1.x. In version 2.x, the Flush option is gone and the Report and Label options are combined into one item.

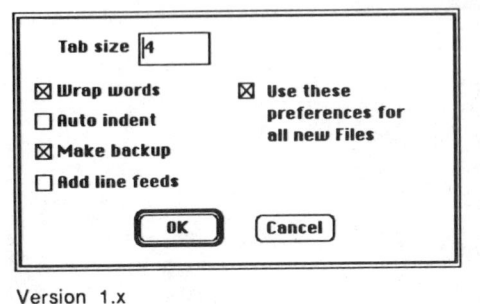

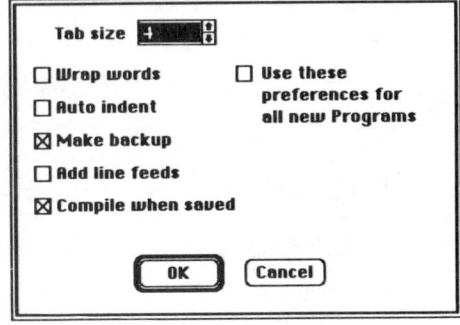

Version 1.x

Version 2.x

Fig. 3-18. The preferences dialog.

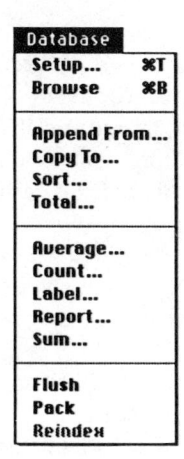

Fig. 3-19. The Database menu.

Setup

The Setup options bring forth an imposing dialog box (see Fig. 3-20) that controls indexes, data filters, and field selectors. This option even has the ability to modify the structure of a database file. The setup options are briefly covered here, but if you want to master this very important tool, read Chapter 5, Working with Data.

The Modify option is the button above the fields list in the setup dialog. If you press it, you will see a screen where you can modify the database file by adding or deleting fields, or by changing their name, width, or data type. Fields in the current database file are listed in the left scrolling window of the setup dialog.

Fig. 3-20. The database setup dialog.

The Database Menu   33

The Index option on the right half of the setup dialog lists up to seven possible index orders. Indexes can be added, modified, removed from the selection list, or selected to control the alphabetic or numeric order of records.

The Set Fields option, a checkbox below the scrolling fields list, is used to pick fields from the larger list for visibility while browsing, entering data, reporting, and so on. After a field selection has been made, the On and Off buttons adjacent to the set fields checkbox determine whether the selected list, or the whole list, is visible.

The Filter option opens a dialog where you can set a condition that limits the visible records to those that meet one or more criteria. If there is an "X" in the checkbox it means that a filter is in effect. In that case, its condition would be listed in the long rectangular box to the right of the filter checkbox.

The Format option opens a dialog where you can determine which format file to use for data entry and editing. FoxBASE has standard, but boring, screens where data can be entered and edited one record at a time. You can exchange these screens with designs of your own by creating a new form file and selecting it here for your database. If there is an *X* in the checkbox it means that a format file has been selected to replace the standard FoxBASE screen, and its name would appear in the long rectangular box to the right of the format checkbox.

Browse

Figure 3-21 shows what the Browse and Change windows look like. Browse lets you locate and change data visually. It's like a fast-scrolling spreadsheet for traversing a file quickly. File relations set in the View window automatically cause the Browse window that's related to a parent to update itself whenever you select it. Once a Browse window is opened, a new menu appears on the screen, allowing you to change the window's appearance and to toggle back and forth with the Change window (see Fig. 3-21).

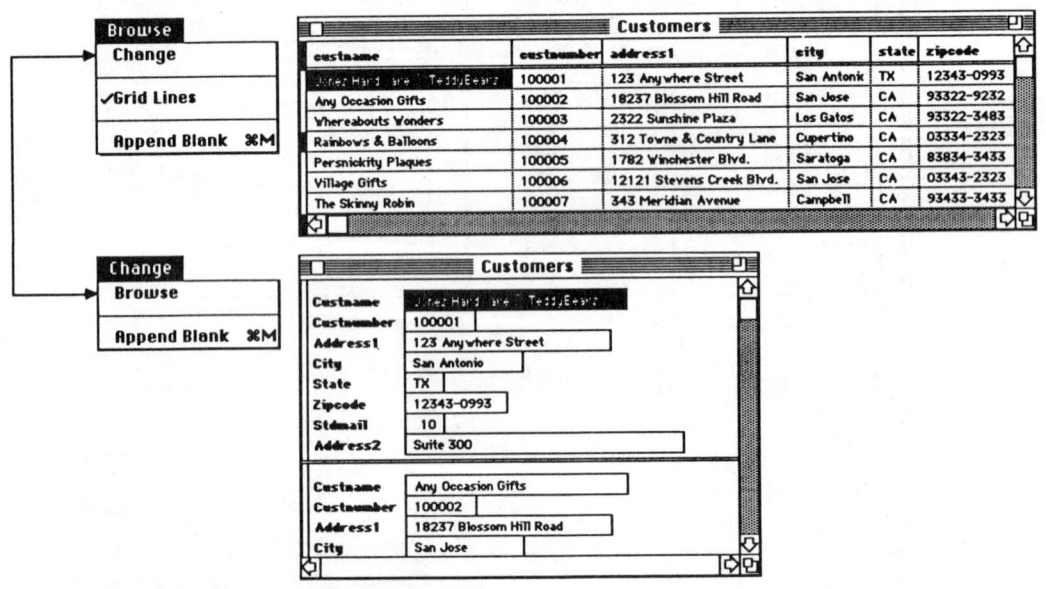

Fig. 3-21. The Browse and Change windows.

Append From

The Append From option imports data from other files, including dBASE files, other FoxBASE files, and ASCII files delimited by tabs, commas and spaces.

There are choices you will have to make before importing a file: tabs work well moving data back and forth between spreadsheets such as Excel. Commas are the most common way to move mail merge data back and forth between word processors.

Chapter 8 includes an entry for the APPEND command that explains and illustrates the technical aspects of importing data. Figure 3-22 shows the dialog that this option brings forward. The process of importing involves the selection of a file to import from, selecting the format of the data to be imported (the types were just mentioned above), and selecting data-discriminating filter criteria.

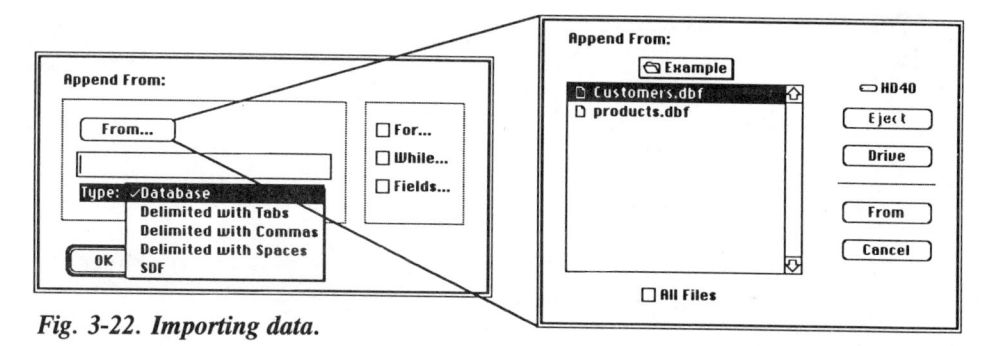

Fig. 3-22. Importing data.

Copy To

The Copy To option is similar to the append from option except that it exports data instead of importing it. You can select which fields to export. You can also export directly to word processors and spreadsheets. See the section *COPY TO* in Chapter 8 for more details on exporting.

Sort

Sorting is especially useful when you want to give someone a selected portion of the data in your file. Sorting a database file doesn't actually sort the file you're working on; it copies the source file into a new file in sorted order, leaving the old file intact. There are options for sorting. You can limit the number of fields from the source file to be copied into the sorted file, and use filters for selecting records to copy, as well as other options. Indexes, which are created in the Database/Setup dialog, are usually preferable to sorts. Figure 3-23 shows what the sort dialog looks like. If you want to learn more about sorting, see the SORT TO entry in Chapter 8.

Total

The Total option lets you create a new database file containing totals from the numeric fields in any open database file. It creates a new record in the output file for each grouping of records that occurs in the source file. Groups are determined by the sort or indexed order of the source file's records. A key field (which is selected by the "Total ON" option) tells FoxBASE which field to group. The numbers in each record of the target file are a sum of each group's numeric fields in the source file. Figure 3-24 shows the total dialog. For further details on totalling, see the *TOTAL* section in Chapter 8.

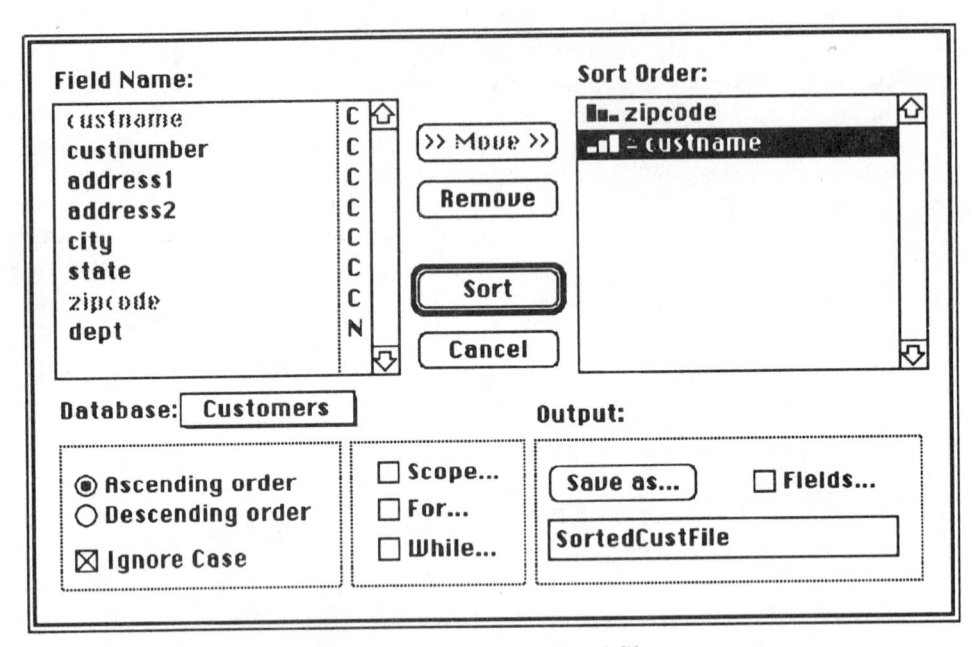

Fig. 3-23. Use the Sort option to make a new, ordered file.

Fig. 3-24. The Total option creates a file containing all totals.

36   **The Database Menu**

Average

The Average option produces numbers that represent the average of every numeric field in a database file and displays them on the screen. You can also use this option to store an average in a memory variable, but the field's name and the variable name must be explicitly identified. See the AVERAGE entry in Chapter 8 for more information.

Count

The Count option simply counts records and displays the result. It can also store the total in a memory variable. What makes count useful is that it can count records in a file that meet a condition, such as, "How many people in the city of Tuskjaw own a pet Yak?" Count works like the average option because you can use it to specify a FOR or WHILE condition. The dialog for counting is shown in Fig. 3-25. See the Chapter 8 entry COUNT for more information.

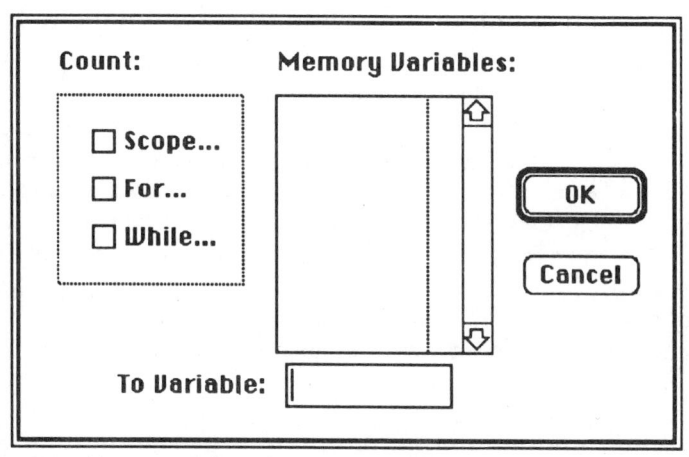

Fig. 3-25. Counting records.

Label (Version 1.x)

The Label option can be used to view or print a predefined label form file that was created using the File/New/Label menu option. (See Fig. 3-26.) Label form files merely format the data in a file for printing on labels. There must be a match between the field names in the label form and the database selected for printing. You can type in a name or you can press the Form button to select a label form that's been saved on disk. The Scope, For, and While options filter the data printed, and the Prompt option, if selected, causes the Macintosh print dialog to appear before printing begins so you can set the number of pages, amount of reduction, etc. See Chapter 5, or the *CREATE LABEL* command section in Chapter 8 for more detailed information.

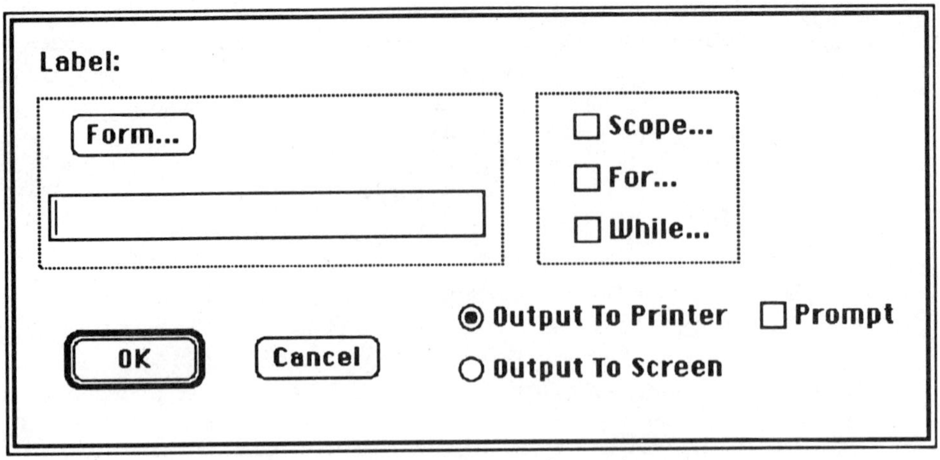

Fig. 3-26. Selecting a label form and which records to print.

Report (Version 1.x)

The Report option prints data using report form files and the currently selected database file (see Fig. 3-27). Use the File/New/Report menu option to create a report form file, and then print data from a selected database file in the prescribed format by the form file. The report can be seen on screen or printed. The Plain and Heading options in the report dialog tell FoxBASE to print a report with or without page numbers and dates, and to include or omit an optional one-line heading. Headings can include data or they can simply consist of text. A summary report includes group totals only as defined in the report form itself. The Prompt option causes FoxBASE to bring forward a standard print dialog before printing so you can set the amount of reduction and number of copies to be printed.

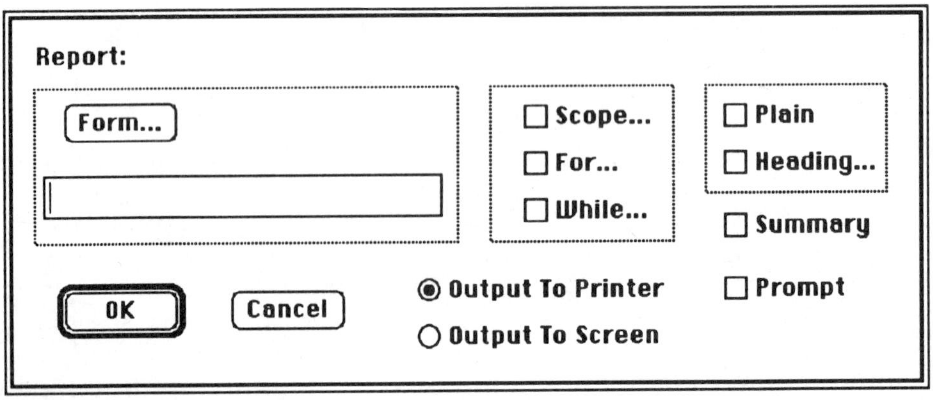

Version 1.x

Fig. 3-27. Selecting report forms and options.

Fig. 3-27. Continued.

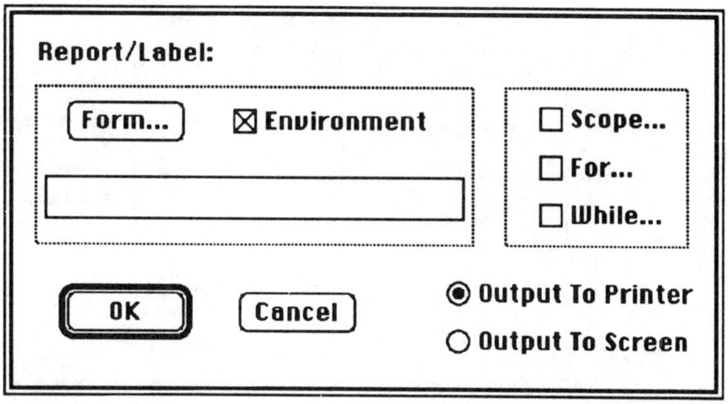

Version 2.x

Report/Label (Version 2.x)

The new generator in Version 2.x does labels and reports in one design environment. It also gives you the completely new ability to print lines, boxes, multiple fonts, and even pictures. Fox discontinued the one that was shipped in version 1.x because it's design was too reminiscent of their DOS database. Consequently, Version 2.x has only one menu item and one option dialog to serve for both labels and reports, and this menu is for invoking reports or printing labels after a report or label file has been defined and saved. Use the file menu to create and define new reports and labels. There is a new environment checkbox that didn't exist in Version 1.x. If it is checked, FoxBASE will look for a View file with the same name as the report or label file. Note that View files can be made automatically if the Save Environment box is checked at the time you save a new report or label file.

Sum

The Sum option adds the numbers in numeric fields (see Fig. 3-28). Sum is most useful when a FOR clause is used to select records for summing. It's rarely useful to sum a whole database, unless it contains homogenous information. WHILE clauses are useful only if you have already placed the database pointer at the top of a sorted group of records. For more information about Expressions, Scopes, FOR and WHILE clauses, see Chapter 6.

Flush

The Flush option is a protective command that can save you grief. Version 2.x automatically flushes data from memory onto the disk where it's safe from power or computer failures. Although version 1.x does this also, it is less frequent. It's wise when using a word processor or spreadsheet to save your work frequently for the same reasons that it's wise to flush data from buffers.

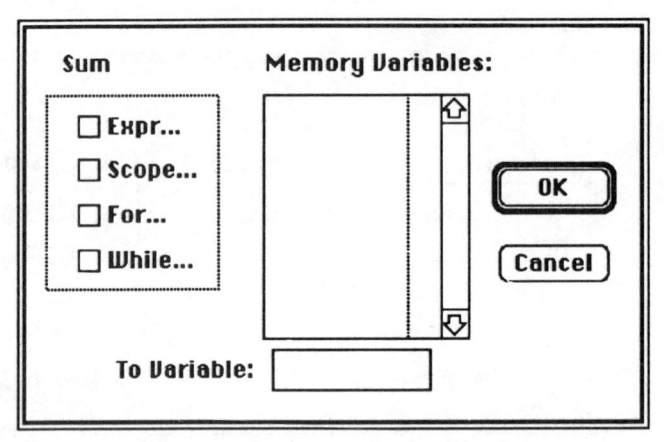

Fig. 3-28. The Sum option produces totals for display or print.

Pack

The Pack option is used after the DELETE command to permanently remove any records that have been marked for deletion. It works on the currently selected database file, one file at a time. In the Browse window you can mark (or delete) records by clicking in the very left-most window column. Once "deleted," records can be removed forever using the Pack command. There are at least two reasons for this kind of record removal. One is obvious—you should be able to change your mind or recover a mistaken deletion. The other is less obvious. When records are removed, the file size changes, a process that takes computer time and effort. If packing was done for each deletion, continual file resizing would slow things down. Consequently, FoxBASE waits until you are sure about deletions and removes them all at once. Then it resizes the file only once for all marked deletions. Records that are marked for deletion can be made invisible by SETting the DELETED switch OFF in the View window.

Reindex

The Reindex option does what its name implies, it rebuilds all of the open indexes associated with a currently selected database file. It's an instant cure for error messages that occur in a Browse window (see Fig. 3-29). Up to 10 database files can be open, and as many as seven indexes can be opened for each one (only one at a time, however, can

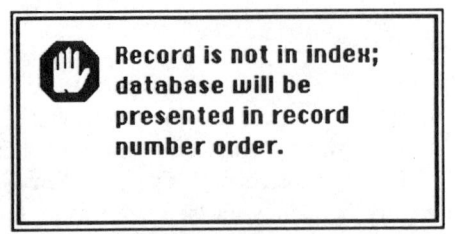

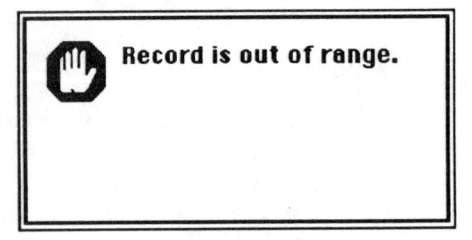

Fig. 3-29. Reindex updates unkempt indexes.

40 *The Database Menu*

control the apparent order of records). Once they are open, and changes are made to their associated database file, indexes are automatically updated. There are times, however, when it is necessary to manually update an index. You can use the Database/Setup menu to create, and open indexes, and to choose a controlling index among the possible seven. This Reindex menu option updates all open indexes so that you can be assured of their accuracy before printing reports, browsing through data, or setting relationships with other files—all of which require accurate record ordering.

THE RECORD MENU

If you are just learning database terminology, the name record on this menu might be confusing. A record is one entry in a database file, such as a name and address are one entry among many in a phone book. This menu offers choices that let you add, change, and delete records from an open database file. It also lets you locate records that meet a special condition, even while browsing in a file (see Fig. 3-30).

Fig. 3-30. The record menu.

Append

The meaning of append is "to add to," so this option lets you add data to a file by opening either the standard entry format screen or a format that you created with the form layout maker (see the File/New/Form menu). Figure 3-31 shows both the FoxBASE standard data entry screen and one I created to replace it. Notice that there is a big difference between the interactive appending screen in Version 1.x and the one in Version 2.x. If you create a nice screen layout (a format file defined from the File/New menu and generated by the Program/Generate menu) that you'd rather use than FoxBASE's standard form, use the setup option under the database menu (also available in the View window) to install it. If you save a view file after installing such a custom for, FoxBASE will use it whenever that view file is open. To learn more about custom format files, see "FoxForm and Fox-Code" in Chapter 5.

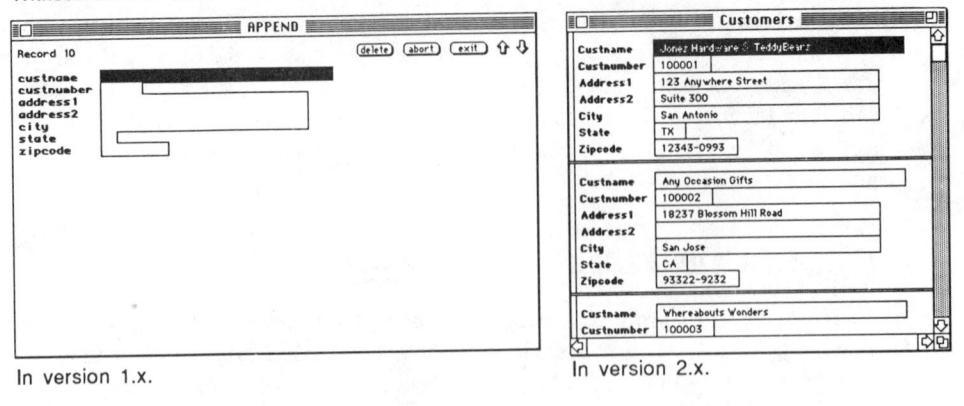

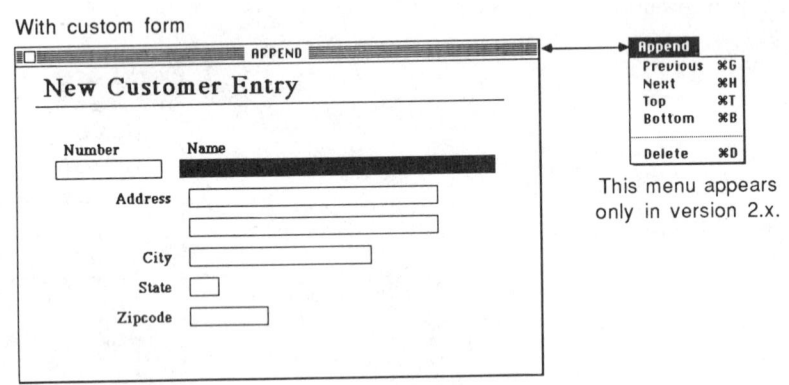

Fig. 3-31. Default and custom data entry forms.

Change

The Change option is for editing data that's already on file. It is particularly useful when you have to make lots of changes by hand. The Browse window also lets you change data, but the Change option is more convenient. It puts one or more records on the screen at a time while displaying the fields vertically (more than one record in Version 2.x). Browse displays records horizontally, which sometimes forces you to scroll back and forth just to see or change records. You can also get to Change from the Browse window, and the field order arranged in the Browse window will stay. Put the fields you want to change at the top of the Change window so that you don't have to use lots of keystrokes to get to them.

Change can use custom screen forms just like the append menu option. Since Fox-BASE lets you filter records (see Fig. 3-32), it's often beneficial to preselect which records and fields you want to change so you won't waste time with those that don't need changing, especially in large files. The Scope, For, While and Fields options can be combined to select, for example, "all of the customers in Texas who are within the next 100 records of the database file."

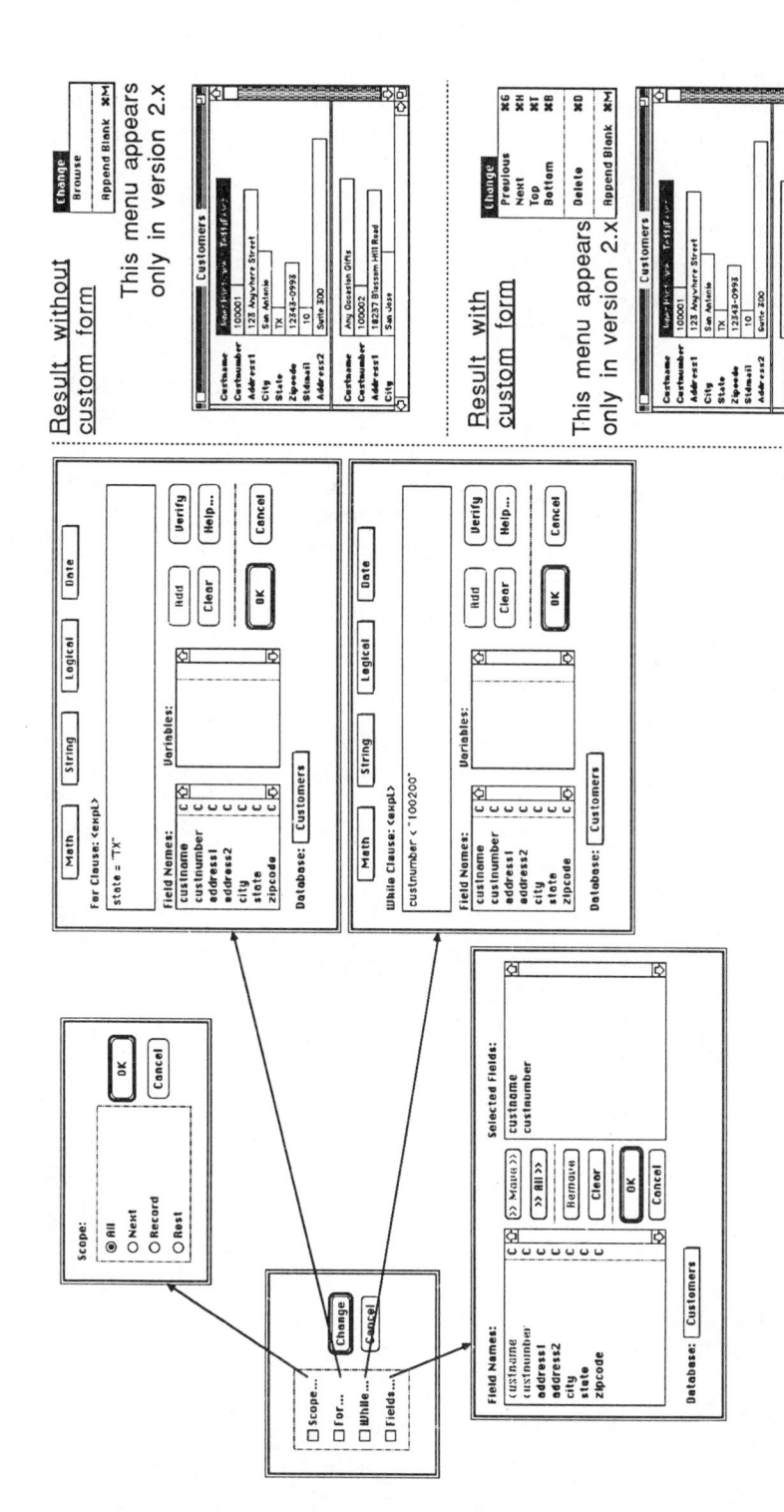

Fig. 3-32. Selecting fields and selecting sets of data.

The Record Menu   43

Scope limits the physical range of records to change from the currently selected record. You could, for example, tell FoxBASE that you want to change the next 100 records, or the rest of the records in the file, or just one record (selected by its record number). All records are selected by default.

For is not the same as scope. Scope sets the number of records from the current point we will consider; For sets a condition within that range selection (usually within the whole file). For acts as a filter regardless of the scope. Look at the example in Fig. 3-32 at the condition that requires that customers be in Texas. That's what the statement *state = TX* means in the "For Clause: <expL>" box. Condition clauses are simple when you understand what they mean.

While tells FoxBASE that you want to skip through the file, changing each record encountered, as long as the customer number is, for example, less than "100200" (as shown in the While box in Fig. 3-32). You could also enter a condition such as *RECNO() < 200* to edit all record numbers under 200. The file should be in a determined order that is established by an index. The While option assumes that the file is in some order, because its condition assumes, by its name, that the condition will be matched for a certain number of records and then change.

Fields let you select the fields you want to see in an append, edit, or change form, data listing, and so on. The fields option also lets you select a new top-to-bottom order of fields, regardless of the physical order they're in. For example, by putting fields in an arbitrary order in the *Selected Fields*: list, you will see only those fields in an append, edit, or change data form, and in the order you selected them. The selected fields will be at the top of the form for quick editing, allowing you to make changes and go quickly on to the next record. For example, if you were just adding new digits to older five-digit zip codes, you could put the zip code field right on top so that you wouldn't have to tab through fields in each customer record.

The fields option does not limit or order fields shown in a custom form of your own making. To do that, you have to make a form in the form layout editor containing the same fields that you select here and establish their entry order. Chapter 5 shows you how. To save the custom form and the field's list together, save them as a view. Using views is a great way to establish a default form of your own and a complementary fields selection. Views are discussed further later in this chapter. For now, just know that you can select the fields that show up when you are changing records.

Goto

The Goto option moves the database pointer to a new location (see Fig. 3-33). You can go to the top of a file, the bottom, any record (by selecting its number), and you can skip any number of records to move forward in the file. Goto has the same effect as scrolling and selecting new records in the Browse window, but it is more useful, for example, when you are changing records.

Locate and Continue

The Locate option is powerful. With it, you can find records that meet a specific condition. Locate uses the same method for searching that Change uses for screening

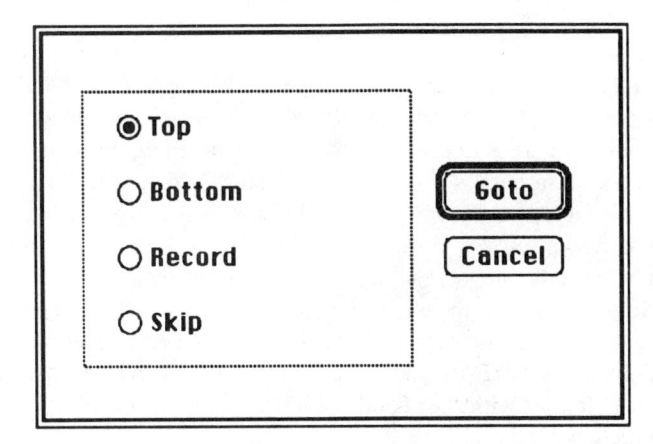

Fig. 3-33. The Goto option moves the record pointer.

records—the "For" clause that is shown in Fig. 3-34. The reason that the Locate dialog includes options for scope, For, and While instead of simply one option for finding records is because Locate is often used with the next menu option, Continue. Continue takes advantage of the condition you set for finding a record and uses it, if you like, to continue finding records that match until no more are found. If a locate attempt was successful, the continue option will become available (it's normally grey) so you can attempt, if you like, to find another record that meets the same condition.

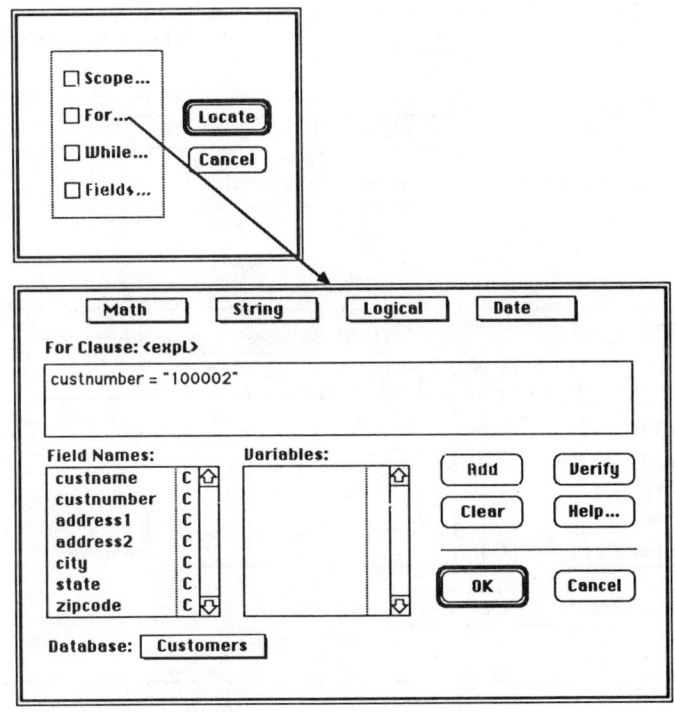

Fig. 3-34. Locating records.

The Record Menu   45

Seek

The Seek option is similar to Locate except that it has the advantage of speed in large files. You must have an index to use Seek because it can only find items based on a condition that is in the active index, whereas Locate can find records based on any condition. For example, if you had created an index for the customer name field, you could seek a customer name in order to find a record; or, if you had an index with the customer number (as in Fig. 3-35), you could seek only a customer number. Because of its index-only restriction, the Seek option has only one method for working and one dialog box. Notice, that in Fig. 3-35 FoxBASE tells you near the top of the box what index is currently active and what field(s) is indexed. You just enter the value to find and FoxBASE does the rest. Lightning speed is the hallmark of FoxBASE, and speed is abundantly evident in whenever you do an indexed Seek. In files with even hundreds of thousands of records, you can find specified records in mere seconds.

Replace

The Replace option is an automatic way to exchange information in a field with new information rather than entering it at the keyboard. Replace can work on one record, or on many records, when used with the Scope, For, or While options.

Replace always takes a field by name and changes values in it with other values. It is a powerful and flexible tool. You can take, for example, all of the customer names and replace them with an uppercase version of the customer name by using the UPPER( ) function (see Fig. 3-36). In another example, you could replace a field value with the record number by entering the RECNO( ) function. The REPLACE command is most

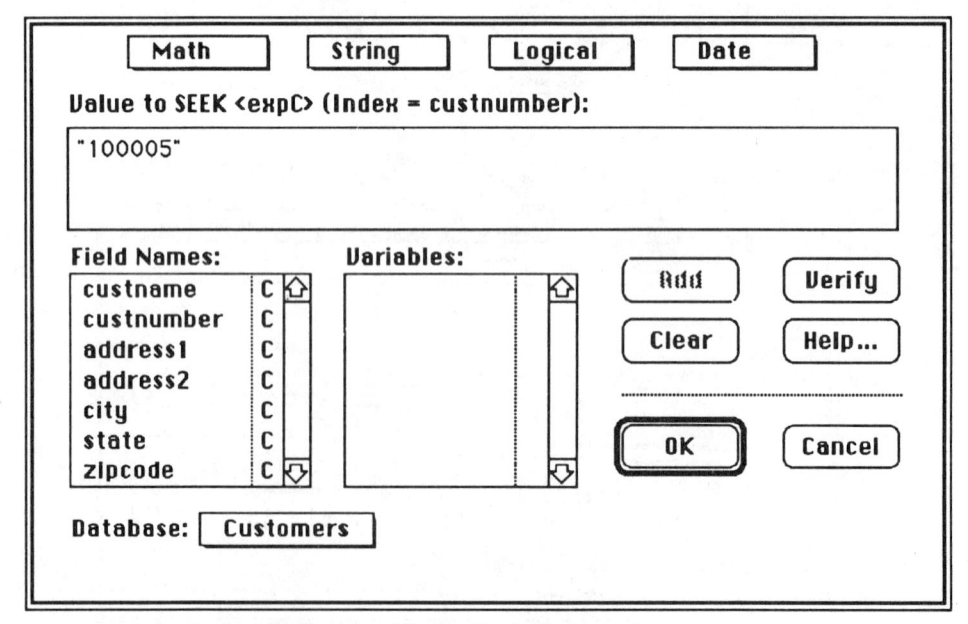

Fig. 3-35. The Seek option uses an index for added speed.

46 *The Record Menu*

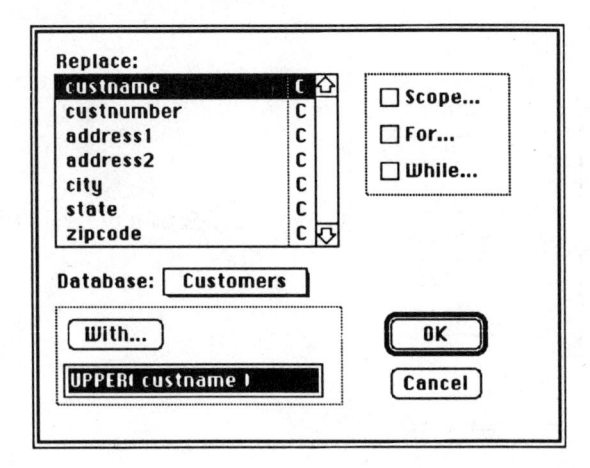

Fig. 3-36. The Replace option changes field contents.

often used by programmers who have no better way to put data into a database, but this menu version of the command is valuable to anyone who wants to change many records at once with a known value. To learn more about this powerful command, refer to Chapter 8.

Delete

The Delete option actually marks records for later deletion by Pack, which is an option on the Database menu. It does not actually remove records by itself, however. The Browse window displays deleted records by marking them with a grey square in the leftmost column. You can also delete (mark) records there, which is advised if single records need to be deleted. Use this option with the Scope, For, and While options to delete batches of records at once. Don't forget to pack.

Recall

The Recall option is the inverse of Delete; it undeletes records that have been marked for deletion.

THE PROGRAM MENU

The Program menu won't be used by everyone, but will be used by most people at one time or another. Developers use the program debugging and compiling options, and interactive FoxBASE users will find that the Do and Generate options are helpful in special situations. Nevertheless, the Program menu is mainly intended for programmers.

Do

The Do option simply tells FoxBASE to run a program you have stored on disk. The dialog shown in Fig. 3-37 appears, asking you to select a program. Format files will show up in the file list because they are technically similar to program files except that they're not executable. Once a program is selected, it runs, performing whatever tasks were

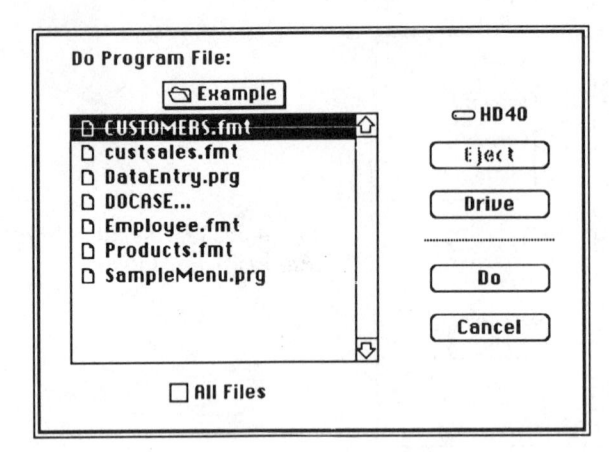

Fig. 3-37. Start a program running.

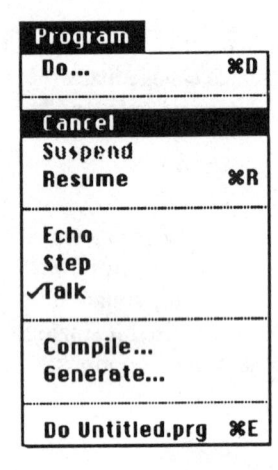

Fig. 3-38. The program menu starts, suspends, and stops programs.

encoded in it. If you went through the exercise at the beginning of this chapter, you know how to save commands in program files and run them later.

Cancel

The Cancel option stops a program's execution permanently. To restart a program after terminating it with cancel, you will have to restart it from the beginning. Use this option when you don't want to resume a program from its current place, or when something is wrong that requires immediate intervention (see Fig. 3-38).

Suspend

Suspend temporarily stops a program's execution so that you can check it for errors, look at values in a database file or in memory variables, and perhaps modify them, then continue execution. To continue execution select the Program/Resume menu. Programmers will like this option because it lets them get into a program while it's running to check things out.

Resume

The Resume option restarts programs after a Suspend.

Echo

The Echo option is one of those check mark menus that's similar to a switch. If a check mark appears next to it, it's on; if not, it's off. Echo plays program commands back to you immediately by making the trace window active when a program runs. In the trace window you can see the commands "echo" as they execute, one line at a time. Echo is usually off, but programmers will turn it on to help them locate problems in programs that are under construction.

Step

Step is another debugging tool like echo—it's either off or on. Step causes programs to execute one step at a time so that program writers can find out which command is doing something wrong, or at what point something happens, and so on. Sometimes there is no way to know what's really happening in a program without "stepping" through it.

Talk

Talk is normally on because it simply tells FoxBASE to let you know what it's thinking when it is doing something such as counting records or summing numbers. If talk is off during these operations, you have no way of knowing what the result is. Programmers turn talk off because they can see the results of operations and progress other than on the screen.

Compile

Compile is just a manual way to do what FoxBASE does automatically when you save a program file. There are times when a text file is created outside of FoxBASE (say, in a word processor, or in dBase on an IBM compatible computer), that requires compilation to turn it into a bona fide FoxBASE program. If you're a programmer, you might need to use this option. Technically, what compiling does is turn readable command statements into computer "tokens," then it stores a tokenized version of the program in a hidden part (the resource fork) of the program file. Then, when FoxBASE runs the program, it's really running the tokens, not the original text.

Generate

Generate is used to take a screen file (a drawinglike file created in FoxForm, the form layout tool described earlier in this chapter) and turn it into a special kind of program called a format (.fmt) file. The Generate step is necessary because the two files are so different. Chapters 5 and 7 discuss form files in some detail.

The Generate option can also be used to create more advanced applications from screen files when it is used with templates. For more information, see the FoxForm and FoxCode sections in Chapter 7.

THE TEXT MENU

The text menu determines the appearance of text in output screens, the Browse window, in program and Command windows, and in custom entry forms. Figure 3-39 displays the options you have for changing text in any active text window. Note that text changes made to any of the main output screens, 1 through 9, affects only the currently active screen. To control the text characteristics of inactive screens, run the SCREEN command from the Command window or a program. The variety of fonts and sizes you can install is endless. You can visit software stores or look through computer magazine ads to get ideas.

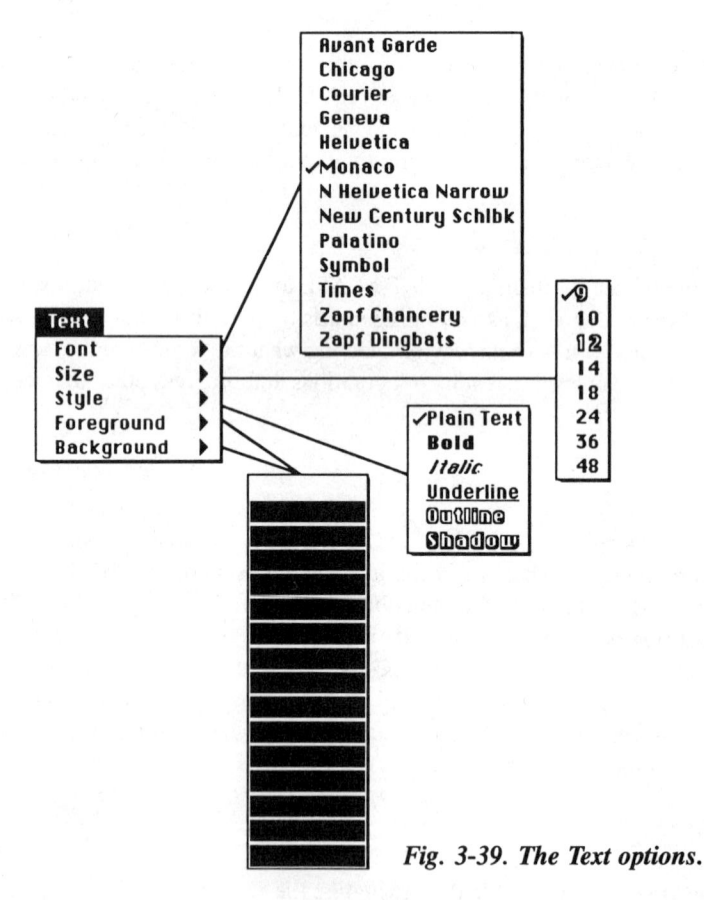

Fig. 3-39. The Text options.

Font

Fonts are the different typefaces installed in your Macintosh, such as the standard fonts, Times and Geneva. Computers differ, but it's common to see Avant Garde, Chicago, Courier, Geneva, Helvetica, Monaco, and Times on a menu's font list. Of them, only Chicago is unavailable on most Laserwriters. Monaco 9 is the best choice for emulating DOS computer screens, because it is mono-spaced, which means that all characters take up the same amount of space. Therefore, you can use it to make the Macintosh screen simulate an IBM-XT-compatible computer screen, which has a fixed 80 × 25 character display.

Size

Each font can have a variety of available sizes. Standard Macintosh fonts come in sizes between 9 and 24 points.

Style

Style controls the appearance of a typeface—bold, underlined, italic, and so on.

THE WINDOW MENU

The window menu is by far the hotbed of activity when working interactively with FoxBASE because it controls all the windows and display screens, it contains the view window where database files are opened, related and browsed, and it controls several screens that are just for programmers. Something that every user can appreciate is that the window menu "grows" a new option for each new named file that is opened, regardless of its type, so if there are too many confusing display layers you can go to the window menu and select the window you want by name (see Fig. 3-40).

Hide Screens

Hide screens closes all of the display screens, one through nine.

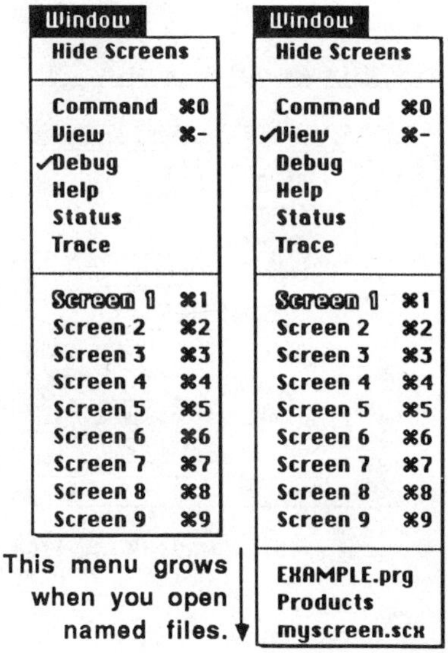

Fig. 3-40. The window menu controls displays.

Command

The Command window is discussed in some length at the beginning of this chapter. FoxBASE gets all of its instructions from the Command window, or from program files. Even menu selections are translated into commands, put here, and then executed. You can reissue commands by clicking on the command line you want and pressing return. Cutting selections of text out of the Command window and pasting them into a Program window for saving is a good way to make "macros" for later use. The keyboard shortcut to open the Command window, or to bring it to the top, is Command-0.

View

Views are discussed in more detail in Chapter 8, because the subject is too large to fit more than a few key points here. Views is the name given to a data-handling environment. A data handling environment consists of all the things you see in the View window, including its five panels. See Fig. 3-41. The five view panels in the View window are called the view panel, the on/off panel, the keys panel, the miscellaneous panel and, finally, the color panel. The following considers each one in turn. Remember that all of the settings and options in the entire View window can be saved in a view file and recalled, later simply by double-clicking the mouse.

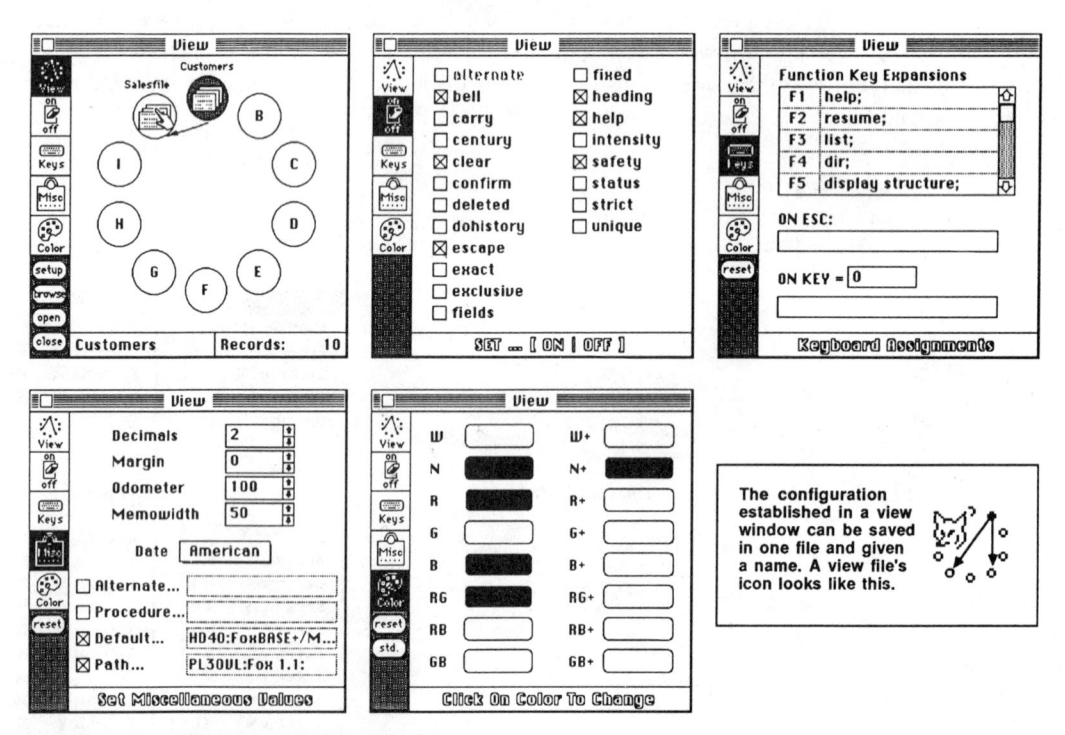

Fig. 3-41. Panels in the View window.

52   The Window Menu

View panel. The main panel is small circles arranged in a clocklike circle. In clockwise order, the smaller circles A-J (or 1-10) can each contain an open database file. If you press the setup button, double-click an empty circle, or select the File/Open menu, you can get a data file from the disk and open it into any of the circles. In Fig. 3-41, the Salesfile has an index (as indicated by the index finger icon over the records) in its circle—J. The Customers file is not indexed, but is related to the Salesfile database file (as indicated by the arrow between them). The direction of the arrow indicates that records located in the Customers file will automatically cause any matching records (based on the key column/field) to be, located in the Salesfile file.

At the bottom right corner of the View window is a digit that represents the number of records in a selected file. To make a selection, simply click on the circle that contains the file you want.

The setup button opens exactly the same dialog as the Setup menu option does under the Database heading in the menubar, and browse the same thing as the Browse option. The open and close buttons open and close database files in any selected circle.

On/Off panel. The on/off panel has lots of settings that affect the way FoxBASE behaves. Every option is explained in Chapter 8 as a SET command, such as *SET BELL*, so I won't explain each option here. Just remember that the settings affect many small, but sometimes important, things that you can take for granted, and which you might want to change from time to time. These settings, like all others in the View window, can be saved inside of a view file for automatic recall when it's reopened.

Keys panel. The third panel provides a way to change the programmable function keys. If your keyboard doesn't have programmable function keys, and you don't plan to write programs for users who do, this panel holds little value for you. Each function key is described in the SET FUNCTION TO entry in Chapter 8. The *ON ESC*: and *ON KEY* boxes are also programmable and are also explained in Chapter 8.

Misc panel. This panel is similar to the on/off panel and is also described in the SET entry of Chapter 8. You might need to change the default folder (second item from bottom) now and then, because it determines where FoxBASE looks first for files. After checking for files in the default folder, FoxBASE checks every folder listed in the path statement (the bottom item).

Color panel. This panel lets you select the hues for each color on a Macintosh II.

Views should be used often to save work settings. It can take time to create some database files, to create indexes for them, or to relate them and set filters, but it is worth it. If the View window is active and you select the File/Save menu, you can save all of the View window options in one file. Just think of the time savings when you turn your computer on at a later time and double-click the view file icon. Everything you stored in this set of five panels will come back just as you left it!

A word of caution about views: don't take view files from one computer to another or rename folders. View files record the location of database and index files, and they can fail if the files are moved into folders that have different names. If you move view files along with databases to another computer, be sure to record all of the folder names so that you can establish the same folder names.

Debug

The Debug window is for program bug extermination. Programmers can use it to watch what happens to memory variables or expressions under a program's control. Figure 3-42 shows the two-sided Debug window. In the left side, you enter variable names or expressions that can include variable names; the right side displays their values. If a running program changes the value of variables, the changes will be reflected in the Debug window. The "break point" dot next to variable1 was placed there by clicking the mouse. The dot tells FoxBASE to halt the program whenever the value of variable1 changes.

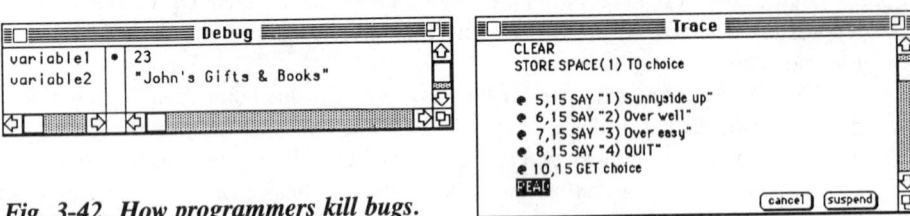

Fig. 3-42. How programmers kill bugs.

Fig. 3-43. The Status window.

Help

This help method is equivalent to the one shown in the early part of the chapter. It brings forth the topical Help window (see Fig. 3-4).

Status

The Status window is a small, horizontal bar window that tells you what database file is open and active, what the default folder is, and what record number the pointer is currently positioned at (see Fig. 3-43).

Trace

The Trace window is for programmers (see Fig. 3-39). It is used to watch program code as it's running. The Trace window lets you set break points to stop execution of a program at any line, and you can cancel or suspend a program from within it. For more information about Trace, see SET ECHO in Chapter 8.

Screens One through Nine

Screens one through nine are identical display screens. When you start FoxBASE, you automatically see screen one. If you select another screen from this menu, it will come to the top and become the default active output screen; other screens that were previously open will remain open, but will be made inactive until they are reselected. If you want to save some displayed information so that you can compare it with some other information, you can use two screens, one just to hold displayed values until you're ready to compare the two. To learn how to program screens see the SCREEN command in Chapter 8.

4
The FoxBASE Data Handling Engine

THE technical tips in this chapter can help you take advantage of FoxBASE+/Mac's flexibility and power. It explains in general terms how FoxBASE is structured, how it handles commands and programs, and how it does the job of managing database files. There's also a section on how to find information to help you configure FoxBASE to suit your needs and make it perform best on your computer. At the very end of the chapter is a list of FoxBASE+/Mac's specifications.

FoxBASE PROGRAM FILES

Program files and commands that are typed in or selected from menus are the only methods you have of communicating with FoxBASE. And, while you might be a wizard at programming, you don't have to be a programmer to get a lot out of FoxBASE. Understanding its command-oriented design is enough to make you a skilled database manager, and programming skills can be a by-product you gain with time.

Interactive or Preprogrammed

Before discussing differences between command compiling and interpreting, it's important to make another distinction between databases that have an interactive mode and those that have a preprogrammed mode. FoxBASE has both. Most database managers are interactive, which means that they let you interact with them directly, and with the database files they manage, and some have a compiler and interpreter built in to handle programs as well.

In preprogrammed mode, which is an optional way to use FoxBASE, your access to data is restricted so that data files cannot be affected in any way that was not predesignated by a programmer. When you decide to run a program, you temporarily loose access to some of FoxBASE's menu options, yet you or another programmer can add other options to replace them. More important, preprogrammed applications don't let you have free access to raw database files the way FoxBASE does interactively. Like a compiler, Fox-BASE can also operate in a non-interactive, preprogrammed mode. It is interactive, and it both interprets and compiles programs, too.

It's almost impossible for strict compilers to be fully interactive as FoxBASE is. Compilers are desirable for their speed, and because they make it easy to distribute finished applications. To do that, they freeze limited menu options into an application and freeze unrestricted interaction with the data out. This kind of limitation is good when you need a complex accounting or inventory control system that would be impossible to organize from scratch, and which would be damaged by someone playing with the data in ignorance. In finished applications, the programmer has organized a difficult job into manageable parts, and simplified your interaction with its processes and with the data itself. So what if a general ledger won't print mailing labels, it wasn't designed to!

Interpreting and Compiling Programs

Interpretation and compiling are the two main ways computers run programs. Because FoxBASE compiles programs before running them, it's a compiler, however, it does allow you to enter commands or modify them any time you like, so its also an interpreter. This hybrid approach that FoxBASE takes toward its commands gives you the speed of a compiler and the flexibility of an interpreter.

Interpreters look at program command lines one at a time and execute them one at a time. By contrast, compilers interpret whole programs in advance, turning commands that humans understand into terse commands for the computer. The difference is like a foreign language interpreter who must follow someone around in order to translate sentences as they are spoken, versus a speech that has been fully and carefully translated before it's read. Compiled programs operate faster than interpreters do because the work of understanding has been done ahead of time.

When you enter single-line commands in the Command window, or you use the menu system to tell it what to do, FoxBASE compiles your instructions into concise tokens and places them into memory before execution. The significance of compilation is noticed most, however, when you're executing commands from a program file. In that case, FoxBASE stores a complete precompiled, or "tokenized" copy of your program in the program file's resource fork (see Fig. 4-1). The data fork, on the other hand, stores the readable, changeable commands that you see. Since resource forks are hidden from view, you might never see a compiled program, only its effects. It is the compiled version of a program that is actually executed when you run it with the DO <program name> command. When you make changes to the program it is automatically recompiled so that the resource fork always has a current version of your commands.

FoxBASE Commands and Expressions

Not only does FoxBASE automatically compile your commands into speedy tokens "on the fly," it also translates most of your menu choices into FoxBASE commands and places them into the Command window where they're compiled and executed. As I dis-

Data fork	Resource fork
Readable, changeable program code is stored here.	Unreadable, hidden machine instructions are stored here.
Whenever you change this program and save it...	it gets recompiled and stored here automatically.
This program is called ASCII code because it's simple text.	This program is called tokens or object code because it's been boiled-down to its functional essence.
You understand version of the program.	FoxBASE understands this version.

Fig. 4-1. Inside a program file.

cussed in Chapter 1, you can learn how to write commands by reading the commands that FoxBASE writes for itself.

It's a good idea to build a library of useful commands, saving them in program files, for those times when you need them. Commands FoxBASE cannot write for itself are those that control a program's action when decisions need to be made, such as IF and DO WHILE commands. Nevertheless, the FoxBASE menus are powerful command builders that you can learn from.

Next to command verbs, expressions are the most powerful single ingredient in any FoxBASE command. You learn about expressions every time you get prompted by the expression builder dialog box, such as the one shown in Fig. 4-2. Expressions can be small or large. As parts of a command that must be evaluated before executing, an expression is a unit unto itself that results in one of several (number, date, character, or logical) value types when evaluated.

The numeric expression 5+7 evaluates to 7. RECNO( ) is a function, but it is also an expression because it can be evaluated—returning the number of the current database row. Combining an expression with the REPLACE command lets you calculate math columns or change the contents of database fields in ways limited only by your imagination.

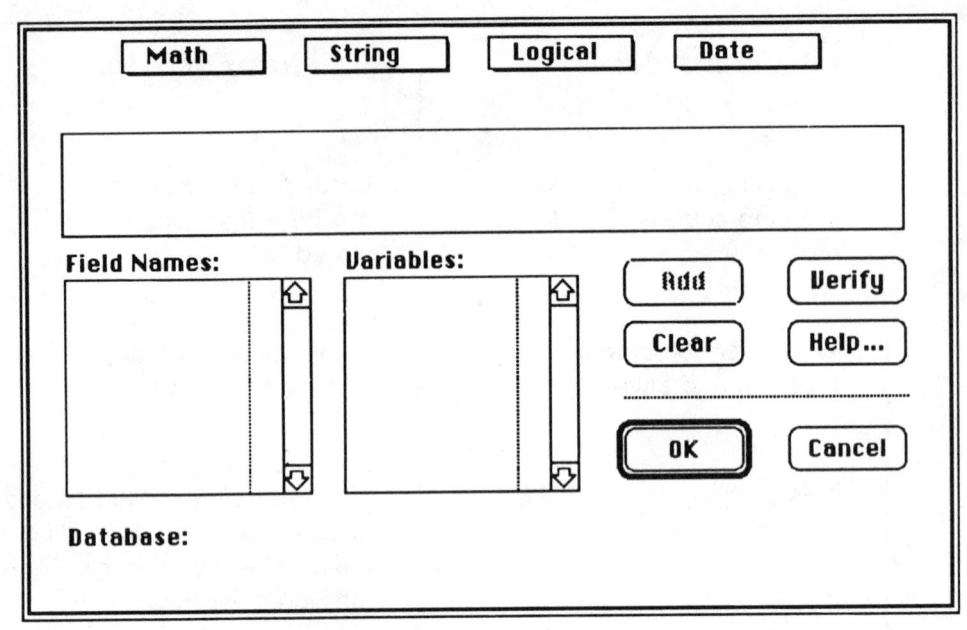

Fig. 4-2. The expression builder.

FoxBASE FILE TYPES SURVEY

Figure 4-3 lists the different types of file that FoxBASE uses, including their default naming extensions. The reason why (.frm) and (.frx) files are listed together is because (.frm) files are created using version 1.x and (.frx) files are created using version 2.x.

In addition to the identifying extension FoxBASE tacks onto the end of its files, there's a distinct icon for each type of file that you'll later become familiar with. There is also something extra you don't see that the Macintosh does. It's the creator and type indication recorded inside the file's hidden header. All FoxBASE files are marked with a creator of "FOX+," and the type is identified as one of the following:

Database file (.dbf)	F+DB
Database memo/picture file (.dbt)	F+DT
Screen file for FoxForm (.scx)	F+FM
Index file (.idx)	F+IX
Memory variable file (.mem)	F+ME
Program and Format files (.prg/.fmt)	F+PR
Report or Label files (.frm/.frx)	F+RP
Resource files like FoxUSER	F+US
View files (.vue)	F+VU
Text or "File" files (.txt)	TEXT

These distinctions are good to know if you plan to use the GETFILE( ) function that's discussed in Chapter 9, or if you are a developer who wants to know what's going on under the surface of things in the Macintosh file system.

Extension	Description
.dbf	- Database file created with CREATE<filename>, or via the File/New.../Database menu option, used by USE <filename>, or via the File/Open.../Database menu option.
.dbt	- Database text file to hold memofield and picturefield data for .dbf file of the same name, managed automatically when its associated .dbf file is created, used and modified.
.frm/.frx	- Report form file created by CREATE REPORT<filename>, or via the File/New.../Report menu option, used by REPORT FORM<filename>, or via the File/Open.../Report menu option.
.fmt	- Format file created by the File/New.../Form menu option and saved via the Program/Generate.../Format File menu option, modified via the File/Open.../Program menu option, used by SET FORMAT TO<filename>.
.idx	- Index file created by INDEX ON...TO<filename>, or via the Database/Setup.../Index:/Add.../New menu option, used by SET INDEX TO<filename>, or USE<filename> INDEX<filename>, or via Database/Setup.../Index:/Add.../Open menu option.
.lbl/.lrx	- Label form file created by CREATE LABEL<filename>, or via the File/New.../Label menu option, used by LABEL FORM<filename>, or via the Database/Label.../Form menu option.
.mem	- Memory variable file created by SAVE TO<filename>, used by RESTORE FROM<filename> (stores all <memvar>s in memory at time of SAVE TO).
.prg	- Program file created by MODIFY COMMAND<filename>, or via the File/New.../Program menu option, used by DO <filename>, or via the Program/Do... menu option.
.scx	- Screen file created by CREATE SCREEN<filename>, or via the File/New.../Form menu option, used via File/Form menu option (saved visual layouts used only to create .fmt files).
.txt	- Text file created by SET ALTERNATE TO<filename> when SET ALTERNATE is ON, formatted via ?... or @ SAY... commands, modified via the File/Open.../File menu option.
.vue	- View file created by CREATE VIEW<filename>, or via File/Save As... when the view window is active, used by SET VIEW TO<filename>, or via File/Open.../View... menu option.

Fig. 4-3. FoxBASE files.

STORING AND MANAGING DATA

Careful design of database files (tables) is important because a bad design can create excess work when the data is being managed in a structure that's already loaded. Chapter 5 discusses database design considerations in some depth. Here, we're concerned with the technical attributes of FoxBASE database files, because careful design should be combined with an understanding of the way FoxBASE "thinks" about data if you want to manage it efficiently.

The Data Files (.dbf)

FoxBASE stores data in tables of rows and columns. The tables must be designed with the intention of storing specific information: each column, called a field, must have a name and a specified width, each row, called a record, has a unique number assigned to it called, appropriately, the record number. Over a billion records can be contained in one file. That's a limit that is rarely reached on even the largest mainframes! I frequently work with files containing several hundred thousand records, but the most common file size we're likely to encounter in offices contain only several hundred to several thousand records.

Each database file contains information about a subject. Inventory, customers and orders are all different subjects, requiring different database files. Each FoxBASE database record, or row, can contain up to 4,000 characters in up to 128 fields. Only 254 characters, however, can be held in any single field. Memo fields are an exception to both rules. They can contain up to 32,000 characters each, yet they count for only 10 characters in the record's character total. Pictures also count for only 10 characters in the record, because like memos, they are stored in a separate file by FoxBASE.

Records are stored in the exact order that they are entered—usually by the APPEND command. Make sure that there is plenty of space on your disk for the files you're working on. It's a good rule of thumb to give a database file twice the space it takes on the disk, or more, so that FoxBASE has working space for manipulations. If a hard disk is available it should be used. Database systems are "disk intensive," so performance and safety increase when the disk is fast and large.

FoxBASE creates temporary files while it's working, which it names *FoxTEMPxxx-xxx*. The *xxxxxx* is a unique number it uses to keep track of which file is which. If power to your Macintosh is shut off while FoxBASE is running you'll probably see some temporary files left on the disk that can be trashed; but more important, you could loose data or damage files permanently. Make backups of your files before using them and use the COPY TO command now and then during a work session to make a backup in another file name.

Memo/Picture Files (.dbt)

Whenever you tell FoxBASE to put a memo or a picture field into a database file it automatically creates another file to store them in (see Fig. 4-4). A memo file is given the same name as its parent, except that it has a (.dbt) extension instead of a database file's standard (.dbf) extension. Incidentally, the text, or memo, name for (.dbt) files comes from the DOS world where picture fields don't exist; otherwise the file might have been called something else.

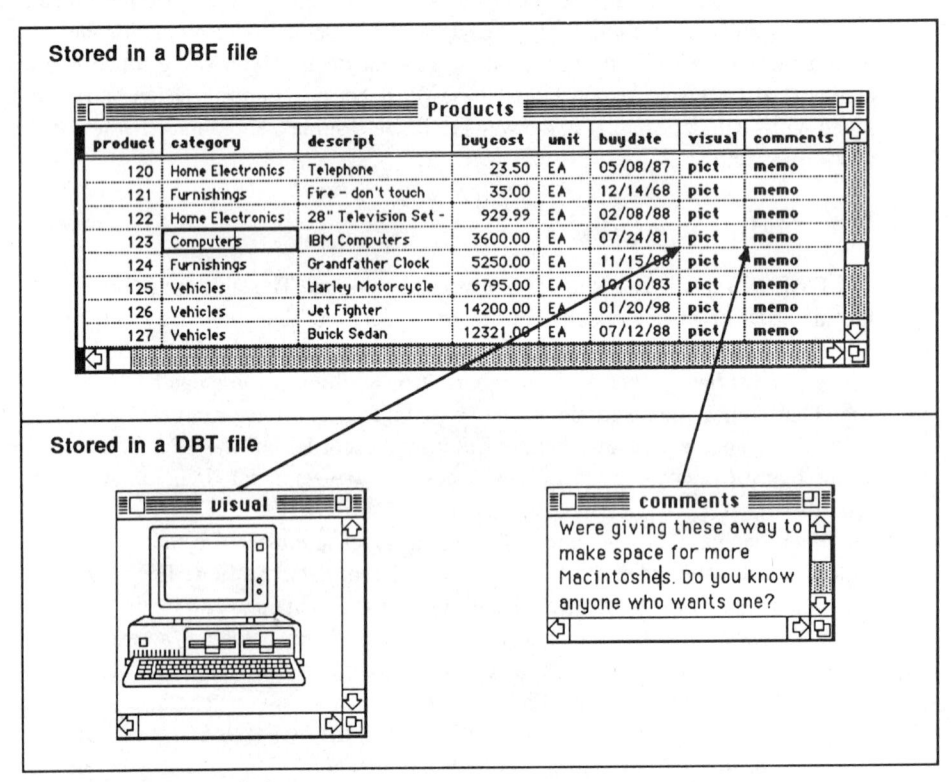

Fig. 4-4. Memos and pictures.

60   *Storing and Managing Data*

Don't remove a database text/memo (.dbt) file from the folder that its parent file is in, and make sure to copy both (.dbf) and (.dbt) files together whenever the database file is copied or moved. If, for any reason, a (.dbt) file is missing or damaged, the message, *MEMO file is missing* will appear when you try to open the associated database file, and the parent file won't open. To remedy the situation, after an unsuccessful search for the file, of course, you must create a new (.dbt) file for the parent file by making the structure of the parent file again. Inside of FoxBASE select the File/New/Database menu, and recreate the file's structure from scratch. Be sure to do so in another folder than the one containing the (.dbf) file so it's not overwritten in the process. After the file has been recreated, quit FoxBASE and copy only the (.dbt) file to the folder containing the database (.dbf) file that won't open. If you did things right it will open, albeit without the memos or pictures you once had.

Index Files

To reorder records alphabetically or numerically, indexes are best. In FoxBASE, sorting physically rearranges the actual database file itself in the desired order. By contrast, indexing creates a special type of file that lets you look at the physical database file as though it were in the order you choose, but without actually reordering the file itself. Refer to Fig. 3-8 in Chapter 3 to see how indexes work.

The advantage of indexing over sorting is obvious. Without indexes, you would have to physically reorder the whole file each time you needed to see it in a new order—an impossible job if you also wanted to switch between different orders frequently or quickly. Sorting would also be required every time new records were added to the file. On the other hand, indexes can be automatically maintained as new records are entered. A single database can have unlimited indexes, however, only seven can be maintained, per file, at one time.

Indexes can be as simple as arranging customers by name, or as complex as a 100-character compound key. Keys are the specification for ordering a database file. You can create multiple column keys, or even keys based on parts of a field or fields. The only restrictions are that the index expression, or key expression, be one data type (character, numeric or date), and that the combined length of the key not exceed 100 characters.

Using functions, you can combine number, date, and character fields into one key of the character data type, so the first restriction is moot. The limit on the number of characters in a key is adequate; you will probably never need more than 100 characters to put a file in order. Use the substring function SUBSTR( ), the DTOC( ) function, and the STR( ) function to make character-type keys. Use the VAL( ) function to convert characters into number values for creating compound numeric keys.

Relations and Views

In addition to simple reordering of mixed up data, indexes are required for two important commands to work: SEEK, and SET RELATION TO. The SEEK command can find a record that matches any index key you create, so you can quickly find records matching complex criteria at lightening speed. With the SET RELATION TO command you can relate files together for multifile browsing, reports, and other uses. Index keys are required for multifile relationships because it would take too long to find matching records in a child file without them. A parent file looks in a child field for matching records, consequently an index is required in the child file for the parent to search. Index files are automatically created with a (.idx) extension so you can tell them apart from other file types.

View files can be created whenever the View window is active. Just use the File/SaveAs menu option. The view file will store the names of all open database, index, and screen format files, along with information about filters, field settings, and interfile relationships. View files have a (.vue) extension. When a view file is double-clicked from the Macintosh desktop, FoxBASE opens, and the previous data handling environment should open too, just as it was when it was saved.

Indexes can save considerable time when you work with multifile arrangements. Be careful, however, when moving view files to new computers, they are not as portable as database files because they store the disk and folder names, along with the other information they need, to restore things to a previous state.

MANAGING MEMORY REQUIREMENTS

Multifinder partitions allow you to run more than one program at a time on a Macintosh. In order to establish the memory needs of each program, it looks at the lower-right corner box in each program's *Get Info* dialog box (see Fig. 4-5). FoxBASE version 1.1 can be set as low as 750(K) and still work. Reducing the memory partition, however, also reduces performance.

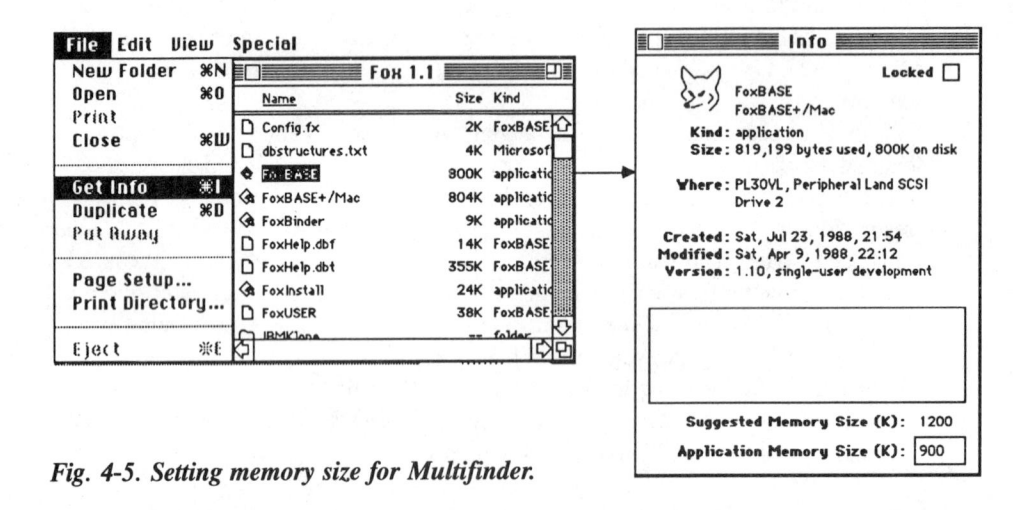

Fig. 4-5. Setting memory size for Multifinder.

The *Get Info* setting has no influence on memory allocated to FoxBASE under the regular Macintosh finder; it's for Multifinder only. If you have lots of memory and are using Multifinder, give FoxBASE as much memory as you can spare. Memory translates directly into performance because the FoxBASE caching system intelligently uses memory to increase performance.

Containing Memory Demands

Keep in mind that fonts and desk accessories take memory away from programs. Ram cache, if set too high (in the Control Panel of your Macintosh), say above 64K, can also take valuable memory needed by programs. Color monitors require more system memory than black and white screens because there's more information to store for each screen pixel. FoxBASE needs lots of memory, and you can run into conflicts if there's not enough. FoxBASE is a full-feature, powerful, database application tool which requires a lot of memory, just as other large program applications do, so give it all you've got.

If FoxBASE won't start, or if you get a *Not enough memory* message, try removing sounds, fonts, or desk accessories from your system file. If you need them, and you also want to run FoxBASE, try using a program such as Suitcase. Suitcase manages fonts and desk accessories by keeping them out of memory until they are needed, and it lets you have many more at your fingertips than you would otherwise be able to load because it loads and unloads them on demand.

If you write programs, the most common low memory message is *No memory for screen of that size* because additional screens (two through eight, for example) take up lots of memory, and because you're likely to want to use them. Try removing some other application or peripherals, and then try to establish optimal default settings in a Config.fx file as outlined below. If you write programs for color Macintosh users, you'll probably need 2 megabytes of memory because color displays require more memory.

ADJUSTING FoxBASE DEFAULTS

FoxBASE provides two places where you can establish setting to affect its behavior, and also some Macintosh options can have an influence on its appearance or performance. All of the settings discussed below can be called environmental settings, or environmental defaults, because they determine the computing environment in which FoxBASE will work.

Macintosh Settings

The most important Macintosh settings are in the control panel under the Apple menu, which is the left-most menu at the top of every Macintosh screen. Control panel device settings are designed to be adjusted. When running FoxBASE, the ram cache, monitor, and display color settings are significant.

The ram cache stores information from the most recent disk and reads it in a pre-allocated portion of memory, which gets checked before the computer reads the disk again in search of data. This saves time in disk I/O (information In and Out) and increases performance. RAM cache can be set as high as 64K to increase the performance of your hard disk. Although higher settings are possible, it's not likely that you'll get improvements with settings greater than 64K, it would compete with FoxBASE's own memory management system for disk I/O that is far more intelligent and more suited for database management than the cache Apple provides. I leave mine off so that it stays out of FoxBASE's way.

The monitor setting determines how many shades of grey, or how many colors your system will use, depending, of course, on its hardware configuration. If you create screen forms or programs using color settings, and then run them on a black and white Macintosh, FoxBASE will do its best to convert the colors to readable black and white.

The color settings in the control panel determine what colors FoxBASE will use. It supports all the colors and shades that you installed and selected, getting its default color settings from the Macintosh control panel. You can change the colors inside FoxBASE by selecting the color panel in the View window, which leaves the default Macintosh system colors unchanged.

The SET Command

The SET command is FoxBASE's main environmental controller. If you look in the view window's second panel, you will see a series of switches that control various program behaviors such as the ones shown in Fig. 4-6. For more information on options, refer to Chapter 8, where the SET commands are discussed in some depth. You can make FoxBASE start up with the switches set any way you like by storing commands in an optional configuration file named config.fx. If you don't, FoxBASE will use the default settings.

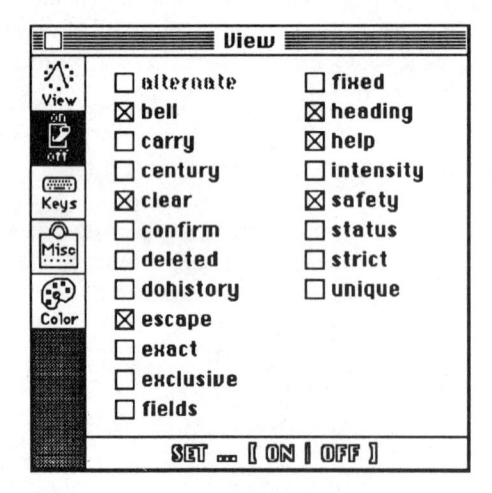

Fig. 4-6. Setting default options.

The Configuration File

If FoxBASE finds a text file named Config.fx in its folder when it starts up, it will read the file for configuration information and startup instructions. Only one Config.fx file can be used at a time. FoxBASE doesn't come with a configuration file, but you can create one any time by selecting the File/New/File menu option, which opens a simple text editor for nonprogram files.

The following list shows which commands and settings can be modified by an entry in the Config.fx file. They can be entered in any order, and like the Config.fx file itself, are optional. If FoxBASE encounters errors in a configuration file it will either ignore it, if the entry is not understandable or in complete error, and it will use the standard default setting; or if a range setting is not within its allowed range, it will use the nearest allowable setting.

64 Adjusting FoxBASE Defaults

The syntax for configuration settings is simply a matter of joining an option and its setting with an equal sign, such as this:

OPTION = SETTING

Don't use quotation marks, enter settings without them. To set the date display, for example, the entry should look like this:

DATE = BRITISH

Table 4-1 shows a list of configurable options, many of which have equivalent settings that are fully described in Chapter 8 as SET commands. Table 4-2 shows specifications.

Table 4-1. Configurable Options.

OPTION	DEFAULT VALUE	ACCEPTABLE VALUES
ALTERNATE An output text file.	—	\<filename\>
BELL The default Macintosh "bell."	ON	ON or OFF
BUCKET Kilobytes for storing GETS.	4	1 to 32
CARRY Carry forward when entering data.	OFF	ON or OFF
CENTURY Shows the century in dates.	OFF	ON or OFF
CLEAR Clears screen when a format file is entered.	OFF	ON or OFF
COLOR Sets colors.	\<colors\>	B & W
COMMAND Runs a program when Fox-BASE starts.		\<command\>
CONFIRM Forces press of return to confirm entries.	OFF	ON or OFF

Table 4-1. Continued.

OPTION	DEFAULT VALUE	ACCEPTABLE VALUES
CONSOLE Echo results to the screen.	ON	ON or OFF
DATE Sets the date display type by nationality.	AMERICAN	<format>
DECIMALS Number of displayed decimals.	2	1 to 14
DEFAULT Selects main folder.	none	<drivename and folder (path) list>
DELETED Hides or shows deleted records.	OFF	ON or OFF
DEVICE Sets active output device.	SCREEN	SCREEN/PRINT
ECHO Turns trace window on.	OFF	ON or OFF
Escape Enables/disables Escape key	ON	ON or OFF
EXACT Sets sensitivity of string comparisons.	OFF	ON or OFF
EXCLUSIVE Enables/disables sharing of opened files.	ON	ON or OFF
F<number> Installs commands into function keys.	none	<command>
FILES Sets number of possible open files.	16	16 to 48
HEADINGS Enables/disables display of field names in file dumps to screen or printer.	ON	ON or OFF

Adjusting FoxBASE Defaults

Table 4-1. Continued.

OPTION	DEFAULT VALUE	ACCEPTABLE VALUES
HELP Enables/disables help access.	ON	ON or OFF
HISTORY Sets number of saved commands.	20	0 to 16,000
HMEMORY Kilobytes for storing historical command lines.	5	0 to 63
INDEX Sets default index file extension.	IDX	3 characters
INTENSITY Turns on fancy colors in edited fields.	ON	ON or OFF
LABEL Sets default extension of label form files. Version 2.x only.	.FRX	3 characters
MARGIN Sets left printer margin, in characters.	0	0 to 254
MEMOWIDTH Sets width of memo field displays.	50	8 to 256
MVARSIZ Kilobytes for memory variables.	6	1 to 64
MVCOUNT Sets number of memory variables.	256	128 to 3,600
ODOMETER Increments record count echo interval during file operations.	100	1 to ?
PATH Sets folders for search.	none	<drivename and folder (path) list>

Table 4-1. Continued.

OPTION	DEFAULT VALUE	ACCEPTABLE VALUES
PRINT Activates dialog with printer.	OFF	ON or OFF
REPORT Sets default extension of report form files. Version 2.x only.	.FRX	3 characters
SAFETY Enables/disables file overwrite warning.	ON	ON or OFF
STATUS Opens/closes small status window.	ON	ON or OFF
STEP Sets single command step in trace window.	OFF	ON or OFF
TALK Enables/disables simple interactive echo to screen.	ON	ON or OFF
TYPEAHEAD Sets keystroke buffer size.	128	0 to 32,000
UNIQUE Forces indexes to be unique.	OFF	ON or OFF
VIEW Reopens view at last quit time.	last setting used	ON or OFF
VOLUME <char> Sets DOS-like drivenames for Macintosh folders.		<drivename and folder (path) list>

Table 4-2. Specifications.

SPECIFICATIONS	
Arrays	Up to 3,600
Cells per array	Up to 32,767
Characters in an index key	Up to 100
Characters in a command line (includes those contained in macros-&)	Up to 254
Characters per character string	Up to 254
Characters in a record	Up to 4,000
Characters in a field	Up to 254
Fields in a record	Up to 128
Files open simultaneously	Up to 48 (set in Config.fx file)
Memory variables	Up to 3,600
Numeric precision	16 digits
Records in a database file	Up to 1,073 billion

5

How to Use FoxBASE

FOXBASE can be used countless ways, but no one will use it the way you will. Nevertheless, like cross-country drivers, all FoxBASE users have some things in common. If you are driving across the country, you need a car, and it wouldn't hurt to know about Interstate 80 before considering lesser alternatives. This chapter is a simple cross-country map to show you how FoxBASE designers expect you to use their product. I want to show you how to get from here to there in FoxBASE without going into details. This short guide should help you to see the big FoxBASE picture well enough to guide you toward your own specific goals. Chapters 6 through 9 contain more specific "how to" information about the topics covered here in this chapter, and you can refer to them if you need to.

EXPRESSIONS

If anything confuses new FoxBASE users most, it is the "sentences" FoxBASE reads called expressions. I suspect that it's partly because they are so flexible and do so many things. You've probably seen these notations: <expr>, <exprC>, <exprN>, <exprD>, and <exprL>. They stand for expression, character expression, numeric expression, date expression and logical expression. While FoxBASE can read almost any kind of "sentence" expression you enter, it does like you to remember the categorical difference between characters, numbers, dates, and logical expressions.

"Cat," for example, is a character expression, and 4 is a numeric expression. Each expression has only one data type. Whenever you need to add an expression, you can enter it directly from the keyboard, but you'll also need to include some of the following information to make it more meaningful:

- Constants—which are literal things you type in.
- Database field names—which tell FoxBASE to use the field's contents.

- Memory variables—see Chapter 6 for a description of memvars.
- Functions—see Chapter 9.
- Operators—such as + − / =.

Complex expressions, such as 4∗4, evaluate to a result, which consist of one answer and one data type. For more technical information about expressions see the discussion in Chapter 6. FoxBASE lets you know whenever it needs an expression by displaying the expression building dialog shown in Fig. 5-1.

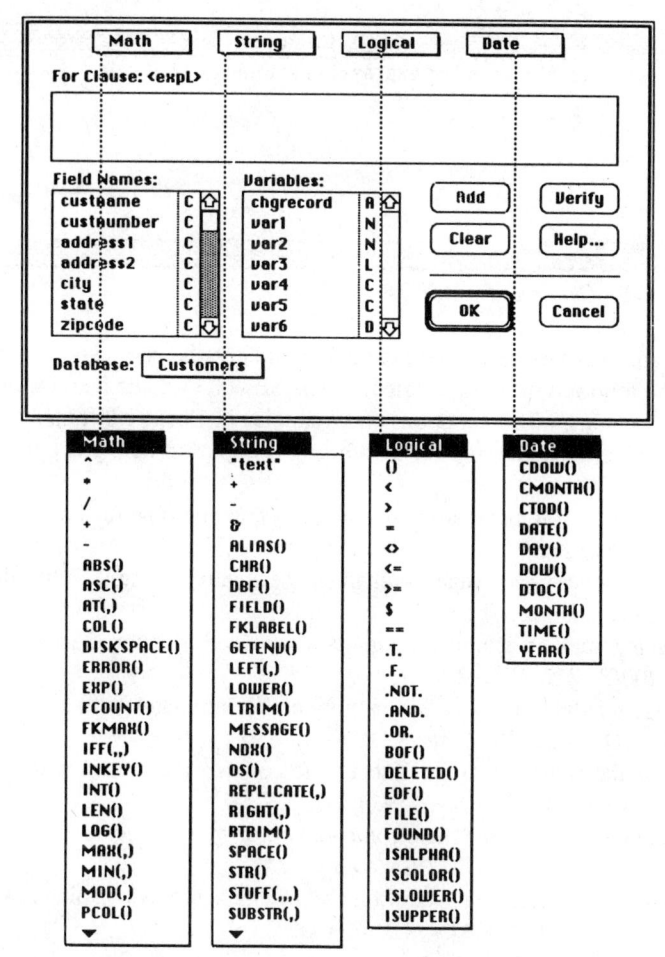

Fig. 5-1. Functions are all at your fingertips.

Because functions can convert one data type into another, they're often a useful part of many expressions. With functions, you can change the data type of one expression to be used by another. Parentheses can be used to determine the order of evaluation in complex expression like they do in algebra expressions (see Chapter 6 for the natural order of evaluation). If you're just learning, it's a good idea to experiment with expressions by using the ? command as demonstrated in Fig. 5-2. Enter expressions freely and learn by exploring.

Expressions 71

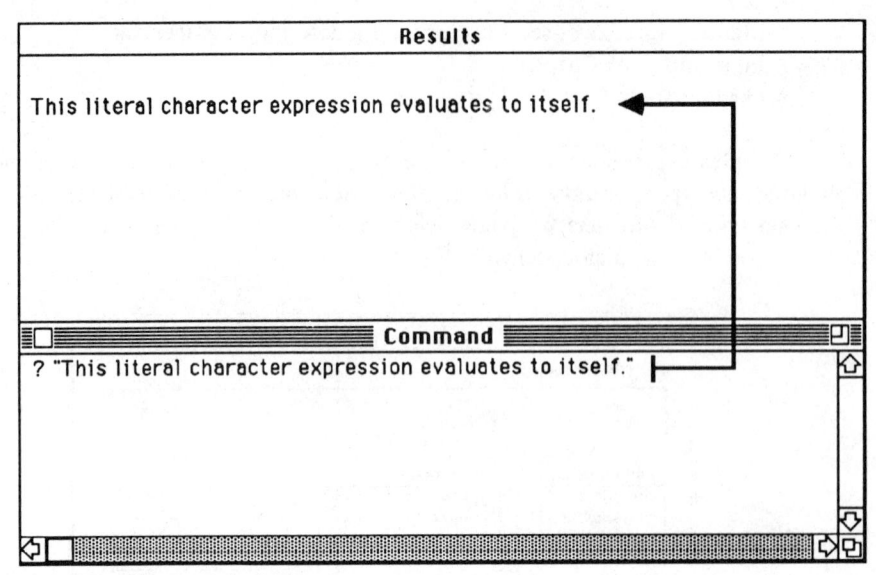

Fig. 5-2. The Command window.

If you want to experiment, start FoxBASE and open the command window, then enter a ? command followed by an expression. FoxBASE will evaluate it and show the result on the screen. Use some of the functions and examples in Chapter 9 to make things interesting. The following are some rules of thumb and examples to help you enter expressions:

- Put quotation marks around characters that you type in: For example, "I like dogs and cats."
- Join (concatenate) separate character sets with a + sign. "I like dogs and cats." + " Animals are my friends."
- Enter numbers plainly, no quotation marks or other markers are needed. 4+2, 1200*3, 822/2, 12-2.
- Use the date-to-character function to compare dates with characters.
    DTOC(DATE()) = "12/25/83"
- Use the character-to-date function to compare characters with dates.
    CTOD("12/25/83") = DATE()
- Logical expressions must compare two or more things.
    1 > 0   "CAT" = "DOG"   "A" < "Z"
- Use the $ operator to see if one set of characters is contained in another.
    "CATS" $ "DOGS CATS COWS PIGS".

WORKING WITH DATA

Just as there are two popular ways to travel across the U.S.A., there are two ways to work with data in FoxBASE+/Mac, with a million variations between. Interactively using FoxBASE is like driving a car. You've got to know where you're going at each turn, and you can't sleep because it's your job to stay on course and reach your destination alive. All

72 *Working with Data*

users start by creating one or more database files, or tables. If you're an interactive user, you'll want to pay careful attention to the section below.

Creating and Using Tables in the View Window

Making database files, or tables, is fundamental. Make one or more tables to store all of the information you need by selecting the File/New/Database menu, or by double-clicking in a View window work area circle. If you don't know how to structure a database file, use established paper forms as a model. Establish a length for each column (field), and remember, character data types are for alphanumeric information, dates are for dates, logical fields for true or false information, and so on. Use numeric fields only when you will calculate the numbers they contain, otherwise consider using the character data type for numbers; after all, who's going to divide zip codes by telephone numbers?

You can store long notes (up to 32,000 characters per record) in memo fields, and pictures (bitmapped images) in picture fields. Fields can also have calculated data. If you want to calculate a column from other numeric columns—such as price * quantity to get a total—you can create a field for it and use the REPLACE command to update the total. (See the Replacing Field Data entry in this chapter.)

The View window has 10 circles, each one a work area that can hold a single database file and associated indexes. The View window lets you open and close database files, and you can even save the memory of open database files for instant recall in a View file. To do this, select the View window so it is active, then select the File/Save As menu option. The name you enter will become a view file name that can be opened, or double-clicked, at any time to restore the open database files exactly as they were before quitting FoxBASE (see Fig. 5-3).

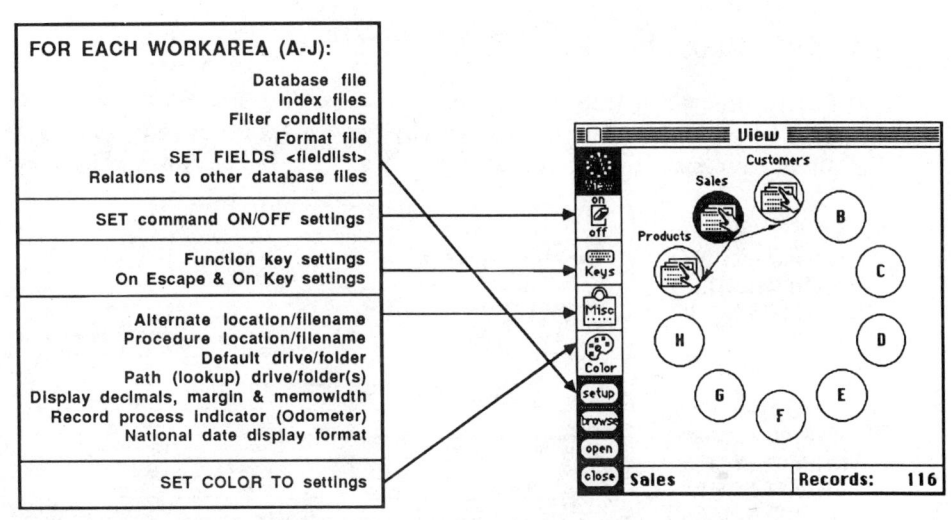

Fig. 5-3. Options available in the View window.

Adding, Browsing, and Changing Records

Add records to tables by selecting the Append option from the Record menu. If you switch the Carry option to on in the View window, the contents of one record you're adding will be carried forward to the next one as you go, so that you only need to type things that are different from one record to the next. The Carry option is useful when all of the records are for one city and state, for example, because you could go nuts typing San Jose, California 200 times in an afternoon.

Another way to add data is to select the Record/Append Blank option several times, to make blank records, and then browse. Browse lets you see, edit, and delete records in a row and column format that's much like a spreadsheet. If there are blanks you can enter new data. The little column on the left side of the Browse window can hold a grey mark, signifying that the record marked can be permanently removed from the database. You can mark records for deletion by clicking in the narrow column on the left side and selecting the Database/Pack menu option, which removes them forever.

To change a record's contents you can use the Browse window, or the menu option Record/Change. Record/Change puts one record on the screen at a time, letting you edit individual field contents in each one. You can scroll up and down to select one record after the next. Remember, you can make custom forms to replace the standard FoxBASE entry and change screens (see Creating your own data entry forms below).

To add to a memo field, simply click on it. It will open up allowing you to make changes. Picture fields work the same way, except that there are no tools for drawing pictures in the edit mode, you've got to paste pictures into the field from another source via the Macintosh's standard clipboard or scrapbook. Cut, copy, and paste functions work with pictures just as they do with text. If you aren't familiar with the clipboard and scrapbook, or how they work, take a look at any Macintosh owners manual.

Deleting Records and Packing Files

Records are not deleted when they're deleted. Deleting a record merely marks it so that it can be removed from the file permanently by use of the PACK command (see Fig. 5-4). You can also make records appear to be deleted (and PACKed) by marking them for

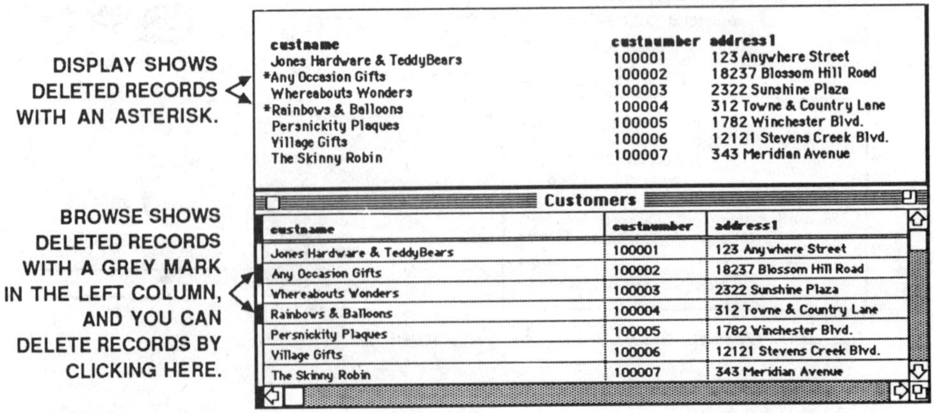

Fig. 5-4. Deleting records.

deletion and then setting DELETED ON—a toggle switch setting in the View window. Mark records for deletion by clicking in the window-splitting bar of the Browse window. It should be on the left side if it hasn't been moved. Grey means the record is deleted, white means it's not.

The most aggressive way to delete records is to ZAP the file, which erases everything but the file's structure! In fact, it's so dangerous that FoxBASE requires that you enter it longhand into the Command window, and even then, it prompts you before actually turning the file into bare bones (see Fig. 5-5).

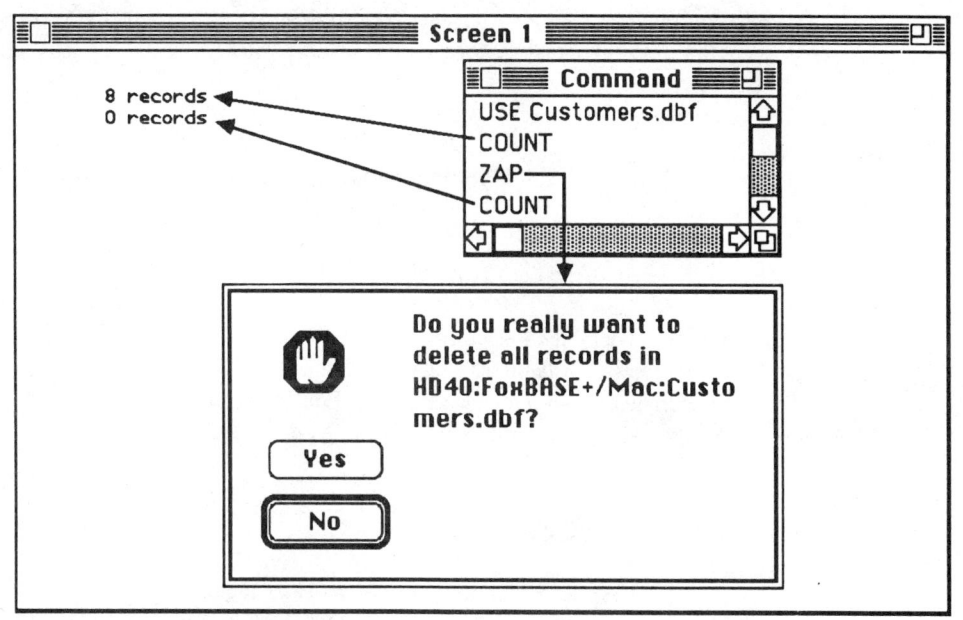

Fig. 5-5. Clearing a database.

INDEXING

If you want to see records in a certain order, make an index. Indexing does not physically rearrange the database file but just appears to put the file in a new order. Indexes are like wearing glasses made out of prism-shaped glass. When you look through an index all of the records are neatly arranged, even though they are physically mixed together in a random order. Look back at Fig. 3-8 in Chapter 3 to see an illustration of what I mean.

Each database file can have up to seven index files, for example, one for state, city and zip, sales volume, company name, etc. You can decide at any time which of the seven files you want to be the "boss," that is, which one will control the current visible order of the database file. All open indexes are updated when you add, delete, or change data. If you open a database file and select the Setup/Add option in the view or database menus, you'll see on the right side of the screen, a place for seven index files. To select the "boss," just darken it with a mouse click and press the Set Order button.

Creating Indexes

You can make a simple index by selecting the Setup/Add option under the view or database menus. If you select one field's name for the index, it will index the database on that field. You can, however, index on more than one field at a time. In fact, ridiculously large indexes can be created by selecting many fields as sort criteria. When you select more than one field, indexes put the first field in order first, the second field in order within the groups created by the first field, and so on.

Indexes must be made with only one type of data. You can't index on number fields and character fields without employing the converting functions to harmonize different types of data. This index expression, for example, won't work:

INDEX ON customers + dollars TO AMOUNTS

Dollars are probably in a numeric field and customers are probably in a character field. Try this instead:

INDEX ON customers + STR(dollars) TO AMOUNTS

The only difference between this command and the one above is that the STR( ) function is used to turn numeric dollars into a character value for the purpose of indexing. The actual data hasn't changed. Rather, we've fooled FoxBASE into accepting numbers as characters so that the index will work. What if you had dates and characters together? Try this:

INDEX ON customers + DTOC(buydate,1) TO AMOUNTS

The *buydate* field has the date data type that will not index with characters. In this case, you would use the date-to-character function, DTOC( ), to fool FoxBASE into thinking that the dates are characters, at least for indexing. The optional *1* that I snuck in there tells FoxBASE to put the dates into an internal order, which makes years most important, months less important, and days least important. This way, I get the outcome to work exactly as planned.

The REINDEX command is also under the Database menu as a mouse-selectable option. If an index is not open, and changes are made to its associated database file, it becomes obsolete. Nevertheless, you can refresh it simply by opening it up and reindexing. You don't have to recreate it from an expression, because the fields that define an index file are stored in its header.

Data-Converting Functions

The thing to remember when selecting an index sequence is that almost any expression of data in the file is legal as long as it isn't too long and so long as the index expression has only one type of data in it. It's a good idea to look at the data-converting functions in Chapter 9, they can help you make indexes with mixed field data types, or to order data using all of the power under FoxBASE's hood.

If you use the "expression builder" method of indexing, you only have to name the index file *AMOUNTS*, and select the field names *customers* and *dollars*. Of course, you'd have to put a + sign between customers and dollars and employ the STR( ) function, which is described earlier in this Chapter. After that, FoxBASE would put the rest of the command together for you. Regardless of how you entered index building commands, the result is the same.

Filtered Indexes

Filtered indexes are created with a FOR clause or, in the expression builder, there's a Filter checkbox you can select. The FOR clause is a conditional scope command that tells FoxBASE which records from the file to include in the index. (The FOR clause is described in greater detail at the end of Chapter 6.) If indexes are like a prism that makes light appear in an orderly array, like a rainbow of colors, filtered indexes are prisms that discriminate against certain colors of light. You can make a filtered index with a command like this one, which will show only records where the dollars are greater than 1000:

INDEX ON customers + STR(dollars) TO AMOUNTS FOR dollars > 1000

Find and Seek

FIND and SEEK are commands that use indexes to locate data quickly. Finding data is like seeking data except that FIND is intended to be an interactively easy way to search for records, and so it works only in the Command window. For example:

FIND Smith

Notice that there are no quotation marks around "Smith." Normally, you would expect to find quotation marks around any character expression. But FIND was made only for ease of use in the Command window, so FoxBASE doesn't require them, or any other delimiters, when using it for character, date, or numeric data. An index is required, however, so FIND won't locate any value that is not inside an active, controlling index.

SEEK is like FIND, because it too needs an index and won't find any values that are not in the index file. Like FIND, SEEK is lightning fast, finding records in large database files of up to 50 megabytes or more in size in less time than it takes to move the mouse from one corner of a mousepad to the other. Unlike the FIND command, SEEK requires that the data you're looking for be properly delimited. You'd use SEEK like this:

SEEK "Smith"

Numbers don't require delimiters, but dates must be entered as character expressions and converted for the purpose of seeking, that is, if the index was made using the date data type. If an index was made with a date data type like this:

INDEX ON buydate TO dateindex

Indexing 77

You would SEEK like this:

SEEK CTOD("12/25/85")

If an index was made with a character data type like this:

INDEX ON DTOC(buydate) TO dateindex

Or this, to make the date's order index properly:

INDEX ON DTOC(buydate,1) TO dateindex

You would SEEK like this, because the index would contain characters:

SEEK "12/25/85"

Numbers are straightforward, because they don't require delimiters. Therefore, if an index was made with a number data type like this:

INDEX ON dollars TO dollarindex

You would SEEK number values in the index like this:

SEEK 1000

The EXACT setting in the View window affects FIND and SEEK. If it is ON, you're required to include the whole character string or data value that you're looking for. If EXACT is OFF, you can enter any part of the value you're looking for and FoxBASE will locate it for you, as long as they match from the left side of the character string or data value and match as far as you go.

SORTING

Sorting sounds attractive because "to sort" means that we're making order out of chaos, but sorting in FoxBASE is probably not what you think. Sorting creates a new file from an old one while putting the new file in a different physical order (see Fig. 5-6). Sorting is not flexible, and it must be redone every time data changes in the file. The options for ordering data are fewer than for indexing, and you end up with two files to manage instead of one.

It is wise to sort very large files so that indexes don't have to work so hard. Sort files that you're giving to someone else so that they'll immediately see that the data is in order. If you sort, don't get an important file confused with sorted copies. If you sort files frequently, the "real" database can easily get lost in the shuffle. Indexes are simpler to create, use, and maintain, and they're helpful for relating two files.

| Observer | Original File | → | Sorted File |

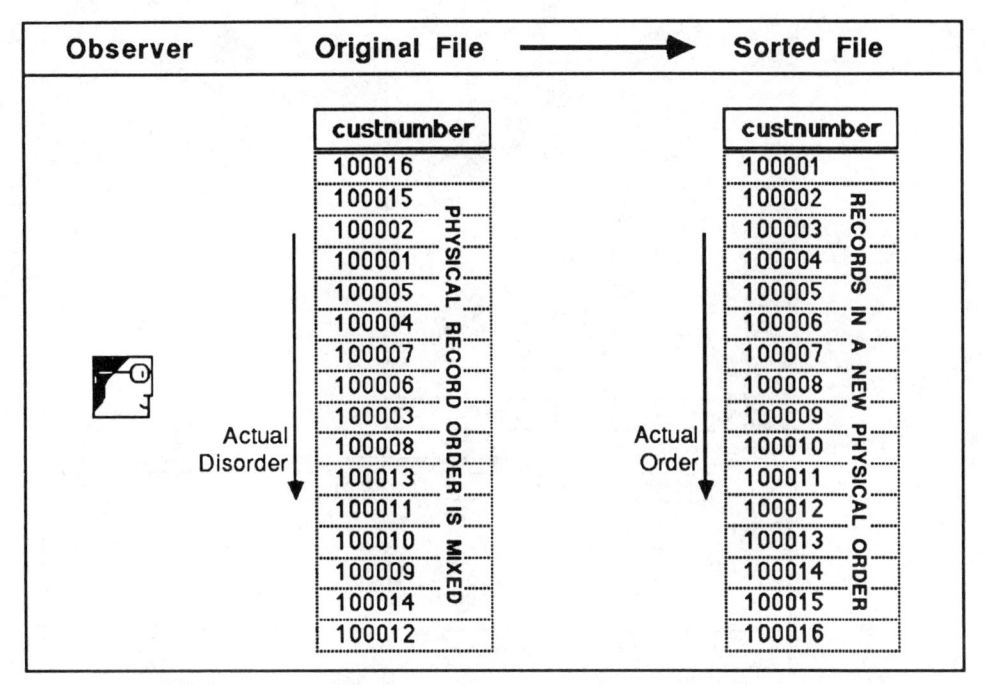

custnumber
100016
100015
100002
100001
100005
100004
100007
100006
100003
100008
100013
100011
100010
100009
100014
100012

Actual Disorder ↓ PHYSICAL RECORD ORDER IS MIXED

custnumber
100001
100002
100003
100004
100005
100006
100007
100008
100009
100010
100011
100012
100013
100014
100015
100016

Actual Order ↓ RECORDS IN A NEW PHYSICAL ORDER

Fig. 5-6. Sorting makes a new file.

SETTING FILE RELATIONSHIPS

Relational databases let you link files together, and as I mentioned above, indexes are essential for this purpose. Relationships are automatic lookups that happen so quickly that you're able to get data from several files as easily as from one. Here are the steps for relating files:

1. Open two files in the View window (see Fig. 5-7).

2. Make sure that both files have one field in common so that a record can be matched—there must be something in one file that can be located in the other file, record for record. The matching field is called a key. If there is no matching key, make one. Their names can be different, but it's a good idea to give them exactly the same length.

3. Decide which file will be the parent and which one will be the child. Parents lead children, so the child file will follow the parent file. It's like gears. If you move one gear, the related gear will move because they match. In database files, some records match, others don't. So you can move through a parent file, and if there's no matching record in the child file, only blanks will be returned when you ask it for data. If you were to look at the child file in such a case, you'd find the record pointer smack at the end of the file—that is where it will land after it has unsuccessfully looked for a record to match the parent.

Setting File Relationships

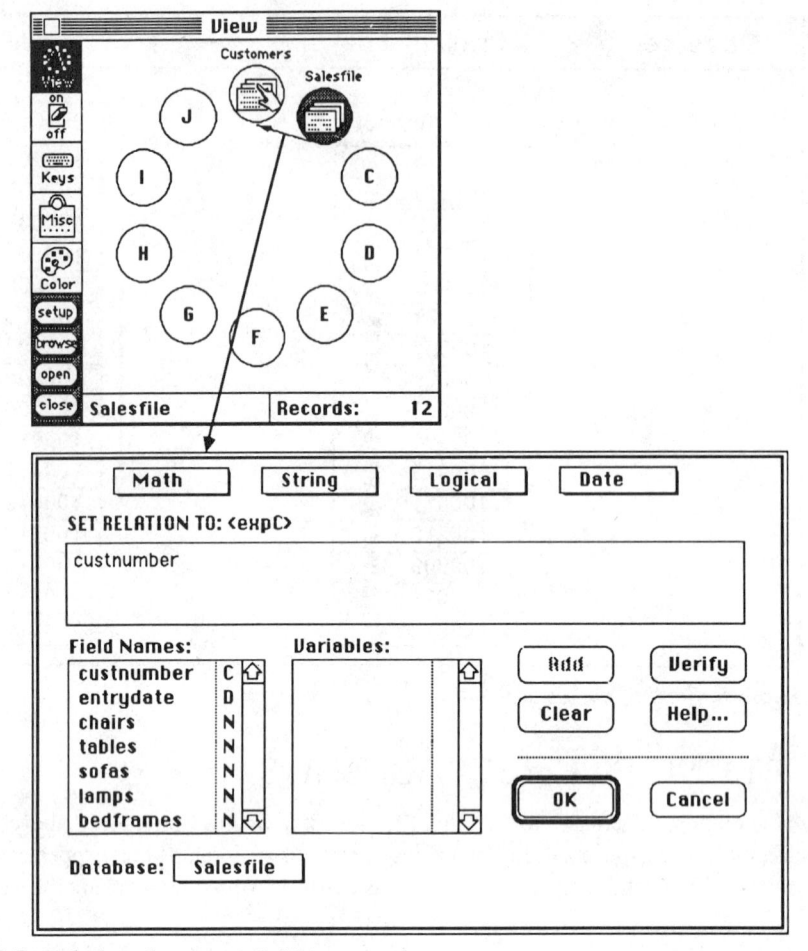

Fig. 5-7. Relations have one field or more in common.

Record pointers are simply the way FoxBASE pays attention to a database file, one record at a time. If you open a Browse window and click on a record, you're placing the record pointer. If you listed all records, deleted all records, and so on, FoxBASE would quickly and automatically move the record pointer from the first record (top of file) to the last (bottom of file), one record at a time.

If there are matching records in a child file, FoxBASE will align them automatically by putting the child's record pointer on the first record that matches the current parent record. Relationships are one way. If you manually moved the child file's pointer by browsing and clicking on different records, the parent file will stay where it is.

4. Whenever possible, relate many records to one, not one to many. It's a good idea to make the shorter file the child, resulting in a relationship of many records to one. If you related invoices (parent) to customers (child) there would be many invoices for one customer. If, however, you related customers (parent) to invoices

(child), there would be one customer (parent record) to many invoices (child records). Without programming, FoxBASE can find only one record in the child file that matches a parent record—so, in the example above, only one invoice would be found for each customer.

Relationships locate only the first child-file match encountered. Programmers can get around this limitation, but even then, it's not automatic. Therefore, to relate multiple records without programming, get in the habit of relating many records (usually longer files) to one (usually shorter files). That way you're sure to get out all the data you put in.

5. Index the child file on a key field—the one that matches the parent you're about to link with. This index is required because FoxBASE can maintain the relationship and in turn assume that the indexed field is the one that you'll relate to the parent file. An index finger will appear in the circle to let you know it's indexed.

6. Click on the parent file's circle and drag the arrow into the indexed child file's circle. When you let go of the mouse button a dialog box will appear like the one in Fig. 5-4 asking you to choose the parent's matching field. Remember, FoxBASE already knows the child file's matching field because it's indexed. Double-click on the field name, or type it in.

The files are related! If you've done your job and there are, indeed, matching records, browsing through them will reveal how they are linked. Browse both files, giving each one a portion of the screen. When you click on a record in the parent file it will align the child file, then select the child file's Browse window to see the relation. If there's no match to a selected parent record, the child file's browse will be at the last record, indicating that the SEEK failed. Try again until you find a record that matches.

You can relate up to 10 files at once, and multiple children per parent file is allowed. Chaining, so that a child can be a parent for other files, can also be done. The SET RELATION command in Chapter 8 contains information on the command syntax and other technical points that might interest programmers.

LISTING DATA ON-SCREEN

The simplest way to see data on the screen is to use the Browse window. You can scroll vertically from the top of a file to the bottom or horizontally through the field columns. What's more, you can split the window so important fields stay on one side of the screen, while you scroll horizontally through the rest. You can even reposition the columns by pushing them around.

Memo and picture data become visible in a browse only when you double-click on the field. Create a database with a memo field and store a few characters in it by double-clicking. Notice that the field name becomes boldface when it's closed so you'll know that it has contents.

The only important thing that Browse windows can't show you are calculated record sums, averages, and others such as those shown in Fig. 5-8. Sums and average are discussed in a later section. Because browse can display any field in a database, it can show

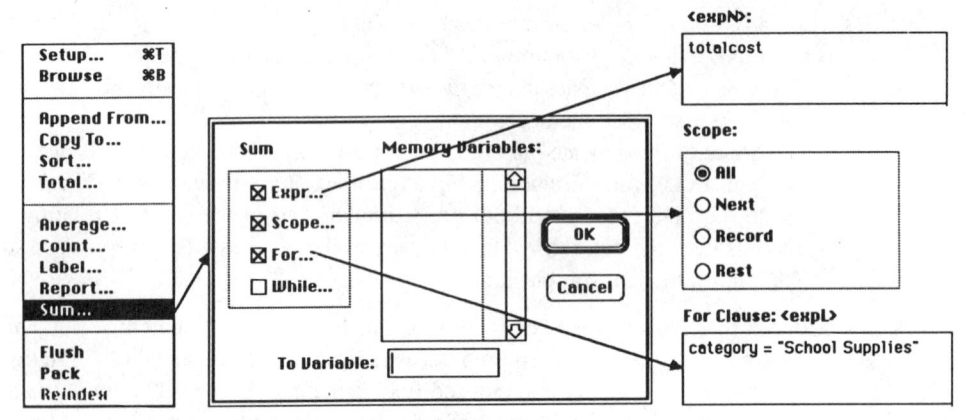

Fig. 5-8. Summing, counting, and averaging.

you a total column if you've made a field (column) for that purpose, such as the one in Fig. 5-9. Use the REPLACE command to calculate totals, like this:

REPLACE ALL totalcost WITH buycost * qtyinstock

Fig. 5-9. A total field.

Another way to view data is to use the LIST or DISPLAY commands. They're not available on a menu, so you'll have to enter them from the keyboard directly into the Command window. They work the same way and produce the same result, with one slight difference, DISPLAY shows records one screen at a time, pausing for you to view them, and continuing to the next screen only when you're ready. LIST waits for no one. It scrolls the display without pauses. Both LIST and DISPLAY can produce cross-field calculations. Take a look at the following examples:

82   *Listing Data On-Screen*

LIST ALL category, descript, buycost * 100 FOR descript = "Edsel"

The result:

Record#	category	descript	buycost*100
2	Automobiles	Edsel	923000.00

This one is almost the same, but with a significant difference. See if you can catch it.

LIST OFF ALL UPPER(descript), buycost * 100 FOR descript = "Edsel"

The result:

UPPER(descript)	buycost*100
EDSEL	923000.00

Did you notice that you can control the display with functions as well as calculations? And the fields listed are also at your control? You decide which ones to see, and in what order. If you don't itemize field names, they will all display. You can also display data from multiple files if a relationship is established. Just be sure to use the alias prefix (remember, it's filename->fieldname?) to name the fields in child files (out of the currently selected work area). If you don't want to see the record number, use the OFF option, it tells FoxBASE not to show or print the record numbers.

LIST OFF TO PRINT is an under-used command because it's not in a menu. Nevertheless, it prints the contents of a database file on your printer quickly and without fuss. The only alternative to it is a fully formatted report form that can take too much time to create if you're in a hurry. Look up the LIST and DISPLAY commands in Chapter 9 and read about how they work. They're powerful and useful tools for displaying and printing data. They can also reveal information about the status of your system or the structure of a database file.

SUMS, COUNTS, AVERAGES, AND TOTALS

Sum, Count and Average are all options in the Database menu. Total is also there but because it works differently, it is discussed separately. Sum, Count, and Average display the results on the screen. If you want to see, say, a sum of the numbers in a numeric database column, you can just execute the Menu option and it happens. If you wanted to limit the sum to only those records that match a condition, you'd need to enter a scope and FOR condition when prompted (see Fig. 5-8).

Using the file shown in Fig. 5-9, I asked FoxBASE to sum the total cost of all school supplies. If displayed records were the only ones with school supplies, FoxBASE would display the sum result as $8,750. In Fig. 5-8, I entered an optional numeric expression, "totalcost." Totalcost is the name of the field I wanted summed. I could have added others to the list simply by separating them with commas, like this:

SUM ALL totalcost, qtyonhand, buycost, reorderqty

If you don't enter a list of field names, which serve as the numeric expressions, Fox-BASE will sum or average every numeric field in the selected file.

Counting records works the same as summing. But why count records? So you can find out how many customers you have in New Jersey, or how many customers bought lamp shades last year. Counting is also useful when you need a divisor to calculate your own averages. Averaging works the same as counting and summing. You select the fields you want to average, FoxBASE does the rest.

These operations can be even more useful when you use record scoping to count only certain records in your calculation. See the entry Pinpointing Records of Interest later in the chapter.

The TOTAL command is special because it creates a summary file with the same structure as the file you're totalling, but with only one record for each group in the file of interest (see Fig. 5-10). The numbers that end up in the new file are group totals. Because the last record from each group shows up in the summary file, only the records that pertain to their whole group are accurate—and the totals, of course, will be accurate. When using TOTAL, group the file with an index or a sort ahead of time so that the grouping field is truly in order.

The TOTAL command also needs to know the name of the summary file you're going to create, and the name of the field that it should group and total. You can select certain fields for inclusion in the summary file, which is a good idea because some fields might be useless when separated from the detailed records in the original file.

REPLACING FIELD DATA AND CALCULATING COLUMNS

The REPLACE command is the most useful way to automatically change what's in a record. It calculates total columns, and does every other kind of automatic field data changing you can think of, all because it can be carefully controlled. This command, for example, would change every state in a database with Florida:

REPLACE ALL state WITH "FL"

Awesome power, isn't it? Consider this command:

REPLACE ALL state WITH UPPER(state)

This command changes all of the state abbreviations into uppercase abbreviations by use of the UPPER( ) function. The following command would scoot all of the names in a first name field to the right side of the field, effectively right-justifying them:

REPLACE ALL firstname WITH RTRIM(firstname)

You are limited only by your imagination in the many ways you can use the REPLACE command. By adding scopes (that's what ALL is because it tells FoxBASE what the scope of affected records is), and conditions (with expressions of your own making), you can tell REPLACE to affect only those records that meet certain conditions. In an example earlier in this chapter, I entered a command that put totals into a field, like this:

REPLACE ALL totalcost WITH buycost * qtyinstock

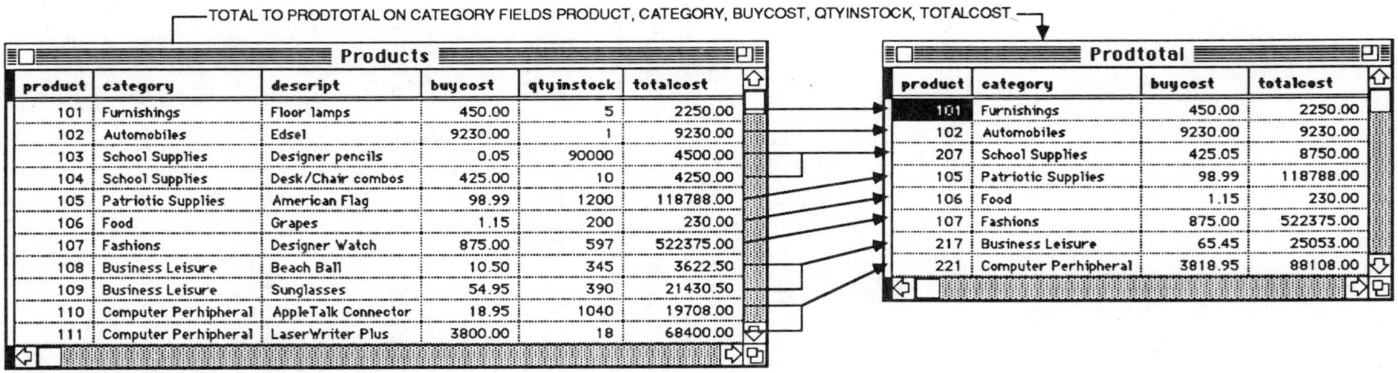

┌─ TOTAL TO PRODTOTAL ON CATEGORY FIELDS PRODUCT, CATEGORY, BUYCOST, QTYINSTOCK, TOTALCOST

Products

product	category	descript	buycost	qtyinstock	totalcost
101	Furnishings	Floor lamps	450.00	5	2250.00
102	Automobiles	Edsel	9230.00	1	9230.00
103	School Supplies	Designer pencils	0.05	90000	4500.00
104	School Supplies	Desk/Chair combos	425.00	10	4250.00
105	Patriotic Supplies	American Flag	98.99	1200	118788.00
106	Food	Grapes	1.15	200	230.00
107	Fashions	Designer Watch	875.00	597	522375.00
108	Business Leisure	Beach Ball	10.50	345	3622.50
109	Business Leisure	Sunglasses	54.95	390	21430.50
110	Computer Perhipheral	AppleTalk Connector	18.95	1040	19708.00
111	Computer Perhipheral	LaserWriter Plus	3800.00	18	68400.00

Prodtotal

product	category	buycost	totalcost
101	Furnishings	450.00	2250.00
102	Automobiles	9230.00	9230.00
207	School Supplies	425.05	8750.00
105	Patriotic Supplies	98.99	118788.00
106	Food	1.15	230.00
107	Fashions	875.00	522375.00
217	Business Leisure	65.45	25053.00
221	Computer Perhipheral	3818.95	88108.00

Fig. 5-10. Making total fields.

Replacing Field Data and Calculating Columns 85

Here are some more sample field calculations:

REPLACE ALL commission WITH (sales * .05) FOR seller = "JOHN"

REPLACE ALL commission WITH (sales * .08) FOR seller = "MARY"

You can calculate any column with this type of command and expression or you can selectively enter new data, like this:

REPLACE ALL tires WITH "PIRELLI" FOR veh__type = "LITETRUCK"

REPLACE ALL tires WITH "MICHELIN" FOR veh__type = "BIGTRUCK"

REPLACE ALL tires WITH "GOODYEAR" FOR veh__type = SPACE(10)

In the last example, the SPACE( ) function checks for an empty, 10-character field. If it finds that there's no vehicle type mentioned in a record, it puts "GOODYEAR" in the tires field. I encourage you to try this command out for yourself. You'll be surprised how easy it is, and the Record/Replace menu options are there to help.

PINPOINTING RECORDS OF INTEREST

If you are in a Browse window you can find information in its file by selecting the Edit/Find menu option. This is the easiest way to locate random information because it searches through all the browsed fields to find what you want. A nice thing about this option is that it isn't picky about data type, so you can search for anything without getting bothersome error messages.

The SEEK command is the fastest way to find data in large files. In order to use it, your file must have an index to serve as the basis for searching because SEEK looks directly into the index to find a match. When a match is found, the record is found, because indexes store direct addresses to records in the form of record numbers. FIND is equivalent to SEEK in the way it works, but it's for interactive use only and doesn't require that you put quotation marks around characters. A SEEK command looks like this:

SEEK "Jones, Davie"

A FIND looks like this:

FIND Jones, Davie

The LOCATE command is useful for small files, searching records sequentially until it is satisfied that what you're looking for is found, or the end of the file has been reached. LOCATE has an advantage over SEEK in that it can look for a record using any condition. SEEK can only find what's been put into an index. A typical LOCATE command would look like this:

LOCATE FOR name = "Jones, Davie" .AND. state < > "CA"

This command says to find the first occurrence of the name "Jones, Davie" that's not in the state of California. The CONTINUE command is LOCATE's compliment, because it continues the same search, looking for the next occurrence that matches the same condition (see Fig. 5-11).

For some people, these data finding commands are easier to use because there are menu options, and they don't have to remember commands.

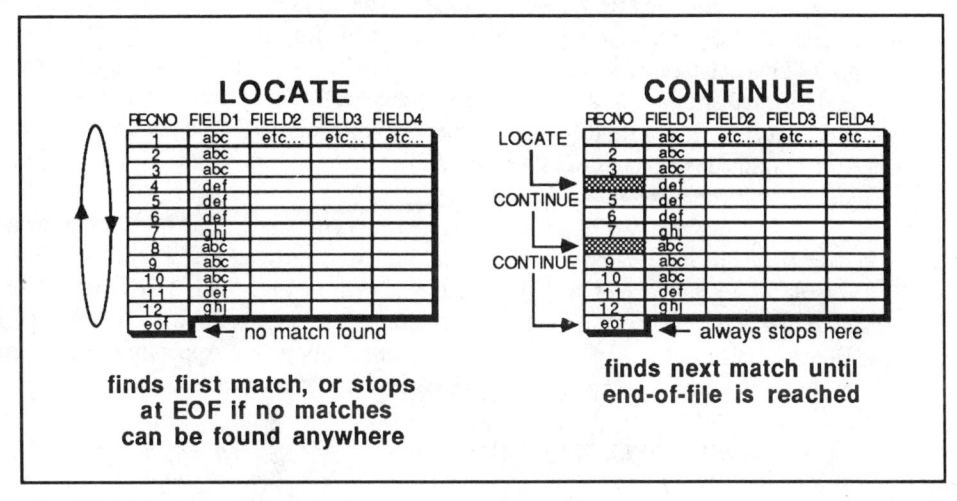

Fig. 5-11. Locate and Continue.

SETTING RECORD RANGES

Ranges can be set to limit or select certain records. Scoping, and the FOR and WHILE command clauses are the best ways to set record ranges. I mentioned deletions above because they can also limit access to records, but their purpose is to remove records, so use them for that purpose alone.

The scopes include ALL, NEXT, RECORD, and REST. ALL is self explanatory. NEXT uses a number, which you supply, that indicates how many records should be affected. RECORD affects only one record that is specified by a record number you supply, and last, REST affects all the records that remain between a current record position and the end of a file.

WHILE is a command modifier that instructs FoxBASE to affect every record from the current position, as long as they meet some condition. Once you have an indexed database, and records are in groups of interest, you can locate a record that meets some condition (with a LOCATE, FIND, or SEEK commands), and then use the WHILE command option to make changes to all of the records that are in the group.

For very large files, this method is much better than using the FOR clause, because it looks through the whole file, at every single record, to see if it should be processed. If only a few records in a large file need to be considered, FOR is a dumb way to go.

FoxBASE is so fast that FOR can be used without performance problems in almost any file that has less than 10,000 records. In larger files that have between 10,000 and 1 million records or more, the SEEK (or FIND) option combined with a WHILE is noticeably faster.

IMPORTING DATA

Data can be imported from several different types of ASCII files. ASCII is the American Standard Code for Information Interchange, which means, practically, that they are stripped-down database files with rows and columns, but without field (column) names or a strictly formal structure. ASCII files can be created by word processors, spreadsheets, other database programs, and by mainframe or minicomputers. The common ASCII formats are delimited (with commas if unspecified), tab delimited, blank delimited, and fixed length (or SDF, for system data format).

To import records, two requisites must be satisfied. There must be a complimentary database structure that matches the records, and you must APPEND records from the import file using the correct ASCII format as shown in Fig. 5-12. Files that are in the standard dBase format on DOS or Macintosh computers are treated natively by FoxBASE and don't need to be imported. You can use them as they are. Appending data from an Excel spreadsheet that has been saved as a text file could be done like this:

APPEND FROM TEXTFILE DELIMITED WITH TAB

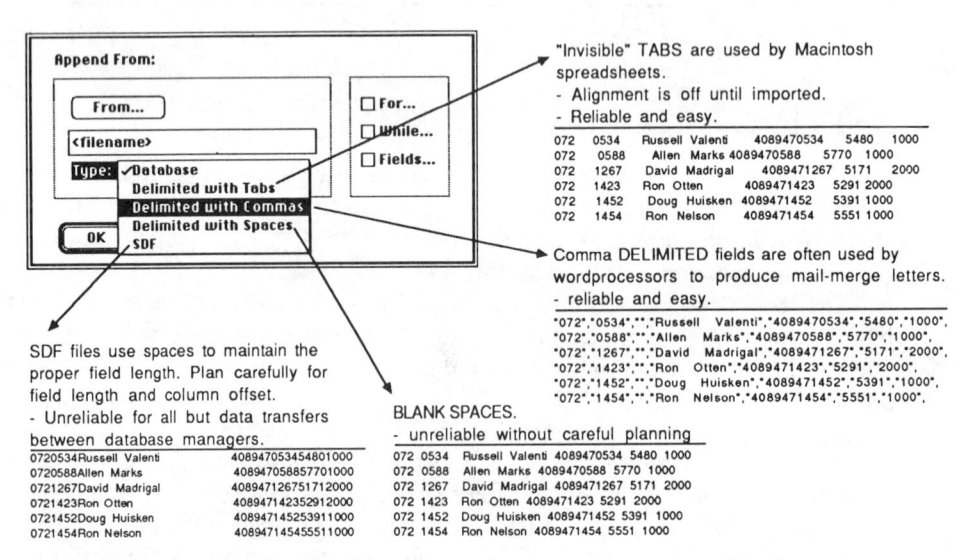

"Invisible" TABS are used by Macintosh spreadsheets.
- Alignment is off until imported.
- Reliable and easy.

```
072  0534  Russell Valenti   4089470534  5480  1000
072  0588  Allen Marks       4089470588  5770  1000
072  1267  David Madrigal    4089471267  5171  2000
072  1423  Ron Otten         4089471423  5291  2000
072  1452  Doug Huisken      4089471452  5391  1000
072  1454  Ron Nelson        4089471454  5551  1000
```

Comma DELIMITED fields are often used by wordprocessors to produce mail-merge letters.
- reliable and easy.

```
"072","0534","","Russell  Valenti","4089470534","5480","1000",
"072","0588","","Allen  Marks","4089470588","5770","1000",
"072","1267","","David  Madrigal","4089471267","5171","2000",
"072","1423","","Ron  Otten","4089471423","5291","2000",
"072","1452","","Doug  Huisken","4089471452","5391","1000",
"072","1454","","Ron  Nelson","4089471454","5551","1000",
```

BLANK SPACES.
- unreliable without careful planning

```
072 0534  Russell Valenti 4089470534 5480 1000
072 0588  Allen Marks 4089470588 5770 1000
072 1267  David Madrigal 4089471267 5171 2000
072 1423  Ron Otten 4089471423 5291 2000
072 1452  Doug Huisken 4089471452 5391 1000
072 1454  Ron Nelson 4089471454 5551 1000
```

SDF files use spaces to maintain the proper field length. Plan carefully for field length and column offset.
- Unreliable for all but data transfers between database managers.

```
0720534Russell Valenti     408947053454801000
0720588Allen Marks         408947058857701000
0721267David Madrigal      408947126751712000
0721423Ron Otten           408947142352912000
0721452Doug Huisken        408947145253911000
0721454Ron Nelson          408947145455511000
```

Fig. 5-12. Import/Export file types.

EXPORTING DATA

Just as information can be imported from outside sources, FoxBASE can export data in the common ASCII formats. The command is COPY TO DELIMITED WITH ???.

The ??? stands for the file format you're exporting to. Excel likes tab delimited files, and common word processors use commas to delimit mail merge records. To export a file for Microsoft Word to use in mail merge you could use a command like this:

    COPY TO mergedata DELIMITED

The result would be a comma-delimited file suitable for processing as a data document by most word processors. For more information about exporting see the entry COPY TO in Chapter 8.

SAVING PROCEDURES

In Chapter 3, I showed you how to save commands for later use. It's as easy as cutting them out of the Command window and pasting them into a new program file. The FoxBASE designers want you to reuse routines that you've created using the menu-driven commands, and certainly, to save those that you toiled over in the Command window so they'd be perfect for a task. Over time, there's no better way to master FoxBASE than to write, collect, and rewrite commands so that they can become your own personal library of tricks.

CREATING DATA ENTRY FORMS

Some people want to know and control everything that FoxBASE does, so Fox Software has obliged them with a program that writes programs. FoxForm lets you draw screens and, like a robot, it writes FoxBASE programs from the screens. Remember, almost everything FoxBASE does is through programs, and nice data entry screens are no exception. Consequently, FoxForm and FoxCode automate the task of program writing for you. FoxCode is the robot's brain that you can change if you want by learning the template programming language. For practical guidance in using FoxForm, see Creating Applications—A Short Tutorial in Chapter 7.

Artificial Intelligence?

If it weren't for the FoxForm screen generator, creating custom entry forms would be impossible for many of us. With FoxForm, it's a routine thing to design screens, save them, and then generate either complete programs or simpler format layouts to be installed as a new way to view data (see Fig. 5-13). Fox Software built intelligence into the format file generating template, and into the simple and advanced application-making templates it ships with every FoxBASE program.

You don't need to know anything about FoxCode templates to use them; the most you'll ever have to do is compile the template programs (.gen files) into finished .cod files so FoxForm can use them (see Fig. 5-14) when you're ready to generate format files or programs. Only (.cod) files can produce form files or programs, so if you get a message while generating your forms that it can't generate from this version, or something similar, try compiling the (.gen) file into a (.cod) file from the Program/ Compile/Template menu. Then you can try to generate the screen into a form again after selecting the newly compiled (.cod) template file.

It's a good idea to try the format template first until you can see how it works. Then try the simple application template because it gives you a complete add, edit, delete program that shows what a FoxBASE program looks like. Once you create a few of these for some related files, you can create a menu for them, and viola, a serious application is born. Look at the menu program example later in this Chapter, or the one in Chapter 7, to learn how to make and change pull-down menu programs.

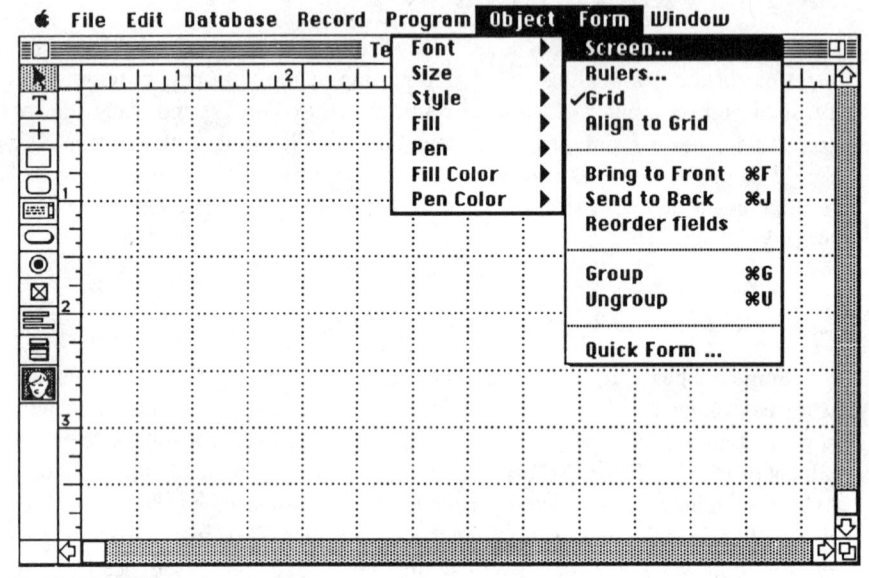

Fig. 5-13. FoxForm.

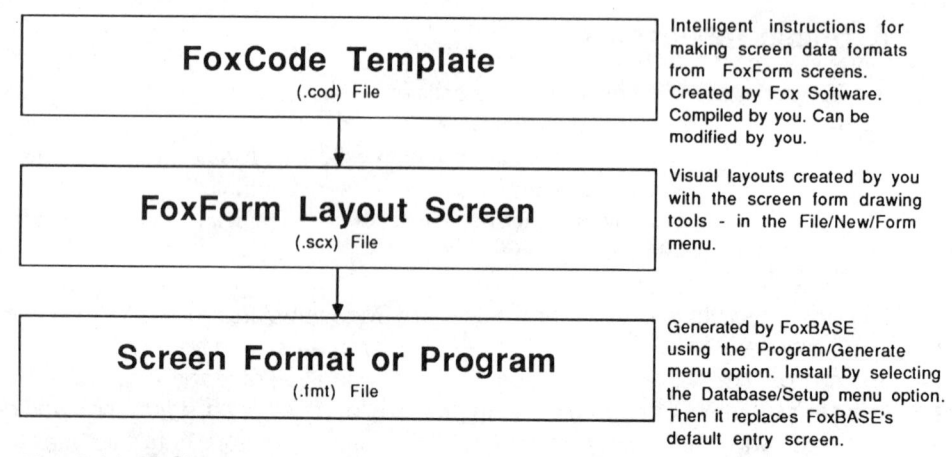

```
FoxCode Template
   (.cod) File
```
Intelligent instructions for making screen data formats from FoxForm screens. Created by Fox Software. Compiled by you. Can be modified by you.

```
FoxForm Layout Screen
   (.scx) File
```
Visual layouts created by you with the screen form drawing tools - in the File/New/Form menu.

```
Screen Format or Program
   (.fmt) File
```
Generated by FoxBASE using the Program/Generate menu option. Install by selecting the Database/Setup menu option. Then it replaces FoxBASE's default entry screen.

Fig. 5-14. Making your own screens.

90 *Creating Data Entry Forms*

DEVELOPING APPLICATIONS

You can start some FoxBASE application programs, press a button and you're done before you know it—the checks are printed and the invoices mailed. The flip side to that simplicity, however, is the complexity of programming. Like airline pilots who carry passengers, programmers take responsibility for the whole journey. They have certain goals in mind and specific methods for reaching them.

Application development starts with understanding the information you're managing and tests that understanding by modeling. Only then can you provide users with ways to add it, see it, change it, and remove it. Finally, success comes when the people using your applications can manage their data with ease.

Creating Successful Database Structures

As discussed in Chapters 1 and 2, databases are a collection of tables that hold information. Sometimes one table is enough, but most applications used in business need more. It's your responsibility to decide how many tables should be used and what information will go into each one. Analyzing the data and devising a model for it out of tables, records, and fields, are important first steps to creating an application. If you're interested, I've discussed each of these steps in more detail below. Then I discuss the inputs and outputs for data, and finally, basic menu design.

Analyzing the Information to be Stored

Study the information to be stored until you know about all of its small and large parts. Discover and define each small part of the information so that database fields can be created to hold them, but don't loose sight of the big picture and how the information flows in and out of the system. Make a simple worksheet for yourself that shows field names, the information each field will hold, how long it needs to be, and what type of data it is—logical, character, numeric, date, and so on. Long text notes can be stored in memo fields, but memos aren't as accessible as fixed-length fields, and you can't sort, index, or calculate them.

Discover how individual data parts are naturally related. Make notes. Ask yourself how the information is currently gathered and managed by its users—there's usually some system already in place to manage most data, even if it's inadequate or primitive. Collecting copies of forms and reports that are already in use is an excellent way to learn about the data. Follow up by discussing your findings with those who will use your application; they can usually tell you if you've left something out or don't have the whole picture. Be thorough. It might be difficult to change things after the application is finished.

Creating a Data Model

The second part of database creation is to divide the information into logical groups or sets. Each unique set of information can reside in a table all its own. Arrange tables (or files) by subject: Customers, invoices, inventory, employees, and so on. What makes modeling different from analysis is that you recreate the relationships in modeling that you studied in their current state during analysis. Accomplished FoxBASE programmers also consider issues of storage efficiency and performance while modeling.

Relating Tables with Key Fields

The third step is to relate the different sets or tables on paper so that you can discover if the model will work when it's put to the test of printing reports, data entry, and so on. Be certain that the key fields in each database file are sufficient to relate them to other files that might need to be joined with it to satisfy a user's needs. Also check for redundancy, making sure that you're not storing similar information in more than one table for no good reason. This process is called normalization by database academics.

Reviewing the Design

After you've come this far, take a look at things and make changes as needed. Check out your design by showing it to users. They might not appreciate the technical aspects, but they will appreciate your interest and understanding of their data, and you'll need their confirmation before starting actual development. It doesn't hurt to know you are going straight before painting lines on a freeway.

Creating Input and Maintenance Forms

The difference between input forms you create and the default FoxBASE screen data formats is great. You will want to shield users from having to look at cryptic field names by making forms that are more human and fitting for the task. Design screens like paper forms. You can use the form layout tool under the File/New/Form menu, or you can create form files from scratch.

The easiest way to create screens is in the layout editor. Turn them into working forms (.fmt files) or programs (.prg files) with the Program/Generate menu, and then customize them in the program editor (File/Open/Program) so that they look exactly the way you want. The difference between finished screen forms and programs is academic. Forms, or format (.fmt) files are used by the command SET FORMAT TO ?, whereas programs (.prg) files are used with the DO ? command. The format file option creates a static screen that merely replaces FoxBASE's own default screen for datafile entry and changing, and the program file option is created when you generate an application instead of a format file. Applications are run with the Program/Do menu option, or they can be run from a menu of your own creation—and they are far more flexible and powerful than screen forms.

If you're not an accomplished programmer, I suggest that you generate screens using the "simple application" template Fox Software provides, because it lets you make screen programs that let your users add, edit, and delete data. Since these "screens" are actual programs that you can combine under a menu later on, you'll be building parts for an application instead of replacing FoxBASE parts. In any case, you should make one screen for each file in the system.

Creating Screen Outputs

Screen outputs can be simple and easy, or complex and impossible. They aren't as important as input and maintenance screens or reports, because most applications get all of the data displaying they need from those options. On-line information systems need screen displays, and one of the easiest ways to give users displayed data is to let them browse a file with the nomodify option, which prevents data from being inadvertently changed, like this:

```
USE FILENAME
BROWSE NOMODIFY
```

Another way to change the screen output is to use the screen painter to design a layout solely for the purpose of displaying data, not changing it. The way to do that is to use the Say option in the screen generator instead of the Get option. Get lets users change data, Say just puts it out there for show. If you're interested in some programming, you can use memory variables to store the results of sums, averages, and so on, and display their results in neat formats on the screen.

Building a Menu System

Menus are not hard once you've made one. If you've created a screen for data entry and maintenance, and a report for output, all you need is a menu to glue them together, and the result is an application! Menus are exciting, too. If you type this example program into a program file and name it TESTMENU, it will produce true FoxBASE menus that you can use to run your report and screen programs:

```
*************
* Testmenu.prg
* A simple menu program for launching other programs
*
SET PROCEDURE TO TESTMENU
SCREEN 1 TOP
CLEAR
DIMENSION TopRow(1)
DIMENSION DownCol1(3)
STORE "Action"   TO TopRow(1)
STORE "One"      TO DownCol1(1)
STORE "Two"      TO DownCol1(2)
STORE "QUIT"     TO DownCol1(3)
MENU BAR TopRow,1
MENU 1,DownCol1,3
ON MENU DO ACTION WITH MENU(0), MENU(1)
DO WHILE .T.
    READ
ENDDO
```

```
PROCEDURE ACTION
PARAMETER zero, one
DO CASE
    *\ MENU SELECTED ACTIONS GO HERE
    CASE zero=1 .AND. one=1
        *\ DO programone
        CLEAR
        ? "You selected menu option one."
    CASE zero=1 .AND. one=2
        *\ DO programtwo
        CLEAR
        ? "You selected menu option two."
    CASE zero=1 .AND. one=3
        *\ DO programthree
        CLEAR
        ? "You selected menu option three."
        CANCEL
ENDCASE
RETURN
**************
```

To use this program, you should replace the lines that look like "*\ DO programone" with your own program names. You can also expand the menu to include as many items as you want. The * symbols causes FoxBASE to ignore the words that follow it, so take them out if you want to put a "DO programname" of your own in the place of the dummy calls I made. Adding additional menu columns is easy too, just refer to the menu section in Chapter 7 for more how-to menu directions.

Part Two
Developing FoxBASE+/Mac Applications

6
Introduction to FoxBASE Programming

APPLICATIONS have structures to hold data, ways of relating those structures, and procedures that automate data manipulation and viewing. This chapter introduces FoxBASE programming—its operators, commands, functions, and constructs—the tools and processes used to make applications for yourself or others to use.

PROGRAMMING FEATURES

It's a good idea to understand FoxBASE's way of handling data, so I've included in this chapter a brief discussion of indexes, record pointers, and other functions. Because many commands and functions are designed to work directly on database files, records, and fields, your time learning the "engine" of FoxBASE will be well spent. User interface issues are a subject of their own, so they are discussed later in Chapter 7.

Commands

FoxBASE commands are issued by using the command verbs (listed in Chapter 8) or by adding expressions and operators to command verbs. Each command starts on its own line, and, almost without exception, each line must start with a command verb. Commands are executed from the top of a program to the bottom, one line at a time. All commands are evaluated and executed, unless there are constructs that instruct FoxBASE to skip them (such as IF, or DO CASE), and others can be executed over and over again, which is what happens with commands inside of a DO WHILE construct. The following outline shows the parts that can go into each command line:

```
COMMAND VERB    —one only, required
EXPRESSION(S)   —one or more, often optional
OPERATOR(S)     —as needed
```

If an expression directly affects the general behavior of a command (or a function) it's called an argument. It's not unusual to see several arguments in a command statement. While some command verbs work alone, others need arguments. The following command would work fine by itself if you were using a database that had a numeric field in it:

SUM

SUM adds the values in each numeric field (column) of a database, displaying the results on your screen. You could add more expressions to the SUM command, for example, to tell it what numeric fields to add (by name), or to indicate which selection of records you want FoxBASE to add. This command does both:

SUM buycost FOR category = "Furnishings"

Unlike SUM, which can take or leave arguments, the TOTAL command requires two arguments in order to work, one to tell it what file to create (by name), and another to tell it what field to group and summarize:

TOTAL TO newfilename ON fieldname

Operators

Operators are like punctuation. They bind or separate parts of command expressions according to the rules of syntax. Another similarity between punctuation and the FoxBASE operators is that some have great power—a period at the end of a sentence, and some have less—a comma. When FoxBASE is reading your commands, it uses this order of importance, or precedence, to determine which operators to evaluate first, second, third, and so on.

The following lists show what operators you have at your disposal for constructing your own expressions and what the order of precedence is, if any, within each type.

For the numeric data type (in order of precedence):

( )	Makes groups, forcing evaluation of innermost first to outermost last.
** or ^	Exponentiation, raises the first number (before ** or ^) to the power of the second number (after ** or ^).
*	Multiplies the first number (before *) with the second number (after *).
/	Divides the first number (before /) by the second number (after /) (has same precedence as *).
+	Adds the first number (before +) with the second number (after +).
-	Subtracts the second number (after -) from the first number (before -) (has same precedence as +).

For the character (string) data type:

( )	Makes groups, forcing evaluation of innermost first to outermost last.

98   Programming Features

+	Concatenates, or joins, two strings while leaving trailing blanks, if any, at the end of each string.
–	Concatenates, or joins, two strings while moving trailing blanks, if any, from the end of first string to the end of the second string.

For any data type—to establish or evaluate relationships:

<	Tests to see if one thing is less than another.
>	Tests to see if one thing is greater than another.
=	Tests to see if one thing is equal to another, also used in place of the STORE command to assign a value to a memory variable.
< > or #	Tests to see if one thing is not equal to another.
< =	Tests to see if one thing is less than or equal to another.
> =	Tests to see if one thing is greater than or equal to another.
$	Tests to see if the first string (before $) is contained in the second string (after $).
= =	Evaluates for equality between two strings with the additional ability (that is compared with the = operator) to ignore trailing blanks when EXACT is set to OFF.

For the logical data type (listed in order of precedence):

( )	Makes groups, forcing evaluation of innermost first to outermost last.
.NOT. or !	Negation, evaluates to true .T. or false .F..
.AND.	AND, evaluates to true .T. or false .F..
.OR.	Inclusive OR, evaluates to true .T. or false .F..

Expressions and ?

Expressions are the customizable part of a command line. They are not the command verb itself, but they add to it. Some of the following examples use the ? command to evaluate expressions. The ? command puts the result of expressions it evaluates on the screen or, if you have used the SET PRINT ON command, on a printed page. Expressions can consist of:

- Constants—literal things you type in.
- Database field names—which tell FoxBASE to use the field's contents.
- Memory variables—Chapter 6 describes memory variables.
- Functions—see Chapter 9.
- Operators—such as + – / =.

Each expression produces a single result:

Expression: ? 45 – 25
Result: 20.00

Expression: ? "I like "+"animals."
Result: I like animals.

Although each expression can have only one result, and data types must match when expressions are combined, several expressions can be evaluated at one time provided each one is separated from the next by commas (see Fig. 6-1).

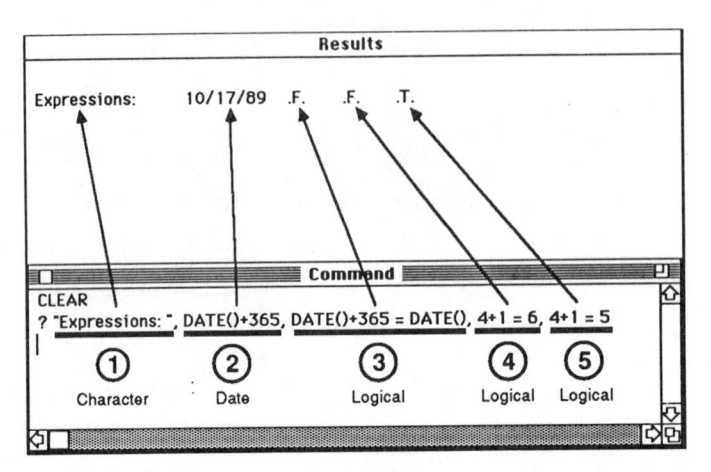

```
                              Results
Expressions:   10/17/89  .F.  .F.  .T.




                            Command
CLEAR
? "Expressions: ", DATE()+365, DATE()+365 = DATE(), 4+1 = 6, 4+1 = 5
        ①              ②             ③            ④       ⑤
    Character         Date         Logical      Logical  Logical
```

Fig. 6-1. Expressions add to the command verb.

Expressions are called "logical" when they evaluate to a true (.T.) or a false (.F.), regardless of whether the data used in the expression led to a logical result. For example, character data elements in the expression "CAT" = "DOG" evaluate to a logical false. In FoxBASE, (.F.) is displayed for logically false results and (.T.) is displayed for true results.

Logical expressions are most useful when filtering data, selecting records for a report, sum, or total, and so on. Logical expressions can be used to test almost any condition in a database file or program. Records will either meet selection criteria, or they won't; or a user either selected a menu option, or he didn't. Here's an example showing what I mean:

LIST ALL FOR "CAT" $ animal

This expression says to list the records that have the word "CAT" anywhere in the animal field. Either "CAT" is contained in (the meaning of $) the ANIMAL database field, or it isn't. You can use this method to create filters, too:

SET FILTER TO "CAT" $ animal

Logical fields can also be tested to see if they are true or false. A T or F with a period on each side is the way FoxBASE programs specify logical values. When you enter a value in a database file, the periods are not used, only T and F are accepted. Programs can test logical fields for an affirmative value, such as this test of the field named "housesold:"

IF housesold

```
    . . . commands
ENDIF
```

To test a logical field for a negative value, ask the question like this:

```
IF .NOT. housesold
    . . . commands
ENDIF
```

Controls and Constructs

Program controls are any commands or program features that you can use to put forks in the road, so to speak, and allow your program to make some of its own decisions. Constructs are the specific commands and language features FoxBASE has for controlling programs. Three of the most important such features are DO WHILE, DO CASE, and IF. There's also a function called IIF( ), for "immediate if," that allows a program to make decisions right inside almost any other command.

Do While...Enddo

The DO WHILE command sets up a loop construct that causes controlled repetition of any commands you want. The loop will re-execute as long as a WHILE clause is true. DO WHILE constructs need at least one logical expression in order to work, even if it's as simple as this:

```
DO WHILE .T.
    . . . commands
ENDDO
```

The .T. in the example above would cause the commands between the DO WHILE and the ENDDO to keep repeating forever until you pressed the Escape key, which is command-period on a Mac Plus or older model computer. More often, you'll see DO WHILE constructs that look something like this:

```
DO WHILE "CAT" $ animal .AND. .NOT. EOF( )
    . . . commands
    SKIP
ENDDO
```

This construct tells FoxBASE to continue repeating all of the commands inside the construct until the end animal of a record is no longer a cat, or the file's end is reached. The SKIP tells FoxBASE to move to the next record for processing. Logical expression conditions following the WHILE can be many and complex. You can use (.OR.), (.AND.), and (.NOT.) operators in various combinations to give your loop construct excellent control over what it's doing. DO WHILE constructs are the workhorse in FoxBASE and are limited only by your imagination. Take a look at the examples in Fig. 6-2 to get more ideas about how you can use these constructs.

```
* Counter.prg
* Counts from 1 TO 50
SET TALK OFF
x = 0
DO WHILE x < 50
  @ 5,x SAY "*"
  x = x + 1
ENDDO
RETURN


* Traverse.prg
* Skips through a database file one record at a time
GOTO TOP
DO WHILE .NOT. EOF()
  <statements - check for this or that and do this or that>
  SKIP 1
ENDDO
RETURN
```

DO WHILE structures always have an ENDDO

Fig. 6-2. A sample DO WHILE construct.

Do Case...Otherwise...Endcase

The DO CASE ENDCASE command is a switch construct. Think of a railroad switch yard where trains can go many ways. That's exactly what DO CASE does. ENDCASE merely ends the construct and nothing else. Consider this example:

```
engine = "Red"
DO CASE
CASE engine = "Black & dirty"
     ? "This is a car"
CASE engine = "Red"
     ? "This is a fire truck"
CASE engine = "Round and noisy"
     ? "This is a jet"
OTHERWISE
     ? "I don't know what it is"
ENDCASE
```

Can you tell which of the four text options would be displayed? The ? command evaluates whatever expression follows it, so the text I entered above would display exactly as it's shown. Engine could be a database field, a memory variable (I'll get to them shortly), or a constant value that you've entered into the program. Most often, case constructs are used to control the flow of a program when a user chooses menu options. For an example, take a look at the sample menu program in *Building a Menu System* near the end of Chapter 5.

The DO CASE construct is useful whenever there are multiple options and a decision needs to be made. If the "case" is true, FoxBASE executes the program statements that follow that "case," and all of the others are ignored, even if they're also true. If none are true, FoxBASE executes the commands that follow the optional OTHERWISE statement. Take a look at the example in Fig. 6-3 where the OTHERWISE option is used to question a user.

```
CLEAR
STORE SPACE(1) TO choice

@  5,15 SAY "1) Sunnyside up"
@  6,15 SAY "2) Over well"
@  7,15 SAY "3) Over easy"
@  8,15 SAY "4) QUIT"
@ 10,15 GET choice
READ

DO CASE
CASE choice = "1"
    @ 14,15 SAY "don't flip the eggs "
CASE choice = "2"
    @ 14,15 SAY "turn up the heat    "
CASE choice = "3"
    @ 14,15 SAY "turn down the heat  "
CASE choice = "4"
    @ 14,15 SAY "Time to go          "
    RETURN
OTHERWISE
    @ 14,15 SAY "What button is that?"
ENDCASE

RETURN
```

DO CASE structures always have an ENDCASE

Fig. 6-3. A sample DO CASE construct.

If...Else...Endif

The IF construct is like DO CASE and ENDCASE constructs, except that it has fewer options. All of these constructs are interchangeable, but the CASE construct should be used whenever there are multiple options for the purpose of clarity. Use the IF and ENDIF constructs to test for a condition or to branch when one condition is tested. If the condition is not true, FoxBASE skips the commands that are inside the construct, or executes those that are inside the ELSE portion of the construct if an optional ELSE has been included. Look at this example:

```
IF engine = "Red"
    ? "Has to be a fire truck!"
ELSE
    ? "Who knows what it is?"
ENDIF
```

IIF( )

The immediate "if" function (IIF( )) is not a command or a construct, but it's so powerful and useful for controlling programs that you should know about it in this context. Consider this use:

```
? "The engine " + IIF(engine = "Red","is a Fire truck","is unknown")
```

Without the IIF( ) function, you would have to do what I just did with five lines of code instead of one, because the alternative is a three line IF and ENDIF construct with one ? command inside the IF and one ? command inside of the ELSE. The IIF( ) function uses a comma to separate the test and a comma to separate the result options, like this:

```
IIF( this is true ,   do this ,   otherwise do this )
```

Functions

Functions are evaluators that can test, modify, or inform. You can easily identify functions because they all have parentheses like the IIF( ) function. Remember that parentheses are where arguments go. Some functions require no arguments at all, such as the DATE( ) function that returns the computer's current date.

It's important to remember one simple thing about functions: They always replace themselves with the result of their work. For example, you can get the current date to put into a database field by combining the REPLACE command with the date function, like this:

```
REPLACE buydate WITH DATE( )
```

As a result of this command, FoxBASE will ask the computer for today's date, replace the DATE( ) function with the date, and the REPLACE command will then put it into the buydate database field.

Some functions are powerful modifiers of data. Functions are like independently operating commands that have a specialized purpose. They can make hard jobs easy once you've learned how to use them in your commands.

While functions cannot replace commands entirely, they do play an important role as command modifiers. They can convert the data types of any data element from character to date, number to character, character to number, etc., and they do so without changing the original data. In the above example, we did not change the computer's date, we just got a copy of it using the Date( ) function. With the STORE command, you can change the value of a memory variable with the result of a function:

```
STORE DATE( ) + 7 TO duedate
```

The result is that there is a variable named "duedate" that contains the date seven days from now.

Most functions take arguments. Arguments are either literal (typed-in) values or expressions. CTOD( ), for example, uses the parentheses to contain characters representing a date. Its function is to convert the characters into a real date, like this:

? CTOD("12/25/89")

Chapter 9 contains mathematical functions to round numbers, return a square root, and so on. Another important group of functions test things for you. They can check to see if the end of a file has been reached EOF( ), when a file was last updated, etc. There is even a function to test for what kind of computer a program is running on and another to tell you how big the screen is.

Functions that manipulate character strings are valuable, because they let you take information from databases or from memory variables to use any way you want. For example, the SUBSTR( ) function lets you select any portion of a string of characters. The AT( ) function finds the location, in any string of characters of the one(s) you might be looking for. The RTRIM( ) and LTRIM( ) functions trim blanks off the right or left sides of character strings so you can create a new one that has just the right spacing in it. What would happen if you wanted to print an address using data from three fields, city, state, and zip code? This could be the result:

Expression: ? city + state + zipcode
Result: Nanty Glo   Pennsylvania   12832

Now try this:

Expression: ? RTRIM(city) + ", " + RTRIM(state) + " " + zipcode
Result: Nanty Glo, Pennsylvania 12832

If you are relatively new to programming or database management, dates can be confusing, mostly because computers like to store dates internally, as numbers. This means that they have their own data type, and that you can't directly mix dates with characters or numbers in expressions. The most important date functions for you to know are CTOD( ) and DTOC( ). These date functions convert characters to dates and the dates to characters respectively. Take a look at Appendix D for a list of the functions you can use with dates to make your programming job easier.

MEMORY VARIABLES

Memory variables are exactly what their name suggests. They store variable information in memory. The information in memory variables can be supplied by a user who types something in or selects a button or menu, or it can be taken out of a database file. Memory variables are temporary. That is, they go away when the computer is turned off if you don't save them.

Naming and Creating Memory Variables

All memory variables have names. Their names become your handle to get hold of them, so you must remember their names if you expect to use them. Memory variables are created like this:

```
STORE 120 TO qtysold
qtysold = 120
```

In the first line, the STORE command is used to put a numeric value of 120 into the variable named qtysold. The qtysold variable did not exist before, it was initialized when you used the STORE command. The second example uses a different approach to do the same thing. It's an assignment. The assignment operator, "=", was used to say "qtysold equals 120." FoxBASE doesn't care which one you use, however, when you use the STORE command, you can create many variables at once, storing the value to each one, like this:

```
STORE 0 TO qtysold, qtybought, qtyused, qtylost
```

Attributes

Memory variables take on the attributes and the data type that you store in them. Consequently, if you want a variable number to have decimal places, be sure to include decimals in the STORE command or the assignment that initializes it. The same is true of character data. Store the length that you want the variable to have, and it will retain the attributes you give it until you STORE something different in it.

If you store a number to a variable, and later store a number to the same name, FoxBASE will remove the first variable and create a new one. No error messages will occur because it assumes that you're the boss and that you know what you're doing.

Public Variables

Memory variables are visible and useable only in the program that created them. If you have several programs in one application that need to use a variable because, for example, you used one program to "Do" another program, you'll need to tell FoxBASE to make it available, by name, to all programs by declaring it to be public (see Fig. 6-4). Therefore, the PUBLIC command should be used in the first program of your application, such as this one:

```
PUBLIC qtysold, qtybought, qtyused, qtylost
STORE 0 TO qtysold, qtybought, qtyused, qtylost
```

This ensures that the variables you named in the Public expression list will be available to all programs, such as the "myarray" variable in Fig. 6-5. In contrast, the "myarray" variable in Fig. 6-6 cannot be seen by other programs.

Saving Variables on Disk

To save memory variables on disk, issue this command:

```
SAVE ALL LIKE qty* TO MEMQTY
```

Public Variables

Private Variables

Undeclared "Private" Variables

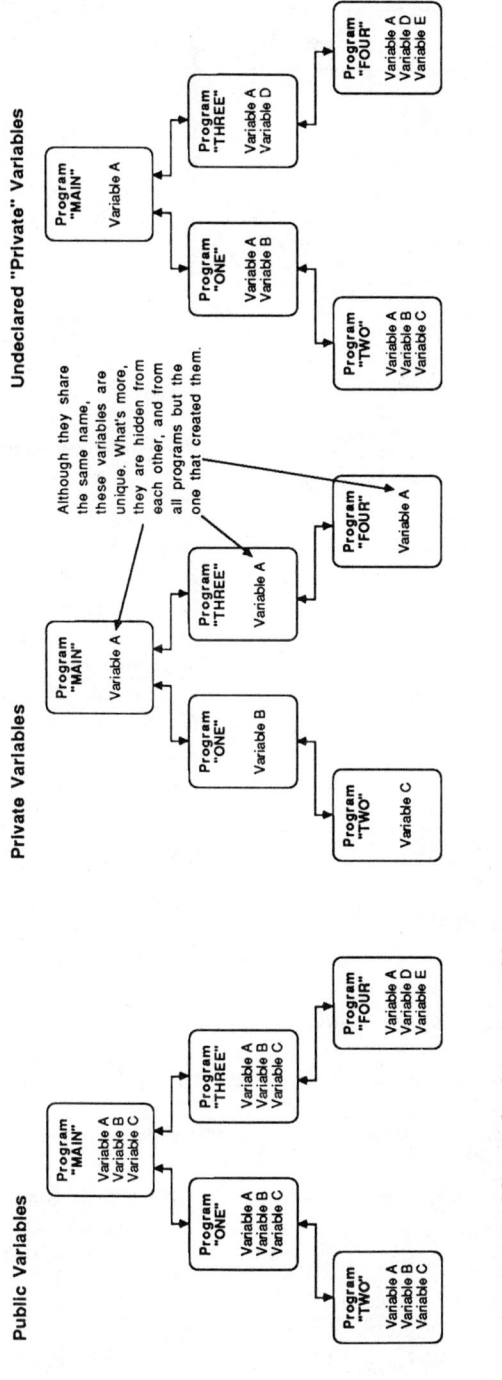

Although they share the same name, these variables are unique. What's more, they are hidden from each other, and from all programs but the one that created them.

Fig. 6-4. Public and private variables.

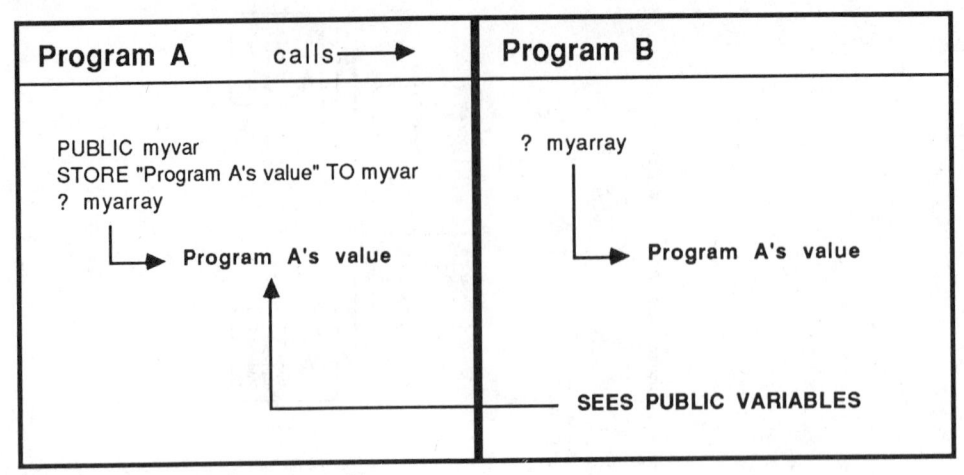

```
┌─────────────────────────────────┬─────────────────────────────────┐
│  Program A      calls ──▶       │  Program B                      │
├─────────────────────────────────┼─────────────────────────────────┤
│  PUBLIC myvar                   │  ? myarray                      │
│  STORE "Program A's value" TO   │      │                          │
│         myvar                   │      └──▶ Program A's value     │
│  ? myarray                      │                                 │
│      │                          │                                 │
│      └──▶ Program A's value     │                                 │
│                   ▲             │                                 │
│                   └─────────────┼── SEES PUBLIC VARIABLES         │
└─────────────────────────────────┴─────────────────────────────────┘
```

Fig. 6-5. Public memory variables.

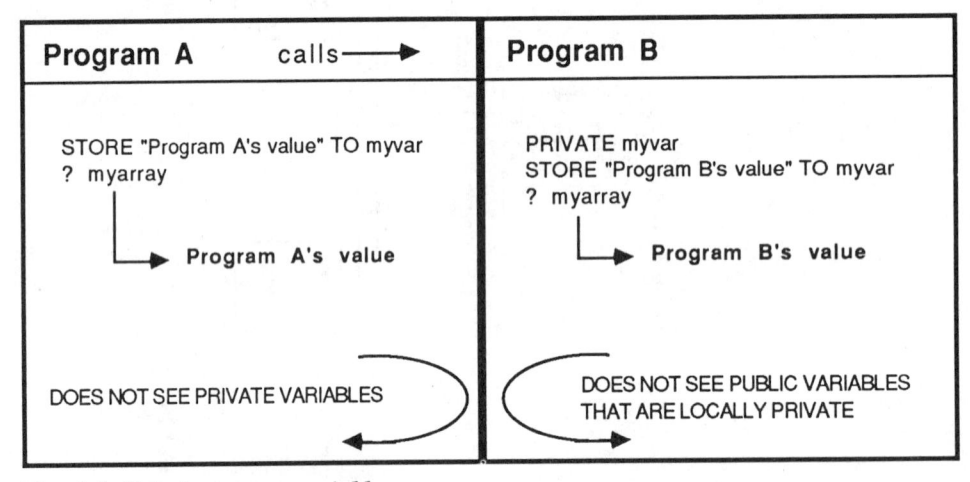

```
┌─────────────────────────────────┬─────────────────────────────────┐
│  Program A      calls ──▶       │  Program B                      │
├─────────────────────────────────┼─────────────────────────────────┤
│  STORE "Program A's value" TO   │  PRIVATE myvar                  │
│         myvar                   │  STORE "Program B's value" TO   │
│  ? myarray                      │         myvar                   │
│      │                          │  ? myarray                      │
│      └──▶ Program A's value     │      │                          │
│                                 │      └──▶ Program B's value     │
│                                 │                                 │
│  DOES NOT SEE PRIVATE VARIABLES │  DOES NOT SEE PUBLIC VARIABLES  │
│                                 │  THAT ARE LOCALLY PRIVATE       │
└─────────────────────────────────┴─────────────────────────────────┘
```

Fig. 6-6. Private memory variables.

To get them back into memory from the disk, issue this command:

```
RESTORE FROM MEMQTY
```

Notice that I used the * wildcard symbol to specify that only certain variables, i.e., those that start with "qty," should be saved. There are lots of saving and restoring options. Look at the SAVE TO and RESTORE commands in Chapter 9 if you want to know more about them.

Exchanging Variable Data with Database Fields

To get information from a database into a memory variable, simply name the variable and the database's field name:

    STORE fieldname TO memvarname

or

    memvarname = fieldname

To put variable information into a database field, reverse the process and use the REPLACE command, like this:

    REPLACE fieldname WITH memvarname

An important use of memory variables is to control conditions. Remember, conditions are used in all of the FoxBASE constructs—DO WHILE, IF, and DO CASE.

Getting Information from Users

If you use the FoxForm screen generator to make a simple application, you will notice, that the program it produced has commands that look like one of these examples:

    @ ROW( ), COL( ) SAY "This thing" GET fieldname
    @ 02,02 SAY "This thing" GET fieldname

The content of any database field can be changed when you "Get" it onto the screen and allow it to be modified with the READ command because GET(s) are activated by a READ command. You can do the same thing with memory variables that you've created. Try entering the following program from your Command window and watch what happens on the active output screen (Note: When you're prompted by a black input box, change the value of 120 to something else):

    STORE 120 TO qtyonhand
    @ 02,02 SAY "How many are left?" GET qtyonhand
    READ
    @ 04,02 SAY qtyonhand

Using Memory Variables in Programs

As mentioned before, variables can be used to control programs. This example lets a user enter the name of a person who's records should be printed:

    STORE SPACE(25) TO persontoprint
    @ 02,02 SAY "Enter the person's name:" GET persontoprint
    READ
    LIST ALL FOR fieldname = persontoprint TO PRINT

Memory variables can also be used in the condition expression of constructs. Let's assume that there's a library database with names and fines in it. Its structure looks like this:

    Library.dbf

1. NAME   Character   15
2. FINE   Numeric   5.2

Now, to find out how much a person owes, you could use this program:

```
* libfines.prg
* adds library fines
SET TALK OFF
STORE 0.00 TO amtdue
STORE SPACE(15) TO person
@ 02,02 SAY "What person should I check for fines?" GET person
READ
LOCATE FOR name = person
DO WHILE name = person .AND. .NOT. EOF( )
     STORE fine + amtdue TO amtdue
     CONTINUE
ENDDO
IF amtdue > 0.00
    @ 04,04 SAY "The fine for " + RTRIM(person) + " is: " + STR(amtdue,5,2)
ELSE
    @ 04,04 SAY RTRIM(person) + " has no book fines."
ENDIF
* eof libfines
```

This example might look complex, but I used some new functions that we have not discussed yet. The TALK command was set off so that FoxBASE won't put any unwanted messages on the screen. Then the program stored a zero dollar amount to the variable "amtdue." We also stored 15 spaces using the blank space function to "person." The user is then asked to enter the name of a person who might have library fines—GETting the variable "person" with a READ command. The LOCATE command then goes to work looking for a match. If it locates the contents of the variable "person" anywhere in the "name" database field, the DO WHILE construct is employed—because its condition is true—to add the "fine" amount in that record to our memory variable "amtdue." The CONTINUE command causes the search to resume. Therefore, the DO WHILE construct will continue to loop until "person" is no longer found in any records. Once done, the IF construct tests to see if "amtdue > 0.00." If it is, a message with the total fine is put on the screen, or, if it's zero or less, a notice will appear saying that there are no fines to pay. (Note: The STR( ) function converts numbers into characters for display, which is necessary because I've joined it with a character string using the "+" operator.)

To view the contents of all memory variables and their private/public status, use the DISPLAY MEMORY command as shown in Fig. 6-7.

Arrays

Arrays are memory variables that have more than one cell for storing data. They're useful when several related items need temporary storage in an organized container. You can put a whole record into an array and put it back again with these commands:

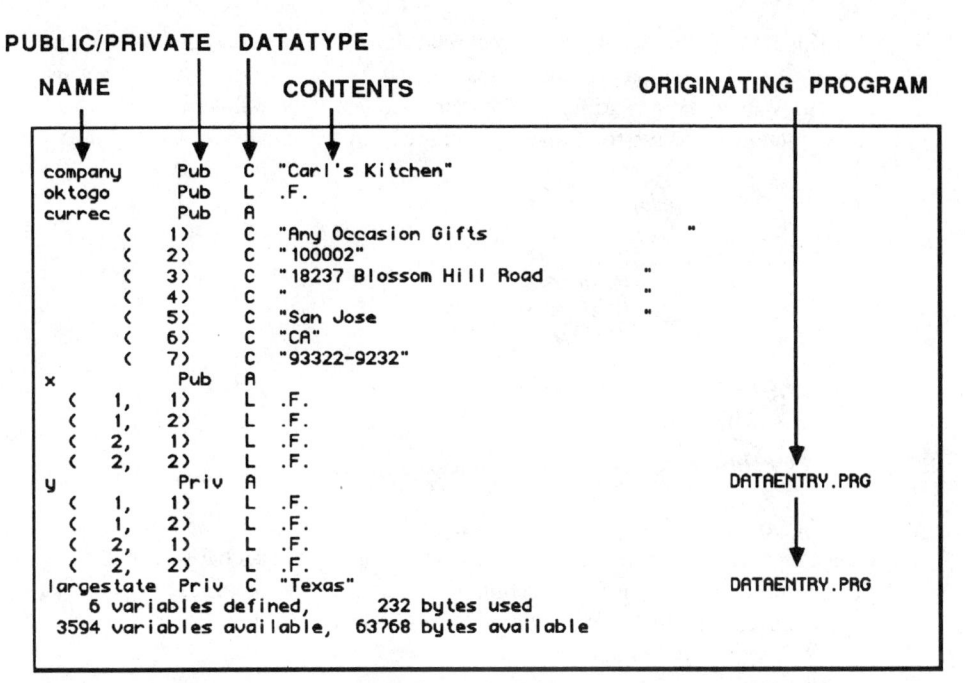

```
PUBLIC/PRIVATE  DATATYPE
   NAME                  CONTENTS              ORIGINATING PROGRAM

  company      Pub    C   "Carl's Kitchen"
  oktogo       Pub    L   .F.
  currec       Pub    A
      (   1)          C   "Any Occasion Gifts"           "
      (   2)          C   "100002"
      (   3)          C   "18237 Blossom Hill Road"      "
      (   4)          C   ""                             "
      (   5)          C   "San Jose"
      (   6)          C   "CA"                           "
      (   7)          C   "93322-9232"
  x            Pub    A
      (  1, 1)        L   .F.
      (  1, 2)        L   .F.
      (  2, 1)        L   .F.
      (  2, 2)        L   .F.
  y            Priv   A                         DATAENTRY.PRG
      (  1, 1)        L   .F.
      (  1, 2)        L   .F.
      (  2, 1)        L   .F.
      (  2, 2)        L   .F.
  largestate   Priv   C   "Texas"               DATAENTRY.PRG
       6 variables defined,      232 bytes used
    3594 variables available,  63768 bytes available
```

Fig. 6-7. Displaying memory variable contents.

SCATTER TO array1
GATHER FROM array1

The SCATTER command automatically creates an array to hold every field in the active database, one record at a time. Take a look at the SCATTER entry in Chapter 9 for more information about this feature.

The DIMENSION command is the most often used command for creating arrays. The syntax it uses helps us to understand how arrays are structured. Arrays have at least one row and, possibly, many columns. To dimension an array, enter a command like this:

DIMENSION array1(3)

This command creates a one-row array with three columns. To put information into the array cells, just use the array name with a subscript reference to the cell, like this:

STORE "Army boots" TO array1(2)

The character value "Army boots" was put into the second cell of the three, and it can be used just like any other memory variable, except that you cannot, reliably, do macro expansions of it (macros are explained soon, so keep reading). Two dimensional arrays work the same way, except that their subscript references have two numbers instead of one:

DIMENSION array2(2,3)

Memory Variables

This DIMENSION command creates an array with two rows and three columns. Otherwise, it's the same as the one above. Arrays are handy because you can use counter loops to write to them or to read from them. Consider the following loop, which puts the entire contents of a five-row, one-column array on the screen:

```
DIMENSION array3(5)
STORE "Cat"        TO array3(1)
STORE "Dog"        TO array3(2)
STORE "Fish"       TO array3(3)
STORE "Fly"        TO array3(4)
STORE "Person"     TO array3(5)
CLEAR
DO WHILE x < 6
    @ x,10 SAY array3(x)
    x = x + 1
ENDDO
```

The counter "x" allows you to change the cell address at the same time it's used to change the screen coordinates! The CLEAR command wipes the screen clear before displaying the results. To use this technique in a two dimensional array (in this case, three rows by three columns), put a loop within a loop, like this:

```
DIMENSION array4(3,3)
STORE "Cat"              TO array4(1,1)
STORE "Dog"              TO array4(2,1)
STORE "Fish"             TO array4(3,1)
STORE "Fur"              TO array4(1,2)
STORE "Fur"              TO array4(2,2)
STORE "Scales"           TO array4(3,2)
STORE "Meow, Purr"       TO array4(1,3)
STORE "Growl, Bark"      TO array4(2,3)
STORE "Bubble Bubble?"   TO array4(3,3)
CLEAR
x = 1
DO WHILE x < = 3
  y = 1
  DO WHILE y < = 3
  @ x,(15 * y) SAY array4(x,y)
    y = y + 1
  ENDDO
  x = x + 1
ENDDO
```

The purpose for the number 15 in the screen column setting (@ ROW( ), COL( )) is to give each column lots of width. If the data is longer, you can put in a higher number to make more room.

SPECIAL FEATURES AND PROGRAM DESIGN

The FoxBASE+/Mac language is enhanced by several powerful features that can add flexibility to your programs. The most important thing about FoxBASE program structures is that programs can be called from other programs, and several programs can be inside of one program file, as you'll soon see. The RETURN command causes any currently operating program to quit, and return control to the program that called it. If the program was called from the Command window or the interactive menu, all of the programs would quit running and the control would revert to the interactive mode of Fox-BASE.

Memory variables are a special feature that free you from restraints, because they can retain values that can be used in any or all programs, as long as you haven't gone back to the interactive mode of FoxBASE. Other special features include variables, which can be stored in an easy-to-remember name that you can call on any time. User-defined functions let you write your own functions, with some limitations, that can return special information on the spot, and finally, macros allow you to use the contents of a memory variable as though they were command-line literals (expressions that you type in when writing a program). Each of these features is explained in the following section.

Subroutines

Modular programming makes large application development possible because it allows one program to call another. Usually, programmers will use one program to call, or "DO," all other programs. It is usually used on a menu program where it is the user who makes decisions about what to do—enter data?, delete it?, and so on. Look at the menu program at the end of Chapter 5 to get an idea of what one looks like.

Not only can you structure programs in modular blocks, one subroutine per file, you can put several subroutines (up to 128 to be exact) inside one program. The following program has several subroutines:

```
* main.prg
* a program that does everything
SET PROCEDURE TO MAIN
. . . main program statement one - setup environment
. . . main program statement two - open database files
. . . main program statement three - puts up nice screen
. . . main program statements - lets a user choose subroutines

DO CASE
CASE this
    DO one
CASE that
    DO two
CASE the other
    DO three
ENDCASE

PROCEDURE one
. . . procedure one commands
RETURN

PROCEDURE two
. . . procedure one commands
RETURN
```

```
PROCEDURE three
. . . procedure one commands
RETURN

* eof main.prg
```

A procedure is no different from a program except that it happens to be inside of a file that contains other programs and has been initialized by the command, SET PROCEDURE TO. If a program contains its own subroutine procedures, just simply SET PROCEDURE TO itself. Once FoxBASE reads a SET PROCEDURE TO command, it looks in the named procedure file for programs before checking the disk. You can have as many procedure files in an application as you want, although one is usually enough! Think of how neat this can make your disks when an application is finished and bound up into one or more procedure files.

It's a good idea to keep a program in its own file until it's working well, because each time you modify a program file, FoxBASE compiles the whole thing. If you keep programs you're working on in separate files until they're done, debugging will go much more quickly because compile times are substantially reduced.

From this point onward, I'll use the terms program and procedure interchangeably. Remember, they're functionally the same, only structurally different.

It is a good idea to keep every major, repeatable, action in a procedure by itself. There's no reason to have the same 10 lines of code scattered throughout an application when it can be in one place, doing the work for all. Maintenance and modifications are much easier when programs are structured like building blocks.

Parameter Passing

Parameter passing makes it possible to reuse codes. A parameter is a chunk of information that you send along to a program when you want to run it. The practical value is enormous. If you want a program to print report titles at the top of a page, you could write it over and over again, once for each report, or you could write it once so that it could receive new report titles each time it printed. Passing parameters is as easy as this:

```
DO one WITH "Cat"
```

"Cat" is the parameter. But in order for the parameter to work, a receiving program must be ready to catch it. To prepare a program to receive parameters, just use the PARAMETERS command to make variables that can catch the parameters (like buckets) being passed. A PARAMETERS command must be the first executable line in a parameter-receiving procedure or you'll get an error. Here's a parameter-receiving procedure:

```
* procedure one
* a routine that likes animals
PROCEDURE one
PARAMETERS animal
@ 02,02 SAY animal
```

```
... other commands in procedure one
RETURN
```

In this example, procedure one treats the variable "animals" like any other variable except that this program didn't originate the value in the memory variable "animals," it received it from another program.

Parameters can be passed as literals, as is the case with the "Cat" in the above example, by value, or by reference. Literals are unchangeable values that you've permanently committed into the program code itself. "Cat" is literal because I named it explicitly and passed it along. Passing parameters by reference is almost the same, but there is a difference:

```
STORE "Cat" TO memvar
DO PROCEDURE one WITH memvar
```

Notice the difference? Instead of saying "Cat," we passed the variable name that contained the value of "Cat." We used a reference to the value "Cat" instead of the literal value of "Cat." Why is this important? Because the program receiving the parameter, now has the opportunity to exchange the memvar value to something else. It could turn your "Cat" into a "Dog" so that any other procedures that need a "Cat" would be at a loss. Its fine to let a subroutine change memory variable values as long as you don't care, or as long as you want them to. If you don't, it's trouble. To pass a variable reference to a subroutine without danger of it changing the variable's value, pass by value like this:

```
STORE "Cat" TO memvar
DO PROCEDURE one WITH (memvar)
```

The one little difference between this example and the one above is that memvar is surrounded by parentheses, which tells FoxBASE to evaluate it as an expression. Consequently, it doesn't pass the name "memvar" along so that a subroutine can change its contents. When you put parentheses around passed memory variable names, FoxBASE evaluates them, extracts their contents, and sends the resulting value along. In this case, "Cat" gets sent instead of the variable's name.

Remember, if a subroutine has a variable's name, it can change its contents. If you put parentheses around a variable, or any expression for that matter, FoxBASE evaluates it and returns the result of its evaluation rather than any named references it finds in the expression.

User-Defined Functions (UDFs)

User-defined functions are procedures you write that can pass values back to the program that called them. What is significant about them is that they can operate almost entirely like functions. What do functions do? They immediately replace themselves in a command with the result of their own work. In some instances, you can write procedures and call them like functions:

- As conditions in constructs: DO CASE...ENDCASE
  DO WHILE...ENDDO
  IF...ENDIF
- When initializing memory variables or changing their contents with a STORE command or the assignment operator "=".
- With the evaluate and display commands, ? and ??.
- With the LIST and DISPLAY commands.
- As a VALID condition in a GET...VALID command.
- In REPLACE commands.

Be careful, however, you could write a command that uses a UDF to close the very file it's using. User-defined functions should be used for situations that don't change any of the underlying assumptions in the program that uses them. Generally, here's the hard part—they should not change the selected database work areas or modify data in databases. It's best to use them for variable manipulation, mathematical formulae or for testing conditions, as is the case when VALIDating a GET. (See the section Validating New Data in Chapter 7 to see how UDFs can be used to protect a database from collecting mistaken or unacceptable values.) The following is a simple decision-making UDF:

```
* udfdemo.prg
* uses the "addorsub" UDF to add 10 if number is negative, or subtract
* 10 if positive
SET PROCEDURE TO udfdemo
PUBLIC testnumber
STORE 000.00 TO testnumber
@ 02,02 SAY "Enter a number" GET testnumber
READ
STORE addorsub(testnumber) TO testnumber
@ 04,02 SAY "The result is " + STR(testnumber)

PROCEDURE addorsub
PARAMETER mynumber
IF mynumber < 0
     RETURN mynumber + 10
ELSE
     RETURN mynumber – 10
ENDIF
RETURN 0
* eof udfdemo.prg
```

The procedure named "addorsub" is the user-defined function. It operates on the parameter "mynumber" when called and returns the value specified when done. UDFs must return a value or an error will result. The difference, as noted above, between UDFs and procedures is that UDFs can be called like functions. They are small kernels of power, because they let your programs make multiline decisions in one line—actually in part of a line—such as this single command line does in the example cited above:

```
STORE addorsub(testnumber) TO testnumber
```

Macro Expansion

To fully understand macros, you have to use them. The name "macro" starts to describe what they do, but the description only makes sense once you've been programming awhile and you've used them. The macro function is an oddball. It's an ampersand (&) that you can put immediately in front of a memory variable's name, like this:

&memvar

You can't start a command line with a macro function, but almost. You could do this:

DO &memvar

FoxBASE would start to run the program named inside of the memvar. Now, in case you haven't caught the technical achievement in this, you are modifying a command. Actually, you are supplying everything a command needs except for the verb from the inside of a memory variable. Is that a big deal? Once you remember that memory variables can get their contents from database files with a simple operation like this:

STORE fieldname TO memvar

The power of macros is astounding. If you carried this to an extreme, you could put 90 percent of a program into database files! I'll leave it to your imagination to use this language feature, but with this note: Macros can slow a program down when run, because they can't be pre-compiled like the rest of your program is. Be very careful that the macros you expand into commands are accurate, or the program will screech to an abrupt halt. Take a look at how macros are used in Fig. 6-8 and Fig. 6-9.

In case you're curious, the technical thing that macro expansion does is to take the quotation marks off the values in the memory variable as it places them on the command line, just as the memory variable name is taken away. Consequently, the variable's contents look like literal commands just entered to FoxBASE.

SCREENS ONE THROUGH NINE

FoxBASE has nine screens. You can look in the window menu to see them. The screens are designed to provide programmers with flexible ways to output information for application users to see, and so interactive users can keep information on one of several screens for instant recall while using another. The flexibility is useful if you don't let it overwhelm you. Programmers can select one of nine different visual types of display screens (see Fig. 6-10). To select each screen type for output screen one:

```
SCREEN 1 TYPE 0
SCREEN 1 TYPE 0 LOCK
SCREEN 1 TYPE 1
SCREEN 1 TYPE 2
SCREEN 1 TYPE 3
SCREEN 1 TYPE 16
```

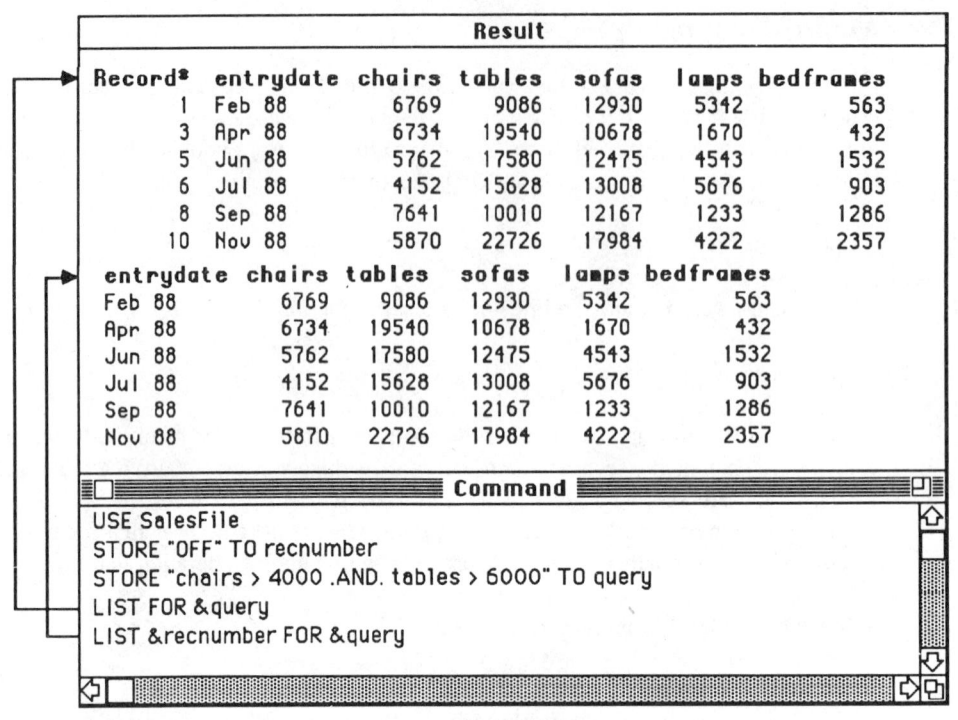

```
                              Result
   Record#  entrydate  chairs   tables   sofas    lamps  bedframes
        1   Feb 88      6769     9086    12930    5342        563
        3   Apr 88      6734    19540    10678    1670        432
        5   Jun 88      5762    17580    12475    4543       1532
        6   Jul 88      4152    15628    13008    5676        903
        8   Sep 88      7641    10010    12167    1233       1286
       10   Nov 88      5870    22726    17984    4222       2357

           entrydate  chairs   tables   sofas    lamps  bedframes
            Feb 88      6769     9086    12930    5342        563
            Apr 88      6734    19540    10678    1670        432
            Jun 88      5762    17580    12475    4543       1532
            Jul 88      4152    15628    13008    5676        903
            Sep 88      7641    10010    12167    1233       1286
            Nov 88      5870    22726    17984    4222       2357
```

```
                             Command
   USE SalesFile
   STORE "OFF" TO recnumber
   STORE "chairs > 4000 .AND. tables > 6000" TO query
   LIST FOR &query
   LIST &recnumber FOR &query
```

Fig. 6-8. Macros are variables that can be used in commands.

```
                              Result
   Filename           Records  Updated      Data    Resource
   Config.bak                                 38         600
   Config.fx                                  37         600
   DOCASE...                                 379        1131
   EXAMPLE.prg                               459        1243
   FoxHelp.dbf           345   09/26/88    14243           0
   FoxHelp.dbt                            363008           0
   JUNK.idx                                 1024           0
   JUNK1.idx                                1024           0
   MENUSEL.BAK            30   01/19/89    12292           0
   MENUSEL.DBF            30   01/22/89    12474           0
   setup.prg                                  63         720

   11 total files/folders                  405041        4294
   4158464 bytes remaining on drive.
   Filename           Records  Updated      Data    Resource
   FoxHelp.dbf           345   09/26/88    14243           0
   MENUSEL.BAK            30   01/19/89    12292           0
   MENUSEL.DBF            30   01/22/89    12474           0

   3 total files/folders                    39009           0
   4158464 bytes remaining on drive.
```

```
                             Command
   STORE "*.*" TO filetypes
   STORE "HD40:FoxBASE+/Mac:&filetypes" TO folder
   DIR &folder
   DIR HD40:FoxBASE+/Mac:
```

Fig. 6-9. Using macros to hold file names.

118 Screens One through Nine

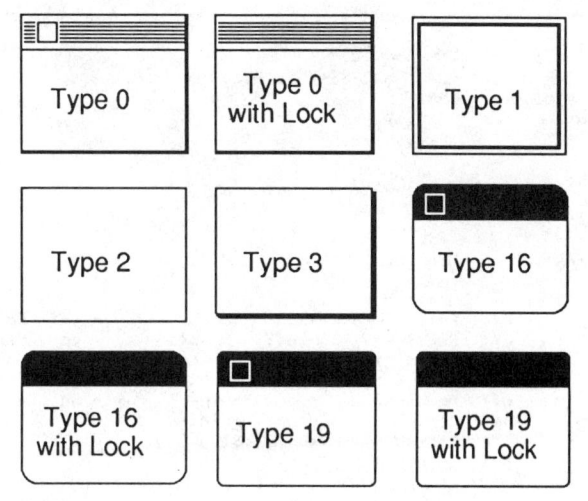

Fig. 6-10. FoxBASE has nine screen types.

```
SCREEN 1 TYPE 16 LOCK
SCREEN 1 TYPE 19 HEADING
SCREEN 1 TYPE 19 LOCK HEADING
```

There are, of course, other options for the screen command that are not shown here (see Chapter 7), but this demonstrates how a screen can take on different visual types. The LOCK argument creates a screen with no close box in the upper-left corner. If an application user inadvertently closed a window they needed, what could you do? This prevents this from occurring when you don't want it to. The runtime version of FoxBASE does not allow users to close windows, you have to do it for them under program control.

THE DATA-HANDLING ENVIRONMENT

Up to ten individual database files can be opened at one time by FoxBASE. The work areas keep open files separate from one another while at the same time letting them share dynamic links. Think of work areas as big desktop areas where separate files can be opened and viewed.

The ten work areas can be seen in the View window, where ten circles, marked A through J, form a clockwise circle. Use the DISPLAY STATUS command for a textual description of what the file-handling environment is like, as shown in Fig. 6-11. You can select the work areas from within a program by using the SELECT command, or from the View window by simply clicking on any circle. The work areas are identified as numbers 1 through 10 as well as characters A through J. Whenever you use a FoxBASE function to refer to a work area, use one of the numbers. To select different files or work areas:

```
SELECT A
SELECT B
SELECT 1
SELECT 2
```

```
File search path:
Default disk drive: HD40:FoxBASE+/Mac:AYequip:
Print file/device:  PRN:
Work area:            1
Margin:              10
Decimals:             2
Memowidth:           50
Typeahead:          128
History:             20

Date format:        American


Alternate    - off   Bell         - on    Carry      - off   Catalog    - off
Century      - off   Confirm      - off   Console    - on    Debug      - off
Deleted      - on    Delimiters   - off   Device     - scr   Dohistory  - off
Echo         - off   Escape       - on    Exact      - off   Fields     - off
Fixed        - off   Heading      - on    Help       - on    History    - on
Intensity    - off   Menu         - on    Print      - off   Safety     - off
Scoreboard   - off   Status       - off   Step       - off   Strict     - off
Talk         - on    Unique       - off


Programmable function keys:
F2   -  resume;
F3   -  list;
F4   -  dir;
F5   -  display structure;
F6   -  display status;
F7   -  display memory;
F8   -  display;
F9   -  append;
F10  -  edit;
F11  -
F12  -
F13  -
F14  -
F15  -
```

Fig. 6-11. Display Status.

The ten files can be opened at once, and related file operations can be performed automatically by some FoxBASE commands so that they're all active at once. Nevertheless, FoxBASE likes you to select a specific file for every operation by selecting the work area it's in. Interfile relationships have a parent, and many commands operate on one file at a time, so it's best to get used to the idea of work areas as file pointers. You need to let FoxBASE know what file you're concerned with at all times when you issue commands.

Relations and Views

Relationships are established between two files when you have:

1. chosen a parent file (usually the one with more records in it) and a child file;

2. indexed the child file on a key field, or expression of data elements, that also exists in the parent file;

3. issued a SET RELATION TO command to consummate the deal.

Once you have done the above, moving the record pointer in the parent file automatically causes a sympathetic movement of the record pointer in the child file, allowing you to read data from, or write data to, the child file as well as the currently selected parent file. For more information about file relationships, see the *File Relationships* section in Chapter 5. For more information about command syntax and technical points see the *SET RELATION* section in Chapter 8.

The Record Pointer

The record pointer acts like a database work area. You must tell it where to go. There is one record pointer per file, and it can be positioned automatically on records because of a file relationship, or you can move it yourself with the SKIP command. Whenever you click on a record in a Browse window, you're moving the record pointer to a record. It's a good idea to understand what level of control, and responsibility, you have to control Fox-BASE's attention. FoxBASE is record oriented; it likes to work on one or more records at a time. The REPLACE command, for example, always assumes that you have already placed the record pointer on the record you want changed. Many other commands and functions work the same way, on one record at a time.

Rather than telling you about every command that moves the record pointer automatically or manually, let me encourage you to read through Chapter 9 and look for commands that you think might move the record pointer. If it looks like one does, it probably does. Whenever you see a command that uses the argument ALL, for example, you can bet that it can operate on every record in the database, from top to bottom, all by itself. The word ALL is called a scope, because it sets a range of records for your chosen operation.

There is no "best" way to move the record pointer. If you can write a command that uses the ALL word to do what you want, perhaps with a condition, that's great. Sometimes you'll need manual, one-record control of the pointer. The SKIP command positions the pointer one record forward, or back, from its current location, and the GOTO command locates records by their number. If you want to locate a specific record that matches something you know, just use the LOCATE or SEEK command.

Record pointers are not hard to learn, you just have to experiment to get the feel of FoxBASE's way of doing things. It's straightforward, because the commands do what they say they do. Scopes, filters, and indexes, which can influence the movement of record pointers, are discussed next.

Scopes Are Record Boundaries

Some commands need to be told what scope, or range, of records they should affect when processing. Scoping commands operate only in one database work area at a time—the work area that's selected when they're used. Blind record scopes affect record pointer movement without thinking about the contents of records. Conditional scopes, however, affect record pointers because of what they "see" in records.

Most FoxBASE+/Mac commands work on one record at a time without a scope to widen their range of effect. The DELETE command, for example, will delete only one record unless you give it a larger scope. The largest scope of all is ALL. The command, DELETE ALL, would do exactly as you asked, so be careful with scopes!

Scopes work predictably unless there are two or more things vying for record pointer control. Commands like SET FILTER, SET DELETED ON|OFF, SET INDEX TO, SET ORDER TO, and INDEX can adversely affect the behavior of other commands when mixed carelessly, because they all try to establish the way records are considered for processing. The scoping commands are described more fully in the remainder of the chapter.

Blind Record Scoping

Blind scoping doesn't look inside each record to determine which ones should be processed (see Fig. 6-12). The following are blind record-scoping commands:

ALL. ALL tells a command that all records should be processed in its operation. If SET DELETED is ON, any records marked for deletion will be ignored.

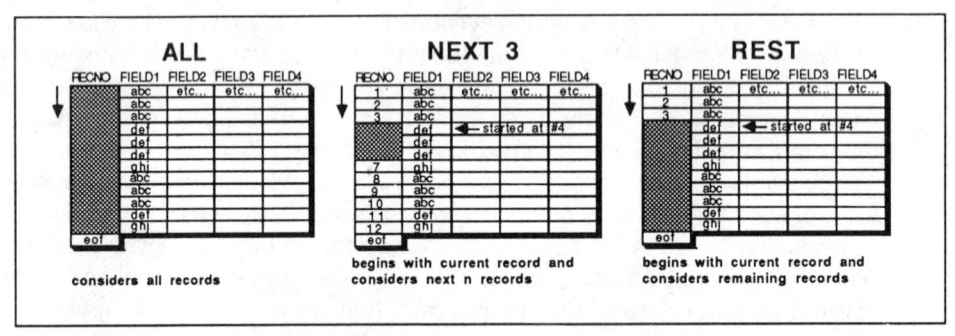

Fig. 6-12. Record scoping sets boundaries.

NEXT <expN>. Next starts with the current record and continues until <exprN> number of records have been operated on. If SET DELETED is ON, any records marked for deletion will be ignored.

RECORD<exprN>. Record operates on the record number identified by <exprN>, whether it has been marked for deletion or not.

REST. Rest begins at the current record and continues until the end-of-file is reached. If SET DELETED is ON, any records marked for deletion will be ignored.

Conditional Record Scoping

The conditional scoping commands select records by matching something in the table's records with a specific condition. Unlike blind scoping, which operates without considering record contents, conditional scoping considers each record (see Fig. 6-13). The FOR and WHILE scoping commands are two such conditional record-scoping commands:

FOR. The FOR scope tells FoxBASE+/Mac to consider records that match condition, even if they are scattered throughout the file. The word FOR means "where" or "wherever." It is like saying, "Where this condition is true, do thus-and-so." FOR limits the command so that the thing you want done to each record is accomplished one record at a time until the FOR condition is no longer true for any more records. If SET DELETED is ON, any records marked for deletion will be ignored.

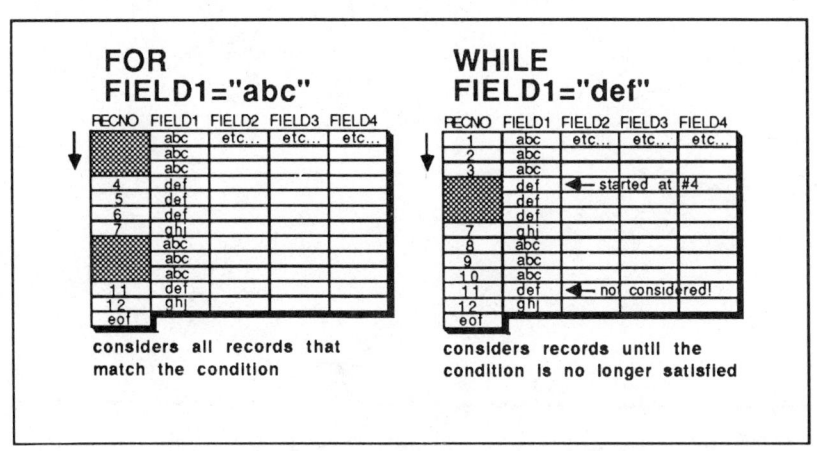

Fig. 6-13. Conditional record scoping considers each record.

WHILE. The WHILE scope assumes that a database file is in a certain physical order or in a logical order because an index is active. If an index put a file in order by customer name, once you locate the first record matching the customer you want to process, you can use WHILE to print, delete, list, and so on, each record that continues to match the customer-name condition. WHILE assumes you've already found the first record meeting the condition and continues with each record in turn until it reaches one that no longer matches. If SET DELETED is ON, any records marked for deletion will be ignored.

7
Developing the User Interface

I expect that those of you who are reading this book have varied levels of programming and interface making experience. Consequently, this chapter offers both simple and complex information about interface making in FoxBASE. We will explore the strengths, limitations, and approaches available to you in terms of your abilities and need for results. First, though, let me explain the purpose of interfaces more carefully.

INTRODUCING INTERFACES

"Impressions are important because what people think of you can make all the difference." While that sentence might sound as if it came from an advice column, computer programs, if they could, should take note. An application that behaves well is more likable and easier to use than one that appears unsocial. While the user interface is a critically important part of any application, it can also be a difficult thing to build.

User interfaces are the side of a program that's seen by its users. They're also called application interfaces or program interfaces. Regardless of what you call them, interfaces have menu options, dialog boxes, screen reports, lists, and so on, that we hope presents a coherent and easy way to control the computer. Interfaces are more than just a pretty face, however. They directly affect what the program does, what the user sees, prints, changes, adds, and removes from the database.

Aesthetic interface features (nice screens) and data manipulations (such as indexing) are intimately related. But there are times, for example, when an interface option can slow the processing of a program, yet appear to make it faster, simply because it tells the user what's going on under the surface. That's good. People like to know that their computer is working for them when they're forced to wait, or any job seems slower than it should.

INTRODUCING FOXFORM AND FOXCODE

Application interface building brings up the question: How can you build the interface of your dreams without first knowing every possibility of FoxBASE or without knowing the techniques for exploiting them? FoxBASE can turn your interface designs into reality, but you'll need a few minor technical skills and the ability to plan ahead.

Programmers eventually learn know how to integrate the gears and the aesthetics of a program so that they're as seamless as a dancer and the dance. They usually learn to manipulate data first then how to put a nice facade of user controls on the gears they've made. If you are just learning FoxBASE programming, take some time to learn FoxForm and let it be your interface making tool. Don't worry about interface programming details. This chapter explains the commands FoxForm creates and the layout tools (see Fig. 7-1) you can use to generate them.

Use FoxForm exclusively before trying the @ SAY...GET commands. Whether you're a programmer, or not, the best way to design is visually. Very complex systems can be created by putting FoxForm screen programs and other procedures together into one seamless application.

CREATING APPLICATIONS—A SHORT TUTORIAL

An application is an active program with screens, not merely an inactive window into the data. In the short tutorial section that follows, I'll show you how to use FoxForm to make an application screen program that can stand by itself to add, locate, edit, or delete records in a database table. At this point, don't worry about how pretty or accurate your design is, the goal is to become familiar with the main steps so you can create screens of your own. Don't spend a lot of time on it, just do the steps. Later on, when you're ready, you can read the rest of this chapter to learn each of FoxForm's tools.

To use FoxForm, you'll need an open database file. If you don't have one opened already, select the File/Open/Database menu option and use one you've already created, or make one by selecting the File/New/Database option. Your database file needs to have one or more records in it for our purposes, so after creating a new file, enter at least one record (it can be blank) using the Record/Append menu option.

Creating a New Form

To create a new form, Select the File/New/Form menu. When the file type dialog appears, select the Form option. When you're done, the screen should look like the one shown in Fig. 7-2. Notice too, that some of the menus on your screen have changed to give you tools for design.

Putting Database Fields in the Layout

Quick Form is an option in the FoxForm layout designer that puts many fields at once from a database onto the screen where you can arrange them. Select Quick Form from the Form menu. If you haven't opened a database file yet, the Quick Form option will not be visible, so open the database file and try again. Figure 7-3 shows what the field placement options look like. You need to decide, at this point, how you want the fields to layout on

Pointer
Use the pointer to select, drag or resize objects, and to make menu choices.

Text
Use the text tool to make labels for fields, or to enter text anywhere you like.

Lines
Use the line tool to draw lines. You can select the line thickness in the Object/Pen menu. To make the line double, double click it.

Rectangles
Using the pointer, click and drag to create a rectangle. Line thickness can be adjusted using the Object/Pen menu. To make the line double, double click it.

Rounded rectangles
Using the pointer, click and drag to create a rectangle. Line thickness can be adjusted using the Object/Pen menu. To make the line double, double click it.

Text regions
Text regions are for memo fields, and they can be used for large database character fields. Click and drag to create a region, then select the field name. See the discussion in Chapter 7 for instructions.

Text buttons
Text buttons are for making controls, like OK, YES, NO, or CANCEL. As such, they'll usually be related to memory variables in a controlling program, not with fields in a database file. See the discussion in Chapter 7 for instructions.

Radio buttons
Radio buttons are for making controls, or for representing exclusive categories, like: On order, Back ordered, In stock, and so on, where one case must be true. Each category is assigned a number from 1 (the first button) to ? (up to 254), for storage in a numeric database field. See the discussion in Chapter 7 for instructions.

Check boxes
Check boxes are for making controls, or for YES/NO information, like: Doors locked, Windows shut, Bolt latched, and so on. When a button is checked, the state is true, when blank, it's false. Numeric or logical database fields (or memvars) are assigned to checkboxes. For numeric fields, checked = 1, not checked = 0. For logical fields, checked = .T., not checked = .F.. See the discussion in Chapter 7 for instructions.

Fields
Fields are for character, numeric, logical, date or memo database fields. If a picture field is used, users will double click to open and see it. The Quck Form option (in the Form menu) places all database fields on screen at once. See the discussion in Chapter 7 for instructions.

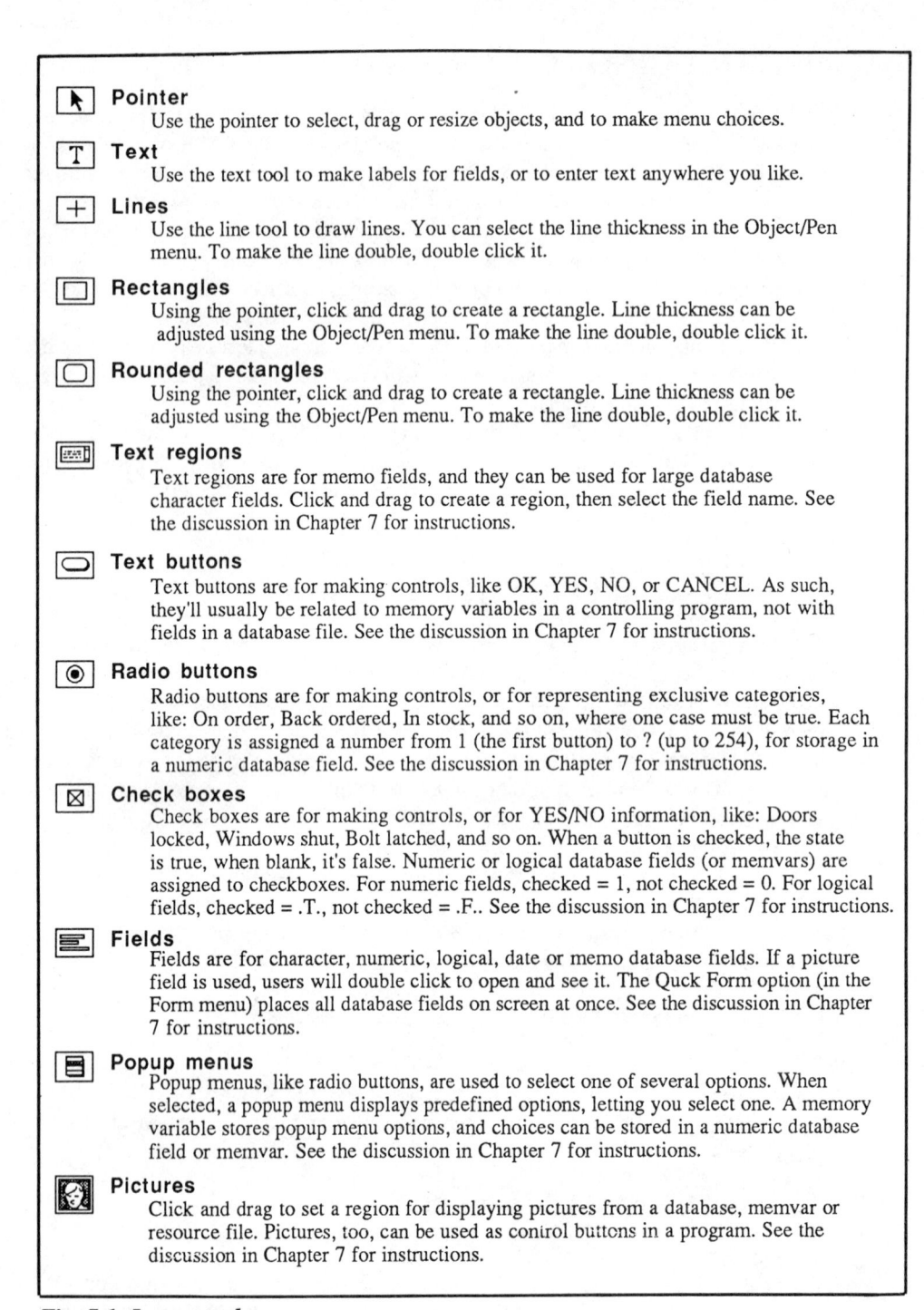

Popup menus
Popup menus, like radio buttons, are used to select one of several options. When selected, a popup menu displays predefined options, letting you select one. A memory variable stores popup menu options, and choices can be stored in a numeric database field or memvar. See the discussion in Chapter 7 for instructions.

Pictures
Click and drag to set a region for displaying pictures from a database, memvar or resource file. Pictures, too, can be used as control buttons in a program. See the discussion in Chapter 7 for instructions.

Fig. 7-1. Layout tools.

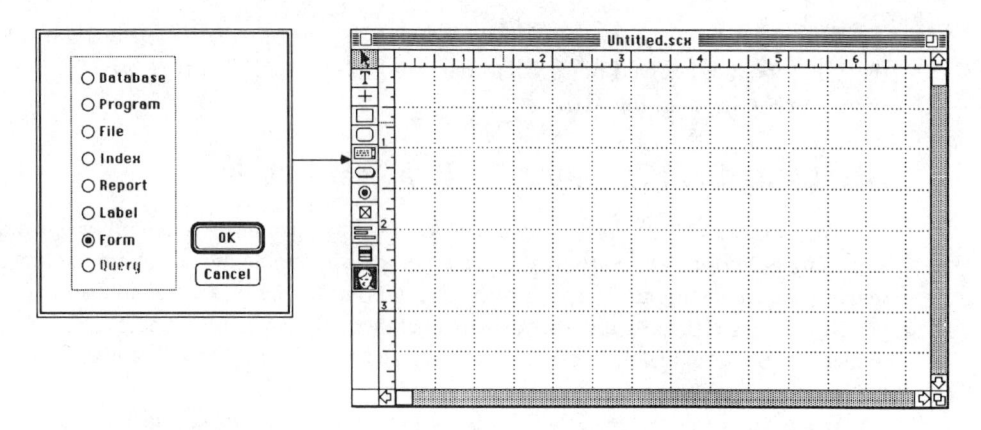

Fig. 7-2. A clean slate.

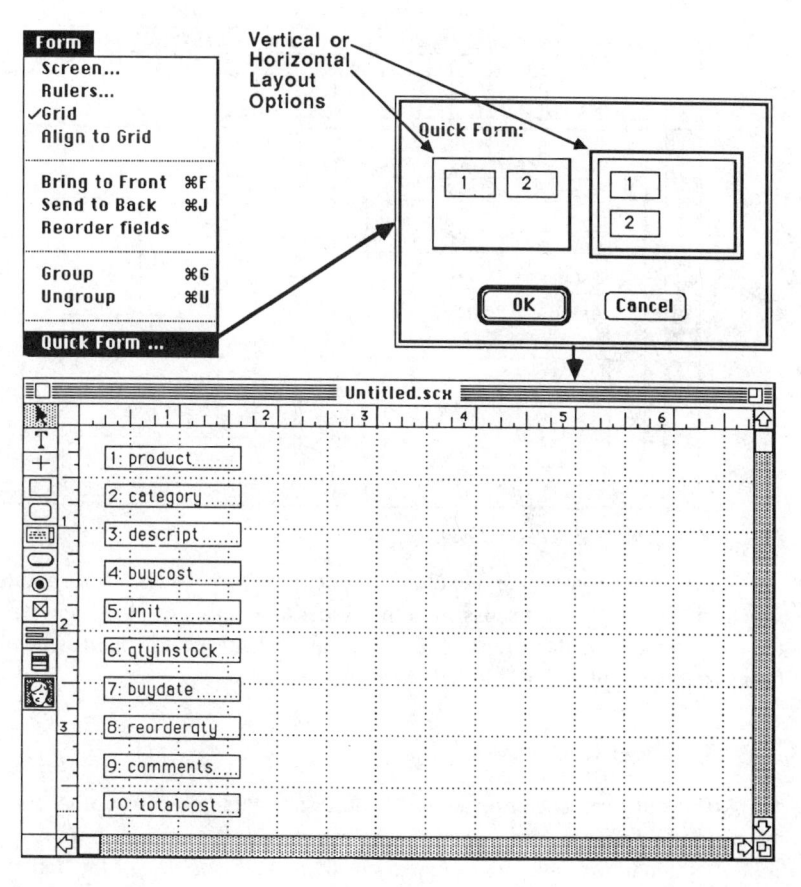

Fig. 7-3. Quick form options.

Creating Applications—A Short Tutorial 127

the screen. Select horizontal or vertical placement by clicking on the left or right side of the dialog box. When you press OK, FoxForm will place the fields. I used the vertical option for the fields in Fig. 7-3.

Arranging the Fields and Adding Text Labels

The next thing to do is to arrange the fields with your mouse in any order you want, stretching fields that are too short, for example, and shortening those that are too long, so that lengths are just right and the finished screen arrangement is pleasing to the eye. After you have arranged database fields, you can label them, describing what each field contains with a text label, and you can even draw boxes and lines to add a touch of class or clarify the layout.

When you're done, select all fields by pressing command-A, and then, select the Reorder Fields option in the Form menu. This reordering step makes the return key move through the fields from top to bottom and left to right when it's finished. After making changes to the sample screen, I ended up with the layout you can see in Fig. 7-4.

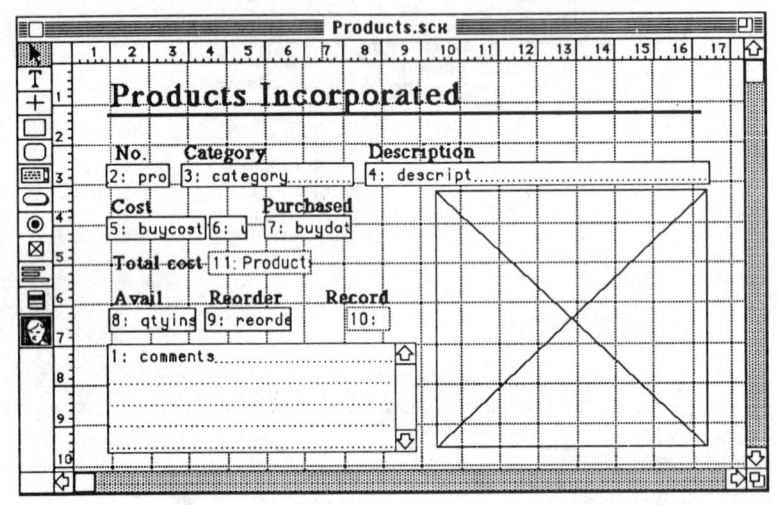

Fig. 7-4. A finished screen design.

Use your imagination and explore. Experiment with the text, line, and rectangle tools shown in Fig. 7-5. I'll discuss the other tools after this exercise. Leave a few different objects you made on the screen so that you can see later what happens when FoxBASE has turned into an application.

Saving the Form

After your form is completed you should save it and give it a name. Figure 7-6 shows the dialog box that appears when you select the File/Save menu option. I want to draw your attention to the Save Environment checkbox at the bottom of the dialog. If you select it before pressing the Save button, FoxBASE will make a view (.vue) file and give it the same name you've chosen for the form (.scx) file. A view file stores everything important

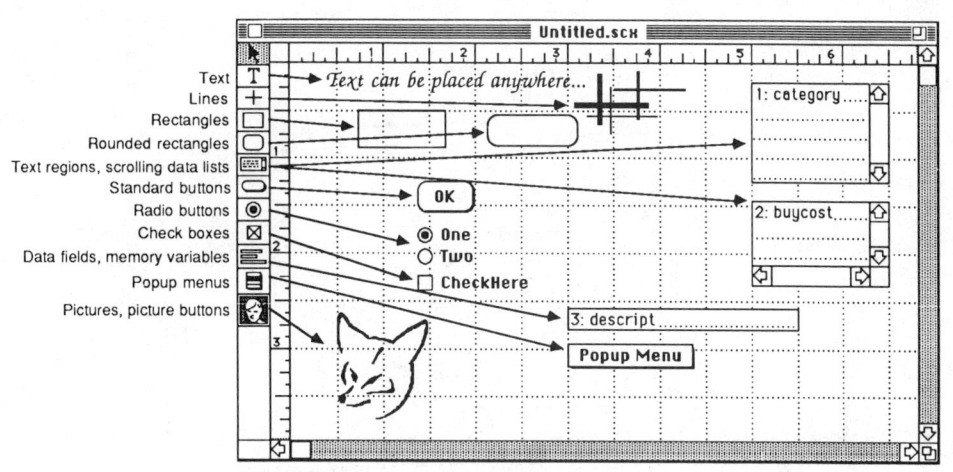

Fig. 7-5. Designing screen layouts.

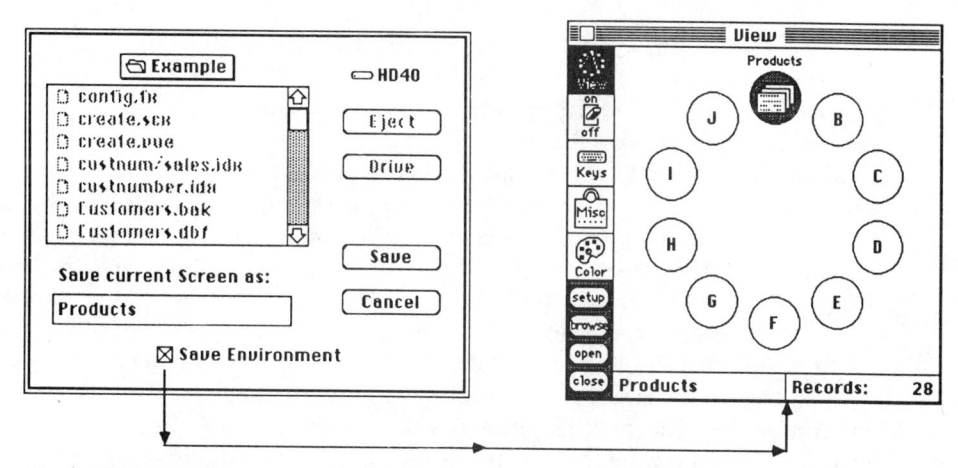

Fig. 7-6. Saving forms.

about database files, like, which ones are open, what indexes are in use, filters, format files installed, and so on.

The benefit of checking the Save Environment checkbox is that you can open the form file later, and the database(s) you are now using will automatically open too. In the event that you delete the view file, FoxBASE will tell you that a "File does not exist.", and you'll have to open the database file(s), again, yourself. The screen form won't be changed or damaged, though.

Generating an Application from the Screen Form

Now that you've saved your design, you can do something with it. Select the Program/Generate menu option that's shown in Fig. 7-7. Although the process shown in Fig. 7-7 looks complex, it's not. There are only two decisions to make: 1, What screen form

Creating Applications—A Short Tutorial **129**

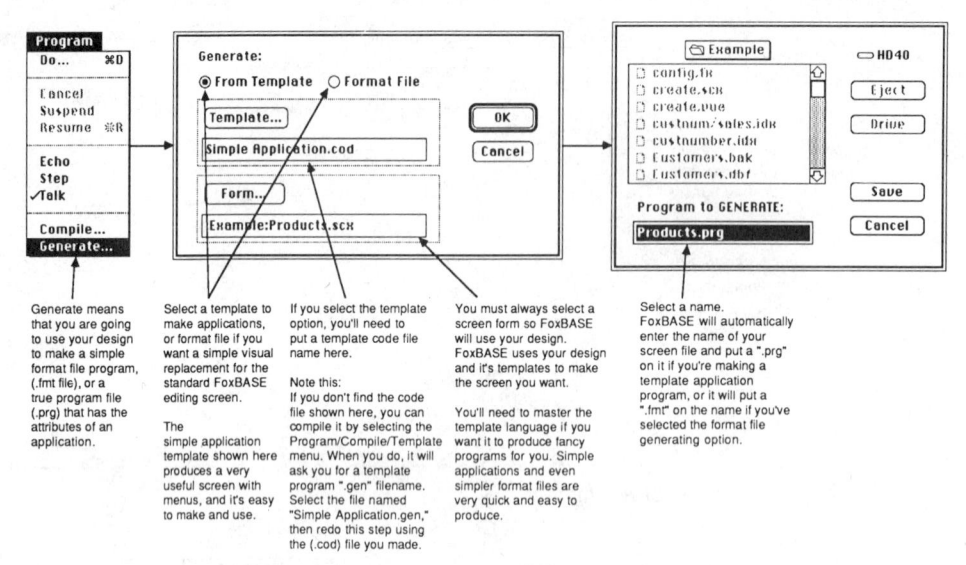

Fig. 7-7. From design, to a working screen program/format.

you want to use (in this case, it's probably the one you just made); and 2, what you want to generate, an application or a format file. I've said it before, and forgive me for the repetition if it's already clear to you, but the point bears repeating—Format files (.fmt) merely replace the bland design FoxBASE has for editing database files when you select the Append or Change menu options, whereas application, or program (.prg) files can do anything that a programmer wants them to do, including, as is the case here, replacing a boring screen format with something that not only displays fields for adding and editing data, but has custom menu options and some control over a database file.

Application templates make automatic program generation via FoxForm possible. Do you remember the discussion in Chapter 5 about templates and their role in FoxForm? FoxForm uses templates to do fancy things with your screen designs, things that you'd otherwise have to program yourself. A few basic templates come with FoxBASE. My favorite is the application template because it produces simple but effective screens that are fun to use and share. If you're a developer, you can make your own templates, but it takes a thorough understanding of programming issues. You will need the FoxCode manual.

Select the simple application template, and the screen file you just made using Fig. 7-7 as a guide. Don't let me dissuade you from trying the Format file generation option, but if you find it boring remember that I warned you. In either case, after you've selected the template and the screen form you made, name the file. When you're done, press the Save button and FoxBASE will generate your program or format file.

If you couldn't find the simple application code file with the (.cod) in its name, the template file (known by the ".gen" in its name) was probably not compiled into a code file (.cod). In this case you'll need to compile it yourself. Select the Program/Compile/Template menu and open the simple application (.gen) file that's in the simple application folder. It will compile letting you continue. Figure 7-7 details the generation process if you need further help.

Running the Program

If you chose the Format File option instead of the From Template option, the next few paragraphs and the *Enhancing Applications by Hand* section below won't apply to you. You'll need to install your new format file. If you used the simple application template, skip this paragraph. To install a format file: Open the Database/Setup menu option and install the file you just created by pressing the checkbox in the lower right corner (see Fig. 7-8). After installing it, just select the Record/Append or Record/Change menu and you'll see your design in action.

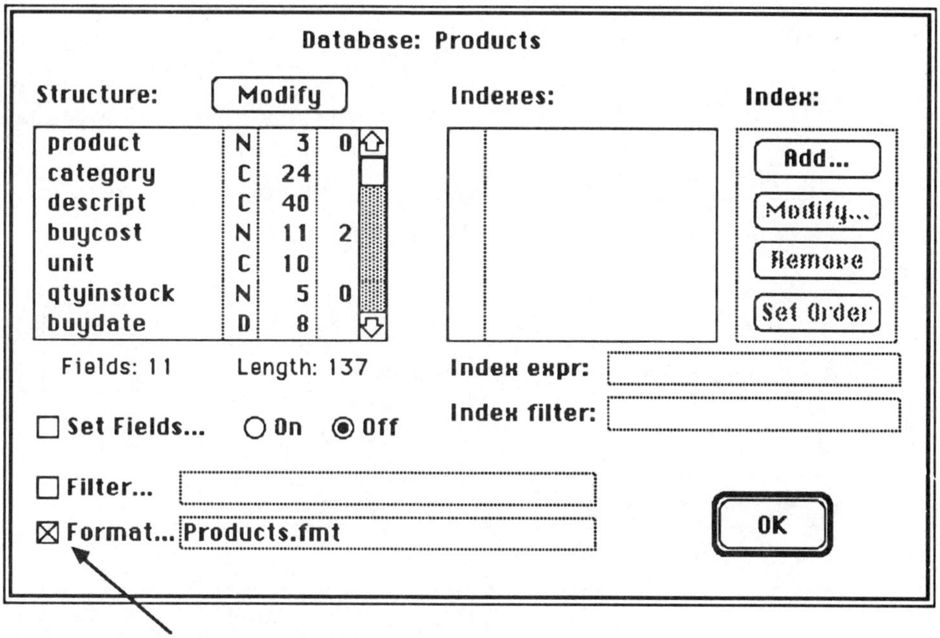

Click in this checkbox to install a Format file. But remember, it won't be active until you append or change data.

Fig. 7-8. Installing finished formats.

Once the program is generated, you can select the Program/Do menu to run it. The (.prg) extension in its name indicates that it is now a FoxBASE program. Press the Do button. If all is well, you'll see a screen that looks something like the bottom illustration in Fig. 7-9. To quit, select the Utilities/Exit menu.

Your screen might not have pictures or a scrolling memo field such as the illustration does; you can add those later. For now, use the mouse to try out the new menus you've made. Add records with the Append menu option and delete one with the Delete menu option. A nice thing about FoxForm's simple application generator is that you need only *DO* the program you created, it does the rest.

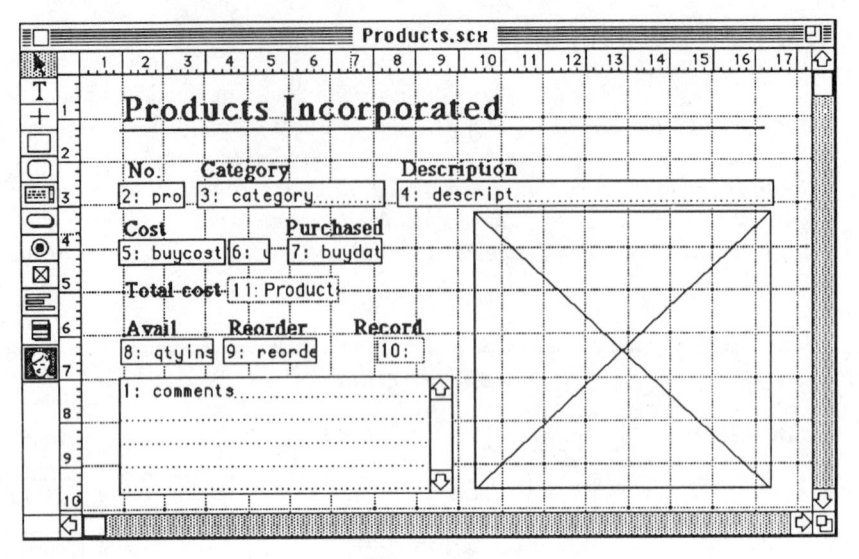

From this

To this

Fig. 7-9. The final results.

PROGRAMMING THE BROWSE AND CHANGE WINDOWS

In addition to supporting all of the basic features of browse, version 2.x lets you specify how the browse window looks and displays when it's invoked by a program. What's more, the interactive change window in version 2.x has been enhanced and made to work with the browse window-allowing users to quickly switch from the browse's table view to

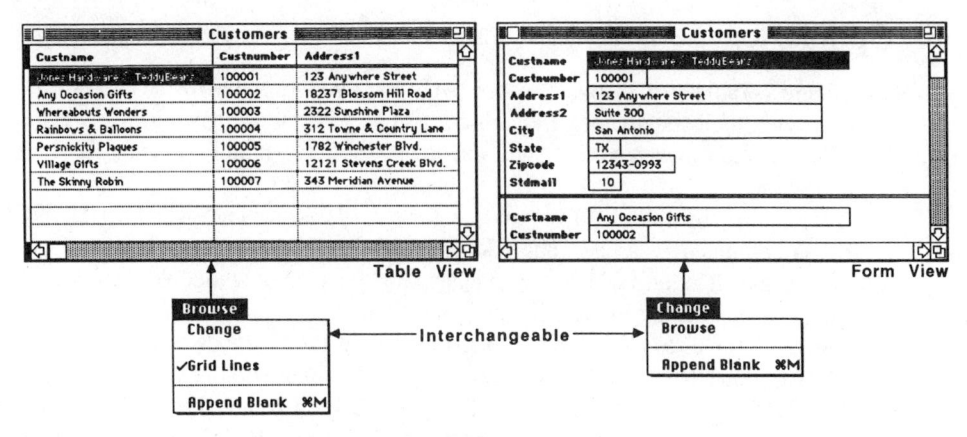

Fig. 7-10. Browse and Change work together.

a form view that's often more appropriate for data entry and for viewing whole-records at a time.

Because of these additions, the browse/change window combination lets programmers save their talent for things other than simple screen lists. In fact, I often use BROWSE commands in programs in the place of programmed add, edit and delete screens. There is a limit of one table per browse/change, but that's often all that's needed to handle typical table maintenance situations. Why do the work when you can get Fox-BASE to do it for you?

The commands

The first thing to notice about the BROWSE and CHANGE commands is that they can be used without options, signified by the [ ] symbols. However, it is precisely because of the options that they become useful inside programs, so I heartily recommend BROWSE over CHANGE for most occasions. Other things to notice are that BROWSE has more options than CHANGE and that either can be invoked in a program. The BROWSE command's syntax is:

```
BROWSE [LAST]
       [FIELDS<fieldlist>]
       [HEADINGS<exprC>[,<exprC>]]
       [NOMODIFY]
       [NOAPPEND]
       [SAVE]
       [AT <exprN1>,<exprN2>
       [SIZE <exprN1>,<exprN2>]
       [NOMENU]
       [FONT   <exprC>[,<exprN>]]
```

The CHANGE command's syntax is:

```
CHANGE [LAST]
       [FIELDS <fieldlist>]
       [HEADINGS <exprC>[,<exprC>]]
```

Options for the BROWSE and CHANGE Commands

Figure 7-TableFormView . . . shows what the two views of browse and change look like and what their menus look like when invoked without an installed format file. The NOMENU option prevents the menus you see in Figure 7-TableFormView from appearing altogether.

The change menu looks different if a format file is in place when a CHANGE or APPEND command is issued. The additional menu options provide for record pointer movement and deletion, which are managed in the default windows, respectively, by scrolling and by clicking in the window-splitter bar.

Since FoxBASE+/Mac stores information about the last browse or change session, the LAST option can be a shorthand way to re-invoke them without further specification.

Use the FIELDS clause with either the BROWSE or CHANGE command to indicate what fields should be seen and in what order. Without the FIELDS option all fields will become visible in the database's natural order.

BROWSE FIELDS customer, number, contact

The HEADINGS option gives you power over the window's title, over field names appearing above each column of data, and even lets you determine the display width, in pixels, of each column.

BROWSE HEADINGS "Window title","Customer name:22;Number:6;Contact:20"

If you specify HEADINGS like this they must be equal in number and in the same order as the FIELDS list. The colons and column width numbers which follow field titles to specify their width are optional.

BROWSE-Only Command Options

Use NOMODIFY if the window will be used only for look-up, and the NOAPPEND option to prevent adding of new records.

SAVE forces a user to close the window by pressing the window's close box (top−left corner), otherwise a mouse click anywhere outside of the window will close it.

AT tells FoxBASE in pixels, where to place the browse window. <exprN1> represents the screen pixel row and <exprN2> the screen pixel column where the window's top−left corner will reside. If you enter 0 for <exprN1> and <exprN2>, the browse window will automatically center on the monitor screen.

SIZE tells FoxBASE how many pixels tall, <exprN1>, and how many pixels wide, <exprN2>, the window will be.

Use the FONT clause to specify its font and size.

FONT "Geneva",9

Using BROWSE and CHANGE in Programs

I recommend that the CHANGE window not be used in a program if the BROWSE command will work just as well. The reasons are because so many more options are available for the BROWSE command that make it useful in programs, and because the change window is so easily reached by menu once the browse window has been opened.

The example procedure, below, finds the first, unused work area and opens a parts database into it. The BROWSE command centers a browse window on the screen (because the AT clause uses 0,0).

```
PROCEDURE editparts
SELECT 0
USE parts
GOTO TOP
BROWSE  FIELDS partnum,partdesc,price,stdcost,units HEADING "Parts;
        Master","Number;Description:30;Price:9;Std. Cost:8;Unit" AT 0,0;
        SIZE 330,618 FONT "Geneva",9
DELETE ALL FOR LEN(TRIM(partnum))=0
COUNT FOR DELETED ( ) TO delcount
IF delcount > 0
        PACK
ENDIF
USE
RETURN
```

If a user appends records but does not use them, they will not have a part number. Consequently, those records are deleted. The last thing to happen before the procedure ends is counting deleted records and PACKing the file if deleted records exist. This method is a clean and simple way to let users control the data entry and editing process without much programming knowledge.

FOXFORM OBJECTS AND FOXBASE COMMANDS

Applications reside as commands in one or more program files. FoxForm's role is to write those programs that make screens for an application, and indeed, it's even capable of making simple applications almost by itself. When designing in FoxForm, it's helpful to remember the relationship between programs, screens, and your database files (see Fig. 7-11). You must make the database tables; while you and FoxForm work together to make screen layouts. The finished results can be controlling programs (in the case of application template generation) with screens, or just screens made for incorporation into a larger controlling program. Finished applications work much like the diagram shown in Fig. 7-11.

Looking at Objects

There are six types of screen objects you'll encounter, and possibly make, in Fox-Form, each with their own distinction. These distinctions are useful because they will make the various FoxForm tool options easier to understand:

1. **Text labels** are objects that describe other objects. Text can be used to describe the contents of a box, add humor, or whatever you like. Text objects can also be inside of buttons or in menu selections, but these uses of text are not the stand-alone text labels I'm describing here.

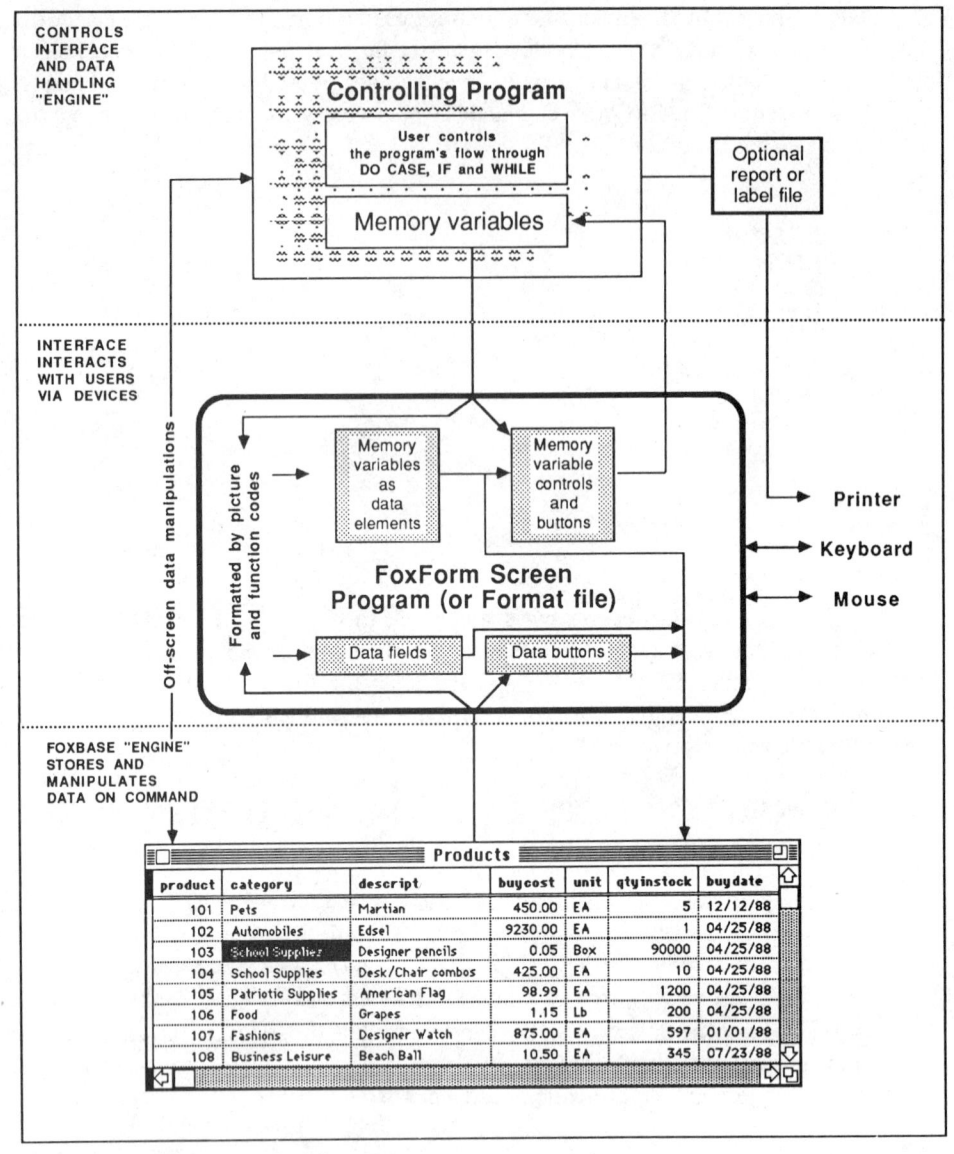

Fig. 7-11. The master plan for screens.

2. **Graphics** objects are boxes, circles, or line art that you create with the drawing tools. Graphics objects can mark regions of the screen so that a form is clear to a user, or for any other design reason you want. Graphics are not pictures.

3. **Pictures** are bitmap, graphical images that you did not draw in FoxForm. Technically, they're data if they come from a database file, or they're picture resources if they come from the FoxUser file (resource files hold icons, pictures, buttons, alerts, and sounds, etc.) that FoxBASE and other Mac programs can use. Pictures are dynamic, graphics aren't. Pictures can be scaled isometrically to retain their

shape and color integrity, and they can be used in several ways: as controls, data, or in lieu of simpler FoxForm-drawn graphics.

4. **Data** comes directly out of a database file. To put data on the screen in FoxForm, you simply pick a database field name from a list when defining an object. This is true for all types of data: character, numeric, date, logical, memo, or picture. Data is usually put on a screen so it can be seen, edited, or both. Data can look differently on screen than it does in a file. Months of the year, for example, can be stored as the numbers 1 to 12 in a database field, and translated into nicely displayed character descriptions. This is done by defining an object that contains the month's names so they don't need storage in the file. Buttons, checkboxes, and pop-up menus can also function this way in lieu of traditional data entry fields.

   The following are the possible data entry objects you can use and their most typical uses: Data entry fields are often used for numbers or for character strings (up to the limit of a field—254 characters), when there's a need for free-form entry. Checkboxes are good for database logical fields (yes or no), while short, exclusive lists of attributes are excellent candidates for numeric storage and representation by radio or text buttons. Memo fields are usually put into scrolling text regions because they have a capacity of 32,000 characters, and finally, pictures have just one kind of on-screen object form that's suitable only for obvious relations to data values.

   When you're defining and placing screen objects, FoxForm will present you with an option called "variable." To FoxForm, a variable is either a database field or a memory variable, which is discussed next. Just remember that data is only one type of variable.

5. **Memory variables** come from programs. It's true that you can create memory variables "on the fly" while using FoxBASE interactively, but variables used in pre-designed screens are almost exclusively created by some kind of program. Memory variables have names just as data fields do, but memory variable contents are more variable because they come and go at will, certainly going when the program quits running (I won't explore the exception to this rule here). A memory variable gets its temporary value, or content, from constants, from a user's mouse or keyboard, or from a database.

Any unchanging value that's written into a program is a constant. In terms of screen design and use, constants aren't special. They are information that's permanently programmed-in because it doesn't change, and it's little enough to easily store in the body of a program. You can assign constant values to memory variables by writing an assignment such as this: <variable> = <constant>

The STORE command is another way to create a memory variable and store some value in it:

STORE <value> TO <memvar>

Memory variable values, like database field values, can be represented in a variety of ways: by checkboxes, radio buttons, text buttons, standard keyboard entry fields, etc.

6. **Controls** are a special way to use memory variables because programs create and use them to control itself! Controls typically take the form of text, radio, or picture buttons, pop-up menus, pull-down menus, or checkboxes. Control variables can also take the form of keyboard entry fields, but that's considered too boring for a Macintosh by some people. After it has placed a memory variable's value on the screen, a controlling program reads its value to find changes, then when the user makes a decision, it takes action. The programmer decides what the program can do by making it capable of certain things, then installs variable values to act as switches, routing FoxBASE's attention to one or another portion of the program for execution. See the DO CASE command in Chapter 8 to see what I mean about switches.

When you are learning to use FoxBASE and FoxForm at the same time, screen object types can be confusing. As a help, ask yourself what type of object you want before putting it on the screen, and refer to Fig. 7-11 to keep the bigger picture in mind. Does the object come from a database file, or does it come from a program variable? The object types and their purposes will be clearer if you take your time and keep the distinctions, outlined above, in mind.

Understanding Commands

Knowing about the commands FoxForm creates can make its tools easier to use. Figure 7-1 explains what each tool is designed for. The commands that tools can make are introduced in the list below. Be sure to look it over before going on to the next section about FoxForm menus.

?	This command evaluates any expression that follows in on the same line (or more than one if separated by commas), placing results on the next line down from the current line. Works in print and on the screen.
??	This command evaluates expressions, placing results on the current line. Works in print and on the screen.
@ row,col SAY	The command that "says" the results of any expression to the screen or printer. The contents of the field or variable cannot be edited because they are only displayed. It will put items at whatever row and column you specify.
@ row,col GET	The command that "gets" memory variables or field values from users by displaying them on the screen. Unlike "SAYing," "GETting" means that the variable or field contents not only becomes visible, but that they can also be edited. It will put items at whatever row or column you specify.

About GET and READ

The GET command must be associated with a variable or a field name because, unlike the SAY command, it lets users change the values. Several GETs can be used in a row, but they must eventually be followed by a READ command, or they won't become active. Activating outstanding GETs with the READ command makes the cursor and its highlight go to the first GET on the screen, and it allows editing by the keyboard or mouse until the READ is ended by a button, menu hit, or other means. Only one READ is needed and allowed at once. Terminating a READ also means that editing is no longer allowed until another READ command is issued, and that changes made to edited fields or memory variables via GETs is permanent (unless, of course, you edit them again with another GET-READ sequence).

Putting Things in Their Place

FoxForm always uses fixed addresses when picking places on the screen to show a button, text, or other object (see Fig. 7-12). To place a screen object at a fixed screen address you, or FoxForm, could write a command that looks like this:

@ 10,20 SAY "This is formatted text on row 10 and column 20."

To put something on the next line down, enter a command like this:

@ 11,20 SAY "This formatted text is on line 11."

Or, like the following, which does the same thing but with relative addressing:

@ ROW( ) + 1,20 SAY "This formatted text is on line 11."

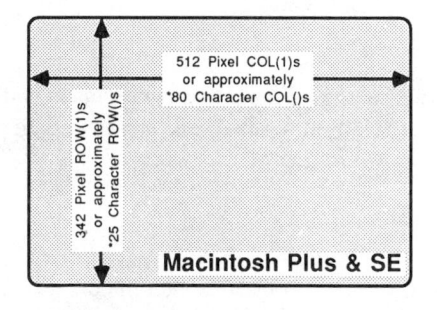

```
                512 Pixel COL(1)s
                 or approximately
                *80 Character COL()s

  342 Pixel ROW()s
   or approximately
  *25 Character ROW()s

          Macintosh Plus & SE
```

```
                640 Pixel COL(1)s
                 or approximately
                *102 Character COL()s

  480 Pixel ROW()s
   or approximately
  *36 Character ROW()s

                   Macintosh II
```

*Note: Character row and column spacing is affected by fonts. The height of all fonts is directly related to their point size. Each point/pixel is approximately 1/72nd of an inch. In proportional fonts, character widths differ, whereas monospaced fonts like Monaco will align vertically because all of their characters have equal width. Also, note that the actual display area is less than the screen size because of the top menubar. The character display numbers shown here reflect what's available while using a recommended font, Monaco 9.

Fig. 7-12. Screen coordinates.

Notice that the ROW( ) function automatically knows where the last line was, so that all you need to do is add 1 to it? That's what's meant by relative addressing. Although FoxForm uses fixed addressing, it's a good idea for you to know the options you have when, and if, you decide to create or modify screen programs.

Pixel rows and columns, instead of character rows and columns, would look like this:

@ PIXELS 10,20 SAY "This is formatted text on pixel row 10 and pixel column 20."

There are 72 pixels per square inch on most Macintosh screens. It's a good idea to use a monospaced font like Monaco 9 when using text-based coordinates. If you want consistent alignment, the Monaco 9 font is roughly equivalent to MS-DOS computer displays and yields predictable, if less than aesthetic results.

When using the Monaco font at 9 points, the translation between pixels and characters is roughly 25 character rows per 286 pixel rows, and 80 character columns per 492 pixel columns. That's on a Macintosh Plus or SE. The coordinates are in English, starting at the top left corner toward the bottom right corner.

If you aren't interested in creating large tabular lists or precisely aligned displays, proportional fonts work fine.

PICTURES and Pictures

There are two types of "pictures" that you'll encounter in FoxForm and in FoxBASE. One is a literal picture that can be seen, the other kind is a template that makes characters appear the way you want them to look. In the command syntax examples and summaries you see in this book, PICTURE refers to the latter character masks, not to pictures that can be buttons or decoration. Literal pictures can be stored in files. FoxBASE refers to them with a special type of SAY and GET command, so don't think literal picture when you see the word PICTURE in uppercase letters.

USING FOXFORM MENUS

Figure 7-13 shows what tools you have for setting up the layout environment and for manipulating most any object. The options are briefly described, one at a time, below.

The File and Program Menus

The file menu opens, saves, and renames screen files. Here you can create new screens and open old ones. The program menu's generate option is the vehicle for making something out of a finished, saved, screen design. Just select it, then go to the templates folder to select a simple or advanced application template. If you don't know which one to use, try the simple application first. Another generating option is for a format file instead of a program file. Formats don't require templates for generating, their only use is to replace FoxBASE's default editing screen, whereas template-generated applications have menus and other features that make the screen easier for FoxBASE novices to use.

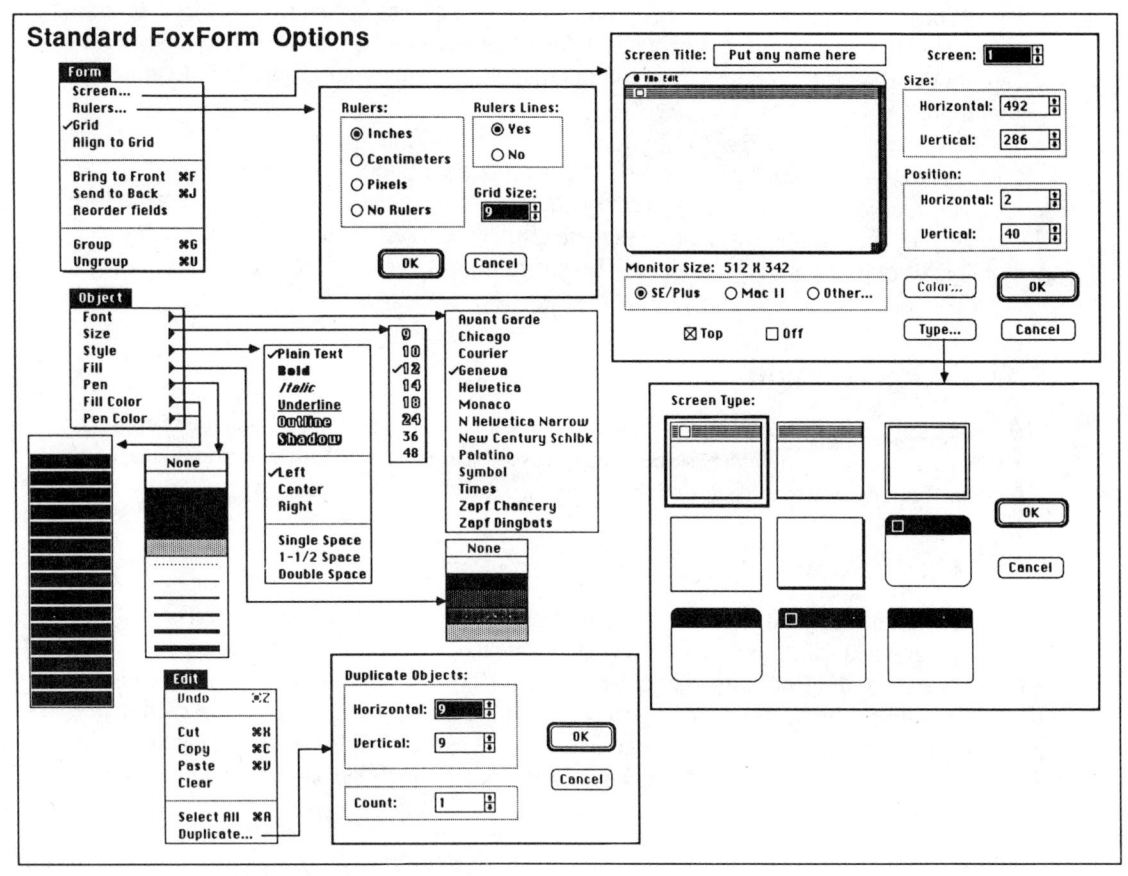

Fig. 7-13. Tools in the drawing environment.

The Form Menu

The form menu is where you establish the screen you'll create (1 through 9 are available), what type of screen you'll use, and what the rule of measure and grid increment will be. Every form maintains its own grid settings until you change them. In addition, a grid alignment option can snap any object into place, as well as a front/back, many-layered object that is in front or in back of another. Use the "bring to front" and "send to back" menus if an object becomes invisible when it should be seen. The view you see of an object on the screen design is the view that will be seen in a generated program.

The re-order fields option works on nonselected fields first, then on those you've selected, in a left to right order. It assigns sequence numbers that are used to determine which field will be read first, second, and so on, when a user presses tab or return while editing data on the finished screen. By selecting most fields, then selecting fewer, and then fewer yet, you can make any field order you like. It's a good idea to establish an order early in the layout process. Changing it later might require reordering GET commands in the final program because the field sequence here decides which GETs are placed top to bottom in the program at generation time.

The group and ungroup commands combine objects into virtual single objects so that they can be moved together. A group is defined as those objects that are selected when the group menu option is chosen. You can ungroup at any time, and groups can be grouped with groups.

If you have an enhanced keyboard, you have a few options that can make life a little easier. You can stretch objects or entry fields pixel – by – pixel simply by pressing the option key and a left or right arrow key. To shrink an object, press both the option and shift keys before pressing an arrow. To nudge an entire object up, down, left or right, simply select an object and press an arrow key.

The Object Menu

The object menu options can all be seen in Fig. 7-13. Pens and Fills can be in color if you have a color Macintosh screen, otherwise the options are presented in black and white. Experiment with each option to learn what it does.

The Edit Menu

All of the standard Macintosh editing features are available to you in FoxForm: Cut, Copy, Paste and Clear, as well as a new Duplicate tool that appears as you enter, create, or open a screen file. Duplicate tools are shown at the bottom of Fig. 7-13. Use the Duplicate menu to repeat lines, boxes, text, or any object that must be precisely in patterned intervals. The Duplicate option uses the grid size you've established in the Rulers menu option to specify offset values. It works with grouped objects, single selections, or with multiple selections.

USING FOXFORM TOOLS

FoxForm generates at least one command for each object you put on the screen. This section discusses each FoxForm tool in turn, and explains the FoxBASE command that FoxForm creates from your design to actually put the object on screen when the screen application program runs. If you aren't interested in the commands themselves, just read as much of this material as you need to understand the FoxForm tool and the type of object you're making.

Text Labels

The first three options in the Form menu (see Fig. 7-13) show what you can do while defining the appearance of text labels created using the text tool (see Fig. 7-14). While the FoxForm Text tool is designed only to display text you enter onto the design screen, it makes exactly the same kind of command that displays database fields when they won't be edited. The only difference is the expression that's put after the SAY command, such as:

```
@ PIXELS 45,35 SAY "This is a text expression, it could be another type though!" STYLE 65536
FONT "Geneva",9
```

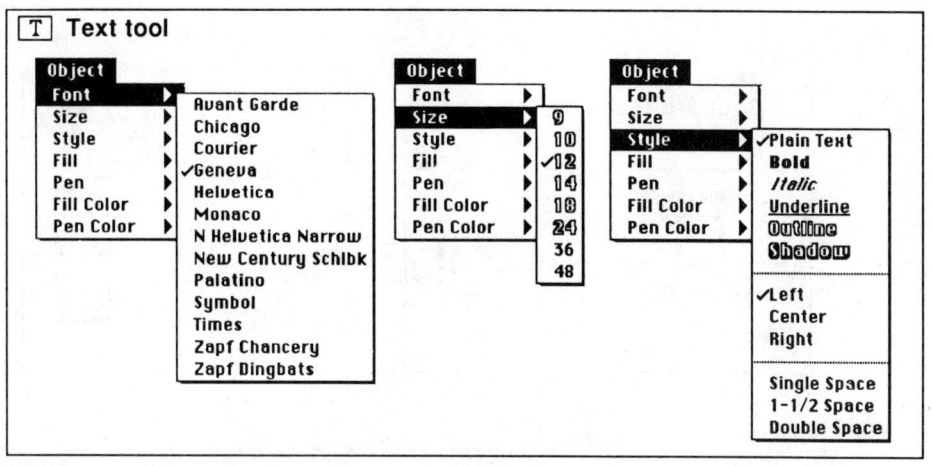

```
┌─────────────────────────────────────────────────────────────────────────┐
│  T  Text tool                                                            │
│                                                                          │
│  Object              Object                  Object                      │
│  Font    ▶           Font    ▶               Font    ▶                   │
│  Size    ▶ Avant Garde  Size    ▶  9         Size    ▶ ✓Plain Text       │
│  Style   ▶ Chicago      Style   ▶ 10         Style   ▶  Bold             │
│  Fill    ▶ Courier      Fill    ▶ ✓12        Fill    ▶  Italic           │
│  Pen     ▶ ✓Geneva      Pen     ▶ 14         Pen     ▶  Underline        │
│  Fill Color ▶ Helvetica Fill Color ▶ 18      Fill Color ▶ Outline        │
│  Pen Color  ▶ Monaco    Pen Color  ▶ 24      Pen Color  ▶ Shadow         │
│             N Helvetica Narrow    36                                     │
│             New Century Schlbk    48                    ✓Left            │
│             Palatino                                    Center           │
│             Symbol                                      Right            │
│             Times                                                        │
│             Zapf Chancery                               Single Space     │
│             Zapf Dingbats                               1-1/2 Space      │
│                                                         Double Space     │
└─────────────────────────────────────────────────────────────────────────┘
```

Fig. 7-14. Fonts, typestyles, and sizes available using the Text tool option.

Refer to the section Anatomy of an Interface Command near the end of this chapter for more information about specifying typestyles and colors in programs you write yourself. You won't need that information unless you program displays in lieu of FoxForm, or you modify FoxForm's programs. The way to print a database field or a memory variable with this command is to put its name where <expr> is, instead of literal text as in the example above.

Text Object Syntax Summary

@ < [PIXELS] row,col> SAY <expr>
[FONT [<exprC>][<,exprN>]]
[COLOR<standard>]

Lines and Boxes

You can draw boxes and lines with the tools shown in Fig. 7-15, then you can modify them with the options shown in Fig. 7-13. If you want even rows or columns of graphic objects, try the Duplicate menu option under the edit menu, and the group/ungroup options under the form menu. They can save you a lot of time and hassle when things need to come together quickly and look balanced. A typical line-making command looks like this:

@ PIXELS 36,18 TO 36,460 STYLE 31 COLOR 0,0,0,0,0

A typical rectangle command looks like this:

@ PIXELS 36,18 TO 208,460 STYLE 3871 COLOR 0,0,0,-1,-1,-1

Rounded rectangle commands are similar to typical rectangle commands, except that their style clause has a different number. For advanced information about the STYLE

Using FoxForm Tools 143

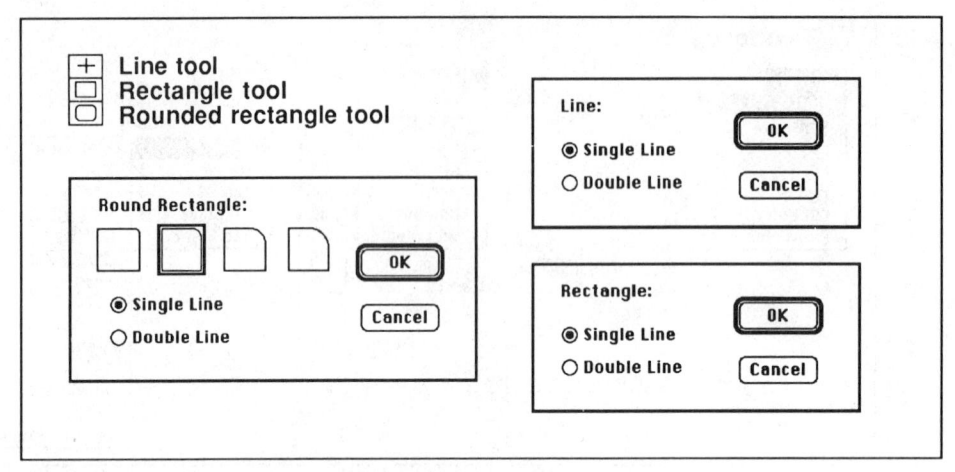

Fig. 7-15. Double, click-on lines for these tools.

clause and what it means in these commands, take a look at Fig. 7-16. The following is the syntax for lines and rectangles.

Line and Rectangle Syntax Summary

@ <[PIXELS] row,col> TO <row,col> [DOUBLE]

Clearing Parts of the Screen

When FoxForm screen programs are run, they completely replace the previously employed screen of the same number. If you want to clear a whole screen without redefining it, use the CLEAR command by itself. If you want to only clear rectangular portions of a screen, use this type of command:

@ PIXELS 36,18 CLEAR TO 208,460

If you want to clear a portion of a screen downward and to the right of any single position while leaving on screen what's above and to the left of that position, use a command like this:

@ PIXELS 36,18 CLEAR

Remember, you don't have to use pixel coordinates. You can use character coordinates instead simply by leaving the PIXELS keyword out of your command. Here's the syntax for screen clearing.

Screen Clearing Syntax Summary

@ <[PIXELS] row,col> CLEAR

Style clause options

For graphics objects

Fill pattern		Pen pattern		Pen width	
Style Number	Fill pattern effect	Syle Number	Pen pattern effect	Style Number	Pen width effect (In Pixels)
0	None	0	None	0	None
1	White	256	White	16	1
2	3% gray	512	3% gray	32	2
3	6% gray	768	6% gray	48	3
4	Light gray	1024	Light gray	64	4
5	Light gray	1280	Light gray	80	5
6	Light gray	1536	Light gray	96	6
7	Gray	1792	Gray	112	7
8	Gray	2048	Gray	128	8
9	Gray	2304	Gray	144	9
10	Dark gray	2560	Dark gray	160	10
11	Dark gray	2826	Dark gray	176	11
12	Dark gray	3072	Dark gray	192	12
13	Black	3328	Black	208	.25
14	Black	3584	Black	224	.50
15	Black	3480	Black	240	.75

For rounded rectangles

Radius

Style number	Radius effect
0	None
4096	16
8192	20
12288	24
16384	28
20480	32
24576	36
28672	40
32768	44
36864	48
40960	52
45056	56
49152	60
53248	64
57344	68
61440	Oval

For all objects

Transfer mode

Style number	Transfer mode effect (B & W)	Transfer mode effect (Color)
0	Copy	Copy
65536	Or	Or
131072	Xor	Xor
196608	Bic	Bic
262144	notCopy	notCopy
327680	notOr	notOr
393216	notXor	notXor
458752	notBic	notBic
524288	Copy	Blend
589824	Bic	addPin
655360	Xor	addOver
720896	Or	subPin
786432	Or	Transparent
851968	Bic	adMax
917504	Xor	subOver
983040	Or	adMin

For all objects:
- Copy - Replaces object behind.
- Or - Foreground only replaces object behind.
- Xor - Foreground inverts foreground of object behind.
- Bic - Foreground mask clears object behind.
- notCopy - Inverts foreground and background to replace object behind.
- notOr - Inverts foreground and background, background replaces object behind.
- notXor - Inverts foreground and background, blends background with foreground of object behind.
- notBic - Inverts foreground and background, background clears object behind.

For color only: Unless otherwise noted, selected and overlayed objects are both compared and affected.
- Blend - Produces weighted average of pixel color values of overlayed objects.
- addPin - Color closest to the sum of RGB values with a maximum of white.
- addOver - Color closest to sum all overlayed objects, not pinned to white so can turn dark.
- subPin - Color closest to sum of RGB values in selected object minus those in object behind, maximum of black.
- Transparent - If not equal to background color, pixels replace pixels in object behind.
- adMax - Replaces pixels in object behind withgreater RGB saturation based on comparison with selected object.
- subOver - Color closest to sum of RGB values in selected object minus those in object behind.
- adMin - Replaces pixels in object behind lesser RGB saturation based on comparison with selected object.

Fig. 7-16. The Style command options.

or

@ <[PIXELS] row,col> CLEAR TO <row,col>

Checkboxes

Checkboxes can be used to change the value of any numeric database field or a memory variable between the values of 0 and 1, or of logical database field or memory variables between the values of true (.T.) and false (.F.). See Fig. 7-17 for an overview of the FoxForm method of defining checkboxes. This is what a checkbox command looks like:

@ PIXELS 63,54 GET saleitem STYLE 65536 FONT "Chicago",12 PICTURE "@*C On Sale" SIZE 15,69

The text label appearing next to this checkbox says "On Sale," and the variable it edits is a database field named "saleitem". Checkboxes are defined one at a time, and they stand alone, operating independently of one another. Notice that the syntax of the sample above, and in the syntax summary, below, that the picture code "C" is used. It, along with the @ symbol, determines that the object will be a checkbox and not something else.

Checkbox Syntax Summary

@ < [PIXELS] row,col>
SAY|GET <varN>|<varL>
PICTURE|FUNCTION "[@]*C <string>"
[FONT [<exprC>][<,exprN>]]
[COLOR<standard>]

Checkboxes Have a "C".

"@*C..." to make a checkbox.

Data Entry Fields

Data entry fields look like little rectangular boxes in which users can see, add, and edit data from a variety of sources, including character, numeric, date, or logical fields. They are, by far, the most common method used to edit numbers and text, and you can even use them for editing logical fields. Checkboxes are better for logical fields, but if you want users to type T, F, Y, and N instead of checking a box, use this tool. Entry fields are so common that the Form/Quick Form menu option uses it by default. Look at Fig. 7-18 to see how the Field tool works to define data entry field objects. This is what a finished FoxForm data entry object command looks like:

@ PIXELS 63,56 GET products->category STYLE 0 FONT "Geneva",12 PICTURE "@A " SIZE 15,151

In this example, "products" is the file and "category" is the field being edited. The font is geneva in a point size of 12, and the picture clause uses a format code specifying

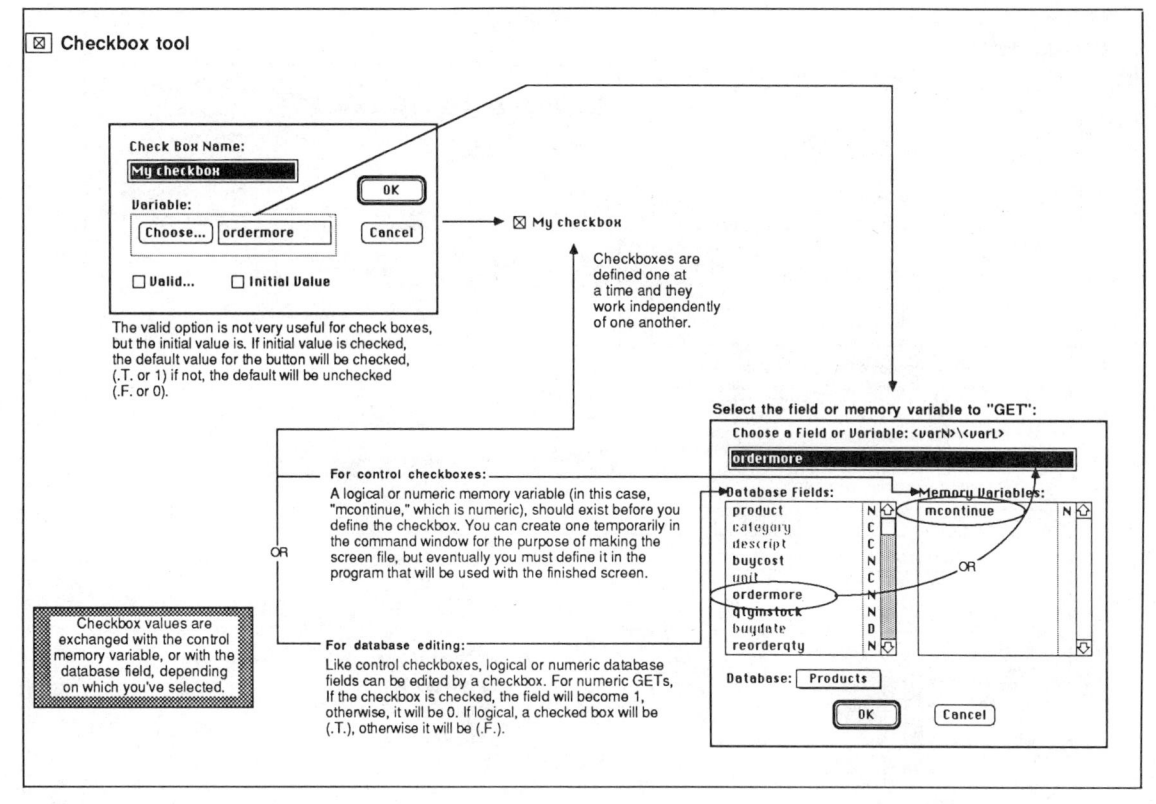

Fig. 7-17. Making checkboxes.

that all characters entered into the field should be converted into uppercase letters as they're entered.

Data Entry Field Syntax Summary:

@ < [PIXELS] row,col> GET <expr>
[PICTURE <template>]
[FUNCTION <code>]
[RANGE [<exprN1>] [,<exprN2>]]
[VALID<exprL>]]
[FONT [<exprC>][<,exprN>]]
[COLOR<standard>]

THE PICTURE CLAUSE

The Picture syntax option can be used to determine what kind of object will be used with an SAY or GET command, and it has special uses that are unique to the data entry object. The PICTURE templates, and FUNCTION codes applied here control how data is seen and edited. They have an uncanny ability to mask data, changing for example, lower-case characters into uppercase characters as they're entered, or allowing only numbers to be entered into a telephone number field.

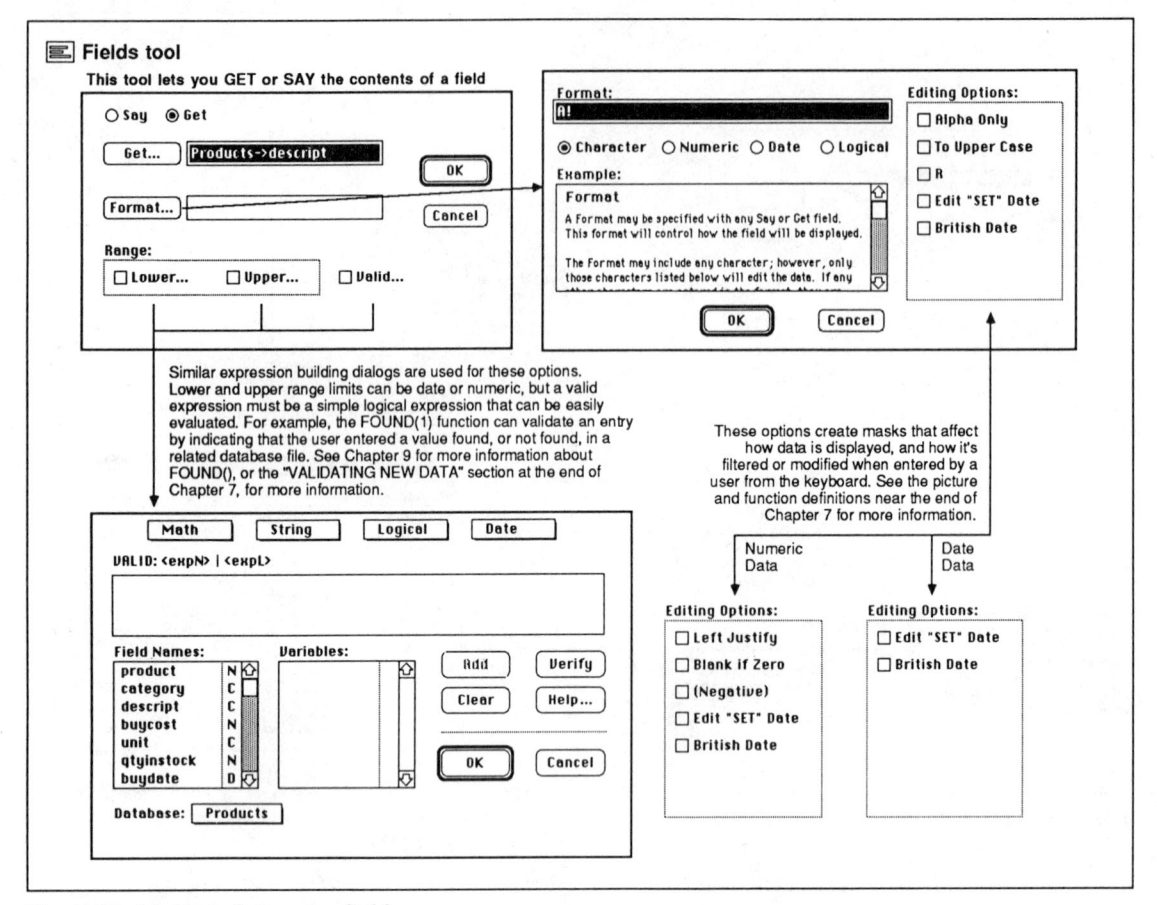

Fig. 7-18. Making data entry fields.

      Picture templates get their name from the ability to provide a general template, or picture, of the data someone will enter. They also prevent a user from entering something that doesn't fit the picture. Picture codes are also called masks, because they can change the data's appearance to match the picture. If you want to restrict numbers from a character editing field, for example, or to make all letters uppercase as they're entered, picture template codes can help. To use them, just enter them in similar to this example:

    @ row,col GET <field or memory variable> PICTURE "0123456789"

      A picture template code can go anywhere. I've put a number in the example immediately above. The number of picture codes can be as many as there are character, or number, positions in the entry field. Each picture code affects one character position in the entry field, so you can specify one code for one character or number position, another code for the next character or number position, and so on, for every position in the field. The following is a list of picture template codes:

148   *The Picture Clause*

A	Only letters of the alphabet are allowed into the position. Example:
	@ GET <variable or field name> PICTURE "AAAAA"
L	Only the logical letters "T", "F", "Y", and "N" are allowed into the position. Example:
	@ GET <variable or field name> PICTURE "L"
N	Only digits and letters are allowed into the position. Example:
	@ GET <variable or field name> PICTURE "NNNNN"
X	Any character is allowed. Example:
	@ GET <variable or field name> PICTURE "XXXXX"
Y	Only the logical letters "Y" and "N" are allowed into the position. Example:
	@ GET <variable or field name> PICTURE "Y"
9	Only numbers are allowed into the position. Example:
	@ GET <variable or field name> PICTURE "99999999"
#	Only blanks, digits, and plus or minus signs are allowed. Example:
	@ GET <variable or field name> PICTURE "99999999"
!	Accepts digits, blanks, signs, etc., but converts characters to uppercase on input. Example:
	@ GET <variable or field name> PICTURE "!!!!!!!!!"
$	Place in first position indicate dollars. Example:
	@ GET <variable or field name> PICTURE "$99999999"
*	Place after $ for check printing security. Prints a line of * between $ and numbers. Example:
	@ GET <variable or field name> PICTURE "$99999999"
.	Use to place a decimal in a memory variable edit field. Also places decimals in entry field for editing database fields that have decimals. Example:
	@ GET <variable or field name> PICTURE "999.99"
,	Separates thousands in number variables. Example:
	@ GET <variable or field name> PICTURE "99,999.99"

Blanks can be used wherever you don't want the effect of codes, but be careful. Characters other than blanks and the codes listed in the next section will be treated literally as data! As such, they will be seen and stored in the variable or field as if they were entered by a user from the keyboard. There is a use for that unique ability, however, which is discussed in the next section.

The FUNCTION Clause

Don't confuse these functions with the functions detailed in Chapter 9. These affect the way an editing field functions. Function codes, unlike picture codes, can't determine what kind of object you'll use for an on-screen GET, they do the kind of input/output masking that the picture template codes do. Even then, function codes aren't true templates because they affect every character or number in an entry field at once, whereas picture codes affect only one character or number position at a time, thereby offering more precise control. Function codes, however, have a unique value: They're shorter and easier to use for some things, because they can be used with picture template codes when general and specific masking is needed in combinations, and they're useful when you need an option that only a special function code can provide.

FoxBASE needs only one function code to affect a whole entry field. This example allows only letters into a field of any size:

@ row,col GET <fieldname> FUNCTION "A"

You can use more than one function code when a combined effect is desired, but only one kind of data can be used in a field, so don't mix function codes that are made for different types of data.

You can use Function codes in PICTURE clauses, but they must appear first in the list and must be preceded by a @ symbol so FoxBASE will know what they are. In fact, the only significant difference between the way a FUNCTION clause works and a PICTURE clause works is that the FUNCTION clause doesn't need a @ symbol to indicate that its codes are functions instead of picture template codes. If you combine picture and function codes, use a PICTURE clause, put the @ symbol first in the list, and separate its function codes from picture template codes by a space. This example uses both clauses to turn letters to uppercase and allow only numbers in the first three of six positions:

@ row,col GET <fieldname> PICTURE "@! 999AAA"

The following is a list of function codes:

A   Only letters of the alphabet are allowed into the field. Example:

        @ GET <variable or field name> FUNCTION "A"

    or

        @ GET <variable or field name> PICTURE "@A"

B   Use this function only with numeric variables or to left justify the numbers as they're entered and displayed in the fields.

150   The Picture Clause

C   Use this function only with numeric variables or fields to put the letters CR immediately after positive numbers to indicate a credit. This doesn't work with the GET clause, but it does work with the SAY clause for display purposes. Be sure to provide additional room for the space and CR.

D   Use this function with dates, characters, and numbers that you're using to represent a valid date. It causes the entered or displayed values to conform to the date format established via the SET DATE TO (American, British, German, etc.) command.E, Edit data as a European (BRITISH) date. May be used with date, character, and numeric data.

E   Like the D code, but works to specify that the date mask is the European (BRITISH) date format.

R   This unusually powerful function works with the PICTURE clause (remember to use it as "@R . . ."), allowing you to put characters into the entry field that won't be stored in the data field or memory variable. A typical use is for telephone numbers where you don't want to waste disk space for the dashes between numbers. Another benefit is that phone numbers can have a standard appearance if you enter them into a database using this function, for example:

@ GET phonenum PICTURE "@R (999)999-9999"

A result is that 9999999999 will be stored in the database, and (123)456-7890 will be seen for editing. Be sure not to use a literal character that's already employed as a picture or function code.

S<n>   Use this function with character data to let users scroll through large character data strings in a shorter area on screen. This function is more useful on a non-Macintosh computer, where character editing is more primitive.

X   Use this function only with numeric variables or fields to put the letters DB immediately after negative numbers to indicate a debit. This doesn't work with the GET clause, but it does work with the SAY clause for display purposes. Be sure to provide additional room for the space and the DB.

Z   Use this code with numbers only to prevent zeroes from displaying when the value is 0, allowing cluttered rows and columns to be more readable.

(Use this function with numeric data only to put ( ) around negative numbers. Make sure to plan for the extra room needed.

!   Like the picture code that does the same thing, this function code will change any alphabetic characters in an entry field to uppercase.

The RANGE Clause

The RANGE clause accepts only numeric and date expressions to prevent entry of values that are not within a specifically desired range. If a user attempts to enter a value outside of the specified range, an informative box alerts the user of the acceptable range. You can use a lower range without an upper range, or the reverse, but you must use one range specification (and the comma if an upper range only) whenever the RANGE clause is present.

The VALID Clause

To understand the VALID clause and how it's used, look at the section Validating New Data near the end of this chapter.

The FONT Clause

To give characters bold, italic, or underlined type styles, you can add the following numbers to the font's point size, FoxBASE will figure out what the combinations are and display the field's data accordingly. See the section near the end of this chapter Anatomy of an Interface Command for more information.

- 256   added to the font number makes it bold
- 512   added to the font number makes it italic
- 1024 added to the font number makes it underline
- 2048 added to the font number makes it outline
- 4096 added to the font number makes it shadow

The COLOR Clause

The COLOR clause determines the display colors following the conventions shown in Fig. 7-19. Also, for more information, see the section near the end of this chapter Anatomy of an Interface Command.

The SIZE Clause

This clause determines how large a data entry field will be on screen in character or pixel height and width. For more information, see Anatomy of an Interface Command near the end of this chapter.

PICTURE BUTTONS

Pictures can be selected from the fields of an open database file, or from the resource fork of the FoxUser file. The FoxUser file, incidentally, can be copied and renamed, and you can add your own pictures and icons to its store (see Fig. 7-20). This is how to get custom pictures for picture buttons that aren't vulnerable like those in a database file. For

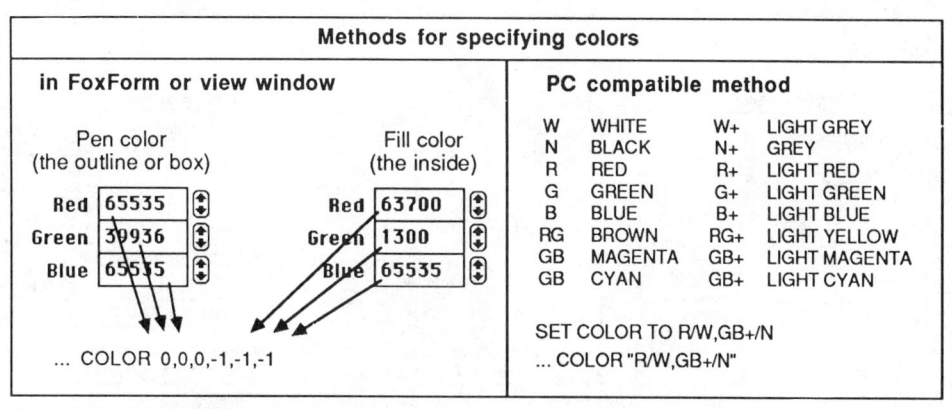

Methods for specifying colors	
in FoxForm or view window	**PC compatible method**
Pen color (the outline or box) — Red 65535, Green 30936, Blue 65535 Fill color (the inside) — Red 63700, Green 1300, Blue 65535 ... COLOR 0,0,0,-1,-1,-1	W WHITE W+ LIGHT GREY N BLACK N+ GREY R RED R+ LIGHT RED G GREEN G+ LIGHT GREEN B BLUE B+ LIGHT BLUE RG BROWN RG+ LIGHT YELLOW GB MAGENTA GB+ LIGHT MAGENTA GB CYAN GB+ LIGHT CYAN SET COLOR TO R/W,GB+/N ... COLOR "R/W,GB+/N"

Fig. 7-19. Specifying colors in FoxForm or the View window.

more information about custom picture resource files, see the section Managing Picture Resources in Chapter 10.

Picture buttons are like text buttons that change the value of numeric control variables or database fields (see Fig. 7-21). FoxForm can make only one button at a time, and because it's alone, it will return a 1 if pressed and a 0 if not pressed. To make multiple buttons that change the value of one numeric variable or database field, say, between 1 and 5, you must create a list in the command's picture clause like this:

"<type>num[;<type>num. . .," etc.

In this sample, each "num" refers to a picture in the FoxUser file, or a database file. Database files can't hold more than one picture per field, so to execute a multipicture button with pictures from a database file, the file must have several picture fields in each record.

The default button layout is horizontal, so insert a "V" after the * if you want a vertical button display. Listed Button values range from 1, for the left-most button, to a high number representing the right-most button in the list. If used with the "N" option, picture buttons won't terminate an active READ when pressed, otherwise, by default they do terminate READs so that no more editing of open GETs can be performed until another set of GET-READs is issued. Notice, as with all buttons, that the mouse pointer changes into a button pusher whenever it's over a hot region defined as a button.

Pictures can be imported directly from MacPaint or MacDraw into a database field by cutting the pictures from them and pasting them in an open picture field. The Picture Mover (see Fig. 7-22) works like the Macintosh Font/DA Mover, letting you move pictures directly from MacPaint or MacDraw files into FoxUser, or another resource file. For more picture moving instructions, see Managing Picture Resources in Chapter 10. Once a picture is installed, you can use it by making an object for it in FoxForm, or making your own command that uses its resource ID number, such as:

@ PIXELS 54,72 GET controlvar STYLE 65536 PICTURE "@* \P3071" SIZE 33,36

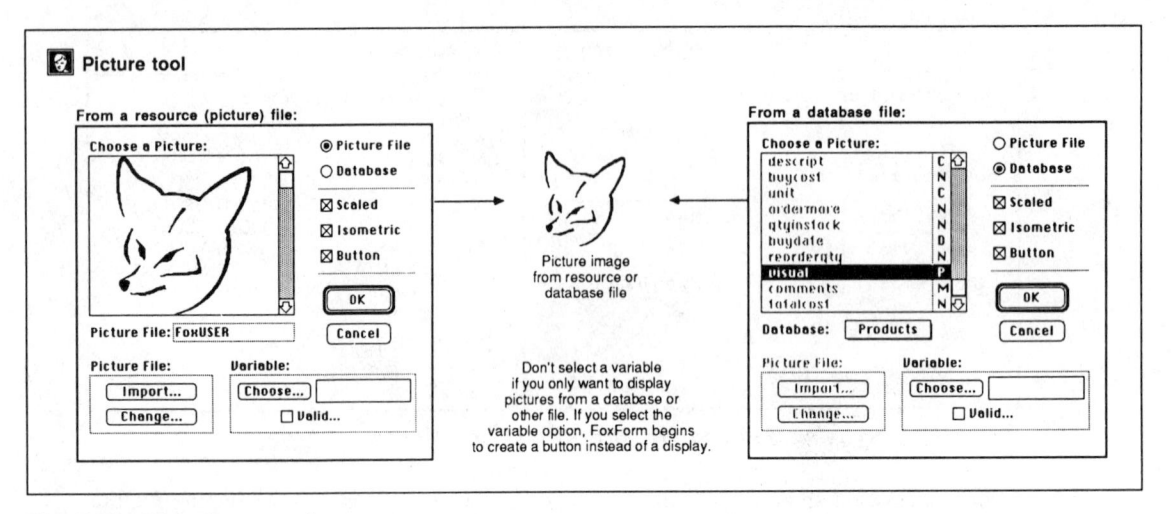

Fig. 7-20. The picture tool.

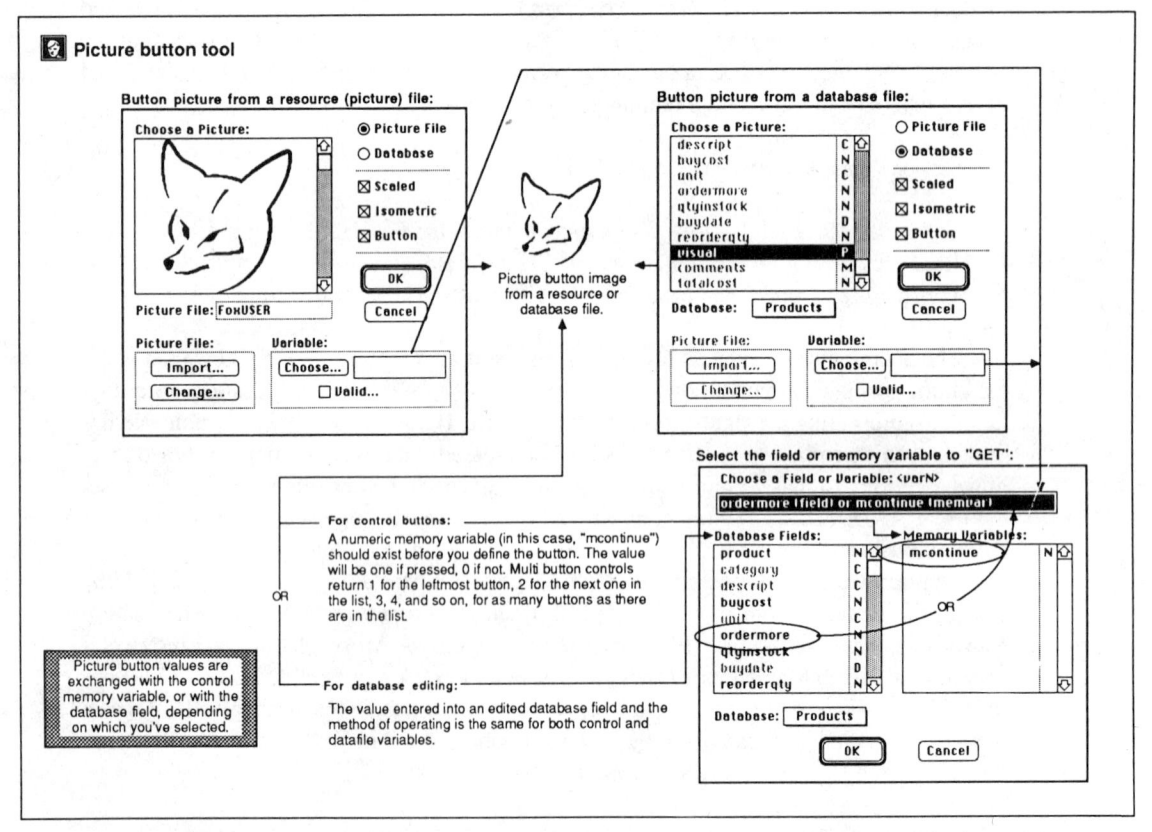

Fig. 7-21. Making picture buttons.

154　Picture Buttons

The following is what a command for a row of horizontal buttons looks like:

```
@ PIXELS 54,72 GET controlvar STYLE 65536 PICTURE "@*
\P3071;\P129;\P5301;\P209" SIZE 33,36
```

The PICTURE clause in all picture button commands has a "@* \" followed by a symbol indicating what kind of picture to display, and possibly (as in the example), numbers that represent the picture's resource ID in the FoxUser, or other, resource file. The picture type "P", used for all the pictures in this example, stands for a PICT type resource in the FoxUser file. For more information about PICTURE clauses and the kinds of pictures, icons, and so on, that you can use with this command, refer to the list below. Note that the picture ID in the command sample immediately above, and the picture ID of the picture in Fig. 7-22, are the same.

Picture Buttons Use PICTURE to Determine Where the Picture Comes From

PICTURE "@*\I..."	from an ICON in the FoxUser file, ends a READ.
PICTURE "@*N\I..."	from an ICON in the FoxUser file.
PICTURE "@*\P..."	from a PICT in the FoxUser file, ends a READ.
PICTURE "@*N\P..."	from a PICT in the FoxUser file.
PICTURE "@*\#..."	from a #ICN in the FoxUser file, ends a READ.
PICTURE "@*N\#..."	from a #ICN in the FoxUser file.
PICTURE "@*\F..."	from a database file, ends a READ.
PICTURE "@*N\F..."	from a database file.

There's simply no way that you will feel comfortable working with picture buttons until you've experimented with them. Take a half hour or more with some clip art, or a painting/drawing tool that can make PICT or PAINT files, and play with picture importing and exporting via the picture mover (see Fig. 7-22) until you're comfortable with the process. Here's the syntax of the picture button command for your reference:

Picture Button Syntax Summary

```
@ < [PIXELS] row,col>
    SAY|GET <varN>
    PICTURE|FUNCTION "[@] * [<options>]
        <type>num[;<type>num][;...][;<type>num]"
    [COLOR<standard>]
```

POP-UP MENUS

Pop-up menus work in a list like picture buttons. Look at the command syntax summary, below. The "<string1>;<string2>"" method is used for building a text list of items that appear in the menu itself (see Fig. 7-23). The value returned by the menu is a number from 1 to ?, which represents the position of the menu option selected from the

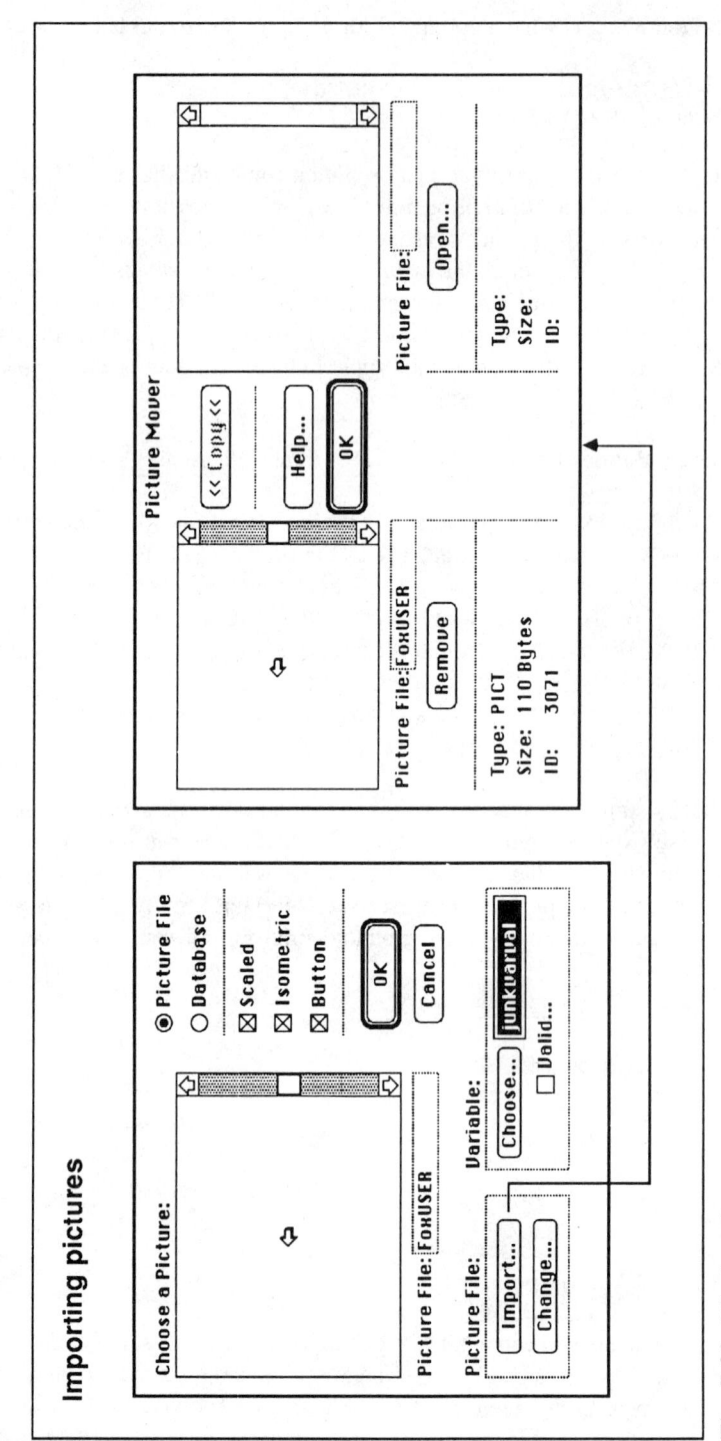

Fig. 7-22. Moving pictures.

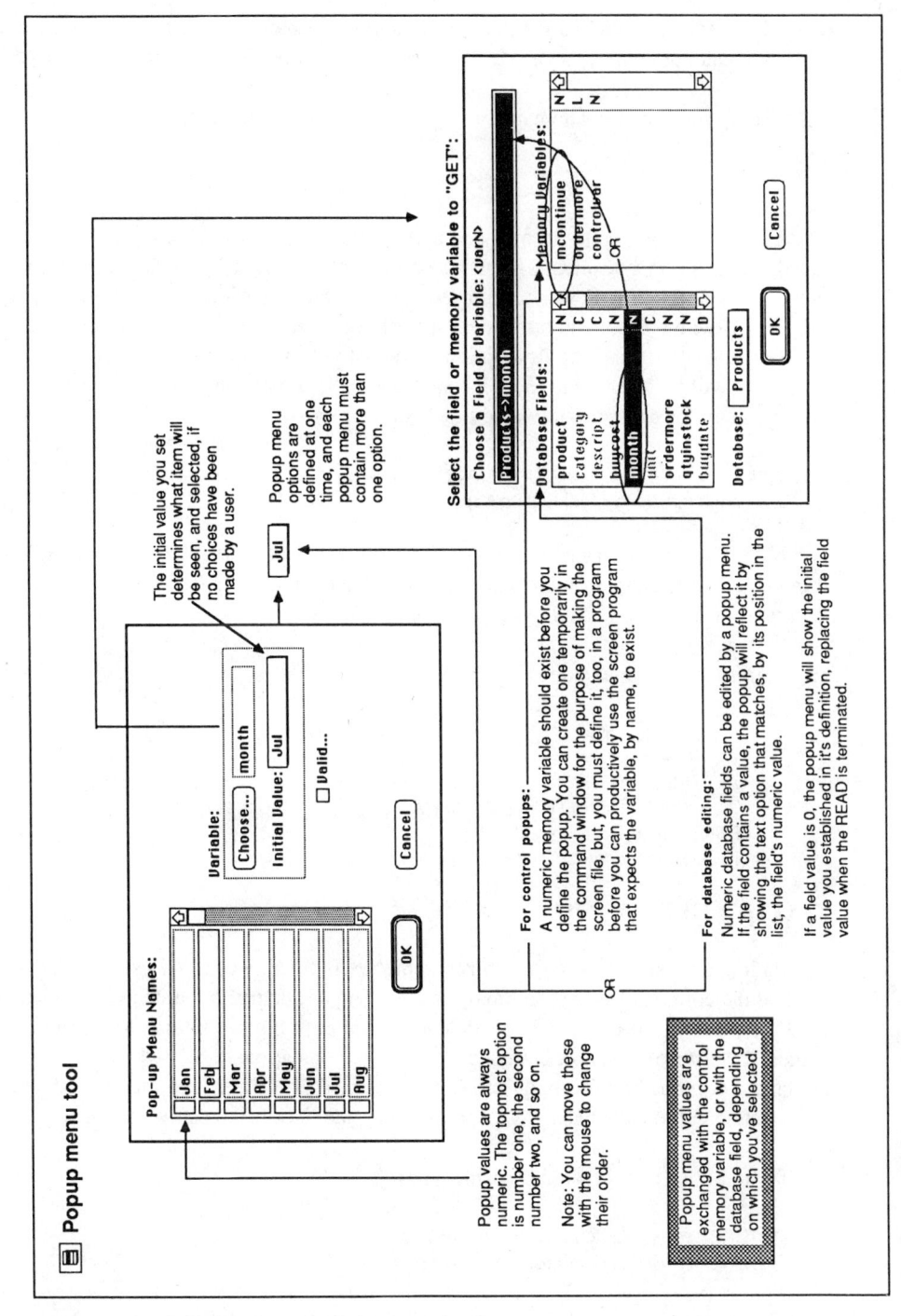

Fig. 7-23. Making pop-up menus.

list. The first item in the list is the topmost item in the menu. The PICTURE clause in all pop-up menu commands has a "@^" symbol followed by the string list of options.

Pop-up menus are made using a ^ symbol that looks like a popup:

PICTURE "@^. . ."

You can change a pop-up menu as many times as you like until the READ is terminated. Popups don't terminate READs, so the value of <varN> will be the last value entered before the READ was terminated. If the value of the variable or field that you're GETting is within the menu's range of options, the menu option text matching that value will be displayed. If not, the first option in the list will be displayed, and if no selection is made, a 0 will be returned to the GET variable or field when the READ is terminated. A pop-up menu for each of the twelve months could look like:

@ PIXELS 71,72 GET month STYLE 0 FONT "Chicago",12 PICTURE "@^;
Jan;Feb;Mar;Apr;May;Jun;Jul;Aug;Sep;Oct;Nov;Dec" SIZE 19,47

Note that each <string> is nothing more than a descriptive item for display. What's important is that you carefully match the number positions, from left to right, with the data field or memory variable you're GETing into.

Pop-up menu syntax summary:

@ < [PIXELS] row,col>
    SAY|GET <varN>
    PICTURE|FUNCTION
        "[@]^ <string1>[;<string2>][;. . .][;<stringN>]"
    [FONT [<exprC>][<,exprN>]]
    [COLOR<standard>]

RADIO BUTTONS

Radio buttons, like pop-up menus and picture buttons, work in a list (see Fig. 7-24). Look at the command syntax summary below. The "<string1>;<string2>" method is used for building a text list of items that appear, at each button in turn. Radio buttons are named so because you can't be tuned into two stations at once, and when you push one, the others pop out because only one can be selected at a time. The picture clause in all radio button commands has a "*R" followed by the list of descriptive options.

Radio buttons are created by using an "R":

PICTURE "@*RV. . ." to make vertical radio buttons
PICTURE "@*RH. . ." to make horizontal radio buttons

The value returned by this command is a number from 1 to ? representing the position of the button selected, which matches its text in the list of strings: "<string-1>;<string2>." The first item in the list is the topmost, or the left-most, displayed.

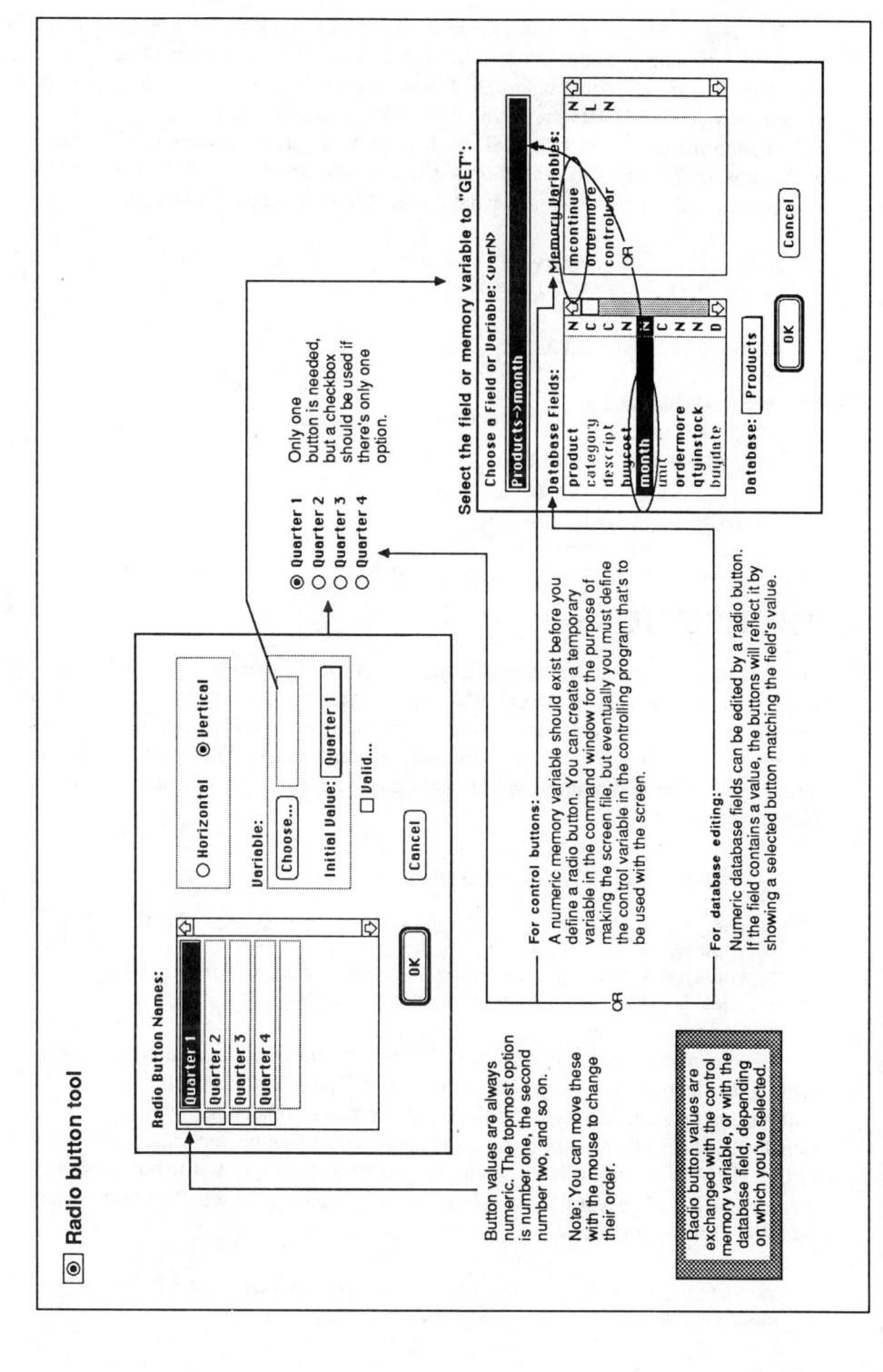

Fig. 7-24. Making radio buttons.

Like pop-up menus, you can change a radio button as many times as you like until the READ is terminated. Radio buttons don't terminate READs, so the value of <varN> will be the last value entered before the READ was terminated. If the value of the variable or field that you're GETting is within the numeric range of options in the string list, the radio button matching that value will be displayed. If not, all of the radio buttons will be visibly unselected; and if no selection has been made when the READ is terminated, a 0 will be returned. The following is what a radio button command looks like:

@ PIXELS 45,72 GET quartervar STYLE 65536 FONT "Chicago",12 PICTURE;
"@*RV Quarter 1;Quarter 2;Quarter 3;Quarter 4" SIZE 784,80

Radio Button Syntax Summary

@ < [PIXELS] row,col >
   SAY|GET <varN>
   PICTURE|FUNCTION "[@]*R[<options>]
      <string1>[;<string2>][;...][;<stringN>]"
   [FONT [<exprC>][<,exprN>]]
   [COLOR<standard>]

TEXT BUTTONS

Text buttons change the value of numeric control variables or database fields. Look at Fig. 7-25 to see how they're made. It's easy to make multiple buttons at one time, and the default display orientation is horizontal. To make a vertical display of buttons, FoxForm inserts a "V" after the * in the command's picture clause. The width of all buttons is determined by the width of the widest one, based on the number of characters you enter as button text.

Text Buttons Can Be Vertical or Horizontal

PICTURE "@*V..."   to make vertical text buttons that end a READ.
PICTURE "@*VN..."   to make vertical text buttons.
PICTURE "@*H..."   to make horizontal text buttons that end a READ.
PICTURE "@*HN..."   to make horizontal text buttons.

Listed button values range from 1, for the left-most button, to a high number representing the right-most or lowest button in the list. If used with the picture option "N", text buttons don't terminate an active READ when pressed, otherwise, by default, they do terminate READs so that no more editing of open GETs can be performed until another set of GET-READs is issued. Notice that, as with all buttons, the mouse pointer changes into a button pusher whenever it's over a hot region defined as a button. Text button commands look like these examples:

@ PIXELS 54,63 GET direction STYLE 0 FONT "Chicago",12 PICTURE "@*V ; North; South;East;West" SIZE 2072,65 COLOR 0,0,0,-1,-1,-1

☐ **Text button tool**

Text Button Names:
- North
- South
- East
- West

○ Shadow
○ Standard
○ Horizontal ● Vertical
☒ Terminating [Spacing...]

Variable:
[Choose...] direction
☐ Valid...

[Cancel] [OK]

Button values are always numeric. The topmost option is number one, the second number two, and so on.

Note: You can move these with the mouse to change their order.

Horizontal, vertical and spacing are display options. Terminating, if checked, causes a READ to terminate when one of the buttons is pushed, which is good for controls and not usually good for database editing.

[North] [South] [East] [West]

Only one text button is needed, several are allowed. The default display is horizontal.

Select the field or memory variable to "GET":

Choose a Field or Memory Variable: <varN>
| direction |

Database Fields:		Memory Variables:
product C		myvar N
category C		direction N
descript C		
buycost N		
unit C		
ordermore N		
qtyinstock N		
buydate D		
reorderqty N		

Database: [Products]

[OK] [Cancel]

For control buttons:
A numeric memory variable should exist before you define a text button. You can create a temporary variable in the command window for the purpose of making the screen file, but eventually you must define the control variable in the controlling program that's to be used with the screen you're making. Terminating text buttons end a READ, so they are great for controls that advance a program.

OR

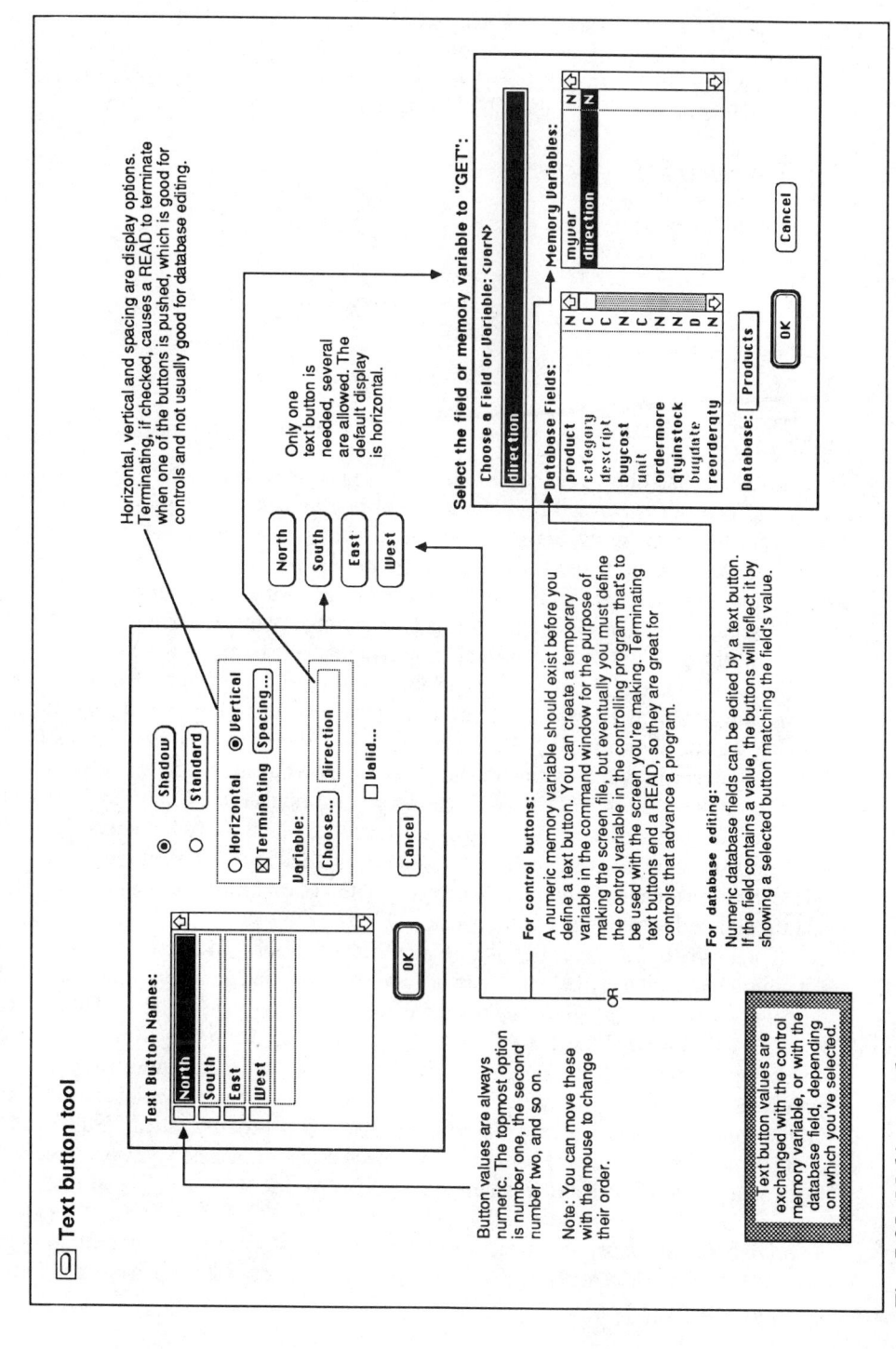

For database editing:
Numeric database fields can be edited by a text button. If the field contains a value, the buttons will reflect it by showing a selected button matching the field's value.

Text button values are exchanged with the control memory variable, or with the database field, depending on which you've selected.

Fig. 7-25. Making text buttons.

Text Buttons 161

This is what a command for a row of horizontal buttons looks like:

@ PIXELS 54,63 GET direction STYLE 0 FONT "Chicago",12 PICTURE "@*H ; North; South;East;West" SIZE 2072,65 COLOR 0,0,0,-1,-1,-1

Text Button Syntax Summary

```
@ < [PIXELS] row,col >
    SAY|GET <varN>
    PICTURE|FUNCTION "[@]*[<options>]
         <string1>[;<string2>][;...][;<stringN>]"
    [FONT [<exprC>][<,exprN>]]
    [COLOR<standard>]
```

SCROLLABLE LISTS

Scrollable lists allow you to scroll through a list of text items and select one by double-clicking. The value returned by their selection is a number that represents the selected item's position in the array. Scrolling pick lists, while they are nice, are the most difficult of the interface options to use because they require that you create an array, that you fill the array with visible text values, and finally, that you display the list. After doing all that, you have to set up a way to make the result (the array number of the item picked) useful to you.

Look at Fig. 7-26 to see an example program that creates an array and puts a scrolling pick list on the screen. If you want to define a scrolling pick list from constant text values, as this program does, I suggest that you first create and run a program to make the array, copying the one shown in Fig. 7-26, then go to FoxForm to define the object's location and size. FoxForm, will then find the array as you have already made it, and it can do the job of positioning the scroll list on screen as you manipulate it. When FoxForm is done and you have generated a format or program file containing the layout command, combine the program you wrote (the one that makes the array), and the command FoxForm made to create the object into one program. When you "DO" it, everything will happen as planned and the finished scrolling list will appear.

If you want to get values out of a database field to display in a scrolling list, try using the program immediately below. It can be used as is, or you can incorporate it as a procedure within your own programs by removing the * in front of the "PROCEDURE" command. It uses any database file you've got open, fetching the values from a field into its own array (that's right, you don't have to bother), and it displays the scrolling pick list anywhere you want on the screen. The item picked gets stored into a variable called "pickedval", and the database record picked gets stored into a variable called "pickedrec". In addition, the file pointer will be left on the selected record in case you want to select the work area and modify record contents.

If you use this program as a procedure in your own programs, make sure to declare "pickedval" and "pickedrec" public so that their values will be available to the program that called it.

Scrollable list tool

○ Text Region ● Scrollable List

Variable:
[Choose...] stdmail

Array:
[POSTAGE]

☐ Valid...

[OK]
[Cancel]

Array is a special memory variable with more than one cell. It contains the text to be scrolled, and its cell address numbers (subscripts) are the way that choices get reported.

Variable is the database field or a memory variable that holds array cell (subscript) numbers after a user has made a choice.

Scrollable lists require programming because they draw upon the values in an array to make displayed, scrolled text. And the only efficient way to make an array is in a program.

```
SET TALK OFF
CLEAR
CLEAR ALL
DIMENSION POSTAGE(10)
STORE "Airline ticket      " TO POSTAGE (1)
STORE "Birth announcement  " TO POSTAGE (2)
STORE "Bond - negotiable   " TO POSTAGE (3)
STORE "Bond - nonnegotiable" TO POSTAGE (4)
STORE "Book                " TO POSTAGE (5)
STORE "Catalog             " TO POSTAGE (6)
STORE "Check               " TO POSTAGE (7)
STORE "Circular            " TO POSTAGE (8)
STORE "Currency            " TO POSTAGE (9)
STORE "Document            " TO POSTAGE (10)
@ PIXELS 31,91 GET STDMAIL FROM POSTAGE SIZE 100,155
READ
CLEAR
@ 8,12 SAY "You picked "+POSTAGE(STDMAIL)
```

Airline ticket
Birth announcement
Bond - negotiable
Bond - nonnegotiable
Book
Catalog
Check

For memory variables:
If you're going to use a numeric memory variable to capture the user's choices, it should exist before you create the scrolling list.
You can make one in the command window in order to create the screen file. Eventually, however, the variable must be available to FoxBASE in the same program that creates the array.

OR

For database editing:
Numeric database fields can be edited with a scrolling pick list. They will GET a value equal to that of the array subscript (the array cell location, in parentheses).
If a number in the database field finds a match in the array, the matching array text option will be highlighted.

Select the field or memory variable to "GET":

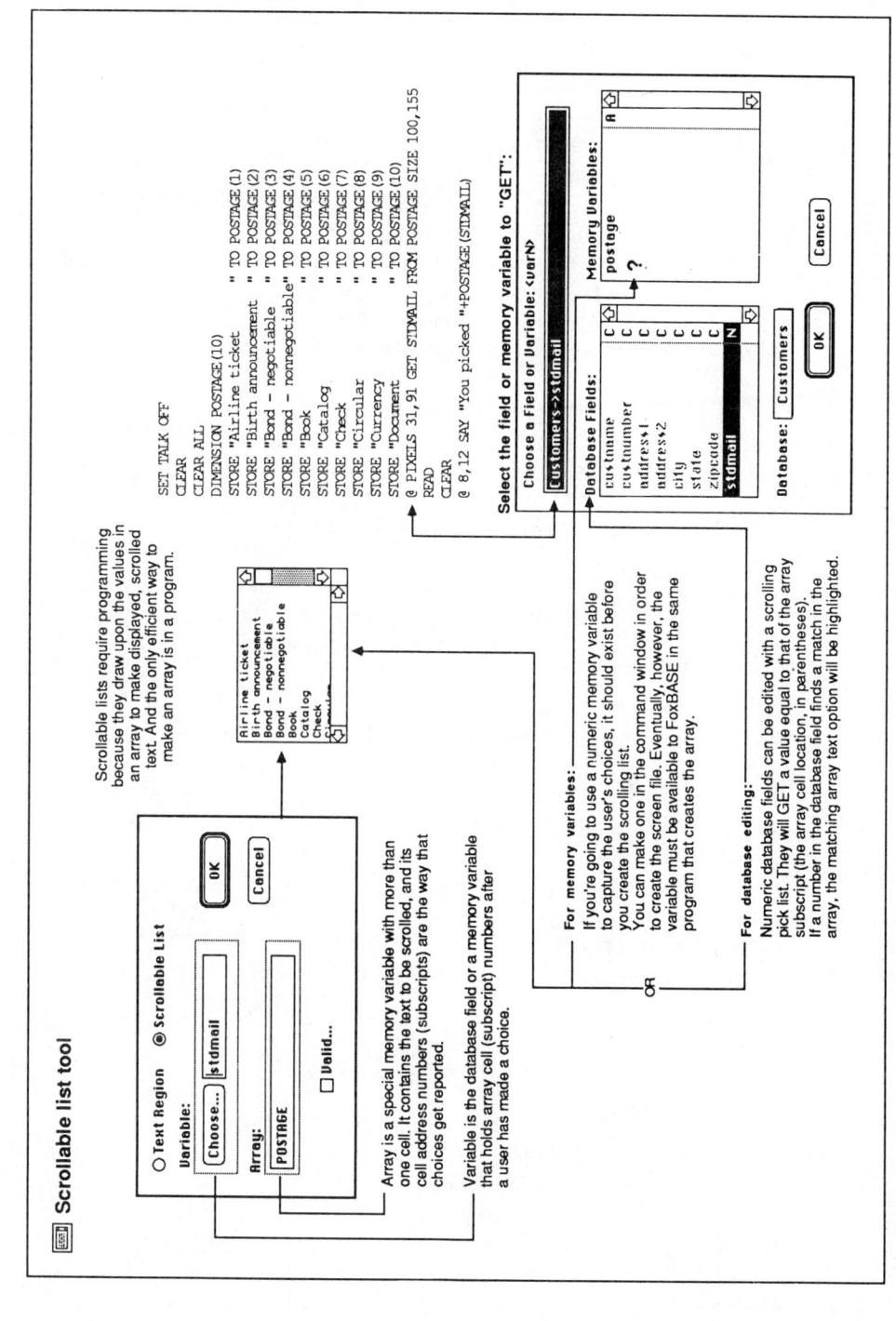

Choose a Field or Variable: <varN>
[Customers->stdmail]

Database Fields: Memory Variables:
custname   C   postage
custnumber   C   ?
address+1   C
address+2   C
city   C
state   C
zipcode   C
stdmail   N

Database: [Customers]

[OK] [Cancel]

Fig. 7-26. *Making a scrollable list.*

```
* * * * * * * * * * * * * * * * *
* Name:            Procedure PickOne
* Author:          Michael P. Masterson
* Date:            November 1988
* Purpose:         Creates a single-item picklist from a database field
*                  that respects deletions.
* Before calling:  1> Declare public variables "pickedrec" & "pickedval"
*                  2> USE a datafile in any workarea.
*                  > Put MVARSIZ=32 or greater in config.fx file
*                  to make memory avail for large array
*                  4> Sort the file, index not allowed.
* Parameters:      "scrollfile" C—the file with the data
*                  toprow        N—the top screen display row
*                  leftcol       N—the left screen display col
*                  boxrows       N—the # of rows to display (5 min)
*                  boxcols       N—the # of cols to display (12 min)
*                  hilite        N—the default selection (0=no none)
*                  "contents"    C—the field to display
* Leaves:          1> The selected workarea is the pickfile's
*                  2> Variable "pickedrec" has the selected RECNO( )
*                  3> Variable "pickedval" has the selection's content
*                  4> The record is positioned on selection
* *
* PROCEDURE PickOne
PARAMETERS scrollfile,toprow,leftcol,boxrows,boxcols,hilite,contents
SET TALK OFF
SELECT &scrollfile
COUNT FOR .NOT. DELETED( ) TO y
DIMENSION scrlarray(y)
x = 1
GO TOP
DO WHILE .NOT. EOF( )
   IF .NOT. DELETED( )
      STORE TRIM(&contents) TO scrlarray(x)
      x = x+1
   ENDIF
   SKIP
ENDDO
@ toprow,leftcol GET hilite FROM scrlarray SIZE boxrows,boxcols
@ toprow,leftcol say "Pick one"FONT,9+256
READ
GOTO hilite
pickedrec = hilite
pickedval = &contents
@ toprow,leftcol CLEAR TO toprow+boxrows,leftcol+boxcols
@ toprow+1,leftcol TO toprow+3,leftcol+boxcols-1 DOUBLE
```

```
@ toprow+1,leftcol+1 SAY "Selected" FONT,9+256
@ toprow+2,leftcol+2 SAY SUBSTR(&contents,1,boxcols-3)
RELEASE ALL LIKE
scrollfile,toprow,leftcol,boxrows,boxcols,hilite,contents,x
RETURN
* * * * * * * * * * * * * * * * *
```

The way to use this program is to enter a command that passes parameters to it, like this: DO PICKONE WITH "filename",5,5,12,20,1,"fieldname" The numbers mean, in order, the top row (in characters) where the scroll list box will display, the left column (in characters) where the scroll list will display, the number of rows to display inside the scroll box, and the number of columns to display in the box, and finally, the default item to highlight when the scroll list first displays. The filename and the fieldname must be inside quotes as shown, and the file must already be open in any of the selected work areas.

The following is a sample scroll list with commands that I've taken from the program above. It receives the parameters you give it when issuing the DO command shown above:

```
@ toprow,leftcol GET hilite FROM scrlarray SIZE boxrows,boxcols
```

Note that the "hilite" variable this command is GETting can be any previously existing numeric variable. It receives the number that's returned when a selection is made. So the number value of the variable "hilite," in this case, becomes the number of the array item selected as determined by its subscript, or cell location. The Size option, for scrolling pick lists, indicates the entire size of the display in coordinates down and right of the @ row,col location. This is the command shown in Fig. 7-26 that actually creates the scrolling list object:

```
@ 31,91 GET stdmail FROM postage SIZE 100,155
```

In this case, the "stdmail" variable will be edited by the user's selection, and the selection will be made from an array named "postage".

Scrollable List Syntax Summary

```
@ < [PIXELS] row,col >
    GET <varN> From <array>
    SIZE <exprN1>,<exprN2>
    [FONT [<exprC>][<,exprN>]]
    [COLOR<standard>/[,<enhanced>]]
```

TEXT EDIT REGIONS

Text editing regions are easy to produce. See Fig. 7-27 to see what I mean. FoxForm puts the SCROLL keyword in by default to make the scroll bar on the right side of the region appear whenever the text you're GETting exceeds the box size. If you leave SCROLL out, you can still edit all text in the box, but the mouse's cursor must do the scrolling inside the text region itself.

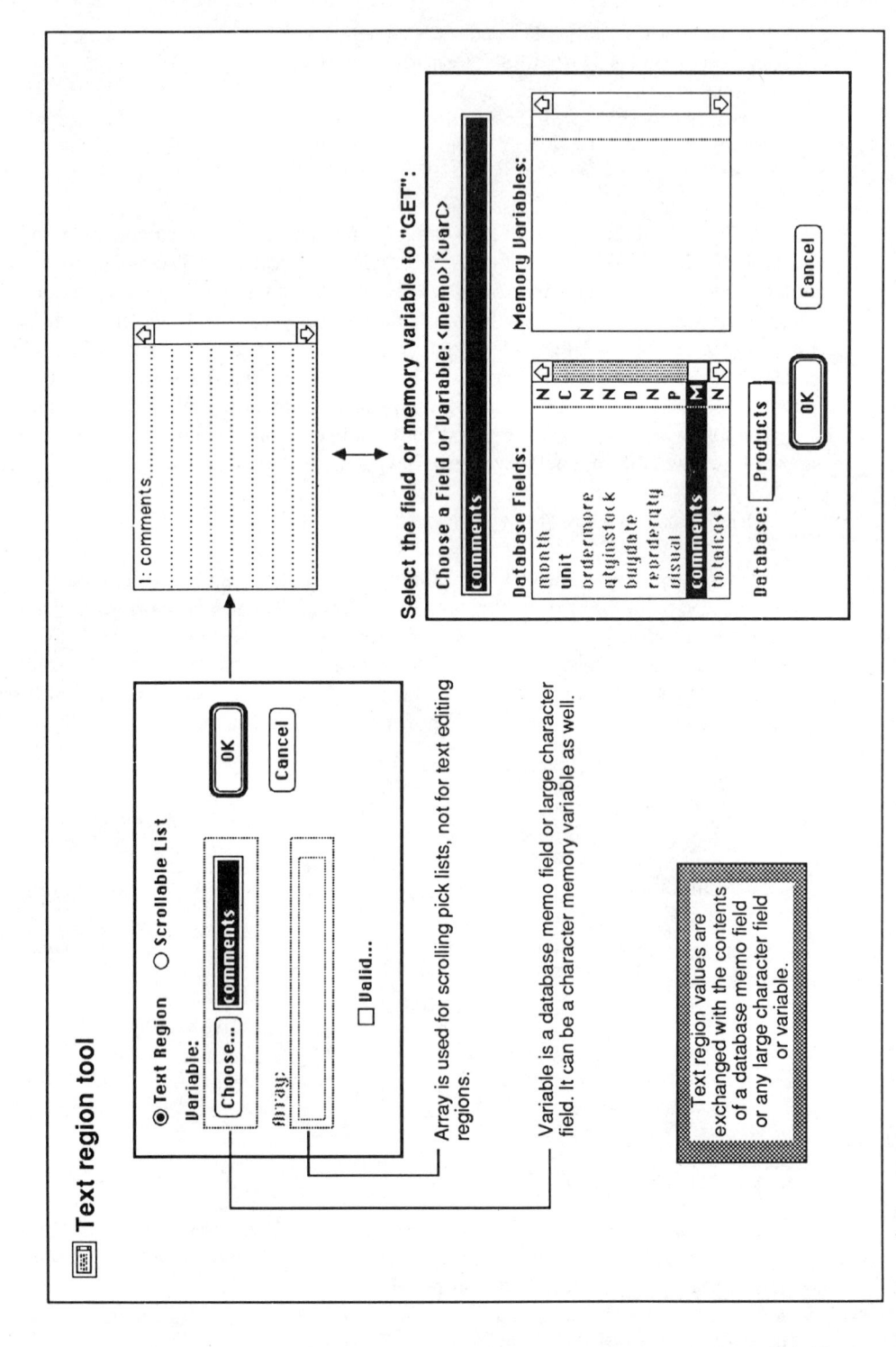

Fig. 7-27. Making regions to edit text or memos.

You can edit text from any source in a text region, but memo fields in a database file are the most common. If you don't use the keyword PIXELS, the region displays in character rows and columns.

```
@ PIXELS 63,56 GET Products->comments STYLE 0 FONT "Geneva",12 SCROLL;
   SIZE 120,214 COLOR 0,0,0,-1,-1,-1
```

Hint: You can specify any type size or style so that large amounts of text can be seen in smaller regions of the screen, or they can be made to stand out.

Text Region Syntax Summary

```
@ < [PIXELS] row,col >
   GET <memofieldname>|<varC>
   SIZE <exprN1>,<exprN2> [SCROLL]
   [FONT [<exprC>][<,exprN>]
   [COLOR<standard>]
```

ANATOMY OF AN INTERFACE COMMAND

There are many options in a @ SAY or @ GET command for controlling the behavior of objects. Let's analyze the different parts of a sample command. Because most of the commands in this chapter follow a pattern, you'll understand what they consist of and what their different parts mean:

```
@ PIXELS 45,35 SAY "This is a text, or character expression." STYLE;
   65536 FONT "Geneva",9 COLOR 0,0,0,-1,-1,-1
```

Essential Command Parts

@	equivalent to "at."
PIXELS	means that the row and column numbers refer to pixels instead of the default columns based on character rows and columns.
45,35	The row and column, respectively, where the left side of the expression should display.
SAY	Means that the expression should be said, or displayed, not gotten. The GET command, by contrast, is used to both display and edit information. Only the SAY command can be used with text objects you make in FoxForm. If you use a GET, instead of a SAY, make sure to use the READ command as well to activate the GET. Many GETs can be put on a screen and then activated all at once with one READ command.

<expr>   In this command, the expression is a literal text object that I entered in FoxForm, so it's a string surrounded by quotes. It could just as well have been a number, or a small calculation such as BUYCOST * QTYINSTOCK, for example. The expression is utterly flexible, following the rules that any expression must follow. See Chapter 4 for a simple explanation of expressions, or Chapter 6 for a more detailed discussion.

Optional Command Parts

STYLE   The STYLE clause is a rather complex numbering system that defines five things: Object fill pattern, object pen pattern, object pen width, the radius of rounded rectangles, and the transfer mode (which determines how objects visually relate to one another when overlayed or adjacent). FoxForm creates STYLE clauses automatically, and I suggest that you use it before trying to hand code the attributes of screen objects. If you decide to code your own styles, pick number values from the appropriate tables shown in Fig. 7-16 and add them like this example that establishes, in order, a pen pattern (15), a fill pattern (256), a pen width (16), a radius (4096), and a transfer mode (65536):

    STYLE 15 + 256 + 16 + 4096 + 65536

If you have trouble getting expected results, it's probably because FoxBASE's internal style word (32 bits long) needs upper bits set to 0, so add at least one clause number that makes the number large, such as an OR transfer mode with its style number of 65536. You can use the STYLE clause for example, to create custom programmed reports that don't use FoxReport. Figure 7-16 has one table of choices for each of the object attributes and their associated style number values.

A note about printing with the STYLE clause: The mere presence of a STYLE clause forces FoxBASE to create whole pages in memory, before printing, so you can use STYLE to prevent page ejects when using @ SAY to format printed output. Normally, a page eject occurs whenever a @ SAY command makes reference to a lower-valued coordinate that might have already been printed. Printers don't like to back up. As a rule, they like to go forward, from left to right, and from top to bottom. STYLE frees you from that page formatting restriction.

FONT   Use FONT to specify any character font installed in the computer. If you leave the FONT clause out of a @ SAY or @ GET command, the most recently used font, or the screen's default font, will be used. There's a catch: If you design with a font that is not installed on a computer that your screen will eventually be used on, the results can be ugly. FoxBASE will make a poor image of the font it can't find. Because of this, it's a good idea to use standard fonts and sizes.

"Geneva" — Font names are character expressions and require quotes around them.

,9 — The font size is numeric, so put a comma and then a number to specify the font's point size. You can change the type style from plain text to a fancier style by adding typographical style numbers to the point size number. The predetermined type style numbers are:

    256   bold text
    512   italics
   1024 underlining text
   2048 outlined text
   4096 shadowed text

Refer to this table whenever you need to specify a typographical style by hand. Using this formula in our sample command line, 265 would be the font number for bold text, 521 for italics, and so on. Typographical style combinations can be created by adding one style to another, and then adding the result to the font's point size number. In this sample, bold, italicized print would be created if you used the number 777, or if you entered 9+256+512. To increase the point size to 12 while printing bold italics, the number would be 780, or easier yet, 12+256+512.

COLOR — COLOR tells FoxBASE how to color the text. There are two methods to use. The example shows the method that's commonly used on a Macintosh, and it's always used by FoxForm when you use it to make layouts. The other method is compatible with other computers running FoxBASE, even with the dBase product from Ashton-Tate. This is what the numbers mean that you see in our sample command:

   0, 0, 0   pen values for a Red, Green, and Blue mix
 -1, -1, -1   fill values for a Red, Green, and Blue mix

Pen is the outline, fill is what's inside. Only pen values affect the color of text objects, whereas pen and fill values affect most other screen objects. If you want to see what color values look like (you must have a color Macintosh), open the color selection panel in the View window. Then, when you double-click on a color, the standard color setting features will appear. The part of the color setting dialog that relates to the RGB color mix in the COLOR clause, here, is shown in Fig. 7-19.

Take a look at the alternate color representations in Fig. 7-19. To specify colors with these characters instead of the Red, Green, and Blue color mixing numbers, follow this format:

@ row,col SAY "Colors" COLOR "R/B"

Red is the foreground color of the pen, blue is the background color that will surround the red text. Remember, this method is most used on other models of computer, but if you're making programs to run on both Macintosh and IBM compatibles, you'll need to specify colors this way. An enhanced color option is available with this method of color specification that I don't need to mention in this context. Look up the SET COLOR command in Chapter 8 if you think it might be useful.

SIZE If you don't specify a size, FoxBASE will make a good guess as to the size of the object and will display it accordingly. The size is entered as two numbers separated by a comma, indicating the number of screen rows, and the number of screen columns the object will occupy. If the keyword PIXELS is used anywhere in the command, the coordinates will be in terms of pixels. If PIXELS is left out, the coordinates will default to character rows and column sizes based on the currently selected text and typestyle.

VALID The VALID clause you see in the syntax of many commands, and as a Checkbox option in FoxForm, prevents unwanted values from being entered by users into a database file. Its usefulness is nearly limited to data entry fields where a user can enter almost anything they want, including accidental or improper values. Pop-up menus, boxes, and so on, have little use, in my opinion, to have a VALID clause associated with them even though it's present in FoxForm. Nevertheless, the VALID clause is very useful for data entry fields, which are the most often employed screen objects. If you want to know how to use the VALID clause, see the next section.

ENHANCING APPLICATIONS BY HAND

This brief exercise is intended to show you how easy it is to make changes in programs generated by FoxForm. If you aren't interested in hands-on programming, or don't

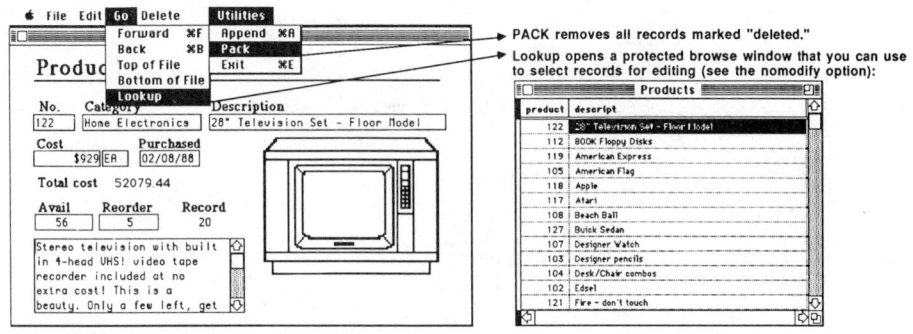

Fig. 7-28. New lookup and pack menus.

have the time, just skip ahead to the section FoxForm Objects and FoxBASE Commands. Otherwise, dive in. You might be surprised at how quickly you can take control of what your programs do. The sample "products.prg" program listed in this section is just an example; modify yours instead—it should look very similar.

In the sample program, I've shortened lines that are not important for illustration, so pay closer attention to the parts printed in bold letters and don't trust the rest except to compare its structure with your own FoxForm generated programs. Make the changes I marked in bold print to your application program, and exchange your own field names for those in the sample. You don't need to understand everything you see to get a valuable feel for the way FoxBASE thinks and works. When you're done, you can rerun the program to see the results of your changes.

This exercise adds two options to your program that FoxForm didn't put in, a Browse window for data lookup, and a packing option that permanently removes records you've marked for deletion. You'll need to select one or two fields out of all those in your own database file to display in the Browse window, putting their names in the command line that starts with "BROWSE FIELDS...". Once you are done modifying all of the program, its menus should look like those in Fig. 7-28.

Command line samples in this chapter might wrap around from one line to the next. In use, however, FoxBASE commands must fit on one line without wrapping unless ended by a semicolon. Semicolons on one line tell FoxBASE that a command's remainder is on the next line down. You can break lines anywhere you like with a semicolon, but it's clearer when you separate whole expressions. An exception to this rule is literal character expressions that cannot wrap around to the next line, but must be broken into two parts for joining by concatenation with a + operator.

```
*************************
* Program.: Products.prg
* Date. . ..: 2/ 2/88
* Notes. . .: Simple database application.
* Created by Fox Software's FoxForm
* Modified by Michael P. Masterson
* ---Set environment.
SET TALK OFF
SET BELL OFF
```

Enhancing Applications by Hand **171**

```
CLOSE ALL
* ---Open procedure file.
SET PROCEDURE TO Products
*
* ---Initialize database file.
SELECT 1
IF FILE("products.dbf")
    USE "products.dbf"
ELSE
    fname = getfile('F + DB','Locate products.dbf:')
    IF fname = = ""
        SET PROCEDURE TO
        RETURN
    ENDIF
    USE &fname
ENDIF

INDEX ON DESCRIPT TO PRODUCTS    && add this to make an index
SET INDEX TO PRODUCTS            && makes sure index is active

DIMENSION mbartop(3)
* DIMENSION mbar1(4)              && change this line to
DIMENSION mbar1(5)                && this - for the lookup menu
DIMENSION mbar2(1)
* DIMENSION mbar3(2)              && change this line to
DIMENSION mbar3(3)                && this - for the pack menu

STORE "Go" to mbartop(1)
IF DELETED( )
    STORE "Recall" to mbartop(2)
    STORE .F. TO isdelete
ELSE
    STORE "Delete" to mbartop(2)
    STORE .T. TO isdelete
ENDIF
STORE "Utilities" to mbartop(3)

STORE "Forward/F" to mbar1(1)
STORE "Back/B" to mbar1(2)
STORE "Top of File" to mbar1(3)
STORE "Bottom of File" to mbar1(4)
STORE "Lookup" to mbar1(5)        && adds the lookup menu
STORE "Append/A" to mbar3(1)
* STORE "Exit/E" to mbar3(2)      && change this to number 3
STORE "Exit/E" to mbar3(3)        && like this
STORE "Pack" to mbar3(2)          && adds the pack menu

IF .NOT.(isdelete)
    STORE "Recall Record/R" to mbar2(1)
ELSE
    STORE "Delete Record/D" to mbar2(1)
ENDIF
```

```
MENU BAR mbartop,3
*  MENU 1,mbar1,4                    && 5 options not 4
   MENU 1,mbar1,5                    && like this
   MENU 2,mbar2,1
*  MENU 3,mbar3,2                    && 3 options not 2
   MENU 3,mbar3,3                    && like this .

*
* ---Display screen format.
SCREEN 1 TYPE 0 HEADING "Screen 1" AT 40,2 SIZE 286,492 PIXELS TOP
CLEAR
ON MENU DO MENUPROC WITH MENU(0),MENU(1)
*
* ---Main execution loop.
DO WHILE .T.
    DO GETSAY
    READ
    IF (DELETED( ) .AND. isdelete) .OR. ((.NOT.(DELETED( ))).AND.;
        (.NOT.(isdelete)))
        DO DELRECL
    ENDIF
ENDDO
*
* ---Closing operations.
CLEAR
SET BELL ON
SET TALK ON
RETURN
* END: Products.prg


*
* Notes...: Procedures for simple database application.
*
PROCEDURE MENUPROC
PARAMETER row,col
DO CASE
    CASE row = 1 .AND. col = 1 && forward
        IF .NOT. EOF( )
            SKIP
        ENDIF
        IF EOF( )
            ALERT NOTE 2 "You are positioned at the bottom of the file."
            SKIP -1
        ENDIF
        RETURN
    CASE row = 1 .AND. col = 2 && backward
        IF .NOT. BOF( )
            SKIP -1
        ENDIF
        IF BOF( )
            ALERT NOTE 2 "You are positioned at the top of the file."
        ENDIF
        RETURN
    CASE row = 1 .AND. col = 3 && top of file
        GO TOP
```

```
            RETURN
    CASE row = 1 .AND. col = 4     && bottom of file
        GO BOTTOM
        RETURN

    CASE row = 1 .AND. col = 5     && lookup action
        BROWSE FIELDS PRODUCT,DESCRIPT NOMODIFY && field names
        RETURN

    CASE row = 2 .AND. col = 1 && delete/recall
        IF .NOT. DELETED( )
            DELETE
        ELSE
            RECALL
        ENDIF
    CASE row = 3 .AND. col = 1 && append
        APPEND BLANK
        RETURN

    CASE row = 3 .AND. col = 2     && pack action
        PACK
        RETURN

    CASE row = 3 .AND. col = 3 && exit, changed number
        SCREEN 1 OFF
        SET TOPIC TO
        CLOSE DATABASE
        CANCEL
ENDCASE
PROCEDURE DELRECL
    IF isdelete
        STORE "Recall Record/R" to mbar2(1)
        STORE 'Recall' TO mbartop(2)
        isdelete = .F.
    ELSE
        STORE "Delete Record/D" to mbar2(1)
        STORE 'Delete' TO mbartop(2)
        isdelete = .T.
    ENDIF

MENU BAR mbartop,3
*   MENU 1,mbar1,4                  && 5 options not 4
    MENU 1,mbar1,5                  && like this
    MENU 2,mbar2,1
*   MENU 3,mbar3,2                  && 3 options not 2
    MENU 3,mbar3,3                  && like this
```

* This part of the program puts all the fields on screen. Not all
* screen objects are listed here as they should be in your program:
```
PROCEDURE GETSAY
@ PIXELS 30,29 SAY "Products Incorporated" STYLE 65536 FONT "Times",280
@ PIXELS 36,27 TO 36,459 STYLE 47 COLOR 0,0,0,0,0
@ PIXELS 83,27 GET Products->product STYLE 0 FONT "Monaco",12

* * * * * * * * * * * * * * * * * * * * * * * * * * * * * * * * * *
```

174   Enhancing Applications by Hand

The * symbol that you see in front of some program lines tells FoxBASE that it's a comment put there by a programmer instead of a command. I've marked some lines in the sample program that way because I want you to replace them with a nearby command in bold print. The && symbols also tell FoxBASE that it should ignore whatever follows on the same line. These && symbols can be used anywhere in a line, whereas * is used in the first column to comment a whole line.

For hackers: If you expect to modify programs frequently, look at the simple application template's main include file *"simmain.inc,"* and the FoxForm template documentation provided by Fox Software. You can add features to the template program. The advantage of this more technical approach is that your changes will automatically go into every program you generate; because it's programming the FoxForm "robot."

VALIDATING NEW DATA

A valid check of an entry is usually done by a simple logical expression that must be found true for the entry to be accepted. This command could look like this:

```
@ 10,10 GET customer VALID FOUND(2)
```

This example uses the FOUND( ) function to discover whether or not the related file (a precondition) in work area 2 (also known as B) has a record that matches what was entered.

The problem with VALID is that free entry and roaming on the screen becomes inhibited when an "Invalid input!" message persistently appears without further explanation to the user, forcing them to press the Escape key for mercy and an exit from the field.

If you use a numeric expression with a VALID clause instead of a logical expression, you have more options at your disposal for control. For one thing, numeric valid expressions let you jump from one entry field to the next, based on the number value that a numeric valid expression returns to the GET. The affect is eerie, yet predictable. Look at the following section of code and see if you can't dream up some uses for the technique in your screens. Remember that the semicolons just tell FoxBASE that one command is on two separate lines.

```
CLEAR && SCREEN
CLEAR GETS
STORE " " TO var1
STORE " " TO var2
STORE " " TO var3
STORE " " TO var4
STORE " " TO var5
STORE " " TO var6
@ 3,2 SAY "Any value....." GET var1
@ 4,2 SAY "Any value....." GET var2
@ 5,2 SAY "Numbers back 1" GET var3 ;
   VALID IIF(var3 $ "0123456789",-1,1)
@ 6,2 SAY "Any value....." GET var4
```

```
    @ 7,2 SAY "Numbers back 4" GET var5 ;
VALID IIF(var5 $ "0123456789",-4,1)
    @ 8,2 SAY "Any value....." GET var6
READ
```

In this example, validation is implemented in such a way that no annoying messages are introduced, and the programmer has complete control over what happens. The IIF( ) is a logical function used here to return one of two numbers for each validated GET. Because it returns a number, however, the IIF( ) comprises a numeric expression.

Another good way to implement validation is to use the SCATTER TO command to make memory variables containing database field values, then to check those with your own, perhaps more sophisticated, routines. You can alert the user as necessary for proper values before using the GATHER FROM command to replace the database field contents with the user-edited variables.

As an alternative, UDFs, or user-defined functions, can be used in VALID clauses where they return a logical value after performing checks of one kind or another. See the discussion of UDFs in Chapter 6.

ALERTS, UDFs, AND VALIDATION

Alerts can be used for many things, but a favorite use of mine is with user-defined functions and the VALID clause to create some powerful entry error-trapping tools. Alerts are made with one line commands using simple resources. An ALERT command looks like this:

```
ALERT NOTE 1 "Hi there!"
```

The "NOTE" keyword indicates what type of symbol will appear in the upper-left corner of the box and the number, in this case it's 1, indicates what type of box you'll get (see Fig. 7-29). Alerts return numbers in response to the button a user presses when an optional clause is added to the command:

```
ALERT NOTE 11 "Hi there!" TO memvar
```

Take a look at Fig. 7-30. The default button (darkened) returns the number 1, and the other buttons return 2, and 3, from left to right respectively. The following program demonstrates the use of alerts and the VALID clause for data entry. The numeric expression in the VALID clause's user-defined function (UDF) not only validates data, but it also alerts users.

```
* * * * * * * * * * * * *
* UdfValid.prg
* Demonstrates UDFs, VALID, Alerts
* by Michael Masterson
*
    SET PROCEDURE TO UDFVALID
    CLEAR && SCREEN
```

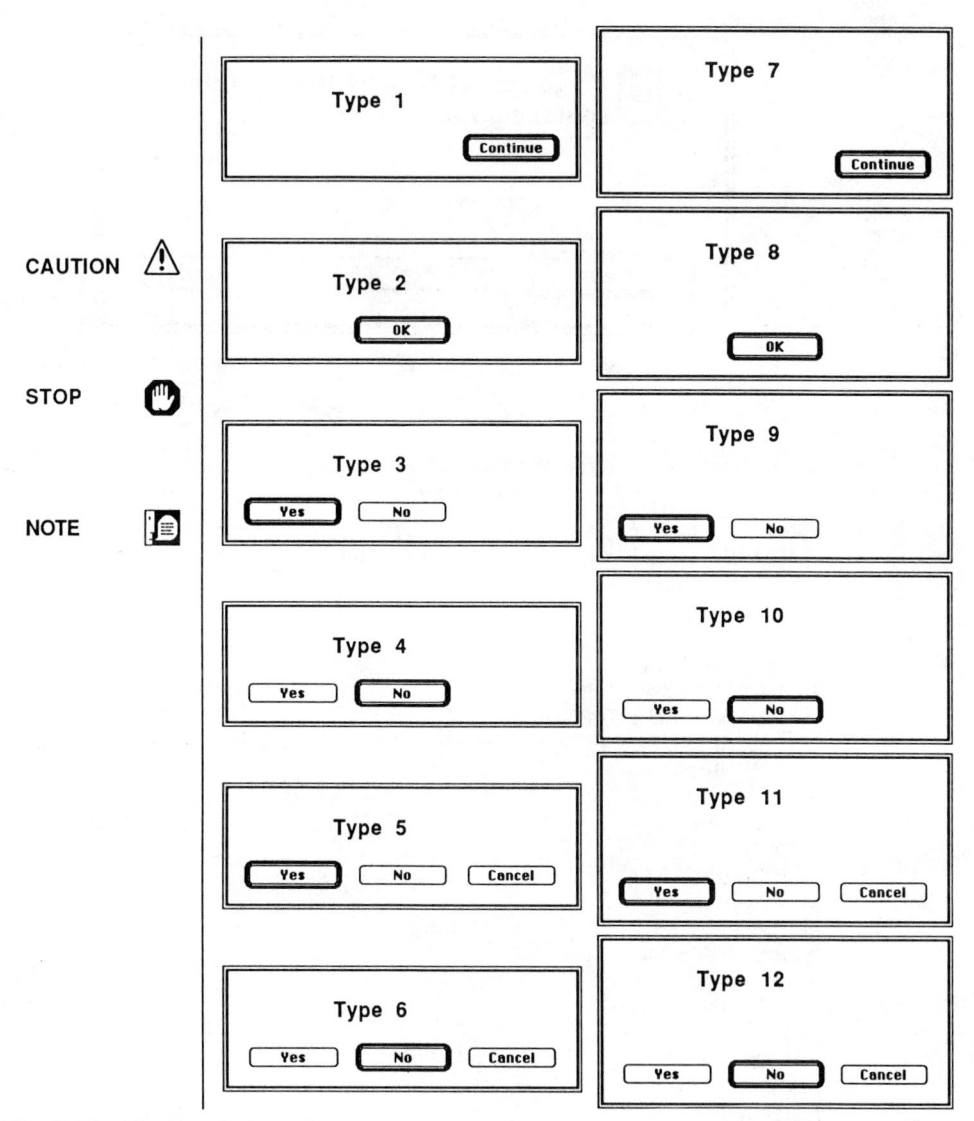

Fig. 7-29. Alert symbols and types.

```
            CLEAR GETS
            SET STRICT ON
            STORE " " TO var1
            STORE " " TO var2
            STORE " " TO var3
            STORE " " TO var4
            STORE " " TO var5
            STORE " " TO var6
            @ 3,2 SAY "No numbers            " GET var1 VALID TEST1(var1)
            @ 4,2 SAY "Number 2 ends READ    " GET var2 VALID TEST2(var2)
            @ 5,2 SAY "Letters send back 1   " GET var3 VALID TEST3(var3)
            @ 6,2 SAY "Letters made uppercase " GET var4 PICTURE "@A!" VALID TEST4(var4)
```

Alerts, UDFs, and Validation **177**

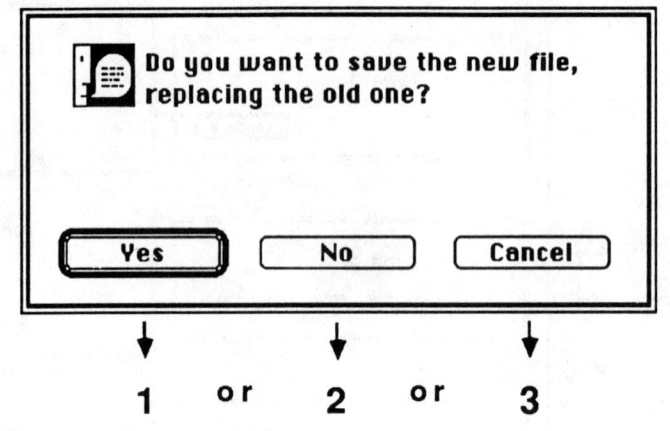

Fig. 7-30. Alerts can change variables.

```
@ 7,2 SAY "Number 3 sends back 4 " GET var5 VALID TEST5(var5)
@ 8,2 SAY "Numbers only!         " GET var6 VALID TEST6(var6)

READ SAVE

PROCEDURE TEST1
PARAMETER testval
        IF testval $ "0123456789"
    ALERT CAUTION 1 "Enter a character, numbers aren't allowed."
    RETURN 0
ELSE
    RETURN 1
ENDIF
RETURN 0

PROCEDURE TEST2
PARAMETER testval
IF testval = "2"
    RETURN 10
ELSE
    RETURN 1
ENDIF
RETURN 0

PROCEDURE TEST3
PARAMETER testval
IF .NOT. testval $ "0123456789"
    IF testval = " "
        ALERT NOTE 1 "I gotta have something!"
        RETURN 0
    ELSE
        ALERT STOP 1 "Number " + testval + ", so back you go!"
        RETURN -1
    ENDIF
ELSE
    RETURN 1
ENDIF
```

178 *Alerts, UDFs, and Validation*

```
        RETURN 0

    PROCEDURE TEST4
    PARAMETER testval
    RETURN 1

    PROCEDURE TEST5
    PARAMETER testval
    IF testval = "3"
        ALERT CAUTION 1 "You typed number " + testval + ", so back you go for
        4!"
        RETURN -4
    ELSE
        RETURN 1
    ENDIF
    RETURN 0

    PROCEDURE TEST6
    PARAMETER testval
    IF testval $ "0123456789"
        RETURN -5
    ELSE
        ALERT CAUTION 1 "Typed a letter you rat! Try again..."
        RETURN 0
    ENDIF
    RETURN 0
    * * * * * * * * * * * * * *
```

In this program, the READ is almost never terminated because the numbers returned by UDFs keep the cursor moving to only active GETs. I set it up that way so you could see the contrast of what happens when the number 10 is returned by the UDF "TEST2." It summarily terminates the READ. This happens any time a number is returned that does not land the cursor on an active GET.

Do not change a program's data handling environment in UDFs; it could easily crash a program that's working on the assumption that files open, indexes, filters, and so on, won't change. Also, on a more positive note, consider opening a Help window when a user makes an error in an entry field. For more information on this, look at the section near the end of this chapter on Customizing Help.

DIALOGS

Dialogs are small screens that appear over the top of the currently selected screen for the purpose of holding, appropriately enough, a conversation with the user. Dialogs give and get specific information that's needed to accomplish the task at hand. FoxBASE lets you define any of nine screens any way you like. When you need a dialog box, use one of those screens. They can be defined in a variety of ways, and the benefit to using them is that you can use them and put them away without messing up the main screen's action. The only drawback to multiple screen usage is the amount of memory each screen requires. Test the machine first for available memory. Users who have lots of fonts, sounds and other functions, might not have enough free RAM for screen-based dialogs. If you don't have enough memory for multiple screens try this:

```
SAVE SCREEN TO <memvarname>
@ row,col CLEAR TO row,col
@ row,col TO row,col DOUBLE
...put dialog commands here but stay inside of row,col
RESTORE SCREEN FROM <memvarname>
```

This method repaints the current screen after its image has been saved in <memvarname>. When you're done, it's easy to put the image back with the RESTORE command.

MENUS

Menus are different on a Macintosh than they are on previous microcomputers because they implement the event-driven, modeless ideal for interfacing computers with people. The idea is that users get to choose what events they want to initiate with as few restrictions as possible, and they should never feel trapped because their computer is stuck in some indiscernible mode of operation from which they cannot either extract it, or proceed through quickly. I'm sure that everyone who's used computers knows what it's like to be uncomfortable because of some mode of operation that's out of their control.

Menu Trees versus Bar Menus

Macintosh style menus can allow a programmer to provide near modeless computer operation to users, but they don't necessarily do so just because they're installed, nor do they make programming any easier. In fact, pull-down, event-sensitive menus are usually harder to manage because users can do unpredictable things when given the opportunity. There is comfort for both programmers, and for some users who like security (and reading manuals), when the options in their application are structured like a tree, with several branches where users must decide what's next, such as the program below:

```
* * * * * * * * * * * * * * * * * * * * * *
Main option one
    Sub option one
        Sub-Sub option one
        Sub-Sub option two
        Sub-Sub option three
    Sub option two
        Sub-Sub option one
        Sub-Sub option two
        Sub-Sub option three
    Sub option three
        Sub-Sub option one
        Sub-Sub option two
        Sub-Sub option three
```

```
            Main option two
                Sub option one
                    Sub-Sub option one
                    Sub-Sub option two
                    Sub-Sub option three
                Sub option two
                    Sub-Sub option one
                    Sub-Sub option two
                    Sub-Sub option three
                Sub option three
                    Sub-Sub option one
                    Sub-Sub option two
                    Sub-Sub option three
            Main option three
                etc...
```

* *

Menu tree program structures are easier for programmers because they provide clearly defined plateaus at which they can open files, rebuild indexes, create screens, and so on. And when a user steps back down off the branches, so to speak, and returns to the main options at the trunk, a programmer can clean up and close files needed for tasks performed while out on a branch.

Modeless, or Nearly So

While the tree structure for programs makes life easier for programmers, it can make life hard for users who want the freedom, for example, to change a customer's address while entering a new invoice, which can't be done if changing a customer's address is allowed only in a mode that's up five, and over three branches. Menu trees are modal. By their very structure they prevent users from dictating what will happen next. Before I get too critical, however, let me say that no program can go without the kind of discipline and structure that branching menus can provide. If a programmer can make menu trees that guide a user through their program's options, they can make event loops instead, because they already know, at least, the basics of modular programming. Also, no program is free of modes. It's an ideal that's worth striving for, but it cannot be perfectly attained within reason.

MENU-EVENT HANDLING

What FoxBASE developers are encouraged to do with the Macintosh is to provide a menubar at the top of the screen, perhaps with several possible variations depending on the program's complexity, that can be used to make an application do everything it was designed to do. The way to make this happen is to establish an event-handling loop instead of a tiered structure with steps or branches going to program functions. This loop should continually lead around a pole so that a user can switch to another application with ease. If a user is already performing a task and decides to launch another, then the user should enter the new task and be returned to the previous state, rather than being forced to restore, with effort, the previous state of a suspended task. While this sort of programming is not impossible on single-screened microcomputers, it's very "doable" on Macintosh computers. FoxBASE has nine screens that can be made into dialog boxes, output devices, and so on, including alerts to make things easier.

Defining, Installing, and Handling Menus

The following commands are used to define and invoke menus in FoxBASE. Syntax information about these commands are discussed throughout this section or see their descriptions in Chapter 8.

DIMENSION	makes arrays to hold menu values
STORE	places text values into arrays
MENU	installs the menus in place of FoxBASE's own
ON MENU	routes menu hits to a handler using MENU( ) functions
READ	reads menu hits continually

The way FoxBASE establishes event loops is through a perpetual READ that's made in an infinite loop. The program below demonstrates how to do this. Look for the DO WHILE .T. construct and you'll understand what I mean. The only command inside it is READ. READs get every type of input from users, and from all types of screen objects. The condition that makes this particular READ special is an event handling command that was issued before the READ:

ON MENU DO ACTION WITH MENU(0), MENU(1)

The ON MENU command is like ON KEY, ON ERROR, or ON ESCAPE, because it traps events regardless of when they occur. Certain conditions satisfy the ON ERROR trap, and other conditions satisfy the ON ESCAPE trap. They don't fire all the time, and the ON MENU needs both a READ and a menu hit to satisfy its condition for operating. Menu hits occur any time a user makes a menu selection with the mouse. When ON MENU and any READ are satisfied that they've got a reason to go to work, they look for an action to perform. In the example both above and in the program below, this action will be to run the ACTION procedure. Menu hits always return two numbers, one to each function: MENU(0) gets the number of the menu column hit, and MENU(1) gets the number of the menu row that was hit.

A gracious thing about FoxBASE's way of handling menus is that it knows when it's too busy to be interrupted, and it lets users hit menus any time they like, so you don't have to turn menu options off and on when there's serious data handling going on. Generally, FoxBASE ignores menu hits when the data handling engine is preoccupied with a task of its own. This allows you to leave menu options up during all phases in a program.

There are times when menus should be shut off, however, such as when a selected option is in conflict with the data handling environment necessary to support an engaged task. In other words, when the data handling environment cannot be restored to the pre-event state. An obvious example is printing. You can't enter new customers while someone is printing customers, unless you've got a shadow table established for entry purposes. You can enter a new customer while viewing inventory, however. To make all the possible combinations, you need to set flags in the event loop to test for conditions and close as few options as possible from a user launching incompatible tasks.

The MENU(0) AND MENU(1) functions are public variables that will return the last menu selected, regardless of where the user is at, although no menu event is recorded when a user attempts to select a deactivated menu option, so the ON MENU command is never invoked by inactive menu selections.

Only one READ command is necessary in a program for menu events, data entry, and so on, but more than one can be employed. If a READ is encountered in a subroutine or in another program off of the main menu handler, the ON MENU event trap will function as it did under control of the first READ. The purpose for putting a READ inside an infinite loop is to ensure that the program will not end until the user wants it to.

You can change menu appearance at any time by redefining a menu option, and reinstalling it, by redefining and installing a whole new set of menus, by turning options on or off with the MENU ON|OFF command, or by changing the menu's event handling routine with the ON MENU DO...?...command. Most of these techniques are demonstrated in the following sample program.

Note: This demonstration menu program will work with all versions of FoxBASE+/Mac. The shorter and easier menu syntax supported in version 2.x is explained in Chapter 8.

A Demonstration Menu

```
* * * * * * * * * * * * *
* DemoMenu.prg
* Demonstrates menu management
* by Michael Masterson
SET PROCEDURE TO DEMOMENU
SET TALK ON
SCREEN 1 TOP
CLEAR
DIMENSION TopRow(4)
DIMENSION DownCol1(5)
DIMENSION DownCol2(6)
DIMENSION DownCol3(3)
DIMENSION DownCol4(6)

? "This list shows menu definitions exactly as STOREd. Look them over before"
? "making any menu selections. P.S. - You'll find QUIT in the Actions menu."
?
STORE "Actions"          TO TopRow(1)
?? " <-Compare these entries with the Actions menu"
STORE "Action1"          TO DownCol1(1)
STORE "Action2"          TO DownCol1(2)
STORE "QUIT/Q"           TO DownCol1(3)
```

```
STORE "Options"            TO TopRow(2)
?? " <-Compare these entries with the Options menu"
STORE "Option1"            TO DownCol2(1)
STORE "Option2 ("                               TO DownCol2(2)
STORE "Option3"            TO DownCol2(3)
STORE "(-"                 TO DownCol2(4)
STORE "Activate #2"                             TO DownCol2(5)
STORE "Deactivate #2"                           TO DownCol2(6)

STORE "Choices"            TO TopRow(3)
?? " <-Compare these entries with the Choices menu"
STORE "Choice1"            TO DownCol3(1)
STORE "Choice2/Z"                               TO DownCol3(2)
STORE "Choice3"            TO DownCol3(3)

STORE "Styles"             TO TopRow(4)
?? " <-Compare these entries with the Styles menu"
STORE "Normal"             TO DownCol4(1)
STORE "Bold<B"             TO DownCol4(2)
*STORE "Underline<U"       TO DownCol4(3)
STORE "Italic<I"           TO DownCol4(4)
STORE "Outline<O"                               TO DownCol4(5)
STORE "Shadow<S"           TO DownCol4(6)

MENU BAR TopRow,4
MENU 1,DownCol1,3
MENU 2,DownCol2,6
MENU 3,DownCol3,3
MENU 4,DownCol4,6

SCREEN 1 HEADING "Menu Management Demo" FONT "Monaco",9 TOP
ON MENU DO ACTION WITH MENU(0), MENU(1)
DO WHILE .T.
    READ
ENDDO

PROCEDURE ACTION
PARAMETER zero, one
DO CASE
        *\ MENU SELECTED ACTIONS GO HERE
    CASE zero=1 .AND. one=1
        *\ DO program one
        CLEAR
        ? "You selected action menu one."
    CASE zero=1 .AND. one=2
        *\ DO program two
        CLEAR
        ? "You selected action menu two."
    CASE zero=1 .AND. one=3
        *\ DO program three
        CLEAR
        ? "You selected action menu three."
        CANCEL

        *\ MENU SELECTED OPTIONS GO HERE
```

```
CASE zero = 2 .AND. one = 1
     * \ DO program one
     CLEAR
     ? "You selected option menu one."
     ? "Divider lines like option #4 are created with the (-
     symbol."
     ? "They take up an array cell for display purposes, but
     cannot be selected."
CASE zero = 2 .AND. one = 2
     * \ DO programtwo
     CLEAR
     ? "You selected option menu two."
     ? "Divider lines like option #4 are created with the (-
     symbol."
     ? "They take up an array cell for display purposes, but
     cannot be selected."
CASE zero = 2 .AND. one = 3
     * \ DO program three
     CLEAR
     ? "You selected option menu three."
     ? "Divider lines like option #4 are created with the (-
     symbol."
     ? "They take up an array cell for display purposes, but
     cannot be selected."
CASE zero = 2 .AND. one = 5
     * \ DO program four
     * This code activates option menu 2
     STORE "Option2" TO DownCol2(2)
     MENU 2,DownCol2,6
     CLEAR
     ? "You selected option menu five."
     ? "Menu option two reactivated by redefinition without the (
     symbol."
CASE zero = 2 .AND. one = 6
     * \ DO program five
     * This code deactivates option menu 2
     STORE "Option2 (" TO DownCol2(2)
     MENU 2,DownCol2,6
     CLEAR
     ? "You selected option menu six."
     ? "Menu option two deactivated by redefinition with the (
     symbol."

* \ MENU SELECTED CHOICES GO HERE
CASE zero = 3 .AND. one = 1
     * \ DO program one
     CLEAR
     ? "You selected choice menu one."
CASE zero = 3 .AND. one = 2
* \ DO program two
     CLEAR
     ? "You selected choice menu two."
     ? "Did you notice that you can press Command-Z to activate
     this option?"
     ? "Use / followed by a letter to make a command key
```

Menu-Event Handling 185

```
                    equivalent for any menu."
        CASE zero=3 .AND. one=3
            * \ DO program three
            CLEAR
            ? "You selected choice menu three."

            * \ MENU SELECTED STYLES GO HERE
        CASE zero=4 .AND. one=1
            * \ DO program one
            CLEAR
            ? "You selected style menu one."
            ? "Normal menu style requires no additional characters."
        CASE zero=4 .AND. one=2
            * \ DO program two
            CLEAR
            ? "You selected style menu two."
            ? "Bold menu style requires a <B in its definition."
        CASE zero=4 .AND. one=3
            * \ DO program three
            CLEAR
            ? "You selected style menu three."
            ? "Underline menu style requires a <U in its definition."
        CASE zero=4 .AND. one=4
            * \ DO program four
            CLEAR
            ? "You selected style menu four."
            ? "Italic menu style requires a <I in its definition."
        CASE zero=4 .AND. one=5
            * \ DO program five
            CLEAR
            ? "You selected style menu five."
            ? "Outline menu style requires a <I in its definition."
        CASE zero=4 .AND. one=6
            * \ DO program six
            CLEAR
            ? "You selected style menu six."
            ? "Shadow menu style requires a <S in its definition."
    ENDCASE
    RETURN
    * * * * * * * * * * * * * *
```

CUSTOMIZING HELP

FoxBASE's own native help facility is really a database file with two fields in it: a twenty-character field called "topic," and a memo field called "details." FoxBASE automatically uses the FoxHELP file that came with FoxBASE so that users can ask for help any time by selecting the Apple menu's Help option, or by pressing the help key on extended keyboards. You can make a custom help facility by creating your own help file. With a few simple commands and a good help file, you can install custom, context-sensitive help that makes any user's job easier.

Helpful Hints

The simplest way to make a help file is to copy the FoxHELP file's structure. In the memo field next to the topic of choice, put help texts that relate directly to the options or problems that a user might encounter in specific sections of your program. Because memo fields can hold up to 32,000 characters, you're not likely to run out of space. Help files aren't indexed, so it's a good idea to organize the topic list in a way that the user can quickly find information. To install a custom help file in place of FoxBASE's native help file, just issue this simple command:

SET HELP TO <filename>

Users will then be able to read your help text by selecting the Help option under the Apple menu.

In programs, there are several ways to customize things even further. Using the following command, you can automatically select topics so that users won't have to scroll through the subjects to find the appropriate help text:

SET TOPIC TO <topic>

If the HELP command is issued after a topic has been set, or the user selects help from the Apple menu, the selected topic will automatically appear. To generalize help again and let users scroll through topics just enter the command:

SET TOPIC TO

Helpful Functions

You can make help more specific using the SYS(16) and/or SYS(18) functions to automatically select help texts for any programmed entry screen—and even for each field in a data entry screen if you want. This method uses SYS(16) to return the name of the currently running program and SYS(18) to return the name of the current get-field location of the cursor. To take advantage of the program and field names, you need to add two additional fields. The file structure recommended by Fox Software has four fields named *topic, helptext, getfield,* and *progname*. The *topic* field can be 20 to 30 characters in length, the *helptext* field must be a memo field, and the *getfield* and *progname* fields should be 10 characters each. Accordingly, enter the exact name of your programs and fields (note that the <fieldname> used with GET might be a memory variable) into the database. To automatically select help from a program, you use the SET TOPIC command like this:

SET TOPIC TO progname = SYS(16) .AND. getfield = SYS(18)

If there is no cursor-selected field for SYS(18) to name during a read operation, such as when only buttons are being READ, it will return the value "@READ". If you want the program to automatically detect that no READ is active, use the IIF( ) function with SET TOPIC like this:

Customizing Help 187

```
SET TOPIC TO IIF(SYS(18)< >"", getfield=SYS(18) .AND. progname=SYS(16),;
progname=SYS(16))
```

Another option for customizing help is to install a button that, when pressed, issues this command:

```
HELP <topic>
```

Still another option is to install a HELP command in a VALID clause so that help opens automatically when a user makes a gross mistake entering data. When he leaves the help screen, he can be right back where he encountered the problem, armed with the knowledge needed to proceed.

PROGRAMMED DATA DISPLAYS

If you have a relationship established between two or more files, the easiest way to view related data is to display rows of data from both by relying on the relationship to align the files, and by relying on the alias operator "->" to call field values out of any child files that are open in non-selected work areas (see the sample program below). The parent file is in work area A, and the child file is in work area B. Remember, the child file should have one record in it compared to the parent file's one or more record(s). This way, the skip command moves through the parent file with more records—one by one—and you'll see all the data that matches in the two files because the child file's record pointer is automatically moved by the parent. Take some time to review this sample program:

```
* * * * * * * * * * *
* MFList.prg
* by Michael Masterson
* Demonstrates controlled multi-file listing
* Note: Substitute valid filenames and fieldnames for the <filename>
* and <fieldname> notations below:
SET TALK OFF
SELECT A
USE <filename1>
SELECT B
USE <filename2> INDEX <filename>
SELECT A
SET RELATION TO <fieldname> INTO <filename2> ADDITIVE
ON ESCAPE EXIT
GOTO TOP
DO WHILE .NOT. EOF( )
    CLEAR
    DO WHILE ROW( ) < 23 .AND. .NOT. EOF( )
        @ ROW( )+1,2 SAY RTRIM(A->  <fieldname>)+", "+B-> <fieldname>
        @ ROW( ),30 SAY B-> <fieldname> +" "+A-> <fieldname>
        @ ROW( ),40 SAY A-> <fieldname>
        SKIP
    ENDDO
```

```
        WAIT "Press any key to continue, Command-period to exit."
    ENDDO
    CLEAR
    RETURN
    * * * * * * * * * * * *
```

In the example above, I used the GOTO command to put the pointer at the top of the parent file in work area A. This way, all of the records in the parent file, and matching records in the child file would be found.

If you only wanted to see records for a single client or vendor, limit the display by finding the first record with a SEEK command, instead of starting at the top of the file as I did in the example above. To automatically stop the list when the records of interest are exhausted by SKIPping, insert an additional condition in the DO WHILE's argument list, like this:

```
    * * * * * * * * * * * *
    * MFList.prg
    * by Michael Masterson
    * Demonstrates controlled multi-file listing
    * Note: Substitute valid filenames and fieldnames for the <filename>
    * and <fieldname> notations below:
    SET TALK OFF
    SELECT A
    USE <filename1>
    SELECT B
    USE <filename2> INDEX <filename>
    SELECT A
    SET RELATION TO <fieldname> INTO <filename2> ADDITIVE

    ON ESCAPE EXIT
    SEEK <memvar>
    IF FOUND( )
    DO WHILE .NOT. EOF( ) .AND. <keyfieldname> = <memvar>
        CLEAR
        DO WHILE ROW( ) < 23 .AND. <keyfieldname> = <memvar>
            @ ROW( )+1,2 SAY RTRIM(A-><fieldname>)+", "+B-><fieldname>
            @ ROW( ),30 SAY B-><fieldname>+" "+A-><fieldname>
            @ ROW( ),40 SAY A-><fieldname>
            SKIP
        ENDDO
        WAIT "Press any key to continue, Command-period to exit."
    ENDDO
    CLEAR
    ENDIF
    RETURN
    * * * * * * * * * * * *
```

Note that the WAIT command was used to pause the records. WAIT produces a visual cue on screen and can optionally gather a user response into a memory variable.

The WHILE command is commonly used by programmers to limit the data displayed to a selection that matches some criteria. All you need to do is create a little routine that lets users enter a value they're wanting to see displayed, SEEK it, and then SKIP until that value is no longer found. Incidentally, it's a good idea to create indexes with UPPER (<keyfieldname>) and to SEEK with UPPER(<memvar>) values so that the user's search isn't in vain because of case sensitivity. Another way to let users pick a record for edit is through a scrolling pick list. For more information, see the example provided in the scrollable lists section of this chapter under the Using FoxForm Tools section.

PRINTING PROGRAMS

To print reports you defined with the report writer, issue a REPORT FORM <filename> command. Developers, however, might want to directly drive the printer from a program. The hints in this section can help you use the ?, ??, and the @ row,col SAY commands for printing.

Printing with ? and ??

If you are printing with ? and ?? to an imagewriter or a laser printer, the reports you print will use the font and point size last defined for screen display. Use the Option-Dash key (character) to make nice horizontal lines and the | key to make vertical lines on the page. You won't be able to use FoxForm graphics such as lines and boxes this way, however. To prepare for printing using ? and ?? insert these commands:

```
SET CONSOLE OFF
SET PRINT ON PROMPT
```

The PROMPT keyword brings forth the print dialog box so a user can select the number of pages they want to print. When you're done, use these commands:

```
SET CONSOLE ON
SET PRINT OFF
```

The screen display will be suspended and a standard Macintosh print dialog box will appear. The printing program will then run and print will begin to appear. When the printing is done, it will be turned off and the console turned back on.

⚠️ If there is an error during the print job, SET PRINT OFF must be executed. If it's not, the print job won't be closed and the Macintosh will remain in a background conversation with the printer.

Printing with the @ SAY Command

The advantage of using the @ SAY command for printing instead of the ? and ?? commands is that @ SAY can print boxes and lines. It also lets you use multiple fonts and typestyles (as long as their supported by the printer!) and graphic objects as well. Printing with the @ SAY command is similar to using the ? and ?? commands, but there are a few extras to note. Make sure that you've used a STYLE clause in each printing command, even if it's STYLE 0. This suppresses the tendency to eject a page whenever a specified printing coordinate is above the last one printed (in some odd cases that's considered a feature). You will also need to issue each of these commands:

```
SET CONSOLE OFF
SET DEVICE TO PRINTER PROMPT
SET PRINT ON
```

When you're done, use these commands:

```
SET CONSOLE ON
SET DEVICE TO SCREEN
SET PRINT OFF
```

The prompt command is optional. I've found that the prompt opens automatically whenever I issue the SET DEVICE TO PRINTER command. Also, like with ? and ?? printing, make sure that the SET PRINT OFF command is used, regardless of how normally or abnormally the printing job ends. Also, be sure to SET DEVICE TO SCREEN.

Printing to a File

You can send output that's normally printed into a text file simply by using these commands:

```
SET ALTERNATE TO <filename>
SET ALTERNATE ON
...printing program or report format goes here...
```

When you're done, use this command:

```
SET ALTERNATE OFF
```

There is another way to create an alternate file and turn file printing on that works fine in lieu of the SET ALTERNATE combination above. It is:

```
SET PRINTER TO <filename>
SET PRINT ON
```

Whenever you print to a file or a printer, it's a good idea to use the SET CONSOLE command to prevent echoes from showing up on the screen. There are some other quirks you should know about before printing to a file:

1. Files are character based, so it's best to use the ? and ?? commands to print. The @ SAY command and graphic images aren't allowed for file printing. Also, use a monospaced font such as Monaco. Nine point Monaco works well with page reductions in the page setup dialog. Nice tabular reports can be generated in the landscape (sideways) and portrait (normal) modes.

2. When you aren't using a version 2 report form (.FRX) file, there's no page setup information available, so FoxBASE uses the character information currently selected for the active grafport to determine how wide the page should be and what font and pitch it should use. Be careful, the grafport is the screen that's selected when the print job begins. If the selected screen is not wide enough to print the widest report line without wrapping, you can select another font (Monaco 4 works well) and another screen.

3. Page ejects can occur only when an EJECT command or form-feed command (? CHR(11)) is encountered in the printing program.

Reports that print require a great deal of patience and skill. The rewards, however, include incredible control over printed output that is unmatched by using any other method, including the powerful report writer that comes with version 2.

8
FoxBASE+/Mac Commands

THIS chapter contains an alphabetical listing of the commands available in FoxBASE+/Mac. All of the commands work in programs, and most of them will work in the interactive command window. You can tell which commands are strictly for programming by their context in the examples, or from their descriptions.

HOW THE COMMAND REFERENCE IS ORGANIZED

Each command verb entry has one or more of the following sections. Note that commands that can be accessed directly from a menu have a menubar at the top of the page with the menu choice highlighted.

- **Syntax.** This section demonstrates acceptable syntax options for the command.
- **Purpose.** This section contains a narrative explanation describing what the command does.
- **Example.** This section describes how commands are used in the context of a program or in the command window. Code samples are included to demonstrate use when appropriate.
- **Note.** This section warns you of common mistakes that can occur when using the command. Special considerations that can adversely affect a command's behavior in a program are mentioned.
- **Tips.** This section offers comments that can help you tap the more powerful uses of the command.
- **Also see.** This section provides a list of other commands and functions that are useful to know because they resemble the function described, or because they are useful in combination with it. Sometimes the items listed here provide a better way to do the same thing.

SYMBOLS USED IN THE COMMAND REFERENCE

The following is a list of the symbols used for each command entry. Refer to this list whenever you're unsure about a command's meaning.

Uppercase Letters Uppercase letters are used for command key words and optional expressions or arguments. The command key words should be entered as shown. Options written in uppercase letters should also be entered exactly as shown.

Angle Brackets< > Angle brackets enclose arguments. Arguments are expressions or elements of expressions. Literally, angle brackets mean, "Something should be supplied by you and put here." You can decide what to put in the place of brackets by studying their context and notation. For example, <exprC> means that you should supply a character expression. The brackets themselves should not be entered.

Parentheses Parentheses are used to arbitrarily group expressions or portions of expressions so they evaluate in a prescribed and predictable order.

Square brackets[ ] Square brackets enclose optional elements that can be used with a command. Do not type or enter the brackets.

Quotation Marks Quotation marks indicate that the items should be enclosed within quotation marks when entered. You can use either single quotation marks or square brackets, but matching pairs must be used for each element in the command expression. Typically, quotation marks are required for literal character strings of any length, like 'A,' or, "123 Almond Street."

Ellipses Ellipses indicate that you can enter the option again, perhaps many times. Do not enter the dots. An ellipsis is also used to join the second required part, or optional parts, of a command construct. IF...ENDIF, DO CASE...CASE...ENDCASE, for example. Occasionally, ellipses are used to indicate that there is a part missing from a sample command that is not necessary for the purpose of demonstration.

Alias Indicator -> The alias indicator is used to let FoxBASE+/Mac know that it might need to look for the named field in another work area. It is entered "alias->fieldname." See alias->fieldname in the next section for more information.

Commas Commas are used to separate parts of an expression. If you are using portions of a command where commas exist, type them exactly as shown in the example.

Semicolons Semicolons are used only in program files to indicate that the command will continue on the next line, which allows long commands to be entered. There is a limit of 255 characters, however, on any single command line, even when a semicolon is used.

SYNTAX OPTIONS

By now, you should be familiar with the following command notations and conventions. Many of the command key words cannot operate by themselves; they need additional information that you supply such as field names, memory variable names, etc. Infrequently used notations are not listed below but are explained in the context of their use. The following is a list of command key words that are used for field names, constants, functions, memory variables, and operators.

alias Alias is an alternate name for a database. When you USE a database file, you can specify that it be referred to by an alias. If no alias is specified, the database file must be referred to by its full name, but an alias can be shorter and easier to remember.

alias->fieldname Alias->fieldname is the way to refer to a field that is not in the currently selected database file, but is in one of the nine other database work areas. To use this feature, enter the database name (or alias) first, the -> symbol, then the name of the field you want to reference. If a field name and a memory variable have the same name (which you should try to avoid), indicate the memory variable by entering "M->memvar."

arrayname Arrayname is the name of an array. Arrays are memory variables that can contain more than one element of data. See the DIMENSION command in this chapter for more information.

col A col is the column coordinate on the screen or printer. Screen coordinates are typically 0-79 across. Printer coordinates are 0-82, 0-132, or sometimes more, depending on the model of the printer and type of font you are using.

commands One, or a series of commands to be performed.

coord The coordinate of a row or column for either the screen or printer.

date A date entered in a format that fits the context.

device The screen or a printer.

drivename An MS-DOS-type drive designator or a Macintosh drive name. For example, DOS drive names are A:, or C:. Macintosh drive names can have about 30 characters.

enhanced Refers to enhanced screen colors, which can be specified.

eof Indicates end-of-file condition.

expr Any type of expression.

exprC An expression that evaluates to a character string or a character literal.

exprL An expression that evaluates to a logical value (.T.) or (.F.).

exprN An expression that evaluates to a numeric data value. Unlike character values that might have numbers in them, numeric values can be added, subtracted, and so on.

exprlist A list of expressions, usually separated by commas.

fieldlist A list of fields that are usually separated by commas.

fieldname The name of a field used to define it when a database file is created or modified. The length of field names is limited to 10 characters.

filelist A list of files that are usually separated by commas.

filename The name of a file on the disk. A file name can include the drive name and/or path(list). File names should not exceed eight characters if you want to be able to port them to an MS-DOS computer.

filetype Filetype is the type of file that is to be operated on. The options are explained with each command that has this option.

Fn Fn is a function key where n is the number of the function key.

folder Folder is a Macintosh file folder. Folder names are preceded by a drive name and a colon, or simply by a colon. Folder names always end with a colon so that FoxBASE can distinguish them from file names.

key Key refers to an index key. Index keys are usually the name of a field used to put a database file in "sorted" order. Because files can be ordered by more than one field at a time, a key can also be an expression such as "fieldname1 + fieldname2" (for example, lastname + firstname).

len Len indicates the length of something, determined by the number of characters.

memofieldname Memofieldname is the name of a memo field. Memo fields follow the same naming conventions as file names.

memvar or memvarname Memvar or memvarname is a memory variable.

memvarlist Memvarlist is a list of memory variables, usually separated by commas.

n N is an integer number.

newfilename Newfilename is a file name that is used to create a new file.

oldfilename Oldfilename is a file name understood by its context.

parmlist Parmlist is a parameter list. Parameters are items of information passed to functions, procedures, or programs. The function, procedure, or program uses the information passed to it as a guideline to do a job and then usually returns a result to the program or procedure that initiated it.

pathlist Pathlist is a single-line listing of drive and folder names that lead to a folder where FoxBASE should look for files.

procedurename Procedurename is the name of a procedure or subroutine within a program file.

resource Resource is the name of an external resource module that's been written in another language and compiled. Usually it is an XCMD (command) or XFCN (function) routine that has been placed inside the resource fork of the FoxUser or other similar resource file.

row Row is a row coordinate on the screen or printer. Screen coordinates are typically 0-25 down. Printer coordinates are typically 0-66 or more rows down. The printer model and type of font you use affects the number of available rows on the screen or printer.

scope Scope is one of the four scoping arguments: ALL, NEXT<exprN>, RECORD <exprN>, or REST, which tells a command what records to process or consider in its operation. See the *Scopes are Record Boundaries* section in Chapter 6.

skeleton A skeleton is a memvar or file name that might contain wildcards to modify its scope of reference. Just as in MS-DOS, allowable wildcards are an *, which stands for a combination of characters, and ?, which stands for a single character.

standard Standard refers to standard screen colors which can be specified.

string String is a literal character string that is enclosed in quotation marks.

value Value is any value (understood by its context).

var Var refers to either a memory variable name or a database field name.

workarea Workarea is one of the 10 possible areas where a database can be opened and manipulated. Work areas are identified by the name or alias of the file they contain, or by reference to the work area itself (as A through J) or numerically (as 1 through 10).

?

Syntax   ? <expr> [,<expr2>,...]
 or
 ?? <expr> [,<expr2>,...]

Purpose   The single ? command evaluates one or more expressions and displays the results on the next line. The double ?? evaluates expressions and displays the results on the current line. The ? and ?? commands are used primarily for screen display, although you can use these commands to print if a printer has been selected as the output device (see the SET DEVICE TO entry near the end of the chapter).

Example   If an expression being evaluated by the ? command results in a number, it's considered to be a "numeric" expression. If it evaluates to characters, it's considered to be a "character" expression. The same is true for all data types. If several expressions are used in one command line, they must be separated from each other with a comma.

Expressions are called "logical" when they evaluate to a true (.T.), or a false (.F.), regardless of what type of data was used in the expression that led to the logical result. For example, character data elements in the expression "CAT" = "DOG" evaluate to a logical false. In FoxBASE (.F.) is displayed for logically false results, and (.T.) is displayed for true results.

Displaying characters. The next few examples show how the ? command displays simple character strings and evaluates expressions. If you want to try these out for yourself, just open the command window and enter commands as you see them in Fig. 8-1.

```
Results
This literal character expression evaluates to itself.
Hello one
Hello two  Hello three

          Enter here...    Results here...

Command
CLEAR
? "This literal character expression evaluates to itself."
? "Hello one"
? "Hello two"
?? "Hello three"
```

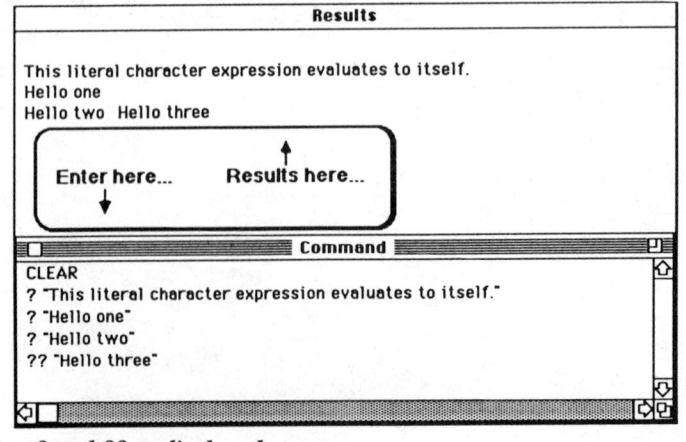

Fig. 8-1. Using ? and ?? to display characters.

Notice that the ?? command puts "Hello there" on the same line, not on the next line down like the single ? does.

Evaluating expressions and displaying results. Because the ? command evaluates expressions before it displays anything, you can use it to solve math problems entered into the command window, or to experiment with functions and expressions before using them in programs or reports. All of the FoxBASE functions are listed in Chapter 9.

Several expressions can be evaluated at one time, as long as each one is separated from the next by a comma.

Displaying database contents. The ? command can also display what's in a database file. You can display the contents of any type of field just by referring to its name, like this, "? fieldname," regardless of whether fieldname is a character, numeric, logical, date, memo, or picture data type. For memo fields, use the SET MEMOWIDTH command to control the width of display. For picture fields use the SET FRAME command to establish the picture's on-screen position and dimensions.

Note	The ? command first evaluates expressions, then it displays the result. Although the ? command does not care what data type it's evaluating, you will nevertheless get an error message if different types of data are improperly mixed within any single expression. Some FoxBASE "functions" (see Chapter 9) let different types of data, such as date, character, and numeric coexist within an expression. Use them to your advantage.
Tips	There is probably no better way to learn about data types and the way functions behave in FoxBASE+/Mac than to spend time playing with the ? command. The question mark simply asks, "What?," making it an excellent way to test any expression before using it on important data. What's more, if an expression works in the command window it can also work in a program. New and experienced FoxBASE users alike can use ? in the command window to experiment with expressions and functions.
	The results displayed by ? and ?? are unformatted, meaning that you have little control over appearance. While there are functions and operators which, combined with ? and ??, provide some formatting power, it is better in most cases to use @ SAY... to display and print.
Also See	@ SAY, LIST, and DISPLAY

Accept

Syntax ACCEPT [< exprC >]
TO < memvar >

Purpose The ACCEPT command waits for you to enter information at the keyboard, then it places whatever was typed into the named < memvar >. ACCEPT creates a variable with up to 254 characters—depending on how long the user's entry is. FoxBASE stops accepting typed characters when the user presses the return or enter keys, then the < memvar > is created and the input is stored. The < exprC > argument can be used to create a customized user prompt.

Example The ACCEPT command gathers a department name from the user and places it into a variable named "response."

The little program below attempts to get a department name from the user and then checks to see if the user entered any characters at all. If characters were entered, they are displayed by the ? command:

```
ACCEPT "What is your department? " TO response
IF response = ""
         ? "No department was entered..."
ELSE
         ? response
ENDIF
```

If a user presses return in response to an ACCEPT command, a character variable is created with nothing in it.

Note There is no way to limit or control what a user enters as there is with the RANGE and VALID clauses of an @ SAY...GET command. ACCEPT puts the burden of data validation on programmers, who must write a testing procedure to ensure that collected information is adequate for processing. Make sure that your programs test the information entered by users before proceeding to use it, unacceptable information could cause a program to function unpredictably or stop altogether.

Input is limited to 254 characters, so an error will result from trying to enter a longer string.

You cannot edit what you've typed as you enter it; the delete key has no effect whatsoever. The only way to correct an entry is to perform a GET...READ on <memvar> after the ACCEPT command is done.

Information is stored in the character data type field only, regardless of what a user enters. If you are collecting any data other than character, it is best to use an alternative to ACCEPT.

Tips

There are other ways to do what ACCEPT does (@ GET...READ, for example), which are usually preferable. The only times ACCEPT is truly useful is when you don't know how long the entered character string will be, and when you want to halt a program to get keyboard input without going through the trouble of setting up a GET...READ sequence.

Also See

INPUT, WAIT, INKEY( ), and READKEY( )

Alert

Syntax ALERT [CAUTION|STOP|NOTE] <exprN>
[TO <memvarN>]
[AT <coord>]
[<exprC1> [,<exprC2> [,<exprC3> [,<exprC4>]]]]

Purpose The ALERT command places one of 12, predefined alert boxes with buttons on the screen to prompt users. You can select what type of symbol appears in the box and what text appears. When a user presses a button in the alert box, a number is put in the memory variable <memvarN>, which is used to elicit responses during program operation. The dark button in each ALERT box is a suggested default, which activates if the enter or return key is pressed. If the default button is pressed, it returns the number 1, and the remaining buttons return 2, 3, and so on, from left to right, until they are all exhausted.

Fig. 8-2. Alert/Caution

The CAUTION alert lets users know that something they are about to do might result in unhappy consequences, and that they should carefully consider the results before they continue.

Fig. 8-3. Alert/Note.

The STOP alert informs users that there is something serious that needs attention, and it provides some choices for dealing with the situation. It is the most serious interactive Macintosh dialog.

Fig. 8-4. Alert/Stop.

The NOTE alert prompts users and gives them some options like, "yes," "no," and cancel. There are no serious consequences from any action the user decides to take, and he normally presses "yes."

Example The 12 basic types of alerts are shown in Chapter 7, Fig. 7-29. The <exprN> tells FoxBASE which alert you want, the variable <memvarN> tells FoxBASE what variable will collect the user's response when a button is pushed, and the expressions <exprC1>

thru <exprC4> tell FoxBASE what prompting text to put into the box.

Tips   ResEdit, a developer's tool from Apple Computer, can be used to clone and modify the standard alerts that come inside the FoxUser file. You can use ResEdit to change, for example, the names of buttons, their sizes, and so on.

Also See   @ SAY...GET, and SCREEN

Append

File	**Edit**	**Database**	**Record**	**Program**	**Text**	**Window**

Record ▸ Append

Syntax   APPEND

or, in version 2 only
APPEND [HEADINGS <exprC1>[<exprC2>]]

Purpose   The APPEND command opens up a full-screen database file editor, allowing you to enter new records by hand keying data.

Example   To use APPEND, you must first open a database, then issue the APPEND command. Figure 8-5 shows what the APPEND command does in version 1.x, version 2.x, and in version 2.x when you've installed a custom format file that was created in FoxForm. APPEND displays one blank record at a time, and new blank records will continue to appear as long as you keep entering new information.

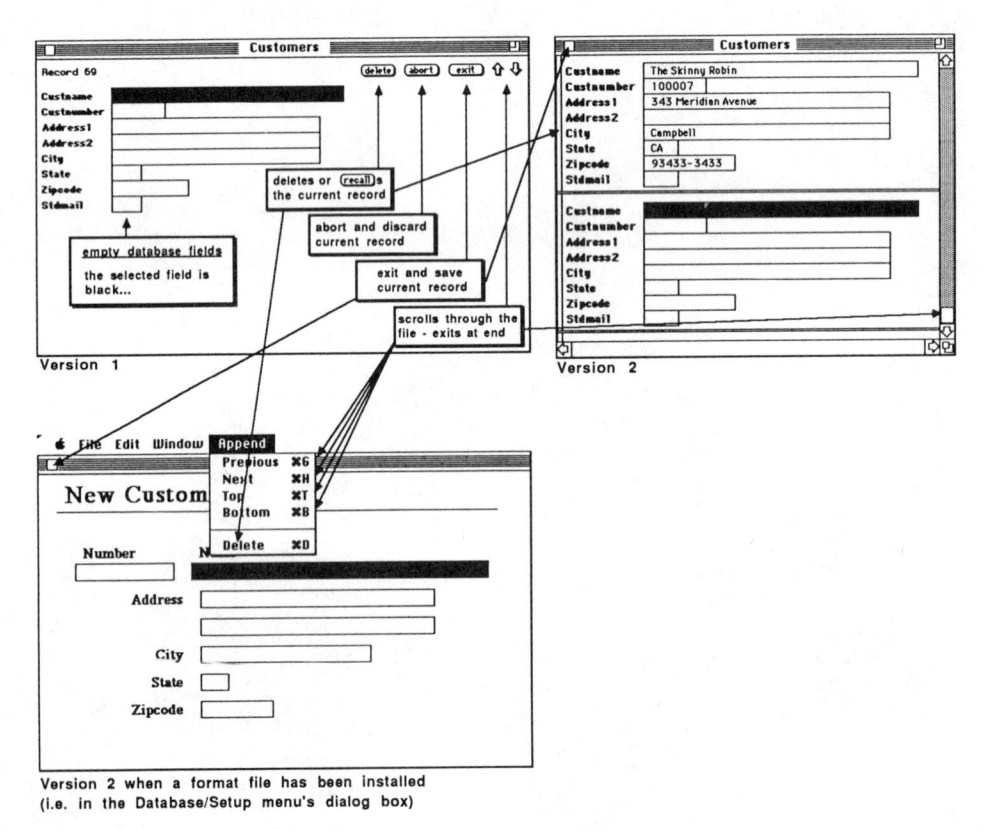

Fig. 8-5. Adding new records.

204   Syntax Options

If SET CARRY is ON, the information entered into each appended record will be carried forward to the next new record. SET CARRY is intended to reduce typing when much of the new data is similar.

If SET FIELDS TO command is active, only those fields specified will be shown.

The headings option is useful when you want to change the append window's title and the label that appears before each data entry field. In this example, the "Window title" is <exprC1> and the field labels for <exprC2> begin with "Customer name."

APPEND HEADINGS "Window title","Customer name:22;Number:6;Contact:20"

The numbers that appear after the semicolons determine how wide, in characters, the displayed field area will be. Fields will temporarily pop open or scroll during edit if the selected width is too short for all of the characters to display at once.

Note Indexes that are associated with a database file should be open during the append process if you want them to be constantly updated. If associated indexes are closed during an append, you will have to reindex them before you can use them.

Tips Use format files to supply users with customized screens for data input as shown in Fig. 8-4. Chapter 7 contains a short discussion of format file creation using FoxForm and how they're installed.

Also See SET CARRY and SET FORMAT

Append Blank

Syntax   APPEND BLANK

Purpose   APPEND BLANK creates a new, blank record at the end of the currently selected database file. Unlike APPEND, APPEND BLANK does not allow you to enter new field information from the keyboard.

Example   APPEND BLANK is used primarily in programs when new data will be entered into a record from other database files or from memory variables. It's often used with the REPLACE Command.

Note   If blanks are left in a file as a primary part of an index key, they will all appear at the top of the file when the index is active. It's a good idea to fill blanks right away or else delete them.

Also See   INSERT

Append From

`🍎 File Edit Database Record Program Text Window`
`   Append From...`

Syntax

APPEND FROM <filename>
[FIELDS <fieldlist>]
[FOR <exprL>]
[WHILE <exprL>]
[TYPE SDF]
[TYPE DELIMITED [WITH <delimiter>|BLANK|TAB]]

Purpose

The APPEND FROM command copies data records into the currently selected database file from another file. New data can be imported from two fundamental types of data files, industry-standard dBase or FoxBASE+/Mac database files that are recognizable by their "DBF" extension, and ASCII text files. ASCII stands for American Standard Code for Information Interchange, and ASCII text files are readable by almost any word processor. They can be created by most database and spreadsheet programs, making them an ideal format for moving data between programs. ASCII files can be arranged in several ways: standard delimited format (SDF), DELIMITED with commas and quotes, DELIMITED with BLANKS (space characters), and DELIMITED with TAB characters.

If the file you are appending data "from" is another FoxBASE+/Mac database file, any fields that are named the same in both will be copied into the file you are appending data "to." If the append-from file is not an industry-standard "DBF" file, you need to use one of the APPEND's TYPE options to identify the data format for FoxBASE.

Example

Unless the optional TYPE clause is used, the data being appended must be a FoxBASE+/Mac database file. No matter what type of original data is used, the file you're putting the data in must be a FoxBASE file, must be open, and it must be in the currently selected work area. The FOR and WHILE clauses can be used to select records from the source file by applying filter conditions, regardless of the data type.

APPEND FROM joesfile

The Database/Appendix menu can also be used to import data from other files as shown in Fig. 5-12.

If the "from" file is in an ASCII file like those shown in Fig. 5-12, you need to tell FoxBASE which specific format the data is in. You should plan ahead by preparing a FoxBASE database file with fields

Syntax Options 207

arranged in exactly the same order as the ASCII file you will append data from.

The APPEND FROM <filename> TYPE DELIMITED WITH TAB command reads an ASCII text file that uses tab characters to separate fields. Field length in the data file receiving data is not critical because tabs align the data field-by-field, but be careful not to make them too short or data can be truncated.

The APPEND FROM <filename> TYPE DELIMITED command reads ASCII text files that use commas to separate fields. By default, commas are placed after every field, effectively separating them. In addition to the commas, character fields are enclosed by quotation marks whenever commas are part of the data itself. Numeric fields are not usually enclosed by quotation marks so that decimals will align automatically. If a numeric field has a minus sign immediately preceding the number, it will import as a negative value. Although commas are required in delimited formats, you can specify an alternate field-enclosing character by entering "...DELIMITED WITH <char>", where <char> is any legal Macintosh character. You can even use the CHR( ) function to install other nonprintable characters as delimiters.

The APPEND FROM <filename> TYPE DELIMITED WITH BLANK command reads an ASCII text file that uses a blank space or a tab to separate fields.

The APPEND FROM <filename> TYPE SDF command reads an ASCII text file that has an equal number of characters in every record and every field. Using a ruler, you could easily draw vertical lines dividing an SDF file into columns. When importing this type of file, be sure to make all of your FoxBASE database fields correspond in sequence and length to the SDF file format.

If a field name exists in both files, it will be appended. If a field name is not the same in both files, its data will be ignored. Memo fields will import from standard DBF files, FoxBASE and others included, if the original DBT file associated with the DBF file was present during the append process. Pictures will append from Fox-BASE+/Mac data files only if the original DBT file associated with the DBF file is present during the append process.

Note: FoxBASE assumes that a ".DBF" file name extension is present in the name of DBF files, and that a ".TXT" extension is present in the name of ASCII text files, unless otherwise specified in your command. You can specify a full pathlist and file name to FoxBASE like this: "diskname:directoryname:filename." The file name should include any extensions. Include the quote marks in your specification and use colons to separate disk names from directory names and from file names.

Note

The natural data type of information in an ASCII file is character, and conversion to FoxBASE data types is usually automatic. You might need to convert some data after it is imported, however. Dates in particular can be troublesome. In case of difficulty, create a character field in your FoxBASE target file to accept the data and attempt to change the field's data type using the MODIFY STRUCTURE command. If that doesn't work, you can add another field to your FoxBASE file and do a REPLACE ALL command to move data from one field (the new one), and convert it in the process. Some knowledge of the data type converting functions will help—for dates see DTOC( ) and CTOD( ); for numbers, see VAL( ) and STR( ). After the data has been moved into the new field and converted, you can remove the old character-type field.

In my experience, a FOR condition applied to TAB and standard DELIMITED (comma) files sometimes allows the first record of an import file to be appended even though it might not meet the filter's condition. This problem does not occur when the source file is already a FoxBASE file.

Tips

APPEND FROM is extremely useful for doing mail merges. Microsoft Word accepts DELIMITED files as mail merge data documents without a hitch. The spreadsheet Microsoft Excel exports and imports tab-delimited files just as easily. Refer to your user manuals to see how FoxBASE data management can complement other programs.

Also See   COPY TO

Average

[menu bar: File Edit Database Record Program Text Window — Average...]

Syntax AVERAGE <exprlist> [<scope>]
[FOR <exprL>]
[WHILE <exprL>]
[TO <memvarlist>]

Purpose The AVERAGE command computes the average values for each numeric field you specify and includes only those records that you include in the scope clause of the command. If no conditions or scopes are specified, AVERAGE computes the numeric average for all numeric fields and records in the file. If SET TALK is ON, the results are displayed. If you include TO <memvarlist>, they are stored in memory.

Example The simplest way to use AVERAGE is by itself, which causes the averaged values of all numeric fields to display on screen. The WHILE option limits the number of ordered records considered in the average.

AVERAGE WHILE STATE = "CA"

The FOR option selects records for consideration, regardless of the file's order.

AVERAGE FOR STATE = "CA"

Use memvars to capture values in memory, and turn SET TALK OFF to prevent an obvious display of the average and its result.

SET TALK OFF
AVERAGE WHILE STATE = "CA" TO mdues, mpaid

Note The syntax supports a <memvarlist> and not array names, so even if all fields are numeric, you cannot average to an <array-name> that was created with the SCATTER command. Instead, AVERAGE to a list in which each array cell reference is separated by commas. If TALK is OFF, a screen display of the returned values will be suppressed.

Also See SET HEADING, SET TALK, SUM, and TOTAL

Browse

File	Edit	Database	Record	Program	Text	Window
		Browse ⌘B				

Syntax
BROWSE
[FIELDS <fieldlist>]
[WIDTH <exprN>]
[NOMODIFY]
[SAVE]

or in version 2
BROWSE [LAST]
[FIELDS <fieldlist>]
[HEADINGS <exprC> [, <exprC>]]
[NOMODIFY]
[NOAPPEND]
[SAVE]
[AT <exprN1>, <exprN2>]
[SIZE <exprN1>, <exprN2>]
[NOMENU]
[FONT <exprC> [, <exprN>]]

Purpose
The BROWSE command opens a full-screen editing window that looks like a fast-scrolling spreadsheet (see Fig. 8-6). Browse windows have a menu of their own, but they behave like other Macintosh windows for closing, resizing, and so on.

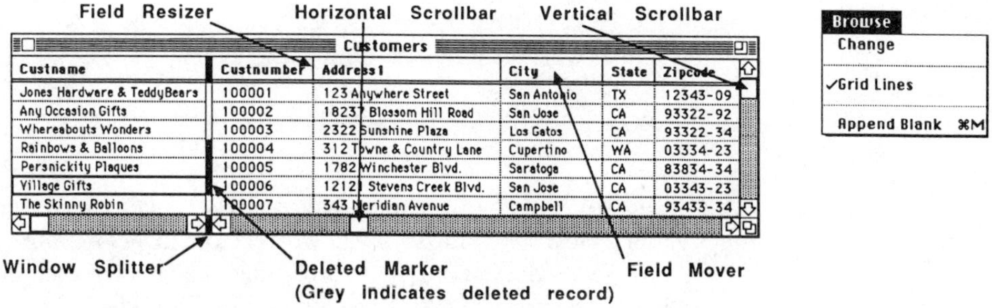

Fig. 8-6. The standard browse window and menu.

Example
The FIELDS <fieldlist> option lets you select which fields will be visible in the browse window, and whether or not the data can be edited by users. This is useful when you want users to be able to look at data, seeing only those fields that make sense at the time.

BROWSE FIELDS customer,address1,city,state,zip

Use the HEADINGS <exprC1> option to tell FoxBASE what

Syntax Options 211

name you want to put at the top of the browse window, and the optional <exprC2> clause to provide a list of names to appear above each column specified in the FIELDS <fieldlist>.

BROWSE FIELDS customer,address1,address2,city,state,zip HEADINGS "Customers", "Name;Address;Suite or PO Box;City;State;Zipcode"

An optional item that can be specified in the fields heading <exprC2> is a number, attached to any of the field headings, specifying (in characters) how wide that field should be when displayed.

BROWSE FIELDS customer,address1,address2,city,state,zip HEADINGS "Customers", "Name:20;Address:20;Suite or PO Box:10;City;State;Zipcode"

Notice that there's a colon between each field name and the number used to indicate its width.

The WIDTH <exprN> option sets a standard display width, in characters, for the first field. If FIELDS <fieldlist> is included, and the HEADINGS option is not used, the WIDTH option sets a standard width for all displayed fields.

BROWSE FIELDS customer,address1,city,state,zip WIDTH 20

The NOMODIFY option prevents data in the browse window to be edited, which makes it useful for display-only purposes.

BROWSE FIELDS customer,address1,city,state,zip NOMODIFY

The SAVE option is for programmers who want to make sure that users close the browse window, because the close box in the browse window's upper-left corner must be pressed to put it away when this option is used. In addition, this option must be specified whenever a programmer wants to open another window over a browse window without closing the browse window.

BROWSE FIELDS customer,address1,city,state,zip SAVE

The AT option, specified in pixels, places the browse window on the screen at any coordinate you desire. The <exprN1> places the window's top pixel on a screen row, and <exprN2>, the window's left on a screen pixel column. AT 0,0 automatically centers the browse window on the monitor.

BROWSE FIELDS customer,address1,city,state,zip AT 0,0

Use the SIZE option to specify how tall <exprN1> and how wide <exprN2> to make the browse window.

The FONT clause is used to specify what font and what size letters should be used inside the fields of a browse window.

BROWSE FIELDS customer,address1,city,state,zip FONT "Geneva",9

The NOAPPEND option tells FoxBASE to prevent new records from being added to the database file by hiding the "Append Blank" menu option, which normally appears in the browse window's own menu. Without the NOAPPEND option, users can add records by selecting "Append Blank" from the browse menu, or by pressing COMMAND-N.

The NOMENU option prevents the browse menu from appearing when the browse window is opened.

As is the case with all optional command key words, these options can be mixed and matched in a variety of ways to suit your needs.

Tips Despite the fact that there's no way to trap errors, such as with VALID and RANGE clauses, in custom record entry forms, browse windows are very useful in programs because the options control what a user can see and do. The menu that automatically appears when a browse window is opened enhances a user's control, and makes application development much easier for programmers who need to provide methods for simple table maintenance.

Also See APPEND, EDIT, and CHANGE

Cancel

🍎 File Edit Database Record Program Text Window
                                    Cancel

Syntax   CANCEL

Purpose   The CANCEL command stops a program from executing and returns you to the interactive mode. With the runtime version of FoxBASE+/Mac, CANCEL causes the application to terminate entirely.

Example   It's sometimes necessary to stop a program from running. If SET ESCAPE is ON, you can press the Escape key, then elect to CANCEL or RESUME the program when the cancel dialog appears. The CANCEL button, an option in the program menu, is accessible during program execution, such as when there are no programmed menus and the current program activity permits menu selection. You can also use CANCEL within a program to terminate it.

Note   Using CANCEL causes private memory variables to be released.

Tips   Use the SUSPEND command instead of CANCEL if you want to check memory variable values or check on another environmental condition, then just RESUME the program. CANCEL stops programs entirely.

Also See RETURN, QUIT, SUSPEND, and RESUME

Change

🍎 File Edit Database Record Program Text Window
                                  Change...

Syntax   CHANGE [<scope>] [LAST]
                  [FIELDS <fieldlist>]
                  [FOR <exprL>]
                  [WHILE <exprL>]
                  [HEADINGS <exprC1>[,<exprC2>]]

Purpose   The CHANGE command has a lot in common with the EDIT and APPEND commands because it also opens up a full-screen, one record-at-a-time editing window for data.

Example   The CHANGE command works beautifully all by itself, and there are extra key words for it that make it even more useful for programmers who are developing applications. Figure 7-10 in Chapter 7 shows what the CHANGE command does.

Use the LAST key word if you want FoxBASE to remember the last change window setting—field widths, font, and type size, etc. Leave LAST out of the command, however, if you want to open a change window with all new settings.

CHANGE LAST

The FIELDS <fieldlist> option lets you select a list of fields and a field order for display in the change window. Fields you list from left to right will display from top to bottom. If you omit the FIELDS option, all fields will display according to the database file's natural field order.

CHANGE FIELDS customer,address1,address2,city,state,zip

The HEADINGS key word allows two options: <exprC1> to set the window's title and <exprC2> to select a meaningful name that will appear above each column/field displayed.

CHANGE FIELDS customer,address1,address2,city,state,zip HEADINGS "Customers"

Window titles <exprC1>, which is named "Customers" in this example, are required whenever the HEADINGS option is used.

The field headings clause <exprC2> is not required, but I recommend you use it. Not only is it useful to name columns, but also because you can specify an optional number for each column that

Syntax Options

tells FoxBASE how wide (in characters) you want each field to be when displayed.

CHANGE FIELDS customer,address1,address2,city,state,zip HEADINGS "Customers", "Name:20;Address:20;Suite or PO Box:10;City;State;Zipcode"

Be sure to use a colon between field names and the number used to indicate width.

Note

If you specify HEADINGS, they must be equal in number and in the same order as the FIELDS list.

If a custom format file has been installed, it will appear instead of the default change window. This is not necessarily a problem, and it might even be desirable in some cases. To prevent a format file from interfering, enter a SET FORMAT TO command without a file name to un-install the format, then enter the CHANGE command.

Also See SET FORMAT TO and EDIT

Clear

Syntax CLEAR

Purpose Entering the CLEAR command without any other options erases the screen that is currently active. In addition, all GETs pending on the screen are released.

Example CLEAR is most often used in programs to clear the entire screen before more information, menus, or other items are displayed. All you have to do is enter CLEAR by itself: CLEAR.

If you want to save GETs, use the GET command with its SAVE option. This way, CLEAR won't remove the GETs from memory, allowing them to be restored simply with another READ command.

Also See @. . .CLEAR, SCREEN and CLEAR GETS

Clear All

Syntax CLEAR ALL

Purpose The CLEAR ALL command returns the data-handling environment to a neutral status by closing all open database files, releasing all memory variables and arrays, closing index files, format files, etc. When CLEAR ALL is done it selects work area 1.

Example To clear the data handling environment simply issue this command: CLEAR ALL.

Note Procedure files that have been established via the SET PROCEDURE TO <filename> command, will not be cleared.

Tips By closing everything associated with the currently active view, CLEAR ALL is as powerful as its near opposite, SET VIEW TO. Remember, VIEW files tell FoxBASE+/Mac to open database files, filters, and indexes, and they even define relations among database files. CLEAR ALL puts views away, and it empties the memory space in FoxBASE that was occupied by data files and data manipulation tasks.

Also See CLOSE, SET VIEW TO, CLEAR MEMORY, RELEASE ALL, and FLUSH

Clear Fields

Syntax   CLEAR FIELDS

Purpose   CLEAR FIELDS undoes what is done by the SET FIELDS TO <fieldlist> command, making all fields in all work areas visible again for display and processing.

Example   Because the SET FIELDS command is useful for limiting the number of fields, by name, that are available for most file operations, including BROWSE, CHANGE, EDIT and APPEND, LIST, DISPLAY, and others, it is a good idea to use it with the CLEAR FIELDS command, which can restore all fields to visibility. To use, just enter this command: CLEAR FIELDS.

Note   CLEAR FIELDS affects all work areas. If you want to make fields visible in only one work area or database, use SET FIELDS OFF or SET FIELDS TO ALL.

Also See   SET VIEW TO, CREATE VIEW, and SET VIEW ON

Clear Gets

Syntax   CLEAR GETS

Purpose   The CLEAR GETS command removes from memory any GETs that are still pending.

Example   CLEAR GETS is useful when you have used the READ command with its SAVE option, because READ/SAVE keeps GETs in memory even when the screen on which the GETS were being edited has been cleared, closed, or another screen has overwritten it.

It works like this: @...GET... makes it possible to edit the contents of memory variables and database fields, and READ activates editing of the GETs on-screen. If a READ has been issued with the SAVE option, GETs are saved so that they can later be reedited with another READ command. When you issue a CLEAR GETS or CLEAR ALL command, the GETS are erased from memory. If a CLEAR GETS command has been issued and you need to edit the GETs again, just issue @...GET and READ again.

Also See   @ SAY...GET, READ [SAVE], and SCREEN

Clear Memory

Syntax	CLEAR MEMORY
Purpose	The CLEAR MEMORY command removes memory variable names, arrays, and any values they hold from memory. The same result can be obtained with the RELEASE ALL command, except that RELEASE is useful for selective memory variable erasure, whereas CLEAR MEMORY is not.
Example	To remove all variables and arrays from memory, enter a command like this: CLEAR MEMORY
Also See	RELEASE ALL, CLEAR GETS, and CLEAR ALL

Clear Program

Syntax	CLEAR PROGRAM
Purpose	Programs take space in memory as they are loaded and run. The CLEAR PROGRAM command frees memory space by removing all programs from memory. When a cleared program is reinvoked with the DO command, however, it must then reload from a disk back into memory before it can run.
Example	CLEAR PROGRAM is useful when you are writing and testing programs. When a program is invoked with the DO command, FoxBASE looks for it in memory first. If there was a recent change to the program on the disk because of editions, FoxBASE will use it instead of the one in memory. If you want to run a different version of a program than the one that is in memory or in the current DEFAULT volume or PATH locations, you must issue CLEAR PROGRAM first. FoxBASE will then allow you to select a program to run, regardless of its name or location.
Tips	FoxBASE programs are always compiled before they are stored in memory so that they can run faster and require less space.
Also See	MODIFY COMMAND

Clear Typeahead

Syntax	CLEAR TYPEAHEAD
Purpose	The CLEAR TYPEAHEAD command removes all keyboard characters from their internal memory buffer. Used with the SET TYPEAHEAD and KEYBOARD commands, CLEAR TYPEAHEAD provides control over what is accepted from the keyboard.
Example	CLEAR TYPEAHEAD is particularly useful for times when you don't want mistaken characters, such as ones used to initiate important events, to be entered into a critical GET. By using CLEAR TYPEAHEAD just before a critical GET, you can keep users from accidentally typing their way into it.
Also See	SET TYPEAHEAD and KEYBOARD

Close

Syntax

CLOSE ALL
or
CLOSE ALTERNATE
or
CLOSE DATABASES
or
CLOSE FORMAT
or
CLOSE INDEX
or
CLOSE PROCEDURE

Purpose

The **CLOSE ALL** command closes all open alternate files, database files, indexes, format files, procedure files and views, then usually returns the internal data-handling environment to a neutral status. Unlike CLEAR ALL, this command does not release memory variables. It does clear any pending GETs, however, and it selects work area A.

The **CLOSE ALTERNATE** command closes any open text or "alternate" file. Alternate files are text files that can be created and written to by FoxBASE+/Mac. You can use them to create log files, report files, and other similar files. See the SET ALTERNATE command for more information about them.

The **CLOSE DATABASES** command closes all database files along with associated index and format files. When done executing, work area A is selected.

The **CLOSE FORMAT** command closes any format file in the current work area (A-J). Format files replace FoxBASE's default format screens for the routine editing and appending of data. See SET FORMAT for more information.

The **CLOSE INDEX** command closes any index files that are open in the currently selected work area. Up to seven indexes can be opened and closed at once with this command.

The **CLOSE PROCEDURE** command closes any procedure file that is open. Procedure files are program files that have one or more subroutines that can be used by other programs. Take a look a at the SET PROCEDURE TO command for more information.

Also See

CLEAR ALL, SET VIEW OFF, and FLUSH

Continue

Syntax CONTINUE

Purpose After you have issued a successful LOCATE command, the CONTINUE command will locate the next record or records that meet your search criteria.

Example The CONTINUE command is like reissuing the LOCATE command for a second time, with one exception—if the file's record pointer has already passed all of the records that match the search condition, a CONTINUE command would go to the bottom of the file and stay there, whereas the LOCATE command will search to the bottom of the file then start again from the top until it finds the match it's seeking. Use LOCATE and CONTINUE together to search a whole file, top to bottom, for every occurrence of a condition. The CONTINUE command will then find all remaining occurrences of the item without starting over again at the top of the file, like this:

```
LOCATE FOR lname = "Smith"
DO WHILE .NOT. EOF( )
    ? lname,address,city,state,zip
    CONTINUE
ENDDO
```

Note The LOCATE and CONTINUE commands work without an index, so it's slower than performing a SEEK with an index. For large database files, the sequential LOCATE and CONTINUE method for retrieval might be too slow.

Tips LOCATE and CONTINUE can be used any time, because no index is necessary, and it will accept complex search conditions based on any information in the file.

Also See LOCATE, FOUND( ), and EOF( )

Syntax Options 225

Copy File

🍎 File Edit Database Record Program Text Window
Copy File...

Syntax COPY FILE <filename1> TO <filename2>

Purpose Use the COPY TO command for database files. The COPY FILE command is for any other type of file, even if it belongs to another application other than FoxBASE+/Mac.

Example This command copies a file and renames it in the process:

COPY FILE "MemoToBob" TO "MemoToMary"

Quotation marks are not always required, but using them can prevent confusion and mistakes when you are copying files to other folders, or when the COPY FILE command gets long and complex, as in the next two examples. Quotation marks are required when file, folder, or disk names contain blank spaces.

This command copies a file and places it in a folder named Folder1 and renames it:

COPY FILE "MemoToBob" TO ":Folder1:MemoToMary"

This command copies a file, placing it in a folder named Folder2 without renaming it. Folder2 is also on the current disk, named HD40:

COPY FILE "MemoToBob" TO "HD40:Folder2:MemoToBob"

This command copies a database file and places it on another disk, in a folder named Folder3:

COPY FILE "MemoToBob" TO "OtherDisk:Folder3:MemoToBob"

Note If there are spaces in the disk, folder, or file names and you have not enclosed them in quotation marks, an "unrecognized phrase" error will occur.

Tips The SET SAFETY OFF command allows you to copy a file anywhere, even when it overwrites an existing file with the same name. If you want to be safe, leave the warning: ". . . already exists. Overwrite it?," intact by using the SET SAFETY ON command.

You can also use the SET SAFETY ON command in programs to create automatic backups of critical data to another folder on a hard disk. You could also write an archive routine for other users so that they won't have to do anything but place a floppy disk in the computer. The backup files would be copied for them at the press of a button.

Also See   SET SAFETY, USE, COPY TO, CLOSE ALL, DIR, RENAME, and ERASE

Copy Structure

Syntax COPY STRUCTURE TO <filename>
[FIELDS <fieldlist>]

Purpose The COPY STRUCTURE command creates an empty database file that has exactly the same fields (structure) as the currently selected database file. If you use the FIELDS clause, COPY STRUCTURE will create a new file that contains only those fields you included in the <fieldlist>.

Example Figure 8-7 shows the Customer file's structure being duplicated. Because only three fields were specified in the FIELDS clause, the new file's structure display is shorter than the original.

```
Screen 1
Structure for database: HD40:FoxBASE+/Mac:Customers.dbf
Number of data records:  8
Date of last update:     11/26/88
Field  Field Name  Type       Width  Dec
    1  custname    Character     36
    2  custnumber  Character      6
    3  address1    Character     32
    4  address2    Character     32
    5  city        Character     32
    6  state       Character      2
    7  zipcode     Character     10
    8  dept        Numeric        1
** Total **                     152

Structure for database: HD40:FoxBASE+/Mac:NewCust.dbf
Number of data records:  0
Date of last update:     11/27/88
Field  Field Name  Type       Width  Dec
    1  custname    Character     36
    2  city        Character     32
    3  state       Character      2
** Total **                      71
```

```
Command
USE Customers
DISPLAY STRUCTURE
COPY STRUCTURE TO NewCust FIELDS custname,city,state
USE NewCust
DISPLAY STRUCTURE
```

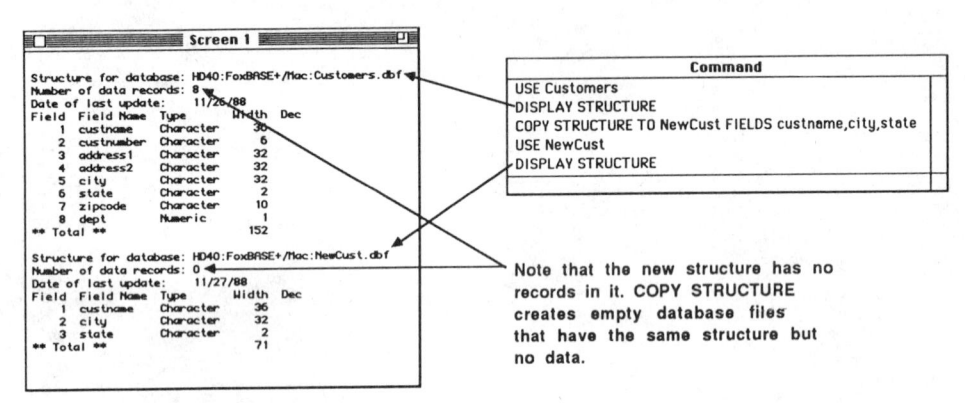

Note that the new structure has no records in it. COPY STRUCTURE creates empty database files that have the same structure but no data.

Fig. 8-7. Copying a database file's structure.

The file being copied must be in the currently selected work area (A-J in the View window), and the newly created file will be saved on disk using the name you provide.

Also See DISPLAY STRUCTURE, SET SAFETY, COPY FILE, and MODIFY STRUCTURE

Copy Structure Extended

Syntax COPY TO <filename> STRUCTURE EXTENDED
or
COPY STRUCTURE EXTENDED TO <filename>

Purpose The COPY STRUCTURE EXTENDED command creates a special type of database file that stores structural information about a regular database file. The special files created by this command always have the structure shown in the second display of Fig. 8-8. After the structure file is created it appends one record to it for each field in the currently selected database file, storing the names, data types, lengths, and decimals (if numeric) for each field in the selected source file.

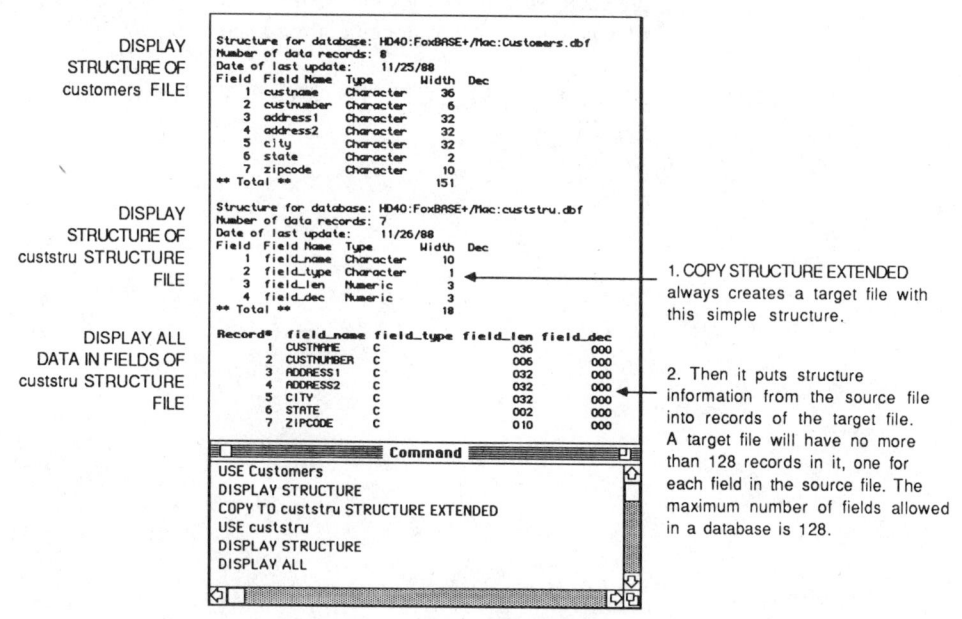

```
                  Structure for database: HD40:FoxBASE+/Mac:Customers.dbf
DISPLAY           Number of data records: 8
STRUCTURE OF      Date of last update:    11/25/88
customers FILE    Field  Field Name  Type       Width  Dec
                    1    custname    Character    36
                    2    custnumber  Character     6
                    3    address1    Character    32
                    4    address2    Character    32
                    5    city        Character    32
                    6    state       Character     2
                    7    zipcode     Character    10
                  ** Total **                    151

                  Structure for database: HD40:FoxBASE+/Mac:custstru.dbf
DISPLAY           Number of data records: 7
STRUCTURE OF      Date of last update:    11/26/88
custstru STRUCTURE  Field  Field Name  Type     Width  Dec
FILE                1    field_name  Character   10
                    2    field_type  Character    1        ◄──── 1. COPY STRUCTURE EXTENDED
                    3    field_len   Numeric      3              always creates a target file with
                    4    field_dec   Numeric      3              this simple structure.
                  ** Total **                    18

DISPLAY ALL       Record#  field_name  field_type  field_len  field_dec
DATA IN FIELDS OF   1      CUSTNAME        c          036         000
custstru STRUCTURE  2      CUSTNUMBER      c          006         000   2. Then it puts structure
FILE                3      ADDRESS1        c          032         000   information from the source file
                    4      ADDRESS2        c          032         000   into records of the target file.
                    5      CITY            c          032         000   A target file will have no more
                    6      STATE           c          002         000   than 128 records in it, one for
                    7      ZIPCODE         c          010         000   each field in the source file. The
                                                                        maximum number of fields allowed
                  ┌─────────────── Command ───────────────┐            in a database is 128.
                  │ USE Customers                          │
                  │ DISPLAY STRUCTURE                      │
                  │ COPY TO custstru STRUCTURE EXTENDED    │
                  │ USE custstru                           │
                  │ DISPLAY STRUCTURE                      │
                  │ DISPLAY ALL                            │
                  └────────────────────────────────────────┘
```

Fig. 8-8. Commands for copying database file structures.

Example See Fig. 8-8 to see how a structure is created. This command is used by programmers along with the CREATE FROM command to make new database files modeled on another file's structure.

Although it's only useful in special situations, there is nothing as easy as this command for making a new file when you need to. Application programmers can use it under program control to make archival backup files with special names, and make new files for receiving data from outside sources.

Another practical use of this command is to store information about files in your database systems instead of saving all of the files themselves. Printing reports from data is more flexible than displaying a structure.

Figure 8-9 shows how advanced programmers can REPLACE values in a structure to change a database file's structure under the control of a program. Under program control, you can also use structure files to determine the name or length of fields in any database. Again, this is not common, but when the facility is needed, there is no better way. Control like this gives you the ability to write programs that can control even the structure of files when you are not around to watch! See the REPLACE and CREATE FROM commands to learn more about this.

Tips   Use this command after creating database systems that have multiple files; storing every field in the entire system inside structure files is a good way to document the system.

Also See   CREATE FROM, COPY TO, MODIFY STRUCTURE, and REPLACE

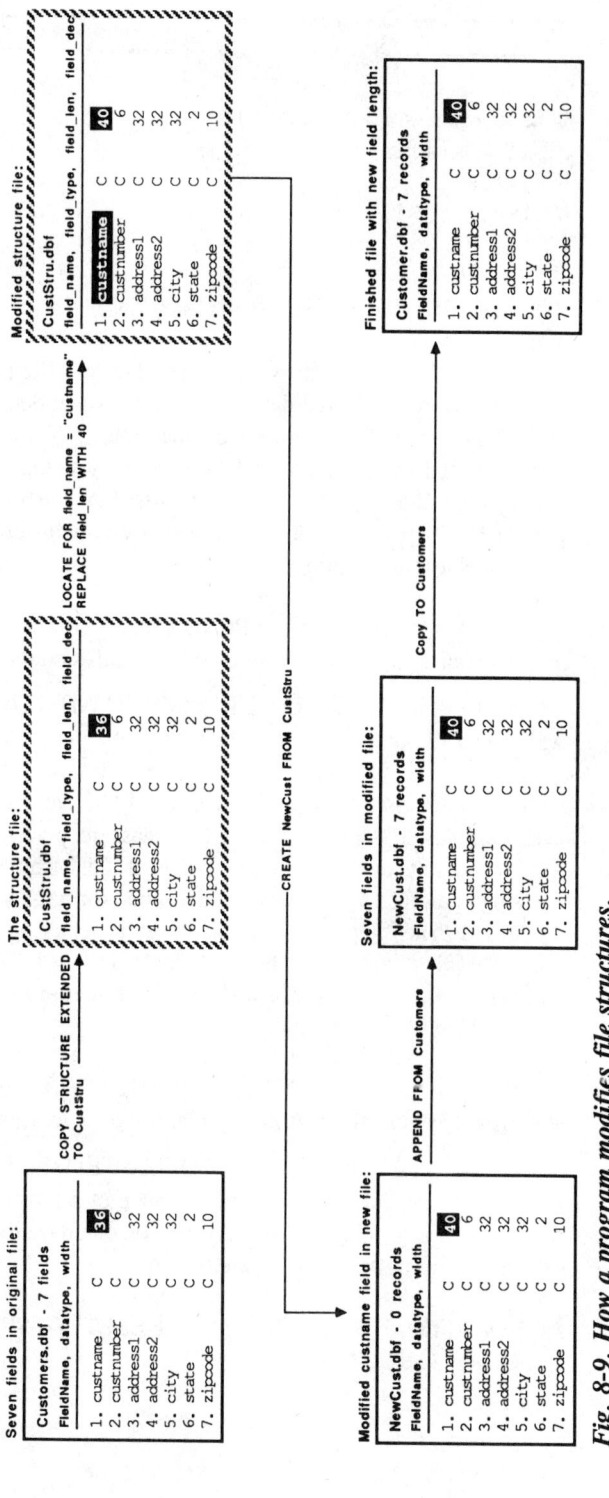

Fig. 8-9. *How a program modifies file structures.*

Syntax Options 231

Copy To

[Menu bar: File Edit Database Record Program Text Window / Copy To...]

Syntax

COPY TO <filename> [<scope>]
[FIELDS <fieldlist>]
[FOR <exprL>]
[WHILE <exprL>]
[TYPE SDF]
   or
[TYPE DELIMITED [WITH <delimiter>|BLANK|TAB]]

Purpose

The COPY TO command creates a new database file that's exactly like the currently selected database file unless you decide that only specific records will be copied using the FOR or WHILE clauses or that a limited set of fields will be copied by using the FIELDS option. The COPY TO command is also how FoxBASE exports files to other formats for use by spreadsheets, word processors, or other database managers.

Example

COPY TO is the reverse of APPEND FROM, so refer to that entry in this chapter for more information about this command's use.

COPY TO <filename> TYPE DELIMITED WITH TAB creates an ASCII text file that uses tab characters to separate fields.

COPY TO <filename> TYPE DELIMITED creates a text file that uses commas to separate fields. Commas are placed after every field by default, effectively separating each field from one another. Although commas are common in delimited formats, you can specify an alternate field-enclosing character by entering "...DELIMITED WITH <char>," where <char> is any legal Macintosh character. You can even use the CHR( ) function to install other nonprintable characters as delimiters.

COPY TO <filename> TYPE DELIMITED WITH BLANK creates an ASCII text file that inserts blank spaces to separate fields.

COPY TO <filename> TYPE DELIMITED SDF creates an ASCII text file that has an equal number of characters in every record and every field. By using a ruler you could easily draw vertical lines dividing an SDF file into columns.

Also See

APPEND FROM, COPY FILE, SET DELETED, SET SAFETY, and COPY STRUCTURE

Count

Syntax	COUNT [<scope>] [WHILE <exprL>] [FOR <exprL>] [TO <memvar>]
Purpose	The COUNT command counts all of the records in the currently selected database file. You can use the WHILE or FOR scoping clauses to count only records that meet a condition. COUNT can also initialize a memory variable and store the record count in it.
Example	The RECCOUNT( ) function always "knows" how many records there are in a selected database file, but it cannot tell you how many there are that meet some condition you've set. The COUNT command meets the need for conditional record counting. To count deleted records:

COUNT FOR DELETED( )

To count deleted records and place the number in a variable:

COUNT FOR DELETED( ) TO delcount

To count nondeleted records:

COUNT FOR .NOT. DELETED( ) TO ndelcount

To count records in an unindexed file for occurrences of the state of Massachusetts using FOR:

COUNT FOR state = "MA" TO mass

To count records in an indexed file for occurrences of the state of Massachusetts using WHILE:

INDEX ON state TO custstate
SEEK "MA"
COUNT WHILE state = "MA" TO mass

Also See	SET DELETED, RECCOUNT( ), SET TALK, and SUM

Syntax Options 233

Create

```
  File  Edit  Database  Record  Program  Text  Window
  New...    ⌘N
```

Syntax CREATE [<filename>]

Purpose The CREATE command allows you to make a new database file by opening a dialog box like the one shown in Fig. 8-10, where you can specify what fields will be in the new file, what they will be named, what data type each new field will hold, and how large each field should be.

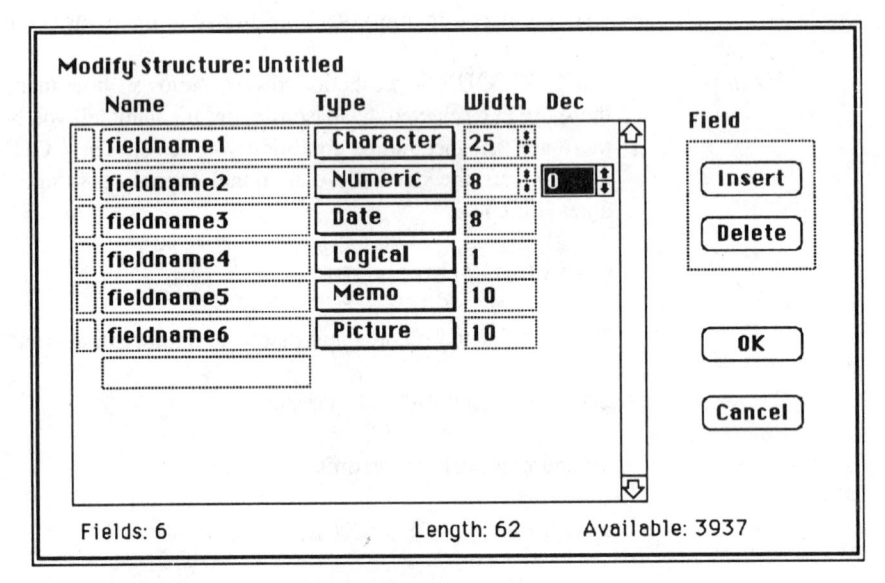

```
Modify Structure: Untitled
    Name            Type         Width  Dec         Field
  fieldname1     Character       25
  fieldname2     Numeric          8       0       [ Insert ]
  fieldname3     Date             8
  fieldname4     Logical          1               [ Delete ]
  fieldname5     Memo            10
  fieldname6     Picture         10
                                                  [   OK   ]

                                                  [ Cancel ]

  Fields: 6           Length: 62      Available: 3937
```

Fig. 8-10. The CREATE database dialog.

Example To make a new database file, simply select the File/New/Database menu, or enter this command:

CREATE mynewfile

If you want to create a file but don't know how, Chapter 2 contains a short tutorial that you can follow in order to learn the steps.

Note Don't throw away a (.dbt) file unless you know what database file owns it. If a memo/picture .dbt file gets trashed, you will no longer be able to open the database file that owns it and a "MEMO file is missing" error will occur, indicating the loss of all of the file's data. If this occurs, there is a way to recover nonpicture and nonmemo data. Create a new database file in another folder using exactly the same memo and picture field names. When you're done, copy only the newly created memo (.dbt) file to the folder where the orphaned database (.dbf) file is. It will then open, albeit without memos or pictures.

Also See USE and MODIFY STRUCTURE

Create From

Syntax CREATE [<filename1>] FROM [<filename2>]

Purpose The CREATE FROM command works only when you have already created a special database file like the one created using the COPY STRUCTURE EXTENDED command. It can create a new database file <filename1> from the fields described in <filename2>.

Example Look at the discussion for COPY STRUCTURE EXTENDED earlier in this chapter for an explanation and examples of its use.

Also See COPY STRUCTURE EXTENDED and MODIFY STRUCTURE

Create Label

Syntax	CREATE LABEL [<filename>]
Purpose	The CREATE LABEL command opens a dialog box that is used to define a label form file. When you're done, it will save your description in a file with a (.lbl) extension if you're using version 1.x, or an (.frx) extension if you're using version 2.x. Label files, also called label form files, contain the names of fields you want to print on the labels, as well as information about the layout of the labels you are printing on.
Example	Chapter 11 contains a thorough discussion of creating reports and report files, which includes labels. Because version 2.x FoxBASE+/Mac treats reports and labels identically, I recommend that you take a look at Chapter 11 to learn how it's done. To print a label select Report/Label from the database menu.
Also See	LABEL FORM and MODIFY LABEL

Create Report

Syntax	CREATE REPORT [<filename>]
Purpose	The CREATE REPORT command produces report form files that have an (.frm) extension in version 1.x and a (.frx) extension in version 2.x. Report form files contain the names of fields you want to have printed in a report, the layout of the report's columns, from left to right, and other information about the report's layout such as header appearance and calculated totals for numbers. CREATE REPORT makes the report form file but doesn't print the report. To print a report, select Report/Label from the Database menu.
Example	Chapter 11 contains a thorough discussion of creating report and report files. Take a look there to learn how it's done. To print a report, select Report/Label from the Database menu.
Also See	REPORT FORM and MODIFY REPORT

Create Screen

Syntax	CREATE SCREEN [<filename>]
Purpose	The CREATE SCREEN command opens the form editor where you can lay out new screens for FoxBASE to use while adding or editing data. You can also design complex screens for use in programs.
Example	For a full description of the layout editor's functions, see the discussion of screen design in Chapter 7. The steps for creating a format file are:

1. Enter CREATE SCREEN to open the form file layout editor.
2. Create a layout using the tools and features of the editor.
3. Save the layout. This creates a screen (or .scx) file.
4. Generate a format (.fmt) file from the screen file by using the Program/Generate menu.
5. Use the SET FORMAT TO <filename> command to install the new form.

The new form can now be used in place of the standard EDIT, APPEND, CHANGE, and INSERT screens of FoxBASE (see SET FORMAT).

Note	You can modify a format file after it has been generated, but use only the @...SAY/GET and READ commands in it. Otherwise, an error will result (see the SET FORMAT TO command entry in this chapter).
Tips	Another way you might be able to create new screens is to generate the form (.fmt) file, cut out its commands, and paste them into a program file instead. Format files are technically the same as program files, but they are far more limited in what they can do. Screen actions such as buttons and menus can be highly customized when a form file is defined from inside a program rather than by a format file. See Chapter 7 for examples.
Also See	SET FORMAT TO

Syntax Options 239

Create View

Syntax   CREATE VIEW [< viewfilename >]

Purpose   The CREATE VIEW command takes a snapshot of all the currently open database and index files, along with all of the other options available in the View window, and stores the information in a view (.vue) file. You can later recall and reinstate all of the settings by double-clicking a saved view file icon, opening a view file from the File menu, or by issuing a SET VIEW TO command.

Example   Views can save a lot of time, because they save whole computer environments for recall at the press of a button. Figure 5-3 in Chapter 5 shows what kind of information view files hold.

To create a view, you can either enter the CREATE VIEW <filename> command in the Command window or in a program, or you can make the View window active and then use the File/Save as... menu option.

Note   Pathlists and default folders are stored in view files, so don't change the names of folders that your files are in if you want the view file to work later. This is a real risk when moving view files from one person's computer to another, because folder names and file locations are likely to change. If a view file doesn't find things where it expects them, it probably won't work. Write down the names and locations of drives and folders in views that will be used on more than one computer, then make sure that those names exist on any computer where you install view files.

Tips   Views are a great way to provide quick programs to application users, because they allow developers a very fast way to swap data-handling environments in response to a user's menu choices. A particularly effective technique is to marry screens with view files that support them. Then it's a simple matter to hop from one screen to another and back again.

There are some potential problems with views, however, that need attention: View files are useful in programs, but settings that go into a view file for later recall are often set interactively by the mouse. Many important settings are saved in view files, so make sure that the SET commands you have established in your programs are not undone by a SET VIEW TO command, which reestablishes a stored environment, and erases the current one. View files should be created as carefully as the application programs. An alternate way to handle views is to establish all of the views parameters through procedures instead of view files.

Also See   SET VIEW TO and SET VIEW OFF|ON

Delete

Syntax DELETE [<scope>]
[FOR <exprL>]
[WHILE <exprL>]

Purpose The DELETE command marks one or more records in a database file to be removed with the PACK command. It's the only selective way to remove records from a database file. PACKing, however, is required to permanently remove the records. DELETE marks them and PACK erases them. DELETE also hides records from many FoxBASE operations when the SET DELETED parameter is ON (refer to the SET DELETED command entry to see which operations are affected). The SORT and INDEX commands are not affected by deleted records; they are sorted or indexed even if marked for deletion.

Example You can DELETE records in the browse window simply by clicking in the left column. The Command window and programming way to delete records is to enter the simple command DELETE when the current record is the one you want affected. The Edit window has a button appropriately marked for that purpose. Once a record, or many for that matter, has been deleted, you can remove it permanently with the PACK command. A deleted record has a grey mark in the left-most column of a browse window as shown in Fig. 5-4. The top half of Fig. 5-4 shows how deleted records look when they are DISPLAYed.

Blind <scope> and conditional <exprL> scopes can be used to DELETE many records at once. See the *Scopes are Record Boundaries* section in Chapter 6 for more information about FOR and WHILE.

Note Do not use DELETE to mark records for reasons other than permanent removal by the PACK command. If you need to mark records for other reasons and find yourself eyeing this as a method, be careful. Consider adding a logical field to your files that can be used for arbitrarily marking records, without placing your data at risk.

Tips Records that have been deleted can be recalled with the RECALL command as long as SET DELETED is OFF. Individual records can be recalled by record number regardless of the SET DELETED setting. Open indexes before deleting.

Also See RECALL, SET DELETED, PACK, DELETED( ), and ZAP

Delete File

	File	Edit	Database	Record	Program	Text	Window
	Delete File...						

Syntax   DELETE FILE <filename>

Purpose   The DELETE FILE command permanently erases any file from any disk attached to your Macintosh. It is the same as ERASE <filename> in FoxBASE and trashing a file at the Macintosh desktop.

Example   Figure 8-11 shows the "Customer.dbf" file before erasure. After erasure, the second DIR command cannot find it. Did you notice that I made a copy of the customer file before erasing the original? Take note, this is a powerful command. The ERASE <filename> command works identically to the DELETE FILE command. The "dBase" language has grown somewhat erratically over the years, so it's my guess that Fox Software has put both ways of erasing files into FoxBASE to accommodate all programmers' tastes.

```
                              Screen 1

Filename                    Records  Updated      Data      Resource
Copy of Customers.dbf             7  11/25/88     1315             0
Customers.dbf                     7  11/25/88     1315             0
FoxHelp.dbf                     345  09/26/88    14243             0

3 total files/folders                            16873             0
6987776 bytes remaining on drive.
File has been deleted.
Filename                    Records  Updated      Data      Resource
Copy of Customers.dbf             7  11/25/88     1315             0
FoxHelp.dbf                     345  09/26/88    14243             0

2 total files/folders                            15558             0
6989824 bytes remaining on drive.
========================== Command ==========================
DIR
DELETE FILE ::FoxBASE+/Mac:Customers.dbf
DIR
```

Fig. 8-11. DELETE FILE lets programs do their own housekeeping.

Note   Make sure that the file you're deleting is not currently in use, or an error message will occur. There is no recovery for a deleted file without quick action and fancy tools, so be careful.

Tips   There are better ways to permanently erase files on a Macintosh than to wrestle with this command's syntax. One of them is to use

242 Syntax Options

the File/Delete File menu option, the other is to wait until you're out of FoxBASE and trash the file from the desktop. This command is useful when you need to make room while in FoxBASE or when a program you've created uses temporary files that are no longer needed after your program quits. Users like their disk space, so don't leave large scratch files around.

Also See   ERASE and PACK

Dimension

Syntax DIMENSION|PUBLIC <arrayname> (<exprN1> [,<exprN2>])
[,<memvar> (<exprN1> [,<exprN2>]),...]

Purpose The DIMENSION command creates named arrays in memory. A named array is a set of rows and columns in which each cell behaves much like an individual memory variable. Arrays are nice because they can hold many separate items of information in a consistent relationship. Just as fields are related to other fields in a database record, each cell of an array is related to other cells in the same row, and rows in an array are related to other rows by row and column numbers called the subscript. See <exprN1> and <exprN2> above.

Example Arrays are useful when you have lists to store in memory, because storing them in many individual memory variables would be too cumbersome. In Fig. 8-12, for example, the array "myarray" could hold three pieces of information about four weeks in the month.

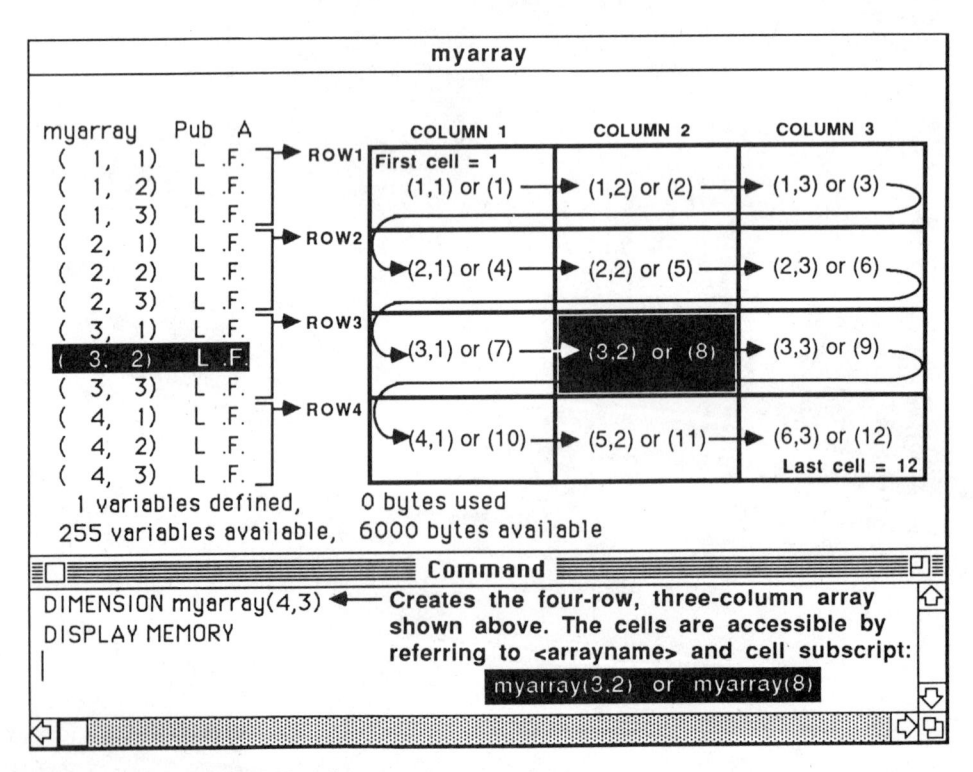

```
                                     myarray
myarray     Pub  A              COLUMN 1      COLUMN 2      COLUMN 3
(  1, 1)    L   .F.  → ROW1  First cell = 1
(  1, 2)    L   .F.          (1,1) or (1) → (1,2) or (2) → (1,3) or (3)
(  1, 3)    L   .F.
(  2, 1)    L   .F.  → ROW2
(  2, 2)    L   .F.          (2,1) or (4) → (2,2) or (5) → (2,3) or (6)
(  2, 3)    L   .F.
(  3, 1)    L   .F.  → ROW3
(  3, 2)    L   .F.          (3,1) or (7) → (3,2) or (8) → (3,3) or (9)
(  3, 3)    L   .F.
(  4, 1)    L   .F.  → ROW4
(  4, 2)    L   .F.          (4,1) or (10)→ (5,2) or (11)→ (6,3) or (12)
(  4, 3)    L   .F.                                       Last cell = 12
  1 variables defined,     0 bytes used
255 variables available, 6000 bytes available
============================== Command ==============================
DIMENSION myarray(4,3) ← Creates the four-row, three-column array
DISPLAY MEMORY           shown above. The cells are accessible by
                         referring to <arrayname> and cell subscript:
                              myarray(3,2)  or  myarray(8)
```

Fig. 8-12. DIMENSION makes arrays.

Column one could hold the week's sales, column two the number of customers served, and column three could contain the cost of goods sold each week.

PUBLIC can be used in lieu of the DIMENSION command when it's desirable to make public arrays.

When arrays are first created with the DIMENSION command, the cells are given a logical value of false (.F.) as shown in Fig. 8-12, although array cells can hold any type of data except memos. Even pictures can be stored in array cells. Although data cannot be stored as a database memo, long character strings can be stored in array cells. In addition, the STORE command can be used to fill a whole array with one value at once as shown in Fig. 8-13. Use the STORE 0 command to set up an array for numbers, or quotes to put an empty character set value in all of the cells. Date cells can be initialized with the CTOD( ) function or by storing the value of DATE( ).

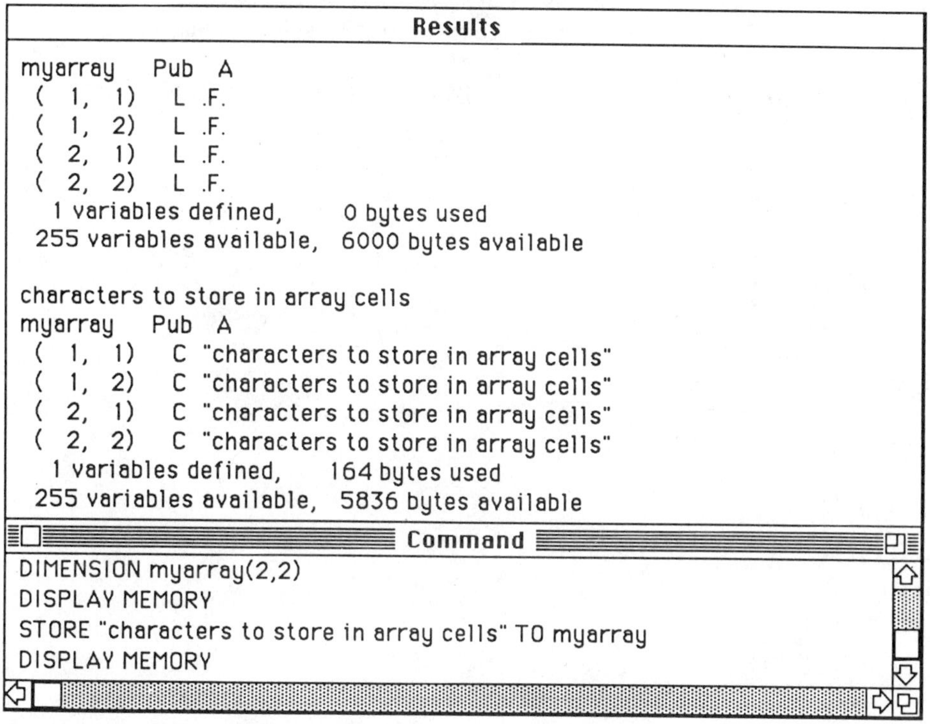

```
                        Results
myarray    Pub  A
 ( 1, 1)    L  .F.
 ( 1, 2)    L  .F.
 ( 2, 1)    L  .F.
 ( 2, 2)    L  .F.
    1 variables defined,      0 bytes used
  255 variables available,  6000 bytes available

characters to store in array cells
myarray    Pub  A
 ( 1, 1)    C  "characters to store in array cells"
 ( 1, 2)    C  "characters to store in array cells"
 ( 2, 1)    C  "characters to store in array cells"
 ( 2, 2)    C  "characters to store in array cells"
    1 variables defined,    164 bytes used
  255 variables available,  5836 bytes available
========================= Command =========================
DIMENSION myarray(2,2)
DISPLAY MEMORY
STORE "characters to store in array cells" TO myarray
DISPLAY MEMORY
```

Fig. 8-13. Viewing array and variable contents.

You can address any array cell individually by using an array name and subscript numbers to identify the cell's exact location within the array. The row <exprN1> and column <exprN2> subscripts for a typical array are shown in Fig. 8-12. Because all arrays are addressed in a rowlike fashion, you can also refer to cells with one subscript number, as long as you don't confuse rows and columns. Rows are first and primary; columns are secondary.

Each cell in an array takes 18 bytes plus the small amount of memory the array takes as an equal among other memory variables. Although an array is treated like one memory variable, its cells can contain a total of 32,767 characters.

Note The STORE, DIMENSION, and PUBLIC commands, and the assignment operator (=) all declare variables. Because of dimensioning differences betweeen regular variables and arrays, a syntax error will result if you declare a variable by using the PUBLIC command and later try to DIMENSION it. This is because the PUBLIC command declares variables, assigns them a logical value of .F., and automatically dimensions them to have one cell. Dimensioning a variable that has already been declared is like trying to redimension an array, which is not possible. For more information about these issues, see the PUBLIC command entry.

Also See STORE, GATHER, SCATTER, and PUBLIC

246 *Syntax Options*

Directory|Dir

Syntax   DIRECTORY|DIR [<drive>]
[<pathlist>]
[<skeleton>]
[TO PRINT]

Purpose   The DIRECTORY command displays the name of all the database (.dbf) files in a folder, including the number of records each file contains, the date it was last changed, and its size. By using the <skeleton> argument, you can view other kinds of files in addition to database files. The TO PRINT option prints the listing. The optional <pathlist> is a way to view files in a drive or folder that's not currently selected.

Example   Figure 8-14 shows the results of three DIR commands. The first command, DIR, shows only database files, the number of records in each, and the date it was last updated. The second command was issued with a <skeleton> argument—DIR *.PRG, which selected only those files that have a .prg extension at the end of their names.

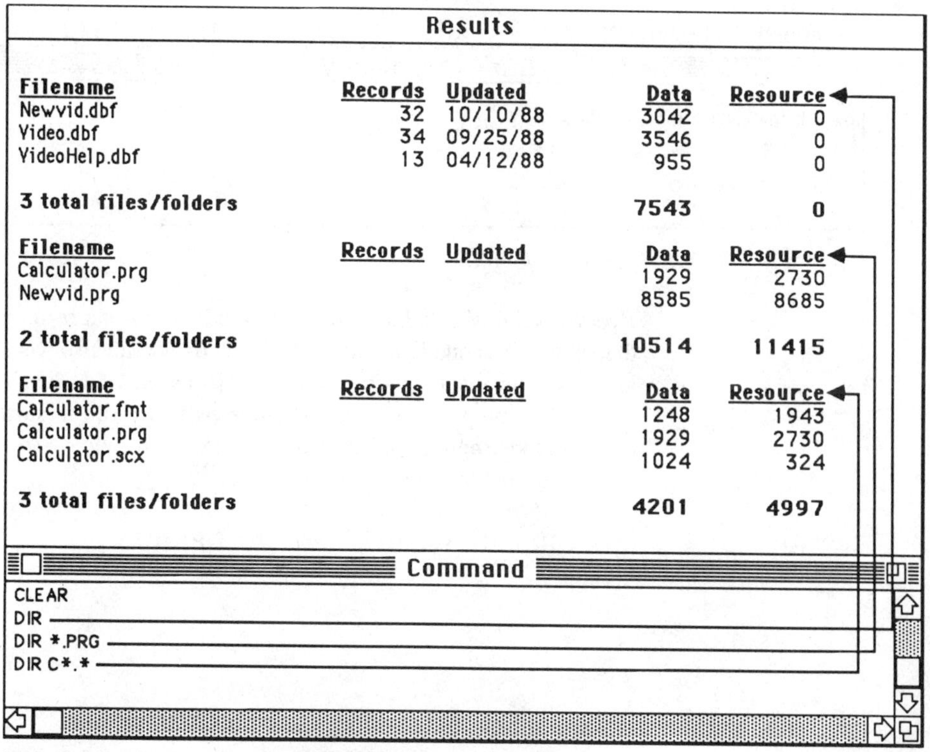

```
                              Results
Filename              Records  Updated     Data    Resource
Newvid.dbf                32   10/10/88    3042       0
Video.dbf                 34   09/25/88    3546       0
VideoHelp.dbf             13   04/12/88     955       0

3 total files/folders                      7543       0

Filename              Records  Updated     Data    Resource
Calculator.prg                              1929     2730
Newvid.prg                                  8585     8685

2 total files/folders                     10514    11415

Filename              Records  Updated     Data    Resource
Calculator.fmt                              1248     1943
Calculator.prg                              1929     2730
Calculator.scx                              1024      324

3 total files/folders                      4201     4997

========================= Command =========================
CLEAR
DIR
DIR *.PRG
DIR C*.*
```

Fig. 8-14. The results of a DIRECTORY command.

Syntax Options 247

The last DIR command also has a <skeleton>, which selects all of files that have a "C" at the beginning of their names. A skeleton of *.* or * selects all files. Note that the DIR command is not sensitive to uppercase and lowercase letters. Folders displayed with DIR show up in bold lettering.

Figure 8-15 shows how to use the optional drive and pathlist arguments. DIR looks in the currently selected folder if you don't specify a drive or pathlist. Quotation marks are not required. The DIRECTORY command looks in the current default folder if there is no drive or pathlist. A partial pathlist is acceptable as long as the first folder has a colon before it and the first folder is located inside the currently selected default drive/folder. For more information about default paths, see the SET DEFAULT command entry in this chapter.

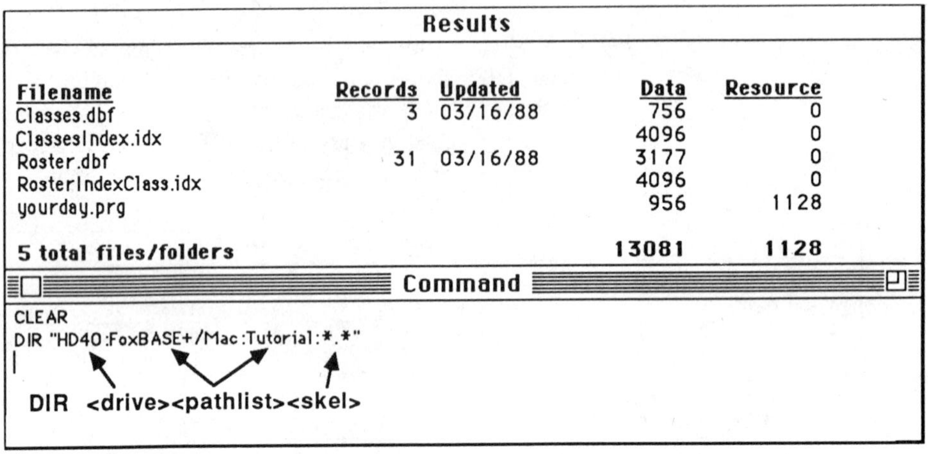

```
                              Results

Filename               Records   Updated    Data    Resource
Classes.dbf                 3    03/16/88    756         0
ClassesIndex.idx                            4096         0
Roster.dbf                 31    03/16/88   3177         0
RosterIndexClass.idx                        4096         0
yourday.prg                                  956      1128

5 total files/folders                      13081      1128
════════════════════════════ Command ════════════════════════════
CLEAR
DIR "HD40:FoxBASE+/Mac:Tutorial:*.*"

     DIR  <drive><pathlist><skel>
```

Fig. 8-15. Filtering a directory listing.

Every Macintosh file has two parts, a data part and a resource part that show up as one icon on the desktop. Every file also has a separate data and resource size, which is displayed by DIRECTORY. Macintosh computers use the resource part of a file to store controls, sounds, and visual information so the resource size varies depending on the type and use of a file.

Also See   SET VOLUME, SET PATH, and SET DEFAULT

Display

Syntax DISPLAY [<scope>]
[[FIELDS] <exprlist>] [FOR <exprL>]
[WHILE <exprL>] [OFF] [TO PRINT]

Purpose The DISPLAY command shows the contents of a database one screen at a time, pausing so you can read the screen before continuing. In addition to showing data from a database file, DISPLAY can calculate numbers from number data in database fields and it can show the contents of picture and memo fields. In addition to screen displays, the DISPLAY command will print if you use the TO PRINT option.

Example Figure 8-16 shows records from a customer's database. Normally, DISPLAY shows only one record at a time, but with an ALL <scope> it shows every record unless DELETED is SET ON. Notice that the asterisk in the topmost display indicates that record number one is marked for deletion, whereas in the bottom display after SET DELETED has been turned ON, the record is not visible at all.

```
                           Results
Record#  custname                        custnumber  address1
    1   *Jones Hardware & TeddyBears     100001      123 Anywhere Street
    2    Any Occasion Gifts              100002      18237 Blossom Hill Rd
    3    Whereabouts Wonders             100003      2322 Sunshine Plaza
    4    Rainbows & Balloons             100004      312 Towne & Country L
    5    Persnickity Plaques             100005      1782 Winchester Blvd.
    6    Village Gifts                   100006      12121 Stevens Creek B
    7    The Skinny Robin                100007      343 Meridian Avenue

Record#  custname                        custnumber  address1
    2    Any Occasion Gifts              100002      18237 Blossom Hill Rd
    3    Whereabouts Wonders             100003      2322 Sunshine Plaza
    4    Rainbows & Balloons             100004      312 Towne & Country L
    5    Persnickity Plaques             100005      1782 Winchester Blvd.
    6    Village Gifts                   100006      12121 Stevens Creek B
    7    The Skinny Robin                100007      343 Meridian Avenue

                           Command
DISPLAY ALL
SET DELETED ON
DISPLAY ALL
```

Fig. 8-16. The results of DISPLAY command.

The FIELDS option is for selecting one or more fields by name. If the FIELDS option is chosen, you can include an <exprlist>. This means that you can do simple algebraic operations in the display or else tailor the field display with FoxBASE functions. Any legal expression goes. For example, if you are interested only in the month from a field's date, you can display it with the CMONTH(<fieldname>). If you had a field with prices and a field for quantities, you could ask FoxBASE to display an expression of "price * quantity" to see the extended price of goods. Just remember that display considers only one record at a time when you write the expression, so anything in a record can be used in an expression, but not things out of a record.

The FOR and WHILE options follow the rules for conditional filtering and scoping of records (see the *Scopes are Record Boundaries* section in Chapter 6 for more information). Using the WHILE option with an indexed or sorted file, you could ask to display all of the customers whose city was Cupertino. FOR or WHILE conditions consider only one record at a time, in either the selected file(s) that have been related with the SET RELATION TO command.

The OFF option causes the record number to not display on the left side of the screen, which is a good idea if you need the space to see data.

Note The screen will truncate the right side of displayed data if there is not enough screen and too much data.

Tips DISPLAY is flexible enough so that developers of applications for others to use can tailor it to list records and calculations without overly complex programming. DISPLAY is practical in applications because of the flexibility that functions can give it and because it stops at each screenfull, waiting for the user to proceed. Interactive users who know how to relate files can use DISPLAY to create useful multifile reports.

Also See LIST, ? and SET HEADING

Display Files

Syntax	DISPLAY FILES [ON <drive|folder>] [LIKE <skeleton>] [TO PRINT]
Purpose	The DISPLAY FILES command does what the DIR command does except that the ON and LIKE options for DISPLAY FILES might be easier for some people to remember and use.
Example	See the DIRECTORY command entry for information about the results of DISPLAY FILES because they are identical.
Also See	DIRECTORY and LIST FILES

Display Memory

Syntax	DISPLAY MEMORY [TO PRINT]
Purpose	The DISPLAY MEMORY command shows the contents and status of all variables and arrays stored in memory.
Example	Figure 6-7 in Chapter 6 shows the results of a DISPLAY MEMORY command. Variable and array names show up in the left-most column followed by the location (public or private), the variable's data type, and if it is not picture data, its actual data contents. The last thing to display on the right side is the name of the program that created the variable.
	The types of data that can be stored in memory include all of the standard database types except for memo: character, numeric, date, logical, and picture. In addition, an array data type and screens that have been saved using the SAVE SCREEN TO command will show up as special memory variables when memory is displayed.
Tips	Not all memory variables can be active at the time you display them.
Also See	LIST MEMORY, SAVE TO, RESTORE FROM, PUBLIC, and PRIVATE

Display Status

Syntax	DISPLAY STATUS [TO PRINT]
Purpose	The DISPLAY STATUS command provides a wealth of information about the status of the data-handling work environment, SET command switch settings, and print/display settings. Like other display commands, DISPLAY STATUS waits after filling the screen so you can read what it has shown before continuing.
Example	Figure 6-11 in Chapter 6 shows the information provided by the DISPLAY STATUS command. For open database files, the display provides its name and alias, filters or indexes in use, name of the current master index (established by SET ORDER), what work area each open database file occupies (A-J in the View window), the name of open memo (.dbt) files associated with database files, and finally, relationship links each database file has to others via the SET RELATION TO command. If you have the multiuser version of FoxBASE, each open file's lock status will also be displayed.
Tips	The TO PRINT option can be very useful because it puts all of the status information, as well as the contents of view (.vue) files, at your fingertips. To capture view file information, just open a view file or issue the SET VIEW TO command and then DISPLAY STATUS TO PRINT.
Also See	LIST STATUS

Display Structure

Syntax DISPLAY STRUCTURE [TO PRINT]

Purpose The DISPLAY STRUCTURE command shows the names of all the fields in the currently selected database file and their data types and widths. In addition, it tells how many records there are in the file and when it was last updated.

Example This command is simple and elegant because it quickly shows the structure and status of any single database file. The TO PRINT option is particularly useful if you want to document the files you've created:

DISPLAY STATUS TO PRINT

Also See LIST STRUCTURE, MODIFY STRUCTURE, and SET FIELDS TO

Do

Syntax	DO <filename> [WITH <parmlist>]
Purpose	The DO command initiates a program command file (.prg) or a procedure.
Example	Once started by the DO command, a program or procedure will run until it is finished or it encounters a RETURN, CANCEL, or QUIT command. When a program or procedure is finished, it returns to where you were before it ran, which means that one program can call another. When that happens, the called program runs until it is done, then it quits, returning control to the program which called it.
	DO myprog
	The WITH <parmlist> option DO can pass information to the program you're calling in the form of variables or literal values. Take a look at the PARAMETERS entry in this chapter for a fuller explanation of parameter passing.
Note	Don't run programs unless you know what they will do to your data and your disk. If you didn't write them, read them before using them.
	It is a good idea to use only one or a very few programs to call all other programs in an application, and to explicitly use the RETURN command in command files at any point where a program should stop running. These habits will keep programs from nesting. Nesting occurs when one program calls another (1 level of nesting), then that program calls another (2 levels of nesting), then that program calls the first program (3 levels of nesting), and so on. When you chain more than 24 programs without returning to a main program or launching point, the allowed nesting level will be exceeded, causing FoxBASE to issue an error message and halt.
	It's not a good idea for a program to call a program that called it, or for it to call a parent of the program that called it. FoxBASE naturally keeps track of every program it runs and the order it runs it in, and it is always prepared to RETURN to the calling program with a simple RETURN command. You should take advantage of that and set up a main program that calls others in order to accomplish tasks. Several levels of nesting are normal, but don't let programs stray. Make them return to a main or subordinate menu before launching another programmed task.

Syntax Options 255

Tips	SUSPEND will temporarily stop a program from running until you enter a RESUME command.
Also See	SET PROCEDURE TO, CANCEL, RETURN, SUSPEND, and RESUME

Do Case...Otherwise...Endcase

Syntax
```
DO CASE
CASE <exprL1>
  <statements>
CASE <exprL2>
  <statements>
  ...
CASE <exprLn>
  <statements>
[OTHERWISE
  <statements>]
ENDCASE
```

Purpose DO CASE...OTHERWISE ENDCASE is more than a command, it's a programming construct as well, which means it acts like an intersection traffic light, controlling the way that the programs themselves will work. Like IF...ENDIF, DO CASE...OTHERWISE ENDCASE evaluates logical conditions so that you can conditionally execute a set of commands based on any condition in the CASE structure that tests true. The practical difference between DO CASE and IF is that DO CASE is designed to evaluate many conditions, where IF can evaluate only one. DO CASE...OTHERWISE ENDCASE goes from the top of its structure to the bottom, checking to see if each subsequent CASE expression is true or false. If it finds one that's true, the command/statements between that CASE expression and the next CASE expression will be executed, the remaining CASEs will be skipped and the DO CASE construct will be exited, returning control to the program line that immediately follows ENDCASE. Only one (the first true) set of CASE statements will be executed if more than one is true. IF none of the CASE conditions is true and an OTHERWISE statement exists, the statements following OTHERWISE will be executed before exiting.

Example The most common use of CASE...ENDCASE is to branch to different programs based on input from users, whether it be from a menu choice or another form of GET variable. Figure 6-3 in Chapter 6 shows how this command works.

Note GETs aren't accurately updated until the READ that activates them is terminated, and some GET options, some popup buttons and some checkboxes, for example, don't terminate a READ. You can't check the value of a GET variable within a CASE...ENDCASE until the READ on it has been terminated. The @...GET command

Syntax Options

for buttons and checkboxes has options for controlling whether or not the buttons terminate a READ. Also, the SET CONFIRM command can cause a deliberate READ termination, allowing a program to continue past an open READ with updated GET-variable values.

Tips Use IF...ENDIF for simple branching, DO CASE...OTHERWISE ENDCASE for more complex branching.

Also See IF...ENDIF

Do While...Enddo

Syntax
DO WHILE <exprL>
<statements>
[LOOP]
<statements>]
[EXIT]
ENDDO

Purpose The DO WHILE command is one of the most powerful commands in FoxBASE, although it's actually a construct more than a command. Because it is an incomplete command by itself, an ENDDO command is required to complete it. DO WHILE...ENDDO constructs are often called loops, because they continue to run from top to bottom through the <statements>, then they loop quickly from the bottom to the top again so that the <statements> can be executed again until <exprL> becomes false. ENDDO signals to FoxBASE that it has reached an end, and that all <statements> should be executed again, but only if <exprL> is still true. The <statements> can be any legal commands or expressions, as long as they combine to return one logical value, either true or false. DO WHILEs can be nested, which means that one DO WHILE can be contained inside another.

LOOP tells FoxBASE to stop executing <statements> and to begin executing <statements> immediately following DO WHILE (at the top of the construct) again.

DO WHILE...ENDDO does what its name implies. It continues doing, over and over, until <exprL> is no longer true.

Example DO WHILE...ENDDO is used whenever an action must be taken over and over again. Two simple examples are given in Fig. 6-2 in Chapter 6. Counter.prg shows how a counting loop is used to place a fixed number of asterisks on the screen, and Traverse.prg shows how a DO WHILE loop can be used to traverse a database file one record at a time, checking for conditions and executing statements at each record until the end of file, EOF( ), is reached.

Note This command/construct is used differently by different programmers, so it's hard to say what common dangers there are or what mistakes users can make using it. The possibilities for success and for problems are too many. Most programmers learn by experimenting. Having said that, take note that <exprL> must eventually become false. Otherwise, the loop will continue endlessly requiring you to press {COMMAND}{PERIOD} or {ESCAPE} to

Syntax Options 259

stop it. You'll have little trouble controlling the "looping" effect if you pay attention to the fact that the condition, <exprL>, is evaluated immediately after the ENDDO and before <statements>.

Tips

Place a DO CASE...ENDCASE construct inside of a DO WHILE...ENDDO to create a menu system. For more about this see the discussion of menus in Chapter 7. The ability of FoxBASE to perform repetitive tasks is one of the features that makes it powerful. Experiment with this command by building on the ideas shown in Fig. 6-2.

Edit

| 🍎 | File | Edit | Database | Record | Program | Text | Window |

Change...

Syntax   EDIT [<scope>]
             [FIELDS <list>]
             [FOR <exprL>]
             [WHILE <exprL>]

Purpose   The EDIT command opens up the same full-screen data editor that CHANGE does, allowing you to edit existing records. This is one of those commands that has become nearly useless over time in the development of the "dBase" language standard.

Example   Use EDIT just like you would the CHANGE command.

Also See   CHANGE, BROWSE, and APPEND

Syntax Options 261

Eject

Syntax EJECT

Purpose The EJECT command causes a page to be ejected from whatever printer you have selected with the chooser. Technically speaking, it sends a form-feed command CHR(12) directly to the printer. Because the PROW( ) and PCOL( ) functions return the current printer row and column, they too are affected by EJECT in that their values are automatically reset to 0 to indicate that the printing is ready to begin, again at the top left corner of a new page—row 0 and column 0. If you are sending output to an alternate file (see the SET ALTERNATE entry later in this chapter), EJECT will put a form-feed command into the designated output file instead of sending it to a printer.

Example EJECT has limited usefulness except in programs that write custom reports. Designed as a command for direct row-by-row control of printing to dumb printers, EJECT provides a high degree of control to programmers. Refer to the SET PRINT commands for more information about controlling programmed print jobs.

Note When writing to Laserwriters on AppleTalk networks, the EJECT command ignores the status of SET PRINT ON/OFF, initiating a request to the Laserwriter no matter what. You can prevent this otherwise harmless paper-waster by using EJECT only when SET PRINT is ON.

Tips REPORT FORM and LABEL FORM commands can automatically eject pages (or labels) both before and after the body of the print job is printed, so EJECTs are not needed when printing labels or reports. This ensures that all printed material is ejected far enough from the bowels of a printing device that you can get it, tear it off, and so on. If you use the REPORT or LABEL FORM commands with the NOEJECT option, an automatic EJECT will not occur, which can save paper when several reports are printed one after another.

Also See SET PRINTER, SET DEVICE TO, REPORT FORM, and LABEL FORM

Erase

Syntax ERASE <filename>

Purpose The ERASE command can permanently remove any file from any disk mounted to your Macintosh, accomplishing the same thing as DELETE FILE or as trashing a file from the Macintosh desktop.

Example Look at Fig. 8-10. ERASE works identically except that you should replace the DELETE FILE command with the ERASE command. The <filename> works the same. Why there are two commands that do exactly the same thing is puzzling, except that it reflects the strange, somewhat erratic, way the dBase language standard has grown. I suspect that the two commands exist to please users who are comfortable with DOS commands and so that FoxBASE+/Mac will be compatible with different dBase dialects.

Note The <filename> you are erasing cannot currently be in use or an error will occur. Also, there is no recovery for an erased file, so be careful.

Tips There are easier ways to permanently erase files on a Macintosh, such as using the File/Delete File menu option, than to type file names in letter for letter. The other is to wait until you are out of FoxBASE, then trash the file at the desktop. This command is useful when you need to make room while you're in FoxBASE or when a program you've created uses temporary files that are no longer needed after your program quits.

Also See DELETE FILE

Exit

Syntax

```
DO WHILE
    <statements>
[EXIT]
    <statements>
ENDDO
```

Purpose

The EXIT command causes a DO WHILE...ENDDO to be terminated, then it passes control of the program to the first command line after ENDDO. EXIT works only inside DO WHILE... ENDDO constructs.

Example

EXIT is a quick way to trap changes or problems inside a DO WHILE...ENDDO loop and exit from it.

EXIT can occur anywhere between a DO WHILE and an ENDDO regardless of how many <statements> are above or below it. When EXIT is encountered, it always ends the DO WHILE.

```
USE members
DO WHILE membership = "Active"
    IF contributions > 200
        DISPLAY lastname
    ENDIF
    SKIP 1
    IF contributions = 0
        EXIT
    ENDIF
ENDDO
```

In this example, DISPLAY shows the names of members who have contributed more than $200, and SKIP 1 moves the record pointer to the next record for consideration. EXIT causes the whole process to end when a record is encountered that has no recorded contributions.

Note

While EXIT is useful, it is better, whenever possible, to put all of the breakout conditions for a DO WHILE...ENDDO loop into the condition itself, like this.

```
USE members
DO WHILE membership = "Active" .AND. .NOT. contributions = 0
    IF contributions > 200
        DISPLAY lastname
    ENDIF
    SKIP 1
ENDDO
```

This makes programs easier to read and understand because the decision points are where people reading your program are more likely to see them. Programs with lots of EXITs are unpredictable and harder to maintain simply because they're harder to follow. Crisp, modular programs are worth the effort, so use EXIT sparingly.

Also See   LOOP

Find

Syntax | FIND <string> | <n>

Purpose | The FIND command was designed for dBase II, and then only for interactive use. As such, it's nearly useless in FoxBASE+/Mac.

Example | FIND locates records very quickly by searching for the first occurrence of <string> or <n> in an active index, but it's nearly the same thing as SEEK, which is more predictable to use. Unlike the SEEK command, quotation marks are not required when you're looking for character strings because FIND was not designed for programming users. Number values entered to locate amounts in numeric fields must be accurate for all decimal places or the search will fail. FIND Thom will find Thom, Thomas, and Thompson.

Also See | SEEK and LOCATE

Flush

Syntax FLUSH

Purpose The FLUSH command empties any memory buffer space that contains database information by forcing a write to the disk.

Example Use FLUSH in programs routinely following any major file operation to guarantee that all changes to data have been committed to disk. Automatic buffer flushing occurs whenever a READ command is encountered, a file is closed, or all programs are terminated, returning a user to the interactive mode.

```
USE customers
CHANGE
FLUSH
```

Also See CLOSE, CLOSE DATABASES, CLOSE ALL, CLEAR ALL, and USE

Gather

Syntax   GATHER FROM <arrayname>
                [FIELDS <fieldlist>]

Purpose   The GATHER command automatically replaces database field contents for the currently selected database file with the contents of an array when a suitable array had previously been made using the SCATTER command. PICTURE and MEMO data fields are not included in the operations of SCATTER and GATHER.

Example   There can be many reasons to use a set of array cells or memory variables containing the contents of a database record. A common use is in networking, where editing memory variables can prevent users from "sitting on" a locked record with a GET...READ, thereby preventing access to other users.

If you want to edit the fields of a database file without holding the record at all, use the SCATTER command to create an array containing the contents of each database field. Suppose a customer file had a customer number in the first field, their name in the second, their balance due in the third, and their credit limit in the fourth, and you wanted to allow editing of that information without disturbing other network users working in the same file. Do this.

```
USE customer INDEX custname
SEEK "Wilson"
IF FOUND( )
    STORE RECNO( ) TO currec
    SCATTER TO myarray
    SCATTER TO myarraychk
ELSE
    ALERT NOTE 1 "Customer Wilson not found."
ENDIF
```

These arrays I created with SCATTER contain one cell for each field in the file or if specified, in the fieldlist. Notice that I made two arrays? One is to edit; the other is a check for my user's edits and to ensure that no one changed the record in the time my user had it on screen.

After the array has been created, you can let the user edit customer balance and limit cells in the array for as long as they like, because the record hasn't been locked, which would prevent access to other network users, for example:

```
@ 2,2 SAY myarray(1)     && custnumber
@ 2,3 SAY myarray(2)     && custname
@ 2,4 GET myarray(3)     && custbaldue
@ 2,5 GET myarray(4)     && custlimit
READ
```

After the user has edited the customer's balance due and credit limit, do this:

```
GOTO currec
gotrec = RLOCK( )
IF gotrec
    IF myarraychk(3) = custbaldue .AND. myarraychk(4) = custlimit
        GATHER FROM myarray
    ELSE
        ALERT STOP 1 "Data changed by another. Try again."
    ENDIF
ELSE
    ALERT STOP 1 "Sorry, another user has record."
ENDIF
UNLOCK
```

Notice that I didn't let the GATHER command work to change data until checking that the original record hasn't changed. I compared it with the values in the myarraychk array, which was not edited, and only if they didn't change since I first took a copy was the GATHER operation performed.

Also See   DIMENSION, SCATTER, and REPLACE

Getexpr

Syntax   GETEXPR [<exprC1>] TO <memvar>
[TYPE <exprC2>[;<exprC3>]]
[DEFAULT <exprC4>]

Purpose   The GETEXPR command opens the standard FoxBASE expression building dialog shown in Fig. 8-17, initializes memory variable <memvar> to contain the resulting expression, and then places the result into <memvar>. If the user presses cancel, an empty character variable will result.

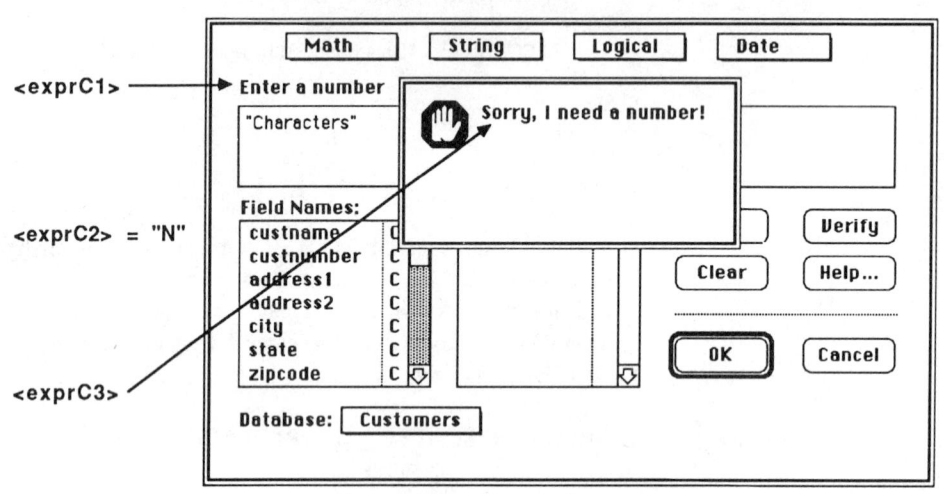

Fig. 8-17. Getting user-entered expressions for use in a program.

Example   Use GETEXPR when you need to ask a user for information, such as an index expression, an index value to SEEK, a value to LOCATE, and so on. The optional string <exprC1> provides the user with a simple prompt above the entry box, while <exprC2> tells FoxBASE what kind of expression, in data type, you want returned. <exprC3> is an optional, and very helpful, error string that appears if the user enters an error. The DEFAULT <exprC4> option will place an expression into the dialog's entry box for the user to change and/or approve. This command will produce the dialog shown in Fig. 8-16.

GETEXPR "Enter a number" TO myvar TYPE "N;Sorry, I need a number!"

Notice that I entered characters into the expression builder's box after indicating in the command, via <exprC2>, that only a numeric expression was valid. That's why the alert appeared bearing a preprogrammed error message (<exprC3>). If I'd entered a number as requested, the error wouldn't appear.

Go/Goto

Syntax GO <exprN> | TOP | BOTTOM
or
GOTO <exprN> | TOP | BOTTOM

Purpose The GOTO TOP or GOTO BOTTOM commands move the record pointer to the first or the last logical record in a database file. If SET DELETED is ON, it will move to the first or last nondeleted record, respectively. If, however, SET DELETED is OFF, the GOTO TOP or GOTO BOTTOM commands send the record pointer to the first or last logical record in the file, regardless of its DELETED( ) status. GOTO TOP and GOTO BOTTOM respect indexes, so the file's TOP might not be record 1 and the file's bottom might not be the last physical record when an index is active.

The GOTO <exprN> moves the record pointer to any physical record in the file, regardless of its DELETED( ) status or index order. If you try to go to a record that is not in the physical file, an error results.

Also See RECNO( )

Help

Syntax   HELP [<topic>]

Purpose   The HELP command opens the FoxBASE help window and allows you or a user to select a topic. All of the topics listed in the "topic" field of the current help file are available for selection. If the <topic> is entered and located, its "details" field will automatically be presented.

Example   Look at the discussion on *Customizing Help* in Chapter 7 for information about how to use help files in custom applications. These commands will open a help text window:

   HELP SET
   HELP BROWSE
   HELP CHANGE

Also See   SET TOPIC TO

If...Else...Endif

Syntax

```
IF <exprL>
    <statements>
[[ELSE]
    <statements>]
ENDIF
```

Purpose

The IF command is a decision-making construct that's capable of evaluating any logical expression and branching depending on the outcome. If the logical expression <exprL> tests true, the first set of <statements> is executed. If an ELSE clause is provided and <exprL> returns false, the second set of <statements> will execute. ENDIF merely marks the construct's end.

Example

Use IF...ENDIF anytime a simple programmed decision must be made. Use CASE...ENDCASE if more than one option must be available for selection, but only one can be selected.

```
X = 1
IF X = 1
    ? "X does equal 1, so this result will show"
ENDIF
IF X = 2
    ? "X equals 1, so this result won't show"
ENDIF
IF X = 2
    ? "X equals 1, so this result won't show"
ELSE
    ? "X is other than 2, so this result will show"
ENDIF
```

Note

Be careful to avoid nesting of IFs inside of one another beyond 13 or 14 layers deep, and make sure that each IF has a matching ENDIF.

Also See

DO CASE...OTHERWISE...ENDCASE

Index

File Edit Database Record Program Text Window
Setup... ⌘T

Syntax INDEX ON <expr> TO <filename>
[FOR <exprL>]
[UNIQUE]

Purpose The INDEX command creates a file that's used to make a database file appear, in all respects, as though it were physically in a well-defined order. Index files can be ordered by any valid expression based on the record contents, as long as the expression returns a value of fixed length from one record to the next.

Example See the *Making Indexes* discussion in Chapter 5 for information about how to make and maintain indexes.

Also See SET ORDER TO, SET DELETED, SET UNIQUE, SET FILTER, and SORT

Input

Syntax INPUT [< exprC >] TO < memvar >

Purpose The INPUT command is one of those commands that most users would do better without, because it was created for use in dBase II on CPM computers and has been functionally replaced by the @ GET...READ. It takes input from the keyboard and stores it in < memvar >, which is initialized and typed according to the data entered. If a user enters no data, it persists in asking for a response.

Example Characters must be entered with quote marks around them, and numbers can be entered directly. Dates must be entered using the CTOD( ) function, and logical values must be entered in their formal (.T.) and (.F.) form.

INPUT "Enter something " TO myvar

Note This command is useful only when the user understands FoxBASE data types and how to enter them properly. The GETEXPR command is preferred because it can trap errors and better prompt users for a proper response.

Also See ACCEPT, WAIT, INKEY( ), READKEY( ), READ, WAIT, and @ SAY...GET

Insert

Syntax INSERT
[BEFORE]
[BLANK]

Purpose The INSERT command makes a new record after the current record in the currently selected database file. If you use the BEFORE option, the new record is inserted before the current record. If you use the BLANK option, the record is inserted and the record pointer is positioned on it, but nothing else happens. If, however, you don't specify the BLANK option, an entry screen appears for keyboard data entry.

Note Because indexes are so good at putting files into an apparent order, and because INSERT physically rearranges a file, it's better to use APPEND for all but the most rare occasions. Don't use INSERT in large files because every record in the file that's after the inserted record will have to be rewritten on disk. That operation can take a long time! Let APPEND and open index files take care of order for you.

Also See APPEND BLANK, EDIT, CHANGE, SET CARRY, and SET FORMAT

Join

Syntax
JOIN WITH <alias>
TO <filename>
FOR <exprL>
[FIELDS <list>]

Purpose
The JOIN command makes a new database file by combining two files based on a logical condition. The product of the JOIN command is the result of the two files. All fields from both files are placed in the new file unless the FIELDS <fieldlist> option limits them by name.

Example
SELECT A
USE customers
SELECT B
USE bills
JOIN WITH A TO allbills FOR custnum = customers->custnum

Note
Think about this command's results before using it! It makes a file containing every occurrence of a value in one file for every occurrence of the value in another. That produces a product, which is more like multiplication than addition. Be careful and think it out first. A genuine need for this command is rare.

Also See
SET RELATION

Keyboard

Syntax KEYBOARD <exprC>

Purpose The KEYBOARD command places characters in the keyboard buffer so that the effect is exactly as though they were entered by hand. The <exprC> can be a character string, a number, a date, a logical value, or even a nonprintable control character supplied via the CHR( ) function.

Example If you combine several items at once for stuffing into the keyboard buffer, place them inside of parentheses so that they will be evaluated at once, otherwise an error will result. Try these in the command window:

```
KEYBOARD ("? 'Hi there'")
KEYBOARD ("? 'Hi there'" + chr(13))
```

CHR(13) is the ASCII value of a carriage return.

Tips The KEYBOARD command has amazing power to automate actions during program execution. You can use it to make self-running demos, enter carriage returns, to move the cursor into a specific GET during screen entry, and more, all without touching the keyboard.

Also See SET TYPEAHEAD, CLEAR TYPEAHEAD, CHR( ), and INKEY( )

Label Form

Syntax
LABEL FORM <filename>
[<scope>]
[SAMPLE]
[WHILE <exprL>]
[FOR <exprL>]
[TO PRINT [PROMPT]]
[TO FILE <filename>]
[ENVIRONMENT]

Purpose
The LABEL FORM command invokes a preexisting label file (.lbl), or Report Form file in version 2.x (.frx) that's been created in FoxReport to display or print. Note that in version 1.x, .frx files were .frm files. They are now combined in version 2.x and only .frx file extensions are used. If you don't specify the output target, labels are displayed to the screen, but by using the PRINT or FILE options, you can send output to the printer or to a file. In a program, you must use the PROMPT option to get the Macintosh print dialog before printing begins; interactively, the print dialog always appears. The ENVIRONMENT option tells FoxBASE to look for a view (.vue) file bearing the same name as the report and open it so that you don't have to remember what files, indexes, and so on to open just so that the report will print. The FOR and WHILE clauses work to filter the data being printed.

Example
See the discussion in Chapter 3 about the Database/Report menu for practical information about how this command is used. In a program, the command can follow one of these examples:

LABEL FORM mylabel TO PRINT PROMPT ENVIRONMENT
LABEL FORM mylabel TO FILE <myfile>
LABEL FORM mylabel SAMPLE TO PRINT PROMPT

The SAMPLE option tells FoxBASE to print a few labels that are suitable for alignment of the printer and paper before asking if you want to continue printing the real thing.

Also See
CREATE LABEL and MODIFY LABEL

List

Syntax LIST [<scope>]
[[FIELDS] <exprlist>] [FOR <exprL>]
[WHILE <exprL>] [OFF] [TO PRINT]

Purpose The LIST command shows the contents of a database on the screen without pausing. Like DISPLAY, LIST can calculate numbers from number data in database fields, and it can show the contents of picture and memo fields. In addition to screen displays, LIST can print if you use the TO PRINT option.

Example LIST works just like the DISPLAY command. The difference is that DISPLAY pauses with each full screen of data, while LIST continues to list data until you press escape or the list is done. For this reason, LIST is a much better command for printing.

Also See DISPLAY and SET HEADING

List Files

Syntax
: LIST FILES
  [ON <drive|folder>]
  [LIKE <skeleton>]
  [TO PRINT]

Purpose
: The LIST FILES command works just like DISPLAY FILES does except that LIST does not pause with each full screen of data. For this reason, LIST FILES is a much better command for printing.

Also See
: DIRECTORY and DISPLAY FILES

List Memory

Syntax LIST MEMORY [TO PRINT]

Purpose The LIST MEMORY command works just like the DISPLAY MEMORY command except that it does not pause with each full screen of data. For this reason, LIST MEMORY is much better for printing memory variable contents.

Also See DISPLAY MEMORY, RELEASE, STORE, and CLEAR MEMORY

List Status

Syntax   LIST STATUS [TO PRINT]

Purpose   The LIST STATUS command works just like the DISPLAY STATUS command except that it does not pause with each full screen of data. For this reason LIST STATUS is a much better command to use for printing.

Also See   DISPLAY STATUS

List Structure

Syntax	LIST STRUCTURE [TO PRINT]
Purpose	The LIST STRUCTURE command works just like the DISPLAY STRUCTURE command except it does not pause with each full screen of data. For this reason LIST STRUCTURE is a much better command to use for printing.
Also See	DISPLAY STRUCTURE, MODIFY STRUCTURE, and SET FIELDS TO

Locate

Menu: File | Edit | Database | Record | Program | Text | Window
Record → Locate... ⌘L

Syntax

LOCATE [<scope>]
[FOR <exprL>]
[WHILE <exprL>]
[commands]
[CONTINUE]

Purpose

The LOCATE command attempts to find the first record in the currently selected database file that meets the condition specified in <exprL>.

Example

Use LOCATE and the CONTINUE command together to search a whole file, top to bottom, for every occurrence of a condition. Look at Fig. 5-11 in Chapter 5 for a visual description of this command's function.

```
LOCATE FOR lname = "Smith"
DO WHILE .NOT. EOF( )
    ? lname,address,city,state,zip
    CONTINUE
ENDDO
```

If the sought value is found, the record pointer will stop at the record matching the search condition in <exprL>, the EOF( ) function will return (.F.) and the FOUND( ) function will return (.T.).

Use the REST option if you want the LOCATE to begin at the current pointer position and stop when the condition is satisfied or the end of file is reached.

Use the ALL option if you want the LOCATE to begin at the current pointer position and continue through the top of file until the condition is satisfied or a match is not found.

Note

LOCATE/CONTINUE works without an index, so it's slower than performing a SEEK with an index. For large database files the sequential LOCATE and CONTINUE method for retrieval might be too slow.

Tips

LOCATE/CONTINUE can be used any time because no index is necessary, and it will accept complex search conditions based on any information in the file.

Also See

CONTINUE, FIND, SEEK, and FOUND( )

Menu

There are several required commands that work together to make every pull-down menubar. The individual menu commands listed and described below are part of a system. The steps for making menus include defining the menubar and its options, and naming the program, which acts on choices made by users. A menu-handling program takes action based on what menu options are selected.

Syntax

The commands explained below make pull-down menus using version 2.x of FoxBASE+/Mac. They automatically replace the normal FoxBASE menubar options to the right of the edit menu that appear when FoxBASE is started up. Chapter 7 includes a discussion of menu-making commands that work in version 1.x and version 2.x. The commands here are preferred if your programs will always be run in version 2.x, because the commands are simpler, and they don't require an array definition.

Technical note: MENU(0|1) is a function and not a command. Nevertheless, it is discussed here because it is only meaningful when used with menu-making commands.

Menu Making Steps

1. Define the menubar:

   MENU BAR [<expC>]

The easiest way to define a menubar is to simply list the options in a line, like this:

MENUBAR "Item1;Item2;Item3"

The text, "Item1;Item2. . .," creates the menu selections users will see at the top of their screen. The first item in the list will appear immediately to the right of the Edit menu, the second next to it, and so on. Each menu has a number for use with the MENU( ) function in order for your program to determine which one a user selected.

The first menu option to the right of the Edit menu is menu 1, the one to its right, menu 2, and so on. The Edit menu is menu 0, the File menu is menu -1, and the Apple menu is menu -2.

2. Define menubar options

   MENU <expN1>,<expC>[,<expN2>]

The easiest way to define a menubar option is to simply identify the menu you want to define and list the options in a line, like this:

MENU 1,"Option1;Option2;Option3;Option4"

This sets up four menu options under menu 1. Now, according to the MENUBAR command just above, these options would appear under a top menubar named "Item1."

Each menubar item should have a numbered MENU command to create the options that will appear below it when the menu is selected. Let's complete the example with these commands:

MENU 2,"Option1;Option2"
MENU 3,"Option1;Option2;Option3"

Now, each of our three MENUBAR items has a list of options for users to select. The first menu to the right of the Edit menu has four options, MENUBAR item 2 has two options, and MENUBAR item 3 has three options.

You cannot change the names of the Apple, File, or Edit menus, but you can install some of your own options and affect what appears below them. To replace the File menu options with your own, put this command line somewhere after the MENUBAR command:

MENU −1,"Quit"

A MENU 1 list like this will put two options under the File menu:

MENU −1,"System Maintenance;Quit/Q"

Notice the "/Q"? It makes a command key shortcut for the Quit menu option. To use it, a user can simply press COMMAND-Q. Keyboard shortcuts can be made with almost any character in a similar fashion.

Edit menu options cannot be replaced, but the options in it that are not useful except in text editing situations can be turned off with a command like this:

MENU 0, ""

You can make a whole new menu option to replace the standard Apple/About option by adding a command line like this one:

MENU −2, "About MyProgram"

Syntax Options 287

Hierarchical submenu options automatically appear next to any menu option that has been designated as hierarchical whenever the mouse is positioned on it. An arrow appears on hierarchical menu options to indicate that there are submenus attached.

To make hierarchical menus, just add one command for each hierarchical menu option list that will be attached to another menu item. The only difference in the command syntax is that the hierarchical menu commands include a number to indicate what option is to get the hierarchical list. These commands, respectively, make option 2 of MENUBAR item 1, and option 1 of MENUBAR item 2 into hierarchical menus.

```
MENU 1,"Hmenu1;Hmenu2;Hmenu3",2
MENU 2,"Hmenu1;Hmenu2",1
```

Now, if you've followed this discussion carefully, you'll notice that there are now two commands that say "MENU 1" and two commands that say "MENU 2". This is because the second "MENU" commands have a number <exprN2> that tells FoxBASE that they aren't for main menu options, but rather, to install submenus under MENU 1 and MENU 2.

Important note: The order of the hierarchical MENU commands is very important. You should issue hierarchical MENU commands, for example, immediately after the MENUBAR and MENU commands. Also, be sure to install them in the order of their attachment to the main menus as shown above. If you do, this example menu setup will cause the MENU(0) function to return a hit on the first and second hierarchical menu as 4 and 5, respectively. It is intended that MENU(0) return hierarchical menu hits as main menu numbers beginning with the first number following the number of installed menubar items. When I make complex menu systems I always test the structure with MENU(0) and MENU(1) functions to determine exactly what's being returned when options are hit.

3. Name the menu-handling program

```
ON MENU [<commands>]
MENU(0|1)
```

The ON MENU command is usually used just before an endless DO...ENDDO loop containing a READ to tell FoxBASE what to do when any menu hit occurs. Menu selections can happen at any time. For that reason alone an ON command is needed, because it is an event trap capable of responding whenever it's needed.

Note: FoxBASE+/Mac allows menu hits and menu handling whenever there's a READ, so you might want to disable the menus during full screen READs, or limit the effect of menu selections by installing an ON MENU <command> line with only a few options that are useful during edits. In a few paragraphs I'll describe the method you can use to turn menus off entirely during any program or operation.

Commands inside of angle brackets usually tell FoxBASE to run a program that's been written to handle a menu hit and act upon it. The MENU( ) function takes two forms, MENU(0) and MENU(1). They indicate, respectively, what menuitem was last hit, and what menuoption was last hit. You can use them with the ON MENU command such as the one below, which tells a menu handling program what the user wants:

```
ON MENU DO menuaction WITH MENU(0),MENU(1)
DO WHILE .T.
    READ
ENDDO

PROCEDURE menuaction
PARAMETERS menuitem,menuoption
DO CASE
CASE menuitem = -2
    DO CASE
    CASE menuoption = 1
        <commands> for "About MyProgram"
    ENDCASE
CASE menuitem = -1
    DO CASE
    CASE menuoption = 1
        <commands> for "System Maintenance"
    CASE menuoption = 2
        <commands> to shutdown and "Quit"
    ENDCASE
CASE menuitem = 1
    DO CASE
    CASE menuoption = 1
        <commands>
    CASE menuoption = 2 && to hierarchical menu 4
    CASE menuoption = 3
        <commands>
    CASE menuoption = 4
        <commands>
    ENDCASE
CASE menuitem = 2
    DO CASE
    CASE menuoption = 1 && to hierarchical menu 5
    CASE menuoption = 2
        <commands>
    ENDCASE
```

```
        CASE menuitem = 3
            DO CASE
            CASE menuoption = 1
                <commands>
            CASE menuoption = 2
                <commands>
            CASE menuoption = 3
                <commands>
            ENDCASE
        CASE menuitem = 4 && hierarchical menu attached to menuitem 1, option 2
            DO CASE
            CASE menuoption = 1
                <commands>
            CASE menuoption = 2
                <commands>
            CASE menuoption = 3
                <commands>
            ENDCASE
        CASE menuitem = 5 && hierarchical menu attached to menuitem 2, option 1
            DO CASE
            CASE menuoption = 1
                <commands>
            CASE menuoption = 2
                <commands>
            ENDCASE
    ENDCASE
    RETURN
```

In this example, the user is always returned to the menus, because they're the only thing FoxBASE has to work with inside the endless READ loop.

4. Enable/disable menus and menu options (optional)

   MENU ON <exprN1> [,<exprN2>]
       and
   MENU OFF <exprN1> [,<exprN2>]

These commands turn menu options on and off. <exprN1> is the menuitem in a MENUBAR, and <exprN2> is any option underneath a menuitem. Whenever a menu or its options are disabled, they appear grey and cannot be selected. Active items appear black. This command turns off an entire menuitem and all of its options:

MENU OFF 1

Likewise, this command will turn it back on:

MENU ON 1

There is a very special use for the MENU ON command, which is associated with a "hidden" menu.

MENU ON −3,1

It makes it possible for mouse clicks inside of a screen to be treated like menu hits so that the menu handling program gets called when it occurs. This allows you to make programs with multiple screens that users can select. To determine what screen a user selects when MENU(0) returns −3 and MENU(1) returns 1, use the SYS(1034), SYS(1035), and SYS(1036) functions inside the menu-handling program. The SYS(1034) function returns a number from one to nine that indicates which of the nine possible screens is currently active for output. The SYS(1035) function returns a number that indicates which screen is front-most, and the SYS(1036) function indicates whether or not a screen is anywhere on the desktop. Refer to Chapter 9 for specifics about these functions, and look at the Fox Software sample program shipped with every version 2.x package. It shows you how to use the −3,1 menu to control multiple screens.

Menu Modifying Characters

Use the characters listed below to modify the appearance or behavior of a menu option. Most of the options can be used together, but it's unusual to need more than one or two of them, if any, for a single menu option. Place these options immediately after the descriptive menu option text you want to modify. If there's no text in a menu option, such as when lone icons are desired, use a single space for fill in lieu of descriptive menu option text.

Character	Effect
<character>	Marks options with <character>. Some programmers use a check mark to indicate that a menu option is turned "on," and the absence of a check mark to indicate that it is "off."
<B	Makes menu letters bold.
<I	Makes menu letters italic.
<O	Outlines menu letters.
<U	Underlines menu letters.
<S	Shadows menu letters.
/ <character>	Makes <character> into a keyboard shortcut.
(	Disables a menu option.

(- Makes a visual divider line out of a menu option. Note: (- takes up a menu location and address number that cannot be selected by users or used for another option.

^   Assigns icons to menu options. To use the circumflex, just insert the ^ followed immediately by a number from one to nine. The icon that displays in the menu will have a resource ID number that is equivalent to the number supplied + 256. Make sure that the icon is installed in a resource file that is accessible to FoxBASE when the menu command is encountered or an error will result.

For specific examples demonstrating the use of these menu modifiers, look at the menu exercise in Chapter 7.

Modify [Command]

Syntax MODIFY COMMAND|FILE [<filename>]

Purpose The MODIFY COMMAND opens the text editor for program writing, and MODIFY FILE opens the text editor for simple text editing. It is the equivalent of selecting Program or File from the File/New or File/Open menus. If the <filename> you specify exists, it will be opened, otherwise this command will create it.

Example MODIFY FILE myfile
MODIFY COMMAND myprog

Modify Label

Syntax	MODIFY LABEL [<filename>]
Purpose	The MODIFY LABEL command lets you change a preexisting label form file. In version 2.x, labels are contained in (.frx) files, in version 1.x they are contained in (.lbl) files.
Example	Chapter 11 explains label making and label files. Because version 2.x FoxBASE+/Mac treats reports and labels identically you should take a look there to learn how it's done.
Also See	CREATE LABEL and LABEL FORM

Modify Report

Syntax   MODIFY REPORT [<filename>]

Purpose   The MODIFY REPORT command lets you change a preexisting report form file. In version 2.x reports are contained in (.frx) files, in version 1.x they are contained in (.frm) files.

Example   Chapter 11 explains report making and report files. Take a look there to learn how it's done.

Also See   CREATE REPORT and REPORT FORM

Modify Screen

Syntax	MODIFY SCREEN [<filename>]
Purpose	The MODIFY SCREEN command opens the form editor where you can modify preexisting screen layouts.
Example	For a full description of the layout editor's functions, see the discussion of screen design in Chapter 7.
Also See	CREATE SCREEN

Modify Structure

Syntax	MODIFY STRUCTURE
Purpose	The MODIFY STRUCTURE command allows you to make changes to the currently selected database file by opening a dialog box like the one shown in Fig. 8-9.
Example	To change the current database file, simply select the Database/Setup/Modify menu or the View/Setup/Modify menu, or enter this command: MODIFY STRUCTURE
Also See	CREATE

Note|*|&&

Syntax NOTE [<comments>]
    or
 * [<comments>]
    or
 && [<comments>]

Purpose The NOTE, *, and && commands allow you to enter comments into a program file.

Example The NOTE and * commands work identically to prevent FoxBASE from considering a line in a program file as program material.

NOTE this is not program text. Rather, it is a comment.
* this line, too, would be ignored if found inside a program.

The && command is a bit different. Use it to insert comments on a line that already has a command, like this.

REPLACE lname with m->lname   && this is a comment

On Error

Syntax ON ERROR [<command>]

Purpose The ON ERROR command causes an error-handling program to run whenever a nonfatal error occurs. This is part of FoxBASE's error management facility that programmers can use in their own programs.

Example Take a look at the thorough discussion of error handling in Chapter 10 for information about the use of the ON ERROR command.

Tips The first step to error management is to trap an error, then you handle it. When a program manages errors, users aren't (unnecessarily) inconvenienced, worried, or annoyed. Creating routines to trap and handle errors takes a little effort, but they can be used over and over again, in different applications.

As a programmer, why manage errors? Suppose, for example, that you've written a program that packs a few database files and rebuilds the indexes those files use. No problem. But what if one of the files weren't there when the program was run because someone moved it. To prevent a crash, you can take two approaches.

1. Prevent the error: Use the FILE( ) function to check for the presence of any file before trying to USE it.

2. Trap the error. Error #1 (File does not exist.) will occur if you try to USE a file that's FoxBASE can't find. If you are trapping and handling errors your program can detect the problem and guide the user to a solution without crashing your program.

Also See ERROR( ) and RETRY

On Escape

Syntax ON ESCAPE [<command>]

Purpose The ON ESCAPE command causes a command to execute whenever the Escape key is pressed. When the <command> is done, FoxBASE resumes execution on the line following the one where it was when interrupted. If, however, the <command> was a DO <programname>, which terminated on a RETRY, FoxBASE will resume on the same line where the interruption occurred. If the command ON ESCAPE is issued without a <command>, it will be entirely disabled.

Example It might be a good idea to use the Escape key as a universal way to "back out" of a program or a series of menu choices. Suppose that menu 4 and menu option 6 were the "exit" option. To exit using the Escape key as well as the menu you could program it like this:

ON ESCAPE DO menuaction WITH 4,6

Note ESCAPE must be set ON if you want it to work.

Also See SET ESCAPE

On Key

Syntax   ON KEY [<command>]
              or
              ON KEY = <exprN> [<command>]

Purpose   The ON KEY command causes a command to execute whenever any key is pressed. Since the key pressed leaves its value in the keyboard buffer when pressed, you can test and remove it with the INKEY( ) function.

              The ON KEY = <exprN> causes a command to execute when a specific key is pressed, where <exprN> designates a printable character "hot key" according to its ASCII value (see Appendix A). Nonprintable keys such as Function keys and Command key combinations are valued by adding 256 to their scan code. For a list of scan codes see the entry for the INKEY( ) function in Chapter 9.

              Using either of these ON KEY approaches, when <command> is done, FoxBASE resumes execution on the line following the one where it was when interrupted. If, however, the <command> was a DO <programname> which terminated on a RETRY, FoxBASE will resume on the same line where the interruption occured.

Also See   INKEY( ), READKEY, and SYS(18)

Pack

File Edit Database Record Program Text Window
Pack

Syntax PACK

Purpose The PACK command permanently removes all records from the currently selected database file that are marked for deletion. In addition, currently open indexes are automatically updated during the PACK operation.

Example To remove all members from the file who are more than 30 days delinquent in dues, a club secretary issues these commands:

```
DELETE ALL FOR date-duedate > 30
PACK
```

Note PACKing is permanent. There's simply no way to recover records that have been permanently removed.

Also See DELETE, RECALL, DELETED( ), SET DELETED, and ZAP

Parameters

Syntax	PARAMETERS <parmlist>
Purpose	The PARAMETERS command is used to indicate what local names will be given to variable or constant information being passed into a program or procedure by another.
Example	PARAMETERS <parmlist> is always, of necessity, the first active line of code in any procedure or program that will receive parameter values. Look at the *Parameter Passing* section in Chapter 6 for examples of parameter passing, or take a look at the sample program under "MENU" in this chapter.
Also See	DO, PUBLIC, PRIVATE, SET PROCEDURE TO, and PROCEDURE

Private

Syntax PRIVATE <memvarlist>
 or
 PRIVATE ALL [LIKE|EXCEPT <skeleton>]

Purpose The PRIVATE command allows called programs to secretly use variable names that were created by another program, and more significantly, variables that have already been declared to be PUBLIC.

Private memory variables are hidden from programs other than the one that created them, so that other programs cannot change or use the values they store.

Variables are private by nature, but they are available to programs called by the program that created them. Consequently, variables created by a main program are private but are still available to "lower" programs. Variables that are public are available to any program, regardless of when it is called.

Example See Fig. 6-4 and Fig. 6-5 to get an idea of what PRIVATE does to declare the locality of memory variables and arrays. Figure 6-5 contains an example of the command in use.

Also See PUBLIC and STORE

Procedure

Syntax PROCEDURE <procedurename>

Purpose PROCEDURE is a command that marks off segments in a larger program file for subprograms. Each subprogram or procedure acts just like it is a program file all by itself on a disk, so that it can be called by another program or from the Command window even though it's imbedded inside a larger program.

Example The one important requisite for using procedures is that you tell FoxBASE where they'll be before you call them. If a program consists of a named file on disk, FoxBASE has no trouble finding it. That's not the case when it's inside another program. So use the SET PROCEDURE TO <filename> command before trying to DO a procedure like a program.

Procedures simplify applications because up to 128 of them can be placed inside of one file, thereby reducing the time needed for disk access, not to mention the simple disk housekeeping that's made easier by virtue of the fact that there are fewer files hanging around.

Look at the Subroutines section in Chapter 6 to learn how the PROCEDURE command is used.

Also See SET PROCEDURE TO

Public

Syntax

PUBLIC <memvarlist>
   or
PUBLIC <memvar> (<exprN1> [,<exprN2>])
[,<memvar> (<exprN> [,<exprN>]),...]

Purpose

Memory variables can be a tough subject when you're first learning them—even without the locality issues raised by the PUBLIC and PRIVATE commands. Simply put, memory variables are names that hold values in memory for storage and reference (see STORE).

The PUBLIC command first initializes variables with a logical (.F.). Then they assign a value and a new data type with a STORE command or by the assignment operator =. PUBLIC causes memory variables to be visible and changeable regardless of what program is running. Private variables are removed from memory when the program that created them finishes execution, public variables are not; they must be removed by command (see RELEASE and CLEAR MEMORY). Figure 6-4 shows the effect of program execution on public and private variables.

Public variables are completely blind to the existence and values of private variables, whereas both private variables and public variables are visible to the currently running program unless a private variable has the same name as a public variable. Again, when a name is used by both a private and a public variable, the public variable is not visible.

Example

The PUBLIC and PRIVATE commands can simplify your life by letting you use the same variable names in different programs. In addition, such control keeps FoxBASE from confusing similarly named variables.

PRIVATE does not declare variables like PUBLIC does, it just hides local variables from other programs. So you can use PRIVATE before a DIMENSION command as long as PRIVATE and DIMENSION are not used in the same program which declared an <arrayname> to be public. Arrays are automatically declared private if they are dimensioned in a called program, and the PRIVATE command is not absolutely necessary if there is no public variable with the same name, but it is strongly advised. The PRIVATE command is always required if there is already a public variable with the same name.

Note   Don't use the usual PUBLIC command for array variables. Use the DIMENSION command instead, but replace the word DIMENSION with the word PUBLIC as shown in the syntax example above. This declares and dimensions the array all at once.

Also See   PRIVATE and STORE

Quit

	File	Edit	Database	Record	Program	Text	Window
	Quit ⌘Q						

Syntax   QUIT

Purpose   QUIT closes all files and ends the current FoxBASE Session.

Note   Don't shut your computer off without QUITting! FoxBASE needs to close files for you before it stops running, otherwise data can be lost.

Also See   RETURN, CANCEL, SUSPEND, and RESUME

Read

Syntax READ [SAVE] [OFF]

Purpose The READ command allows you or a user to edit memory variables or database fields that have been placed on the screen by the @...GET command. Typically, READ clears GETs from memory so that they need to be restated in order to become active again. The SAVE option causes GETs to be saved in memory so that only another READ is required to reactivate them. The OFF option prevents the standard box from appearing around GETs when they are being READ.

Example The number of possible GETs that you can maintain and READ at once is determined by the BUCKET option in the configuration file. See the SET BUCKET command for information. See the GET and READ section in Chapter 7 for more information and examples.

Also See @...GET, CLEAR GETS, CLEAR MEMORY, and SET FORMAT TO

Recall

```
  File   Edit   Database   Record   Program   Text   Window
                           Recall...
```

Syntax   RECALL [<scope>]
             [FOR <exprL>]
             [WHILE <exprL>]

Purpose The RECALL command is the inverse of DELETE because it unmarks records that have been marked for deletion.

Example RECALL ALL
             RECALL ALL FOR DELETED( )
             RECALL FOR state = "CO"
             RECALL WHILE custname = "Wilson"

Also See DELETE, DELETED( ), SET DELETED, PACK, and ZAP

Reindex

Syntax REINDEX

Purpose The REINDEX command simply rebuilds all currently open index files in the selected work area.

Example To rebuild an index:

```
USE customers INDEX custname
REINDEX
```

Also See INDEX, SET INDEX TO, SET UNIQUE, and SET ORDER TO

Release

Syntax RELEASE <memvarlist>
  or
  RELEASE ALL [LIKE|EXCEPT <skeleton>]

Purpose The RELEASE command selectively removes memory variables from memory, freeing the space for use by other tasks. RELEASE <memvarlist> lets go of variables named in the list, whereas RELEASE ALL LIKE <skeleton> releases all that match a pattern. RELEASE ALL EXCEPT identifies variables that are to be spared, while releasing all others. You can use the * wildcard for a contiguous string of characters in the LIKE and EXCEPT options.

Also See CLEAR MEMORY, LIST MEMORY, RESTORE FROM, SAVE TO, PUBLIC, and PRIVATE

File	Edit	Database	Record	Program	Text	Window
Rename File...						

Rename

Syntax   RENAME <oldfilename> TO <newfilename>

Purpose   Use the RENAME command to change the name of any file on an attached disk volume. The <oldfilename> and <newfilename> designations can contain full pathlists, including disk/drive and folders.

Example   This command renames a file:

RENAME "MemoToBob" TO "MemoToMary"

See the COPY FILE command for relevant examples that use full pathlists.

Also See   COPY FILE, DIRECTORY, and ERASE

Replace

🍎 File Edit Database Record Program Text Window
                            Replace...

Syntax   REPLACE [<scope>] <field>
                 WITH <expr>
                 [,<field2> WITH <expr2>...]
                 [FOR <exprL>]
                 [WHILE <exprL>]

Purpose   The REPLACE command is a particularly powerful command and a good friend of programers, because it is the most common method used for changing the contents of database fields under control of a program. Simply put, it replaces what's in a named field, or list of fields, with any value that's indicated, whether it be a constant, or the result of a formula expression, or a reference to a variable or other field in the same or another database work area. When used with FOR or WHILE options, REPLACE can make many replacements in a file's records at one time.

Example   Like most commands that work with data, the data type of the field you're replacing must be taken into consideration. For example, you can't replace the contents of a character data field with the result of a numeric formula. Aside from that restriction, there's hardly anything that limits REPLACE's operations.

This command REPLACEs the value in one record, which just happens to be the one where the record pointer is currently located.

REPLACE custname WITH "Edison Lighting"

If the file containing the customer name field were in another work area, you could still replace its contents by using the alias operator like this:

REPLACE customers->custname WITH "Edison Lighting"

To conditionally replace many values at once, consider this command:

REPLACE ALL custzip WITH "12345" FOR custzip = "23456"

Consider the use of REPLACE as a housekeeper,

REPLACE ALL custstate WITH UPPER(custstate)

or as an incrementing device.

314   Syntax Options

REPLACE ALL datedue WITH datedue − 2

Note   It is extremely risky to do global REPLACEs of a key field in a database when the key is part of a currently active index. This is because you cause the index to update every time a field's value is changed, which can be hundreds of times per second! Not only will an index slow things down, but thrashing the record pointer this way can cause file damage in extreme cases and is most certainly going to result in data errors. Turn off indexes when doing a REPLACE ALL or REPLACE WHILE.

Also See   UPDATE

Report Form

	🍎 File Edit **Database** Record Program Text Window
	Report...

Syntax   REPORT [FORM <filename>]
[<scope>]
[FOR <exprL>]
[WHILE <exprL>]
[PLAIN|HEADING <exprC>]
[NOEJECT]
[TO PRINT|TO FILE <filename>]
[PROMPT]
[SUMMARY]

Purpose   The REPORT FORM command invokes display or printing of a preexisting report file (.frx) that's been created in FoxReport. If you don't specify the output target it presents reports to the screen, but using the PRINT or FILE options you can send output to the printer or to a file. In a program the PROMPT option must be used to get the Macintosh print dialog before printing begins; interactively the print dialog always appears. The ENVIRONMENT option tells FoxBASE to look for a view (.vue) file bearing the same name as the report and open it so that you don't have to remember what files, indexes, and so on to open just so that the report will print. FOR and WHILE clauses work to filter the data being printed.

Example   See the discussion in Chapter 3 about the Database/Report menu and look at Fig. 3-27 for practical information about how this command is used. In a program the command can follow one of these examples:

REPORT FORM myreport TO PRINT PROMPT ENVIRONMENT
REPORT FORM myreport TO FILE <myfile>
REPORT FORM myreport SAMPLE TO PRINT PROMPT

Also See   CREATE REPORT and MODIFY REPORT

Syntax Options

Restore From

Syntax   RESTORE FROM <filename> [ADDITIVE]

Purpose   RESTORE FROM is the inverse of SAVE TO. As such, it opens a (.mem) file on disk that contains saved memory variables. If the ADDITIVE optional key word is used, RESTORE FROM adds the memory variables in the disk memory variable save file to those already in memory. Without the ADDITIVE key word, RESTORE FROM removes all current memory variables from memory before it restores to memory those in the file.

If variables are restored under program control, they'll be private to the program that restored them, unless they've been declared to be PUBLIC beforehand and are restored with the ADDITIVE key word. If variables are restored in the interactive mode, they'll be PUBLIC regardless.

Example   Suppose that you stored the last member number your system issued in a memory variable and saved it with the SAVE TO command whenever it was issued and incremented by one. You could use the RESTORE FROM command to collect this number from the disk whenever your system starts up.

```
PUBIC membernum
RESTORE FROM sysvars
<program commands>
SAVE TO sysvars
QUIT
```

Also See   SAVE TO, RELEASE, CLEAR MEMORY, LIST MEMORY, and PRIVATE

Restore Screen

Syntax RESTORE SCREEN [FROM <memvar>]

Purpose The RESTORE SCREEN command is the inverse of SAVE SCREEN. If a SAVE SCREEN command had been issued at any time previously in a session, the RESTORE SCREEN command would replace all of the screen's contents with the image saved. If the SAVE SCREEN TO <memvar> command had been used, RESTORE SCREEN FROM <memvar> would replace the screen's current image with the one saved in that picture memory variable.

Example Both commands, SAVE SCREEN and RESTORE SCREEN, work on the currently active output screen device (1-9). Screens can be RESTORED FROM picture type memory variables as well as from variables created by screen saves. This is because the image type is PICT.

```
SAVE SCREEN TO screenone
<commands that change the screen>
RESTORE SCREEN FROM screenone
```

Note Make sure that color screens are not saved in a memory variable and file, then restored on a black and white monitor. To cause this problem one would have to use the SAVE TO command, the RESTORE FROM <filename> command, then RESTORE SCREEN FROM <memvarname> command.

Tips Use SCREEN SAVING and RESTORATION as a way to quickly rewrite screens that need frequent updating to a constant condition, such as during GET...READs that when there are many SAYs that you'd otherwise have to issue over and over again.

Also See SAVE SCREEN and SCREEN

Resume

Syntax	RESUME
Purpose	The RESUME command works only with SUSPEND. SUSPEND causes a program to stop executing without CANCELing it entirely. SUSPENDed programs can be RESUMEd where they left off using this command. When SUSPENDed programs are RESUMEd, they continue executing on the line following the last line executed before suspension.
Example	While a SUSPEND command can be placed in a program to stop execution at a certain point, both SUSPEND and RESUME are best issued from the program menu or from within the trace window. They are primarily used by programmers to debug programs, because lots of things can be examined at the time a program is suspended—things that reveal what's really going on as the program runs. You can check memory variable values, print a list of memory variable names with their contents, view the position of a record pointer and examine records, and so on, all during SUSPENSION.
Note	Make sure that you don't change variables, database files, work areas, record pointers, or other things that the program expects to find in place when it RESUMEs. An unexpected change that occurs when SUSPENDed can cause an error at best, and can damage data in the worst case.
Tips	SUSPEND and RESUME are buttons in the Trace window. If ECHO is turned on, the Trace window will open, allowing you to see program lines as they run and SUSPEND programs quickly. For programmers these features are handy and, sometimes, indispensable.
Also See	CANCEL, RETURN, SUSPEND, and RETRY

Retry

Syntax RETRY

Purpose The RETRY command, like RETURN, passes control of the currently running program to the one that was last under control. Most often, this is the program that called the currently running program. The difference between RETRY and RETURN is that RETRY causes the line last executed in the calling program to be reexecuted, whereas RETURN continues execution on the line that immediately follows the last one executed.

Example Use the RETRY command in an error-handling routine to RETRY an option that causes an error. If the error cannot be corrected, or the user wants to quit trying, a suitable course of action can then be taken. For more information about error-handling routines, see the *Multiuser Issues* section in Chapter 10.

Also See RETURN, ON ERROR, and ERROR( )

Return

Syntax RETURN [TO MASTER| <expr>]

Purpose The RETURN command is most often used to mark the end of a program or procedure, giving control to the program that called the currently running program. If a running program was called by a user from the Program/Do menu, or from a command in the Command window, RETURN causes the program to terminate and return control to the interactive mode.

RETURN TO MASTER causes the first program in any series to regain control. This is usually a menu program that calls other menus, and so on. The TO MASTER option is not often used by programmers because its behavior is much less predictable than simple RETURNs, and it can make programs harder to analyze.

The <expr> option of RETURN is used only in user-defined functions, or UDFs, to send a value back to the program that called the UDF. For examples see the *Alerts, UDFs, and Validation* section in Chapter 7.

Example The following little program uses RETURN to mark its end. If it were called by another program the RETURN statement would cause the calling program to regain control.

```
* sayhi.prg
* a demonstration program
CLEAR
@ 2,2 SAY "Hi"
RETURN
```

See the *Subroutines* section in Chapter 6 for more information about program design and the usefulness of RETURN.

Also See QUIT

Syntax Options 321

Save Screen

Syntax	SAVE SCREEN [TO <memvar>]
Purpose	The SAVE SCREEN command is the inverse of RESTORE SCREEN. If a SAVE SCREEN command was issued earlier in a session, the RESTORE SCREEN command would replace all of the screen's contents with the image saved. If the SAVE SCREEN TO <memvar> command was used, RESTORE SCREEN FROM <memvar> would replace the screen's current image with the one saved in that picture memory variable.
Example	Both commands, SAVE SCREEN and RESTORE SCREEN, work on the currently active output screen device (1-9). Screens can be RESTORED FROM picture type memory variables as well as from variables created by screen saves.
	For more information see the RESTORE SCREEN command entry in this chapter.
Also See	RESTORE SCREEN, and SCREEN

Save To

Syntax SAVE TO <filename>
[ALL LIKE|EXCEPT <skeleton>]

Purpose The SAVE TO command is the inverse of RESTORE FROM. It creates a (.mem) file on disk that contains saved memory variables. The ALL and EXCEPT options specify what memory variables will be saved.

Example To save all current memory variables issue this command:

SAVE TO memfile

To save only those memory variables that begin with "cust", enter a command that looks like this:

SAVE TO memfile ALL LIKE can*

The * <skeleton> indicates a character string with any values and any length. The ? <skeleton> indicates any values of one character in length for each ? used.

Use the EXCEPT option like the LIKE option when you need to make an exclusive list of variables.

Also See RESTORE FROM, RELEASE, CLEAR MEMORY, and LIST MEMORY

Scatter

Syntax SCATTER [FIELDS <fieldlist>] TO <arrayname>

Purpose The SCATTER command works only with GATHER. It makes an array containing the same number of fields as the currently selected database file (minus memo and picture fields, which it ignores), and it copies the contents of the current record into the array cells. If a FIELDS list is included, SCATTER makes an array containing only the fields listed.

Example Look at the GATHER command entry in this chapter for examples of how SCATTER is used.

Also See GATHER, DIMENSION, and REPLACE

Screen

```
 File   Edit   Database   Record   Program   Text   Window
                                    Screen 1      ⌘1
```

Syntax	SCREEN [<exprN>] [HEADING <exprC>] [TYPE <exprN>] [LOCK] [AT <exprN1>,<exprN2>] [SIZE <exprN>,<exprN> [PIXELS]] [FONT <exprC>,<exprN>] [COLOR <standard>,<enhanced>] [OFF] [TOP] [DELETE]
Purpose	The SCREEN command is used to open, size, control, and modify the appearance and behavior of FoxBASE+/Mac's nine programmable screens. The screens are FoxBASE's console output devices, and as such, only one can be truly active at any given moment. They act like normal Macintosh screens in that the one which is selected is the current output device for display, and so on, and the programmer has a high degree of control over what happens to screens.
Example	SCREEN 1

makes screen 1 the active output device. The last used SCREEN command, regardless of what options are used with it, determines which one is active. If you're in the interactive mode, the specified screen will also be displayed, unless the OFF option is used to hide it.

A screen's number (one to nine) will be its title if you don't specify another title, like this:

SCREEN 1 HEADING "My screen title"

You can use almost any of the SCREEN command options together, as in the following command, which prevents a user from closing it.

SCREEN 1 HEADING "My screen title" LOCK

The TYPE option allows you to select a screen type. Some screens types have no close box, and some have no resize box. Look at Fig. 6-10 in Chapter 6 to see what types of screens you can use. Type eight is the standard default output screen TYPE that appears if no other one is explicitly specified.

Syntax Options

SCREEN 1 HEADING "My screen title" TYPE 4

The AT option allows you to place a screen anywhere on the computer monitor by selecting the vertical pixel row, from the top, as <exprN1> and the horizontal pixel column, from the left, as <exprN2> where the screen's top-left corner will appear. To determine a screen's location and size, use AT and SIZE together like this:

SCREEN 1 TYPE 4 AT 40,25 SIZE 100,200 PIXELS

Note that the AT command is always specified in terms of pixels, whereas the SIZE clause is in terms of character rows and columns (using the current or last used screen font for measure) unless the PIXELS option is included. Like AT, SIZE arguments <exprN1> and <exprN2> are specified as vertical rows and horizontal columns, respectively. If you enter the AT command like this,

SCREEN 1 AT 0,0

it will automatically center itself on the computer monitor, regardless of what kind it is, Mac II, SE, Plus, and so on.

Use the FONT option to declare what default font will be used in all screen output. The default font is used whenever a ? or ?? command is used, or whenever an @ SAY or @ GET command is used without a FONT clause of its own. Using a FONT clause in @ SAY and @ GET commands does not change the screen's default font, it only temporarily overrides it for that one command.

SCREEN 1 HEADING "My screen title" FONT "Geneva",9

The COLOR option sets a default output display attribute to override the black on white that is standard on Macintosh monitors. You must, of course, have a color monitor to see the results. If a color setting is made and a black and white monitor is in use, FoxBASE will do its best while mapping the color attributes to black or white. Consider this command syntax:

SCREEN 1 COLOR <standard>,<enhanced>]

The <standard> color setting determines what colors will be used for all normal screen displays, and the <enhanced> setting determines what colors will be used inside of programmed data entry fields when SET INTENSITY is ON. If SET INTENSITY is OFF, the <standard> colors are used inside of programmed data entry fields.

For black text on a white background in normal displays, and for blue letters inside of a yellow data entry background enter this command:

SCREEN 1 COLOR "N/W","B/RG+"

For red text on a white background in normal displays enter this command:

SCREEN 1 COLOR "R/N"

The available color settings are:

White	W	Light Grey	W+
Black	N	Grey	N+
Red	R	Light Red	R+
Green	G	Light Green	G+
Blue	B	Light Blue	B+
Brown	RG	Yellow	RG+
Magenta	RB	Light Magenta	RB+
Cyan	GB	Light Cyan	GB+

Use the OFF option to remove a screen from view:

SCREEN 1 OFF

Note that the OFF option does not clear the screen or prevent it from being the active output device! OFF merely hides a screen. In fact, you can make a screen invisible and still "paint" on it, and use the TOP option at a later time to make what was "painted" visible.

SCREEN 1 OFF

Also See ALERT, GETEXPR( ), GETFILE( ), PUTFILE( ), @ SAY...GET, SAVE SCREEN, RESTORE SCREEN, and MENU

Syntax Options 327

Scroll

Syntax SCROLL [PIXEL]
<coord1>,<coord2>,<exprN1>,<exprN2>

Purpose The SCROLL command moves the display in any rectangular portion of the screen outlined by <coord1> (upper left) and <coord2> (lower right) to a new location determined by distance from <coord1> and <coord2> in vertical measure <exprN1> and in horizontal measure <exprN2>. If the PIXELS key word is used, the measure is in pixels, otherwise it is in the default measure of characters as determined by the current font.

Example The only use I know of for this command is for pseudo animation. This command takes a rectangle whose upper left corner is at pixel row 50 and column 20, and whose lower-left corner is at pixel row 120 and column 100, and moves it upward 20 pixels.

SCROLL PIXELS 50,20,120,100,+20,0

Seek

Syntax SEEK <expr>

Purpose The SEEK command is the command to use for super fast data searches. The <expr> can be any type of data that's contained in the active index of the currently selected database file. The required index is directly responsible for the speed of SEEK's searches. In fact, SEEK is so fast that programmers consider it instant for all practical purposes.

Example First, you must have an accurate, open index on the file you want to SEEK.

```
USE CUSTOMERS
INDEX ON city TO custcity
```

Then you can SEEK a value that's contained in the index like this:

```
SEEK "San Francisco"
```

If the data value you SEEK was found, the FOUND( ) function will return true (.T.), and the file pointer will not be at the end of the file. If the SEEK failed to find a matching value in the index file, FOUND( ) will return (.F.) and the end-of-file function, EOF( ), will return (.T.).

You can seek any value contained in an index, even if it's comprised of data from more than one field.

```
USE CUSTOMERS
INDEX ON city+custname TO custcityname
SEEK "San Francisco" + "Merrit Enterprises"
```

Note that literal character searches are enclosed inside of quotation marks. You can use single quotation marks and brackets as well to delimit a sought character string. When searching for a value in a memory variable, just supply the variables name like this:

```
SEEK mymemvar
```

Also See FIND, LOCATE, and SET INDEX TO

Syntax Options 329

Select

```
  File   Edit   Database   Record   Program   Text   Window
                                                    View      ⌘-
```

Syntax   SELECT <workarea|alias>

Purpose   The SELECT command is like clicking on a circle in the view window. Grey circles are SELECTed, others are not. Only one database file work area can be SELECTed at a time.

Example   Whenever a work area is selected, the database commands you use will affect the file in that work area. In programs it's important to be careful when SELECTing files/work areas so that commands that modify data operate on the proper file!

This series of commands selects each of the possible work areas in turn:

```
SELECT A      SELECT F
SELECT B      SELECT G
SELECT C      SELECT H
SELECT D      SELECT I
SELECT E      SELECT J
```

SELECT 1, SELECT 2, and so on, through number 10 are exchangeable with the letters A through J. File alias names are also acceptable in lieu of letters A through J.

SELECT customers

This command causes the "customers" file to become SELECTED regardless of what work area it's in.

Also See   SET VIEW ON, LIST STATUS, and SET RELATION

Set

The SET commands that follow control the way many FoxBASE features behave. Most of the SET commands can be accessed interactively—through programs, buttons, or menu options. Others can become default parameters when a change is made in a file named "Config.fx." See the section in Chapter 4 (*Adjusting Fox-BASE Defaults*) for more information about the configuration file and how to use the syntax below marked "(Config.fx)."

ALTERNATE = <filename>	(Config.fx)
SET ALTERNATE TO [<filename>]	(interactive)
Default: None	
Accepts: <filename>	

Creates a file to catch screen output using the ? or @ SAY...GET commands. Use SET ALTERNATE TO <filename> to create a file, and SET ALTERNATE TO by itself to close the file. See also, LIST STATUS and MODIFY FILE.

SET ALTERNATE OFF|ON   (interactive only)

If ALTERNATE is ON, screen output is directed to a previously named alternate file. If it's OFF, output is disabled. Create and close output files using the SET ALTERNATE TO <filename> command. See also, LIST STATUS and MODIFY FILE.

BELL = ON|OFF	(Config.fx)
SET BELL ON|OFF	(interactive)
Default: ON	
Accepts: ON or OFF	

The default Macintosh "bell" sounds when a selected option is not available, when a process is finished, and so on. This is also affected by the volume setting.

BUCKET = <exprN>   (Config.fx only)
Default: 4
Accepts: 1 to 32

This command is not interactive and it works only when FoxBASE finds it in the Config.fx file. Sets the number of kilobytes available for storing pending GETS in memory. This allocation includes memory for everything associated with GETS, such as VALID and RANGE clauses, as well as PICTURE statements and functions.

Syntax Options 331

CARRY = ON|OFF   (Config.fx)
SET CARRY ON|OFF   (interactive)
Default: OFF
Accepts: ON or OFF

Do you want the information in a record to carry forward from one record to the next when entering (APPENDing) data so that you won't have to retype repeated field entries over and over? See also, APPEND, INSERT, and EDIT.

CENTURY = <ON|OFF>   (Config.fx)
SET CENTURY <ON|OFF>   (interactive)
Default: OFF
Accepts: ON or OFF

Do you want to see the 19 in 1990?, or the 20 in 2001? Unless it's overridden by a PICTURE clause within an @ SAY...GET command, this option can make the century portion of a date visible in all displays and printouts.

CLEAR = ON|OFF   (Config.fx)
SET CLEAR ON|OFF   (interactive)
Default: OFF
Accepts: ON or OFF

Do you want the selected background screen to be cleared when a format (entry) screen is used?

COLOR = <standard>[,<enhanced>]] (Config.fx)
SET COLOR TO <standard>[,<enhanced>]] (interactive)
Default: Black and white
Accepts: <colors>

The standard color setting determines what colors will be used for all normal screen displays, such as text, boxes, lines, and so on, unless overridden with an individual @ SAY or @ GET command. The enhanced color setting determines what colors will be used inside of programmed data entry fields. Note: The SET INTENSITY ON|OFF command affects enhanced color settings because it turns the enhanced effect on and off without changing the color selection. When INTENSITY is ON, the enhanced colors display in programmed data entry fields. When INTENSITY is OFF, the standard colors are used inside of programmed data entry fields. See also, ISCOLOR( ).

For black text on a white background in normal displays, and for blue letters inside of a yellow data entry background, enter this command:

SET COLOR TO N/W,B/RG+

For red text on a white background in normal displays enter this command:

SET COLOR TO R/N

The possible color settings are:

White	W	Light Grey	W+
Black	N	Grey	N+
Red	R	Light Red	R+
Green	G	Light Green	G+
Blue	B	Light Blue	B+
Brown	RG	Yellow	RG+
Magenta	RB	Light Magenta	RB+
Cyan	GB	Light Cyan	GB+

Note: The FoxForm screen painter allows you to access up to 256 colors using an alternate, and more complex, color syntax. If you need to identify and install a set of default colors from the 256 colors possible on your monitor, use FoxForm to make your selection and to create the commands.

COMMAND = <command>   (Config.fx only)
Default: None
Accepts: <command>

This entry in a configuration file tells FoxBASE to run a specific program when it starts up.

CONFIRM = ON|OFF   (Config.fx)
SET CONFIRM ON|OFF   (interactive)
Default: OFF
Accepts: ON or OFF

Do you want to press return to confirm entries into database fields when you've filled them in? If OFF, this option causes the cursor to go to the next field when a field has been filled by typing.

CONSOLE = ON|OFF   (Config.fx)
SET CONSOLE ON|OFF   (interactive)

Default: ON
Accepts: ON or OFF

Do you want output from the ? command and from most printing to be echoed to the screen? See also, SET DEVICE, SET PRINT, and SET TALK.

DATE = SET DATE   (Config.fx)
SET DATE <format>   (interactive)
Default: AMERICAN
Accepts: <format>

This sets the type of date display you want to use on the screen and in printed output. Possible formats are AMERICAN, ANSI, BRITISH, ITALIAN, and FRENCH. See also, SET CENTURY, CDOW( ), and DTOC( ).

DECIMALS = <exprN>   (Config.fx)
SET DECIMALS TO <exprN>   (interactive)
Default: 2
Accepts: 1 to 14

This establishes the number of numeric decimals displayed by LIST, DISPLAY and the @ SAY...GET commands. See also, SET FIXED.

DEFAULT = <path list>   (Config.fx)
SET DEFAULT TO <path list>   (interactive)
Default: None
Accepts: <drivename and folder (path) list>

Where should FoxBASE expect to find database and index files? This option sets a drive and folder as the default operating folder if it's not the one you double-clicked a document in at start-up time. You can use the miscellaneous button in the view window to set a default folder or enter a command in the command window like this:

SET DEFAULT TO "HD40:FoxBaseSamples:Example:"

See also, SET VOLUME and SET PATH.

DELETED = ON|OFF   (Config.fx)
SET DELETED ON|OFF   (interactive)
Default: OFF
Accepts: ON or OFF

Do you want to see and process records that are marked for deletion, or treat them as though the database files were already PACKed? If you want to see them, leave this setting OFF. See also, DELETE, DELETED( ), and RECALL.

DEVICE = SCREEN|PRINT	(Config.fx)
SET DEVICE TO SCREEN|PRINT [PROMPT]	(interactive)
Default: SCREEN	
Accepts: SCREEN/PRINT	

This setting determines where all output from @ SAY commands will go. If you set it to PRINT, FoxBASE will attempt to print anything formatted by an @ SAY command. If you don't want to see the result on the screen as well, make sure to enter a SET CONSOLE OFF command. The optional PROMPT keyword is important only in programs, telling FoxBASE to also show the print dialog so you, or a user, can set the number of copies, etc. In interactive mode, the prompt is not necessary. See also, SET CONSOLE and SET PRINTER.

SET DOHISTORY ON|OFF	(interactive only)
Default: OFF	
Accepts: ON or OFF	

Dohistory makes a record of commands in the command window while a program runs, much like command windows that automatically make a history of commands during interactive use. It should be used only by developers who want to record the program path a user takes, because it slows programs down too much to justify its use for anything but debugging.

ECHO = ON|OFF	(Config.fx)
SET ECHO ON|OFF	(interactive)
Default: OFF	
Accepts: ON or OFF	

Echo determines whether or not the trace window is opened up and active when a program runs. The trace window shows you the program as it's running and gives you control over executing programs. See the *The Mac as a Development Environment* section in Chapter 10 and Fig. 3-42 for more information. See also, SET TALK.

ESCAPE = ON|OFF	(Config.fx)
SET ESCAPE ON|OFF	(interactive)
Default: ON	
Accepts: ON or OFF	

The Escape key is a valuable way to interrupt an executing program or operation. Setting this OFF prevents the Escape key (and the alternative keystrokes, Command period) from stopping things. Developers might want to use an OFF setting when they've programmed more graceful ways to stop a process. See also, ON ESCAPE.

EXACT = ON|OFF   (Config.fx)
SET EXACT ON|OFF   (interactive)
Default: OFF
Accepts: ON or OFF

If you set any string in comparison with another, a shorter one that matches a longer one (as far as it goes, that is) will be considered a match. If, however, you set EXACT to ON, comparisons consider the full length of each string before a match is made.

EXCLUSIVE = ON|OFF   (Config.fx)
SET EXCLUSIVE ON|OFF   (interactive)
Default: ON
Accepts: ON or OFF

Do you want exclusive access to any database file that you use? The single-user version of FoxBASE always works in an exclusive mode that prevents file sharing, but setting EXCLUSIVE OFF in the multiuser version allows files over a local area network to be shared. For more information about multiuser file access and programming see the *Networking* section in Chapter 10.

SET FIELDS ON|OFF   (interactive only)
Default: ON
Accepts: ON or OFF

This determines whether or not the list specified by a SET FIELDS TO <fieldlist> command is able to limit the visible fields for processing. See also, SET FIELDS ON|OFF and CLEAR FIELDS.

SET FIELDS TO [ALL|<fieldlist>]
Default: last saved
Accepts: ALL or any specific field names separated by commas

SET FIELDS limits the number of fields, by name, that are available for most file operations, including BROWSE, CHANGE, EDIT and APPEND, LIST, DISPLAY, and so on. A field list is saved for each open database file (work area) when view files get saved so that you don't have to look at every field in a database when you're interested in only a few of them. Another advantage of the fields list is that it limits the fields used to process import and export files. To set fields interactively use the Database/Setup menu or the View/Setup menu. If you enter the command from the keyboard or into a program, the <fieldlist> can include any open database file as long as the "->" indicator is used to identify the work area/file alias. Otherwise, FoxBASE assumes that the field list includes only fields that are in the currently selected work area. See also, SET FIELDS ON|OFF and CLEAR FIELDS.

SET FILES   (Config.fx only)
Default: 16
Accepts: 16 to 48

How many files can FoxBASE open at once? Don't forget to count indexes for each database, program files, and so on. It's not unusual to need a setting of 24 or more files.

SET FILTER TO [<exprL>]   (interactive only)
Default: None
Accepts: a logical expression

The SET FILTER command limits the records that are visible for processing to those that meet a condition specified in the <exprL>. For this reason, filters can powerfully affect the behavior of all data processing commands. Filters are specific to a work area, so one can be set for each and every open file. It is very useful when you want, for example, to mail only to those customers who live within local zip code zones, or those who have purchased more than $1,000 worth of goods in the last year. If SET FILTER TO is used without any conditional <exprL>, FoxBASE will turn off any previously established filter and allow you to process all records. Like most data handling parameters, filter conditions can be saved in view files. See also, INDEX ON <expr> FOR <exprL>.

SET FIXED ON|OFF   (interactive only)
Default: OFF
Accepts: ON or OFF

The SET FIXED command determines whether or not the SET DECIMALS setting is in effect. If SET FIXED is OFF, FoxBASE displays numeric data from fields or variables in the highest decimal resolution that it can, regardless of what that might be. See also, SET DECIMALS TO <exprN>.

SET FORMAT TO [<filename>]   (interactive only)
Default: None
Accepts: The name of any valid format (.fmt) file

SET FORMAT installs a screen format that was previously designed in FoxForm and generated with the Program/Generate/Format menu option. Once installed, a format file becomes visible whenever an APPEND, CHANGE, EDIT, INSERT, or READ command is issued, which effectively replaces the standard Fox-BASE data entry forms. Up to one format file can be installed per database work area.

Suppose you had a large database file to record survey responses and it simply wouldn't all fit on one screen? You could create several format files and combine them in one text file by separating each format with a READ command. When this type of format file is used, you can flip through the multiple format pages by pressing the PgUp and PgDn keys. Up to 128 pages, or formats, can be joined this way. SET FORMAT TO without a <filename> releases any format file previously installed in the current work area. See also, SCREEN.

SET FRAME TO [<exprN1>,<expN2>] [CLIP] (interactive only)
Default: None
Accepts: Numbers indicating the picture display area in pixels.

SET FRAME establishes the default area of the screen that will be used to display pictures from a database picture field. The <exprN1> is the height of the display area in pixels and <exprN2> is the width in pixels. The CLIP option tells FoxBASE to truncate pictures that are too large to fit in the specified area. If the CLIP word is not used, FoxBASE will scale (by enlargement or reduction) the pictures to fit the area.

Note that the frame is not placed at a specific coordinate via the <exprN> numbers. The @ SAY command takes care of the frame's placement:

SET FRAME TO 50, 50
@ PIXELS 202,104 SAY picture

See also, SET PICTURE.

```
F<number> = <command>                      (Config.fx file)
SET FUNCTION <expr> TO <commands>          (interactive)
Default:    None
Accepts:    <commands>
```

Use this command if you want to program another FoxBASE command into one of the function keys, other than one that's already there. Use the keys panel in the View window or enter the command into the Command window with quotation marks around the <command>. FoxBASE interprets the semicolon as a carriage return, so use a semicolon whenever you need a return at the end of a command or between several commands that you're installing into one key. No command string, however, can exceed 254 characters in total length. Figure 8-18 shows what the View window function display looks like.

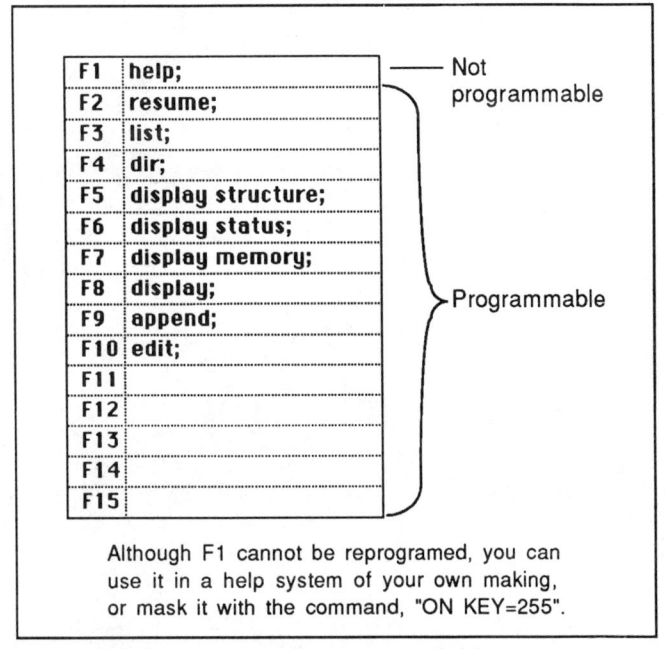

```
┌─────────────────────────────────────────┐
│  F1   help;        ─── Not              │
│  F2   resume;          programmable     │
│  F3   list;                             │
│  F4   dir;                              │
│  F5   display structure;                │
│  F6   display status;                   │
│  F7   display memory;                   │
│  F8   display;         Programmable     │
│  F9   append;                           │
│  F10  edit;                             │
│  F11                                    │
│  F12                                    │
│  F13                                    │
│  F14                                    │
│  F15                                    │
│                                         │
│  Although F1 cannot be reprogramed,     │
│  you can use it in a help system of     │
│  your own making, or mask it with the   │
│  command, "ON KEY=255".                 │
└─────────────────────────────────────────┘
```

Fig. 8-18. The View window function display.

Note: On nonextended keyboards, Command-2, Command-3, Command-4, etc., are function key equivalents. F1 is not programmable, but you can use an "ON KEY=225" command to block help from being called whenever a READ is in effect. See also, FKLABEL( ) and FKMAX( ).

```
HEADINGS = ON|OFF                          (Config.fx)
SET HEADINGS ON|OFF                        (interactive)
```

Default: ON
Accepts: ON or OFF

This setting is intended to establish the number of commands from the command buffer that will be displayed or printed by the DISPLAY or LIST HISTORY command. It's most useful in the DOS version of FoxBASE, which has no Command window. See also, SET DOHISTORY.

HELP = ON|OFF   (Config.fx)
SET HELP ON|OFF   (interactive)
Default: ON
Accepts: ON or OFF

While help is always available when using FoxBASE interactively, it can be turned off while running programs.

SET HELP TO <filename>   (interactive only)
Default: FoxHelp
Accepts: The name of any valid database file containing help texts.

FoxBASE allows you to create your own help files modeled after its own. Developers in particular will make use of this feature so that they can provide application users with custom help screens. To see how it's done, take a look at the *Customizing Help* section in Chapter 7.

HISTORY = <exprN>   (Config.fx only)
Default: 20
Accepts: 0 to 16,000

This setting is intended to establish the number of commands from the command buffer that will be displayed or printed by the DISPLAY or LIST HISTORY command. It's most useful in the DOS version of FoxBASE, which has no Command window. See also, SET DOHISTORY.

HMEMORY = <exprN>   (Config.fx only)
Default: 5
Accepts: 0 to 63

In kilobytes, this setting tells FoxBASE how much memory to make available for storing command histories. Use low numbers to save memory if you don't LIST or DISPLAY previously executed commands.

INDEX = <3 character extension>   (Config.fx only)
Default: IDX
Accepts: 3 characters

Do you want to change the extension on index file names from the default of "idx" to something else? This setting is useful if you want to run programs that were written to run on dBase III Plus, where the "ndx" index file extension has already been included in the program. See also, INDEX ON <fieldlist> TO <filename>, CLOSE INDEX.

INTENSITY = ON|OFF   (Config.fx)
SET INTENSITY ON|OFF   (interactive)
Default: ON
Accepts: ON or OFF

The color setting (see SET COLOR TO in this chapter) can specify special colors for fields being edited. The INTENSITY option determines whether the established special color attribute will be used during programmed field edits. Another effect of INTENSITY is a bold border that appears around each on-screen get field.

MARGIN = <exprN>   (Config.fx)
SET MARGIN TO <exprN> [PIXELS]   (interactive)
Default: 0
Accepts: 0 to 254

This setting establishes the left printer margin in characters, or if the optional keyword PIXELS is used, in pixels. See also, SET DEVICE, SET PRINT, and SET PRINTER.

MEMOWIDTH = <exprN>   (Config.fx)
SET MEMOWIDTH TO <exprN>   (interactive)
Default: 50
Accepts: 8 to 256

How much of the screen or page's width, in characters, do you want memo fields to use when they're printed or displayed? They'll wrap within the area you set with this option.

MVARSIZ = <exprN>   (Config.fx only)
Default: 6
Accepts: 1 to 64

Character strings take up memory when they're stored in variables. This option sets a (kilobytes) limit on the amount of memory available.

Syntax Options 341

MVCOUNT = <exprN>   (Config.fx only)
Default: 256
Accepts: 128 to 3,600

How many memory variables will you simultaneously maintain? This setting establishes a limit. Arrays count for one, regardless of the number of cells they contain, but they are affected by the MVARSIZ setting.

ODOMETER = <exprN>   (Config.fx)
SET ODOMETER TO <exprN>   (interactive)
Default: 100
Accepts: 1 to ?

At what count intervals, during whole file operations, do you want to be informed of the progress FoxBASE is making as it moves through records? Lowering this number lets you know more frequently, but it can slow things down, too. See also, SET TALK.

SET ORDER TO <exprN>   (interactive only)
Default: 1
Accepts: 0-7 (representing index files in the order they were opened)

The SET ORDER TO <exprN> tells FoxBASE which index you want to control the currently visible order of data and to control the movement of the record pointer when record-processing commands take over. An <exprN> of 0 keeps all indexes open for updating, but causes them to be dormant as far as the ordering of records is concerned. See also, USE...INDEX <filename> and SET INDEX TO <filename>.

PATH = <drive and folder pathlist>   (Config.fx)
SET PATH TO <drive and folder pathlist> (interactive)
Default: None
Accepts: <drivename and folder (path) list>

What folders do you want checked for files if they aren't found first in the current working folder? Specify the full path to folders starting with the drive name, and separate path lists with semicolons or commas. See the SET DEFAULT entry above for syntax examples. See also, SET VOLUME and SET DEFAULT.

PRINT = ON|OFF   (Config.fx)
SET PRINT ON|OFF   (interactive)
Default: OFF
Accepts: ON or OFF

Do you want the results of all ? commands to print as well as display on the screen? If so, set PRINT ON. Make sure to SET PRINT OFF when you're done printing so that your computer will be disengaged from the printer. For more information about printing with the ? and @ SAY commands look at the *Programs that Print* section in Chapter 7. See also, SET DEVICE and SET PRINTER.

SET PRINTER TO [<device> | <filename>]   (interactive only)
Default: The current chooser-selected printer.
Accepts: Nothing, COM1, COM2, or a file name.

Printing is very flexible because of the control you have over where printed output goes. If you enter SET PRINTER TO without any arguments, FoxBASE will send output to the currently selected printer, which can be chosen in the Macintosh chooser.

If you enter SET PRINTER TO <filename>, FoxBASE will open a file for you to receive the contents of the report, or whatever it is that you are printing. For more information on this, see the SET PRINT ON|OFF command, because it will affect the printing behavior. Also, take a look at the discussion of printing in the *Programs That Print* section in Chapter 7.

If you enter SET PRINTER TO <device>, by specifying COM1 or COM2, FoxBASE will manage serial communications with any device that's installed at the selected port. COM1 is the phone port and COM2 is the printer port. This command demonstrates the command's syntax and shows what the default values are when you enter a simple SET PRINTER TO COM1 (or COM2) without further arguments:

SET PRINTER TO COM2, 9600, N, 8, 1, H, RL

The arguments mean: print to the printer port (COM2), communicate at the rate of 9600 baud, don't use a parity check (N), transmit and receive eight-bit words (8), use one bit to signify stops (1), use the hardware ClearToSend handshake method (H), and include return and line feed characters (RL) with each line transmitted. The full syntax of the device printing command is:

SET PRINTER TO <COM1|COM2>
[, <baud>] [, <parity>] [, <databits>]
[, <stopbits>] [, <handshake>] [, <endline>]   (interactive only)

Note that all but the COM1|COM2 arguments are optional. If any are omitted the comma must still be present in the finished com-

Syntax Options 343

mand statement. The argument possibilities are listed below. (See also, SET DEVICE and SET PRINTER.)

<baud>	300, 600, 1200, 1400, 3600, 4800, 7200, 9600, 19200, 57600
<parity>	N for none, O for odd, E for even
<databits>	5, 6, 7, 8
<stopbits>	1, 1.5, 2
<handshake>	H for hardware (ClearToSend), S for software (Xon/Xoff), N for none
<endline>	R for carriage return, L for line feed (you can use up to four returns and line feeds in any order)

SET PROCEDURE TO <filename>   (interactive only)
Default: None
Accepts: Any valid program file name.

The SET PROCEDURE TO <filename> command identifies the name of a file that FoxBASE should look in for subroutine procedures before it looks on the disk for a program of the same name. Procedure files are collections of smaller programs that have been placed into one file for the sake of organization, convenience, and speed. The procedure file name must be a valid FoxBASE program file. If the command is issued more than once, only the last procedure file specified will be used, because only one can be active at a time. See the *Special Features and Program Design* section in Chapter 7 for information about how to use procedure files. See also, DO <programname>.

SET RELATION OFF INTO <filename>
SET   RELATION   TO   [<expr>   INTO
<alias>]
[, <expr> INTO <alias>]. . .[, <expr>
INTO <alias>]
[ADDITIVE]   (interactive only)

Note: The *Setting Relationships Between Files* section in Chapter 5 contains practical information on how to relate database files.

The SET RELATION command is a very powerful command because it causes otherwise independent database files to work together by relating them. It ties the currently selected database to any other open, indexed database file by linking a field or expression in the currently selected database with information contained in the other file's index. In this case, the currently selected database is called the *parent* file and the linked database is called the *child* file. As such, an index is required in all child files. The effect of linking is that the child database file automatically aligns its records with any selected record in the parent database file the moment that a parent record is located by the pointer, whether it is done manually by a mouse pointer or automatically by a command that considers many records at a time. If there is no matching record in a child database's index, the pointer goes to the end of the file where empty field values are returned on query.

One parent file can support many direct, child database files as long as the contents of some field, or group of fields, matches the contents of the child file's active index, and you use the ADDITIVE key word when specifying the relationships. Parent files don't need an index, but they can have them for organizational purposes.

Child files can be related to other files in a chaining fashion, making them both parent and child at once. The only taboo is that a chain cannot return to the top-most parent. When the pointer of a file moves, the pointer in related child files will also move. Child files cannot move the pointer in parent files to align matches. Relationships are one-way, and only the first matching record in a child file will be automatically aligned when the parent file's pointer moves. For this reason it's wise to relate files containing more matching records (parent files) to those that contain fewer records (child files). This way, you're sure to find all possible matches between the files.

If the SET RELATION TO command is issued without an expression, it will turn off any established relations going from the currently selected work area into the child files.

There is one exception to the rule: that child files must be indexed. If there is no index, FoxBASE will assume that you want to link the parent and child file by record number. While this establishes an arbitrary relationship, it is highly impractical for all but rare cases when you keep two or more nearly identical files.

The following are a few examples of the relation command. I suggest that you relate a few of your own files using the guidelines in Chapter 5, then study the command that FoxBASE places in the command window. Experimentation is the best way to learn.

```
* RELATOR1.PRG
SELECT A
USE customers
INDEX ON custnum TO custnum
SELECT B
USE invoices INDEX invdate
SET RELATION TO invcustnum INTO customers
```

```
LIST ALL A->custname, A->custnum, B->amtdue, B->datedue FOR over-
due
SELECT C
USE orders INDEX prdcustnum
SET RELATION TO prdcustnum INTO invoices
LIST ALL A->custname, A->custnum, C->prodname, C->qty FOR .NOT.
overdue
* EOF RELATOR.PRG
```

In the example that follows, the customer file is the grandchild of the orders file and the child of the invoices file, because it is the recipient of their relationships. The first LIST command worked because the invoices file was a parent to the customer file. It wouldn't have worked in this program, however, because here I make both the invoice and customer files children of one, the product file:

```
*RELATOR2.PRG
SELECT A
USE customers
INDEX ON custnum TO custnum
SELECT B
USE invoices INDEX invdate
SELECT C
USE orders
SET RELATION TO prdcustnum INTO invoices
SET RELATION TO prdcustnum INTO customers ADDITIVE
LIST ALL A->custname, A->custnum, C->prodname, C->qty FOR .NOT.
overdue
* EOF RELATOR.PRG
```

You can explore the effect of relations by opening a browse window for each of the related files. Click the pointer in one browse window and then in the next to graphically view the relationship's effect. See also, SET VIEW.

SET RESOURCE TO <filename> [NOMODIFY]   (interactive only)
Default: FoxUSER
Accepts: Any valid resource file name modeled after the FoxUSER file.

Resource files contain pictures, sounds, XCMDs, and other things that you can manipulate with FoxBASE if you're an adventurous and technical programmer. This command establishes a second resource file for FoxBASE to use, it does not replace the FoxUser file, which should be kept on the disk with the main FoxBASE program. See the resource file discussion and the discussion about FoxRUN in Chapter 10 if you are interested in developing applications that use custom resources.

SAFETY = ON|OFF   (Config.fx)
SET SAFETY ON|OFF   (interactive)
Default: ON
Accepts: ON or OFF

If you want to be warned before overwriting an existing file, leave this setting ON. When running programs that overwrite existing files intentionally, SAFETY should be set OFF.

STATUS = ON| OFF   (Config.fx)
SET STATUS ON|OFF   (interactive)
Default: ON
Accepts: ON or OFF

The small STATUS window shows what file is currently selected, how many records it has, and what record the pointer is currently on. Also shown is the current working folder. You can use this command, or open the status window directly from the window menu.

STEP = ON|OFF   (Config.fx)
SET STEP ON|OFF   (interactive)
Default: OFF
Accepts: ON or OFF

Do you want the trace window to open whenever programs execute, and then to step through them one command at a time? This option opens the trace window if it's not already open, and it is best to set it after starting FoxBASE. Use it to find problems in a program. You can SET STEP ON and OFF in the program menu.

SET STRICT ON|OFF   (interactive only)
Default: OFF
Accepts: ON or OFF

Do you want the press of the tab key to end editing of data when the cursor is in the last field of a record, or do you want the tab key to cause the cursor to circle back to the first field of the current record instead? With SET STRICT ON, the cursor will stay within the current record and you'll have to press return to exit the edit. With SET STRICT OFF, the tab key also causes programmed edits to terminate.

SET TOPIC TO [<exprL>|<exprC>]   (interactive only)
Default: None
Accepts: Any LOCATE-like search argument.

The SET TOPIC command tells FoxBASE what to search for in the current help file whenever help is requested with either the HELP command, or when the user selects the help menu option. The easiest way to enter topics is to enter the actual help topic that's in the topic field of the help file, however, any search can be formed using the same search mechanism that's used by the LOCATE command. Take a look at the LOCATE command to see how searches are formed. See also, SET HELP TO, SET HELP ON|OFF, SYS(16), and SYS(18).

TALK = ON|OFF   (Config.fx)
SET TALK ON|OFF   (interactive)
Default: ON
Accepts: ON or OFF

Do you want FoxBASE to let you know what it's doing when it performs database operations? If so, leave this setting on. Turn it off if you're running a program that explicitly tells users what's going on, because performance can suffer when FoxBASE takes time out to inform you of operation progress. See also, SET ODOMETER.

TYPEAHEAD = <exprN>   (Config.fx)
SET TYPEAHEAD TO <exprN>   (interactive)
Default: 128
Accepts: 0 to 32,000

How many keys can you press to enter commands or data while FoxBASE is doing something else? This setting establishes the number of characters that can be entered in anticipation of entry prompts. See also, CLEAR TYPEAHEAD and INKEY( ).

UNIQUE = ON|OFF   (Config.fx)
SET UNIQUE ON|OFF   (interactive)
Default: OFF
Accepts: ON or OFF

Set this ON if all of the index files must contain unique values, and unique values only, because it causes only one of each kind to be recorded in, and therefore found by, an index file. It's useful as a filter against duplicates, but it's best established after starting FoxBASE and then turned OFF when no longer needed. See also, INDEX.

VIEW = ON|OFF   (Config.fx)
SET VIEW ON|OFF   (interactive)
Default: last setting used
Accepts: ON or OFF

FoxBASE remembers whether the View window was open or not when you last quit and it reopens it if it was previously open. If this setting is used in the configuration file, it overrides the automatic memory response. If it is used interactively, it opens or closes the View window.

SET VIEW TO <filename>   (interactive only)
Default: last setting used
Accepts: any valid view (.vue) file name

The SET VIEW TO command opens a previously saved view file. View files remember all of the important settings for data management, such as database files, indexes, relationships, filters, other SET command settings, and so on.

VOLUME <exprC>   (Config.fx)
SET VOLUME <exprC> TO <drivename/folder> (interactive)
Default: None
Accepts: <drivename and folder (path) list>

If you're running programs written for DOS computers that have drive letters inside of commands, you can use this option to assign Macintosh drive and folder paths to those already-programmed drive letters. The advantage is that older MS-DOS programs won't need to be rewritten for the Macintosh because they refer to MS-DOS drive letters instead of Macintosh names.

Syntax Options

Skip

Syntax SKIP [<exprN>]

Purpose The SKIP command moves the record pointer by one or more records forward or backward in a file.

Example Without any arguments, SKIP moves the record pointer forward one record, or it can be used like this:

```
SKIP +1
SKIP -1
SKIP +10
SKIP -10
```

SKIP respects the order imposed by an active index, and moves the pointer through an index if one is in use.

Note Any attempt to SKIP past the logical boundaries of a file will result in an error, so use the EOF( ) and BOF( ) testing functions to prevent this problem from occurring.

Also See GOTO, SET DELETED, RECNO( ), and SET FILTER

Sort To

Menu: File | Edit | **Database › Sort...** | Record | Program | Text | Window

Syntax

SORT TO <filename>
ON <fieldname> [/A][/C][/D]
[,<fieldname> [/A][/C][/D]...]
[<scope>]
[FOR <exprL>]
[WHILE <exprL>]
[FIELDS <fieldlist>]

Purpose

The SORT command creates a new file from the currently selected database file. The file it creates is ordered by the <fieldname> specified. Several <fieldnames> can be included in the sorting order as long as they all have the same data type. The <filename> is the name of the file you want to create.

Example

SORT can sort in ascending order and in descending order.

SORT TO newfile ON custname /A
   or
SORT TO newfile ON custname /D

It can even be told to ignore the case of characters in the sorted field:

SORT TO newfile ON custname /C

The A and C, or D, options can be used together, for example:

SORT TO newfile ON custname /AD

Note

Be sure that there's enough space on the disk to hold the newly sorted file, and make sure that you don't confuse the new file with the original file after SORTing.

Also See

INDEX and SET DELETED

Syntax Options 351

Store

Syntax STORE <expr>
TO <memvarlist> | <arrayname>
   or
<memvar> | <arrayname> = <expr>

Purpose The STORE command takes values from database fields, expressions, or constants and places them in memory variables or arrays. It initializes memory variables, but it does not initialize arrays, which must be DIMENSIONed ahead of time with the DIMENSION or PUBLIC commands.

Example STORE "Merrill Enterprises" TO custvar

Storing values into memory variables can be done without the STORE command by using the alternate syntax shown above. Look at this example:

custvar = "Merrill Enterprises"

The <memvarlist> can be a list like this:

STORE 0 TO var1,var2,var3

Array cells must be STOREd just like memory variable names are, so use the cell subscript references when identifying them:

STORE 0 TO myarray(1)
STORE 0 TO myarray(2,4)

Note Be sure that there's enough room in memory for the combined variable contents and that you don't specify more variable names than are allowed. Look at the *Adjusting FoxBASE Defaults* section in Chapter 4 for specifics.

Also See DIMENSION, ACCEPT, INPUT, WAIT, and DISPLAY MEMORY

Sum

Syntax SUM [<scope>]
[exprlist]
[TO <memvarlist>]
[FOR <exprL>]
[WHILE <exprL>]

Purpose The SUM command takes the contents of fields, even if they are modified by an expression, and displays their sum or places the result in memory variables. Only records that fall within the commands <scope> and those meeting the FOR and WHILE conditions will be included in the sum. More than one field can be in the exprlist, but the number of items in the exprlist must match those in the <memvarlist>.

Example The exprlist can have field names, which allow you to limit the numeric fields being SUMmed, like this:

SUM fieldname1,fieldname2 TO var1,var2

Array cells can receive the summed values, but they must be referenced individually and with full subscript references as though they were variable names. If the TO <memvarlist> option is not used, the result of the SUM will automatically be displayed on the screen.

Also See AVERAGE, TOTAL, COUNT, SET HEADING, and SET TALK

Syntax Options 353

Suspend

```
 File  Edit  Database  Record  Program  Text  Window
                                        Suspend
```

Syntax SUSPEND

Purpose The SUSPEND command causes a running program to stop and return FoxBASE to the interactive mode. Runtime versions of FoxBASE+/Mac cannot be SUSPENDed because they have no interactive mode with menus and a Command window. Unlike CANCEL, which permanently terminates a program's execution until it is rerun, SUSPENDed programs can be RESUMEd.

Example The main purpose of SUSPEND is to allow programmers to stop a program just before or during a spot where trouble occurs. SUSPEND leaves all of the database, memory variable, and other environmental conditions intact as it exits a program, so you can use the "suspended" state as an opportunity to examine things, and then RESUME or CANCEL the program.

Also See RESUME, CANCEL, RETRY, and RETURN

Text...Endtext

Syntax TEXT
                <string>
                ENDTEXT

Purpose The TEXT command sends <string> to the current output device or devices. The interesting thing about TEXT is that the contents of <string> can include carriage returns and other light formatting.

Example TEXT is often used in other FoxBASE environments (other than Macintosh, that is) to display menu options in one simple sweep.

```
TEXT
           Main Menu—Consolidated Companies
           1) Enter/edit customer information
           2) Enter/edit invoices
           3) Print reports
           4) Maintain system
           5) Exit
ENDTEXT
```

Whenever a TEXT...ENDTEXT construct is encountered in a program, the things between the TEXT and ENDTEXT commands are displayed or printed on the current output devices.

Total

File Edit Database Record Program Text Window
                    Total...

Syntax   TOTAL TO <file> ON <key>
                [<scope>]
                [FIELDS <list>]
                [FOR <exprL>]
                [WHILE <exprL>]

Purpose   The TOTAL command makes a new file with a structure like the one you're totalling except there is a TOTAL value for each numeric group in the source file.

Example   To use TOTAL effectively, make sure that the file is in an order that places records into groups, such as an index or a SORTed file. When the TOTAL command goes to work, it will add up all of the records matching the first value it finds in a field specified by the <key> until it encounters a new value in the <key> field. When a <key> group is finished, one new record containing a numeric sum of numeric fields will be added to the <file>.

```
USE INVOICES
INDEX ON custname
TOTAL ON custname TO custtotals FIELDS custname,invamount
```

To filter the records going into the <file>, use the FOR clause.

The TOTAL ON <key> must be one field name that is sure to signal changes in grouping. If there is no such field in the file, you must make one and fill it with information from other fields that will guarantee that the group breaks will occur where they should.

Also See   AVERAGE, SUM, COUNT, SET HEADING, and SET TALK

Type

Syntax   TYPE <file> [TO PRINT]

Purpose   The TYPE command is a simple command that lists the contents of a text file to the screen for viewing or to the printer.

Example   There are better ways to display or print text file information. This command is a holdover from the roots of FoxBASE.

```
TYPE textfile
TYPE textfile TO PRINT
```

Unlock

Syntax UNLOCK [ALL]

Purpose The UNLOCK command releases all record and/or file locks on the currently active database file. If used with the ALL option, all locks are released on all files.

Update

Syntax   UPDATE ON <key>
FROM <alias>
REPLACE <field> WITH <expr>
[,<field> WITH <expr>...]
[RANDOM]

Purpose   The UPDATE command takes information in one file and places into another, usually similar, file. The best way to understand UPDATE is to consider that it relates two files and performs REPLACEs of data in one file based on contents in the related file. Memo and picture fields are not included in UPDATE REPLACE operations.

Example   The currently selected database is the one being UPDATEd, and it must be indexed or sorted (unless RANDOM is used) on a <key> field that has a matching data value in the FROM file.

USE members
UPDATE ON membnum FROM membentry REPLACE dues WITH membentry->dues

The RANDOM clause allows you to use the command with an indexed FROM file while the selected target file is in random order, but it's best to place both files in order.

Also See   REPLACE

Use

```
  File   Edit   Database   Record   Program   Text   Window
  Open...      ⌘O
```

Syntax

USE [<filename>]
[INDEX <filelist>]
[ALIAS <alias>]
[EXCLUSIVE]

Purpose

USE is the only command that can open a database file. When you select the File/Use/Database menu option or double click an empty circle in the View window, you're using the USE command without knowing it. The file you open with USE gets placed in the currently selected database work area.

Example

To open a file, simply select the work area you want it in and USE it, like this:

SELECT A
USE custfile

To open a file so that other users on a network cannot get access to it for any reason, issue a command like this:

USE custfile EXCLUSIVE

Exclusive use is important for some operations that cannot support simultaneous multiple-user access. For more information about EXCLUSIVE, see the *Multiuser Commands* section in Chapter 10.

To USE a file with an index in one command, do this:

USE custfile INDEX custcity

To USE a file while assigning a new alias name, do this:

USE custfile ALIAS customers

Also See

SET VIEW TO and SELECT

Wait

Syntax WAIT [string] [TO <memvar>]

Purpose The WAIT command stops any program and puts "Waiting..." or a custom message prompt <string> into a box at the upper-right corner of the screen until the user presses the mouse button or any other key. If the TO <memvar> option is used, the key pressed will be placed into the named memvar.

Example This command is particularly useful when several screens of information will be put on the screen one after another because it can pause the display program at each screenful of information until the user is ready to continue. A prompt <string> for such a use could say, "Press the mouse to see next screen. . .." A <memvar> will automatically be created by the WAIT command so there is no need to declare one ahead of time.

Note It's not a good idea to use this command to gather important responses from users into the <memvar>, because it's easy for them to press a wrong key that would advance the program with no way of reversing their response. Use @...GET with a VALID clause or in a loop that can test and re-request the user's response if it is not within a correct range of values for processing.

Tips Use this command to halt and continue programs, and use your own dialog boxes or ALERT to gather responses from users. (Remember, dialogs are small boxes appearing in the center of the screen that ask a question and gather a response from users when they check inside checkboxes or push buttons that are inside the dialog box. Dialog boxes can be made with the SCREEN command and @...GETs.) When a dialog is used, the users are very deliberate in their responses, making them much more reliable than any WAIT TO <memvar> response.

Also See ACCEPT and INKEY(0)

Zap

Syntax   ZAP

Purpose   The ZAP command is equivalent to DELETE ALL followed by a PACK. It removes every record from the selected database file and reindexes any open index files. ZAP is not like ERASE or DELETE FILE because those commands destroy the file itself. ZAP just permanently removes all of the records while leaving the file in its selected work area.

Note   IF SET SAFETY is ON you will be warned before a ZAP is performed. Otherwise, FoxBASE assumes that you know what you're doing. There is no way to reverse a ZAP but to restore a backup file, so use SET SAFETY and be careful.

Also See   DELETE ALL, PACK, and SET SAFETY

9
FoxBASE+/Mac Functions

THIS chapter contains an alphabetical listing of all the FoxBASE functions. Functions are easy to distinguish from commands because their names have parentheses ( ). The only two exceptions to this rule are the & and the $ functions, which are the first ones listed in this chapter.

HOW THE FUNCTION REFERENCE IS ORGANIZED

Each function entry contains the following information:

- **Syntax.** This section demonstrates acceptable syntax options for the function.
- **Purpose.** This section contains a narrative explanation describing what the function does.
- **Example.** This section describes how the function is used in the context of a command statement and/or program. I've included code samples where appropriate to demonstrate their use. Suggestions might also be included for a particularly useful or popular application.
- **Requirements.** Most functions require arguments, and arguments come in different varieties (characters, numbers, logical values, dates, etc.). This section tells whether or not arguments are accepted by the function and what data type(s) they must be.
- **Results.** All functions return something in their place after testing a condition or modifying an argument of data or an expression supplied by them. This section describes the type of information returned by the function and what data type the returned value possesses.
- **Also See.** This section provides a listing of functions or commands that are useful to know because they work similarly as the function described, or because they are

useful in combination with it. Sometimes, the items listed can provide an alternative or better way to do the same thing as the function.

SYMBOLS USED IN THE FUNCTION REFERENCE

The following is a list of the symbols used for each function entry. Refer to this list whenever you are unsure about a function's meaning.

Uppercase Letters Uppercase letters in bold print are used for function names and 'key words. Functions should be entered as printed, although FoxBASE accepts either uppercase or lowercase letters.

Angle Brackets < > Angle brackets enclose arguments. Arguments are expressions or elements of expressions. Literally, angle brackets mean: "something should be supplied by you and put here." You can decide what to put in the place of brackets by studying their context and notation. For example, <exprC> means that you should supply a character expression. The brackets themselves should not be entered.

Vertical Bar | An exclusive OR. Symbolizes that you should select only one of the options separated by the bar. The bar itself should not be typed.

Parentheses Parentheses are used to arbitrarily group expressions or portions so that expressions are evaluated in a prescribed and predictable order.

Square Brackets [ ] Brackets enclose optional elements that can be used with a function. Don't type the brackets themselves.

Quotation Marks Quotation marks indicate that the items should be enclosed within quotation marks when entered. You might use single quotation marks or square brackets, but matching pairs must be used for each element in the command expression. Typically, quotation marks are required for literal character strings of any length, like 'A', or, "123 Almond Street."

Ellipses Ellipses indicate that you can enter the option again, often many times.

Alias Indicator -> The alias indicator is used to let FoxBASE+/Mac know that it might need to look for the named field in another work area. It is entered "alias->fieldname."

Commas Commas are used to separate parts of an expression. If you are using portions of a function where commas exist, type them exactly as shown in the example.

$

$ (the string comparison function)

Syntax   <exprC1> $ <exprC2>

Purpose   The $ function compares one string with another. Literally, it means, "Is the <exprC1> string contained anywhere in the <exprC2> string?" If so, (.T.) is returned; otherwise, (.F.) is returned.

Example
```
? "Jan" $ "JanFebMar"
.T.                              && result
? "Jan" $ "AprMayJun"
.F.                              && result
```

Requirements   Two character expressions to compare.

Results   A logical (.T.) or (.F.).

&

& (the macro substitution/expansion function)

Syntax &<memvar>
or
&<memvar>.<exprC>

Purpose The & function places the literal contents of a memory variable <memvar> directly into a command statement so that the command operates as though the memory variable contents are part of the command statement itself. Memory variables can be used, therefore, to change a command statement by including in it variable information that might change from time to time. The contents of variables that are used in commands with the & function are called macros. Macro expansion is the name given to the effect & produces, because a small variable name can expand into a larger portion of a command.

Example STORE "chaircount > 4000" TO macrovar
LIST FOR &macrovar

By storing "chaircount > 4000" in a memory variable, we made it available for use in the LIST command.

Rules & cannot begin a command line, only to add arguments to an existing, valid, command verb. More than one & can be used in a command, but only 255 characters are allowed in any command line whether or not macros are included.

An optional period (.) can be placed at the end of <memvar> to eliminate spaces that might otherwise enter between the expanded macro and the literal characters in <exprC>. A period thus used results in concatenation of the expanded macro to any characters that follow.

Modifying commands with the contents of memory variables is a particularly powerful way to affect the behavior of programs. Macros also add to the programmer's responsibility because he must ensure that the results command will always execute without producing errors.

Requirements The name of a character or numeric memory variable that contains an expression(s) that will be used directly in one or more commands.

Results Expanded command statements.

366   Symbols Used in the Function Reference

Abs( )

Syntax ABS(<exprN>)

Purpose ABS( ) returns the absolute value of <exprN>, which is, effectively, a number's difference from 0.

Example
```
? ABS(-123.88)
123.88                          && result
? ABS(123.88)
123.88                          && result
```

Requirements A number or numeric expression.

Results A number.

Also See INT( )

Alias( )

Syntax ALIAS([< exprN >])

Purpose ALIAS( ) returns the alias name, or full name if an alias hasn't been declared, of any open database file.

Example An alias is the name a file goes by. If a file is USE without the ALIAS option (see "USE < filename > ALIAS < alias name > "), its full name becomes its alias. In any case, ALIAS( ) returns a name that can be used in programs or interactively to identify the file.

Suppose that a database file name in the currently selected work area "A" is "Tables.dbf," and that the database file name in work area "C," also designated "3," is "Chairs.dbf." To discover the names of these files, enter the commands:

```
? ALIAS( )
Tables                          && result
? ALIAS(3)
Chairs                          && result
```

You can use both the ALIAS( ) function and the & function in programs like this:

```
STORE ALIAS( ) TO priorarea
. . . commands that select another workarea
SELECT &priorarea
```

In this example, the ALIAS( ) function is used to place the name of the currently selected database file into a memory variable named "priorarea." After other program tasks have been run, the SELECT command returns us to the previously selected work area by using the macro variable expansion facility of the & function.

Requirements None, or a number indicating which work area to query.

Results An empty character string ("") if no file is in use.

Also See USE (its ALIAS option) and SELECT

Asc( )

Syntax ASC(<exprC>)

Purpose ASC( ) returns the numeric decimal ASCII (American Standard Code for Information Interchange) value of the first character in <exprC>. ASC( ) does the opposite of CHR( ), which converts ASCII numbers into characters.

Example You can use ASC( ) to discover what key a user has pressed. Here's a little program that shows you the ASCII value of any key you press. Pressing Escape or Command-Period quits the program.

```
SET TALK OFF
SET ESCAPE ON
CLEAR
STORE 0 TO showascii
DO WHILE .T. .AND. showascii < > 27
   WAIT "Press a key or ESC" TO showascii
   CLEAR
   ? "You pressed: " + showascii
   ? "Which is ASCII: ", ASC(showascii)
ENDDO
```

The IBM and Macintosh ASCII code tables in Appendix A show the full range of possible ASCII values that can be returned.

Requirements Any character or character expression.

Results A number.

At( )

Syntax AT(<exprC1>,<exprC2>)

Purpose AT( ) returns a number indicating where, in characters from the left, the characters in <exprC1> are located in <exprC2>. If 0 is returned it means that the <exprC1> characters were not found anywhere inside the <exprC2> character string. AT( ) returns only the first location of a match. AT( ) works in memo fields as well as in other valid character expressions.

Example
```
STORE "JanFebMarAprMayJunJulAugSepOctNovDec" TO allmonths
? AT("Jan",allmonths)
1                          && result
? AT("Feb",allmonths)
4                          && result
? AT("Mar",allmonths)
7                          && result
? AT("Apr",allmonths)
10                         result
```

Another powerful use of AT( ) is to let it find records that have a memo field containing a particular word or phrase.

```
LOCATE FOR AT("SoughtString",memofieldname) > 0
CONTINUE
```

The LOCATE command works because AT( ) will search the memo field "memofieldname" of each record until it reaches the end of the file or it finds a record that returns a value greater than 0, indicating that it has found "SoughtString." The CONTINUE command then finds the next occurrence.

Requirements Two character expressions or literal strings. <exprC2> will be searched to find <exprC1>.

Results A positive number indicating the distance in characters from the first character where <exprC1> begins, or 0 if <exprC1> is not contained in <exprC2>.

Also See $, LEFT( ), RIGHT( ), SUBSTR( ), and STUFF( )

Bof( )

Syntax BOF([< exprN >])

Purpose BOF( ) is a testing function that tells you if the record pointer in a selected database file is at the beginning or top of a file. If it is, BOF( ) returns a logical (.T.); otherwise, it returns (.F.).

The actual beginning of a file (BOF) is encountered when any attempt is made to SKIP past the first record with the SKIP -1 command. This is because BOF( ), and its counterpart EOF( ), are designed to let programmers know when they have traversed a whole file. If you try to skip past BOF( ) an error message will occur.

Example BOF( ) is most often used as a DO WHILE or IF condition to stop record processing.

```
USE <file name>
GOTO BOTTOM
DO WHILE .NOT. BOF( )
   . . .commands that affect each record encountered
   SKIP -1
ENDDO
```

In this example, all records will be processed from the bottom/end of the file to the top/beginning. SKIP -1 can eventually put the record pointer at the first record, but because BOF( ) does not return (.T.) at record #1, the loop will be entered once more, allowing record #1 to be processed. SKIP -1 will then attempt to move the pointer past record #1 but will not succeed. At that point, the BOF( ) condition will return (.T.) and the loop will break. Here's another example showing the behavior of record pointers when you're traversing the file backwards.

```
USE Customers
GOTO TOP
? RECNO( )
1                         && result
? BOF( )
.F.                       && result
SKIP -1
Record No. 1              && result
? BOF( )
.T.                       && result
```

```
SKIP -1
Beginning of file encountered.        && result
```

Optionally, BOF( ) allows you to enter a number telling it which work area to query. BOF(1), for example, queries work area (A), BOF(2) queries (B), and so on. If there are no files open in the area being queried, (.F.) is returned.

Requirements Nothing, or an optional number indicating which work area to query.

Results A logical (.T.) or (.F.).

Also See GOTO and SKIP

Cdow( )

Syntax CDOW(< exprD >)

Purpose CDOW( ) is the "character day of week" function. It can tell you the day of the week: Monday, Tuesday, and so on, for any known date.

Example Because CDOW( ) accepts any date expression, dates in memory variables, or database fields, even the system date can be queried.

```
? CDOW(DATE( ))
Monday, Tuesday, etc.              && result
```

CDOW( ) can confuse literally entered dates as numeric division problems, so put quotation marks around character dates and use the CTOD( ) function to turn them into date types for use by CDOW( ).

```
? CDOW(CTOD("01/25/89"))
Wednesday                          && result
```

Requirements Any valid date expression.

Results The day of week as a character string.

Also See CTOD( ), DAY( ), and DOW( )

Chr( )

Syntax CHR(<exprN>)

Purpose CHR( ) is almost opposite of the ASC( ) function. The ASC( ) function turns characters into their numeric ASCII equivalents, whereas the CHR( ) function turns numeric ASCII values into the characters they represent.

Example ASCII stands for American Standard Code for Information Interchange. ASCII codes have been adapted from their use in the days of teletypes for use as computer input and output codes via keyboards, displays, and printers. Macintosh and IBM computers have their own ASCII code equivalents, which are included in Appendix A. On Macintosh computers, the first 32 ASCII values are reserved for nonprintable control codes. The displayed results of CHR( ) are affected by the default display font.

In report forms using version 1.x of FoxBASE+/Mac, CHR( ) can be used to make more than one database field appear in a column. For example, placing a suite or post office box number underneath a street address can be accomplished by inserting the ASCII carriage return code:

```
address1 + CHR(13) + address2
```

You can even cause the "bell" to ring by entering its ASCII control code, CHR(7):

```
? CHR(7)
```

For programmers, another more important use of CHR( ) is its ability to send control signals to a printer or other device. CHR(27), for example, can send an escape code to a printer and on some printers, CHR(15) invokes the condensed character mode. Because printers are very different, you should consult a user's manual to get the correct codes.

Requirements Any decimal number that represents an ASCII code.

Results The display or control effect desired.

Also See ASC( ) and INKEY( )

Cmonth( )

Syntax	CMONTH(<exprD>)
Purpose	The character month function, CMONTH( ), returns the name of the month in the date <exprD>.
Example	CMONTH( ) accepts any date expression, so <exprD> can be a memory variable, a date database field, or a literal. Even the system date can be queried by placing CMONTH( ) around the DATE( ) function.

```
? CMONTH(DATE( ))
January, February, etc.          && result
? CMONTH(CTOD("01/25/89"))
January                          && result
```

Requirements	Any valid date expression.
Results	The month as a character string.
Also See	CTOD( ), DAY( ), and DOW( )

Col( )

Syntax COL([1])

Purpose COL( ) provides relative addressing of the cursor's character-column position by returning a number that indicates the cursor's current position. The column number returned is a reference to pixels instead of characters whenever the optional number 1 is used.

On a Macintosh, the mouse moves the cursor, but that's not the kind of location reporting that COL( ) provides. Instead, it tells you where the "painting" cursor stopped last when something was written on the screen. If nothing has been written on a clear screen, the COL( ) function will tell you that the cursor is at column 0, which is the left-most screen column.

Example The COL( ) function is especially useful when you are painting screens under a program's control. It allows you to "step" across the screen in even or measured increments, or to specify any pixel or character-column position relative to the current.

```
@ 0,0 SAY "*"
 *                                          && result
@ 1,COL( ) + 2 SAY "*"
 *                                          && result
@ 2,COL( ) + 2 SAY "*"
 *                                          && result
@ 3,COL( ) + 2 SAY "*"
 *                                          && result
@ 4,COL( ) + 2 SAY "*"
 *                                          && result
```

Proportional fonts do not perfectly align across all columns because the width of characters differs. Monospaced fonts should be used when running programs that were originally designed to run on an IBM screen, because its text map is 25 character rows by 80 character columns. Number columns also require character-based alignment. The Monaco font used with a pitch of nine works well. Monaco is installed automatically so that it's available on most Macintosh computers, and it can be installed on others using the Font/DA Mover.

Requirements None or, optionally, the number 1.

Results   A number representing the current character-column position of the cursor, or a number representing the current pixel-column position of the cursor.

Also See   @, PCOL( ), PROW( ), ROW( ), and SET SCREEN

Ctod( )

Syntax CTOD(<exprC>)

Purpose CTOD( ) is called the character to date function because it turns a character expression, represented here by "<exprC>," into a date.

Example
```
? CTOD("01/02/88")
01/02/88                                   && result
```

An important feature of dates is that they can be added and subtracted with numbers to produce new results. This allows you to perform date math where each 1 is equivalent to a day.

```
? CTOD("01/02/88")—365
01/02/87                                   && result
```

Requirements A character literal or expression that accurately represents a FoxBASE date.

Results A date.

Also See SET DATE, SET CENTURY, and DTOC( )

Date( )

Syntax	DATE( )
Purpose	DATE( ) tells you what the current date is by checking the computer's clock calendar.
Example	? DATE( ) 11/12/89, etc. && result
	Note that the SET DATE command affects the appearance of the result by applying one of several national display standards.
Requirements	None.
Results	The current system date.
Also See	SET CENTURY and SET DATE

Day( )

Syntax DAY(< exprD >)

Purpose DAY( ) lets you know what day of the month (1–31) is represented by the date < exprD >. Like other such functions, DAY( ) accepts any valid date expression, regardless of its source. You can submit any valid date type, including memory variables, character dates that have been converted by CTOD( ), and date fields from a database file.

Example
```
? DAY(CTOD("01/20/89"))
20                                          && result
```

Because the value returned by the DAY( ) function is numeric, you can add or subtract a DAY( ) directly from other dates or numbers.

Requirements Any date literal or expression.

Results A number representing the day of the month (1-31).

Also See CDOW( ) and DOW( )

Dbf( )

Syntax DBF([<exprN>])

Purpose DBF( ) queries a database work area to find out the name of the database file that is open there. It is different from the ALIAS( ) function because, unlike ALIAS( ), DBF( ) tells you the full database file name, including its drive and folder names (path of the file).

The optional number <exprN> tells DBF( ) what work area to query, where 1−10 represents work areas A−J. If no number is specified, the currently selected work area will be queried.

Example DBF( ) can be used to support file operations because it returns the complete path and name of a file. DBF( ) and ALIAS( ) return different results.

```
? DBF( )
HD40:Example:Customers.dbf      && result
? ALIAS( )
CUSTOMERS                       && result
```

Requirements None or, optionally, a number indicating what work area to query (1−10 for work areas A−J).

Results A character string representing a fully qualified path and file name.

Also See FIELD and NDX( )

Deleted( )

Syntax DELETED([<exprN>])

Purpose DELETED( ) asks whether or not the current record is marked for deletion. If so, (.T.) is returned, otherwise (.F.). is returned. The optional number <exprN> tells DELETED( ) what work area to query (1–10 for work areas A–J). If <exprN> is not entered, the currently selected work area's database file is tested.

Example In FoxBASE, records are not removed when they are deleted with the DELETE command. They are merely marked for removal at a later time by the PACK command. DELETED( ) is most often used with the IF command to decide the disposition of a record.

```
SEEK FOR lastname = "Jones"
IF DELETED( )
   RECALL
ENDIF
```

If the PACK command had been used before the RECALL command, the record containing "Jones" would be irretrievably removed from the file.

Requirements None or, optionally, a number indicating which work area to query.

Results A logical (.T.) or (.F.).

Also See DELETE, RECALL, SET DELETED, and PACK

Diskspace( )

Syntax DISKSPACE( )

Purpose DISKSPACE( ) returns a number indicating how much space in bytes remains on the default disk drive. A byte is roughly equivalent to one character's worth of space.

Example DISKSPACE( ) looks at the default drive volume, which can be any physical or logical disk mounted to your computer. Some commands require that lots of disk space be available, so it's wise to check before launching some tasks—sorts and on-disk data backups among them.

```
SET DEFAULT TO "HD20"
? DISKSPACE( )
3423450                        && result (3.5 MB)
SET DEFAULT TO "FloppyDisk1"
? DISKSPACE( )
290212                         && result (300 KB)
```

Requirements None.

Results A number representing available bytes of space on the default volume.

Dow( )

Syntax DOW(<exprD>)

Purpose DOW( ) returns a number representing the day of the week (one through seven for Sunday through Saturday). The date expression can be from any source: a date memory variable, a database field that contains a date data type, or a literal that has been transformed into a date by the CTOD( ) character-to-date function.

Example DOW( ) gives you the ability to perform date math within a week, such as when expired days of the week are important and you want to track them one day at a time.

```
? DOW(DATE( ))
1,2,3,4,5,6, or 7                && result
```

To prove that the first day of 1989 fell on a Sunday, try this:

```
? DOW(CTOD("01/01/89"))
1                                && result
```

Now, add three days and see what happens.

```
? DOW(CTOD("01/01/89")) + 3
4                                && result
```

Requirements Any valid date expression.

Results A number representing the day of the week where 1 = Sunday and 7 = Saturday.

Also See CDOW( ) and DAY( )

Dtoc( )

Syntax DTOC(<exprD>[,1])

Purpose DTOC( ) is the date-to-character function. It takes any valid date in the form of a date expression <exprD>, regardless of its location—memory variable, database file, or literal—and returns a character string. The SET DATE command directly affects the display format of character dates returned by DTOC( ).

The optional argument [1], instructs DTOC( ) to return a character string in which the year appears before the month, and the month appears before the day. This provides a consistent way to index dates in chronological order, regardless of the format established by the SET DATE command.

Example An important thing to know about printing to the screen or to a printer is that date data type information and character data type information cannot be joined (concatenated) with the + operator as attempted in this example:

@ 10,10 SAY "The date is " + DATE( )

However, by converting the date expression into a character expression you can get this result:

@ 10,10 SAY "The date is " + DTOC(DATE( ))
The date is 08/12/89   && result

Use DTOC( ) to create a date INDEX, which is guaranteed to be in chronological order regardless of the SET DATE format. This example results in a properly ordered index of dates:

? DTOC(datefieldname,1)
19890131   && result
INDEX ON DTOC(datefieldname,1) TO indexfile name

Requirements Any valid date expression.

Results A character string representing the date in the SET DATE specified format, or, optionally, in a format designed for accurate indexing.

Also See CTOD( ), SET CENTURY, and SET DATE

Eof( )

Syntax EOF([<exprN>])

Purpose EOF( ) tests for an end-of-file condition, returning a logical (.T.) if the end of a tested database file has been reached and (.F.) if not. An end-of-file condition is created when the FIND, SEEK, or SET RELATION commands fail to find a matching record or when you SKIP past the last logical record in a file. EOF( ) respects the order imposed by an index, exhibiting the same behavior regardless.

The optional number <exprN> tells the function to test a file in any work area, 1–10 for work areas A–J. EOF( ) returns (.F.) if no database file is open in the tested work area.

Example EOF( ) is often used as a DO WHILE condition when a program traverses a file one record at a time.

```
USE <filename>
GOTO TOP
DO WHILE .NOT. EOF( )
   ...commands that affect each record
   SKIP 1
ENDDO
```

For a fuller understanding of EOF( ), take a look at BOF( ). They perform similarly except that BOF( ) becomes true when the pointer is still located on the file's first record, whereas EOF( ) is true only when the pointer has passed the last record. This is so that empty field values instead of erroneous data will be returned in the event that FIND, SEEK, or SET RELATION commands fail to find a match.

Requirements Nothing, or an optional number indicating which work area to query.

Results A logical (.T.) or (.F.).

Also See FIND, GOTO, SEEK, and SKIP

Error( )

Syntax	ERROR( )
Purpose	ERROR( ) checks to see what the last error condition was and returns the number that relates to that particular condition. The error table listing in Appendix C explains the number and meaning of each possible error. Requires the ON ERROR <command> in order to work, or only 0 will be returned.
Example	ERROR( ) is intended for use as part of an error-trapping and handling system that includes an error-handling program or procedure, and the ON ERROR command, which tells FoxBASE to invoke the error handler whenever an error is encountered. The ERROR( ) function works inside an error-handling routine to identify the error condition so that it can be managed gracefully.
	The significant thing about programmed error-handling is that you can trap almost any nonfatal error. If no error handling has been established, FoxBASE issues alert dialogs when errors are encountered and it sometimes has no recourse but to halt application programs from running altogether.
	Take a look at the discussion of error handling in Chapter 7 for examples.
Requirements	None.
Results	A number representing the type of error encountered. See the error message table in Appendix C for specifics.
Also See	MESSAGE( ) and ON ERROR

Exp( )

Syntax   EXP(<exprN>)

Purpose   EXP( ) calculates the base natural logarithm value of 2.71828183, or e, raised to the number represented by <exprN>.

Example   EXP( ) is a mathematical function that can be used at any time to return a number in its place. The number that it returns will be the result of e, the natural logarithm base raised to <exprN> as shown in these examples:

```
? EXP(1.325)
3.762                           && result
? EXP(2.1)
8.17                            && result
? EXP(3.5)
33.12                           && result
```

EXP( ) is the inverse of the LOG( ) function.

```
? EXP(LOG(2))
2.00                            && result
? EXP(LOG(45))
45.00                           && result
```

Requirements   A number.

Results   A number.

Also See   LOG( ) and SET DECIMALS

Fcount( )

Syntax   FCOUNT([<exprN>])

Purpose   FCOUNT( ) checks a database file to see how many fields it has and lets you know by returning a number indicating the count. The optional number <exprN> tells FCOUNT( ) to test a file in any work area, 1–10 for work areas A–J. If there is no database file in the selected work area, FCOUNT( ) returns 0.

Example   FCOUNT( ) has little utility by itself. However, when it is combined with a function like FIELD( ), the FCOUNT( ) function can be very useful.

```
USE <filename>
? FCOUNT( )
1,2, etc.                        && result
```

Requirements None, or an optional number indicating which work area to query.

Results   A number indicating the number or records in the file.

Also See   DBF( ) and NDX( )

Field( )

Syntax FIELD(<exprN1> [, <exprN2>])

Purpose FIELD( ) lets you or your program know the name of any field in any database file that's currently open. It requires that you know what work area the file is in and what position the field occupies from left to right. If no database file is opened, or the field queried doesn't exist, the returned value will be "", an empty string.

Example FIELD( ) requires that you specify the number of a field's position before it can return its name. <exprN1> is that number. <exprN2> is an optional number indicating the work area to check, 1−10 for work areas A−J. Without <exprN2>, the file in the currently selected work area will be tested.

```
USE <filename>
? FIELD(3)
lastname                        && result
```

The following example, using FCOUNT( ) and FIELD( ) lists all of the fields in the currently active database file by checking each in turn.

```
SET TALK OFF
USE <filename>
STORE 1 TO fieldnum
DO WHILE fieldnum <= FCOUNT( )
     ? FIELD(fieldnum)
        STORE fieldnum + 1 TO fieldnum
ENDDO
SET TALK ON
```

Requirements A number indicating what field to query, and optionally, a number indicating which database work area to query (1−10 for work areas A−J).

Results An uppercase character string representing the name of a database field.

File( )

Syntax FILE(<filename>)

Purpose FILE( ) checks to see if a known <filename> exists on the disk and then lets you know by returning (.T.) or (.F.). The <filename> must be a valid character expression that represents a complete file name, including its extension, if applicable.

Example
```
? FILE("Customers.dbf")
.T.                                                      && result
? FILE("HD40:Example:Products.dbf")
.T.                                                      && result
STORE "HD40:Example:Products.dbf" TO isfile
HD40:Example:Products.dbf                                && result
? isfile
.T.                                                      && result
STORE "Customers.dbf" TO isfile
Customers.dbf                                            && result
? FILE("HD40:Example:" + isfile)
.T.                                                      && result
SET PATH TO HD40:IMPORT:
? FILE("EXCELTXT")
.T.                                                      && result
```

This example demonstrates several possibilities for using FILE( ). Note that the first two commands show <filename> enclosed in quotation marks. This is because they are required whenever <filename> is a literal character string. The third command stores a <filename> into a memory variable, then the next two commands use the memory variable "isfile" as an argument for FILE( ).

The "EXCELTXT" file is a text file in the "IMPORT" folder. By establishing a path to the import folder with the SET PATH command it becomes easier to use FILE( ). The last command demonstrates that the FILE( ) function can find any file as long as it is in the default (SET PATH) path list.

Requirements Any valid character string representing the file name sought.

Results A logical (.T.) or (.F.).

Fklabel( )

Syntax FKLABEL(<exprN>)

Purpose FKLABEL( ) tells you the system's name for any of the programmable function keys. This is useful because function keys can have different label names on different computers, and they can be reprogrammed with the SET FUNCTION command when you know their label names. Typically, <exprN> starts at 1 and goes to FKMAX( ), which is another function that returns the maximum number of keys available to a program. Since F1 is permanently programmed with the command "HELP," FKLABEL(1) returns the label for the second function key—usually "F2."

Example The command examples here show what the default FoxBASE labels are, but the labels are not useful in themselves. Make sure to look at the entry in Chapter 8 for "SET FUNCTION TO" if you want to better understand how programmable function keys are used.

```
? FKLABEL(1)
F2                              && result
? FKLABEL(2)
F3                              && result
? FKLABEL(3)
F4                              && result
? FKLABEL(4)
F5                              && result
? FKLABEL(5)
F6                              && result
? FKLABEL(6)
F7                              && result
? FKLABEL(7)
F8                              && result
? FKLABEL(8)
F9                              && result
? FKLABEL(9)
F10                             && result
? FKLABEL(10)
F11                             && result
? FKLABEL(11)
F12                             && result
? FKLABEL(12)
F13                             && result
? FKLABEL(13)
F14                             && result
? FKLABEL(14)
F15                             && result
```

Function key labels, by themselves, are meaningless except that they allow you to assign new commands to the keys with SET FUNCTION TO. Extended keyboards have actual function keys like IBM computers do, and the standard SE keyboard equivalents for F2 through F10 are achieved by pressing Ctrl-2 through Ctrl-0. Unfortunately, Mac Plus and earlier models don't provide function key equivalents.

The extended keyboard is still required if you want to program and use function keys F11 through F15. FoxBASE does not use them by default, but you can.

Requirements   A number indicating which key's label to return.

Results   A character string representing the label name of the function key queried. Typically, in a range between F2 and F15.

Also See   SET FUNCTION TO and FKMAX( )

Symbols Used in the Function Reference   393

Fkmax( )

Syntax FKMAX( )

Purpose FKMAX( ) checks to see how many programmable function keys there are on the host computer and returns a number indicating the total.

Example
```
? FKMAX( )
14                          && result (ext keyboard)
? FKMAX( )
9                           && result (std keyboard)
```

Requirements None.

Results A number representing the count of programmable function keys.

Also See FKLABEL( ) and SET FUNCTION

Flock( )

Syntax	FLOCK( )
Purpose	FLOCK( ) is a programmer's multiuser command that attempts to lock a database file, returning (.T.) if it succeeds and (.F.) if it fails. If a user's computer has locked a file to itself, it can be released with an UNLOCK command or by closing the file.
Example	FLOCK( ) is useful when you need to do something that can change several records at once, such as APPEND FROM, DELETE <scope> and so on. For a fuller explanation and examples of its use see the discussion of multiuser issues in Chapter 10.
Requirements	None.
Results	A logical (.T.) or (.F.) indicating whether or not a file lock is in place.
Also See	RLOCK( ), UNLOCK, QUIT, USE, CLEAR ALL, CLOSE, and SET EXCLUSIVE

Found( )

Syntax FOUND([<exprN>])

Purpose The FOUND( ) function performs a check to see if the database record pointer has located what was sought using the CONTINUE, FIND, LOCATE or SEEK commands. If so, it returns (.T.). If the record pointer gets moved after finding a match, FOUND( ) will return (.F.).

The optional argument <exprN> tells FOUND( ) what work area to query, allowing you to check any files related to the currently selected file to see if there is a match with a parent file. To better understand relations, take a look at the entry for the SET RELATION TO command in Chapter 8.

Example FOUND( ) is applied, for example, in programs that allow users to add new records to a database.

```
STORE SPACE(20) TO newcust
USE Customers INDEX Custname
@ ROW( ),COL( ) SAY "Enter customer name " GET newcust
READ
SEEK newcust
IF FOUND( )
        @ 24,0 SAY custname + " is already on file."
        EDIT
ELSE
        APPEND
ENDIF
```

In this example, FOUND( ) returns (.T.) if the named customer already exists, preventing the APPEND from adding another entry for the same customer. The program also displays the found record so that the user can edit it, or just to verify that it was entered properly in the first place.

The optional argument <exprN> is a number telling FOUND( ) to look in any database work area, 1–10 for work areas A–J. This feature is useful when an automatic relation has been established between two or more files, as is the case in this example:

```
SELECT A
USE Customers
```

```
SELECT B
USE Sales INDEX custnumber
SELECT A
SET RELATION TO custnumber INTO Sales
LOCATE FOR custname = "Village Gifts"
IF FOUND(2)
      SET FORMAT TO custsales
      EDIT
ELSE
      @ 24,0 SAY custname + " has no sales to edit."
ENDIF
```

Here, FOUND( ) checks the "Sales" file in work area 2, for "B," to see if a customer number for "Village Gifts" was found. If "Village Gifts" was not found in the "Customers" file, its pointer would go to the end of the file as would the pointer in the "Sales" file. This happens because of the relationship set between them. However, if the "Customers" file had a record for "Village Gifts" its customer number would automatically be sought in the "Sales" file because of the relationship established between the customer numbers in each file. FOUND(2) looks at the "Sales" file to see if a record was found to match the customer's number. If a record is found, an editing screen format is set and the user is allowed to edit the sales information. If not, the program puts a message on line 24 informing him that no sales were found for that customer.

Requirements   None, or optionally a number representing what work area to query.

Results   A logical (.T.) or (.F.).

Also See   EOF( ), FIND, LOCATE-CONTINUE, and SEEK

Getfile( )

Syntax GETFILE([<exprC1>] [, <exprC2>])

Purpose GETFILE( ) is used in programs when the programmer wants a user to select a file using the standard Macintosh file-picker. The optional argument <exprC1> sets the type of file that a user can see in the dialog for picking, and <exprC2> is a text message that appears inside the dialog to prompt the user. If no file is selected, GETFILE( ) returns "", the null string.

Example When a file selection has been made, GETFILE( ) returns its name. <exprC1> is four characters that indicate what type of file you want the user to select. When you replace <exprC1> with a file type selection from the list below, only files of that type will be visible to the user for selecting.

<exprC1>	Files shown for selection
F+DB	Database
F+IX	Index
F+ME	Memory variable file
F+FR	Report form (version 1.x)
F+LB	Label form
F+RP	Report and Label form (version 2.x)
F+VU	View file
TEXT	ASCII text
Nothing	All files

I recommend only one method for using GETFILE( )—to store the name of the selected file in a memory variable and then open it in a second step.

```
STORE GETFILE("F+RP") TO labelfile
IF LEN(TRIM(labelfile)) > 0
     MODIFY LABEL &labelfile
ENDIF
```

It's a good idea to add the step, shown in the example above, that checks the variable's file name, making sure that the user did not cancel, in which case the variable would be a character string with zero length. If the value returned by GETFILE( ) is 0, you know that the user pressed the cancel button.

Database, text, report, label, and index files are the most likely candidates for use with the GETFILE( ) file-opening dialog, but there are a variety of file types beyond those mentioned that can be selected.

In addition to the file types that the Macintosh records, are each file's creator. This signature, as it is called, tells the Macintosh what program to run when document icons are double-clicked from the desktop. All FoxBASE+/Mac files bear the signature "FOX+."

Requirements	None, or characters to indicate a file type to open, and characters to form a user prompt.
Results	A character string representing the full path and file name of the file selected by a user inside the file open dialog.
Also See	PUTFILE( )

Iif( )

Syntax	IIF(<exprL>,<expr1>,<expr2>)
Purpose	IIF( ) is called the "immediate if" function, because it can select between two options immediately, at any spot inside of any command statement following a valid command verb. If <exprL> is true, IIF( ) returns <expr1>, if <exprL> is false, IIF( ) returns <expr2>.
Example	Use IIF( ) whenever a decision between two or more options must be made on one command line, such as in reports or labels, or in lieu of IF...ENDIF constructs.

```
STORE 1200 TO sales
@ 2,2 SAY IIF(sales > 1000, "Good job!","Keep trying.")
Good job!                           && result
STORE 900 TO sales
@ 2,2 SAY IIF(sales > 1000, "Good job!","Keep trying.")
Keep trying.                        && result
```

Requirements	Three arguments, one logical expression to test, and two result expressions that can be of any data type.
Results	The expression selected after evaluating <exprL>.
Also See	IF...ENDIF and DO CASE

Inkey( )

Syntax INKEY([< exprN >])

Purpose INKEY( ) returns a number between 0 and 255 that represents the ASCII code of the key just pressed. If no key has been pressed, the value returned will be 0. INKEY( ) also removes the keystroke it evaluates from the keyboard buffer so that it will have no effect on a program. A good way to make a program wait for users while trapping all keyboard events is to place INKEY( ) in a continual DO WHILE loop. The optional numeric argument tells INKEY( ) how long to wait for keystrokes before testing the keyboard buffer. 0 makes INKEY( ) wait forever to receive a keystroke or menu hit. Any positive number, including single decimals, make INKEY( ) wait for that number of seconds before testing the buffer.

Example Take a look at the discussion of multiuser commands in Chapter 10 to see examples that use the INKEY( ) function for making a program wait for an event. INKEY( ) can recognize most of the keys on the keyboard, and you can use it to "program" keys other than recognizable, visible, ASCII value keys. Here's a sample list of values:

ASCII	Key pressed
−1	F2
−2	F3
−3	F4
−4	F5
−5	F6
−6	F7
−7	F8
−8	F9
−9	F10
1	Home or Command-A
2	Command-Right Arrow or Command-B
3	Page Down or Command-C
4	Right Arrow or Command-D
5	Up Arrow or Command-E
6	End or Command-F
7	Delete or Command-G
8	Command-H
9	Command-I

10	Command-J
11	Command-K
12	Command-L
13	Command-M
14	Command-N
15	Command-O
16	Command-P
17	Command-Q
18	Page Up or Command-R
19	Left Arrow or Command-S
20	Command-T
21	Command-U
22	Insert or Command-V
23	Command-End or Command-W
24	Down Arrow or Command-X
25	Command-Y
26	Command-Left Arrow or Command-Z
28	F1
29	Command-Home or Command-]
30	Command-Page Down or Command-^
31	Command-Page Up or Command-_

Requirements   None, or optionally, a number indicating how long to wait before testing for keystrokes.

Results   A number representing the ASCII code value of the last key pressed.

Also See   CHR( ), ON KEY, READKEY( ), and SET TYPEAHEAD

Int( )

Syntax   INT(<exprN>)

Purpose   INT( ) returns the integer portion of numbers, which is really the same as removing any decimals from a number that contains them.

Example
```
? INT(78.9123)
78                                && result
STORE 1234.56 TO number
? INT(number)
12345                             && result
```

Requirements A number.

Results   A number without decimal places.

Isalpha( )

Syntax   ISALPHA(<exprC>)

Purpose   If the first character in <exprC> is one of the 26 alphabetic characters or a space, ISALPHA( ) will return (.T.), otherwise it returns (.F.).

Example
```
STORE "ABC" TO string
? ISALPHA(string)
.T.                              && result
STORE "1AB" TO string
.F.                              && result
```

Requirements   Any character string or expression.

Results   A logical (.T.) or (.F.).

Iscolor( )

Syntax   ISCOLOR( )

Purpose   ISCOLOR( ) returns (.T.) if the host computer is poised to support color, and (.F.) if it is not.

Example   Use ISCOLOR( ) to make a program that works in black and white on one color computers and in full color on computers with color support.

```
IF ISCOLOR( )
      SET COLOR TO R+/N
ELSE
      SET COLOR TO N/W
ENDIF
```

Requirements   Nothing.

Results   A logical (.T.) or (.F.) depending on whether or not color support is currently available in the host computer system.

Also See   SET COLOR

Islower( )

Syntax   ISLOWER(< exprC >)

Purpose   ISLOWER( ) checks character expressions to see if the first letter in the expression string is a lowercase alphabetic character, returning (.T.) if it is and (.F.) if it is not.

Example   Use ISLOWER( ) to determine, for example, whether or not a name field contains a proper name or some other information (which might be in lowercase).

```
IF ISLOWER(name)
    ? "This is not a proper name or title."
ELSE
    ? "This is probably a proper name or title."
ENDIF
```

Requirements A character expression or literal string.

Results   A logical (.T.) or (.F.) depending on whether or not the first character in the supplied expression is a lowercase letter.

Also See   ISUPPER( )

Isupper( )

Syntax ISUPPER(< exprC >)

Purpose ISUPPER( ) checks character expressions to see if the first letter in the expression string is an uppercase alphabetic character, returning (.T.) if it is and (.F.) if it is not.

Example Use ISUPPER( ) to determine, for example, whether or not a name field contains a proper name or some other information (which might be in lowercase.)

```
IF ISUPPER(name)
    ? "This is probably a proper name or title."
ELSE
    ? "This is not a proper name or title."
ENDIF
```

Requirements A character expression or literal string.

Results A logical (.T.) or (.F.) depending on whether or not the first character in the supplied expression is an uppercase letter.

Also See ISLOWER( )

Left( )

Syntax LEFT(<exprC>,<exprN>)

Purpose LEFT( ) returns a selected number of characters from a character expression beginning with the left-most character. <exprN> determines how many characters should be returned. If the number of characters is 0 or less than 0, an empty character string, " ", is returned.

Example Use LEFT( ) to consistently truncate a string for printing in a small space, or to extract a portion of any character field or variable for processing.

```
STORE "The dog has big black spots." TO string
? LEFT(string,7)
The dog
? LEFT(string,11)
The dog has
? LEFT(string,15)
The dog has big
```

Requirements A character string or expression and a number.

Results A character string selection.

Also See SUBSTR( ) and LEN( )

Len( )

Syntax LEN(< exprC >)

Purpose LEN( ) tests any character string or expression for its length and returns a number indicating how many character positions it contains. LEN( ) counts blank spaces as characters.

Example Use LEN( ) with TRIM( ) to test whether or not a user has entered something into a character data entry field or to see if a database field contains data. TRIM( ) removes blanks from an expression before evaluation so that only the valuable portion of a string is measured by LEN( ).

```
STORE SPACE(20) TO string
@ 2,2 GET string
READ
IF LEN(TRIM(string)) < 0
        ? "No data was entered into the string memory variable."
ELSE
        ? "Data was entered into the string memory variable."
ENDIF
```

Use LEN( ) to center text on the screen in character values.

@ 10,(80-LEN(string))/2 SAY string

Use LEN( ) to center text on the screen in pixel values.

@ pixels 100, (VAL(SYS(1024))/2)-(VAL(SYS(1030,string))/2) SAY string STYLE;
   65536 FONT "Geneva",14

Requirements A character string or expression.

Results A number representing the length of the character string or expression.

Also See AT( ) and TRIM( )

Lock( )

Syntax	LOCK( )
Purpose	LOCK( ) is a programmer's multiuser command that attempts to lock the current record in a database file, returning (.T.) if it succeeds and (.F.) if it fails. Only when such an explicit lock is used is programmed editing and entry of data allowed in mulitiuser systems.
Example	For an explanation and examples of LOCK's use, see the discussion of multiuser functions in Chapter 10.
Requirements	Nothing.
Results	A logical (.T.) or (.F.) indicating whether or not a record lock is in place.
Also See	FLOCK( ), RLOCK( ), UNLOCK, QUIT, USE, CLEAR ALL, CLOSE, and SET EXCLUSIVE

Log( )

Syntax LOG(<exprN>)

Purpose LOG( ) calculates and returns the natural logarithm of a number greater than 0, which you supply as <exprN>.

Example LOG( ) is a mathematical function that can be used at any time to return a number in its place.

```
? LOG(.2)
-1.6094              && result
? LOG(.3)
-1.2040              && result
? LOG(.4)
-0.9163              && result
? LOG(.5)
-0.6931              && result
? LOG(1)
-0.0000              && result
? LOG(2)
-0.6931              && result
```

Requirements A number.

Results A number.

Also See EXP( ), SET DECIMALS

Lower( )

Syntax	LOWER(< exprC >)
Purpose	LOWER( ) changes all uppercase letters in a character string or expression with lowercase letters.
Example	STORE "Alphabetic Characters" to string ? LOWER(string) alphabetic characters && result
Requirements	A character string or expression.
Results	A lowercase character string.
Also See	ISLOWER( ), ISUPPER( ), and UPPER( )

Ltrim( )

Syntax   LTRIM (< exprC >)

Purpose   LTRIM returns what remains of a character string or expression after it removes all blanks from its left-most side.

Example   This example shows how LTRIM( ) can repair a string returned by the SUBSTR( ) function.

```
STORE "The cat and the dog went out to play." TO string
? LTRIM(SUBSTR(string,4,3))
   cat                                          && result
? STR(string,4,3)
   cat                                          && result
```

This example demonstrates, perhaps more graphically, how LTRIM( ) works.

```
STORE   " Ambulance driver." TO string
? string
 Ambulance driver.                              && result
? LTRIM(string)
Ambulance driver.                               && result
```

Requirements A character string or expression.

Results   A character string.

Also See   LEFT( ), RIGHT( ), RTRIM( ), STR( ), SUBSTR( ), and TRIM( )

Lupdate

Syntax	LUPDATE( )
Purpose	LUPDATE( ) returns the last date when changes were made to the currently active database file.
Example	This example uses LUPDATE( ) to determine which of two files was last modified.

```
USE FileOne
STORE LUPDATE( ) TO mOneDate
USE FileTwo
STORE LUPDATE( ) TO mTwoDate
DO CASE
CASE mOneDate = mTwoDate
    ? "Both files were changed on the same day."
CASE FileOne > FileTwo
    ? "FileOne was the last file changed."
OTHERWISE
    ? "FileTwo was the last file changed."
ENDCASE
```

Another use of this function is to use the basic method demonstrated above to compare archived files with working files to determine the necessity of a backup on a file-by-file basis.

Requirements	Nothing.
Results	A date.

Max( )

Syntax MAX(<exprD>,<exprD>)
 or
 MAX(<exprN>,<exprN>)

Purpose MAX( ) checks two numbers or two dates, returning the bigger or later value.

Example This example checks to see if more widgets or whamos were sold.

```
STORE 350 TO widgets
STORE 340 TO whamos
? MAX(widgets, whamos)
350                                    && result
```

Requirements Two numbers or numeric expressions, or two date expressions.

Results Either a date or a number representing the later or the larger of the two.

Also See MIN( )

Menu( )

Syntax MENU(0)
or
MENU(1)

Purpose MENU( ) returns a number to indicate what pull-down menu item was selected by an application user. As such, this function is useful only in programs. MENU(0) returns the main menu's number from left to right, and MENU(1) indicates the particular row, or option, on the menu that was selected.

Example Most often, MENU(0) and MENU(1) are used to pass numbers to a menu-handling program, which in turn causes programmed actions to occur by means of IF...ENDIF or DO CASE... ENDCASE logic. For an example of MENU( ), look at the *On Menu-Event Handling* section in Chapter 7. You might also want to explore the discussion of menu making and handling in Chapter 8 under the *Menu* topic.

Requirements Only one of two numbers, 0 or 1.

Results A number indicating which menu option or which option on a menu was selected by a user.

Also See ON MENU, MENU BAR, READ, and MENU (command)

Message( )

Syntax MESSAGE([1])

Purpose MESSAGE( ) returns the character message string of any current FoxBASE error conditon that exists when it is used. If no error condition exists, an empty string is returned. If used with the optional argument 1, MESSAGE( ) will return the character string line of program code that was the last one executed. Normally, this line is responsible for generating the error.

Example See the discussion of error handling in Chapter 10 for examples using the MESSAGE( ) function.

Requirements Nothing, or a 1.

Results A character string.

Also See ERROR( ), ON ERROR, and RETRY

Min( )

Syntax	MIN(<exprD>,<exprD>) or MIN(<exprN>,<exprN>)
Purpose	MIN( ) returns the earlier of two dates or the smaller of two numbers.
Example	The MAX( ) function performs exactly the opposite function as MIN( ), so take a look at the examples given for MAX( ) and reverse the comparisons.
Requirements	Two numbers or numeric expressions, or two date expressions.
Results	Either a date or a number representing the earlier or the smaller of the two.
Also See	MAX( )

Mod( )

Syntax	MOD(<exprN1>,<exprN2>)
Purpose	MOD( ) returns the numeric remainder that would exist were <exprN1> to be divided by <exprN2>. The answer's sign will always match that of <exprN1>.
Example	Suppose you wanted to know how many tennis balls would be left in the locker room after dividing 175 of them among your students. This example tells you how many each student will get and how many will be left over.

```
STORE 175 TO balls
STORE 20 TO students
? INT(balls/students)
8                              && result, 8 each
? MOD(balls,students)
15                             && result, 15 left
```

Requirements	Two numbers.
Results	A number indicating the remainder of a division.
Also See	INT( )

Symbols Used in the Function Reference

Month( )

Syntax MONTH(<exprD>)

Purpose MONTH( ) returns a number from 1 to 12 indicating the month, from January to December, of <exprD>.

Example If you wanted to find out how many months were remaining of a club membership for a particular member you could use the MONTH( ) function to return a number suitable for numeric comparison.

```
STORE CTOD("12/01/89") TO expires
STORE CTOD("06/01/89") TO current
? MONTH(expires) - MONTH(current)
6                                        && result
```

Requirements Any date expression.

Results A number.

Also See CMONTH( ), DAY( ), YEAR( ), and SYS( )

Ndx( )

Syntax NDX(<exprN>)

Purpose NDX( ) returns the fully qualified path and file name of any index open in the currently selected work area. <exprN>, a number from one to eight, indicates which of a possible seven index names to retrieve. The eighth position will always return a null string, "", without triggering an error, which is the same thing that happens if there is no index in the list at a position specified by <exprN>.

Example If you wanted to find out if a certain index was open so you could make it the controlling index by means of the SET ORDER command, you could use a program like this one:

```
STORE "lastname" TO desiredorder
tested = 1
DO WHILE tested < 8
    tested = tested + 1
    IF desiredorder $ NDX(tested)
        SET ORDER TO tested
        EXIT
    ENDIF
ENDDO
IF tested = 8
    STORE GETFILE("F+IX","Select the desired index.") TO newdex
    IF LEN(TRIM(newdex)) > 0
        SET INDEX TO &newdex
        . . .commands to process file
    ELSE
        ALERT NOTE 1 "Desired index not available."
    ENDIF
ELSE
    . . .commands to process file
ENDIF
RETURN
```

There are two places where this program can establish a new index order. The first is via the SET ORDER command, which would execute if the desired index ("desiredorder") character string is contained anywhere in the index names found by NDX( ) as it checks each of the seven possible open indexes. The "tested" variable will not reach 8 if the index is successfully found because of the EXIT command, so the file processing commands following ELSE will also execute.

The other place where an index order can be set is where you see the SET INDEX command. To understand what's going on there, look at the GETFILE( ) function reference earlier in this chapter. If the desired index is not open, but is found on disk by the user, the processing commands beneath SET INDEX are executed. Otherwise, an alert appears and the user is returned to the calling program.

Requirements A number from one to eight—any others generate an error.

Results A character string.

Also See USE <filename> INDEX <indexfilelist> and SET ORDER TO

Os( )

Syntax OS( )

Purpose OS( ) returns a character string that identifies the computer operating system that is host to FoxBASE+/Mac.

Example Here are some simple OS( ) queries:

```
? OS( )
Apple Macintosh - System 6.03        && result
? OS( )
DOS 03.10                            && result
```

If you wrote a program that was to run on an IBM PS/2 as well as a Macintosh, you could use OS( ) to let your program select between different color settings.

```
IF "Macintosh" $ OS( )
    SET COLOR TO N/W
ELSE
    SET COLOR TO W/B
ENDIF
```

If you have Macintosh running on a network file server, such as Novell 2.15, you can use the OS( ) function with the SET VOLUME command to determine if the computer running your program is a Macintosh, and if it is, map Macintosh path names to drive letters. The benefit of this approach is that one program, which accesses the file server's volumes using MS-DOS drive letters, can be run on both Macintosh and MS-DOS computers.

```
IF "Macintosh" $ OS( )
    SET VOLUME C TO "Novell2:SalesDep:DataDir"
    SET VOLUME E TO "Novell2:SalesDep:Archives"
ENDIF
```

Requirements None.

Results A character string.

Also See DISKSPACE( ) and VERSION( )

Symbols Used in the Function Reference 423

Pcol( )

Syntax	PCOL([1])
Purpose	PCOL([1]) returns the current column position on a printed page. If you leave the optional number 1 out, PCOL( ) returns the current position in terms of character columns. If you include the number 1, the columns are returned in pixels. Character column widths are taken to be the width of the letter "n" in the selected font and type style.
Example	PCOL( ) is useful whenever you already know what column the printhead is in and you want something else printed relative to it. PCOL( ) works relative to the left margin, so that PCOL( ) will return 0 if the printhead is resting on a left margin that's 10 characters from the page edge. If the SET PRINTER TO <filename> command is in effect, PCOL( ) will let you format text entering a file.

```
STORE "Austin, Texas" TO storecity
@ 5,5 SAY "JOHNSON'S FEED AND GRAIN, "
@ PROW( ), PCOL( )+25 SAY storecity
```

Requirements	None, or an optional number 1.
Results	A number representing the printhead's column position.
Also See	@, COL( ), ROW( ), PROW( ), and SET MARGIN

424 Symbols Used in the Function Reference

Prow( )

Syntax PROW([1])

Purpose PROW([1]) returns the current printhead row position on a printed page. If you leave the optional number out, PROW( ) returns the current position in characters. If you include the number 1, the rows are returned in pixels. If you specify a previously printed row, or one above the current position, FoxBASE will eject the page and reset the PROW( ) TO 0 before it prints what you want on the next page. The EJECT command also sets PROW( ) to 0.

Example As a companion to PCOL( ), PROW( ) is useful whenever you know what row the printhead is on and you want something else printed relative to it. If the SET PRINTER TO <filename> command is in effect, PROW( ) will let you format text entering a file.

```
STORE "Austin, Texas" TO storecity
@ 5,0 SAY "JOHNSON'S FEED AND GRAIN, "
@ PCOL( ), PROW( )+1 SAY storecity
```

Requirements None, or an optional number 1.

Results A number representing the current printhead row position.

Also See @, COL( ), PCOL( ), and ROW( )

Putfile( )

Syntax PUTFILE([< exprC1 >] [, < exprC2 >] [, < exprC3 >])

Purpose PUTFILE( ) returns the complete path and file name selected by a user when saving a file. If the CANCEL button is pressed, an empty string is returned. To do this, PUTFILE( ) opens a file-save dialog box, which is the standard Macintosh method of saving files. Here, users can select any drive or folder they like and enter the name of the file that's being saved.

If the < exprC2 > file name option is used, PUTFILE( ) displays the file name it suggests in the dialog box, allowing the user to change it if desired. The optional < exprC1 > argument is a short message that is displayed immediately above the file name text-entry box. Optional argument < exprC3 > tells FoxBASE what extension to put on the file name the user enters. If the user enters their own extension the < exprC3 > extension is ignored.

Example Every Macintosh file has a:

Finder file type	*Extension < exprC3 >*	*Common file types*
F+DB	dbf	Database
F+IX	idx	Index
F+ME	mem	Memory variable file
F+FR	frm	Report form (ver 1.x)
F+LB	lbl	Label form (ver 1.x)
F+RP	frx	Label and Report form (ver 2.x)
F+VU	vue	View file
TEXT	txt	ASCII text
Nothing		All files

Requirements None, or as many as three optional character string arguments.

Results A fully qualified path/file name, or a null string when the CANCEL button is pressed.

Also See GETFILE( )

426 *Symbols Used in the Function Reference*

Readkey( )

Syntax READKEY( )

Purpose READKEY( ) assumes that there were open GETs in an on-screen edit of variables or data, and that a READ of one form or another has just been terminated. It returns one of two possible integer numbers, depending on which of several keys was pressed and whether or not changes were made in any of the open GETS during the recently terminated READ operation. The commands that can take advantage of READKEY( ) include: APPEND, BROWSE, CHANGE, CREATE, EDIT, INSERT, MODIFY, and READ.

Example The keys most likely to terminate READs are listed in the table below. If you write a program that is used to edit data, it might be useful to know how the user ended the editing process. READKEY( ) is most useful in advanced applications where you can use this information to initiate special processes or to create powerful, friendly, and highly customized editing screens where each GET has its own READ. This allows users to select what field they want to edit by pressing arrow keys, or go back to the last screen by pressing the Home key, and so on.

Number if unchanged	Number if changed	Key
0	256	Delete
0	256	Left arrow
1	257	Right arrow
2	258	Home
3	259	End
4	260	Up arrow
5	261	Down arrow
6	262	PgUp
7	263	PgDn
8	264	Control-Left arrow
9	265	Control-Right arrow
12	268	Esc
14	270	Control-End
16	272	Return
34	290	Control-PgUp
35	291	Control-PgDn

In the following little program, pressing the Home key tells our program that the user wants to end editing and return to the menu without accepting any changes made to the edited variable. If the Home key is not pressed and the READ is terminated by some other means, the REPLACE occurs and the editing program continues.

```
@ 2,2 GET editvar
READ
IF READKEY( ) = 2 .OR. READKEY( ) = 258
        RETURN
ELSE
        REPLACE dbfield WITH editvar
ENDIF
... COMMANDS TO CONTINUE EDITING DATA, ETC.
```

Requirements   None.

Results   A number (see table above).

Also See   INKEY( ), ON KEY, and READ

Reccount( )

Syntax   RECCOUNT([<exprN>])

Purpose   RECCOUNT( ) returns a number that indicates how many physical records there are in the currently selected database file/work area. If no records exist, or if there is no file in use in the work area selected, a 0 is returned. The <exprN> option tells Fox-BASE which of the ten work areas to query. Enter a number from 1 to 10 for work areas A to J. Deleted records are always included in the count regardless of the SET DELETED status.

Example   There are many possible uses for RECCOUNT( ). Here's one that uses it to create a file containing exactly the number of blank records needed for a particular purpose.

```
DO WHILE RECCOUNT( ) < 100
     APPEND BLANK
ENDDO
```

Requirements   None, or an optional number indicating what work area to query.

Results   A number.

Recno( )

Syntax	RECNO([< exprN >])
Purpose	RECNO( ) returns a number indicating what physical record the record pointer is currently at. If an unsuccessful SEEK or another command sends the record pointer to the end of the file, RECNO( ) will return a number that's one more than the last actual record in the file. For this reason RECNO( ) is always 1 and EOF( ) is always (.T.) in an empty database file. Only when there is no database in use will RECNO( ) return 0.
	Use the optional number argument < exprN > if you want to query a database outside of the currntly selected work area, 1 to 10 for files in work areas A to J.
Example	Use RECNO( ) to record the location of a record that must be returned to before launching another process or program.

```
SAVE VIEW TO curview          && store environment
STORE ALIAS( ) TO curarea     && store work area
STORE RECNO( ) TO currec      && store pointer
... commands that change the databases or even close them
SET VIEW TO curview           && restore environment
SELECT &curarea               && restore work area
GOTO currec                   && restore pointer
```

This method works even with indexes that mix up the physical record numbers so that RECNO( ) no longer represents the position of a record in a sequentially ordered file. In other words, regardless of index orders, record numbers remain unchanged and always relate to the same physical record unless the file is sorted or packed.

Requirements	None, or an optional number representing the work area to be queried.
Results	A number representing the number of the current record.
Also See	RECCOUNT( )

Recsize( )

Syntax RECSIZE([<exprN>])

Purpose RECSIZE( ) returns a number that indicates how many character spaces are available in a record of a database file. If the <exprN> argument is used with a number from 1 to 10 for work areas A to J, the number represents the record size for the database in the work area specified. Otherwise, RECSIZE( ) returns the value for the currently selected work area. If no database is open in the selected area, 0 is returned.

Example
```
USE small
? RECSIZE( )
41                        && result
USE medium
? RECSIZE( )
262                       && result
USE large
? RECSIZE( )
2132                      && result
```

Requirements None, or an optional number.

Results A number.

Also See RECCOUNT( )

Replicate( )

Syntax REPLICATE (<exprC>,<exprN>)

Purpose REPLICATE( ) returns a character string where <exprC> is multiplied as many times as indicated by <exprC> <exprN>. The value returned will not exceed 254 because the length limit for a character expression is 254 characters.

Example REPLICATE( ) is very useful for drawing lines, underscores, and so on, when printing or painting screens with any of the special ASCII characters. For a list of these values look at Appendix A. Also, you can use it to issue several carriage returns (ASCII 13), line feeds (ASCII 10), tabs (ASCII 09), and so on.

This command uses the ". . ." character to place a dotted line across the screen:

? REPLICATE(CHR(201),80)

The following command uses the KEYBOARD command to tab forward three spaces as though the tabs were entered directly at the keyboard by a user.

KEYBOARD REPLICATE(CHR(9),3)

Requirements A character expression or string and a number.

Results A character string.

Right( )

Syntax RIGHT(<exprC>,<exprN>)

Purpose RIGHT( ) returns a portion of the <exprC> string or expression beginning with the right-most character and extending into the string as many characters as specified by <exprN>. An empty character string is returned if <exprN> is less than, or equal to, 0. The whole string is returned if <exprN> is larger than the number of characters in <exprC>.

Example
```
STORE "This is a character string." TO string
? RIGHT(string,7)
string.                        && result
? RIGHT(string,17)
character string.              && result
```

Requirements A character expression or string and a number.

Results A character string.

Also See AT( ), LEFT( ), LTRIM( ), RTRIM( ), SUBSTR( ), STUFF( ), and TRIM( )

Rlock( )

Syntax RLOCK( )

Purpose RLOCK( ) is a programmer's multiuser command that attempts to lock the current record in a database file, returning (.T.) if it succeeds and (.F.) if it fails. Programmed editing and entry of data is allowed in multiuser systems only when such an explicit lock is used.

Example For an explanation and examples of RLOCK's use, see the multiuser discussion in Chapter 10.

Requirements None.

Results A logical (.T.) or (.F.) indicating whether or not a record lock is in place.

Also See FLOCK( ), LOCK( ), UNLOCK, QUIT, USE, CLEAR ALL, CLOSE, and SET EXCLUSIVE

Round( )

Syntax   ROUND(<exprN1>,<exprN2>)

Purpose   ROUND( ) returns a number that is the rounded version of <exprN1> to the number of decimals indicated in <exprN2>. If <exprN2> is negative, ROUND( ) returns a rounded integer value that has been rounded to 10s, 100s, thousands, and so on, as specified by the absolute value of <exprN2>.

Example
```
? ROUND(1735.1735,3)
1735.1740                        && result
? ROUND(1735.1735,2)
1735.1700                        && result
? ROUND(1735.1735,1)
1735.2000                        && result
? ROUND(1735.1735, - 3)
2000.0000                        && result
? ROUND(1735.1735, - 2)
1700.0000                        && result
? ROUND(1735.1735, - 1)
1740.000                         && result
```

To get a rounded integer, use ROUND( ) with an <exprN2> of 0 and apply the INT( ) function to the result, like this.

```
? INT(ROUND(1735.1735, - 1))
1740                             && result
```

Requirements   Two numbers, one to be rounded and another to specify the significant digits or decimals.

Results   A rounded number.

Also See   INT( ), MOD( ), SET DECIMALS, STR( ), and VAL( )

Row( )

Syntax ROW([1])

Purpose ROW( ) provides relative addressing of the cursor's character-row position by returning a number that indicates the cursor's current position. Whenever the optional number 1 is used, the row number returned is a reference to pixels instead of characters.

Character positions are taken by dividing the screen into rows. The size and quantity of these rows is derived from a font size table that comes from measuring the small letter "n" in the current screen font. The current screen font is the one that is declared in the last SCREEN command, not the last one used in a @ SAY or @ GET command. A default screen font of Monaco in nine points, most closely emulates the MS-DOS 80 × 25 display where there are 25 rows in a standard Macintosh Plus or SE screen.

The SET SCREEN command discussed in Chapter 8 is a better way to divide the screen up into rows and columns, because you can specify where any @ SAY or @ GET command will start, even when proportional fonts are used.

On a Macintosh, the mouse moves the cursor, but that's not the kind of location reporting that ROW( ) provides. Instead, it tells you where the "painting" cursor stopped last when something was written on the screen. If nothing has been written on a clear screen, the ROW( ) function tells you that the cursor is at row 0, which is the top-most screen row.

Example The ROW( ) function is especially useful when you are painting screens under a program's control. It allows you to "step" down the screen in even or measured increments, or to specify any pixel or character row's position relative to the current one. ROW( ) also works when printing.

Requirements None or, optionally, the number 1.

Results A number representing the current character row position of the cursor, or a number representing the current pixel row position of the cursor.

Also See @, COL( ), PCOL( ), PROW( ), and SET SCREEN

Rtrim( )

Syntax	RTRIM (< exprC >)
Purpose	RTRIM( ) returns what remains of a character string or expression after it removes all blanks from its right-most side.
Example	See the entry in this chapter for LTRIM( ) because it functions almost identically.
Requirements	A character string or expression.
Results	A character string.
Also See	LEFT( ), LTRIM( ), RIGHT( ), STR( ), SUBSTR( ), and TRIM( )

Select( )

Syntax SELECT( )

Purpose SELECT( ) returns a number that indicates what work area is currently selected where numbers 1 to 10 represent work areas A to J.

Example
```
SELECT A
? SELECT( )
1                            && result
SELECT B
? SELECT( )
2                            && result
SELECT C
? SELECT( )
3                            && result
SELECT D
? SELECT( )
4                            && result
```

Requirements None.

Results A number.

Also See ALIAS( ) and DBF( )

Soundex( )

Syntax SOUNDEX(<exprC>)

Purpose SOUNDEX( ) is a uniquely powerful function that reads a character string or expression and returns a small alphanumeric (character) string that roughly identifies its phonetic value.

Example SOUNDEX( ) is useful when you need to search for a name, for example, and you, or the person making the query, don't know how it's spelled.

```
? SOUNDEX("Jones")
J520                    && result
? SOUNDEX("James")
J520                    && result
? SOUNDEX("Johnson")
J525                    && result
? SOUNDEX("Mike")
M200                    && result
? SOUNDEX("Nike")
N200                    && result
? SOUNDEX("Nielsen")
N425                    && result
```

Soundex is useful for making indexes that can be used for phonetic searches, like this:

```
INDEX ON SOUNDEX(lastname) TO namesound
SET INDEX TO namesound
SEEK SOUNDEX("Miller")
```

Requirements A character string or expression.

Results A four-position character string.

Also See SEEK, RECNO( ), and INDEX

Space( )

Syntax SPACE(<exprN>)

Purpose SPACE( ) makes blank characters like those created by the space-bar on a computer keyboard. The number of spaces it generates is determined directly by <exprN>.

Example SPACE( ) is particularly useful when you want to initialize character-typed memory variables.

```
STORE SPACE(2) TO zipcode
STORE SPACE(30) TO company
```

Space can also be used as an alignment tool when monospaced displays or printing is being created. Notice how these two commands create the same horizontal displacement for the word "Cat."

```
@ 2,20 SAY "Cat"
                                        Cat       && result
STORE SPACE(20) TO buffer
@ 2,0 SAY buffer + "Cat"
                                        Cat       && result

SET INDEX TO namesound
SEEK SOUNDEX("Miller")
```

Requirements A character string or expression.

Results A four-position character string.

Also See SEEK, RECNO( ), and INDEX

Sqrt( )

Syntax   SQRT(<exprN>)

Purpose   SQRT( ) figures and returns the square root of a positive number or numeric expression that contains as many decimals as there are in <exprN>, or as many as specified by SET DECIMALS, whichever is larger.

Example
```
? SQRT(25)
5.00                      && result
SET DECIMALS TO 0
? SQRT(25)
5                         && result
? SQRT(25.000)
5.000                     && result
SET DECIMALS TO 2
? SQRT(64)
8.00                      && result
? SQRT(68)
8.25                      && result
```

Requirements A positive number or numeric expression.

Results   A number.

Str( )

Syntax STR(<exprN1>[,<exprN2>] [,exprN3])

Purpose STR( ) is an extremely useful function that simply converts a number or numeric expression into a character string. VAL( ) is its counterpart, which converts character expressions into numeric ones. STR( ) also has the ability to format the character string it returns, which is useful because numbers can have different decimal values, which can easily cause misalignment of printed columns, and so on. The expression or numeric literal to be converted is <exprN1>.

The <exprN2> option indicates how many total characters there can be in the output, beginning with the least significant decimal digit, including the decimal point and any spaces that might be added to pad the left portion of the string as its output. If this number is greater than the number of characters output, leading blanks are inserted ahead of them, effectively padding them with space.

The last expression, <exprN3>, is an option that indicates how many decimals you want output. Any decimals included in the overall output length must be included in the allocation of space made via <exprN2>, or they are truncated from the right-most to left-most in order to fit.

Example STR( ) is most often used when numbers must be included with character expressions in printed or displayed outputs.

```
STORE 1234.5678 TO number
1234.5678                                              && result
? "Your reward this month is $ " + STR(number)
Your reward this month is $           1234             && result
? "Your reward this month is $ " + STR(number,10,4)
Your reward this month is $      1234.5678             && result
? "Your reward this month is $ " + STR(number,10,3)
Your reward this month is $       1234.568             && result
? "Your reward this month is $ " + STR(number,10,2)
Your reward this month is $        1234.57             && result
? "Your reward this month is $ " + STR(number,10,1)
Your reward this month is $         1234.6             && result
? "Your reward this month is $ " + STR(number,10,0)
Your reward this month is $           1234             && result
? "Your reward this month is $ " + STR(number,6,4)
Your reward this month is $         1234.6             && result
```

Notice that STR( ) rounds the numbers it truncates.

Requirements One required numeric expression and two optional numeric arguments.

Results A formatted character string.

Stuff( )

Syntax STUFF(<exprC1>,<exprN1>,<exprN2>,<exprC2>)

Purpose STUFF( ) puts characters into an existing character string at any position you specify within the string. It can also be used to remove characters from a string.

In the syntax example above, <exprC1> represents a character string you want to modify. The <exprN1> expression is a number indicating where in <exprC1> you want to make changes, and <exprN2> tells FoxBASE how many characters you want to extract from <exprC1> for replacement by <exprC2>. <exprN2> cannot be less than 1, so 1 is substituted by FoxBASE in the event that a number less than 1 is used. To remove characters without stuffing any back into the string, use an empty string, "", for <exprC2>. To insert characters without removing any make <exprN> 0. Keep in mind that any characters overflowing a variable or database field will be truncated.

Example
```
STORE "The dog has a bad babit of chasing rabbits." TO string
? STUFF(string,AT("babit",string),LEN("babit"),"habit")
The dog has a bad habit of chasing rabbits.              && result
```

Requirements Two character expressions and two numeric expressions.

Results A single character string.

Also See AT( ) and SUBSTR( )

Substr( )

Syntax SUBSTR(<exprC>,<exprN1>[,<exprN2>])

Purpose SUBSTR( ) returns characters from within the <exprC> character expression or string starting at <exprN1> and continuing until the optional character located by <exprN2>. If <exprn2> is omitted, SUBSTR( ) returns the remainder of <exprC>.

Example Use SUBSTR( ) to extract any known characters from a string.

```
STORE "The dog has a bad habit of chasing rabbits." TO string
? SUBSTR(string,1,3)
The                          && result
? SUBSTR(string,5,3)
dog                          && result
? SUBSTR(string,9,3)
has                          && result
? SUBSTR(string,13,1)
a                            && result
? SUBSTR(string,19,5)
habit                        && result
```

Requirements A character string and up to two numeric expressions.

Results A character string.

Also See LEFT( ), RIGHT( ), and STUFF( )

Sys( ) Functions

SYS( ) functions, or system functions, are special because they can give you, or a program you've written, information about the computer it's running on, about the status of the operating environment—such as printer status, monitor type, and so on. SYS functions can also call forth the print and page setup dialogs, and to do other, less useful things. There's a good chance that something you need to know can be found out by a creative use of standard and system functions.

Note: If you expect your programs to run on MS-DOS versions of FoxBASE as well as on Macintosh computers, check the MS-DOS documentation before using a Macintosh SYS function, most Macintosh SYS functions have an equivalent under DOS, but some don't.

SYS(0) SYS(0) tells you what kind of Macintosh your program is running on by returning a character string that looks like: "Mac Plus," "Mac II," "Mac SE," and so on.

SYS(1) SYS(1) returns a character string of numbers that represent Julian dates in the format used by the original version of FoxBASE. Its main use is to allow conversion of older FoxBASE database files into the new FoxBASE format. If you aren't supporting database files created by dBASE II or the earliest version of FoxBASE, you won't need this function.

SYS(2) SYS(2) counts the seconds since midnight and returns the value to you in the form of a character string consisting of numbers.

SYS(3) When you need to create a temporary file, i.e., one that you'll erase when you're done with it, and you need to give it a name, this function can help. It returns a unique name each time you call it. You can store the name in a variable, using the & macro function to create and erase the file.

SYS(5) SYS(5) lets you know what the currently selected default output device is, PRINT or SCREEN. See also, SET DEVICE TO.

SYS(6)

SYS(6) lets you know what the current print device setting is, which is useful because printed output such as reports and labels can be routed to the printer (which is the normal case) or to a file. See also, SET PRINT TO.

SYS(7[,work area])

Installable format files can replace FoxBASE's standard EDIT or CHANGE screen layout with a format of your own design. To create a format, use the FoxForm editor. To install a format use the SET FORMAT TO command. SYS(7) lets you know the name of any current format file. If none has been installed, an empty character string is returned. An option you can specify with SYS(7) tells it what work area you want to check. Remember, one format file can be installed for each of the 10 possible database files. Therefore, to check work area "C," you would enter the function like this:

SYS(7,3)

The number three stands for area "C." Use numbers 1 through 10 for work areas A through J.

SYS(9)

SYS(9) tells you what your FoxBASE serial number is. You might be able to find a creative use for this function, I haven't yet.

SYS(10, <exprD>)

SYS(10) is like SYS(1), because its purpose is to provide a way to convert older date formats into the new FoxBASE type. Technically, it does the opposite of SYS(1) by converting a Julian day number, represented by "d," into a character-type number that represents a date.

SYS(11, <exprD>)

SYS(11) makes conversion from older FoxBASE database files possible by converting a character date (<exprD>) into the kind of date number used by earlier FoxBASE versions and Ashton-Tate's dBASE II.

SYS(12)

SYS(12) lets you know how much memory is left unused in your computer. Use it to prevent memory problems by installing it in programs you're writing. After you've finished the program, take it out. Large screens take a lot of memory. Use this function to help you configure the memory allocation settings in the "Config.fx" file.

Symbols Used in the Function Reference 447

SYS(14, <exprN1> [, <exprN2>])	SYS(14) returns the name of the index in the index list (from one to seven) indicated by <exprN>. The index list by . <exprN2> is an optional argument to specify what work area, from 1 to 10 for work areas A to J, to query. If omitted, SYS(14) returns the name of an index in the currently selected work area.
SYS(16[, <exprN>])	SYS(16) returns the name of the program that is currently executing. If <exprN> is included, it returns the name of the program that ran before the current program, or the one before it, based on how many lexical levels are indicated by <exprN>. Omit <exprN> to return the name of the currently running program, and use 0 to retrieve the name of the first, or "master," program.
SYS(17)	SYS(17) returns a character string of numbers indicating the processor in use: (68000, 68020, or 68030).
SYS(18)	SYS(18) returns the name of the GET field where the user's cursor is currently positioned so that help can be provided via the ON KEY event command during a READ. This gives users help about the field being entered.
SYS(100)	SYS(100) returns the console setting (ON or OFF). Use it with SYS(101), SYS(102), and SYS(103) to recover from serious errors.
SYS(101)	SYS(101) returns the device setting (SCREEN or PRINT).
SYS(102)	SYS(102) returns the print setting (ON or OFF).
SYS(103)	SYS(103) returns the current TALK setting (ON or OFF).
SYS(1020)	SYS(1020) returns the full path and folder name of the last folder accessed via a directory dialog.
SYS(1021)	SYS(1021) returns a character string of numbers indicating how many vertical pixels are available on the currently running computer.
SYS(1022)	SYS(1022) returns a character string of numbers indicating how many horizontal pixels are available on the currently running computer.
SYS(1023)	SYS(1023) returns a character string of numbers that indicate how many vertical pixels are available in the current

	grafport as determined by the device setting (SCREEN, PRINT, or FILE). File ports use the current screen, whether hidden or not, to gain output specifications.
SYS(1024)	SYS(1024) returns a character string of numbers that indicate how many horizontal pixels are available in the current grafport as determined by the device setting (SCREEN, PRINT, or FILE). File ports use the current screen, whether hidden or not, to gain output specifications.
SYS(1025)	SYS(1025) returns a character string of numbers that indicates how many pixels there are in the ascent of the currently selected font. Ascent is from a character's baseline to its top.
SYS(1026)	SYS(1026) returns a character string of numbers that indicate how many pixels there are in the descent of the currently selected font. Descent is from a character's baseline to its bottom.
SYS(1027)	SYS(1027) returns a character string of numbers indicating how many pixels there are in the leading (the vertical space between characters.)
SYS(1028)	SYS(1028) returns a character string of numbers indicating how many pixels there are in the width of the letter "n" of the currently selected font, which is a useful approximation of the horizontal space proportional fonts require.
SYS(1029)	SYS(1029) returns a character string of numbers indicating how many pixels there are in the widest character in the current font.
SYS(1030, <exprC>)	SYS(1030, <exprC>) returns a character string of numbers indicating how many pixels there are in the character string or expression <exprC>.
SYS(1031)	SYS(1031) makes the pointer (cursor) disappear until someone moves the mouse. Available only in version 2.
SYS(1032)	SYS(1032) changes the cursor into a spinning ball. Available only in version 2.
SYS(1034)	Only one of the nine possible output screens can be active at once. SYS(1034) returns a character string number that

indicates the currently active screen. Note that active output screens are not always visible or in front of all other screens and windows, see SYS(1035). Available only in version 2.

SYS(1035) This function is available only in version 2. Windows are Help, Status, Form/Report, View, Trace, and Debug. SYS(1035) returns a character string containing one number, and sometimes a sign, that indicates (see the table) what window, or output screen, is in front of all the others.

−7	Debug window	2	Output screen 2
−6	Trace window	3	Output screen 3
−5	View window	4	Output screen 4
−4	Form (report) window	5	Output screen 5
−3	Status window	6	Output screen 6
−2	Help window	7	Output screen 7
−1	None visible	8	Output screen 8
0	Command window	9	Output screen 9
1	Output screen 1		

SYS(1036,<exprN>) This function is available only in version 2. SYS(1036,<exprN> lets you know if an output screen has been opened and is presently on the desktop, even if it's hidden by other output screens or one of the FoxBASE windows. Use <exprN> to select which screen (one through nine) you want checked. A 1 is returned if the window is on the desktop, or a 0 if it is not.

SYS(1037) This function is available only in version 2. SYS(1037) is useful because it opens the Macintosh Page Setup dialog screen so a user can set print formatting options and margins for the currently selected printer. Note: Open the page setup dialog only before using the SET PRINT ON or SET DEVICE TO PRINT commands, not after, and when the print job is done, make sure to SET PRINT OFF or SET DEVICE TO SCREEN. SYS(1037) returns a character string of −1 if a print job is already in progress; 0 if the user pressed the CANCEL button; and 1 if the user pressed the OK button.

SYS(1038) This function is available only in version 2. SYS(1038) is like SYS(1037), except that it opens the Print dialog, allowing users to set the number of pages to print and to start or abort the print job. If the user presses OK, printer communication is established and must eventually be terminated by a SET PRINT OFF command. You can use the character numbers this function returns (with DO CASE or IF) to start a print job, or to prevent a print job from starting. SYS(1038) returns a character string of −1 if a print job is already in progress; 0 if the user pressed the CANCEL button; and 1 if the user pressed the OK button.

SYS(1039)   SYS(1039) is available only in version 2. This function returns the printer's horizontal resolution in pixels per inch. It tests whatever printer is currently selected in the Chooser.

SYS(1040)   SYS(1040) is available only in version 2. This function returns the printer's vertical resolution in pixels per inch. It tests whatever printer is currently selected in the Chooser.

SYS(1041)   SYS(1041) is available only in version 2. You can specify the name of your own help file with the SET HELP TO <filename> command. This function will return the name of the currently selected file.

SYS(1042)   SYS(1042) is available only in version 2. You can specify the name of the help file topic with the SET TOPIC TO <exprC> command. This function will return the name of the currently selected help topic.

SYS(1043)   SYS(1043) is available only in version 2. This function is useful because it opens the Imagewriter Page Size dialog screen so a user can set page size and paper type options. Note: It only works when one of the Imagewriter series printers has been selected. SYS(1043) returns these character numbers: −1, if an Imagewriter is not currently selected; 0, if the user pressed the CANCEL button; and 1, if the user pressed the OK button.

Time( )

Syntax   TIME([1])

Purpose   TIME( ) returns an eight-digit character string that represents the system time in the format of a 24-hour clock. Use the optional argument one if you want an 11 digit string that includes hundredths of a second.

Example

```
? TIME( )
17:59:28                        && result
? TIME(1)
17:59:28.51                     && result
```

Requirements   Nothing, or an optional number 1.

Results   An eight or 11-character string.

Transform( )

Syntax	TRANSFORM(<expr>,<exprC>)
Purpose	TRANSFORM( ) formats character or numeric expressions in the same way that @ SAY or @ GET does when a PICTURE or FUNCTION clause is used. The expression you want to format is <expr> and the formatting specification is provided by <exprC>. To learn how to use pictures and functions see the discussion of data entry fields in the Using FoxForm section of Chapter 7.
Requirements	A character or numeric expression for input and a character expression as the picture or function mask.
Results	A character string.

Trim( )

Syntax   TRIM(<exprC>)

Purpose   TRIM( ) removes all blanks from the end of <exprC>.

Requirements   A character string or expression.

Results   A character string or expression.

Also See   STUFF( ) and SUBSTR( )

Type( )

Syntax   TYPE(<exprC>)

Purpose   TYPE( ) returns a character string with a length of one, which indicates what type of expression is represented by <exprC>. Note that the expression you supply, if not already a character expression, must be inside of quotation marks to qualify as a character expression. Returned values have these meanings:

    C - character
    N - numeric
    L - logical
    M - memo
    U - unknown

Note: The unknown type is returned when an expression cannot be evaluated to one type. If this occurs, you can be assured that FoxBASE will return an error message whenever it actually encounters such an expression.

Requirements   A character expression containing any kind of expression.

Results   A single character from the table above.

Updated( )

Syntax	UPDATED( )
Purpose	UPDATED( ) returns a logical value (.T.) or (.F.) to indicate whether or not any changes were made to GETs during the last READ operation.
Example	Use UPDATED( ) soon after a READ command to determine whether or not to write memory variables to a file after a user has had a chance to edit them. This can sometimes save processing time because the user made no changes worth processing.
	Caution: All variables are considered by UPDATED( ), including those used by control buttons, menus, and so on. This can cause you to misinterpret UPDATED( ) if a user has pressed a control button instead of changing data as you might think.
Requirements	None.
Results	A logical (.T.) or (.F.).

Upper( )

Syntax UPPER(<exprC>)

Purpose UPPER( ) converts any lowercase letters within <exprC> into uppercase letters.

Example While you can use UPPER( ) to change the appearance of letters, it has another, less obvious purpose. Indexes are sensitive to the difference between uppercase and lowercase letters so that you can't succeed while seeking, for example, if any character in the sought string differs from the query string. In this case, you can use UPPER( ) to make them equal for the sake of argument.

```
INDEX ON UPPER(company) TO company
STORE company TO string
"Wilson Gas & Electric Company"
? string
Wilson Gas & Electric Company
? UPPER(string)
WILSON GAS & ELECTRIC COMPANY
SEEK string
? FOUND( )
.F.
SEEK UPPER(string)
? FOUND( )
.T.
```

Requirements A character string or expression.

Results An uppercase character string.

Also See LOWER( ), ISLOWER( ), and ISUPPER( )

Val( )

Syntax	VAL(<exprC>)
Purpose	VAL( ) converts character numbers into numeric numbers where <exprC> is the character number you want to convert. If the first characters in <exprC> are alphabetic and not numbers, VAL( ) will return 0. Otherwise, it will return a number after converting the first numbers it encounters in <exprC>, up and until it encounters spaces or nonnumber characters. Leading blanks are ignored and signs are also converted, as long as they immediately precede the numbers being converted.
Example	Sometimes information stored as characters contain numbers that must be used in calculations. For this purpose VAL( ) is indispensable.

```
STORE "01234.56" TO string
? string
    01234.56                    && result = character
? VAL(string)
      1234.56                   && result = numeric
STORE " -01234.56" TO string
? string
   -01234.56                    && result = character
? VAL(string)
    -1234.56                    && result = numeric
```

Requirements	A character string containing numbers and, optionally, a sign.
Results	A number.

Version( )

Syntax VERSION( )

Purpose VERSION( ) returns the version of your copy of FoxBASE+/Mac.

Example If you write programs that must run on several types of computers, or with several different versions of FoxBASE, use VERSION( ) to let your program know what the host system is.

? VERSION( )
Multi-User FoxBASE+/Mac Version 2.00

On another computer, this might result in a different response.

? VERSION( )
Single-User FoxBASE+/Mac Version 2.00

Requirements None, or an optional argument 1, which provides revision information in addition to the version.

Results A character string.

10
Distributing Applications and Sharing Data

MACINTOSH computers running FoxBASE+/Mac can run virtually any program written to run under FoxBASE+ or dBase III Plus® on an IBM compatible. They may not look as great as an application that was written with the Macintosh in mind, but they'll work.

MOVING DATA BETWEEN MACS AND IBM COMPATIBLES

You can use networking software from Tops, AppleShare for the PC, Novell 2.15, or from 3Com to move files from PCs to Macs or back, and there are several good file transfer packages that include a serial cable that works between two computers on a desktop or over a modem. I've used most of the popular Macintosh and PC networking systems and some of the file transfer kits. My personal favorite is MacLink Plus. It lets the Macintosh control what happens on both sides of the connection and it can double as a text converter between different word processing formats.

When you first view an imported PC file on a Macintosh it can look generic and sickly compared to the nice icons appearing on FoxBASE documents. This happens because the Macintosh hasn't yet assigned a creator name and icon (picture). PC files, when first received, are orphans. As such, they can't be double-clicked like other documents, and they don't even show up when you try to view them from inside FoxBASE. To overcome this temporary blindness, select the All Files option in the FoxBASE file picker. Then FoxBASE will see the file and allow you to open it. This process is needed only once, after that documents will be adopted by FoxBASE+/Mac and the Macintosh will recognize them.

Swapping Files

Binary file transfers move a file from one computer to the other in a straightforward copy operation that doesn't change file contents. That's how all transfers of data and indexes should be done. Futhermore, indexes (.idx files) are the same to FoxBASE+/Mac and on FoxBASE+ 2.10 on PCs, but no FoxBASE index will work under dBase III Plus® from Ashton-Tate. Despite the fact that dBase indexes won't run in FoxBASE, FoxBASE will read them and make its own version of them without hardly slowing down. Consequently, you can put dBase indexes on your Macintosh disk until FoxBASE automatically replaces every ".ndx" file with its own ".idx" file by the same name.

Text and program files are almost as easy to transfer as database and index files, but there's one catch. PCs use a special "line feed" character to mark the beginning of each new line and Macintoshes don't. To adjust for this difference, FoxBASE has two options you should know about. One to remove line feeds in a text/program file received from a PC, and one to add them (if you're sending a file from a Mac to a PC). These options might not be necessary at all, because most file transfer tools, like MacLink, can convert them during transfer.

If you need to, you can strip line feeds from a PC file by selecting the Edit/Find (or replace) menu option. Just enter Option-D (to indicate special character) followed by a "L" for line feed. Replace all occurrences with nothing. Adding line feeds for PC use is even easier. You simply select the "Add Line Feeds" option in the Edit/Preferences dialog and save the file.

Another thing to know and remember about files is how limited DOS file names are. IBM-compatible computers running DOS can handle only eight-character file names, so be cautious if you're planning to move files frequently and take care that the names are comparable to both systems.

With the exceptions just mentioned, format files, program files, data files, and index files are fully interchangeable between FoxBASE+/Mac and FoxBASE+ 2.10 on a PC. I've been told that resource files have limited interchangeability that will be increased when FoxPRO for the PC is released, but I haven't tried to swap them myself and don't yet see any reason to until pictures and other resources will be useful on both platforms.

Sharing Data

If you want to share files between the multiuser versions of FoxBASE for the PC and the Macintosh, you'll need a network that supports both. The most popular networks for cross-computer sharing are from Apple, Novell, and 3Com. Tops, from Sun Microsystems might be the best bet for installations involving just a few users, because it's designed as a peer-to-peer system that doesn't require a dedicated central computer. Tops had some compatibility problems with FoxBASE, but they'll probably be cleared up by the time this book hits the shelf.

The rule of thumb for sharing data across multiple platforms is to follow good multiuser programming practice, as outlined later in this chapter, and to use FoxBASE+ version 2.10 on the PC, since earlier versions did not support sharing with Macs. FoxBASE+ 2.10 is not as flexible as FoxBASE+/Mac version 2.x, so you can't interactively share database files as easily as two Macintosh users can; programmed locks are required for simultaneous reading and writing from the PC. Also, there is no picture data type in the PC version, so FoxBASE+ for the PC will ignore them.

THE MAC AS A DEVELOPMENT ENVIRONMENT

FoxBASE+/Mac introduced some development features that have not been available in any other dBase compatible language product for IBM compatibles. Most notable is the windowing interface that lets you decide what to do next while it keeps histories of where you've recently been so that bouncing back to suspended work is easy and quick. Several years ago I would have given something precious for as many cut and paste text windows as I've got now for program writing. The View window concept was first developed by Fox Software for FoxBASE+/Mac, along with the incredible Debug and Trace windows that work interactively during the development phases of a project.

Debugging

The debugger discussed in Chapter 3 is an excellent snooping tool for discovering problems. You can use the Program/Debug menu to locate problems simply by opening it and entering the names of variables causing grief. Put any variable name or any legal expressions on the left side of the Debug window. Its result will be displayed on the right side, even reflecting changes in real time as they occur. If a particular variable value is causing problems or is related to a programming event that is, you can place a break point (marked by a dot) in the bar separating the left and right sides of the Debug window immediately opposite the variable or expression. FoxBASE will then stop and open the Trace window (showing the program code) whenever the value in that expression changes, allowing you to discover the source of the problems.

Tracing

The Trace window shown in Fig. 3-42 appears whenever you select the menu option, or more important, whenever the SET ECHO ON command is encountered in a program. It will also appear automatically if you've got the Debug window open and a marked variable or expression changes value while a program is running. Use the Trace window to see the source code running and its immediate effects.

Once the Trace window has opened, you can cancel the running program, suspend it temporarily, or resume a suspended program by pressing appropriate buttons. If you want to have a program stop at a predetermined point, simply place a break point on any line of code by holding the command key down and then press the mouse button on the line. A dot will appear showing that a break point has been set on that line.

CREATING PROGRAMS THAT RUN ON MACS AND IBM COMPATIBLES

The FOX variable is an example of computer portability that's been built into Fox-BASE for developers. It's automatically available as long as your program declares it as a public variable. If you are running FoxBASE, the FOX variable will initialize as true instead of false, letting you run programs in more than one dBase language product.

```
PUBLIC fox, othervars
? fox         && result = .T.
? othervars   && result = .F.
```

Another, perhaps more useful, feature is the SYS(17) function that returns the CPU manufacturer's model number for the microprocessor in use. On Macintosh computers, the value returned will be a text string representing one of the Motorola 68000 series chips (68000, 68020, or 68030, etc.), and on IBM compatible computers, the result will represent an Intel chip (8088/86, 80286, or 80386, etc.).

```
? SYS(17)   && result = "68030" or another Mororola chip on Macintosh
? SYS(17)   && result = "80286" or another Intel chip on IBM compatibles
```

You can put these environmental tests in programs to sense what kind of computer is running, and switch (using IF, CASE, etc.) to screens and menus that are compatible with that computer.

Fonts

Use the IBM Clone Font shipped with FoxBASE+/Mac if your programs use the IBM character set for screen displays. While that font makes the Mac work almost perfectly as a DOS computer, the ASCII characters 8, 9, 10, and 127 won't be exact equivalents. If you can, it's even better to use Macintosh graphics for boxes and lines and use the Monaco 9 font instead of the IBM Clone Font, because of it's better software and firmware support. Monaco is a monospaced, proportional font, which means that all characters have the same width, just like IBM characters. As such, its the ideal Macintosh font for character alignment, and decimal number columns in particular, on screen and in print.

If you want to use proportional fonts (most Macintosh fonts are proportional) you should use the SET SCREEN TO <exprN, exprN> command to establish invisible screen grid lines:

```
SET SCREEN TO 11,6
```

In this example, the number 11 indicates how high each row should be in pixels. The number 6 indicates how wide each column will be. Incidentally, eleven and six divide a Macintosh Plus or SE screen into a nearly perfect 80 by 25 grid, which is what the IBM PC uses. After setting a screen grid like this, you can enter it's coordinates without counting pixels. More useful is that the grid works with monospaced and with proportional fonts.

If you use custom fonts for applications, put them into the resource fork of the resource file (FoxUser or another custom resource file) that will be shipped with the application to its users. The reason is obvious when you consider it. The fonts may not be installed in the receiving user's system, which can spell disaster for your application if it depends on them for nice screen or print displays. By putting them directly into the resource fork of an available file, you're guaranteeing that they'll be there when needed.

Keystrokes

If you want a program to run in both environments it's not a bad idea to plan the keystrokes that will be required, that is, if you make use of function keys or if you trap keystrokes with the ON KEY command, or with the INKEY( ) or READKEY( ) functions. For more information on these functions, see the respective entries for these commands and functions in Chapters 8 and 9. Note that Mac Plus keyboards and earlier Macintosh computers don't have function keys at all, and that extended keyboards, which are options with the SE and Mac II lines, have keyboards that mimick PCs almost perfectly.

THE FoxBASE RUNTIME SYSTEM

The FoxBASE runtime system, FoxRUN, is a stripped-down version of FoxBASE that has all the features of the regular version except menus and the screen form editor. As such, it won't work without an application program to run, no matter how large and complex or small and simple it is. Consequently, you can't use FoxRUN to build applications or to work with database files interactively, but you can use it to make programs for sale or even to give away. FoxRUN comes in single and multiuser versions for a reasonable one-time fee that requires no subsequent royalties when distributed with your applications as some database vendors sell copies of their runtime program for a fee.

Packaging Applications for Distribution (FoxPackage)

The FoxPackage program comes with FoxRUN. By joining FoxRUN with your programs, FoxPackage lets you make special purpose, double-clickable applications that fit, essentially, under one icon. Still, database (.dbf and .dbt), index, (.idx) and report (.frm under version 1.x and 2.x, and .frx under version 2.x) files must be included separately.

Build Application

Before building an application, it's a good idea to make a folder to keep the new files you'll make for distribution, then select the Build Application menu option. You'll be asked to locate the FoxRUN file and the program files you want included in the application. FoxPackage will then make a copy of the FoxRUN program and insert your application programs into its resource fork, removing the readable ASCII source code from the source program. Your original programs won't be altered. When it's done, there will be a Fox icon bearing the name of your double-clickable application.

Add Resources

The Add Resources menu option of FoxPackage copies all of the resources inside a custom resource file, such as the FoxUser file, into the hidden resource part of the FoxRUN application file you're building. Because you can store pictures, sounds, XCMDs, and fonts in the resource fork, this makes them accessible to your program while hiding them from users. Be careful though. Lots of resources, or large resources, can increase the size of the FoxRUN application considerably. Don't let it get too large to fit on one 800 kilobyte diskette. For this reason, I often give the FoxUser file a new name and keep it separate from the main application file.

If you add a custom resource file to the application be sure your program does not use the SET RESOURCE TO <filename> command. Conversely, if you use an external resource file other than the FoxUser file, the SET RESOURCE TO <filename> command must be included so the application can locate the resources it needs.

Add Config.fx...

The Add Config.fx menu option takes the configuration information you have included in any existing Config.fx file and inserts it into the application file, where it works without being seen. FoxBASE will read the information in a Config.fx file when it starts. This way, you can adjust many things, including memory requirements, environmental adjustments, and so on. For more information about the configuration file, see the Adjusting FoxBASE Defaults section in Chapter 4. If your application does not have, or need, a Config.fx file, this option is not very useful. However, if it needs a Config.fx file, this option can keep users from changing values in a Config.fx file that's vulnerable sitting alone on the disk.

Remove Source

The Build Application option of FoxPackage automatically removes your source code from an application being built. This option is available for times when you want to keep the programs separate from the runtime system, rather than inserting them into its file and icon. Use it to strip codes from application programs when the source code should not be visible to a prying user. If a user already owns FoxBASE, for example, they don't need a runtime version. They can run your programs using their own FoxBASE program.

Be careful to make copies of your application programs before stripping code. The compiled resource-code that remains after stripping the readable code cannot be turned into readable source code without extreme difficulty. As further insurance that your source code will be protected from theft, include a SET ECHO OFF command very early in your program. Without it, your code is vulnerable to hackers who know how to crack the program and read its compiled tokens.

> Don't keep completed, runtime applications around on the same disk that FoxBASE occupies, because the Macintosh finder can reassign the creator name of FoxBASE files to your new application program. If this happens, double-clicking a FoxBASE document can cause a runtime application to launch rather than the interactive version of FoxBASE you intended to use for development purposes.

MULTIUSER ISSUES

While differences between the multiuser version of FoxBASE and the regular version are few, they are significant. Multiuser versions allow a user to change records in a database only when no one else can make simultaneous changes. To make sure that two people won't make changes at once, the multiuser version prevents two users from getting the same record at one time. When a user opens a record by placing their cursor on it, or when a program gets a record for a user to edit, the multiuser version "locks" it until the user is done. Contention by two or more users over records in a file can be rare, but it will eventually occur in every, active mulituser system and must be managed.

Why Lock Records or Files?

If two people have a word processing document, such as a letter or memo, and are making changes simultaneously, the result could be two, incomplete documents instead of one coherent document. Worst yet, imagine what would happen if the word processors automatically merged the two changed documents without consulting you. Or what would happen if the computer were to overwrite the first one saved by replacing it with the one saved last? Record locks prevent such things from occurring to your database files because each change of data in any row or record of a database file is treated like a complete transaction. The changed portion gets locked whenever a user is making changes so that all subsequent users can see the most recent information. The inconvenience of being temporarily locked out of records in a file is worthwhile when you consider the importance of data integrity.

Version 1.x and Version 2.x

With version 1.x, you can put data on a shared fileserver disk and individual users can access it one at a time. For multiple users to make changes to a data program, they must request locks, using the programming language's explicit locking functions, which are explained fully a little later in this chapter. In short, you must program to take advantage of the multiuser features of version 1.x, because interactive data sharing is not possible. Because version 2.x is a more adept platform for multiple users, the examples in this chapter will assume that you're using it.

Version 2.x is more sophisticated. It allows multiple users to change data without the need of programming. Locks are effected automatically whenever a user places their cursor in a data field. If you are creating applications that use screen forms or have programmed data entry and editing methods, however, explicit record and file locking might be needed, regardless of the version of FoxBASE you have. Before discussing explicit programmed locking commands and functions, you must first understand the purposes of locking and how FoxBASE (version 2.x) performs multiuser locking automatically.

The Nature of Locks

Because a user can lock only one record at a time (the one currently selected), the chance that two or more users will contend for the same record is small. When two users contend for one record, the first user gets it, and the second user receives an appropriate message until the first user moves their pointer to another record.

Despite the thoroughness of record locks in FoxBASE, they aren't always enough. Sometimes you need to have a file all to yourself, such as when you are removing deleted records with the PACK command, or changing a file's structure. There are two types of "lock" for a whole file. One prevents all access to the file by other users, and the other allows users to read the file but not change anything until you're done. To see what the locking status is for any files that are currently used, use the DISPLAY STATUS or LIST STATUS commands. The DISPLAY STATUS command pauses on-screen, and the LIST STATUS TO PRINT command sends status information to the printer.

Where to Put the Files

FoxBASE can be shared, but it's a better idea to put a local copy of FoxBASE on every computer that can access centrally stored database files because then the network traffic is limited to data. When FoxBASE itself must be transferred over the network, along with the data it's managing, things can slow down. Put indexes, reports, and label files on the shared network disk in the same folder as the database files.

The FoxUser file can be placed on a shared network disk with the database files, but it's recommended that each user have a copy of the FoxUser file in their local FoxBASE folder, or in the event that users are sharing FoxBASE, in the system folder of their local disk. If you share another resource file for picture storage, or other reasons, it must be in the shared network folder and the SET RESOURCE TO <filename> command must include the optional NOMODIFY keyword:

SET RESOURCE TO myresfile NOMODIFY

Again, it's preferable to put a copy of custom resource files on the local user disks for performance reasons.

Exclusive Use of Database Files

If you will share files, SET EXCLUSIVE ON|OFF is the single most important command to know. If exclusive is ON, only the first user to open a file can have it, and all others will be denied until it is closed by the one user who got it first. In multiuser situations, it's best to set exclusive OFF right away after entering FoxBASE. To permanently enable file sharing, you can create a text file in the FoxBASE folder named "Config.fx"

Multiuser Issues **467**

(see Chapter 4 for more information about default settings and the configuration file). The File/New/File menu option can be used to make this file, and all you have to do is put this line in it:

EXCLUSIVE = OFF

Thereafter, every time FoxBASE starts up, it will read the configuration file and you'll automatically be able to share a file that's in use by someone else, unless, of course, the file is for exclusive use. Having said that, you should know that there are some things that require exclusive use of a file because they would "pull the rug," so to speak, out from underneath unsuspecting users:

INSERT [BLANK]	It resizes a file by inserting a record.
MODIFY STRUCTURE	It changes a file's very structure.
PACK	It resizes a file by removing deleted records.
REINDEX	It rebuilds an existing index that others might need.
ZAP	It permanently removes all records from a file.

Plan ahead if you want exclusive use of a file. Absolutely no one else can be using it when you attempt to open it for exclusive use. The exclusive switch in the View window must be set ON (see Fig. 10-1) by clicking in the box, or you can enter the following command into the Command window:

SET EXCLUSIVE ON

Another way to use a file exclusively is to open the file using this command:

USE <filename> EXCLUSIVE

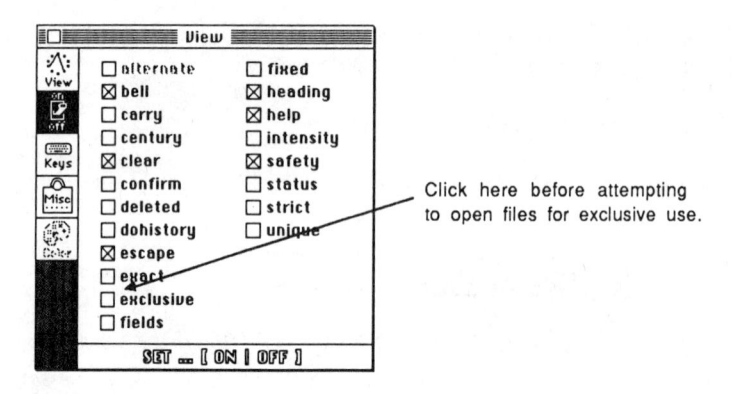

Fig. 10-1. Setting exclusive "on."

Automatic File Locks

Exclusive use of a file and a file lock are not the same thing. Some file operations do not require exclusive use, yet temporarily prevent other users from changing data anywhere in the file. If a user tries to access a record when one of these commands is working a "File is in use by another" message will result. The following operations, for example, automatically lock the file, allowing others to read data but not to make any changes until they are finished:

```
APPEND BLANK
APPEND FROM <filename>
DELETE (if scope includes more than one record)
INDEX
JOIN
RECALL (if scope includes more than one record)
REPLACE (if scope includes more than one record)
UPDATE
```

Automatic Record Locks

The following commands lock one record at a time:

```
CHANGE
DELETE (if scope includes only one record)
EDIT
GATHER
RECALL (if scope includes only one record)
REPLACE (if scope includes only one record)
```

If a user tries to access a record that has already been locked for editing by another user, the message, "Cannot lock" will appear.

Programmed Locking Concepts

Automatic record and file locking works great while using FoxBASE interactively, but application programs can be rudely terminated when automatic record locks fail to secure a record that's needed for an operation to complete. To prevent these types of problems, programmers can install routines to lock records, and even make error-handling routines to manage any other networking error event. There are two record-locking functions in FoxBASE that work identically. The reason why there are two is so that FoxBASE can run programs written for a different language dialect. The record locking functions are:

```
LOCK( )
RLOCK( )
```

If you are writing a program that uses any of these commands, use LOCK( ) or RLOCK( ) and make sure it returns a ".T." before actually performing the command:

```
APPEND BLANK (after appending the blank use RLOCK( ) before adding data)
CHANGE
DELETE (if scope includes only one record)
EDIT
GATHER
RECALL (if scope includes only one record)
REPLACE (if scope includes only one record)
```

Using the Record-Locking Function

In one simple step, the RLOCK( ) and LOCK( ) functions lock the current record and return a ".T." if successful. If another user has already locked the current record for editing, a ".F." is returned to indicate that attempts to edit the record will fail. Whenever attempts to edit a locked record are made errors are generated:

```
STORE RLOCK( ) TO gotrec
IF gotrec
    <commands>
ENDIF
```

Or

```
IF RLOCK( )
    <commands>
ENDIF
```

You should create a method to let the user know that the record is currently in use, such as this:

```
USE <filename>
SET FORMAT TO <formatfilename>
STORE RLOCK( ) TO gotrec
IF gotrec
    EDIT
    UNLOCK
ELSE
    ALERT NOTE 1 "Record is already in use by another. Try again later."
ENDIF
```

Or

```
USE <filename>
IF RLOCK( )
    <commands like @ SAY...GET>
    READ
    UNLOCK
ELSE
    ALERT NOTE 1 "Record is already in use by another. Try again later."
ENDIF
```

The above methods are sufficient, but they have no patience and force the user to try again, perhaps several times, until the record is successfully locked. The INKEY( ) function, or a simple counter, can make a program wait for a predetermined length of time, therefore, you can place them inside of a DO WHILE...ENDDO loop that "waits" until the locking user either releases the record or someone's patience is exceeded.

The following is an example of more sophisticated record locking using this technique. It does the waiting for the user and lets them know when several locking attempts were unsuccessful. Use this method to get a lock *before* entering an edit mode:

```
STORE reclock( ) TO gotrec
IF gotrec
   <editing commands>
ELSE
   <commands to gracefully return the user to another option>
ENDIF
```

If this user-defined function called "reclock" returns a ".T.", all is well. Otherwise, editing is never attempted, and the user is informed to try again:

```
PROCEDURE reclock
PRIVATE delay, times, attempts, count
prevscrn = SYS(1034)
STORE 15 TO delay, times
STORE 0 TO attempts, tcount
DO WHILE delay > 0
    IF RLOCK( )
        RETURN (.T.)   && successfully locked record
    ENDIF
    IF times > 1
        attempts = attempts + 1
        IF attempts = 1
            SCREEN 9 TYPE 19 LOCK     HEADING "A Record is Busy" AT ;
58,84 SIZE 188,299 PIXELS    FONT "Geneva",12 COLOR 0,0,0,-1,-1,-1 TOP
            CLEAR
        ENDIF
        @ 3,7 SAY "The record you need is in use."
        @ 4,7 SAY "Please wait while I try to get"
        @ 5,7 SAY "it for you."
        @ 7,7 SAY "Attempt " + LTRIM(STR(attempts,2)) + " of " + ;
LTRIM(STR(times,2))
        STORE INKEY(1) TO tcount
    ENDIF
    delay = delay-1
ENDDO
CLEAR
SCREEN 9 OFF
ALERT NOTE 1 "That record is tied up. Try again later."
SCREEN &prevscrn TOP
RETURN (.F.)   && couldn't lock record
```

Multiuser Issues **471**

Programmed File Locks

The file-locking function works identically like the record-locking functions except that the result is to lock the whole file. Use the FLOCK( ) command before doing any of these operations:

```
APPEND BLANK (either FLOCK( ) or use an error handling routine)
APPEND FROM <filename>
BROWSE (BROWSE NOMODIFY does not need a file lock)
DELETE (if scope includes more than one record)
INDEX
JOIN
RECALL (if scope includes more than one record, otherwise RLOCK( ))
REPLACE (if scope includes more than one record, otherwise RLOCK( ))
UPDATE
```

Notice that this procedure is just like the one used to lock records except that the RLOCK( ) has been replaced by FLOCK( ), and some of the names have been changed:

```
STORE fillock( ) TO gotfile
IF gotfile
    <editing commands>
ELSE
    <commands to gracefully return the user to another option>
ENDIF
```

If the following user-defined function called "fillock" returns a ".T.," all is well. Otherwise, editing is never attempted, and the user is informed to try again:

```
PROCEDURE fillock
PRIVATE delay, times, attempts, count
prevscrn = SYS(1034)
STORE 15 TO delay, times
STORE 0 TO attempts, tcount
DO WHILE delay > 0
    IF FLOCK( )
        RETURN (.T.)   && successfully locked file
    ENDIF
    IF times > 1
        attempts = attempts + 1
        IF attempts = 1
            SCREEN 9 TYPE 19    LOCK HEADING "A File is Busy" AT ;
58,84 SIZE 188,299 PIXELS    FONT "Geneva",12 COLOR 0,0,0,-1,-1,-1 TOP
            CLEAR
        ENDIF
        @ 3,7 SAY "The file you need is in use."
        @ 4,7 SAY "Please wait while I try to get"
        @ 5,7 SAY "it for you."
        @ 7,7 SAY "Attempt " + LTRIM(STR(attempts,2)) + " of " + ;
```

472 *Multiuser Issues*

```
        LTRIM(STR(times,2))
                STORE INKEY(1) TO tcount
            ENDIF
            delay = delay-1
ENDDO
CLEAR
SCREEN 9 OFF
ALERT NOTE 1 "That file is tied up. Try again later."
SCREEN &prevscrn TOP
RETURN (.F.)   && couldn't lock file
```

Error-Handling Routines

Sometimes multiuser errors can occur even when you've applied locking techniques to prevent them. One condition that can create an error now and then is when two users append a blank at the same time. You cannot always foresee or prevent error-causing events, but you can manage them with this command:

```
ON ERROR <command>
```

The ON ERROR command is wonderful at preventing errors from crashing your programs, because it stops error messages in their tracks and passes control to any command, program, or procedure you want before grief sets in. Here's an example:

```
ON ERROR DO traper
```

After this command has been issued, and a multiusing error occurs, a custom error-handling routine ("traper" in this example) gets a shot at fixing things so that the program doesn't halt. FoxBASE has several powerful functions that can be used with the ON ERROR command to give you full control in error-network conflict situations.

ERROR( )	(returns error numbers, see Appendix C for a full list of all the errors that can be trapped)
MESSAGE( )	(returns an appropriate error message)
MESSAGE(1)	(returns the line of code that generated the error)
SYS(16)	(returns the name of the program that generated the error)

The following is a list of the error numbers and messages that can occur and be trapped by ERROR() when multiuser concurrency issues arise:

108   File is in use by another. This error occurs when exclusive use of a file is attempted by more than one user.

- 109 Record is in use by another. This error occurs when RLOCK( ) or LOCK( ) requests cannot lock a record.
- 110 Exclusive open of file is required. This error occurs when an operation requiring exclusive use of a file is attempted without it.
- 111 Cannot write to a read-only file. This error occurs when an attempt is made to write to a file that has been protected by being on a locked disk or through a Macintosh or network write-protection mechanism such as access privilege controls.
- 130 Record is not locked. This error occurs when an attempt is made to edit a record without first locking it with RLOCK( ) or LOCK( ).
- 2013 Connection to a server has been interrupted. FoxBASE can report this problem but not fix it. It's best to CLOSE DATA immediately if this error occurs and notify the network administrator.

Here's an example of our error-handling routine:

```
PROCEDURE traper
times = 0
DO CASE
CASE ERROR( ) = 108
    ALERT NOTE 1 "A needed file is currently in use by another."
    DO WHILE .NOT. FLOCK( ) .AND. times < 1000
        times = times + 1
    ENDDO
    IF times < 1000
        RETRY
    ELSE
        ALERT NOTE 8 "The file cannot be used at this time. Try again later."
    ENDIF
CASE ERROR( ) = 109
    ALERT NOTE 1 "A needed record is currently in use by another."
    DO WHILE .NOT. RLOCK( ) .AND. times < 1000
        times = times + 1
    ENDDO
    IF times < 1000
        RETRY
    ELSE
        ALERT NOTE 2 "The record cannot be used now. Try again later."
    ENDIF
CASE ERROR( ) = 130
    ALERT NOTE 1 "An attempt was made to edit a busy record."
    DO WHILE .NOT. RLOCK( ) .AND. times < 1000
        times = times + 1
    ENDDO
    IF times < 1000
```

```
                RETRY
            ELSE
                ALERT NOTE 2 "The record is still busy. Try again later."
            ENDIF
        OTHERWISE
            ALERT STOP 7 MESSAGE( ) + " at " + MESSAGE(1) + " in program: " + SYS(16)
            CLEAR GETS
            RETURN TO MASTER
        RETURN
```

RETRY is like RETURN except that it re-executes the last command that was executed in the calling program. Unlike RETRY, RETURN always resumes on the next line down from the last line that was executed in the calling program. RETRY is useful in multiuser programs because you can use it to attempt record locking more than once. However, you should provide a way that allows a user to exit the process entirely.

As an alternative to the error-handling program shown above, you can use functions to pass parameter values to an error-handling routine, such as the one below. This is a better method for using SYS(16) because it returns the name of the currently running program. Since the currently running program is the offending program, you'll most easily get the result you want, which is to identify the problem and resolve it.

```
            * * * * * * * * * * * * * * * * * * * * *
            ON ERROR DO traper WITH ERROR( ), MESSAGE( ), MESSAGE(1), SYS(16)

            PROCEDURE traper
            PARAMETERS errnum, errmsg, errline, errprog
            times = 0
            DO CASE
            CASE ERROR( ) = 108
                ALERT NOTE 1 "Error #" + errnum + "-" + errmsg
                DO WHILE .NOT. FLOCK( ) .AND. times < 1000
                    times = times + 1
                ENDDO
                IF times < 1000
                    RETRY
                ELSE
                    ALERT NOTE 8 "The file cannot be used at this time. Try again later."
                ENDIF
            CASE ERROR( ) = 109
```

Multiuser Issues **475**

```
        ALERT NOTE 1 "Error #" + errnum + "-" + errmsg
        DO WHILE .NOT. RLOCK( ) .AND. times < 1000
            times = times + 1
        ENDDO
        IF times < 1000
            RETRY
        ELSE
            ALERT NOTE 2 "The record cannot be used now. Try again later."
        ENDIF
    CASE ERROR( ) = 130
        ALERT NOTE 1 "Error #" + errnum + "-" + errmsg
        DO WHILE .NOT. RLOCK() .AND. times < 1000
            times = times + 1
        ENDDO
        IF times < 1000
            RETRY
        ELSE
            ALERT NOTE 2 "The record is still busy. Try again later."
        ENDIF
    OTHERWISE
        ALERT STOP 7 errmsg + " at " + errline + " in program: " + errprog
        CLEAR GETS
        RETURN TO MASTER
RETURN
* * * * * * * * * * * * * * * * * * * * * * * * * * * * * *
```

It's harder to recover from errors than it is to prevent them, so don't use error-handling routines to replace record-locking routines. In the error-handling routines above, who knows what will happen when the user is returned to the program that generated the error? Nothing beats experimentation. I suggest that you take an hour or so to experiment with these techniques and become familiar with their behavior before trying to write finished applications that depend on locks.

Editing Memory Variables

There are many ways to write multiuser programs, but it's always a good idea to limit the time that a user can lock a record. One popular method for doing this is to place the contents of data records into memory variables or arrays for editing instead of allowing users to edit the data record itself. This way, locks aren't required except for the very brief moment when the edited memory variable contents are written back into the record's with a REPLACE or GATHER command, such as this program:

```
* * * * * * * * * * * * * * * * * * * * * *
PROCEDURE variabledit
chgcondition = .F.
SCATTER TO memrecord
```

```
        SCATTER TO refrecord
        STORE RECNO( ) TO currec
        ...format file or other commands to display and edit the memrecord variables
        GOTO currec
        ...commands to compare the contents of the refrecord array with the original
        ...if it's ok to replace the original with memrecord make chgcondition true
        IF chgcondition .AND. RLOCK( )
            GATHER FROM memrecord
        ELSE
            IF .NOT. chgcondition
                ALERT NOTE 1 "Another user has changed that record."
            ELSE   && cannot lock record
                ALERT NOTE 1 "That record is currently in use."
            ENDIF
        ENDIF
* * * * * * * * * * * * * * * * * * * * * * * * * * * * * *
```

The SCATTER command puts a whole record, except memo fields, into a memory variable array. Note that the *memrecord* gets edited and the *refrecord* doesn't. Also, note that a variable, *currec,* was created to hold the number of the edited record. Before replacing the original record's contents with the edited *memrecord,* it's a good idea to GOTO *currec,* so that *refrecord* contents can be compared with the original. This prevents an overwrite of the wrong record in case another user completely changes its contents while you are editing. If changes do occur, it's a good idea to prevent further changes until the user looks at the changes someone else made in the interim.

MANAGING RESOURCES

Resources, like alerts, pictures, sounds, and so on, are stored either in FoxBASE itself, in the FoxUser resource file, or in custom resource files of your own making, which are much like the FoxUser file. Do not remove the FoxUser file from the FoxBASE folder unless you will ship a runtime application and have used the FoxUser file as a base for your own custom resource file. It's important that all its resources be available.

Fonts can be moved from one resource file to another with the Font/DA Mover application that comes with every Macintosh. Normally, Font/DA Mover opens only the system file and files with the suitcase icon. If you hold the Option-Command keys down when the Open button is pressed, however, Font/DA Mover will reveal the font contents of any file on your disk, and allow you to insert custom fonts into the FoxUser or other custom resource file.

XCMDs and XFCNs can also be stored in a resource file, but they almost always require that you use a tool like ResEdit, a resource editor, to install or remove them. Make sure that the XCMDs and XFCNs you use are guaranteed to be compatible with Fox-BASE, or test them yourself before relying on them in an application. Many are written to be used with Hypercard and some of them require the presence of Hypercard to perform reliably.

ResEdit is produced by Apple Computer for Macintosh developers. Using it, you have access to the innards of any file's resource fork. Registered Apple developers get ResEdit to use, and it might even be available in computer stores or on bulletin boards. I use ResEdit to copy PICT images, sounds, icons and other things from one file to another.

ResEdit is a dangerous tool when used carelessly. It opens up Macintosh resources making them vulnerable for tampering. It's an equally powerful tool, however, when handled with care and skill. You don't need ResEdit, I just mention it because there are always hackers who want to know how other hackers do it. Use FoxForm's picture tool to move pictures into and out of the resource fork of custom resource files if you don't have, or want, to use ResEdit. Its prompts and dialogs are straightforward and its easy to use.

11
Using FoxReport

FOXREPORT—available only in version 2.x—is Fox Software's answer to a new call from users for an easier and more powerful way to publish reports. Before the desktop publishing revolution, few people thought of database information and proportional fonts in the same context. Now, in FoxReport, we have a high quality *database* publishing tool that matches the power and ease of some *desktop* publishing tools.

FoxReport so easily combines pictures, lines, and boxes with stored data that nearly any user can make striking reports that look as though they were created and typeset by professionals. What's more, its page previewing feature presents reports on the screen just as they'll appear on a page, saving both the time and paper it takes to print proof sheets.

FoxReport can show its stuff on paper, on the screen, and even send character output to a file. Read the REPORT FORM command entry in Chapter 8 to learn how each of these outputs work and how they differ from one another. Continue reading in this chapter if you want to learn how to make and print reports and labels.

MACINTOSH PRINTING

In order to control how a page printed on a Macintosh laser printer will look, you must be able to work with high degrees of resolution that don't exist on character-based computer screens such as those found on mainframes and on most IBM compatible PCs. It's easy to use FoxReport on a Macintosh using laser printers and connecting them with several other users on AppleTalk. It is not uncommon in modern offices to see this type of setup, or these services can be purchased by the hour in photocopy shops and desktop graphics stores all over the world. Although not as good as LaserWriters, Apple Image-Writers are also good output devices, because they were designed to work with the fonts and images produced by the Macintosh computer as well as any dot matrix printer can.

Characters and Bitmaps

The first, and most well-used IBM compatible computer screens have a working resolution of 80 columns by 25 rows. The advantage to this 80 by 25 grid is that it can be quickly occupied by one of many characters, because the characters are pre-formed and the coordinates where they can appear are fixed.

The Macintosh can use character-based coordinates, but it does so only as an afterthought. Its characters are not pre-formed, but are created in pixel bits. A poor analogy of this difference is the difference between an impact printer, with its pre-formed characters on a wheel, and a dot-matrix printer, which must form each character from memory as it's printed. The Macintosh, like a dot-matrix printer, has many more coordinate positions to remember, and it must think about each bit in its coordinate map individually. The advantage is its flexibility, the kind needed to produce bitmapped graphics and pictures.

FoxReport has two modes. In standard mode, it takes advantage of the Macintosh's bit map of 72 dots (or pixels) per inch. In character mode, it uses a monospaced font that mimics the fixed grid of character printers and character displays where each character occupies the same amount of space, regardless of whether it's an I or a W. In standard mode, FoxReport uses all of the resolution in a Macintosh screen—72 dots per inch—for graphics and layout alignment.

AppleTalk and Device Drivers

Another power advantage of the Macintosh that FoxReport takes advantage of are printer drivers that automatically make adjustments whenever a printer is selected. This lets you design and test reports on an ImageWriter, for example, and a LaserWriter, as long as the LaserWriter driver is present for selection in the chooser.

AppleTalking is another lesser known but well used feature of Macintosh printer drivers. You can send a report to an AppleTalk ImageWriter, to a locally connected ImageWriter, cancel it, start it again, and so on, all because the printer driver intercedes for you.

REPORT FEATURES

Version 1.x of FoxBASE+/Mac sports the same report writer that was available in FoxBASE+, a program made for IBM compatible PCs. Without the ability to use Macintosh graphics, however, its reports are *boring* at best. The following sections discuss those features that only the FoxReport feature of version 2.x can offer.

Quick Report

Quick Report is a menu option under the Report menu that appears when you first make a new report. It automatically places as many fields as will fit on the screen for you so that you won't have to spend time selecting each field just to get started. Figure 11-1 shows the Quick Report dialog box and what happens when you press OK.

If you want to get all of the fields in a database on the form at once, just make the body band larger by dragging it down, then select a small font size and Quick Report.

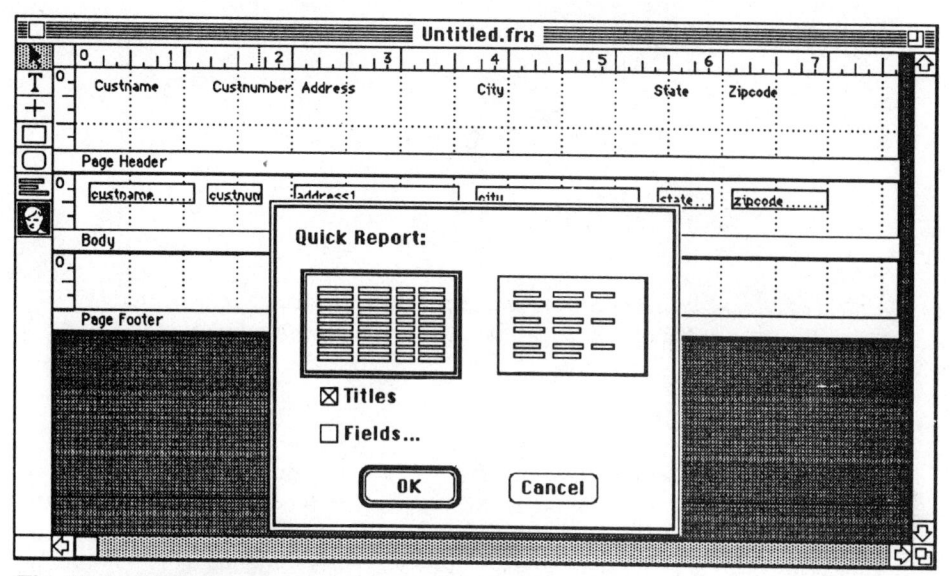

Fig. 11-1. Quick Report automatically places fields.

When the dialog in Fig. 11-1 appears, select the Field Wrapping option on the right and press OK. After the fields appear on-screen, you can move them anywhere.

If the option Titles is checked, field names appear as titles in the page header as shown in Fig. 11-1. The Fields option lets you select which fields will appear and in what order they'll be in.

Bands and Body

Bands are the horizontal lines across the page called Page Header, Body, and Page Footer. The bands take space only on the screen. Above them is where you can place text, data fields, graphic objects you create, and pictures for printing. You don't have to use every band on the screen. In fact, they come in pairs as header and footer, title and summary, and so on. There will be times when you have no use for a band at all. If that's the case, just squeeze all of the room out of it and then abandon it.

If there is no room between bands that you want to use, you can resize them to make as much room as you need. Just put the mouse pointer over a band's left end, then click and drag it. You'll know that the cursor is in a position to move a band when it turns into a little hand. Another, more precise, way to move a band is to double-click when the little hand appears (see Fig. 11-2) and select a band size.

The body band is special because it gets printed many times on each page, repeating for each new record. If the body band is wide, fewer records can be printed and there'll be more white space around them. If it is narrow, more records can be printed and they'll be closer together. Group records work similarly except that they repeat whenever there's a change of group, not of record.

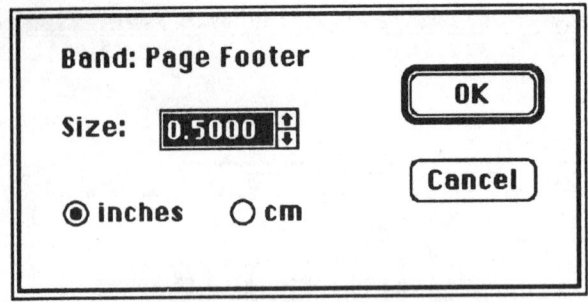

Fig. 11-2. Setting accurate vertical band dimensions.

Page Header and Footer

Almost without exception, any object that's visible in the page header on your screen will be printed at the top of each and every page when the report is run. The same thing is true of the footer, except that fields entered there can be set to print only when certain totals have been accumulated. When you first create and double-click on a data field, a dialog box such as the one shown in Fig. 11-3 will appear, allowing you to modify its contents. You can use the Totalling option to calculate the amount that's printed there by counting, summing, averaging, and so on. If a total is not ready for printing when the field is encountered, such as when the data group is not yet exhausted, it won't print.

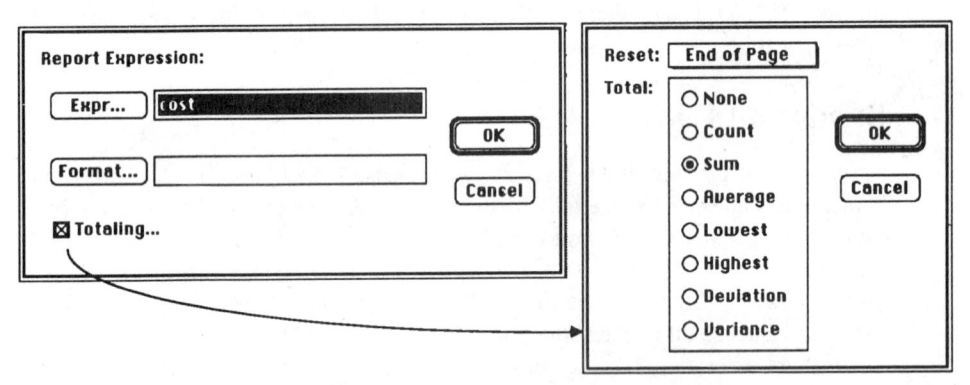

Fig. 11-3. Making computed fields.

Pages, like columns, don't group data by themselves. Group bands do that. Figure 11-4 shows you the boxes to check for quitting on one page and starting on a new one whenever a group is exhausted and another starts. In addition, you can check Reset page to make page numbers start over at 1 whenever this occurs.

Column Header and Footer

Column headers are automatically created when you decide to use two or more columns in the Page Layout dialog as shown in Fig. 11-5. The result is another set of bands, one for a column header and one for a column footer, both of which will be

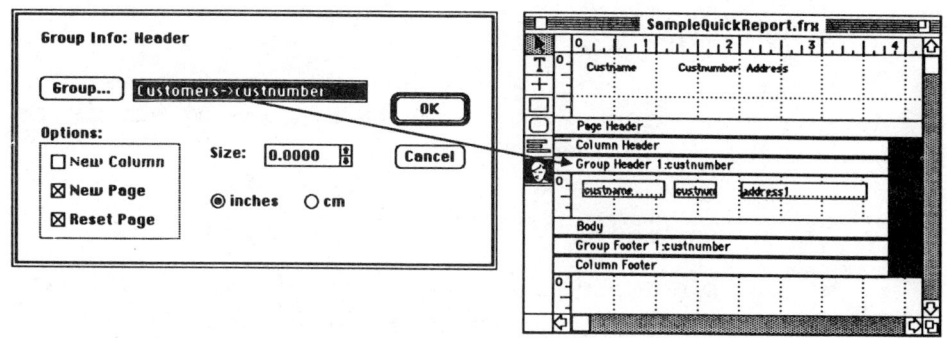

Fig. 11-4. Groups segment reports for readability.

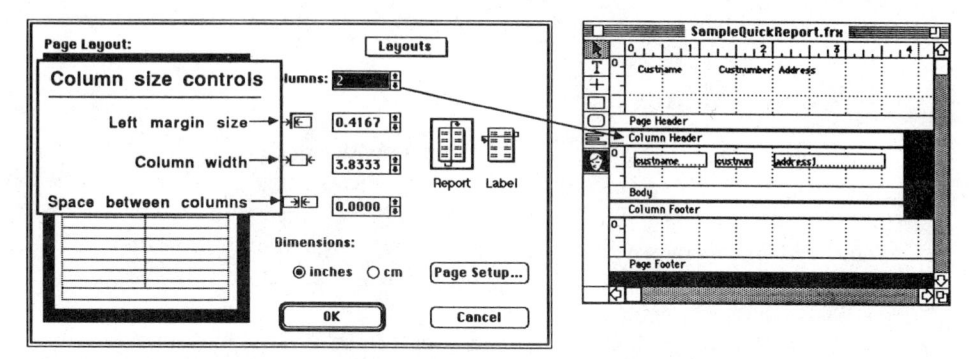

Fig. 11-5. Creating and adjusting columns.

repeated across each page as many times as there are columns. Later, all you need to do to get print to appear in multiple columns is to decide what goes into one column.

Columns come in two basic types, one for reports and one for labels. Report columns wrap data from the bottom of one column up to the top of the next in newspaper column fashion. Label columns wrap data in a tabular fashion from the left column to the next one on its right, and so on, reaching the bottom of the page only when the last entry is printed on the bottom-right page corner. Label reports are read from left to right.

Columns don't group data, you will have to create a data group for that. You can, however, tell a data group to quit printing in the current column when a group ends and to start printing the next group in a new column. Figure 11-4 shows how easily this is done. Simply check the box New Column and you're set.

Group Header and Footer

Group headers and footers are created by selecting the Data Grouping option under the Report menu. Groups are natural breaking points in data, such as invoice number, zip code, company name, and so on, where you want to create totals or indicate where an old group has ended and a new one begins. Groups are as wide as the page's columns. Note, in Fig. 11-4, that grouping changes can trigger a new column or a new page, and page numbers can even be reset to start on page one. You simply select these actions for each group when you define it.

Title and Summary

Title and summary bands always come together like headers and footers. You don't have to use both just because they come in pairs, however. Titles and summaries print only once per report—at the beginning and the end.

WORKING ENVIRONMENTS AND OBJECTS

Working with FoxReport, like anything else, is easier if you know a little about the environment you'll work in. I have already discussed the difference between character-based and bitmapped screens earlier in the chapter, but you need to know about the menu options, the types of objects FoxReport understands and manipulates, and the benefits and restrictions in a band approach to report layout.

FoxReport Menus

There are only two special menus in FoxReport, Object and Report. As you might guess, the Object menu is for manipulating individual things on the report. The Report menu is for making changes that affect more than one object at a time or the report as a whole. The File menu is where you open, create, and save report form files (.frx), just as you do other types of files. To save a report file, make the report window active and select the File/Save menu option.

You can control the font, size, and style of text, select a filling pattern or color for the inside region of graphic objects, and even select the line (pen) width and texture of lines in graphic objects in the Object menu. Finally, the object menu has a set of options called transfer modes that control how objects appear when they overlap.

The Report menu is where you decide basic things about each report. Page Layout establishes columns, page setup information such as paper orientation, column count, width, and so on. Use Page Preview to see an on-screen replica of the page as it will appear in print and the Rulers, Grid, Align to Grid, and the Front/Back options all make object manipulations easier. Finally, use Title/Summary and Data Grouping to create new bands.

Thinking in Bands

FoxReport "thinks" in bands, so it's a good idea to understand how to make them work for you and not against you when you're trying to implement a report design. The most important thing to know about any band is in its name. This is because a band's name tells you where and how often its information will print. Remember that the space immediately above each band is what prints, and that the named band marker that crosses the page or column takes no space on the page when previewed or printed.

The body band, though small, is really the largest band of all when printed. This is because it's space and what's in it gets "printed" for each database record. You should use body bands for the most detailed information in a report.

Now, suppose that a database field, for example, has a few records that contain too much information to fit in the little space showing in the body band. To handle this situation, you would not enlarge the band, because doing so would cause all of records to take up more space. Instead, double-click on the field, which might overflow the band's space and a dialog box such as the one shown in Fig. 11-6 will appear. Select the band stretching option in the field expresion dialog. This will make the band grow larger to accommodate those records that need extra vertical space without enlarging it for every record. The bottom illustration in Fig. 11-6 illustrates the effect that stretching has when a record contents exceeds the width of a field. Stretching works in other bands just like it does in the body band, and it works for pictures as well as for alphanumeric data.

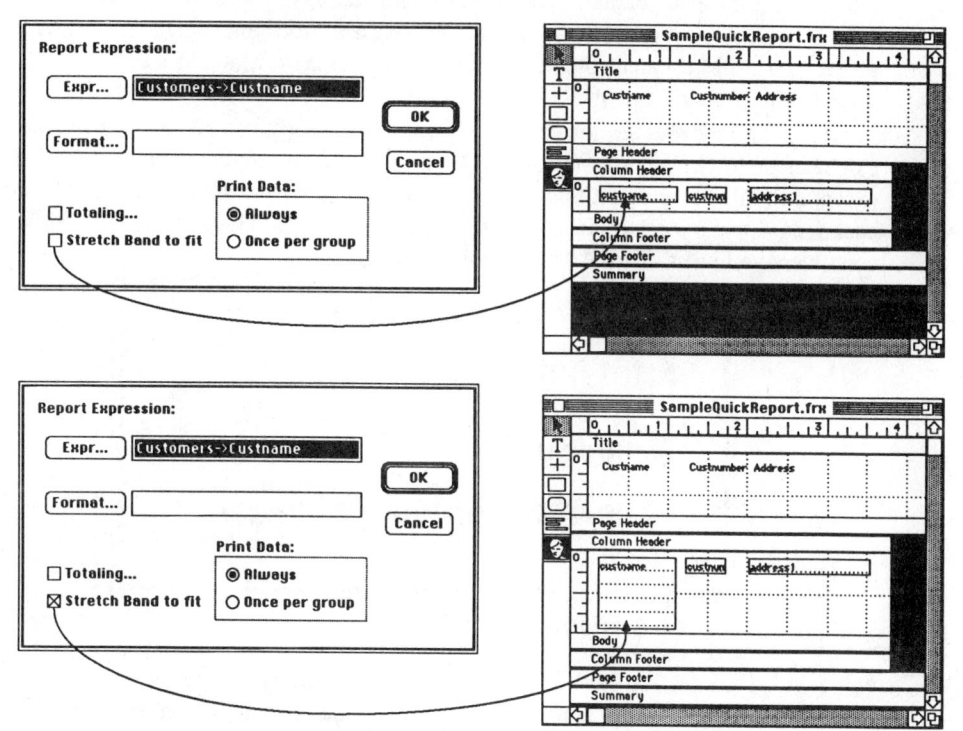

Fig. 11-6. Making flexible space for lengthy data fields.

For me, the one most bothersome limitation of bands is that each page, except the first and last page, which can have a Title and Summary band of their own, is made from one specification. This means that multipage forms, where each page is unique, must be created using separate report format (.frx) files. Consequently, the best you can do is to get three different pages out of one report where a Title band prints one page, the Body band another, and the Summary band another. This objection aside, bands are the most flexible way to make reports from tabular data.

FOXREPORT OBJECTS

There are only four types of object known to FoxReport—Text, Data fields, Graphics, and Pictures. Although that may not sound like an impressive list, what a skilled person can do with them is impressive. Figure 11-8 shows the tools FoxReport gives you to create, select, and manipulate these objects.

Text

You can think of text as labels that don't move and cannot be changed once placed. You can make text objects by selecting the text tool and placing an insertion marker in any band on the page. Once you place an insertion point, simply type the text you want. After a text object has been created, you can change its contents with the text tool and move it anywhere you like by selecting it with the selection tool and dragging. As with other objects, text objects can be duplicated through the standard Macintosh copy and paste features found in the Edit menu.

Text can be displayed for each occurrence (or record) within its band's group, or it can be made to display only once at the beginning of each group (see Fig. 11-7). The only exception to this rule is text that you've put into the body band—it will always print with each record that's printed. To get the dialog shown in Fig. 11-7, just double-click on the text object you want affected.

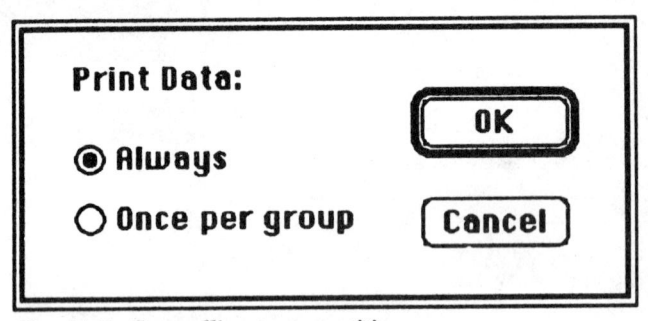

Fig. 11-7. Controlling text repetition.

Text is flexible. You can use proportional fonts, size them, and set the style by selecting options in the Object menu. Style options include bold, italic, underlined, and so on, and you can justify the text left, right, or even center it. Spacing options include single, space and a half, and double spacing. The fonts you can use depends entirely on what fonts are installed in your computer's system file and what fonts will be in the system of others who will use the report.

Be sure to use fonts your report users have, or install them yourself, so that printed reports will look the way you want them to. If a font you select is not available when a report is printed, a substitute might be selected that's not at all what you intended.

Data Fields, Groups, and Totals

Data fields are what their name suggests—regions where data from within a database is printed. Data fields can also be used to print simple text, because they can contain any valid expression, including a simple character expression. Because of this flexibility, they're useful for text label printing when they are to be joined with data.

Data fields can include memory variables, functions used to calculate numbers, dates, and so on, and can even be made conditional by using the IIF( ) function. The most powerful use of data fields comes when they're combined with user-defined functions which I'll discuss a bit later.

Group totals don't show up just because a group band exists, you must place a field in the band, and then select a totalling option to get totals to appear in print. You can place a data field in any band of a report and decide whether or not it should display record-level detail or a total value from one of the report's groups. It's most common to print a group total inside a group band, although it doesn't have to be that way. You can also print data field totals in other bands, such as in page headers or footers.

Groups must be created. If a group exists, it will show up as a band, and conversely, if there's no band, there's no group. But group bands don't have to be used for printing. At times, a group can be incidental except that it makes a break point for use by calculations, user-defined functions, and so on.

Graphics

Graphics are not pictures. They are lines, boxes, and other effects you create to enhance reports using the graphic tools shown in Fig. 11-8. To establish basic attributes for each graphic, simply double-click it on and one of the dialog boxes shown in Fig. 11-9 will appear. If the object is in a body band, one dialog box will appear, if not, the other will appear. Single and double lines can be selected on lines and rectangles regardless of their location.

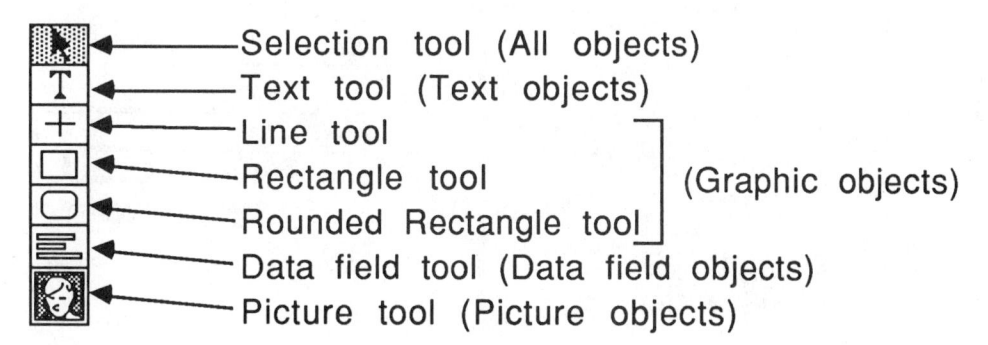

```
Selection tool (All objects)
Text tool (Text objects)
Line tool
Rectangle tool         ┐
Rounded Rectangle tool ┘ (Graphic objects)
Data field tool (Data field objects)
Picture tool (Picture objects)
```

Fig. 11-8. FoxReport tools and the objects they control.

Graphics in a body band can be printed each time a detail record is printed, or you can make them print only when there's a change in the group. The only group that affects graphics is the first, or most detailed grouping of data. If any group's value changes, this level is sure to change with it just as there will usually be a change in zip code data when states change. If no groups are established, no effect will result from selecting the Once per group option button in any of the dialogs shown in Fig. 11-9.

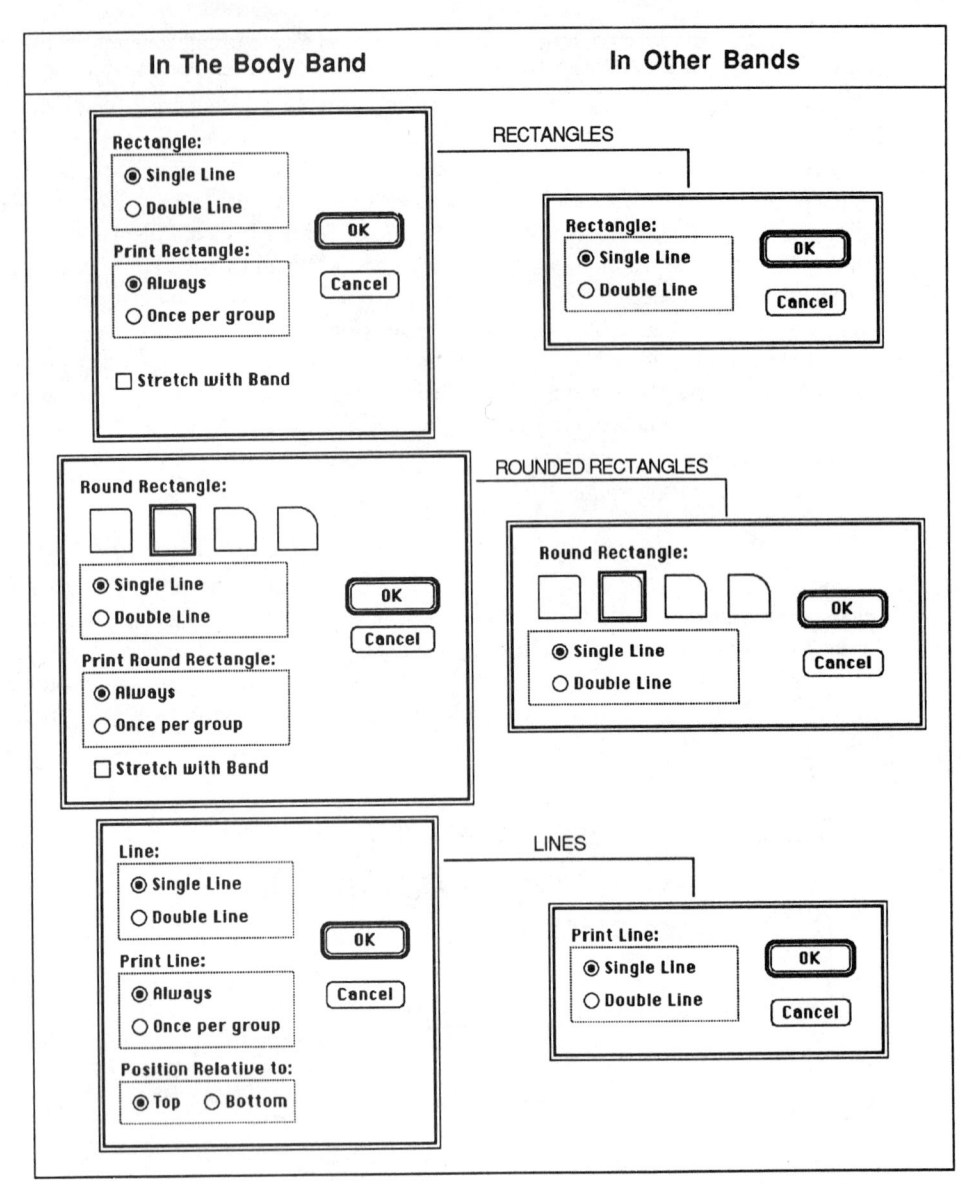

Fig. 11-9. Graphic printing options.

Pictures

Pictures are Macintosh bitmapped images or PICT images (either PICT 1 or PICT 2) that can be stored in database files or in the resource fork of a special resource file like FoxUser, or in the resource fork of a runtime application program. To place a picture, select the picture tool (see Fig. 11-8) then click and drag open the rectangular area in any band where you want the picture to print. The dialog box shown in Fig. 11-10 will show up, allowing you to select picture resource files or database pictures as the source. To

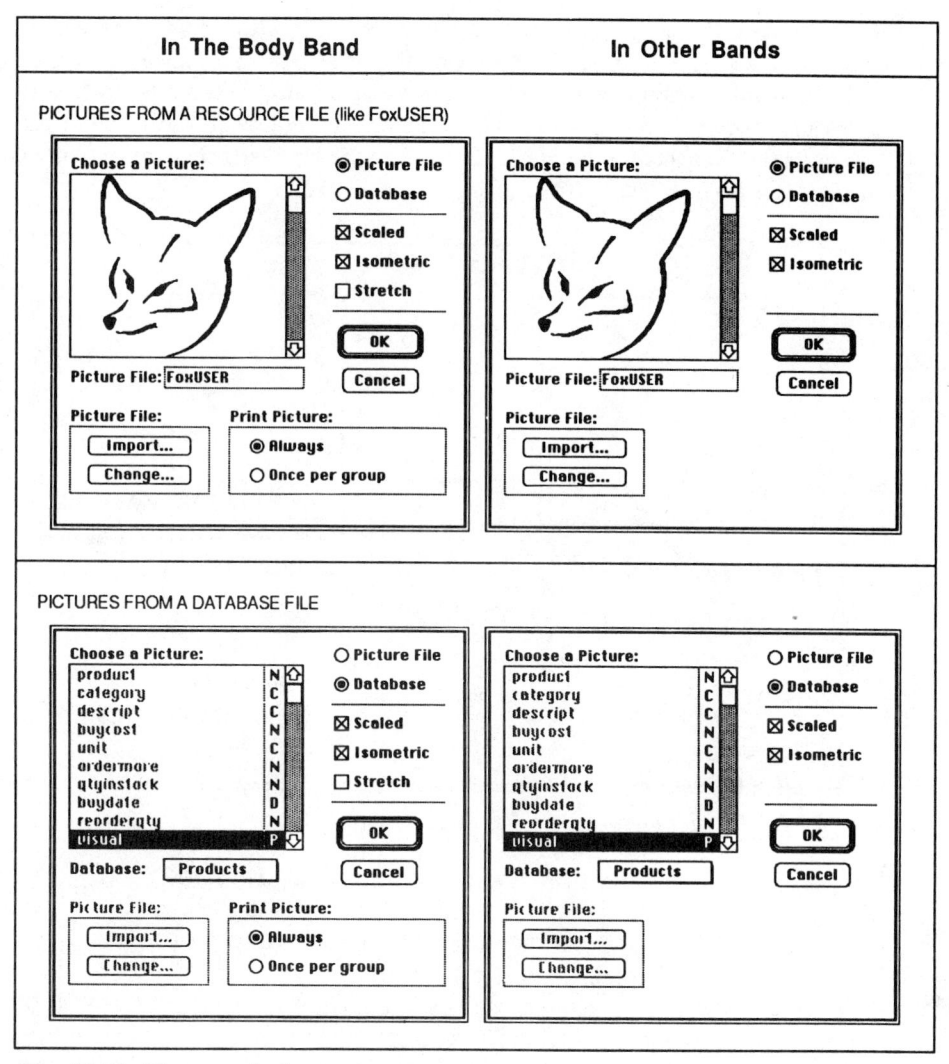

Fig. 11-10. Picture printing options.

choose, press the button on the top right-most portion of the dialog box. If you need to adjust pictures after they have been placed, select tool and change their attributes by double-clicking.

The *Scaled* option allows you to size pictures by using the selection tool. The *Isometric* option instructs FoxReport to maintain the pictures own vertical and horizontal proportions to prevent distortion.

Pictures placed in the body band can keep their isometric integrity and still be stretched with the band, whereas pictures in other bands cannot stretch dynamically. Another thing you'll notice looking at Fig. 11-10 is that you can suppress duplicates when printing pictures in the body band simply by pressing the Once per group button.

The *Import* and *Change* buttons are available only when you've selected a picture

FoxReport Objects   489

resource file as the source of the pictures, because the *Database* pop-up menu is available to select whenever a database file has been selected as a picture source.

The *Import* option (see Fig. 11-10) lets you grab any valid pictures stored in other applications or resource files and put them into the current FoxBASE resource file when you press the Copy button. Figure 11-11 shows a picture that's about to be imported into the FoxUser from an outside file.

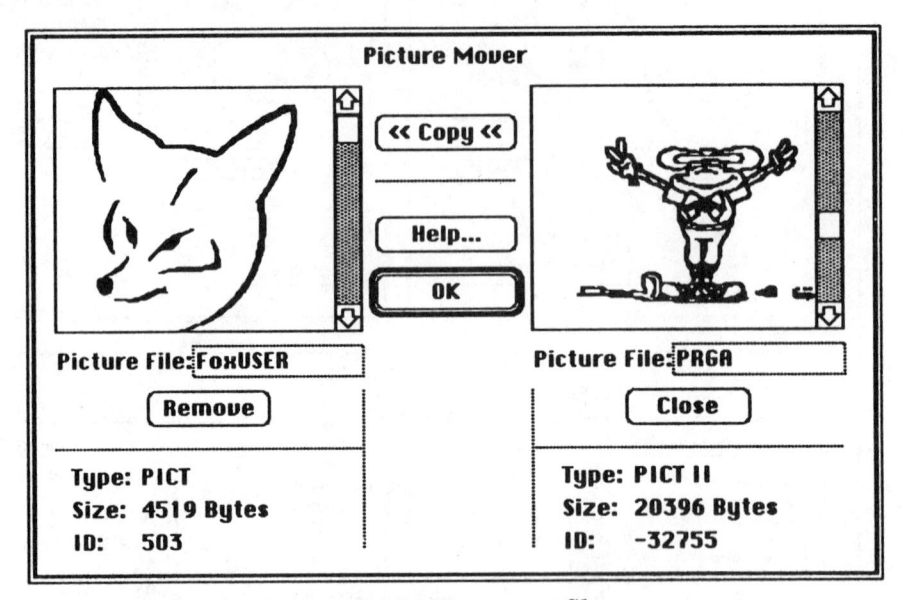

Fig. 11-11. Moving pictures into FoxBASE resource files.

The pictures you save to use in reports can also be used in screens when using Fox-Form, so it's a good idea to make a special copy of the FoxUser file to become a repository of pictures you want to use in reports and in application screens. ResEdit, an application from Apple Computer for managing all resource types, is invaluable for developers who want to manage many pictures, especially if pictures will be used for buttons and other fancy things in application programs.

The *Change* option in Fig. 11-12 brings forth a dialog box that looks like the bottom illustration—the Macintosh file picker—so that you can select another file as a default repository of picture resources. Take note of what happens when you select a different file. The picture selection changes and the Picture File name changes too, indicating that FoxUser is no longer in use as the default picture source. FoxReport will not let you leave a resource file if it is currently using one of its pictures. In this case, you'll have to import the pictures you need in order to get access to them.

MANIPULATING OBJECTS

I've discussed many of the things you can do to manipulate objects, but there are more of them hiding in the Object and Report menus. The options I haven't mentioned, except

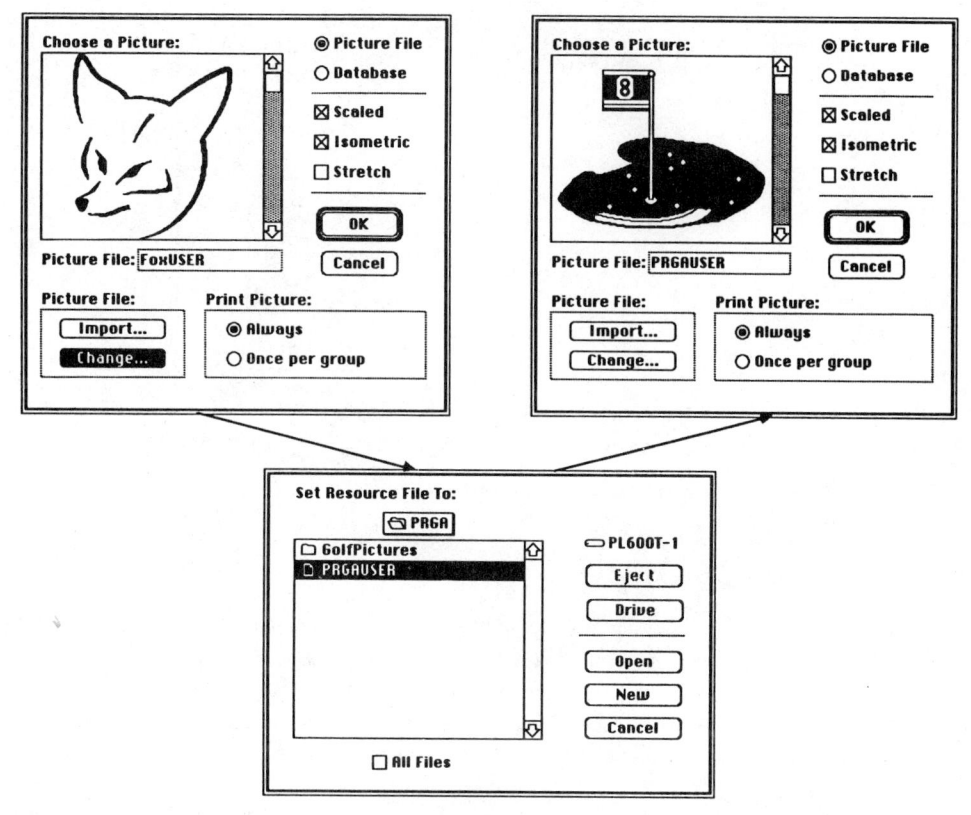

Fig. 11-12. Changing the picture resource file.

in passing, include those used to set grid resolution on the drawing plane and to create different levels of grey in rectangles or lines. Let's discuss the drawing environment first.

Adjusting the Drawing Environment

The Rulers, Grid, and Align to Grid options under the Report menu are all important tools for controlling how things line up and how easy or hard alignments are. Figure 11-13 shows the dialog box that appears when you select the Report/Rulers menu option. You can select among inches, centimeters, and pixels as the rule of measure.

Don't confuse the ruler option with the grid. The ruler is a rough, visual tool for aligning objects, whereas the grid is a physical constraint to objects. If lines appearing in the main section of the report annoy you, just set the ruler lines off. If you want to move objects in full freedom without the grid enforcing alignments on them as you work, just select the Report/Grid menu option. If a check mark is present, the grid is on.

Grid size is very important because it establishes invisible lines in which objects align. Grid pixel numbers should be set low enough to allow enough freedom of placement, yet high enough that you can see the alignment between objects when they've snapped onto the grid.

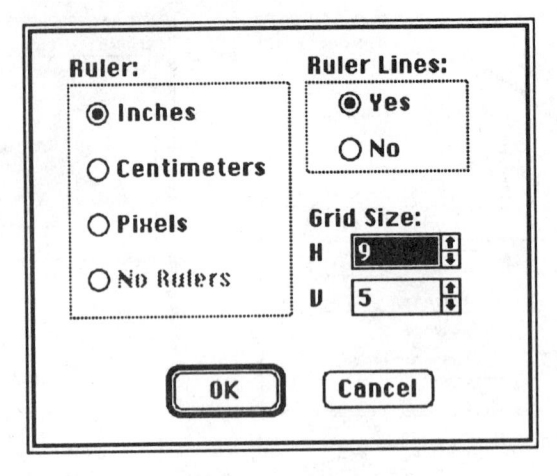

Fig. 11-13. Setting up the working grid and rulers.

Nudging and Micro-Sizing

Nudging is a way to carefully, meticulously, and quickly align objects pixel-by-pixel. Nudging works even when the grid is on: it ignores the grid's constraints.

To nudge an object, just select it and press an arrow key on the keyboard. Each time the arrow key is pressed, the object will move one pixel in the direction you selected. If you select several objects at once, nudging will move all of them. It won't work, however, on grouped objects.

To move objects quickly while nudging, press the command key down and hold it while pressing an arrow. This accelerates the nudging action so that objects can be quickly moved over a greater distance, and in a straight line. Once an object has been nudged, it might not align with the pre-established grid. To restore grid alignment, just select the object, or objects, and select the Report/Align to grid menu option.

Another option related to nudging is what I call micro-sizing, which allows you to adjust the vertical and horizontal size of an object in a manner similar to nudging. To increase the size of an object, just press the Option-Command keys while pressing an arrow. The effect is to "grow" the object in the direction of the arrow key you've pressed. To shrink an object's size, press the Shift-Option keys while pressing an arrow.

Bring to Front and Send to Back

Bring to Front and Send to Back are options in the Report menu that do exactly what they say—they stack objects in their relation to one another, just as you would ingredients going into a bologna sandwich. To use the Front and Back options, just select the object you want affected and then the Menu option. Most times, the result will be immediate and visually obvious.

Fill, Pen, and Transfer Mode

The Fill, Pen, and Transfer mode options are available under the Object menu. Fill and Pen are most useful for graphic objects, while Transfer modes are important to all types of objects.

The Fill option determines what will appear in the inside region of a graphic object. The Pen option determines what the outside line of a graphic object will look like, and the Transfer mode option determines how any two overlapping objects will appear in relation to one another. Take a look at the bottom portion of Fig. 7-16 in Chapter 7 for information about the visual behavior imposed by Transfer modes. Note that the printers don't support as many Transfer modes as are available on-screen, even inside of FoxReport. If transfer modes are important to you, you'll need to experiment for yourself.

CALCULATING AND COMPUTING

FoxReport can perform almost any reasonable numeric calculation on your data. In fact, there's no reason to store a number if it can be calculated during the printing of a report, and because it's band oriented, FoxReport is particularly good at computing group numbers in columns for display or further consolidation.

Calculated Fields

Calculated fields are those which are present, in most cases, one per record. They usually appear to a report viewer just like any other database field, even though they're produced by a formula. Calculated fields can be made from a variety of parts: data from database fields, mathematical functions, memory variable information, constants, and formulas you've created. The calculating power of FoxReport is enormous when you consider all of the functions and operators that FoxBASE has, nearly all of which can be used directly within FoxReport.

Computed Fields

Computed fields are column-wise operations that FoxReport performs on groups of data. Computations can be done on any grouping level, and on the report whole in the form of grand totals, averages, and so on. FoxReport computations can count records in a group, sum, average, figure deviations or variances, and even discover the highest or lowest value in any numeric field's column.

User-Defined Functions

Group computations and field calculations can be enhanced by the power of your own functions. User-Defined Functions, or UDFs, can be "called" by FoxReport just as they can be called by programs. See the section Alerts, UDFs, and Validation in Chapter 7 for more information on how they are made and used. FoxReport can use UDFs with the provision that you don't move the record pointer in any of the files FoxReport is using, or that you return them to the place where they were when the UDF began before returning control to the report form.

DATABASES AND REPORT SPECIFICATIONS

Reports almost always have a sequential approach to data. They start with one company number and end with another, and so on. For this reason, it's important that you take record order into account before creating a report, and that you re-establish the database handling environment's indexes, filters, and relations before printing it. Fortunately, Fox-BASE+/Mac has some tricks up its sleeve that can help you with these things.

Indexes and Relations

The simplest and probably the most important effect of an index while reporting is that it orders a file in some natural way so that the reader can understand what it means. Another, perhaps more technical, reason to use indexes is that they can order a file for grouping. Grouping bands are useless if the data itself is not presented to the report form in an order that's consistent with their breakpoints. For example, you'd create an index on company number to get group totals, by company, of all outstanding invoice records.

Another important reason for using indexes with report files is to establish relationships between database files. If you are having any trouble because multifile reports are missing data, check out the indexes and file relations and follow this advice: Relate files with more matching records to the ones with fewer records. Do this as many times as necessary to include all of the files you're printing from (child files can be parent files to other files). Order the controlling file (the highest parent in a relational hierarchy) in the order you want the final report to appear. This will assure you that all report groups will match the record order, so long as you've been careful.

Views and the (.frx) Report Form File

FoxBASE saves indexes, relations, and so on, in view files so they can later be recalled. Report format files (.frx) can remember the name of a view file for you if you check the environment option when you save them. See the left-most dialog box in Fig. 11-14. When the Environment option is checked, two things happen. FoxBASE records the name of the current view file inside the report form, so you can recall it when you're ready to print, and it makes a view file for you if one does not already exist.

To recall a view file, just select the Database/Report menu or enter this command in the Command window, "REPORT FORM <filename> ENVIRONMENT". The Environment option tells FoxBASE to recall and restore the database handling environment, or view, that existed when you first created the report.

Page Layouts

In addition to saving database information, FoxReport (.frx) files can store page setup information to save you the work of remembering what page size, orientation, and so on is

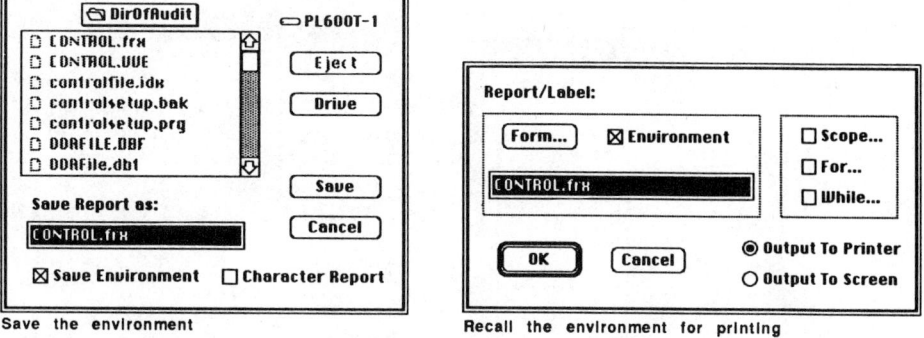

Fig. 11-14. Dialogs to save and restore data views for reporting.

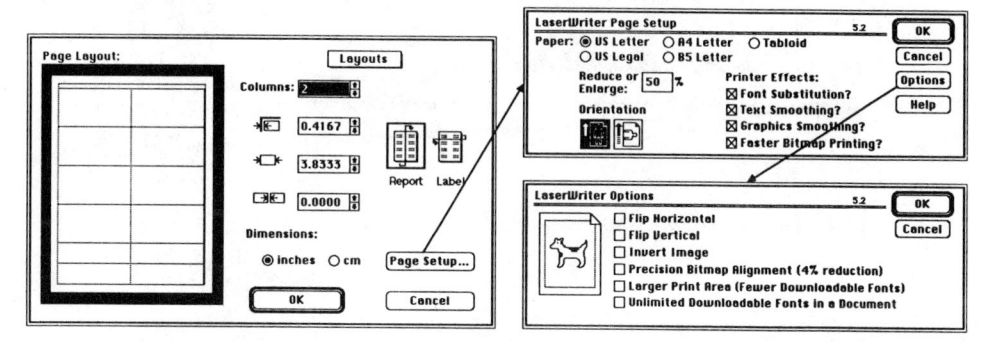

Fig. 11-15. Setting page setup information for each report.

needed for printing (see Fig. 11-15). It is not uncommon for reports to go unused for 30 days at a time, only to be printed at the end or beginning of every fiscal or calendar month. Nothing I can think of would be more frustrating for report printing than to have to recall and re-establish page layout information each and every time it was needed.

LABELS

Labels are no different than reports except in the size of their "page." FoxReport has a special label-sizing menu, shown in Fig. 11-16, that can save you some time when first setting up labels for printing.

New and Old Operators

There are a few new operators in FoxReport that can make labels a lot easier for non-programmers to create than they ever were able to in any "dBASE" language before. These operators are "," and ";". The comma can be used to separate one field from another whenever one space is needed between them in the final printed product. For example, joining first and last names when they are each in a separate field. The semicolon is useful to end one line of a label so that the field that immediateley follows it is printed on the next line down. Figure 11-17 is an acutal example that demonstrates how

Labels   495

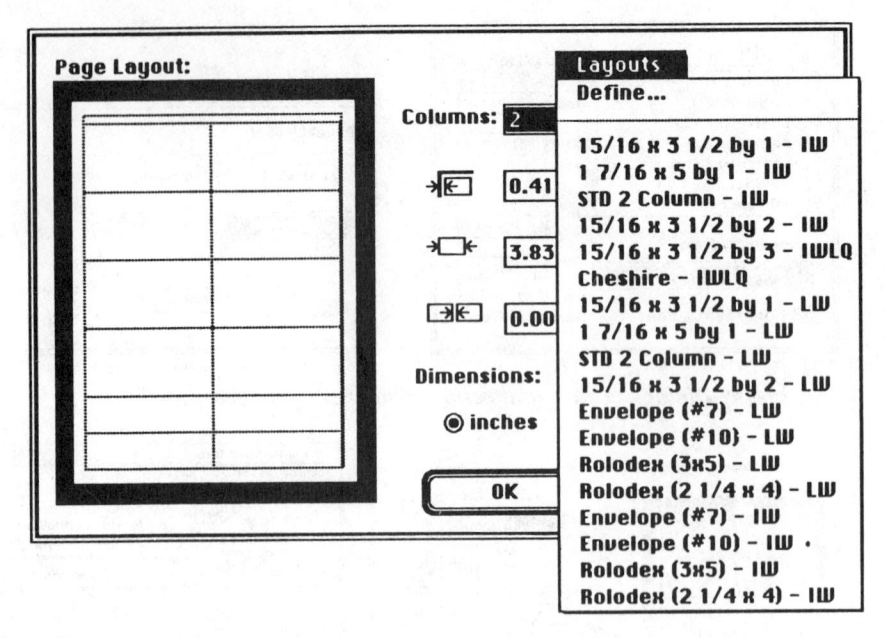

Fig. 11-16. Selecting a standard label dimension.

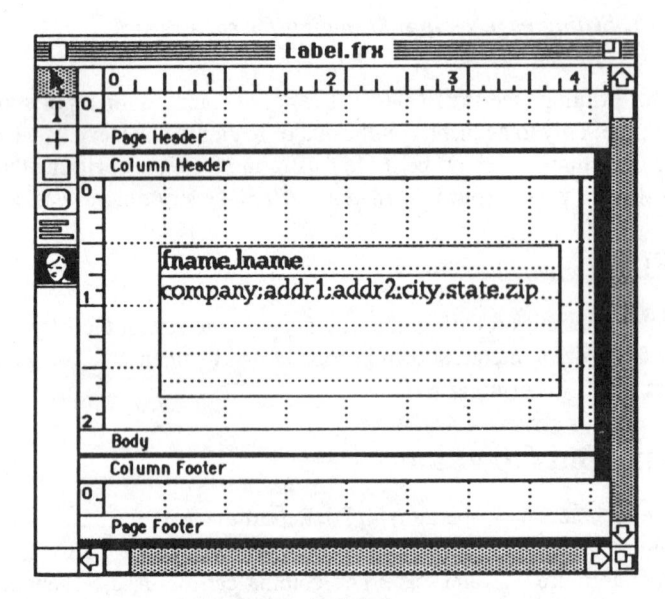

Fig. 11-17. The comma and semicolon in labels.

496   Labels

these operators work. Note that you can put every field that you want printed on a label into one label output field. I've used two fields so that the name can be in large bold print.

Another advantage to using the ; operator is that it causes any blank lines that would be produced by empty fields to be "squeezed" out of the label. Without this feature, annoying gaps occur in labels.

Wide Margins and Exact Sizes

Labels need to be accurately sized, so if you don't find a label format that matches your labels in the predefined label listing shown in Fig. 11-16, enter the dimensions directly into the column box shown in Fig. 11-5 in the Report Layout dialog box and double-click on the body band to open its vertical sizing box (see Fig. 11-2).

Appendix A
ASCII Codes

MACINTOSH ASCII CODES

0	1	2	3	4	5	6	7	8	9	10	11	12	13	14	15
NULL	SOH	STX	ETX	EOT	ENQ	ACK	BEL	BS	HT	LF	VT	FF	CR	SO	SI

16	17	18	19	20	21	22	23	24	25	26	27	28	29	30	31
DLE	DC1	DC2	DC3	DC4	NAK	SYN	ETB	CAN	EM	SUB	ESC	FS	GS	RS	US

32	33	34	35	36	37	38	39	40	41	42	43	44	45	46	47
SPACE	!	"	#	$	%	&	'	(	)	*	+	,	-	.	/

48	49	50	51	52	53	54	55	56	57	58	59	60	61	62	63
0	1	2	3	4	5	6	7	8	9	:	;	<	=	>	?

64	65	66	67	68	69	70	71	72	73	74	75	76	77	78	79
@	A	B	C	D	E	F	G	H	I	J	K	L	M	N	O

80	81	82	83	84	85	86	87	88	89	90	91	92	93	94	95
P	Q	R	S	T	U	V	W	X	Y	Z	[	\	]	^	_

96	97	98	99	100	101	102	103	104	105	106	107	108	109	110	111
`	a	b	c	d	e	f	g	h	i	j	k	l	m	n	o

112	113	114	115	116	117	118	119	120	121	122	123	124	125	126	127
p	q	r	s	t	u	v	w	x	y	z	{	|	}	~	

128	129	130	131	132	133	134	135	136	137	138	139	140	141	142	143
Ä	Å	Ç	É	Ñ	Ö	Ü	á	à	â	ä	ã	å	ç	é	è

144	145	146	147	148	149	150	151	152	153	154	155	156	157	158	159
ê	ë	í	ì	î	ï	ñ	ó	ò	ô	ö	õ	ú	ù	û	ü

160	161	162	163	164	165	166	167	168	169	170	171	172	173	174	175
†	°	¢	£	§	•	¶	ß	®	©	™	´	¨	≠	Æ	Ø

176	177	178	179	180	181	182	183	184	185	186	187	188	189	190	191
∞	±	≤	≥	¥	µ	∂	Σ	Π	π	∫	ª	º	Ω	æ	ø

192	193	194	195	196	197	198	199	200	201	202	203	204	205	206	207
¿	¡	¬	√	ƒ	≈	Δ	«	»	…		À	Ã	Õ	Œ	œ

208	209	210	211	212	213	214	215	216	217	218	219	220	221	222	223
–	—	"	"	'	'	÷	◊	ÿ							

224	225	226	227	228	229	230	231	232	233	234	235	236	237	238	239

240	241	242	243	244	245	246	247	248	249	250	251	252	253	254	255

IBM PC ASCII CODES

0	1	2	3	4	5	6	7	8	9	10	11	12	13	14	15
	☺	☻	♥	♦	♣	♠	•	◘	○	◙	♂	♀	♪	♫	☼

16	17	18	19	20	21	22	23	24	25	26	27	28	29	30	31
►	◄	↕	‼	¶	§	▬	↨	↑	↓	→	←	∟	↔	▲	▼

32	33	34	35	36	37	38	39	40	41	42	43	44	45	46	47
	!	"	#	$	%	&	'	(	)	*	+	,	-	.	/

48	49	50	51	52	53	54	55	56	57	58	59	60	61	62	63
0	1	2	3	4	5	6	7	8	9	:	;	<	=	>	?

64	65	66	67	68	69	70	71	72	73	74	75	76	77	78	79
@	A	B	C	D	E	F	G	H	I	J	K	L	M	N	O

80	81	82	83	84	85	86	87	88	89	90	91	92	93	94	95
P	Q	R	S	T	U	V	W	X	Y	Z	[	\	]	^	_

96	97	98	99	100	101	102	103	104	105	106	107	108	109	110	111
`	a	b	c	d	e	f	g	h	i	j	k	l	m	n	o

112	113	114	115	116	117	118	119	120	121	122	123	124	125	126	127
p	q	r	s	t	u	v	w	x	y	z	{	|	}	~	

128	129	130	131	132	133	134	135	136	137	138	139	140	141	142	143
Ç	ü	é	â	ä	à	å	ç	ê	ë	è	ï	î	ì	Ä	Å

144	145	146	147	148	149	150	151	152	153	154	155	156	157	158	159
É	æ	Æ	ô	ö	ò	û	ù	ÿ	Ö	Ü	¢	£	¥	₧	ƒ

160	161	162	163	164	165	166	167	168	169	170	171	172	173	174	175
á	í	ó	ú	ñ	Ñ	ª	º	¿	⌐	¬	½	¼	¡	«	»

176	177	178	179	180	181	182	183	184	185	186	187	188	189	190	191
░	▒	▓	│	┤	╡	╢	╖	╕	╣	║	╗	╝	╜	╛	┐

192	193	194	195	196	197	198	199	200	201	202	203	204	205	206	207
└	┴	┬	├	─	┼	╞	╟	╚	╔	╩	╦	╠	═	╬	╧

208	209	210	211	212	213	214	215	216	217	218	219	220	221	222	223
╨	╤	╥	╙	╘	╒	╓	╫	╪	┘	┌	█	▄	▌	▐	▀

224	225	226	227	228	229	230	231	232	233	234	235	236	237	238	239
∝	β	Γ	π	Σ	σ	µ	τ	Φ	θ	Ω	δ	∞	ø	∈	∩

240	241	242	243	244	245	246	247	248	249	250	251	252	253	254	255
≡	±	≥	≤	⌠	⌡	÷	≈	°	•	·	√	ⁿ	²	■	

Appendix B
Categorical Cross-Reference of Commands

INTERACTIVE and advanced FoxBASE+/Mac commands are listed below in groups by their purpose. I've done my best to separate interactive and advanced commands so you can become familiar with FoxBASE without learning commands you might never use. This approach is helpful, at first, because the interactive commands are essential building blocks for all programmer-developers. This section is intended to be a quick command locater, not a syntax reference. Refer to Chapter 8 for a full explanation of a command's syntax, options, and behavior.

THE MOST USEFUL INTERACTIVE COMMANDS

Interactive commands are used by everyone, so their purpose is explained below for those who just need a reminder. There are too many commands to learn all at once, so I've listed commands in groups by function and then in their order of usefulness.

An * by a command means that you don't need to type it into the Command window because it's in a menu, in which case its name and menu location will be listed in parentheses. A | symbol separates alternative ways of using the command, while options displayed inside of square brackets are not required at all.

Adding Records

* APPEND (Record/Append)—lets you add a new record with data
* APPEND FROM (Database/Append From)—imports data
  APPEND BLANK—adds blank record

Changing Data

* BROWSE (Database/Browse)—full screen scroll and edit
* CHANGE (Record/Change)—edits records
* REPLACE (Record/Replace)—modifies and computes data in fields

Creating and Copying Data Files

* CREATE (File/New)—makes a new database file
* COPY TO (Database/Copy To)—exports data
  COPY STRUCTURE—makes new file from old empty
* COPY FILE (File/Copy File)—makes copy of file

Filtering Data Records

* INDEX ON FOR <condition> and SET INDEX ON | OFF (Database/Setup/Index/Add/Filter)—makes an index that filters and orders data
* SET FILTER TO <condition> and SET FILTER ON | OFF (Database/Setup/Filter)—filters data
* SET FIELDS ON | OFF and FIELDS TO <condition> (Database/Setup/Set Fields)—sets the fields you want to see and lets you choose their order from left to right

Finding Data

* FIND (Edit/Find)—in the Browse window it searches the whole file
* LOCATE (Record/Locate)—finds records that meet any condition
* SEEK (Record/Seek)—requires an index, finds key field data by matching
* GOTO (Record/Goto)—locates the pointer on a record number
* CONTINUE (Record/Continue)—used after LOCATE only to find more

Modifying Data

* MODIFY STRUCTURE (Database/Setup/Modify)—changes fields
* RENAME (File/Rename File)—changes name

Ordering Records

* INDEX (Database/Setup/Index/Add)—orders data without physically changing the database file
* REINDEX (Database/Reindex)—rebuilds the index from scratch
* SORT (Database/Sort)—physically rearranges the database file

Relating Database Files

* SET RELATION TO (Window/View)—by moving around in one file, a second, related file, will stay synchronized with it because it shares a field (or more) of information

that's also in the first file. This "key" field allows FoxBASE to match records quickly and automatically, making them available to you regardless of what file

Removing Records

* DELETE (Record/Delete)—marks records for removal by PACK, also done by a mouse click in the window splitter (Browse)
* RECALL (Record/Recall)—unmarks deleted records, also done by a mouse click in the window splitter (Browse)
* PACK (Database/Pack)—permanently removes deleted records
  ZAP—empties a file of records

Viewing and Printing

* BROWSE (Database/Browse)—scrolls rows and columns on-screen
  CLEAR—clears the active output screen
  LIST OFF ALL TO PRINT—a fast way to print records, very useful when used with filters
* COUNT (Database/Count)—counts records, very useful when used with filters
* LABEL FORM | TO PRINT (Database/Label)—prints labels
* REPORT FORM | TO PRINT (Database/Report)—prints reports
* SUM (Database/Sum)—totals numeric fields, very useful when used with filters
* AVERAGE (Database/Average)—averages numeric fields, very useful when used with filters
  LIST STRUCTURE TO PRINT—prints database file structure
  ?—evaluates expressions and displays result

To Create Database Support Files

* CREATE LABEL or MODIFY LABEL (File/New or Open/Label)—makes label form
* CREATE REPORT or MODIFY REPORT (File/New or Open/Report)—makes report form
* MODIFY COMMAND (File/New or Open/ Label)—opens a new or existing program or "macro" file to edit
* CREATE VIEW (File/Save As)—when the view window is active, saves memory of open files and file relations in a view file for instant recall at any later time
* CREATE SCREEN or MODIFY SCREEN (File/New or Open/Form)—makes data entry screens

COMMANDS FOR ADVANCED USERS AND USES

Advanced commands are used by those of you who already know the interactive commands. Accordingly, these commands are grouped by function, so you can look them up in Chapter 8 to compare them with commands you might already know. Some of the commands listed above are duplicated here; the idea is to give you a way to quickly select a command(s) when you're learning advanced use of FoxBASE+/Mac. Unlike the interactive commands above, this listing is alphabetical within each group.

Database Management

APPEND
APPEND BLANK
APPEND FROM
AVERAGE
CHANGE
CLEAR FIELDS
CLOSE ALL, CLOSE DATABASES, and CLOSE INDEX
COPY STRUCTURE TO
COPY TO
COUNT
CREATE [LABEL] [REPORT] [VIEW]
COPY STRUCTURE EXTENDED and CREATE FROM
DELETE | RECALL and PACK
DISPLAY
DISPLAY STRUCTURE [TO PRINT]
EDIT
FIND
GOTO <recordnum> [TOP] [BOTTOM]
INDEX | REINDEX
INSERT [BLANK] [BEFORE]
JOIN
LABEL FORM [TO PRINT]
LIST [TO PRINT]
LIST STRUCTURE [TO PRINT]
LOCATE and CONTINUE
MODIFY LABEL | REPORT | STRUCTURE
REPLACE
REPORT FORM [TO PRINT]
SEEK
SET ORDER TO
SET RELATION INTO | OFF
SET UNIQUE ON | OFF
SKIP
SORT TO
SUM
UPDATE
USE
ZAP

Event Processing

@ SAY...GET and READ
KEYBOARD
MENU, MENU BAR, MENU ON | OFF, and ON MENU

ON ERROR
ON ESCAPE
ON KEY

Interface Management

@ SAY...GET and READ (options include Macintosh interface features)
ACCEPT TO
ALERT
CLEAR
CLEAR PROMPT
CLEAR TYPEAHEAD
CLOSE FORMAT
GENERATE FROM
GETEXPR
HELP
MENU, MENU BAR, MENU ON | OFF, and ON MENU
SAVE SCREEN and RESTORE SCREEN
SCREEN (1–9)
SET BELL ON | OFF
SET CENTURY OFF | ON
SET COLOR OFF | ON and SET COLOR TO
SET CONFIRM OFF | ON
SET DATE
SET DECIMALS TO
SET DEVICE TO SCREEN | PRINTER
SET EXACT OFF | ON
SET FIXED OFF | ON
SET FORMAT TO
SET FRAME TO
SET FUNCTION
SET HELP ON | OFF, SET HELP TO, and SET TOPIC TO
SET INTENSITY ON | OFF
SET ODOMETER TO
SET STRICT ON | OFF
SET TALK ON | OFF
SET TYPEAHEAD TO

Memory Variables

ACCEPT TO
CLEAR ALL
RELEASE
CLEAR GETS
CLEAR MEMORY
DIMENSION

DISPLAY MEMORY and LIST MEMORY TO PRINT
GATHER FROM and SCATTER TO
GET and READ
INPUT
RELEASE
PUBLIC and PRIVATE
STORE TO
SAVE TO and RESTORE FROM
WAIT TO

Networking

SET EXCLUSIVE ON | OFF (multiuser only)
UNLOCK
USE <filename> EXCLUSIVE

Other Environment Controls and Commands

COPY FILE
DIR
ERASE
LIST FILES [TO PRINT]
RENAME
SET CARRY OFF | ON
SET CLEAR OFF | ON
SET DEFAULT TO and SET PATH TO
SET DELETED OFF | ON
SET DOHISTORY OFF | ON
SET HISTORY ON | OFF and SET HISTORY TO
SET STATUS OFF | ON
SET VIEW TO and SET VIEW ON | OFF
SET VOLUME TO
TYPE [TO PRINT]

Passing and Receiving Parameters

DO...WITH
PARAMETERS

Print Control

SET PRINT ON | OFF
SET DEVICE TO SCREEN | PRINTER
SET MARGIN TO
SET MEMOWIDTH TO

Categorial Cross-Reference of Commands 507

EJECT
SET HEADING HEADING ON | OFF

Program Writing and Program Controls

*
&
&&
CANCEL
DO
DO CASE...CASE...[OTHERWISE]...ENDCASE
DO WHILE...[EXIT] [LOOP]...ENDDO
FOXCODE
FLUSH
IF...[ELSE]...ENDIF
MODIFY COMMAND
NOTE
QUIT
RETRY
RETURN [TO MASTER]
PROCEDURE
SELECT
SET PROCEDURE TO
SET RESOURCE TO
SET SAFETY ON | OFF
TEXT...ENDTEXT
WAIT

Status Checking and Program Debugging

CLEAR PROGRAM
CLOSE PROCEDURE
DISPLAY MEMORY
DISPLAY STATUS and LIST STATUS [TO PRINT]
SET ECHO ON | OFF
SET STATUS ON | OFF
SET STEP OFF | ON
SET TALK ON | OFF
SUSPEND and RESUME

XCMDs and XCFNs

CALL
LOAD
SET RESOURCE TO

Appendix C
Error Codes and Messages

ERROR codes are listed below in two forms. The first is ordered by code numbers, the second listing is alphabetically with an explanation of each error. Both lists contain codes and messages.

Error *messages* are designed to help you know where something has gone off track so you can put it back on and keep going. Error *codes*, on the other hand, are for programmers to use in error handling routines. Errors have a reason and a source, so those that can only occur within programs won't be encountered by an interactive FoxBASE user, and errors that result from interactive use aren't likely to be encountered by program user. Errors 108 through 111, for example, will only occur if you're using a local area network.

Many application generated errors can be trapped and fixed by a programmer. See the error handling discussion in Chapter 7 for an explanation of the error trapping and error handling process.

ERROR CODES LISTED BY NUMBER

Code	Message
1	File does not exist
4	End of file encountered
5	Record is out of range
6	Too many files open
7	File already exists
9	Data type mismatch
10	Syntax error
11	Invalid function argument value, type, or count
12	Variable not found
13	ALIAS not found

Code	Message
15	Not a database file
16	Unrecognized command verb
17	Invalid database number
18	Line too long
19	Index file does not match database
20	Record is not in index
21	String memory variable area overflow
22	Too many memory variables
23	Invalid key length
24	ALIAS name already in use
26	Database is not indexed
27	Not a numeric expression
28	Too many indices
30	Position is off the screen
31	Invalid subscript reference
34	Illegal operation for MEMO field
36	Unrecognized phrase/keyword in command
37	FILTER requires a logical expression
38	Beginning of file encountered
41	MEMO file is missing
42	CONTINUE without LOCATE
43	Insufficient memory
44	Cyclic relation
45	Not a Character expression
47	No fields to process
50	Report file invalid
54	Label file invalid
55	Memory Variable file is invalid
56	Out of disk
58	LOG domain error
61	SQRT domain error
62	Beyond string
66	Internal consistency error
67	Expression evaluator fault
78	** or ^ domain error
91	File was not LOADed
94	Wrong number of parameters
95	Statement not allowed in interactive mode
96	While nesting error
101	Not suspended
103	Do nesting too deep
104	Unknown function key
107	Operator/operand type mismatch
108	File is in use by another

Code	Message
109	Record is in use by another
110	Exclusive open of file is required
111	Cannot write to a read-only file
112	Index expression is too big
114	Index damaged
124	Printer not ready
125	Invalid printer redirection
130	Record is not locked
138	No fields were found to copy
1001	Feature not available
1101	Cannot open file
1102	Cannot create file
1103	Illegal seek offset
1104	File read error
1105	File write error
1108	Relational expression is too long
1111	Invalid file descriptor
1112	File close error
1113	File not open
1115	Database record is trashed
1117	Wrong length key
1119	No database is in USE
1124	Key too big
1126	Record too long
1127	FOR and WHILE need logical expressions
1134	Variable must be in selected database
1140	FILTER expression too long
1141	Invalid index number
1145	Must be a character, date, or numeric key field
1147	Target is already engaged in relation
1148	Too many relationships
1149	No memory for buffer
1150	No memory for file map
1151	No memory for file name
1152	Cannot access selected database
1153	Attempt to move file to a different device
1156	Duplicate field names
1157	Cannot update field
1160	HFS error—code in SYS(21)
1161	Volume does not exist
1162	Ambiguous relation—all outgoing relations cleared
1201	Attempt to use more than 2048 names
1202	Program too large
1206	Recursive macro definition

Code	Message
1211	IF/ELSE/ENDIF mismatch
1212	Structure nesting too deep
1213	Mismatched case structure
1214	Endtext without text
1217	Picture error in GET command
1220	Invalid character in command
1221	Required clause not present in command
1223	Invalid variable reference
1225	Must be a memory variable
1226	Must be a file variable
1227	Missing expression
1229	Too few arguments
1230	Too many arguments
1231	Missing operand
1232	Must be an array definition
1234	Subscript out of bounds
1235	Structure invalid
1238	No PARAMETER statement found
1241	Improper data type in group expression
1242	Syntax error in field expression
1243	Internal error: Too many characters in report
1244	Label field type must be character, numeric, or date
1245	Error in label field definition
1246	Total label width exceeds maximum allowable size
1249	A READ is currently in effect
1250	Too many PROCEDURES
1252	Complied code for this line too long
1300	Missing)
1304	Missing (
1305	Illegal value
1306	Missing ,
1307	Division by 0
1309	Not an object file
1310	Too many PICTURE characters specified
1410	Unable to create temporary work file(s)
1503	File cannot be locked
1600	Not enough memory to USE database
1604	No menubar is defined
1605	Menu titles/items must be character type
1606	Menu specified is not in menubar
1705	File access denied
1903	String too long to fit
1908	Bad width or decimal place argument
1999	Function not implemented
2000	Screen number out of range 1-9

Code	Message
2001	No memory for screen
2002	No memory for offscreen bitmap
2003	Screen too small for editing (Also, error 2004)
2005	Checkboxes require logical or numeric GETs
2006	Buttons may be used only with numeric GETs
2007	Checkboxes may have only one button
2008	Not enough room for scroll bars
2009	Memo too big for on-screen editing
2010	Resource not found
2011	Buttons do not fit on screen
2012	Not enough room for one line of text
2013	Connection to server has been interrupted
2014	A REPORT is currently in effect
2015	Not a Format file. GENERATE a Format from .scx file

ERROR CODES LISTED ALPHABETICALLY

** or ^ domain error
Check the number you're attempting to exponentiate. It's probably negative, which is not legal. [Error #78]

A READ is currently in effect
You cannot issue a READ, @...GET, or CLEAR GET command from within a user-defined function that's in use by a VALID clause, or in a program/procedure that's been called by ON KEY. [Error #1249]

A REPORT is currently in effect
Only one report can be executed at once. This error indicates that an attempt to run two at once has occurred. [Error #2014]

ALIAS name already in use
You cannot USE a database, assigning it an alias name that's already in use. The letters A-J are also reserved, because they identify database file work areas (aliases). [Error #24]

ALIAS not found
This error occurs when you attempt to SELECT a database file that does not exist in one of the ten work areas, or by referring to an alias that does not exist. [Error #13]

Ambiguous relation—all outgoing relations cleared
Check the relation you're attempting to establish. It's likely that it's cyclic. If not, FoxBASE is unable to understand the field names you're entering. Be sure that the selected database file is correct and that alias names are used, where appropriate. [Error #1162]

Attempt to move file to a different device
> RENAME works only on one disk at a time with Macintosh files. Use COPY TO or COPY FILE to move files from one disk to another and to rename them in the process if you want. [Error #1153]

Attempt to use more than 2048 names
> FoxBASE has an internal limit on the number of variables and field names it can simultaneously manage. If you encounter this error, use the RELEASE command, or split programs into procedures so that variables are released automatically. [Error #1201]

Bad width or decimal place argument
> STR( ) converts numbers into character strings. If you get this error, it indicates that either the <LEN> or the [,decimals] argument, is inappropriate for the number being converted. [Error #1908]

Beginning of file encountered
> This error indicates that an attempt was made to move the record pointer above the first record in the file. The first SKIP-1, while positioned on the first record of a file, will not generate an error. Subsequent attempts, however, will cause an error. [Error #38]

Beyond string
> Using a string-length location or length function, an attempt was made to reference a nonexisting part of a variable string or database character field. Check the length or offset references of the function causing this error. [Error #62]

Buttons do not fit on screen
> The buttons do not entirely fit on the screen, so that at least one of them is off the edge. [Error #2011]

Buttons may be used only with numeric GETs
> You cannot return a character value from a button, or store its numeric values in a character variable or field. Check the GET variable, any associated PICTURE clause, and the button itself to resolve that only numeric values are used. [Error #2006]

Cannot access selected database
> Make sure that you are referencing an open database file, and that all field references to unselected databases include an alias. [Error #1152]

Cannot create file
> This error indicates that the Macintosh has told FoxBASE that it cannot create a new file as requested. Check to see that the disk has room on it and that the file's name is correct. Incorrect path statements preceding a file name can be a cause. [Error #1102]

Cannot open file

This error usually indicates that the operating system cannot open a secured file, a nonexistent file, or a damaged file. Check the spelling of the file's name, and, on networks, check the file's security permissions. [Error #1101]

Cannot update file

This is a serious error. If it occurs you should perform a thorough check of the disk before using it further. If the disk checks ok, open the offending file by itself and attempt to use it in FoxBASE. If the file is defective, install a backup copy. [Error #1157]

Cannot write to a read-only file

This error occurs when a network has established read-only access to a file, or when the "Locked" box in the Finder's Info dialog has been checked and you attempt to make changes to it. [Error #111]

Checkboxes require logical or numeric GETs

This error indicates that you have used an inappropriate PICTURE function or template when specifying an input mask for a checkbox. Only numeric and logical data types are allowed. [Error #2005]

Checkboxes may have only one button

If you establish more than one button with a PICTURE clause (in an @...GET command), this error will occur. [Error #2007]

Complied code for this line too long

Some command lines can produce, when compiled, a statement that is internally too big for FoxBASE's preallocated command space. To remedy the problem, turn the offending command into two or more commands. [Error #1252]

Connection to server has been interrupted

This problem is due to a problem with the network. If it occurs, shut down the Macintosh and notify your network administrator. [Error #2013]

CONTINUE without LOCATE

You cannot issue a CONTINUE command unless a LOCATE preceded it. Check the program again to see that CONTINUE closely follows a LOCATE. [Error #42]

Cyclic relation

File relationships cannot depend on themselves. This error indicates that an attempt to make a relationship can't work because it completes a circular reference, effectively removing the necessary master relationship of one file. [Error #44]

Data type mismatch
> This common error indicates that functions and, or, commands, are attempting to manipulate or evaluate different data types in one expression. Check the functions you're using and make all expressions evaluate to only one type data. [Error #9]

Database is not indexed
> This error can occur when you try to do something that requires an index, and an index to support the operation is not in use. SET ORDER TO 0 can also cause open indexes to be ineffective, precipitating the error. [Error #26]

Database record is trashed
> This error occurs when a database file has internal errors. Try closing all other files and then open the offending file by itself. Then try to copy it using the COPY TO <filename> command. If the error still occurs, install a backup datafile. [Error #1115]

Division by 0.
> The computer cannot divide any number by 0. Check the command line that generated the error and rewrite it so that a division cannot be attempted with a divisor of 0. [Error #1307]

Do nesting too deep
> You can allow one program to DO other programs, but only 24 levels of "nesting" are permitted. Rewrite the programs so that there are enough RETURN commands to "undo" the DOs, or use one or two programs to call the others. [Error #103]

Duplicate field names
> The offending command lists a single field name more than once in an expression that does not allow it. [Error #1156]

End of file encountered
> This error indicates that an attempt was made to position the record pointer past the last record in a database file. If this error occurs while running a program, consider using the EOF( ) function to prevent it. [Error #4]

Endtext without text
> The ENDTEXT command presumes that a TEXT command preceded it. If an ENDTEXT command appears without a complimentary TEXT command, this error can appear. Add a TEXT command or remove the ENDTEXT command. [Error #1214]

Error in label field definition
> This error occurs when FoxBASE has a problem finding a field named in a label file or evaluating an expression. A common reason for the problem is forgetting to use an alias when referring to database files that are in a nonselected work area. [Error #1245]

Exclusive open of file is required
   This error indicates that an operation is being attempted in multiuser mode that requires exclusive use by the user. Operations that can trigger this error are INSERT, MODIFY STRUCTURE, PACK, REINDEX and ZAP. [Error #110]

Expression evaluator fault
   This error is generated when FoxBASE encounters problems in a program file it's running. Try recompiling the program. [Error #67]

Feature not available
   In addition to the Macintosh version of FoxBASE, there are versions of FoxBASE for MS-DOS and Unix computers. This error occurs when an attempt is made to use a feature not supported by the Macintosh version. [Error #1001]

File access denied
   The Macintosh finder's Get Info dialog features an option that allows you to lock a file. Locking a file prevents changes to it until it's unlocked. This error occurs when FoxBASE attempts to change such a file. [Error #1705]

File already exists
   You're required to provide a file name when using the SORT or RENAME commands. When a selected file name already exists, this error can occur. [Error #7]

File cannot be locked
   This error occurs when a needed file is locked in the finder's Info dialog. Get the file's name and unlock it. [Error #1503]

File close error
   The operating system reported to FoxBASE that it could not close a file. This error can be serious if all of the information in the file has not been written to disk. Check the offending disk for errors. [Error #1112]

File does not exist
   FoxBASE cannot find a file you've selected. Make sure that its actual name matches your specification. [Error #1]

File is in use by another
   If another user has already opened a file for exclusive use, this error can occur when a second user tries to open it. [Error #108]

File not open
   The file you're trying to read or write hasn't been opened. [Error #1113]

File read error
   The Macintosh reports to FoxBASE that it was unable to read an existing file as requested. Check the file. [Error #1104]

File was not LOADed
    This error can occur on MS-DOS computers when a binary file was CALLed but not LOADed. On the Macintosh it can only occur when an XCMD or XFCN was not LOADed. [Error #91]

File write error
    An attempt to write to a file or to create a file on a write-protected diskette can cause this error. [Error #1105]

FILTER expression too long
    SET FILTER expressions allow 160 characters. This error occurs when the limit is exceeded. [Error #1140]

FILTER requires a logical expression
    Records can be selected by specifying almost any criteria in a filter expression. However, filters can only be made using expressions that evaluate to a logical (.T.) or (.F.) value. Records will, or won't, match the filter's condition. [Error #37]

FOR and WHILE need logical expressions
    FOR and WHILE record selections can be made by specifying almost any criteria. However, selections can only be made using expressions that evaluate to a logical (.T.) or (.F.) value. Records must match, or fail to match a FOR or WHILE condition. [Error #1127]

Function not implemented
    This unlikely error indicates that a planned but unimplemented feature has been called; because it's not yet available, this error will occur. [Error #1999]

HFS error—Look for code in SYS(21)
    This error indicates that a Macintosh Hierarchical Filing System (HFS) error has occurred. The SYS(21) function can trap many such errors if used in an error-handling routine with the ON ERROR command. The list below is a sample of Macintosh HFS error numbers that can be used in an error trapping routine. [Error #1160]

    File system error codes:

-33	Directory full
-34	Disk fully allocated, disk full
-35	Unable to locate volume, doesn't exist
-36	Disk I/O error, read/write problem
-37	Bad file or volume name
-38	File not open
-39	End-of-file reached in course of file read
-40	Attempt to position before start of file
-42	Too many open files
-43	File not found
-44	Disk/volume is write-protected by a hardware lock

-45	File is locked by software (usually in Get Info box)
-46	Volume is locked by software
-47	File is busy
-48	File name already exists
-49	File is already open for writing
-50	Error in system information about file or volume
-51	Path reference is nonexistent
-53	Volume not on-line
-54	File locked by permission setting, can't write
-55	Volume already mounted and on-line
-56	Drive doesn't exist
-57	Not a Macintosh disk or directory trashed
-58	Foreign file system type
-59	Can't rename file as requested
-60	Bad file directory on volume
-61	Can't write, permission denied

IF/ELSE/ENDIF mismatch
This error indicates that an attempt was made to issue an ENDIF command without an IF. Because IF...ENDIF is a construct, it needs a beginning and an end. [Error #1211]

Illegal operation for MEMO field
This error occurs when an attempt was made to use a memo field in an index key expression. Indexes cannot be created using memo fields. [Error #34]

Illegal seek offset
This error indicates that an attempt was made to position a database record pointer before the beginning of a file using a SEEK command. [Error #1103]

Illegal value
This general error indicates that an illegal reference value was supplied to a command: @...TO, BROWSE, DISPLAY or SET HISTORY or SET MEMOWIDTH. Check the offending command. [Error #1305]

Improper data type in group expression
This error indicates that a group or sub-group expression in a REPORT FORM was supplied with a logical or memo data type. Check the group expressions in the REPORT FORM file, and replace it with a character or numeric or date expression. [Error #1241]

Index damaged
The index file is damaged. REINDEX it before trying to use it. If it cannot be repaired, recreate it with the INDEX ON <key> TO <filename> command. [Error #114]

Index expression is too big
This error indicates that you've attempted to build an index with an expression that's too long. Index expressions can be no longer than 220 characters. [Error #112]

Index file does not match database
If this error occurs, check the index key expression; it depends on information or fields in the database that cannot be found. [Error #19]

Insufficient memory
This error means that something you wanted FoxBASE to do could not be completed because it doesn't have enough memory for it. Screens take an inordinate amount of memory. If opening a new screen caused the error, consider using fewer screens. [Error #43]

Internal consistency error
This error means that FoxBASE has a damaged internal table. Try quitting, rebooting the computer, and running the process again. If that doesn't fix the problem, reinstall FoxBASE+/Mac. [Error #66]

Internal error: Too many characters in report
Use fewer characters in the report, if possible. The combination of headings and expressions has grown too large for the standard REPORT FORM file to hold. [Error #1243]

Invalid character in command
The most common reason for this error is the presence of a control character in a command line. Check the program and rewrite the command from scratch if necessary. [Error #1220]

Invalid database number
The SELECT command needs a file alias in the form of a file name, a specific alias name, a letter from A to J to indicate the work area to select, or a number from 1 to 10. If a number greater than 10 in entered, this error can occur. [Error #17]

Invalid file descriptor
This error indicates that FoxBASE has an internally damaged file descriptor and that it has attempted to use it. Quit FoxBASE and try again. [Error #1111]

Invalid function argument value, type, or count
Some functions accept arguments to provide necessary references or to modify the function's behavior. If one of the function's arguments is in error, this error can occur. [Error #11]

Invalid index number
This error occurs when using the SET ORDER TO <exprN> command. Because seven indexes can be in use for one database file, seven is the highest number that can

be passed as an argument. The error also occurs if there is no index in a position between one and seven. [Error #1141]

Invalid key length
After final evaluation of an index expression, an index key cannot exceed 100 bytes. The SUBSTR( ) function can usually be used to reduce the length of character-based index keys. [Error #23]

Invalid printer redirection
The printer that FoxBASE is trying to use cannot be attached, or a path to it cannot be found. [Error #124]

Invalid subscript reference
This error can occur when a wrong value is supplied for an array subscript, or when one and two dimensional subscripts are misapplied. [Error #31]

Invalid variable reference
FoxBASE expected a variable or array name, but received a function name or abbreviation instead. [Error #1223]

Key too big
The index key is too long. After compilation, the index key cannot exceed 150 bytes. Shorten the key by using the SUBSTR( ) function (if the key is based on characters), or consider another alternative to such a lengthy key. [Error #1124]

Label field type must be character, numeric, or date
LABEL FORMs cannot print memo and logical data. Check and correct the problem in the LABEL FORM file. [Error #1244]

Label file invalid
The LABEL FORM file was probably created by FoxBASE or by a compatible. It could be damaged. [Error #54]

Line too long
Lines of text cannot exceed a length of 254 bytes. The & macro substitution command can easily create a line exceeding this limit because it's sometimes difficult to predict the length before expansion. Use & carefully. [Error #18]

LOG domain error
The numeric argument provided to the LOG( ) function cannot be 0 or less than 0. [Error #58]

MEMO file is missing
FoxBASE automatically creates memo (.dbt) files to store memos and pictures instead of trying to store them in the (.dbf) file. Don't throw them away, move or rename them! If you do, you might need to create a new, empty memo file to replace the miss-

ing one. Instead, create a new database file structure that matches the one you can't open but with a different name. Quit FoxBASE, then rename the (.dbt) file to match the affected database file. FoxBASE will accept the new memo file in lieu of the missing one. [Error #41]

Memo too big for on-screen editing
The memo you're trying to edit on-screen is larger than the 32-kilobyte limit. [Error #2009]

Memory Variable is invalid
Memory (.mem) files can hold memory variables that have been saved with the SAVE TO command; and they can be retrieved again with the RESTORE FROM command. If a (.mem) file cannot be RESTORED because of damage or because it's not a true (.mem) file, this error can occur. [Error #55]

Menu specified is not in menubar
This error can occur if a user-defined menu item does not exist when reference is made to it by name. [Error #1606]

Menu titles/items must be type character
Only character data can be used as menu item names in a menu definition array. [Error # 1605].

Mismatched case structure
The error can occur if a DO CASE command does not precede a CASE, OTHERWISE, or ENDCASE. [Error #1213]

Missing (
This error occurs when functions are not properly composed. In this case, a required left parenthesis has been omitted. [Error #1304]

Missing)
This error occurs when functions are not properly composed. In this case, a required right parenthesis has been omitted. [Error #1300]

Missing ,
This error indicates that FoxBASE did not encounter a required comma where one was expected, probably in a function argument list. [Error #1306]

Missing expression
Look at the offending command again. There's no expression where one is required. [Error #1227]

Missing operand
Operators usually required two operands (things to operate on). If one or more is missing where it's expected, this error can occur. [Error #1231]

Must be a character, date or numeric key field
　　The UPDATE command requires a character, date, or numeric key field. This error occurs if an attempt to UPDATE is made without such an index key. [Error #1145]

Must be a memory variable
　　FoxBASE encountered a database field name where there should be an array or regular memory variable. [Error #1225]

Must be a file variable
　　FoxBASE encountered a memory variable or array variable where there should be a field name. [Error #1226]

Must be an array definition
　　Required subscript arguments that dimension the array being declared are missing. Make sure that the numeric information is provided when DIMENSIONing an array. [Error #1232]

No databases is in USE
　　No database was opened when you attempted to use a command designed to affect a database. [Error #1119]

No fields to process
　　The SET FIELDS TO command can hide all of the fields in a database without any arguments. Therefore, this error can result when a command tries to find fields to process. The command, SET FIELDS TO ALL makes all fields in an open database file visible again. [Error #47]

No fields were found to copy
　　Make sure that a database file is open and that if the SET FIELDS TO command was used, it has specified at least one field. [Error #138]

No memory for buffer
　　This rare error indicates that FoxBASE cannot find enough memory for its own use. Add more memory, or reduce the number of desk accessories or fonts in the system. If you're using Multifinder, consider running FoxBASE without it. [Error #1149]

No memory for file map
　　This rare error indicates that FoxBASE cannot find enough memory for its own use. Add more memory, or reduce the number of desk accessories or fonts in the system. If you're using Multifinder, consider running FoxBASE without it. [Error #1150]

No memory for filename
　　This rare error indicates that FoxBASE cannot find enough memory for its own use. Add more memory, or reduce the number of desk accessories or fonts in the system. If you're using Multifinder, consider running FoxBASE without it. [Error #1151]

No memory for screen
> This error means that FoxBASE cannot find enough memory to create a new screen as requested. Screens take a lot of memory, so it's a good idea when you encounter this problem, to use fewer screens for output. The other option is to add more memory. [Error #2001]

No memory for offscreen bitmap
> This error indicates that FoxBASE cannot create output on an inactive screen because of limited memory. [Error #2002]

No menubar is defined
> You cannot use the MENU BAR command to install a menu if it has not yet been defined. The order of steps is important. Use the DIMENSION and MENU commands to declare variable arrays and to define the menu contents. The last thing to do is to install the menu using the MENU BAR command. [Error #1604]

No PARAMETER statement found
> A PARAMETER statement must be the first line in a program that was called using the WITH <parameterlist> option. If it is missing there will be no way for the called program to receive the parameters, and this error will result. [Error #1238]

Not a Character expression
> FoxBASE expected a character expression and found a numeric, date, or logical expression instead. [Error #45]

Not a database file
> FoxBASE looks at the header of a file when it attempts to open or use it. This error occurs when it's trying to use what it thought was a database file, and another type of file was found. [Error #15]

Not a Format file. GENERATE a Format from .scx file
> If someone confuses an (.scx) file for a format (.fmt) file, this error is sure to occur. .scx files are preliminary screen files saved in a drawlike format so that they can be changed again, or made into finished .fmt files by selecting the Program/Generate/Format menu option. [Error #2015]

Not a numeric expression
> The SUM command requires that all specified fields be of the numeric data type. This error indicates that FoxBASE encountered other data types when trying to perform a SUM. [Error #27]

Not an object file
> This error can occur if FoxBASE expects to find a compiled program in response to a DO <programname> command, if it finds a program that is not compiled (Runtime versions), or one that is not already compiled or cannot be compiled "on the fly." [Error #1309]

Not enough memory to USE database
Each database in use requires a minimum amount of memory so that FoxBASE can manage it. This error indicates that the minimum amount of such memory was not available when a USE command was issued. [Error #1600]

Not enough room for scroll bars
Scrollable text editing regions have scroll bars. This error indicates that a region was defined that was too small in total size to provide room for the scroll bars. [Error #2008]

Not enough room for one line of text
The size of a line of text for editing is too big for the edit region specified for it by default. You can change the font, its size, or redefine the size of the edit region itself (if the region was created with FoxFORM). [Error #2012]

Not suspended
The RESUME command assumes that the program is currently SUSPENDed. If this error occurs, it indicates that the program was not SUSPENDed when the RESUME command was issued. [Error #101]

Operator/operand type mismatch
This error indicates that an operation is being attempted using an incompatible data type, ? 3+"CAT", for example, would create this error because you cannot add a numeric and a character value. [Error #107]

Out of disk
A disk write command attempted by FoxBASE was not completed because the target disk has no room for the change. [Error #56]

Picture error in GET command
Some PICTURE options support one or two specific data types. This error indicates that the PICTURE clause in a @ GET command is inconsistent with the data being formatted for input. [Error #1217]

Position is off the screen
When using a @ SAY or @ GET command, a screen coordinate outside the boundaries of the active screen was used. [Error #30]

Printer not ready
This error indicates that the selected printer was not available when printing started, or that it's taking too long to indicate its readiness to the computer. Try adjusting the "time" option in a CONFIG.FX file. [Error #124]

Program too large
This error means that there is not enough memory for the program to fit, not that there is not enough memory. FoxBASE imposes a 65,000 byte limit on the size of any

Error Codes and Messages   525

single procedure or program file without procedures. The answer to this problem is to write modular, structured programs instead of programs that are overly large. [Error #1202]

Record is in use by another

This error occurs when a second user attempts to lock a record that is already in use and, therefore, locked by another. [Error #109]

Record is out of range

This error can come from a damaged database file header, which can sometimes be repaired by using the COPY TO command to make a new file from the old one. It can also be caused if the demonstration version of FoxBASE is used with files larger than it's intended to hold. The answer for this problem is to install FoxBASE using the "live" activation key. [Error #5]

Record is not in index

Reindex the file if this error occurs. It means that changes were made to the database file when the offending index was not in use. [Error #20]

Record is not locked

In multiuser mode, records should be locked before an attempt is made to change their contents with the @ SAY, GET, or REPLACE commands. This error indicates that FoxBASE has not updated the record as requested because such a lock was not found. [Error #130]

Record too long

The combined length of all the fields in a database file cannot exceed 4000 bytes. This error can occur when a user is making a new database file, but FoxBASE will not allow an overly long record to be created and saved. [Error #1126]

Recursive macro definition

If a macro makes a reference to itself, this error can occur. Check the offending command line for such a problem. [Error #1206]

Relational expression is too long

This error indicates that the compiled version of code FoxBASE is running has an overly long SET RELATION TO command statement (more than 60 bytes). Shorten the offending statement and rerun the program. [Error #1108]

Report file invalid

Check the REPORT FORM file for errors. [Error #50]

Required clause not present in command

Some commands require an argument or clause in order to work. This error indicates that such a required clause has been omitted from a command. [Error #1221]

Resource not found
Custom resources are stored in the FoxUser file or in another file of your choice. If a required resource, such as a picture button, cannot be found, this error will occur. [Error #2010]

Screen number out of range 1-9
Nine screens are accessible at all times in FoxBASE, provided if you have enough memory for them. If you select a screen that is outside of a range of one to nine, this error will occur. [Error #2000]

Screen too small for editing
FoxBASE puts editing regions on screens, therefore, the screen must be large enough to contain the whole text editing region. This error indicates that the screen is too small. Use the SCREEN command to enlarge the screen, or select a larger screen for output. [Error #2003, #2004]

SQRT domain error
The number supplied to the SQRT( ) function must be a positive number. This error occurs if it's not. [Error #61]

Statement not allowed in interactive mode
Some commands are made for programs only: DO CASE, ENDCASE, DO WHILE, ENDDO, EXIT, IF, ELSE, ENDIF, RETRY, RETURN, SUSPEND, TEXT, and ENDTEXT. [Error #95]

String memory variable area overflow
The MVARSIZ and MVCOUNT options you put in the CONFIG.FX file can determine the amount of memory available for memory variables. If the allocation is exceeded by too many or too large variables, this error will occur. [Error #21]

String too long to fit
Up to 254 characters can be placed in a FoxBASE character string. A macro expansion with the & command, REPLICATE, and other commands can cause a situation where a string is too large. Check the offending command. [Error #1903]

Structure nesting too deep
FoxBASE allows no more than 64 programs to be run in serial fashion. Use the RETURN command to prevent this error. [Error #1212]

Structure invalid
This error occurs when you're using the CREATE FROM command and the structure that's defined is not correct. Specifications that follow those outlined with the COPY STRUCTURE EXTENDED command will work. Refer to the COPY STRUCTURE COMMAND for help. [Error #1235]

Subscript out of bounds
>This error means that you or a program has made reference to a cell that does not exist in a named array. The term "subscript" refers, specifically, to the cell address that's in the parenthesis. [Error #1234]

Syntax error
>Check that all command, expression, field, and variable names are correct in the offending command and the way it's constructed. [Error #10]

Syntax error in field expression
>This error occurs when you use the REPORT command and the report form file has a column definition in it that cannot work with the database(s) that are in use at the time. Check the correspondence between the database fields and the report form. [Error #1242]

Target is already engaged in relation
>Only one direct relationship can exist between two open database files. This error occurs when there's an attempt to establish more. [Error #1147]

Too few arguments
>This error occurs when a function is being used without enough arguments. Arguments are the bits of information that you supply to a function inside its parentheses, usually separated by commas. [Error #1229]

Too many arguments
>This error occurs when a function is being used with more arguments than it allows. Arguments are the bits of information that you supply to a function inside its parentheses, usually separated by commas. [Error #1230]

Too many files open
>This error occurs when too many files are opened at once. The FILES setting in the optional CONFIG.FX file can sometimes remedy the problem. Up to 48 open files can be specified, which includes the program, index, data, and other files. The Macintosh might have reached its limit of the number of simultaneously open FoxBASE files it can have. [Error #6]

Too many indices
>Only seven index files can be opened at one time to support a database file. This rare error indicates that an eighth index file opening is being attempted. [Error #28]

Too many memory variables
>The MVCOUNT setting in the optional CONFIG.FX file controls the number of variables that you can have at one time. The default number is 256, but it can be set anywhere between 128 and 3600. [Error #22]

Too many PROCEDURES
The maximum number of procedures FoxBASE allows in any single procedure file is 128. If you must have more, consider using two or more procedure files and switching between them with the SET PROCEDURE TO command. [Error #1250]

Too many PICTURE characters specified
About 4,000 characters is set aside in memory to store information related to pending GETS by default. Picture information is included there, along with VALID and RANGE validation information. To increase the capacity, change the BUCKET statement in the optional CONFIG.FX file. It can be adjusted between 1 and 32K bytes. [Error #1310]

Too many relationships
The limit of 15 interfile relationships has been exceeded. [Error #1148]

Total label width exceeds maximum allowable size
This error indicates that a label file's character count exceeds the amount of characters that can fit on a label. Try reducing the label width by using functions like SUBSTR ( ). [Error #1246]

Unable to create temporary work file(s)
FoxBASE makes its own temporary files to handle jobs like SORT and INDEX. If it cannot make them because of an overfull disk, write-protected network volume, etc., this error is sure to occur, and the process will halt. [Error #1410]

Unknown function key
Check your use of the SET FUNCTION TO command. This error indicates that the named key does not exist. [Error #104]

Unrecognized command verb
The first word in any command line must be a valid FoxBASE command. Functions are not allowed, except as expressions or parts of an expression following a command. Check the command verb on the offending line. [Error #16]

Unrecognized phrase/keyword in command
This error indicates that FoxBASE cannot make out some part of a command, particularly, that it has encountered an unknown word or group of words. [Error #36]

Variable must be in selected database
A variable that you or a program used in a REPLACE command does not exist in the selected database file. Check the command and the database for a mismatch. [Error #1134]

Variable not found
The TOTAL, UPDATE, and CHANGE commands can accept a FIELDS clause that

defines which fields to use. If a named field does not exist in the selected database, this error can occur. [Error #12]

Volume does not exist
Check the path and file name in the offending command. FoxBASE cannot find the disk/volume that was named. [Error #1161]

While nesting error
If DO and ENDDO statements do not exist in matching pairs in the offending program, this error can occur. Look for a missing partner. [Error #96]

Wrong length key
Index keys are the basis for SET RELATION TO and UPDATEs. If an UPDATE or SET RELATION is attempted with a key that does not match the existing index, this error can occur. [Error #1117]

Wrong number of parameters
Parameters are bits of information that can be passed from one program to another as the first program launches, or "calls," the second. The number of acceptable parameters is fixed by the PARAMETERS statement, which is required in the "called" program. Passing fewer or more is not allowed. [Error #94]

Appendix D
XCMDs and XFCNs

FoxBASE+/MAC accepts external commands (XCMDs) and functions (XFCNs) through a special resource interface. External code segments allow you to do things that you can't normally do with FoxBASE alone. There are XCMDs that play sounds, manipulate memory, and even animate speaking characters on screen. "Albert," for example, in Disney Studio's remake of *The Absent Minded Professor,* was created with HyperAnimator—a Hypercard XCMD from BrightStar Technology that I've used with FoxBASE+/Mac.

The difference between XCMDs and XFCNs isn't important, so I'll refer to them both as XCMDs. A good way to try XCMDs is to get them from a developer or from starter stacks designed for Hypercard. You can ask Macintosh dealers or check with friends at a local Macintosh user group. While there's no guarantee that every Hypercard XCMD will work, general purpose XCMDs and those that don't depend on Hypercard-only features should be ok.

Use ResEdit to move XCMDs into FoxUSER or any FoxBASE resource file. If you use another resource file be sure to use the SET RESOURCE command prior to LOADing. The following is an example of the syntax and use of the LOAD, CALL and RELEASE MODULE commands.

```
LOAD
LOAD <resource> [FUNCTION]
```

LOAD finds an XCMD resource by its <resource> name and places it in memory so that it can be CALLed. If the resource is an XFCN, include the FUNCTION word in your command. Up to 16 can be loaded at one time. Suppose there is an XCMD named "bounceball" in the FoxUSER file that displays a bouncing ball. To load it into memory, you could issue this command:

```
LOAD bounceball
CALL
CALL <resource> [TO <memvar>] [WITH <exprlist>]
```

Call executes an XCMD that has been loaded into memory where <resource> is the XCMD's name. Some XCMDs return data to FoxBASE, so <memvar> is the name of a memory variable you've created to receive any such value. If the XCMD needs information from FoxBASE, such as the name of a sound file, for example, use the WITH <exprlist> clause to pass it along. If file names are included in the parameter list, provide full pathnames. Character-type parameters must be enclosed in quotation marks.

To actually use the "bounceball" XCMD, you would issue a command like the one below. Notice the two parameters, a number to tell it how fast to bounce the ball, and a second parameter to indicate the bounce direction.

```
CALL bounceball WITH 15, "left_to_right"
RELEASE MODULE
RELEASE MODULE <resource>
```

RELEASE MODULE removes a LOADed XCMD from memory so that the memory can be reused. Be sure to do the following when you don't need an XCMD, because it frees valuable memory. Example:

```
RELEASE MODULE bounceball
```

Index

A

ABS( ), 367
absolute values, 367
ACCEPT command, 200-201, 275, 352, 361, 506
active screens, 450
addressing
  fixed, 139
  relative, 376, 436
ALERT, 176, 202-203, 327, 506
alert boxes, 176-178, 202
alias indicator, 368
  commands, 194-195
  functions, 364
alias operator, 188
ALIAS( ), 368, 438
ALL, 87, 121
allocating memory, 65, 331
alternate files, 22, 65, 191, 331
angle brackets
  commands, 194
  functions, 364
APPEND, 35, 88, 134, 204-205, 213, 261, 502, 505
APPEND BLANK, 206, 276, 502, 505
APPEND FROM, 207-209, 232, 502, 505
append screens, 15
AppleTalk, 480
arguments, 104
  scope, 197
artificial intelligence, 89
arrayname, commands, 195
arrays, 69, 110-112, 195, 244-246
  clearing, 221
  copy field contents into, 324
  copy record contents into, 324
  creation of, 244
  dimensioning, 111
  display contents of, 252
  record contents into, 110
  releasing, 218
  replace fields with, 268
  values into, 352
ASC( ), 369, 374
ASCII code, 35, 88, 369, 374, 401
ASCII codes, 374, 401
  special characters, 500-501
AT( ), 105, 370, 409, 433, 444
attributes, 106
AVERAGE, 37, 210, 353, 356, 504, 505
averaging, 82-86, 210, 356

B

backup files, 32
bands, report, 481, 484
bell sound, 65, 331
bitmaps, 480
blank characters, 440

remove from string or expression, 454
blind scoping, 122
body, report, 481
BOF( ), 371
boldface, 51, 291
borders, screen, 67, 341
boxes, 39, 143
branching, 273
bring to front, reports, 492
BROWSE, 133-135, 211-213, 261, 503, 504
Browse window, 4, 5, 18, 34, 40, 44, 47, 74, 81, 132-135, 211
buttons, 18, 126, 152-155, 158-165, 331
bytes, 383

C

cache memory, 63
calculated fields, 493
CALL, 508
CANCEL, 214, 256, 308, 319, 354, 508
carry forward, 65
CASE READ, 257
CASE...ENDCASE, 257, 259
categorical data, 12-13
CDOW( ), 373, 380, 384
CHANGE, 133-135, 213, 215-216, 261, 276, 503, 505
Change window, 34, 132-135
character data types, 10
character string, 455
characters, 9, 69, 480
  alphabetic, 404
  blanks, 440
  formatting, 453
  insert or delete to string, 444
  lowercase, 406, 412
  phonetic values of, 439
  position of, 105
  uppercase, 407, 457
check boxes, 126, 146
child files, 62, 68, 79-81, 120, 188, 344-346
CHR( ), 278, 374, 402
CLEAR, 112, 217, 504, 506
CLEAR ALL, 218, 221, 224, 267, 395, 410, 434, 506
CLEAR FIELDS, 219, 505
CLEAR GETS, 217, 220, 221, 309, 506
CLEAR MEMORY, 218, 221, 282, 309, 312, 317, 323, 506
CLEAR PROGRAM, 222, 508
CLEAR PROMPT, 506
CLEAR TYPEAHEAD, 223, 278, 506
CLOSE, 218, 224, 267, 395, 410, 434
CLOSE ALL, 227, 267, 505

CLOSE DATA, 474
CLOSE DATABASES, 267, 505
CLOSE FORMAT, 506
CLOSE INDEX, 505
CLOSE PROCEDURE, 508
CMONTH( ), 375, 420
col, commands, 195
COL( ), 109, 376, 424, 425, 436
color panel, 52-53, 73
colors, 53, 64, 65, 67, 152, 195-197, 326-327, 332, 341, 405
columns, 9, 10, 18, 195
  calculation of, 84-86
  coordinates of, 195
  headers and footers for, 482
  position of, 424
  relative addressing, 376
  width of, 18
Command key, 18
Command window, 4, 6, 19, 20, 27, 52, 56, 66, 339
  recording commands from, 335
commands, 5, 6, 56, 97-98, 193-362
  categorical cross-reference, 502-508
  compiling, 55
  database management, 505
  debugging, 508
  display or print, 67, 340
  echo to screen, 49, 66
  environment control, 507
  event processing, 505
  execute on Escape key, 300
  execute on keypress, 301
  interactive, 502
  interface management, 506
  interface, anatomy of, 167-170
  interpreting, 55
  library of, 57
  memory variables, 506
  networking, 507
  parameter passing and receiving, 507
  printing, 507
  programming, 508
  recording, 19, 66, 335
  status checking, 508
  symbols used in, 194
  syntax options, 195
  user-interface development, 138
  XCMDs and XCFNs, 508
commas
  commands, 194
  functions, 364
  labels, 495
comments (see also notes)
  files, 298
comparison function, 365
compilation, 49
  commands, 55
  programs, 56
computed fields, 493

533

computer storage, 3, 4
concatenation, 72
conditional scoping, 122
configuration files, 64, 331, 447
  data sharing, 465
consoles, 448
constants, 70, 99
  local, 303
constructs, 101
CONTINUE, 87, 110, 225, 285, 503, 505
Control key, 18
controls, 101, 138
coord, commands, 195
coordinates, 139, 195
COPY FILE, 226-228, 232, 313, 503, 507
COPY STRUCTURE, 228, 232, 503, 505
COPY STRUCTURE EXTENDED, 229-231, 236, 505
COPY TO, 88, 89, 209, 227, 230, 232, 503, 505
COUNT, 233, 353, 356, 504, 505
counting, 49, 67, 82-86, 233, 342, 429
CREATE, 234-235, 297, 503
CREATE FROM, 230, 236, 505
CREATE LABEL, 37, 237, 279, 294, 504, 505
CREATE REPORT, 238, 295, 316, 504, 505
CREATE SCREEN, 239, 296, 504
CREATE VIEW, 219, 240, 504, 505
CTOD( ), 104, 105, 373, 375, 378, 385
cursors, 18, 449
custom forms, 44

D

data, flush from memory to disk, 39, 267
data entry, 41, 72-75, 200, 275, 278
  changes, 42
  confirm, 65, 333
  data-converting functions, 76
  editing, 261
  fields for, 146
  format of, 34
  forms for (see forms)
    on-screen, 81
  pause for processing, 361
  screens for, 504
  terminate READ, 427
  validating, 175-176
data fields, reports, 486
data files (see databases)
data fork, 23, 56, 57
data handling environment, 52-53, 55-67
  status of, 253, 283
data sharing (see also networking), 460-478
  Add Config.fx menu, 465
  Add Resources menu, 465
  automatic locks, 469-473
  Build Application option, 464
  debuggin, 462
  error-handling routines for, 473-476
  exclusive use of database files, 467-468

file storage, 467
fonts, 463
FoxPackage, packaging applications for distribution, 464
locking, 466
memory variable editing, 476-477
moving data between Macs and IBM compatibles, 460
programs for, 462
remove source code, 465
resource management for, 477-478
runtime system for, 464
sharing files, 461
swapping files, 461
tracing, 462
data tables, 6-7, 10-11
  creating and using, View window for, 73
  key fields to relate, 92
  normalization of, 11
data types, 10, 12-15, 99, 199
data-handling environment, 119
database management, commands for, 505
Database menu, 32-41
  Append Form, 35
  Average, 37
  Browse, 34
  Copy To, 35
  Count, 37
  Flush, 39
  Label, 27, 37
  Pack, 40, 74
  Reindex, 40
  Report, 27, 38, 39
  Setup, 33-34, 131
  Sort, 35
  Sum, 39
  Total, 35
databases, 3-15, 22, 32-41, 58-60, 69, 137
  add fields, 33, 39
  adding information to, 15
  adding records, 204, 206, 276
  averaging fields in, 37, 210
  blank record at end of, 206
  browsing and changing, 34
  changing data in, 215, 314, 503
  closing, 218, 224
  copying, 207, 226, 228, 232, 503
  count records, 37
  creation of, 13, 234, 503
  data tables in, 10-11
  data types in, 10, 33
  default location for, 66, 334
  delete fields, 33
  delete records, 40
  design of, 8-15
  display contents of, 81, 199, 249, 280
  exclusive access to, 66, 336, 467-468
  export data from, 35, 88
  fields in, 9-10, 33, 125, 197, 389
  filtering records, 503
  flush data from memory to disk, 39, 267
  format of, 34
  goto new location in, 44, 122, 123, 271

import data to, 35, 88
indexes, 11-12, 23, 24, 34
join files to create, 277
layout tools, 126
list fields, 33
locking, 119, 434
menu system for, 16-54
naming, 15, 195, 368, 381
normalization of data tables in, 11
notes in, 10
opening, 54, 360
operational vs. categorical data in, 12-13
records in, 10
reindex, 40, 311, 503
relational, 6-7
saving, 15
selecting work areas, 34, 330
snapshots of, 240
sorting, 35
structure of, 91
structure of, change, 33, 297
structure of, copying, 229, 236
total fields of, 35-36
updating, 414
width of fields, 33
work area for, 197
date data types, 10
DATE( ), 104, 379
dates, 38, 65, 72, 105, 195, 332, 378, 379, 384, 385, 414, 446, 447
  day of week, 373, 380, 384
  formats for, 66, 334, 385
  month, 375, 420
DAY( ), 373, 375, 380, 384, 420
dBASE, 35
DBF( ), 381, 389, 438
Debug window, 450
debugging, 49, 462, 508
decimal places, 66, 334, 337
defaults, 63-68, 331
DELETE, 40, 75, 121, 241, 302, 310, 382, 504, 505
DELETE ALL, 121, 362
DELETE FILE, 242-243
DELETED( ), 75, 241, 302, 310, 382
descent, fonts, 449
device drivers, 480
devices, 195, 448
dialog boxes, 5, 6, 17, 179-180
  abort, 13
  create databases with, 234
  label creation, 237
DIMENSION, 112, 244-246, 269, 324, 352, 506
DIR, 227, 247-248, 251, 281, 313, 507
disk drives, free space on, 383
DISKSPACE( ), 383, 423
DISPLAY, 27, 82, 83, 199, 249, 280, 505
DISPLAY FILES, 251, 281
DISPLAY MEMORY, 110, 252, 282, 352, 507, 508
DISPLAY STATUS, 119, 253, 283, 508
DISPLAY STRUCTURE, 228, 254, 284, 505
distributed applications (see data sharing)

534   Index

DO, 92, 113, 255-256, 303, 508
DO CASE, 97, 101, 109, 400
DO CASE...OTHERWISE...END-CASE, 102-103, 257, 273, 508
DO WHILE, 57, 97, 101, 109, 110, 189, 371, 508
DO WHILE...ENDDO, 101-102, 259, 264, 471
DO...ENDDO, 288
DO...WITH, 507
DOW( ), 373, 375, 380, 384
drive designators, 68, 195, 349
drivename, commands, 195
DTOC( ), 61, 76, 105, 378, 385

E

echoing commands to screen, 49, 66, 334
EDIT, 213, 216, 261, 276, 505
Edit menu, FoxForm, 142
EJECT, 192, 262, 508
ellipses
  commands, 194
  functions, 364
end of file, 196
ENDCASE, 102
ENDDO, 508
ENDIF, 104
enhanced, command, 195
enhancing applications, 170-175, 170
environmental control, 63-68, 119, 507
eof, commands, 196
EOF( ), 105, 225, 386, 397
ERASE, 227, 243, 263, 313, 507
error codes and messages, 40, 387, 417, 509-530
ERROR( ), 299, 320, 387, 417, 474
error-handling programs, 299, 417, 473-476
Escape key, execute programs on, 66, 300, 336
event processing, 505
EXIT, 264
EXP( ), 388, 411
expansion, macro, 117, 366
exponents, 388
exporting data, 35, 88, 503
expr, commands, 196
expressions, 39, 56, 57, 68, 70-72, 99-101, 196, 198, 270, 344-346

  character position in, 105, 370, 413, 433, 437, 445
  character string or literal, 196
  evaluate and display results, 198
  formatting, 453
  length of, 409
  list of, 196
  logical values, 196
  lowercase characters, 406, 412
  numeric values, 196
  pixels in, 449
  remove blanks from, 454
  uppercase characters, 407, 457
extensions, 58, 341

F

FCOUNT( ), 389
field selectors, 33

FIELD( ), 390
fieldlist, commands, 196
fieldname, commands, 196
fields, 9-10, 69, 125, 126, 128
  adding, 15, 33, 39
  aliasing, 195
  averaging, 37, 84, 210
  calculation in, 249, 280, 493
  changing, 15, 215, 314, 503
  clearing, 219
  computed, 493
  confirm data entry to, 333
  contents to array, 268, 324
  contents to memory variable, 108
  data entry, 146
  data types in, 15, 33, 254, 284
  delete, 33
  display contents of, 81
  editing, 309
  headings from names of, 340
  limit use of, 66, 336
  list, 33, 196
  naming, 13, 14, 33, 66, 70, 99, 196, 197, 254, 284, 340, 390
  number of, 389
  ordering of, 44, 122, 123
  rename, 33
  replacing data in, 46, 84-86
  select, 34, 44, 122, 123
  sorting, 35
  summing, 83, 84, 353
  total of, 35-36
  width of, 15, 33, 254, 284
Fields option, 44-45, 122, 123
File menu
  Close, 25
  Copy File, 27
  Delete File, 27
  FoxForm, 140
  New, 21-24, 27
  Open, 24-25
  Page Setup, 26
  Page Size, 25-26
  Print, 27
  Quit, 27, 29
  Rename File, 27
  Revert, 25
  Save, 25
  Save As, 25
file ports, 449
FILE( ), 391
filelist, commands, 196
filename, commands, 196
files, 20-27, 69
  add data to, 41
  backing up, 32
  change data in, 42
  closing, 25, 218, 224, 308
  copying, 27, 28, 226, 232, 503
  creation of, 21, 503, 504
  date of, 247
  default location for, 66, 334
  deleting, 27, 28, 74, 242, 263
  end of, 386
  exclusive access to, 66, 336, 467-468
  find data in, 86, 503
  go back to last saved version, 25
  joining, 277
  kinds of, 22, 58-59, 196
  limit to, 66

  listing, 68, 196, 247, 251, 281, 347
  locking, 119, 395, 410, 434, 466, 469-473
  move record pointer back and forth, 350
  naming, 196, 197, 313, 368, 391, 426
  new, 197
  opening, 24, 337, 360
  ordering, 274
  overwriting, 68, 347
  packing, 74
  paths, 67, 342, 421, 426
  printing, 25-27, 191
  relating, 68, 79-81, 120-121, 344-346, 359, 503
  renaming, 25, 27, 28, 313, 503
  resizing, 40
  saving, 25, 426
  selecting, 330, 398
  sharing, 461
  size of, 247
  sorting, 78, 351, 503
  storage of, data sharing, 467
  swapping, 461
  unlocking, 358
  updating from another, 359
  wildcards, 197
filetype, commands, 196
fill mode, reports, 493
filters, 33, 34, 42-44, 66, 68, 77, 337, 348, 503
FIND, 77, 86, 266, 285, 329, 386, 397, 503, 505
fixed addresses, 139
FKLABEL( ), 392, 394
FKMAX( ), 393, 394
FLOCK( ), 395, 410, 434, 472
FLUSH, 218, 224, 267, 508
Fn, commands, 196
folders, 67, 196, 342, 448
FONT, 152
fonts, 39, 50, 326, 449, 463
footers, 482, 483
FOR, 37, 39, 45, 83, 87, 233
For option, 44-45, 122, 123
form feed, 262
form files, 23
Form menu, FoxForm, 141
Form window, 450
format files, 34, 41, 47, 49, 58, 59, 66, 218, 224, 338, 447
forms, 34, 89-94
  analyzing information to be stored on, 91
  application development, 91
  creation of, 125
  data model creation, 91
  data tables related with key fields, 92
  database structure and, 91
  design review, 92
  input, 92
  maintenance, 92
  menu system for, 93
  saving, 128
  screen layout for, 239
  screen output for, 93
  templates for, 89-90
FOUND( ), 225, 285, 396
FoxBase+/Mac, exiting, 13, 27, 308
FoxCode, 125, 508

Index **535**

FoxForm, 125
FoxPackage, 464
FoxReport (see reports)
FUNCTION clause, user-interface development, 150-151
function keys, 53, 66, 196, 339
 programmable, 392, 394
functions, 5, 6, 57, 71, 99, 104-105, 363-459
 arguments for, 104
 data conversion, 76
 symbols used with, 364
 user-defined, 115-116, 176-179

G

GATHER, 111, 176, 246, 268-269, 324, 476, 507
GENERATE FROM, 506
GET, 109, 110, 116, 139, 147, 176, 179, 257, 507
GET..READ, 201
GETEXPR( ), 270, 327, 506
GETFILE( ), 327, 398, 426
GOTO, 121, 189, 271, 350, 372, 386, 477, 503, 505
grafport, 449
graphics
 reports, 487
 user-interface development, 136
groups, reports, 486

H

headers, 482, 483
headings, 38, 66, 340
HELP, 272, 506
Help system, 4, 18, 21, 54, 67, 272, 340, 348, 450
 customizing, 20, 67, 186-188, 340, 451
Hypercard, 477

I

icons, 292
IF, 57, 97, 101, 104, 109, 257, 371, 400
IF...ELSE..ENDIF, 103, 273
IF...ENDIF, 257, 258, 400, 508
IIF( ), 101, 104, 400
immediate if, 400
importing data, 35, 88, 503
indentation, 32
INDEX, 122, 274, 311, 351, 422, 439, 440, 503, 505
indexes, 11-12, 23, 24, 33-36, 58, 59, 61, 69, 75-83, 196, 274, 341, 348, 448
 change extension, 67, 341
 closing, 218, 224
 creation of, 41, 76
 data-converting functions and, 76
 default location for, 66, 334
 duplicate entries, 68, 348
 filtered, 77
 FIND and SEEK, 77
 naming, 421
 opening, 41
 reindexing, 40, 311, 362, 503
 relating, 61, 68, 79-81, 344-346
 reports, 494
 seeking, 46, 329
 SET EXACT, 78
 snapshots of, 240
 sorting and, 78
 unique values in, 68
 updating, 41, 67, 342
INKEY( ), 201, 275, 278, 301, 361, 374, 401, 428, 464, 471
INPUT, 201, 275, 352, 507
input forms, 92
INSERT, 206, 276, 505
insert mode, 18
INT( ), 367, 403, 419, 435
integers, 197
interactive commands, 55, 502
interactive interface, 4
interface management, commands for, 506
interfaces (see user interfaces)
interpreting
 commands, 55
 programs, 56
ISALPHA( ), 404
ISCOLOR( ), 405
ISLOWER( ), 406, 407, 412, 457
ISUPPER( ), 406, 407, 412, 457
italics, 51, 291

J

JOIN, 277, 505
Julian dates, 446

K

key, commands, 196
key fields, 11, 12, 36, 61, 69, 81, 196
 relating data tables with, 92
KEYBOARD, 223, 278, 464, 505
 ASCII codes represented, 401
 characters in memory buffer from, 278, 348
 data entry from, 275
 execute commands from, 301
 remove characters from memory buffer, 223
keyboard shortcuts, 291
keys panel, 52-53, 66, 73, 339
keystrokes, 464

L

label files, 23, 58, 59
LABEL FORM, 237, 262, 279, 294, 504, 505
labels, 128, 135, 262, 279, 495-497, 504
 changing form of, 294
 creation, 237
 exact sizing, 497
 margins for, 497
 operators for, 495
 printing, 26, 27, 37, 39
 view, 37
landscape printing, 26
layout tools, 126
leading, fonts, 449
LEFT( ), 370, 408, 413, 433, 437, 445
len, commands, 196
LEN( ), 408, 409
length, 196
line feeds, 32
lines, 39, 126, 143
linking, 68, 79, 344-346
LIST, 27, 82, 83, 199, 250, 280, 505
LIST FILES, 251, 281, 507
LIST MEMORY, 252, 282, 312, 317, 323, 507
LIST STATUS, 253, 283, 330, 508
LIST STRUCTURE, 254, 284, 504, 505
LOAD, 508
local variables and constants, 303
LOCATE, 86, 87, 110, 121, 225, 266, 285, 329, 503, 505
LOCATE-CONTINUE, 397
LOCK, 119
LOCK( ), 410, 434, 470, 474
locking, 119, 358, 395, 410, 434, 466, 469-473
LOG( ), 388, 411
logarithms, 411
logical conditions, evaluation of, 257
logical data types, 10
logical expressions, 72
 evaluate and branch, 273
logical string, 455
lookups, 79
LOOP, 265
loops, 101-102, 471
 Do...While, 259
 exiting, 264
LOWER( ), 412, 457
lowercase, 406, 412
LTRIM( ), 105, 413, 433, 437
LUPDATE( ), 414

M

macros, 6, 19, 118, 504
 expansion of, 117, 366
 substitution function, 366
mail merging, 22
maintenance forms, 92
margins, 67, 341, 497
matching strings, 66, 336
MAX( ), 415, 418
maximum values, 415
memo data types, 10
memo fields, 28, 60, 81, 199, 455
 display contents of, 249, 280
 naming, 196
 width of, 67, 341
memofieldname, commands, 196
memory, 62-64, 447
 allocation of, 65, 331
 cache, 63
 characters placed into buffer from keyboard, 278, 348
 clearing, 221
 command histories use, 67, 340
 display contents of, 110, 252, 282
 flush data to disk from, 39, 267
 limit memory variables, 67
 memory variables in, 341
 partitioning, 62
 remove GETs from, 220
 remove keyboard characters from buffer, 223
 remove programs from, 222
 requirements of, 63
memory variables, 58, 59, 69, 71, 99, 105-113, 196, 197, 306, 506
 add to memory, 317
 arrays, 110-112
 attributes, 106

contents of field to, 108
creating, 105
display contents of, 110
editing, 309, 456, 476-477
getting information from users for, 109
listing, 196
memory available to, 341
naming, 105
number of, 67, 342
private, 108
programming with, 109-110
public variables, 106
releasing, 218, 312
saving, 106, 323
user-interface development, 137, 138
values into, 352
wildcards, 197
memvar, commands, 196
memvarlist, commands, 196
memvarname, commands, 196
MENU, 182, 183, 327, 416, 505, 506
menu bars, 180
MENU( ), 182, 183, 288, 289, 291, 416
menu-event handling, 181
MENUBAR, 416, 505, 506
menubars, commands for creation of, 286-292
menus, 4, 6, 180, 286-292, 331
   building system of, 93
   commands for creation of, 286-292
   Database menu, 32-41
   defining, 182
   demonstration of, 183-186
   dialog boxes, 17
   File menu, 20-21
   FoxForm, 140
   FoxReport, 484
   handling, 182
   Help system, 20
   icons for, 292
   installing, 182
   keyboard shortcuts to, 18, 291
   menu-event handling, 181
   modeless, 181
   modifying characters for options, 291
   options, 17, 291, 416
   pop-up, 126, 155-158
   Program menu, 47-50
   Record menu, 41-47
   recording choices and playing back, 19
   saving program files, 19-20
   switches, 17, 291
   Text menu, 27-32, 50-51
   trees vs. bars, 180
   Window menu, 51-54
MESSAGE( ), 387, 417
micro-sizing, reports, 492
MIN( ), 415, 418
minimum values, 418
miscellaneous panel, 52-53, 73
MOD( ), 419, 435
MODIFY COMMAND, 222, 293, 504, 508
MODIFY LABEL, 237, 279, 294, 504, 505
MODIFY REPORT, 238, 295, 316, 504, 505
MODIFY SCREEN, 296, 504
MODIFY STRUCTURE, 228, 230, 235, 236, 254, 284, 297, 503, 505
modulus, 419
MONTH( ), 420
months, 375, 420
mouse, 15, 18, 18, 449
multifinder partitions, 62

N

n, commands, 197
NDX( ), 381, 389, 421
networking (see also data sharing), 460, 507
newfilename, commands, 197
NEXT, 87
normalization, 11
NOTE, 298, 508
notes, 10, 298
nudging, reports, 492
number data types, 10
numbers, 9, 72
   character into numeric, 458
   integer, 197, 403
   operators for, 98
   string conversion of, 442
numeric precision, 69
numeric string, 455

O

Object menu, FoxForm, 142
objects, FoxForm, 135
odometer, 67, 342
oldfilename, commands, 197
ON ERROR, 182, 299, 320, 387, 417, 473-476, 506
ON ESCAPE, 182, 300, 506
ON KEY, 182, 301, 402, 428, 506
ON MENU, 182, 183, 288, 289, 416, 505, 506
on/off panel, 52-53, 73
operating systems, 423
operational data, 12
operators, 71, 98, 99, 495
options, 17, 18, 291, 331, 416
ordering, 67, 342, 503
orientation, 26
OS( ), 423
outline text, 291
output device, default, 446
overwrite mode, 18, 68, 347

P

PACK, 40, 47, 66, 74, 241, 243, 302, 310, 335, 362, 382, 504
page numbers, 38
page size, 451
paper selection, printing, 451
parameter lists, 197
parameter passing and receiving, 114-115, 507
PARAMETERS, 114-115, 303, 507
parent files, 61, 62, 68, 79-81, 120, 188, 344-346
parentheses
   commands, 194
   functions, 104, 364
parmlist, commands, 197
partitioning, 62
pasting, 29
pathlist, commands, 197
paths, 67, 197, 342, 421, 426
PCOL( ), 262, 377, 424, 425, 436
pen mode, reports, 493
phonetic values, 439
PICTURE, 140, 147-150
picture data types, 10
picture fields, 81, 199, 249, 280
picture files, 60
pictures, 39, 126, 140, 346
   buttons, 152-155
   default area of, 66, 338
   reports, 488-490
   user-interface development, 136, 147-150
pixels, 448, 449
point sizes, 51
pointer, record, 80, 121, 126
pop-up menus, 126, 155-158
portrait printing, 26
ports, 449
precision, 69
preprogrammed commands, 55
printing, 25-27, 66, 190-192, 249, 343, 479-480, 504
   aborting, 450
   boxes, 39
   characters and bitmaps, 480
   commands for, 507
   copies, number of, 27
   device drivers, 480
   device name for, 195, 335
   eject page from printer, 262
   fonts, 39
   form feed, 262
   horizontal and vertical resolution of, 451
   labels, 26, 27, 37, 39
   lines, 39
   margins, 67, 341
   number of pages for, 450
   orientation: landscape vs. portrait, 26
   page setup, 26-27, 450
   page size, 25-26, 451
   pictures, 39
   printer settings, 68, 343, 447, 448
   reports, 26, 27, 38-39
   specified pages only, 27
   starting, 450
   to file, 191
PRIVATE, 252, 303, 304, 307, 312, 317, 507
private memory variables, 108
PROCEDURE, 303, 305, 508
procedure files, closing, 224
procedurename, commands, 197
procedures, 68, 89, 114, 197, 305, 321, 344
processing, 18, 505
   pause for, 361
processors, 448
program files, 22, 27, 55-58
   data and resource fork, 57
   DOS users, line feeds for, 32
   procedures in, 197
   saving, 19-20
   subroutines in, 197
   text file to, 23
Program menu, 47-50
   Cancel, 48
   Compile, 49
   Do, 47, 131
   Echo, 49

FoxForm, 140
Generate, 49, 129-131
Resume, 49
Step, 49
Suspend, 48
Talk, 49
programmable function keys, 392, 394
programmed data displays, 188-190
programming, 97-123
  ? command, 99
  commands in, 97-98
  controls and constructs, 101
  data-handling environment for, 119
  DO CASE...OTHERWISE...END-CASE, 102-103
  DO WHILE...ENDDO, 101-102
  expressions, 99-101
  functions, 104-105
  IF...ELSE..ENDIF, 103
  IIF( ), 104
  loops, 101-102
  macros, 117
  memory variables (see memory variables)
  operators, 98
  parameter passing and receiving, 114-115
  procedures, 114
  screens one through nine, 117-119
  special features for, 112-117
  subroutines, 113
  user-defined functions (UDFs), 115-116
programs, 5-6, 47-50, 58, 59, 331, 446, 448, 504
  coding, 54
  commands for, 508
  compiling, 49, 56
  debugging, 54
  display results of, 49, 68, 348
  echo commands to screen, 49
  error-handling program for, 299
  execute from Escape key, 66, 336
  format files for, 49
  interpreting, 56
  Mac and IBM compatible, 462
  macros, 117
  notes and comments, 298
  parameter passing and receiving, 114-115
  pass control to another, 320
  pause, 48, 354, 361
  procedures in, 68, 89, 114, 305, 344
  remove from memory, 222
  resume execution of, 49, 319
  running, 47-48, 65, 131, 255-256, 333
  screen files, 49
  screen layout for, 239
  step-by-step execution of, 49, 68, 347
  subroutines, 113, 305
  templates for, 49
  terminate, 48, 214, 321
  testing, 20
  text editor for, 293
  tokenized, 56
  variable names from other programs used by, 304
PROW( ), 262, 377, 424, 425, 436
PUBLIC, 106, 245, 246, 252, 303, 304, 306-307, 312, 507

public variables, 106
PUTFILE( ), 327, 399, 426

Q

Quick Report, 480
QUIT, 13, 214, 308, 321, 395, 410, 434, 508
quotation marks, 72
  commands, 66, 194, 339
  functions, 364

R

radio buttons, 13, 126, 158-160
RANGE, 152
ranges, record, 87
READ, 109, 110, 139, 179, 182, 183, 275, 288, 289, 290, 309, 416, 428, 507
READKEY( ), 201, 275, 301, 402, 427, 464
RECALL, 241, 302, 310, 382, 504
RECCOUNT( ), 233, 429, 430, 431
RECNO( ), 46, 57, 271, 350, 430, 439, 440
RECORD, 87
Record menu, 41-47
  Append, 41, 74, 131
  Append Blank, 74
  Change, 42-44, 74, 131
  Delete, 47
  Goto, 44
  Locate and Continue, 44-45
  Recall, 47
  Replace, 46
  Seek, 46
record pointers, 80, 121
records, 10, 41-47, 69
  adding, 74, 204, 502
  blank, 206
  browsing, 74
  carry forward for, 65, 332
  change range of, 44, 122, 123
  changing data in, 44, 122, 123, 74, 503
  contents into arrays, 110, 324
  copy to database, 207
  counting, 37, 67, 84, 233, 342, 429
  creation of, 276
  deleting, 40, 47, 66, 74, 241, 302, 335, 382, 504
  editing, 261
  filter, 34, 42-44, 503
  goto new location of, 44, 122, 123, 271
  index, 34
  limit to, 66, 337
  locate and change by condition, 44, 86, 122, 123, 225, 266, 285, 503
  locking, 410, 466, 469-473
  move pointer backward or forward, 350
  number of, 54, 254, 284, 430
  number to change, 44, 122, 123
  ordering, 61, 67, 342, 503
  ranges for, 87
  replace data in, 46
  scoping, 84, 87, 121-123
  seeking, 46, 329, 396
  size of, 431
  top of file, 371
  undeleting, 47, 310
  unlocking, 358

RECSIZE( ), 431
rectangle tool, 126
REINDEX, 76, 311, 503, 505
reindexing, 40, 311, 362, 503
relational databases, 6-7
relations (see files, relating)
relative addressing, 376, 436
RELEASE, 282, 312, 317, 323, 506, 507
RELEASE ALL, 218, 221
remainders, 419
RENAME, 227, 313, 503, 507
reow, commands, 197
REPLACE, 46, 57, 82, 84, 104, 109, 121, 230, 269, 314-315, 324, 359, 476, 503, 505
REPLICATE( ), 432
report files, 22, 23, 58, 59
REPORT FORM, 238, 262, 295, 316, 504, 505
reports, 262, 316, 479-497, 504
  adjusting drawing environment for, 491
  bands and body of, 481, 484
  bring to front and send to back options for, 492
  calculated fields, 493
  changing form of, 295
  column headers and footers, 482
  computed fields, 493
  creation, 238
  data fields, groups, totals in, 486
  databases and specifications, 494
  dates, 38
  fill, pen and transfer modes for, 493
  graphics, 487
  group headers and footers, 483
  headings, 38
  indexes, 494
  manipulating FoxReport objects in, 490-493
  menus for, 484
  micro-sizing, 492
  nudging, 492
  objects in, 485-490
  page header and footers, 482
  page layout, 494
  page numbers, 38
  pictures in, 488-490
  printing, 26, 27, 38-39, 479-480
  Quick Report, 480
  relations, 494
  summary, 38, 484
  text in, 486
  titles, 484
  user-defined functions, 493
  views, 494
ResEdit, 478
resource, commands, 197
resource files, 346
resource fork, 23, 56, 57
resource modules, 197
REST, 87
RESTORE, 108
RESTORE FROM, 108, 252, 312, 317, 323, 507
RESTORE SCREEN, 318, 322, 327, 506
RESUME, 214, 256, 308, 319, 354, 508
RETRY, 299, 319, 320, 354, 417, 475, 508

RETURN, 113, 214, 256, 308, 319, 320, 321, 354, 475, 508
RIGHT( ), 370, 413, 433, 437, 445
RLOCK( ), 395, 410, 434, 470, 474
round numbers, 435
ROUND( ), 435
rounded rectangle tool, 126
ROW( ), 109, 377, 424, 425, 436
rows, 9, 197
   coordinates of, 195
   position of, 425
   relative addressing of, 436
RTRIM( ), 105, 413, 433, 437
runtime system, data sharing, 464

S

SAVE ALL, 106
SAVE SCREEN, 318, 322, 327, 506
SAVE TO, 108, 252, 312, 317, 323, 507
SAY, 139, 147
SCATTER, 111, 176, 246, 269, 324, 477, 507
Scope option, 44-45
scoping, 39, 83-84, 87, 121-123, 197, 233
   blind, 122
   conditional, 122
SCREEN, 54, 203, 217, 220, 318, 322, 325-327, 506
screen files, 23, 49, 50, 58, 59
screens, 449
   active, 325, 450
   borders for, 67, 341
   change appearance of, 296
   clear, 65, 144, 332
   color, 64, 65, 67, 326, 327, 332, 341, 405
   commands to control, 325-327
   coordinates for, 139
   data entry, 504
   default area of, 66, 338
   designing, 239
   echo commands to, 66, 334
   fonts for, 326
   hide, 327, 450
   one through nine, 117-119
   positioning, 326
   replace contents, 318
   resizing, 325
   saving contents of, 322
   scrolling, 328
SCROLL, 328
scrolling, 44, 81, 211
search and replace text, 30-31, 396
SEEK, 61, 77, 81, 86, 121, 189, 190, 266, 285, 329, 386, 397, 439, 440, 503, 505
SELECT, 119, 330, 360, 368, 508
SELECT( ), 438
semicolons
   commands, 66, 194, 339
   labels, 495
send to back, reports, 492
serial numbers, 447
SET commands, 43, 64-65, 331-349
SET ALTERNATE, 64, 65, 191, 331
SET BELL, 64, 65, 331, 506
SET BUCKET, 64, 65, 331
SET CARRY, 64, 65, 205, 276, 332, 507

SET CENTURY, 64, 65, 332, 378, 379, 385, 506
SET CLEAR, 64, 65, 332, 507
SET COLOR, 65, 332, 405, 506
SET CONFIRM, 64, 65, 333, 506
SET CONSOLE, 66, 191, 333
SET DATE, 66, 334, 378, 379, 385, 506
SET DECIMALS, 66, 334, 388, 411, 435, 506
SET DEFAULT, 66, 248, 334, 507
SET DELETED, 64, 66, 122, 232, 233, 241, 274, 302, 310, 334, 350-351, 382, 507
SET DEVICE, 66, 191, 262, 335, 506, 507
SET DOHISTORY, 64, 335, 507
SET ECHO, 54, 66, 335, 508
SET ESCAPE, 64, 66, 300, 335
SET EXACT, 64, 66, 78, 336, 506
SET EXCLUSIVE, 64, 66, 336, 395, 410, 434, 467, 507
SET F, 66
SET FIELDS, 64, 254, 284, 336, 503
SET FILES, 66, 337
SET FILTER, 122, 274, 337, 350, 503
SET FIXED, 64, 337, 506
SET FORMAT TO, 92, 205, 216, 239, 276, 309, 338, 506
SET FRAME, 199, 338, 506
SET FUNCTION, 53, 339, 393-394, 506
SET HEADING, 64, 66, 210, 250, 280, 339, 353, 356, 508
SET HELP, 64, 67, 340, 506
SET HISTORY, 67, 340, 507
SET HMEMORY, 67, 340
SET INDEX, 67, 122, 311, 329, 341
SET INTENSITY, 64, 67, 341, 506
SET LABEL, 67
SET MARGIN, 67, 341, 424, 507
SET MEMOWIDTH, 67, 199, 341, 507
SET MVARSIZ, 67, 341
SET MVCOUNT, 67, 342
SET ODOMETER, 67, 342, 506
SET ORDER TO, 122, 274, 311, 342, 422, 505
SET PATH, 67, 248, 342
SET PRINT, 68, 191, 342, 507
SET PRINTER, 262, 343
SET PROCEDURE TO, 114, 256, 303, 305, 344, 508
SET RELATION, 61, 81, 120-121, 277, 330, 344, 503, 505
SET REPORT, 68
SET RESOURCE, 346, 508
SET SAFETY, 64, 68, 227, 228, 232, 347, 362, 508
SET SCREEN, 377, 436
SET STATUS, 64, 68, 347, 507, 508
SET STEP, 68, 347, 508
SET STRICT, 64, 347, 506
SET TALK, 68, 210, 233, 348, 353, 356, 506, 508
SET TOPIC TO, 272, 347
SET TYPEAHEAD, 68, 223, 278, 348, 402, 506
SET UNIQUE, 64, 68, 274, 311, 348, 505
SET VIEW, 68, 218, 219, 224, 240, 348, 360, 507

SET VOLUME, 68, 248, 349, 507
sets, 6, 11
Setup menu, Add, 75
shadow text, 291
sharing files (see data sharing)
Shift key, 18
SIZE, 152
skeleton, commands, 197
SKIP, 121, 189, 350, 372, 386, 505
snapshots, 240
SORT, 35, 274, 351, 503, 505
sorting, 35, 36, 61, 78, 351, 503
SOUNDEX( ), 439
sounds, 65, 331, 346
source code, removing from distributed applications, 465
SPACE( ), 440
special characters, 500-501
SQRT( ), 441
square brackets
   commands, 194
   functions, 364
square roots, 441
standard, commands, 197
status checking, 508
Status window, 450
STORE, 104, 106, 137, 246, 282, 304, 307, 352, 507
STR( ), 61, 110, 413, 435, 437, 442
strings, 69, 72, 197
   character position in, 105, 370, 408, 413, 433, 437, 445
   commands, 197
   compare, 365
   error messages, 417
   insert or delete characters, 444
   length of, 409
   lowercase, 412
   matching, 66, 336
   numeric data converted to, 442
   operators for, 98
   phonetic values of characters in, 439
   pixels in, 449
   remove blanks from, 454
   replication of, 432
   sending to output device, 355
   trimming, 105
   types of, 455
   uppercase, 457
STUFF( ), 370, 433, 444, 445, 454
subprograms (see procedures; subroutines)
subroutines, 68, 113, 197, 305, 321, 344
substitution, macros, 366
SUBSTR( ), 61, 105, 370, 408, 413, 433, 437, 444, 445, 454
SUM, 210, 233, 353, 356, 504, 505
summary reports, 38, 484
summing, 39, 49, 82-86, 353
SUSPEND, 214, 256, 308, 319, 354, 508
swapping files, 461
switches, 17, 291
syntax, commands, 195
SYS( ), 291, 301, 420, 446-451, 475
system functions, 446-451

T

tab keys, 347
tables (see data tables)

Index 539

templates, 49, 50, 89-90, 147-150
temporary files, 446
text, 27-32, 50-51, 355
  backup files, 32
  boldfaced, 51
  copy, 29, 31
  delete, 29
  editing, 293
  fonts, 50
  indentation, 32
  italic, 51
  line feeds, 32
  move, 28, 29, 31
  reports, 486
  search and replace, 30-31
  size of, 51
  style of, 51
  underlined, 51
  undo changes to, 29
  viewing (TYPE command), 357
  word wrap, 32
text buttons, 126, 160-165
text editor, 22, 293
text files, 22, 27, 58, 58, 59
  compilation of, 49
  program files from, 23
text labels, 135, 142
Text menu, 27-32, 50-51
  Clear, 29
  Copy, 29
  Cut, 29
  Find Again, 31
  Find, 30-31
  Font, 50
  Paste, 29
  Preferences, 32
  Replace All, 31
  Replace and Find Again, 31
  Select All, 31
  Style, 51
  Undo, 29
text regions, 126, 165-167
text tool, 126
TEXT...ENDTEXT, 355, 508
time, 446, 452
TIME( ), 452
titles, 484
tokens, 56
toolbox, 126, 142
TOTAL, 36, 84, 210, 353, 356
totalling, 35-36, 82-86, 356, 486
trace windows, 66, 68, 335, 347, 450, 462
tracing, 462
transfer mode, reports, 493
TRANSFORM( ), 453
TRIM( ), 105, 409, 413, 433, 437, 454
trimming, 105
triple clicking, 18
true/false statement data types, 10
TYPE, 357, 507
TYPE( ), 455
typefaces, 50

U

underlined text, 51, 291
unique values, 68, 348
unknown string, 455
UNLOCK, 358, 395, 410, 434, 507
UPDATE, 315, 359, 505
UPDATED( ), 456
UPPER( ), 46, 84, 190, 412, 457
uppercase, 407, 457
  commands, 194
  functions, 364
USE, 227, 235, 267, 360, 368, 395, 410, 422, 434, 505, 507
user-defined functions, 115-116, 176-179, 493
user-interface development, 123-192, 141
  alerts, 176
  arranging fields and adding text labels, 128
  Browse window programming, 132-135
  Change window programming, 132-135
  checkboxes, 146
  clearing part of screen, 144
  COLOR, 152
  commands, 138
  controls, 138
  create new form, 125
  data, 137
  data entry fields, 146
  database fields in layout, 125
  defining, installing, handling menus, 182
  demonstration menu, 183-186
  dialog boxes, 179-180
  Edit menu, 142
  enhancing applications by hand, 170-175
  File menu for, 140
  fixed addresses, 139
  FONT, 152
  Form menu for, 141
  FoxCode, 125
  FoxForm, 125, 140
  FUNCTION clause, 150-151
  generating application from form, 129-131
  GET and READ, 139
  graphics, 136
  Help system customizing, 186-188
  interface command anatomy, 167-170
  layout tools, 126
  lines and boxes, 143
  memory variables, 137, 138
  menu-event handling, 181
  menus, 180
  modeless menus, 181
  Object menu for, 142
  objects, 135
  picture buttons, 152-155
  PICTURE clause, 140, 147-150
  pictures, 136, 140
  popup menus, 155-158
  Program menu for, 140
  programmed data displays, 188-190
  Quick Form option, 127
  radio buttons, 158-160
  RANGE, 152
  running program from, 131
  saving form, 128
  SIZE, 152
  STYLE options, 145
  templates, 147-150
text buttons, 160-165
text edit regions, 165-167
text labels, 135, 142
toolbox, 142
user-defined functions, 176-179
VALID, 152
validating new data, 175-176
Utilities menu, Exit, 131

V

VAL( ), 61, 435, 442, 458
VALID, 116, 152, 175, 176
validation, 176
values, 197
  commands, 197
  clearing, 221
var, commands, 197
variables (see also memory variables)
  clearing, 221
  display contents of, 252
  local, 303
  naming, 304
VERSION( ), 423, 459
vertical bar, functions, 364
view files, 41, 62
view panel, 52-53, 73
View window, 4, 19, 32, 34, 52, 66, 68, 73, 240, 330, 339, 349, 450, 504
views, 6-7, 44, 52, 58, 59, 61, 120-121, 240, 504
  closing, 224
  color, 53
  function keys, 53
  moving, 53
  reports, 494
  select, 53
  settings for, 53
virtual files, 24

W

WAIT, 189, 201, 275, 352, 361, 507, 508
WHILE, 37, 39, 87, 189, 233
While option, 44-45, 122, 123
wildcards, 197
windows, 4, 18, 51-54, 450
  close all, 51
  Command, 52
  Debug, 54
  Display, 54
  Help, 54
  Hide Screens, 51
  move text between, 28
  screens in, 54, 117-119
  split, 81
  Status, 54
  Trace, 54
  View, 52
word wrap, 32
work areas, 197, 330, 381, 438

X

XCFNs, 477, 508
XCMDs, 346, 477, 508

Y

YEAR( ), 420

Z

ZAP, 75, 241, 302, 310, 362, 504, 505